# WEARING OF THE GRAY

*Yours to count on.*

*J. E. B. Stuart*

# WEARING OF THE GRAY

## BEING PERSONAL PORTRAITS, SCENES, AND ADVENTURES OF THE WAR

## BY JOHN ESTEN COOKE

formerly of General Stuart's staff
and author of "Surry of Eagle's-Nest,"
"Stonewall Jackson," etc.

*With a New Introduction by Emory M. Thomas*

LOUISIANA STATE UNIVERSITY PRESS
*Baton Rouge and London*

Editorial notes and index copyright © 1959 by Indiana
   University Press
Introduction copyright © 1997 by Louisiana State University
   Press
Manufactured in the United States of America

Louisiana Paperback Edition, 1997
06  05  04  03  02  01  00  99  98  97    5  4  3  2  1

Library of Congress Cataloging-in-Publication Data

Cooke, John Esten, 1830–1886.
   Wearing of the gray : being personal portraits, scenes,
and adventures of the war / by John Esten Cooke ; with a
new introduction by Emory M. Thomas. — Louisiana
paperback ed.
      p.   cm.
   Originally published : New York : E.B. Treat & Co., 1867.
   Includes index.
   ISBN 0-8071-2216-5 (pbk. : alk. paper)
   1. Cooke, John Esten, 1830–1886.   2. United States—
History—Civil War, 1861–1865—Personal narratives,
Confederate.   3. Confederate States of America—Biography.
I. Title.
E605.C77   1997                                   97-30013
973.7 ' 82—dc21                                        CIP

The paper in this book meets the guidelines for permanence and
durability of the Committee on Production Guidelines for Book
Longevity of the Council on Library Resources. ⊚

The blessed and ever-glorious dead are not here to defend their memories from the taint of the reproach of rebellion and treason. Alas! I am alive and here, and am bound at every hazard to declare that these men were no rebels and no traitors . . . that they were patriots, loyal citizens, well tried and true soldiers, brave, honest, devoted men, who proved their faith in their principles by the deaths which canonized them immortal heroes and martyrs.

HENRY A. WISE

# CONTENTS

ix

Part 5. LATTER DAYS.

PUBLISHER'S NOTE: The index and editorial notes in the text of this edition are by Philip Van Doren Stern and are reprinted with permission of the heirs of Philip Van Doren Stern, © 1959 by Philip Van Doren Stern. The text of the present edition is from the Indiana University Press Civil War Centennial Series edition of 1959 and is reproduced with permission of Indiana University Press.

# Illustrations

All illustrations are reproduced from the original edition of
*Wearing of the Gray.*

# INTRODUCTION

## EMORY M. THOMAS

JOHN ESTEN COOKE served on the staff of his relative, J. E. B. Stuart, and so rode with Confederate cavalry on Stuart's justly famous "Ride Around McClellan." On this protracted reconnaissance in the hamlet of Talleysville during the predawn hours of June 14, 1862, Cooke claims to have consumed "in succession figs, beef-tongue, pickle, candy, tomato catsup, preserves, lemons, cakes, sausages, molasses, crackers, and canned meats." If in fact he did eat all these items—spoils from Federal sutlers— the feat was likely the greatest of Cooke's entire military career. [1]

A warrior Cooke was not. He professed, "I never liked the business of war," and explained, "there is nothing intellectual about fighting. It is fit work for brutes and brutish men. And in modern war, where men are organized in masses and converted into insensate machines, there is really nothing heroic or romantic or in any way calculated to appeal to the imagination." [2]

But such candor was rare in Cooke. However much he found

1. John Esten Cooke, *Wearing of the Gray.* (Bloomington, Ind., 1959), 175. Future references will be indicated in text by page numbers.
2. This statement, made originally to George Cary Eggleston, is in John O. Beaty, *John Esten Cooke, Virginian* (New York, 1922), 109. Beaty's is the only biography of Cooke, whose papers and diary are at the Perkins Library, Duke University. The Virginia Historical Society also has Cooke materials, and portions of Cooke's diary are in print as Jay B. Hubble, ed., "The War Diary of John Esten Cooke," *Journal of Southern History,* VII (1941), 526–40.

it distasteful, once the American Civil War was over Cooke made a modest career of writing about the conflict. He wrote novels, biographies, and articles based on his wartime experience. And dominant in Cooke's prose is romance, gaiety, and gallantry. The war, in Cooke's mind, and in his introduction to *Wearing of the Gray*, "was a mighty drama, all life, passion, movement, incident, and romance—a singular melange, wherein tears, laughter, sighs, and smiles, rapidly followed each other, communicating to the bitter and determined struggle all the profound interest of a tragedy whose scenes sweep on before the spectator to the catastrophe." After the fact, Cooke's comrades, those "brutes and brutish men," became "brave, honorable, courageous, social—quick in resentment, proud, but placable; and these conspicuous traits were everywhere seen in their actions and daily lives"(4–5). Cooke was much more a writer than he was a fighter.

Born November 3, 1830, in Winchester, Virginia, John Esten Cooke was one of many children—thirteen—of whom only five lived to maturity. His mother, Maria Pendleton Cooke, died when John Esten was nineteen; his father, John Rogers Cooke, survived her by several years, dying in debt in 1854. During most of his youth, however, John Esten lived in comfort—on his mother's plantation, Glengary, near Winchester until he was nine; and thereafter in Richmond, where his father was a prominent lawyer and sometime politician.

Educated at private academies and informally trained in law, Cooke never realized his early goal of attending the University of Virginia. He was several times poised to do so, but by then John senior lacked the financial resources to support his son in Charlottesville. Higher education might have made Cooke a much better writer than he became. He might have benefited from the confidence, scholarly rigor, and the discipline university training offered. Then again, he might not. Cooke did suffer from the lack of all these things in his writing, and so he never fully developed his skills. [3]

After a brief, unfulfilling attempt to practice law, Cooke sold a story to *Harper's* in March, 1852, and thereafter committed himself to earning his living with his pen. Though that living was

3. Beaty, *Cooke*, 1–29.

never lavish, his biographer suggests that Cooke likely earned more money than any other southern writer before 1870. Certainly he produced a prodigious volume of work—seven novels between 1854 and 1859, plus numerous stories, poems, and essays. And Cooke published in prestigious places—finding homes for his novels at Harper and Brothers as well as D. Appleton and Company, and other, shorter pieces at the *Southern Literary Messenger, Putnam's,* and *Harper's.* Cooke usually wrote on five-by-eight-inch paper, and during a productive frenzy claimed "repeatly" to have written a hundred (!) such pages per day. Most often, Cooke's first draft was what appeared in print. He did not like to revise his work, and his early success in the marketplace gave Cooke no reason to begin the practice. [4]

Literary critics then and since have lamented Cooke's haste in the transit from pen to print. One of Cooke's best friends, John R. Thompson, wrote in 1856 of *The Last of the Foresters* (Cooke's fourth novel):

> It does not indicate any higher degree of talent, or farther reach of genius, than the very first novel Mr. Cooke ever wrote. He is wonderfully facile with the pen, and with his fun; his pathos, his eye for pictorial effects in the external world, and his quick apprehension of the superficial in character, we believe he could produce just such books every ninety days—books doing him great credit and affording us no small degree of entertainment, but not such as we have reason to believe him capable of writing with greater care and more painful elaboration. Mr. Cooke writes too rapidly and revises too little. By devoting a longer time to the construction of his plots, and by studying the subtler workings of the human heart, he would be able . . . to enrich the literature of his country with works of fiction that would long survive the period that brought them forth. [5]

Over a century later the critical verdict regarding Cooke's work was quite similar: "[Cooke's literary] path, strewn with millions of words, a host of frail heroines and scheming villains, a goodly dose of fortunate coincidence led forth up to the Civil

4. *Ibid.,* 17–29, 40. A bibliography of Cooke's writings is on 164–67.
5. Thompson's review is in *Southern Literary Messenger,* XXIII (No. 2; August, 1856), 158.

War and after to locate Cooke finally in a secure, if minor, position in the realm of Southern Letters." [6]

The general consensus among scholars holds that Cooke's
best work of fiction was his second novel, *The Virginia Come-
dians; or, Old Days in the Old Dominion* (1854). In this as in
his other romantic novels, Cooke elevated the past as a golden
age in contrast to a tawdry present. This theme provoked
George W. Bagby, fellow Richmonder and editor of the *Southern Literary Messenger*, to write, "Mr. Cooke's eyes are not only
in the back of his head, but they are also afflicted with a pair of
rose-colored goggles & enormous magnifying powers." Bagby's
observation about Cooke's fiction was also true to some extent
of his nonfiction, including *Wearing of the Gray.* [7]

From the beginning Cooke embraced the Confederate States
of America and southern independence. Cooke's uncle, Philip St.
George Cooke, the most distinguished professional soldier in the
family at the time (he was a colonel in the U.S. Army), elected
to fight for the Union. Colonel Cooke's son, John Rogers Cooke,
became a brigadier general in the Confederate army, and the
colonel's son-in-law was J. E. B. Stuart. [8]

Writing in the capacity of "Our Virginia Correspondent" for
the Charleston *Courier*, Cooke said of Stuart in the fall of 1861,
"Probably no man in the South is more hated and more feared
by the Yankees." Nor was this the only instance in which Cooke
praised his cousin-in-law in print. Stuart returned these favors
by appointing the novelist to his staff, where Cooke served, off
and on, during much of the war as voluntary aide, ordnance officer, and assistant adjutant general.

Though Cooke had been an enlisted soldier with the Richmond Howitzers throughout 1861, his experience on Stuart's
staff was the basis of most of his memoir material first issued as
articles, then collected in *Wearing of the Gray* and a subsequent

6. Matthew C. O'Brein, " John Esten Cooke, George Washington, and the
Virginia Cavaliers," *Virginia Magazine of History and Biography*, LXXXI (July,
1976), 265.

7. The Bagby quotation appeared in the Richmond *Whig*, August 4, 1858.
Critical studies of Cooke's works include Louis D. Rubin, Jr., ed., *The History of
Southern Literature* (Baton Rouge, 1985) and Jay B. Hubbell, *The South in
American Literature; 1607–1900* (Durham, 1954).

8. Beaty, *Cooke*, 75.

collection of anecdotes, *Hammer and Rapier.* Cooke also published biographies of Stonewall Jackson and Robert E. Lee as well as a history of Virginia. And his military service certainly inspired most of his post-war novels. [9]

Cooke must have been a better soldier than he admitted in his diary. Stuart would not have allowed an incompetent to remain on his staff. Cooke wrote on February 1, 1893, "My philosophy is to give myself as little trouble as possible." His entry in his diary for March 15, 1863, demonstrates Cooke's philosophy in action.

> Wake about 8—find my fire burning . . . dress leisurely, gazing into fire with one boot on, or cravat in hand—an old weakness, this. Finish, and read the Bible. Then say my prayers. Then if breakfast isn't ready, read a novel or paper or anything.
>
> 'Lige [a servant] then rushes in violently with a coffee pot—breakfast follows—of steak and biscuits nearly invariably: a strong cup of coffee—no molasses now—and I commence the real business of the day, and charm of life, smoking and reading something.
>
> This over I go to writing and write away till three or four—or I don't write. I ride out, to Col. Baldwin's, or elsewhere, and come back, and smoke and lounge in the tents till toward dark when dinner is ready—pretty much the same—a little stewed fruit being the sole addition.
>
> After dinner, smoke—chat chat—or read read! Ma vie!— The storm rages and I must smoke!

Of course, the armies were still in winter quarters during this period; but only two days after Cooke's entry quoted above, a portion of Stuart's command fought the Battle of Kelly's Ford. [10]

Cooke dedicated *Wearing of the Gray* to Stuart's "illustrious memory" and claimed in the dedication that he "loved him living and mourns him dead." A certain irony attends Cooke's tribute here and (elsewhere) his unbridled admiration for his com-

---

9. The quotation is from the Charleston *Courier,* September 21, 1861. For more about Cooke as a staff officer, see Robert J. Trout, *They Followed the Plume: The Story of J. E. B. Stuart and His Staff* (Mechanicsburg, Penn., 1993), 89–94.

10. Hubbell, ed., "War Diary," 528–29.

mander. For Stuart, though he surely tried to relate to Cooke, wrote his wife, Flora (Cooke's cousin), "Jno Esten is a case & I'm afraid I can't like him." Stuart considered his aide a colossal bore and assigned him tasks that took him away from headquarters, though some evidence suggests that the general eventually warmed to Cooke. During the winter of 1864 he invited Cooke to rejoin his staff to help write overdue reports. But Stuart and Cooke were about as unlike as men could be—the "Flower of Cavaliers" and his scribe who sought "as little trouble as possible." [11]

It is frustrating that the two soldiers did not have a Boswell and Johnson relationship, and lamentable that such a talented writer imposed so much romantic hindsight upon the war he witnessed alongside some of the greatest commanders in American history. But *Wearing of the Gray* is an important book, despite these limitations. Thompson was right; Cooke was "wonderfully facile with the pen," and he displays his special abilities in this work just as in his fiction. As a consequence, *Wearing of the Gray* remains good reading long after the author's novels have faded to obscurity.

Cooke divided his book into five parts, but really it consists of eleven "Personal Portraits" and then four collections of descriptions and stories drawn from the war. The verbal portraits focus on famous figures—Stuart, Jackson, etc.—and men mostly forgotten: William Farley, Hardeman Stuart, and Jennings Wise. The descriptions and stories vary enormously in quality. "Stuart's 'Ride around McClellan' in June, 1862," "A Deserter," and "Stuart on the Outpost: A Scene at 'Camp Qui Vive,'" to mention only three examples, are fascinating firsthand accounts. "Longbow's Horse," on the other hand, reads like some leftover prose from *Surry of Eagles'-Nest,* the novel Cooke published a year earlier. And some of the anecdotes in *Wearing of the Gray* may have interested veterans when the work was first published, but now these yarns and vignettes seem garrulous at best.

Stuart suffered a mortal wound at Yellow Tavern near Richmond and died in the capital on May 12, 1864. Cooke, however, fought the good fight to the end and left a moving descrip-

11. Emory M. Thomas, *Bold Dragoon: The Life of J. E. B. Stuart* (New York, 1986), 94, 280.

tion of Lee and the Army of Northern Virginia at Appomattox. Legend holds that Cooke buried his silver spurs at the surrender. Whether he actually did is unimportant; Cooke certainly lived out the romantic faith, regardless of whether he acted out this gesture.

After the war Cooke returned to his writing, producing a plethora of memoirs, articles, stories, and novels. He wed Mary Francis Page on September 18, 1867, and she bore three children. The Cookes established themselves at a farm called The Briers near Millwood in the lower (northern) Shenandoah Valley, where John Esten attempted to become a "gentleman farmer." He was much more successful being a gentleman than a farmer, and the family depended upon income from his writing. Mary Francis died in 1878, and Cooke apparently spent lonely times during what should have been his comfortable midlife. He eventually contracted typhoid fever and died at the age of fifty-five on September 27, 1886. His son noted later that the family could take greater pride in Cooke's Christian character than in his reputation as a writer, and he was right. John Esten Cooke was a good and honorable man who wrote books and stories read and enjoyed by his contemporaries. [12]

One final observation needs to be made about *Wearing of the Gray*. During the campaign that culminated the Battle of Gettysburg in the summer of 1863, Stuart's cavalry endured prolonged action and extensive travel. Confederate horsemen fought the Battle of Brandy Station, the largest cavalry battle ever on American soil, on June 9. Very soon thereafter Stuart's troopers spent five days of nearly constant combat in the battles of Aldie, Middleburg, and Upperville (June 17–21). Then at one o'clock on the morning of June 25, Stuart launched his long ride into Pennsylvania. The Confederates captured a huge wagon train and, encumbered by 150 wagons, conducted an extensive foray that ended circuitously at Gettysburg. On July 3, while the rest of the army focused on George Pickett's disastrous infantry charge on Cemetery Ridge, Stuart's men fought desperately in another part of the field. And then the southern cavalry had to escort the defeated Rebels out of Pennsylvania, back across the Potomac River into Virginia. Conventional wisdom heaps upon

12. Beaty, *Cooke*, 139ff. The son's observation is on p. 157.

Stuart considerable blame for the failure of Lee's campaign in Pennsylvania, because Stuart was not available to scout the enemy and keep Lee informed about Federal movement, strength, and location. Most of the men who survived this march with Stuart recalled the campaign as torment. The Confederate troopers rode at least 210 miles in eight days and then fought a major battle. Men slept as they rode, slept next to artillery pieces while the guns fired, and one man fell asleep while he climbed a fence. A regiment containing 713 officers and men in May rode into the July 3 battle with 80 troopers. One historian of the campaign concluded, "To those who participated, Stuart's expedition around the Army of the Potomac was a horrible experience with the nightmarish qualities of a bad dream." [13]

Cooke remembered things a bit differently. His account in *Wearing of the Gray*, "To Gettysburg and Back Again," says nothing of Stuart's lapse in communicating with Lee. Cooke does note that men slept in their saddles, but his memory is very merry. In twenty-five pages Cooke uses the word "gay" eleven times, "gallant" six times, and some variant of the word "laugh" or "laughter" twelve times. He writes of "high glee," of young women who were the "fairest specimens of the gentler sex that eye ever beheld," and soldiers so honorable in the enemy country that "the very necks of chickens went unwrung." Cooke concludes that he prefers to suppress the "hard and brutal business." Instead, "Let me remember rather the gay laugh of Stuart; the voices of Fitz Lee, [Wade] Hampton, and their noble comrades; the fun, the frolic, and the adventure of the long journey, when so much lit up the dark horizon of war" (251).

Especially does Cooke reflect upon the epicurean delights of the Gettysburg campaign. He accounts the "Cherry-Pie Breakfast" that prompted "exclamations of rapture," laments having to abandon his "excellent supper of hot bread, milk, coffee, and eggs fried temptingly with bacon," and lauds the "fair girl" who "insisted upon presenting nine cups of coffee with every delicacy" (232, 238–39, 243). But Cooke never again could equal the gorge he experienced in Talleysville during Stuart's "Ride Around McClellan."

13. See Thomas, *Bold Dragoon*, 232–56, and Robert Krick, *9th Virginia Cavalry* (Lynchburg, Va., 1982), 22. The quotation is from Edwin B. Coddington, *The Gettysburg Campaign: A Study of Command* (New York, 1968), 202.

## PART 1

# PERSONAL PORTRAITS

# INTRODUCTION

THESE "Personal Portraits" were undertaken with the design of making better known and understood the great actors in the recent struggle who are the subjects of them.

It is a matter of grave importance that the illustrious figures of the war should not be obscured by the mists of ignorance or falsehood. Nor can they be. Dulness and slander do not long blind the eyes of men; and sooner or later the light of truth makes all things visible in their natural colours and proportions. To the good work of placing upon record the actual truth in relation to the lives and characters of Stuart and some other noble soldiers of the Southern army, the writer of this page has here brought a few of his recollections—aiming to draw these "worthies" rather as they lived and moved, following their various idiosyncrasies, than as they performed their "official" duties on the public stage. This seemed best calculated to display their real individuality—the embodiment of their personal characteristics in a portrait with the pen, as a painter draws the form and features of his sitter with the brush.

Such personal details of the characters of these eminent men will not be uninteresting to the lovers of noble natures of whatever "faction;" nor is the fondness for such particulars either trivial or ignoble. They elucidate biography and history—which are the same—for they present the likeness of the actor in the drama, his character and endowments; and to know what great men *are*, is better than to know what they *perform*. What Lee, Jackson, Johnston, Stuart, and their associates accomplished, history will record; how they looked, and moved, and spoke, will attract much less attention from the "historian of the future." The august muse of history will make her partial and passionate, or fair and dignified, summary of the events of the late war; will discuss the *causas resum* with learned philosophy; and mete out in rounded periods what she thinks the due amount of glory or shame to the actors, in gray or in blue. But meanwhile the real personages disappear, and the colours fade; figures become historical personages, not men. And events, too, "suffer change." They are fused in the mass; generalization replaces the particular incident as it does the impressive trait;—the terrible dust of "official documents" obscures personages, characters, and events.

This is trite, but it is true; and the fact thus lamely stated is one of the "chiefest spites of fate." For what is the picture worth unless drawn in its actual colours?—what the value of the figures unless they are likenesses? The war just ended was not an "official transaction," only to be calmly narrated with dignified generalization, philosophic reasoning, and commonplace comment upon peace conferences, grand tactics, and the political bearing of the result. It was a mighty drama, all life, passion, movement, incident, and romance—a singular mèlange, wherein tears, laughter, sighs and smiles, rapidly followed each other, communicating to the bitter and determined struggle all the profound interest of a tragedy whose scenes sweep on before the spectator to the catastrophe. Nor were the actors in the tragedy blocks of wood, or merely "official personages" playing coldly their stage parts. They were men of flesh and blood, full of high resolve, vehement passion; subject to hope, fear, rejoicing, depression; but faithful through all to the great principles which drove them on—principles in which they believed, and for which they were ready to die. They were noble types of the great Norman race of which the Southern people come—brave, honourable, courteous, social; quick in resentment, proud, but placable; and these conspicuous traits were everywhere seen in their actions and daily lives.

The portraits here presented of a few of these men may be rude and incomplete, but they are likenesses. No personage is spoken of with whom the writer was not more or less acquainted; and every trait and incident set down was either observed by himself or obtained from good authority. Invention has absolutely nothing to do with the sketches; the writer has recorded his recollections, and not his fancies. The "picturesque" is a poor style of art, when truth is sacrificed to it. To represent General Lee decked out in a splendid uniform bedizzened with gold lace, on a "prancing steed," and followed by a numerous and glittering staff, might "tickle the ears of the groundlings;" but the picture would be apt to "make the judicious grieve." The latter class would much prefer the actual man, in his old gray cape and plain brown coat, riding, unattended, on his sober iron-gray along the lines; would rather hear him say amid the storm of Gettysburg, in his calm brave voice, "Never mind; it is not your fault, General; I am to blame," than read the most eloquent sentences which the imagination could invent for him. And in regard to others, the truth would possess an equal superiority over fiction. Jackson was a noble human soul; pure, generous, fearless, of imperial genius for making war; but why claim for him personal graces, and the charm of social humour? Stuart ranked justly with the two or three greatest cavalry commanders of the world, and in his character combined gaiety, courage, resolution, winning manners, and the purest traits of the gentleman and Christian; but why draw the gallant cavalier as utterly faultless, never moved by anger, ever serious and devout as was Jackson? By such a process the actual characters disappear; the real men, with faults and virtues, grand traits and foibles, become mere lay-figures to hang uniforms upon. The pictures should either be made likenesses, or not be painted; events should be represented in their real colours, or not at all.

These few words will explain the character of the sketches here presented, and the theory upon which the writer has proceeded in drawing them. They are conscientious "studies," and the result of an honest desire to elucidate the characters of their subjects, who are here described in rapid outline as they lived and moved before all eyes upon the stage of the war. Eulogy has not magnified them, as partisan rancour has not blackened their adversaries. They appeared as they are here drawn to the eyes of the writer; if the portraits are unfaithful, it is not because he lacked the fairness, but wanted the ability, to "denote them truly."

# I

## STUART

### I.

STUART, chief of the Confederate cavalry in Virginia, was one of the *Dii Majores* of the recent conflict—his career rather a page from romance than a chapter of history. Everything stirring, brilliant, and picturesque, seemed to centre in him. There was about the man a flavour of chivalry and adventure which made him more like a knight of the middle age than a soldier of the prosaic nineteenth century, and it was less the science than the poetry of war which he summed up and illustrated in his character and career.

With the majority of those who took part in it, the late revolution was a hard and bitter struggle, which they entered upon resolutely, but with unconcealed distaste. To this soldier, however, it seemed to be a splendid and exciting game, in which his blood coursed joyously, and his immensely strong physical organization found an arena for the display of all its faculties. The affluent life of the man craved those perils and hardships which flush the pulses and make the heart beat fast. A single look at him was enough to convince anybody that Stuart loved danger and adventure, and that the clear blue eyes of the soldier, "with a frolic welcome took the thunder and the sunshine." He swung himself into the saddle, at the sound of the bugle, as the hunter springs on horseback; and at such moments his cheeks glowed, and his huge moustache curled with enjoyment. The

7

romance and poetry of the hard trade of arms seemed first to be inaugurated when this joyous cavalier, with his floating plume and splendid laughter, appeared upon the great arena of the war in Virginia.

This gay bearing of the man was plainly unaffected, and few persons could resist its influence. There was about Stuart an inspiration of joy and youth. The war was evidently like play to him—and he accepted its most perilous scenes and cruellest hardships with the careless abandon of a young knight-errant seeking adventures. Nothing seemed strong enough to break down his powerful organization of mind and body; and danger only aroused and brought his full faculties into play. He greeted it with ardour and defied it with his joyous laughter—leading his column in desperate charges with a smile upon the lips. Others might despond, but Stuart kept his good spirits; and while the air around him was full of hissing balls and bursting shell, he would hum his gay songs. In Culpeper the infantry were electrified by the laughter and singing of Stuart as he led them in the charge; and at Chancellorsville, where he commanded Jackson's corps after that great man's fall, the infantry veterans as they swept on, carrying line after line of breastworks at the point of the bayonet, saw his plume floating in front—"like Henry of Navarre's," one of them said—and heard his sonorous voice singing, "Old Joe Hooker, will you come out of the Wilderness!"

This curious spirit of boyish gaiety did not characterize him on certain occasions only, but went with him always, surrounding every movement of the man with a certain atmosphere of frolic and abandon. Immense animal health and strength danced in his eyes, gave elasticity to the motions of his person, and rang in his contagious laughter. It was hard to realize that anything could hurt this powerful machine, or that death could ever come to him; and the perilous positions from which he had so often escaped unharmed, appeared to justify the idea of his invulnerability. Although he exposed his person recklessly in more than a hundred hot engagements, he was never wounded in any. The rosebud in his button-hole, which some child or girl had given him, or rather say his mother's Bible, which he always carried, seemed to protect him. Death appeared to shrink before him and avoid him; and he laughed in the grim face, and dared it for three years of reckless fighting, in which he seemed every day to be trying to get himself killed.

His personal appearance coincided with his character. Everything about the man was youthful, picturesque, and brilliant. Lee, Jackson, and other eminent soldiers of the South, seemed desirous of avoiding, in their dress and accoutrements every species of display, and to aim at making themselves resemble as closely as possible their brave soldiers, whose uniforms were sadly deficient in military gewgaws. Stuart's taste was exactly the opposite. He was as fond of colours as a boy or a girl. His fighting jacket shone with dazzling buttons and was covered with gold braid; his hat was looped up with a golden star, and decorated with a black ostrich plume; his fine buff gauntlets reached to the elbow; around his waist was tied a splendid yellow silk sash, and his spurs were of pure gold. The stern Ironsides of Cromwell would have sneered at this "frivolous boy" as they sneered at Prince Rupert, with his scarlet cloak, his waving plume, his white dog, and his twenty-three years—all the more as Stuart had a white dog for a pet, wore a cape lined with scarlet, had a plume in his hat, and—to complete the comparison—is said to have belonged to that royal family of Stuarts from which Rupert sprang.* Many excellent people did not hesitate to take the Ironside view. They regarded and spoke of Stuart as a trifling military fop—a man who had in some manner obtained a great command for which he was wholly unfit. They sneered at his splendid costume, his careless laughter, his "love of ladies;" at his banjo-player, his flower-wreathed horses, and his gay verses. The enemy were wiser. Buford, Bayard, Pleasanton, Stoneman, and their associates, did not commit that blunder. They had felt the heavy arm too often; and knew too well the weight of that flower-encircled weapon.

There were three other men who could never be persuaded

---

* Prince Rupert was the nephew of Charles I., and the son of Elizabeth Stuart. [J.E.C.]

that Stuart was no cavalry officer, and who persisted in regarding this boyish cavalier as their right-hand man—the "eye and ear" of their armies. These men were Lee, Johnston, and Jackson.

## II.

Stuart's great career can be alluded to but briefly here. Years crammed with incident and adventure cannot be summed up on a page.

He was twenty-seven when he resigned his first-lieutenancy in the United States cavalry, and came to offer his sword to Virginia. He was sprung from an old and honourable family there, and his love of his native soil was strong. Upon his arrival he was made lieutenant-colonel, and placed in command of the cavalry on the Upper Potomac, where he proved himself so vigilant a soldier that Johnston called him "the indefatigable Stuart," and compared him to "a yellow jacket," which was "no sooner brushed off than it lit back." He had command of the whole front until Johnston left the valley, when he moved with the column to Manassas, and charged and broke the New York Zouaves; afterwards held the front toward Alexandria, under Beauregard; then came the hard falling back, the struggle upon the Peninsula, the battle of Cold Harbour, and the advance which followed into Maryland. Stuart was now a general, and laid the foundation of his fame by the "ride around McClellan" on the Chickahominy. Thenceforth he was the right hand of Lee until his death.

The incidents of his career from the spring of 1862 to May, 1864, would fill whole volumes. The ride around McClellan; the fights on the Rapidan; the night march to Catlett's, where he captured General Pope's coat and official papers; the advance to Manassas; the attack on Flint Hill; the hard rear-guard work at South Mountain; holding the left at Sharpsburg; the circuit of McClellan again in Maryland; the bitter conflicts near Upperville as Lee fell back; the fighting all along the slopes of the Blue Ridge; the "crowding 'em with artillery" on the night at

Fredericksburg; the winter march upon Dumfries; the battle of Chancellorsville, where he commanded Jackson's corps; the advance thereafter, and the stubborn conflict at Fleetwood Hill on the 9th of June; the hard, obstinate fighting once more to guard the flanks of Lee on his way to Gettysburg; the march across the Potomac; the advance to within sight of Washington, and the invasion of Pennsylvania, with the determined fights at Hanovertown, Carlisle, and Gettysburg, where he met and drove before him the crack cavalry of the Federal army; the retreat thereafter before an enraged enemy; the continuous combats of the mountain passes, and in the vicinity of Boonsboro'; the obstinate stand he made once more on the old ground around Upperville as Lee again fell back; the heavy *petites guerres* of Culpeper; the repulse of Custer when he attacked Charlottesville; the expedition to the rear of General Meade when he came over to Mine Run; the bitter struggle in the Wilderness when General Grant advanced; the fighting all along the Po in Spotsylvania; the headlong gallop past the South Anna, and the bloody struggle near the Yellow Tavern, where the cavalier, who had passed through a hundred battles untouched, came to his end at last—these are a few of the pictures which rise up before the mind's eye at those words, "the career of Stuart." In the brief space of a sketch like this, it is impossible to attempt any delineation of these crowding scenes and events. They belong to history, and will sooner or later be placed upon record—for a thousand octavos cannot bury them as long as one forefinger and thumb remains to write of them. All that is here designed is a rough cartoon of the actual man—not a fancy figure, the work of a eulogist, but a truthful likeness, however poorly executed.

## III.

I have supposed that the reader would be more interested in Stuart the man than in Stuart the Major-General commanding. History will paint the latter—my page deals with the former chiefly. It is in dress, habits, the tone of the voice, the demeanour in private, that men's characters are read; and I have never seen a man who looked his character more perfectly than Stuart.

He was the cavalier *par excellence*; and everything which he did, or said, was "in character." We know a clergyman sometimes by his moderation, mild address, black coat, and white cravat; a merchant by his quick movements and "business-like" manner; a senator by his gravity; and a poet by his dreamy eye. You saw in the same manner, at a single glance, that Stuart was a cavalry-man—in his dress, voice, walk, manner, everything. All about him was military; and, fine as his costume undoubtedly was, it "looked like work." There was no little fondness, as I have said, for bright colours and holiday display in his appearance; and he loved the parade, the floating banner, the ring of the bugle, "ladies' eyes"—all the glory, splendour, and brilliant colouring of life; but the soldier of hard fibre and hard work was under the gallant. Some day a generation will come who will like to know all about the famous "Jeb Stuart"—let me therefore limn him as he appeared in the years 1862 and 1863.

His frame was low and athletic—close knit and of very great strength and endurance, as you could see at a glance. His countenance was striking and attracted attention—the forehead broad, lofty, and indicating imagination; the nose prominent, and inclining to "Roman," with large and mobile nostrils; the lips covered with a heavy brown moustache, curled upward at the ends; the chin by a huge beard of the same colour, which descended upon the wearer's breast. Such was the rather brigandish appearance of Stuart—but I have omitted to notice the eyes. They were clear, penetrating, and of a brilliant blue. They could be soft or fiery—would fill with laughter or dart flame. Anything more menacing than that flame, when Stuart was hard pressed, it would be difficult to conceive; but the prevailing expression was gay and laughing. He wore a brown felt hat looped up with a star, and ornamented with an ebon feather; a double-breasted jacket always open and buttoned back; gray waistcoat and pantaloons; and boots to the knee, decorated with small spurs, which he wore even in dancing. To proceed with my catalogue of the soldier's accoutrements: on marches he threw over his shoulders his gray cavalry cape, and on the pommel of his saddle was strapped an oil-cloth overall, used as a protection in rain, which, instead of annoying him, seemed to raise his spirits. In the midst of rain-storms, when everybody was riding along grum and cowering beneath the flood pouring down, he would trot on, head up, and singing gaily. His arms were, a light French sabre, balanced by a pistol in a black holster; his covering at night, a red blanket, strapped in an oil-cloth behind the saddle. Such was the "outer man" of Stuart in camp and field. His fondness for bright colours, however, sometimes made him don additional decorations. Among these was a beautiful yellow sash, whose folds he would carefully wrap around his waist, skilfully tying the ends on the left side so that the tassels fell full in view. Over this he would buckle his belt; his heavy boots would be changed for a pair equally high, but of bright patent leather, decorated with gold thread; and then the gallant Jeb Stuart was ready to visit somebody. This love of gay colours was shown in other ways. He never moved on the field without his splendid red battle-flag; and more than once this prominent object, flaunting in the wind, drew the fire of the enemy's artillery on himself and staff. Among flowers, he preferred the large dazzling "Giant of Battles," with its blood-red disk. But he loved all blooms for their brilliance. Lent was not his favourite season. Life in his eyes was best when it was all flowers, bright colours, and carnival.

He was a bold and expert rider, and stopped at nothing. Frequently the headlong speed with which he rode saved him from death or capture—as at Sharpsburg, where he darted close along the front of a Federal regiment which rose and fired on him. The speed of his horse was so great that not a ball struck him. At Hanovertown, in 1863, and on a hundred occasions, he was chased, when almost unattended, by Federal cavalry; but, clearing fence and ravine, escaped. He was a "horse-man" in his knowledge of horses, but had no "passion" for them; preferred animals of medium size, which wheeled, leaped, and moved rapidly; and, mounted upon his "Skylark," "Star of the East," "Lady Margaret," or "Lily of the Valley," he was the picture

of a bold cavalier, prepared to go into a charge, or to take a
gallop by moonlight—ready for a fight or a frolic.

It was out of the saddle, however, that Stuart was most attractive. There he was busy; in his tent, when his work was once
over, he was an *insouciant* as a boy. Never was there a human
being of readier laughter. He dearly loved a joke, and would
have one upon everybody. They were not mild either. He loved
a horse-joke, and a horse-laugh. But the edge of his satire, although keen, was never envenomed. The uproarious humour
of the man took away anything like sarcasm from his wit, and
he liked you to "strike back." What are called "great people"
sometimes break their jests upon lesser personages, with a tacit
understanding that the great personage shall not be jested at in
return. Such deference to his rank was abhorrent to Stuart. He
jested roughly, but you were welcome to handle him as roughly
in return. If you could turn the laugh upon him, you were perfectly welcome so to do, and he never liked you the less for it.
In winter-quarters his tent was a large affair, with a good chimney and fireplace; in the summer, on active service, a mere
breadth of canvas stretched over rails against a tree, and open
at both ends. Or he had no tent, and slept under a tree. The
canvas "fly" only came into requisition when he rested for a
few days from the march. Under this slight shelter, Stuart was
like a king of rangers. On one side was his chair and desk; on
the other, his blankets spread on the ground: at his feet his two
setters, "Nip" and "Tuck," whom he had brought out of Culpeper, on the saddle, as he fell back before the enemy. When
tired of writing, he would throw himself upon his blankets, play
with his pets, laugh at the least provocation, and burst into some
gay song.

He had a strong love for music, and sang, himself, in a clear,
sonorous, and correct voice. His favourites were: "The bugle
sang truce, for the night cloud had lowered;" "The dew is on
the blossom;" "Sweet Evelina," and "Evelyn," among pathetic
songs; but comic ones were equal or greater favourites with
him: "If you get there before I do;" "The old gray horse;"
"Come out of the wilderness," and "If you want to have a good

time, join the cavalry," came from his lips in grand uproarious merriment, the very woods ringing with the strains. This habit of singing had always characterized him. From the days in the valley when he harassed Paterson so, with his omnipresent cavalry, he had fought and sung alternately. Riding at the head of his long column, bent upon some raid, or advancing to attack the enemy, he would make the forest resound with his sonorous songs; and a gentleman who met him one day, thus singing in front of his men, said that the young cavalier was his perfect ideal of a knight of romance. It might almost, indeed, be said that music was his passion, as *Vive la joie!* might have been regarded as his motto. His banjo-player, Sweeny, was the constant inmate of his tent, rode behind him on the march, and went with him to social gatherings. Stuart wrote his most important dispatches and correspondence with the rattle of the gay instrument stunning everybody, and would turn round from his work, burst into a laugh, and join uproariously in Sweeney's chorus. On the march, the banjo was frequently put in requisition; and those "grave people" who are shocked by "frivolity" must have had their breath almost taken away by this extraordinary spectacle of the famous General Stuart, commanding all the cavalry of General Lee's army, moving at the head of his hard-fighting corps with a banjo-player rattling behind him. But Stuart cared little for the "grave people." He fought harder than they did, and chose to amuse himself in his own way. Lee, Johnston, and Jackson, had listened to that banjo without regarding it as frivolous; and more than once it had proved a relaxation after the exhausting cares of command. So it rattled on still, and Stuart continued to laugh, without caring much about "the serious family" class. He had on his side Lee, Jackson, and the young ladies who danced away gaily to Sweeny's music—what mattered it whether Aminadab Sleek, Esq., approved or disapproved!

The "young lady" element was an important one with Stuart. Never have I seen a purer, more knightly, or more charming gallantry than his. He was here, as in all his life, the Christian gentleman, the loyal and consistent professor of religion; but with this delicacy of the chevalier was mingled the gaiety of the boy. He was charmed, and charmed in return. Ladies were his warmest admirers—for they saw that under his laughing exterior was an earnest nature and a warm heart. Everything drew them towards him. The romance of his hard career, the adventurous character of the man, his mirth, wit, gallantry, enthusiasm, and the unconcealed pleasure which he showed in their society, made him their prime favourite. They flocked around him, gave him flowers, and declared that if they could they would follow his feather and fight with him. With all this, Stuart was delighted. He gave them positions on his staff, placed the flowers in his button-hole, kissed the fair hands that presented them, and if the cheek was near the hand, he would laugh and kiss that too. The Sleek family cried out at this, and rolled their eyes in horror—but it is hard to please the Sleek family. Stuart was married, a great public character, had fought in defence of these young ladies upon a hundred battlefields, and was going to die for them. It does not seem so huge an enormity as the Sleeks everywhere called it—that while the blue eyes flashed, the eyes of women should give back their splendour; while the lips were warm, they should not shrink from them. Soon the eyes were to grow dim, and the lips cold.

Stuart was best loved by those who knew him best; and it may here be recorded that his devotion towards his young wife and children attracted the attention of every one. His happiest hours were spent in their society, and he never seemed so well satisfied as when they were in his tent. To lie upon his camp-couch and play with one of his children, appeared to be the summit of felicity with him; and when, during the hard falling back near Upperville, in the fall of 1862, the news came of the death of his little daughter Flora, he seemed almost overcome. Many months afterwards, when speaking of her, the tears gushed to his eyes, and he murmured in a broken voice: "I will never get over it— never!" He seemed rough and hard to those who only saw him now and then; but the persons who lived with him knew his great kindness of heart. Under that careless, jesting, and often curt demeanour, was a good, true heart. The fibre of the man was tough under all strain, and his whole organization was masculine; but he exhibited, sometimes, a softness of feeling which might almost be called tenderness. A marked trait of his character was this: that if he had offended anybody, or wounded their feelings, he could never rest until he had in some way made amends. His temper was irascible at times, and he would utter harsh words; but the flaming eyes soon softened, the arrogant manner disappeared. In ten minutes his arm would probably be upon the shoulder or around the neck of the injured individual, and his voice would become *caressante*. This was almost amusing, and showed his good heart. Like a child, he must "make up" with people he had unintentionally offended; and he never rested until he succeeded. Let it not be understood, however, that this placability of temperament came into play in "official" affairs. There Stuart was as hard as adamant, and nothing moved him. He never forgave opposition to his will, or disobedience of his orders; and though never bearing malice, was a thoroughly good hater. His prejudices were strong; and when once he had made up his mind deliberately, nothing would change him. He was immovable and implacable; and against these offenders he threw the whole weight of his powerful will and his high position, determined to crush them. That, however, was in public and official matters. In all the details of his daily life he was thoroughly lovable, as many persons still living can testify. He was the most approachable of major-generals, and jested with the private soldiers of his command as jovially as though he had been one of themselves. The men were perfectly unconstrained in his presence, and treated him more like the chief huntsman of a hunting party than as a major-general. His staff were greatly attached to him, for he sympathized in all their affairs as warmly as a brother, and was constantly doing them some "good turn." When with them off duty, he dropped every indication of rank, and was as much a boy as the youngest of them—playing marbles, quoits, or snowball, with perfect abandon and enjoyment. Most charming of all in the eyes of those gentlemen was the fact that he would not hesitate to decline invitations to entertainments, on the plainly stated ground

that "his staff were not included"—after which I need give myself no further trouble to explain why he was the most beloved
of generals!

I have spoken of his reckless exposure of his person in battle.
It would convey a better idea of his demeanour under fire to say
that he seemed unaware of the presence of danger. This air of
indifference was unmistakable. When brave men were moving
restlessly, or unconsciously "ducking" to avoid the bullets show-
ering around them, Stuart sat his horse, full front to the fire, with
head up, form unmoved—a statue of unconsciousness. It would
be difficult to conceive of a greater coolness and indifference
than he exhibited. The hiss of balls, striking down men around
him, or cutting off locks of his hair and piercing his clothes, as at
Fredericksburg, did not seem to attract his attention. With shell
bursting right in his face and maddening his horse, he appeared
to be thinking of something else. In other men what is called
"gallantry" is generally seen to be the effect of a strong will; in
Stuart it seemed the result of indifference. A stouter-hearted
cavalier could not be imagined; and if his indifference gave way,
it was generally succeeded by gaiety. Sometimes, however, all
the tiger was aroused in him. His face flushed; his eyes darted
flame; his voice grew hoarse and strident. This occurred in the
hot fight of Fleetwood Hill, in June, 1863, when he was almost
surrounded by the heavy masses of the enemy's cavalry, and
very nearly cut off; and again near Upperville, later in the same
year, when he was driven back, foot by foot, to the Blue Ridge.
Stuart's face was stormy at such moments, and his eyes like "a
devouring fire." His voice was curt, harsh, imperious, admitting
no reply. The veins in his forehead grew black, and the man
looked "dangerous." If an officer failed him at such moments, he
never forgave him; as the man who attracted his attention, or
who volunteered for a forlorn hope, was never forgotten. In his
tenacious memory, Stuart registered everybody; and in his command, his word, bad or good, largely set up or pulled down.

To dwell still for a few moments upon the private and personal
character of the man—he possessed some accomplishments unusual in famous soldiers. He was an excellent writer, and his

general orders were frequently very striking for their point and eloquence. That in which he called on his men after the ride around McClellan to "avenge Latanè!" and that on the death of Major Pelham, his chief of artillery, are good examples. There was something of the Napoleonic fervour in these compositions, and, though dashed off rapidly, they were pointed, correct, and without bombast. His letters, when collected, will be found clear, forcible, and often full of grace, elegance, and wit. He occasionally wrote verses, especially parodies, for which he had a decided turn. Some of these were excellent. His letters, verses, and orders, were the genuine utterances of the man; not laboured or "stiff," but spontaneous, flowing and natural. He had in conversation some humour, but more wit; and of *badinage* it might almost be said he was a master. His repartee was excellent, his address ever gay and buoyant, and in whatever society he was thrown he never seemed to lose that unaffected mirthfulness which charms us more perhaps than all other qualities in an associate. I need scarcely add that this uniform gaiety was never the result of the use of stimulants. Stuart never drank a single drop of any intoxicating liquid in his whole life, except when he touched to his lips the cup of sacramental wine at the communion. He made that promise to his mother in his childhood, and never broke it. "If ever I am wounded," he said to me one day, "don't let them give me any whiskey or brandy." His other habits were as exemplary. I never saw him touch a card, and he never dreamed of uttering an oath under any provocation—nor would he permit it at his quarters. He attended church whenever he could, and sometimes, though not often, had service at his headquarters. One day a thoughtless officer, who did not "know his man," sneered at preachers in his presence, and laughed at some one who had entered the ministry. Stuart's face flushed; he exhibited unmistakable displeasure, and said: "I regard the calling of a clergyman as the noblest in which any human being can engage." This was the frivolous, irreverent, *hard-drinking* personage of some people's fancies—the man who was sneered at as little better than a reprobate by those whom he had punished, and who, therefore, hated and slandered him!

## IV.

Such, in brief outline, was this "Flower of Cavaliers," as he moved in private, before the eyes of friends, and lived his life of gentleman. An estimate of the military and intellectual calibre of the man remains to be made—a rapid delineation of those traits of brain and nerve combined which made him the first cavalry officer of his epoch—I had nearly written of any epoch.

Out of his peculiar sphere he did not display marked ability. His mind was naturally shrewd, and, except in some marked instances, he appeared to possess an instinctive knowledge of men. But the processes of his brain, on ordinary occasions, exhibited rather activity and force than profoundness of insight. His mental organization seemed to be sound and practical rather than deep and comprehensive. He read little when I knew him, and betrayed no evidences of wide culture. His education was that of the gentleman rather than the scholar. "Napoleon's Maxims," a translation of Jomini's Treatise on War, and one or two similar works, were all in which he appeared to take pleasure. His whole genius evidently lay in the direction of his profession, and even here many persons doubted the versatility of his faculties. It will remain an interesting problem whether he would have made a great infantry commander. He was confident of his own ability; always resented the *dictum* that he was a mere "cavalry officer;" and I believe, at one time, it was the purpose of the Confederate authorities to place him in command of a corps of infantry. Upon the question of his capacity, in this sphere, there will probably be many opinions. At Chancellorsville, when he succeeded Jackson, the troops, although quite enthusiastic about him, complained that he had led them too recklessly against artillery; and it is hard for those who knew the man to believe that, as an army commander, he would ever have consented to a strictly defensive campaign. Fighting was a necessity of his blood, and the slow movements of infantry did not suit his genius. With an army under him, it is probable that he would either have achieved magnificent successes or sustained overwhelming defeats. I confess I thought him equal to anything in his profession, but competent judges doubted it. What every one agreed about, however, was his supreme genius for fighting cavalry.

He always seemed to me to be intended by nature for this branch of the service. Some men are born to write great works, others to paint great pictures, others to rule over nations. Stuart was born to fight cavalry. It was only necessary to be with him in important movements or on critical occasions, to realize this. His instinct was unfailing, his *coup d'œil* that of the master. He was a trained soldier, and had truly graduated at West Point, but it looked like instinct rather than calculation—that rapid and unerring glance which took in at once every trait of the ground upon which he was operating, and anticipated every movement of his adversary. I never knew him to blunder. His glance was as quick, and reached its mark as surely as the lightning. Action followed like the thunder. In moments of great emergency it was wonderful to see how promptly he swept the whole field, and how quickly his mind was made up. He seemed to penetrate, as by a species of intuition, every design of his opponent, and his dispositions for attack or defence were those of a mastermind. Sometimes nothing but his unconquerable resolution, and a sort of desperation, saved him from destruction; but in almost every critical position which he was placed in during that long and arduous career, it was his wonderful acumen, no less than his unshrinking nerve, which brought him out victorious.

This nerve had in it something splendid and chivalric. It never failed him for a moment on occasions which would have paralysed ordinary commanders. An instance was given in October, 1863. Near Auburn his column was surrounded by the whole of General Meade's army, then retiring before General Lee. Stuart massed his command, kept cool, listened hour after hour as the night passed on, to the roll of the Federal artillery and the heavy tramp of their infantry within a few hundred yards of him, and at daylight placed his own guns in position and made a furious attack, under cover of which he safely withdrew. An earlier instance was his raid in rear of General Mc-

Clellan, in June, 1862, when, on reaching the lower Chickahominy, he found the stream swollen and unfordable, while at
every moment an enraged enemy threatened to fall upon his rear
with an overpowering force of infantry, cavalry, and artillery.
Although the men were much disheartened, and were gloomy
enough at the certain fate which seemed to await them, Stuart
remained cool and unmoved. He intended, he said afterwards,
to "die game" if attacked, but he believed he could extricate his
command. In four hours he had built a bridge, singing as he
worked with the men; and his column, with the guns, defiled
across just as the enemy rushed on them. A third instance was
the second ride around McClellan in Maryland, October, 1862;
when coming to the Monocacy he found General Pleasanton,
with a heavy force of cavalry, infantry, and artillery, in his path,
but unhesitatingly attacked and cut his way through. Still another at Jack's Shop, where he charged both ways—the column
in front, and that sent to cut him off—and broke through. Still
another at Fleetwood Hill, where he was attacked in front, flank,
and rear, by nearly 17,000 infantry and cavalry, but charging
from the centre outwards, swept them back, and drove them
beyond the Rappahannock.

Upon these occasions and twenty others, nothing but his stout
nerve saved him from destruction. This quality, however, would
not have served him without the quick military instinct of the
born soldier. His great merit as a commander was, that his conception of "the situation" was as rapid and just as his nerve was
steady. His execution was unfaltering, but the brain had devised
clearly what was to be done before the arm was raised to strike.
It was this which distinguished Stuart from others—the promptness and accuracy of his brain work "under pressure," and at
moments when delay was destruction. The faculty would have
achieved great results in any department of arms; but in cavalry,
the most "sudden and dangerous" branch of the service, where
everything is decided in a moment as it were, it made Stuart
one of the first soldiers of his epoch. With equal—or not largely
unequal—forces opposed to him, he was never whipped. More
than once he was driven back, and two or three times "badly

hurt;" but it was not the superior genius of Buford, Stoneman, Pleasanton, or other adversaries, which achieved those results. It was the presence of an obstacle which his weapon could not break. Numbers were too much for brain and acumen, and reckless fighting. The hammer was shattered by the anvil.

## V.

Stuart was forced, by the necessities of the struggle, the nature of the country, and the all-work he had to perform, to depend much upon sharp-shooting. But he preferred pure cavalry fighting. He fought his dismounted skirmishers with obstinacy, and was ever present with them, riding along the line, a conspicuous target for the enemy's bullets, cheering them on. But it was in the legitimate sphere of cavalry that he was greatest. The skirmishing was the "hard work." He had thus to keep a dangerous enemy off General Lee's flanks as the infantry moved through the gaps of the Blue Ridge towards Pennsylvania, or to defend the line of the Rappahannock, when some Federal commander with thousands of horsemen, "came down like a wolf" on General Lee's little "fold." It was here, I think, that Stuart vindicated his capacity to fight infantry, for such were the dismounted cavalry; and he held his ground before swarming enemies with a nerve and persistence which resembled Jackson's.

It was in the raid, the flank movement, the charge, and the falling back, with cavalry proper, however, that he exhibited the most conspicuous traits of the soldier. The foundation of his successes here was a wonderful energy. The man was a war-machine which never flagged. Day or night he was ready to mount at the sound of the bugle. Other commanders, like the *bonus Homerus*, drowsed at times, and nodded, suffering their zeal to droop; but Stuart was sleepless, and General Lee could count on him at any instant. To that inexhaustible physical strength was united a mentality as untiring. The mind, like the body, could "go day and night," and needed no rest. When all around him were broken down, Stuart still remained fresh and unwearied; ready for council or for action; to give his views and suggest important movements, or to march and make an attack. His organization was of the "hair-trigger" kind, and the well-tempered spring never lost its elasticity. He would give orders, and very judicious ones, in his sleep—as on the night of the second Manassas. When utterly prostrated by whole days and nights spent in the saddle, he would stop by the roadside, lie down without pickets or videttes, even in an enemy's country— as once he did coming from Carlisle, Pennsylvania, in July, 1863—sleep for an hour, wrapped in his cape and resting against the trunk of a tree, and then mount again, as fresh apparently, as if he had slumbered from sunset to dawn.

As his physical energies thus never seemed to droop, or sprang with a rebound from the weight on them, so he never desponded. A stouter heart in the darkest hour I have never seen. No clouds could depress him or disarm his courage. He met ill-fortune with a smile, and drove it before him with his gallant laughter. Gloom could not live in his presence, and the whole race of "croakers" were shamed into hopefulness by his inspiring words and demeanour. Defeat and disaster seemed to make him stronger and more resolute, and he rose under pressure. In moments of the most imminent peril to the very existence of his command, I have seen him drum carelessly with his fingers on the knee thrown over the pommel of his saddle, reflect for an instant without any trace of excitement, and then give the order to cut a path through the enemy, without the change of a muscle. At such moments, it was plain that Stuart coolly made up his mind to do his best, and leave the rest to the chances of arms. His manner said as plainly as any word: "I am going to make my way out or die—the thing is decided upon—why make a to-do about it?" So perfect was his equanimity upon such occasions, that persons ignorant of the extent of the peril could not realize that any existed. It was hard to believe, in presence of this "heart of oak," with his cool and indifferent manner, his composed tones and careless smile, that death or capture stared the command in the face. And yet these were just the occasions when Stuart's face of bronze was most unmoved. Peril brought out his strength. The heaviest clouds must obscure the landscape before his splendid buoyancy and "heart of hope" were fully revealed. That stout heart seemed invincible, and impending ruin could not shake it. I have seen him strung, aroused, his eye flaming, his voice hoarse with the mingled joy and passion of battle; but have never seen him flurried or cast down, much less paralysed by a disaster. When not rejoicing like the hunter on the traces of the game, he was cool, resolute, and determined, evidently "to do or die." The *mens æqua in arduis* shone in the piercing blue eye, and his undaunted bearing betrayed a soul which did not mean to yield—which might be crushed and shattered, but would not bend. When pushed hard and hunted down by a swarm of foes, as he was more than once, Stuart presented a splendid spectacle. He met the assault like an athlete of the Roman amphitheatre, and fought with the ferocity of a tiger. He looked "dangerous" at such moments; and those adversaries who knew him best, advanced upon their great opponent thus standing at bay, with a caution which was born of experience.

These observations apply with especial justice to the various occasions when Stuart held with his cavalry cordon the country north of the Rappahannock and east of the Blue Ridge, while General Lee either advanced or retired through the gaps of the mountains. The work which he did here will remain among his most important services. He is best known to the world by his famous "raids," as they were erroneously called, by his circuits of McClellan's army in Virginia and in Maryland, and other movements of a similar character. This, however, was not his great work. He will live in history as the commander of Lee's cavalry, and for the great part he played in that leader's most important movements. What Lee designed when he moved Northward, or fell back from the valley, it was a matter of the utmost interest to the enemy to know, and persistent efforts were made by them to strike the Confederate flank and discover. Stuart was, however, in the way with his cavalry. The road to the Blue Ridge was obstructed; and somewhere near Middleburg, Upperville, or Paris, the advancing column would find the wary cavalier. Then took place an obstinate, often desperate struggle—on Stuart's part to hold his ground; on the enemy's part to break through the cordon. Crack troops—infantry, cavalry, and artillery—were sent upon this important work, and the most determined officers of the United States Army commanded them.

Then came the tug of war. Stuart must meet whatever force was brought against him, infantry as well as cavalry, and match himself with the best brains of the Federal army in command of them. It was often "diamond cut diamond." In the fields around Upperville, and everywhere along the road to Ashby's Gap, raged a war of giants. The infantry on both sides heard the distant roar of the artillery crowning every hill, and thought the cavalry was skirmishing a little. The guns were only the signal of a hand-to-hand struggle. Desperate charges were made upon them; sabres clashed, carbines banged; in one great hurly-burly of rushing horses, ringing sabres, cracking pistols, and shouts which deafened, the opposing columns clashed together. If Stuart broke them, he pressed them hotly, and never rested until he swept them back for miles. If they broke Stuart, he fell back with the obstinate ferocity of a bull-dog; fought with his sharpshooters in every field, with his Horse Artillery upon every knoll; and if they "crowded him" too closely he took command of his column, and went at them with the sabre, resolved to repulse them or die. It was upon this great theatre that he displayed all his splendid faculties of nerve, judgment, dash, and obstinacy—his quickness of conception, rapidity of decision, and that fire of onset before which few opponents could stand. The infantry did not know much about these hot engagements, and cherished the flattering view that they did all the fighting. General Lee, however, knew accurately what was done, and what was not done. In Spotsylvania, after Stuart's fall, he exclaimed: "If Stuart only were here! I can scarcely think of him without weeping."

The great cavalier had protected the Southern flanks upon a hundred movements; guarded the wings upon many battle-fields, penetrated the enemy's designs, and given General Lee information in every campaign; and now when the tireless brain was still, and the piercing eyes were dim, the country began to comprehend the full extent of the calamity at Yellow Tavern, in May, 1864, and to realize the irreparable loss sustained by the cause when this bulwark fell.

## VI.

I have noticed Stuart's stubbornness, nerve, and coolness. His dash and impetuosity in the charge have scarcely been alluded to, and yet it was these characteristics of the man which chiefly impressed the public mind. On a former page he has been compared to Rupert, the darling of love and war, who was never so well satisfied as when dashing against the Roundhead pikes and riding down his foes. Stuart seems to have inherited that trait of the family blood—for it seems tolerably well established that he and Rupert were descended from the same stock, and scions of that family which has given to the world men of brain and courage, as well as *faineans* and libertines. To notice briefly this not uninteresting point, the "family likeness" in the traits of Stuart and Prince Rupert is very curious. Both were utterly devoted to a principle which was their life-blood—in Rupert it was the love of royalty, in Stuart the love of Virginia. Both were men of the most impetuous temper, chafing at opposition, and ready at any instant to match themselves against their adversaries, and conquer or die. Both were devoted to the "love of ladies," gallant to the echo; of a proud and splendid loyalty to their word; of unshrinking courage; kind and compassionate in temper, gay and smiling in address; fonder of fighting than of looking to the commissariat; adored by their men, who approached them without fear of a repulse; cavalry-men in every drop of their blood; fond of brilliant colours, splendid pageants, the notes of the bugle, the glitter of arms: Rupert with his snowy plume, Stuart with his black one;—both throwing over their shoulders capes of dazzling scarlet, unworn by men who are not attached to gay colours; both taking a white dog for a pet; both proud, gay, unswerving, indomitable, disdainful of low things, passionately devoted to glory; both men in brain and character

at an age when others are mere boys; both famous before thirty—
and for ever—such were the points of resemblance between these
two men. Those familiar with the character of the greatest cavalry-man of the English struggle, and with the traits of Stuart,
the most renowned of the recent conflict, will not fail to see the
likeness.

But I pass to "Stuart in the charge." Here the man was superb.
It was in attack, after all, that his strongest faculties were exhibited. Indeed, the whole genius and temperament of the Virginian were for advancing, not retreating. He could fall back
stubbornly, as has been shown; and he certainly did so in a masterly manner, disputing every inch of ground with his adversary,
and giving way to an enemy's advance under bloody protest. At
these times he displayed the obstinate temper of the old Ironsides
of Cromwell, when they retired in serried ranks, ready to turn
as they slowly retreated, and draw blood with their iron claws.
But when advancing upon an adversary—more than all in the
impetuous charge—Stuart as no longer the Roundhead; he was
the Cavalier. Cavalier he was by birth and breeding and temperament; and he sprang to meet an enemy, as Rupert drove forward
in the hot struggle of the past in England. You could see, then,
that Stuart was in his element. Once having formed his column
for the charge, and given his ringing order to "Form in fours!
draw sabre!" it was neck or nothing. When he thus "came to
the sabre," there was no such word as fail with him. Once in
motion to hurl his column against his adversary, he seemed to
act upon the Scriptural precept to forget those things which
were behind, and press on to those which were before. That
was the enemy in front; and to ride over, and cut right and left
among them, was the work before him. At such moments there
was something grand in the magnificent fire and rush of the
soldier. He seemed strong enough to ride down a world. Only a
glance was needed to tell you that this man had made up his
mind to break through and trample under foot what opposed
him, or "die trying." His men knew this; and, when he took
personal command of the column, as he most often did, prepared
for tough work. His occasional roughness of address to both

officers and men had made him bitter enemies, but the admiration which he aroused was unbounded. The men were often heard to say, in critical places: "There goes old Jeb to the front, boys; it's all right." And an officer whom he had offended, and who hated him bitterly, declared with an oath that he was the greatest cavalry commander that had ever lived. The reported words of General Sedgwick, of the United States Army, may be added here: "Stuart is the greatest cavalry officer ever *foaled* in North America."

The impetuosity here noted was undoubtedly one of the most striking traits of the man. In a charge, Stuart seemed on fire, and was more the Chief of Squadron than the Corps Commander. He estimated justly his own value as a fighting man, when he said one day: "My proper place would be major of artillery;" and it is certain that in command of a battalion of fieldpieces, he would have fought until the enemy were at the very muzzles of his guns. But in the cavalry he had even a better field for his love of close fighting. To come to the sabre best suited his fiery organization, and he did come to it, personally, on many occasions. He preferred saying, "Come on" to "Go on." The men declared that he was reckless, but no one could say that he had ever sent his column where he was not ready to go himself. If he made a headlong and determined attack upon an overpowering force—a thing common with him—he was in front himself, or fighting among the men. He never seemed to feel, as far as my observation went, that his life was any more valuable than that of the humblest private soldier. After one of these occasions of reckless exposure of himself, I said to him: "General, you ought not to put yourself in the way of the bullets so; some day you will be killed." He sighed and replied: "Oh, I reckon not; but if I am, they will easily find somebody to fill my place." He had evidently determined to spend and be spent in the Southern struggle, which had aroused his most passionate sympathies. This love of native land came to add a magnificent fervour to the natural combativeness of the man. As a "free lance," Stuart would have been careless of his person; but in the Southern struggle he was utterly reckless.

This indifference to danger was evidently a trait of blood, and wholly unaffected. Nor, for a long time, did his incessant exposure of himself bring him so much as a scratch. On all the great battle-fields of Virginia, Maryland, and Pennsylvania, as well as in the close and bitter conflicts of his cavalry at Fleetwood, Auburn, Upperville, Middleburg, South Mountain, Monocacy, Williamsport, Shepherdstown, Paris, Barbee's, Jeffersonton, Culpeper Court-House, Brandy, Kelly's Ford, Spotsylvania—in these, and a hundred other hotly-contested actions, he was in the very thickest of the fight, cheering on the sharpshooters, directing his artillery, or leading his column in the charge, but was never hurt. Horses were shot under him, bullets struck his equipments, pierced his clothes, or cut off curls of his hair, as at Fredericksburg, but none ever wounded him. In the closest *mêlée* of clashing sabres the plume of Stuart was unscathed; no sword's edge ever touched him. He seemed to possess a charmed life, and to be invulnerable, like Achilles. Shell, canister, and round-shot tore their way through the ranks around him, overthrowing men and horses—many a brave fellow at his side fell, pierced by the hissing bullets of Federal carbines—but Stuart, like Rupert, never received a wound. The ball which struck and laid him low at the Yellow Tavern on that black day of May, 1864, was the first which touched him in the war. In a hundred battles they had passed to the left and right of him, sparing him.

## VII.

The foregoing presents as accurate an outline of Stuart as the present writer, after a close association with him for two or three years, could draw. No trait is feigned or fanciful, and the picture is not exaggerated, though it may seem so to some. The organization of this man was exceptional and very remarkable. The picture seems a fancy piece, perhaps, but it is the actual portrait. The gaiety, nerve, courage, dash, and stubborn resolution of that man were as great as here described. These were the actual traits which made him fill so great a space in the public eye; and as what he effected was not "done in a corner," so what he was became plain to all.

He was hated bitterly by some who had felt the weight of his hot displeasure at their shortcomings, and some of these people tried to traduce and slander him. They said he was idle and negligent of his duties—he, the hardest worker and most wary commander I ever saw. They said, in whispers behind his back—in that tone which has been described as "giggle-gabble"—that he thought more of dancing, laughing, and trifling with young ladies than of his military work, when those things were only the relaxations of the man after toil. They said that ladies could wheedle and cajole him—when he arrested hundreds, remained inexorable to their petitions, and meted out to the "fairest eyes that ever have shone" the strictest military justice. They said that he had wreaths of flowers around his horse, and was "frolicking" with his staff at Culpeper Court-House, so that his headquarters on Fleetwood Hill were surprised and captured in June, 1863, when he had not been at the Court-House for days; sent off every trace of his headquarters at dawn, six hours before the enemy advanced; and was ready for them at every point, and drove them back with heavy loss beyond the river. In like manner the Sleeks sneered at his banjo, sneered at his gay laughter, sneered at his plume, his bright colours, and his merry songs. The same good friends invented stories of rebukes he had incurred from General Lee, when he uniformly received from that great friend and commander the highest evidences of regard and confidence. These winged arrows, shot in secret by the hand of calumny, which in plain Saxon are called lies, accompanied Stuart everywhere at one period of his career; but the Southern people could not be brought to believe them. They flushed the face of the proud and honest cavalier, sometimes, and made the blue eyes flash; but what could he do? The calumnies were nameless; their authors slunk into shadow, and shrank from him. So he ended by laughing at them, as the country did, and going on his way unmindful of them. He answered slander by brave action—calumny by harder work, more reckless exposure of himself, and by grander achievements. Those secret enemies might originate the falsehoods aimed at him from their safe refuge in some newspaper office, or behind some other "bomb-proof" shelter—*he* would *fight*. That was his reply to them, and the scorn extinguished them. The honest gentleman and great soldier was slandered, and he lived down the slander—fighting it with his sword and his irreproachable life, not with his tongue.

When death came to him in the bloom of manhood, and the flush of a fame which will remain one of the supremest glories of Virginia, Stuart ranked with the *preux chevalier* Bayard, the knight "without reproach or fear."

The brief and splendid career in which he won his great renown, and that name of the "Flower of Cavaliers," has scarcely been touched on in this rapid sketch. The arduous work which made him so illustrious has not been described—I have been able to give only an outline of the man. That picture may be rude and hasty, but it is a likeness. This was Stuart. The reader must have formed some idea of him, hasty and brief as the delineation has necessarily been. I have tried to draw him as the determined leader, full of fire and force; the stubborn fighter; the impetuous cavalier in the charge; the, at times, hasty and arrogant, but warm-hearted friend; the devoted Christian, husband, and father; the gayest of companions; full of fun, frolic, laughter, courage, hope, buoyancy, and a certain youthful joyousness which made his presence like the sunshine. Upon this last trait I have dwelt much—the youth, and joy, and hope, which shone in his brilliant eyes and rang in his sonorous laughter. He passed before you like an incarnate spring, all mirth and sunshine; but behind was the lightning. In those eyes as fresh and blue as the May morning, lurked the storm and the thunderbolt. Beneath the flowers was the hard steel battle-axe. With that weapon he struck like Cœur de Lion, and few adversaries stood before it. The joy, romance, and splendour of the early years of chivalry flamed in his regard, and his brave blood drove him on to combat. In the lists, at Camelot, he would have charged "before the eyes of ladies and of kings," like Arthur; on the arena of the war in Virginia he followed his instincts. Bright eyes were ever upon the daring cavalier there, and his floating plume was like Henry of Navarre's to many stout horsemen who looked to him as their chosen leader; but, better still, the eyes of Lee and Jackson were fixed on him with fullest confidence. Jackson said, when his wound disabled him at Chancellorsville, and Stuart succeeded him: "Go back to General Stuart and tell him to act upon his own judgment, and do what he thinks best—I have implicit confidence in him." In Spotsylvania, as we have seen, General Lee "could scarcely think of him without weeping." The implicit confidence of Jackson, and the tears of Lee, are enough to fill the measure of one man's life and fame.

Such was Stuart—such the figure which moved before the eyes of the Southern people for those three years of glorious encounters, and then fell like some "monarch of the woods," which makes the whole forest resound as it crashes down. Other noble forms there were; but that "heart of oak" of the stern, hard fibre, the stubborn grain, even where it lies is mightiest. Even dead and crumbled into dust, the form of Stuart still fills the eye, and the tallest dwindle by his side—he seems so great.

# II

## JACKSON

### I.

AT FIVE in the evening, on the 27th of June, 1862, General Stonewall Jackson made his appearance on the field of Cold Harbour. Fresh from the hot conflicts of the Valley—an athlete covered with the dust and smoke of the arena—he came now with his veteran battalions to enter upon the still more desperate conflicts of the lowland.

At that time many persons asked, "Who is Jackson?" All we then knew of the famous leader was this—that he was born a poor boy beyond the Alleghanies; managed to get to West Point; embarked in the Mexican war as lieutenant of artillery, where he fought his guns with such obstinacy that his name soon became renowned; and then, retiring from active service, became a Professor at the Lexington Military School. Here the world knew him only as an eccentric but deeply pious man, and a somewhat commonplace lecturer. Stiff and rigid in his pew at church, striding awkwardly from his study to his lecture-room, ever serious, thoughtful, absent-minded in appearance—such was the figure of the future Lieutenant-General, the estimate of whose faculties by the gay young students may be imagined from their nickname for him, "Fool Tom Jackson."

In April, 1861, Fool Tom Jackson became Colonel of Virginia volunteers, and went to Harper's Ferry, soon afterwards fighting General Patterson at Falling Water, thence descending to

34

Manassas. Here the small force—2,611 muskets—of Brigadier-General Jackson saved the day. Without them the Federal column would have flanked and routed Beauregard. Bee, forced back, shattered and overwhelmed, galloped up to Jackson and groaned out, "General, they are beating us back!" Jackson's set face did not move. "Sir," he said, "we will give them the bayonet." Without those 2,611 muskets that morning, good-by to Beauregard! In the next year came the Valley campaign; the desperate and most remarkable fight at Kernstown; the defeat and retreat of Banks from Strasburg and Winchester; the retreat, in turn, of his great opponent, timed with such mathematical accuracy, that at Strasburg he strikes with his right hand and his left the columns of Fremont and Shields, closing in from east and west to destroy him—strikes them and passes through, continuing his retreat up the Valley. Then comes the last scene—*finis coronat*. At Port Republic his adversaries strike at him in two columns. He throws himself against Fremont at Cross Keys and checks his advance; then attacks Shields beyond the river, and after one of the hottest battles of the war, fought nearly man to man, defeats him. Troops never fought better than the Federals there, but they were defeated; and Jackson, by forced marches, hastened to fall upon McClellan's right wing on the Chickahominy.

These events had, in June, 1862, attracted all eyes to Jackson. People began to associate his name with the idea of unvarying success, and to regard him as the incarnate genius of victory. War seemed in his person to have become a splendid pageant of unceasing triumph; and from the smoke of so many battle-fields rose before the imaginative public eye, the figure of a splendid soldier on his prancing steed, with his fluttering banner, preceded by bugles, and advancing in all the pride, pomp, and circumstance of glorious war. The actual man was somewhat different; and in this sketch I shall try to draw his outline as he really looked. In doing so, an apparent egotism will be necessary; but this may be pardoned as inseparable from the subject. What men see is more interesting than what they think, often; what the writer saw of this great man will here be recorded.

It was late in the afternoon of this memorable day, and A. P. Hill had just been repulsed with heavy slaughter from General McClellan's admirable works near New Cold Harbour, when the writer of this was sent by General Stuart to ascertain if Jackson's corps had gone in, and what were his dispositions for battle. A group near a log cabin, twenty paces from Old Cold Harbour House, was pointed out to me; and going there, I asked for the General. Some one pointed to a figure seated on a log —dingy, bending over, and writing on his knees. A faded, yellow cap of the cadet pattern was drawn over his eyes; his fingers, holding a pencil, trembled. His voice, in addressing me, was brief, curt, but not uncourteous; and then, his dispatch having been sent, he mounted and rode slowly alone across the field. A more curious figure I never saw. He sat his rawboned sorrel —not the "old sorrel," however—like an automaton. Knees drawn up, body leaning forward; the whole figure stiff, angular, unbending. His coat was the dingiest of the dingy; originally gray, it seemed to have brought away some of the dust and dirt of every region in which he had bivouacked. His faded cap was pulled down so low upon the forehead that he was compelled to raise his chin into the air to look from beneath the rim. Under that rim flashed two keen and piercing eyes—dark, with a strange brilliancy, and full of "fight." The nose was prominent; the moustache heavy upon the firm lip, close set beneath; the rough, brown beard did not conceal the heavy fighting jaw. All but the eye was in apparent repose; there was no longer any tremor of anxiety. The soldier seemed to have made all his arrangements, "done his best," and he evidently awaited the result with entire coolness. There was even something absent and abstracted in his manner, as he rode slowly to and fro, sucking a lemon, and looking keenly at you when you spoke, answering briefly when necessary.

Twice more I saw him that day—first in the evening, in the midst of a furious shelling, riding slowly with General Stuart among his guns; his face lit up by the burning brushwood—a face perfectly calm and unmoved. And again at midnight, when, as I slept in a fence corner, I felt a hand upon my shoulder, and a voice said, "Where is the General?" It was Jackson, riding about by himself; and he tied his horse, lay down beside General Stuart, and began with, "Well, yesterday's was *the most terrific* fire of musketry I ever heard!" Words of unwonted animation coming from Jackson—that most matter-of-fact of speakers, and expressing much.*

From this time, Jackson became the idol of his troops and the country. Wherever he moved among the camps he was met by cheers; and so unvarying was this reception of him, that a distant yell would often draw from his men the exclamation, "That's Jackson or a rabbit!" the sight of the soldier or the appearance of a hare being alone adequate to arouse this tremendous excitement. From the day of Cold Harbour, success continued to crown him—at Cedar Mountain, the second Manassas, Harper's Ferry, Sharpsburg, where he met the full weight of McClellan's right wing under Hooker, and repulsed it, and Chancellorsville. When he died, struck down by the hands of his own men, he was the most famous and the most beloved of Southern commanders.

## II.

His popularity was great in degree, but more singular in character. No general was ever so beloved by the good and pious of the land. Old ladies received him wherever he went with a species of enthusiasm, and I think he preferred their society and that of clergymen to any other. In such society his kindly nature seemed to expand, and his countenance was charming. He would talk for hours upon religious subjects, never weary, it seemed, of such discourse, and at such moments his smile had the sweetness and simplicity of childhood. The hard intellect was resting, and the heart of the soldier spoke in this congenial converse upon themes more dear to him than all others. I have seen him look serene and perfectly happy, conversing with a venerable lady

* Jackson's remark about "*the most terrific* fire of musketry I ever heard" evidently made a great impression on Cooke, for his original notes on the incident are very detailed.—ED.

upon their relative religious experiences. Children were also great favourites with him, and he seldom failed to make them love him. When at his headquarters below Fredericksburg, in 1863, he received a splendid new cap, gorgeous with a broad band of dazzling gold braid, which was greatly admired by a child one day in his quarters. Thereupon Jackson drew her between his knees, ripped off the braid, and binding it around her curls, sent her away delighted. With maidens of more advanced age, however, the somewhat shy General was less at his ease. At "Hayfield," near the same headquarters, and about the same time, the hospitable family were one day visited by Generals Lee, Jackson, and Stuart, when a little damsel of fourteen confided to her friend General Lee her strong desire to kiss General Jackson. General Lee, always fond of pleasantry, at once informed Jackson of the young lady's desire, and the great soldier's face was covered with blushes and confusion. An amusing picture, too, is drawn of the General when he fell into the hands of the ladies of Martinsburg, and they cut off almost every button of his coat as souvenirs. The beleaguered hero would have preferred storming a line of intrenchments.

Jackson had little humour. He was not sour or gloomy, nor did he look grimly upon "fun" as something which a good Presbyterian should avoid. He was perfectly cheerful, liberal and rational in this as in everything; but he had *no ear* for humour, as some persons have none for music. A joke was a mysterious affair to him. Only when so very "broad" and staring, that he who ran might read it, did humour of any sort strike Jackson. Even his thick coating of matter-of-fact was occasionally pierced, however. At Port Republic a soldier said to his companion: "I wish these Yankees were in hell," whereupon the other replied: "I don't; for if they were, old Jack would be within half a mile of them, with the Stonewall Brigade in front!" When this was told to Jackson, he is said to have burst out into hearty laughter, most unusual of sounds upon the lips of the serious soldier. But such enjoyment of fun was rare with him. I was never more struck with this than one day at Fredericksburg, at General Stuart's headquarters. There was an indifferent brochure published in those days, styled "Abram, a Poem," in the comic preface to which, Jackson was presented in a most ludicrous light, seated on a stump at Oxhill and gnawing at a roasting ear, while a whole North Carolina brigade behind him in line of battle was doing likewise. General Stuart read it with bursts of laughter to his friend, and Jackson also laughed with perfect good-humour; but no sooner had the book been closed than he seemed to forget its existence, and said with an irresistibly matter-of-fact expression which made this writer retire to indulge his own laughter: *"By the by, in going to Culpeper, where did you cross the Rapidan?"* His manner was unmistakable. It said: "My dear Stuart, all that is no doubt very amusing to you, and I laugh because you do; but it don't interest me." On one occasion only, to the knowledge of the present writer, did Jackson betray something like dry humour. It was at Harper's Ferry, in September, 1862, just after the surrender of that place, and when General Lee was falling back upon Sharpsburg. Jackson was standing on the bridge over the Potomac when a courier, out of breath, and seriously "demoralized," galloped up to him, and announced that McClellan was within an hour's march of the place with an enormous army. Jackson was conversing with a Federal officer at the moment, and did not seem to hear the courier, who repeated his message with every mark of agitation. Thereupon Jackson turned round and said: "Has he any cattle with him?" The reply was that there were thousands. "Well," said Jackson, with his dry smile, "you can go. My men can whip any army that comes well provisioned." Of wit, properly speaking, he had little. But at times his brief, wise, matter-of-fact sentences became epigrammatic. Dr. Hunter McGuire, his medical director, once gave him some whiskey when he was wet and fatigued. Jackson made a wry face in swallowing it, and Dr. McGuire asked if it was not good whiskey. "Oh, yes," replied Jackson, "I like liquor, the taste and effect—*that's why I don't drink it.*"

## III.

I have endeavoured to draw an outline of Jackson on horseback —the stiff, gaunt figure, dingy costume, piercing eyes; the large, firm, iron mouth, and the strong fighting-jaw. A few more words upon these personal peculiarities. The soldier's face was one of decided character, but not eminently striking. One circumstance always puzzled me—Jackson's lofty forehead seemed to indicate unmistakably a strong predominance of the *imagination and fancy*, and a very slight tendency or aptitude for *mathematics*. It was the forehead of a poet!—the statement is almost a jest. Jackson the stern, intensely matter-of-fact mathematician, a man of fancy! Never did forehead so contradict phrenology before. A man more guiltless of "poetry" in thought or deed, I suppose never lived. His poetry was the cannon's flash, the rattle of musketry, and the lurid cloud of battle. Then, it is true, his language, ordinarily so curt and cold, grew eloquent, almost tragic and heroic at times, from the deep feeling of the man. At Malvern Hill, General —— received an order from Jackson to advance and attack the Federal forces in their fortified position, for which purpose he must move across an open field swept by their artillery. General —— was always "impracticable," though thoroughly brave, and galloping up to Jackson said, almost rudely, "Did you send me an order to advance over that field?" "I did, sir," was the cold reply of Jackson, in whose eyes began to glow the light of a coming storm. "Impossible, sir!" exclaimed General —— in a tone almost of insubordination, "my men will be annihilated!—annihilated, I tell you, sir!" Jackson raised his finger, and in his cold voice there was an accent of menace which cooled his opponent like a hand of ice.

"General ——," he said, "I always endeavour to take care of my wounded and to bury my dead. Obey that order, sir!"

The officer who was present at this scene and related it to me, declares that he never saw a deeper suppression of concentrated anger than that which shone in Jackson's eye, or heard a human voice more menacing.

There were other times when Jackson, stung and aroused, was driven from his propriety, or, at least, out of his coolness. The winter of 1861-2 was such an occasion. He had made his expedition to Morgan county, and, in spite of great suffering among the troops, had forced the Federal garrisons at Bath and

Romney to retire, and accomplished all his ends. General Loring was then left at Romney, and Jackson returned to Winchester. All that is well known. What follows is not known to many. General Loring conceived an intense enmity for Jackson, and made such representations at Richmond, that an order was sent to Loring *direct*, not through Jackson, commanding in the Valley, recalling him. Jackson at once sent in his resignation. The scene which took place between him and his friend Colonel Boteler, thereupon, was a stormy one. The Colonel in vain tried to persuade him that he ought to recall his resignation. "No, sir," exclaimed Jackson, striding fiercely up and down, "I will not hold a command upon terms of that sort. I will not have those people at Richmond interfering in my plans, and sending orders to an officer under me, without even informing me. No soldier can endure it. I care not for myself. If I know myself I do not act from anger—but if I yield now they will treat better men in the same way! I am nobody—but the protest must be made here, or Lee and Johnston will be meddled with as I am." It was only after the resignation had been withdrawn by the Governor of Virginia without his authority, and explanations, apologies, protestations, came from the head of the War Office, that the design was given up. Such is a little *morceau* of private history, showing how Jackson came near not commanding in the Valley in 1862.

With the exception of these rare occasions when his great passions were aroused, Jackson was an apparently commonplace person, and his bearing neither striking, graceful, nor impressive. He rode ungracefully, walked with an awkward stride, and wanted ease of manner. He never lost a certain shyness in company; and I remember his air of boyish constraint, one day, when, in leaving an apartment full of friends, he hesitated whether to shake hands with every one or not. Catching the eye of the present writer, who designed remaining, he hastily extended his hand, shook hands, and quickly retired, apparently relieved. His bearing thus wanted ease; but, personally, he made a most agreeable impression by his delightfully natural courtesy. His smile was as sweet as a child's, and evidently sprang from his goodness of heart. A lady said it was "angelic." His voice in ordinary conversation was subdued, and pleasant from its friendly and courteous tone, though injured by the acquired habit—a West Pointism—of cutting off, so to speak, each word, and leaving each to take care of itself. This was always observable in his manner of talking; but briefest of the brief, curtest of the curt, was General Stonewall Jackson on the field of battle and "at work." His words were then let fall as though under protest; all superfluities were discarded; and the monosyllables jerked from his lips seemed clipped off, one by one, and launched to go upon separate ways. The eccentricities of the individual were undoubtedly a strong element of his popularity; the dress, habits, bearing of the man, all made his soldiers adore him. General Lee's air of collected dignity, mingled with a certain grave and serious pride, aroused rather admiration than affection—though during the last years of the war, the troops came to love as much as they admired him: to arrive at which point they had only to know the great warm heart which beat under that calm exterior, making its possessor "one altogether lovely." Jackson's appearance and manners, on the contrary, were such as conciliate a familiar, humorous liking. His dingy old coat, than which scarce a private's in his command was more faded; his dilapidated and discolored cap; the absence of deorations and all show in his dress; his odd ways; his kindly, simple manner; his habit of sitting down and eating with his men; his indifference whether his bed were in a comfortable headquarter tent, on a camp couch, or in a fence corner with no shelter from the rain but his cloak; his abstemiousness, fairness, honesty, simplicity; his never-failing regard for the comfort and the feelings of the private soldier; his oddities, eccentricities, and originalities—all were an unfailing provocative to liking, and endeared him to his men. Troops are charmed when there is anything in the personal character of a great leader to "make fun of"—admiration of his genius then becomes enthusiasm for his person. Jackson had aroused this enthusiasm in his men—and it was a weapon with which he struck hard.

One of the most curious peculiarities of Jackson was the strange fashion he had of raising his right hand aloft and then letting it fall suddenly to his side. It is impossible, perhaps, to determine the meaning of this singular gesture. It is said that he had some physical ailment which he thus relieved; others believed that at such moments he was praying. Either may be the fact. Certain it is that he often held his hand, sometimes both hands, thus aloft in battle, and that his lips were then seen to move, evidently in prayer. Not once, but many times, has the singular spectacle been presented of a Lieutenant-General commanding, sitting on his horse silently as his column moved before him—his hands raised to heaven, his eyes closed, his lips moving in prayer. At Chancellorsville, as he recognised the corpses of any of his old veterans, he would check his horse, raise his hands to heaven, and utter a prayer over the dead body.

There were those who said that all this indicated a partial species of insanity—that Jackson's mind was not sound. Other stories are told of him which aim to show that his eccentricities amounted to craziness. Upon this point the philosophers and physiologists must decide. The present writer can only say that Jackson appeared to him to be an eminently rational, judicious, and sensible person in conversation; and the world must determine whether there was any "craze," any flaw or crack, or error, in the terribly logical processes of his brain as a fighter of armies. The old incredulity of Frederick will obtrude itself upon the mind. If Jackson was crazy, it it a pity he did not bite somebody, and inoculate them with a small amount of his insanity as a soldier. Unquestionably the most striking trait of Jackson as a leader was his unerring judgment and accuracy of calculation. The present writer believes himself to be familiar with every detail of his career, and does not recall one blunder. Kernstown was fought upon information furnished by General Ashby, a most accomplished and reliable partisan, which turned out to be inaccurate; but even in defeat Jackson there accomplished the very important object of retaining a large Federal force in the Valley, which McClellan needed on the Chickahominy. For instances of the boldness, fertility, and originality of his conceptions, take the campaigns against General Pope, the surprise of Harper's Ferry, the great flank attack at Chancellorsville, and the marvellous success of every step taken in the campaign of the Valley. This is not the occasion for an analysis of these campaigns; but it may be safely declared that they are magnificent illustrations of the mathematics of war; that the brain which conceived and executed designs so bold and splendid, must have possessed a sanity for all practical purposes difficult to dispute.

IV.

Jackson's religious opinions are unknown to the present writer. He has been called a "fatalist." All sensible men are fatalists in one sense, in possessing a strong conviction that "what will be, will be." But men of deep piety like Jackson, are not Oriental in their views. Fate was a mere word with Jackson, with no meaning; his "star" was Providence. Love for and trust in that Providence dwelt and beat in every vein and pulse of his nature. His whole soul was absorbed in his religion—as much as a merchant's is in his business, or a statesman's in public affairs. He believed that life "meant intensely, and meant good." To find its meaning was "his meat and drink." His religion was his life, and the real world a mere phantasmagoria. He seemed to have died rejoicing, preferring death to life. Strange madness! This religious dreamer was the stern, practical, mathematical calculator of chances; the obstinate, unyielding fighter; the most prosaic of realists in all the commonplaces of the dreadfully commonplace trade of war.

The world knocks down many people with that cry of "eccentric," by which is really meant "insane." Any divergence from the conventional is an evidence of mental unsoundness. Jackson was seen, once in Lexington, walking up and down in a heavy rain before the superintendent's quarters, waiting for the clock to strike ten before he delivered his report. He wore woollen clothes throughout the summer. He would never mail a letter which to reach its destination must travel on Sunday. All these things made him laughed at; and yet the good sense seems all on his side, the folly on that of the laughers. The Institute was a military school; military obedience was the great important lesson to the student—rigid, unquestioning obedience. Jackson set them the example. He was ordered to hand in his report at ten, and did not feel himself at liberty to present it before ten, in consequence of the rain. He was ordered to don a woollen uniform in the winter, and having received no order prescribing or permitting another, continued to wear it. He considered it wrong to travel or carry mails on Sunday, and would not take part in the commission of wrong. This appears logical, however eccentric.

In truth, the great soldier was an altogether *earnest* man, with little genius for the trivial pursuits of life, or its more trivial processes of thought and opinion. His temper was matter-of-fact, his logic straightforward; "nonsense" could not live in his presence. The lighter graces were denied him, but not the abiding charm. He had no eye for the "flower of the peas," no palate for the bubble on the champagne of life; but he was true, kind, brave, and simple. Life with him was a hard, earnest struggle; duty seems to have been his watchword. It is hard to find in his character any actual blot—he was so true and honest.

Jackson has probably excited more admiration in Europe than any other personage in the late revolution. His opponents even are said to have acknowledged the purity of his motives—to have recognised the greatness of his character and the splendor of his achievements. This sentiment springs naturally from a review of his life. It is no part of my design to present a critical analysis of his military movements. This must sooner or later be done; but at present the atmosphere is not clear of the battle-smoke, and figures are seen indistinctly. The time will come when the campaigns of Jackson will become the study of military men in the Old World and the New—the masterly advances and retreats of the Valley; the descent against McClellan; the expedition to Pope's rear, which terminated in the second battle of Manassas; and the great flank movement at Chancellorsville, which has made the tangled brakes of the Spotsylvania wilderness famous for ever.

Under the grave exterior, the reserved demeanour, the old

faded costume of the famous soldier, the penetrating student of human nature will discern "one of the immortals." In the man who holds aloft his hand in prayer while his veteran battalions move by steadily to the charge, it will not be difficult to fancy a reproduction of the stubborn Cromwell, sternest of Ironsides, going forth to conquer in the name of the Lord. In the man who led his broken lines back to the conflict, and charged in front of them on many fields, there was all the dash and impetus of Rupert. The inscrutable decree of Providence struck down this great soldier in the prime of life and the bloom of his faculties. His career extended over but two years, and he lives only in memory. But history cannot avoid her landmarks; the great proportions of Stonewall Jackson will sooner or later be delineated.

The writer of these lines can only say how great this man appeared to him, and wait with patience for the picture which shall "denote him truly."

# III

## HAMPTON

### I.

THERE was a gentleman of South Carolina, of high position and ample estate, who in 1861 came to take part in the war in Virginia, at the head of a "Legion" of six hundred infantry. This body of men, it was said, he had equipped from his own purse; as he had sent to England and purchased the artillery with which he was going to fight.

The "Legion" was composed of brave stuff, and officered by hard-fighting gentlemen—the flower indeed of the great South Carolina race; a good stock. It first took the field in earnest at the first battle of Manassas—as an independent organization, belonging neither to Beauregard's "Army of the Potomac" nor to Johnston's "Army of the Shenandoah." But there it was, as though dropped from the clouds, on the morning of that fiery twenty-first of July, 1861, amid the corn-fields of Manassas. It made its mark without loss of time—stretching out to Virginia that firm, brave hand of South Carolina. At ten o'clock in the morning, on this eventful day, the battle seemed lost to the Southerners. Evans was cut to pieces; Bee shattered and driven back in utter defeat to the Henry-House hill; between the victorious enemy and Beauregard's unprotected flank were interposed only the six hundred men of the "Legion" already up, and the two thousand six hundred and eleven muskets of Jackson not yet in position. The Legion occupied the Warrenton road

47

near the Stone House, where it met and sustained with stubborn
front the torrent dashed against it. General Keyes, with his division, attacked the six hundred from the direction of Red-House
ford, and his advance line was forced back by them, and compelled to take refuge beneath the bluffs near Stone bridge. The
column of General Hunter, meanwhile, closed in on the left of
the little band, enveloped their flank, and poured a destructive
artillery fire along the line. To hold their ground further was
impossible, and they slowly fell back; but those precious moments had been secured. Jackson was in position; the Legion
retreated, and formed upon his right; the enemy's advance was
checked; and when the Southern line advanced in its turn, with
wild cheers, piercing the Federal centre, the South Carolinians
fought shoulder to shoulder beside the Stonewall Brigade, and
saw the Federal forces break in disorder. When the sun set on
this bloody and victorious field, the "Legion" had made a record
among the most honourable in history. They had done more
than their part in the hard struggle, and now saw the enemy in
full retreat; but their leader did not witness that spectacle. Wade
Hampton had been shot down in the final charge near the Henry
House, and borne from the field, cheering on his men to the last,
with that stubborn hardihood which he derived from his ancestral blood.

Such was the first appearance upon the great arena of a man
who was destined to act a prominent part in the tragic drama of
the war, and win for himself a distinguished name. At Manassas,
there in the beginning of the struggle, as always afterwards, he
was the cool and fearless soldier. It was easily seen by those
who watched Hampton "at work" that he fought from a sense
of duty, and not from passion, or to win renown. The war was
a gala-day full of attraction and excitement to some; with him
it was hard work—not sought, but accepted. I am certain that
he was not actuated by a thirst for military rank or renown.
From those early days when all was gay and brilliant, to the latter years when the conflict had become so desperate and bloody,
oppressing every heart, Hampton remained the same cool, un-

WADE HAMPTON'S CAVALRY FIGHT AT GETTYSBURG.

excited soldier. He was foremost in every fight, and everywhere did more than his duty; but evidently martial ambition did not move him. Driven to take up arms by his principles, he fought for those principles, not for fame. It followed him—he did not follow it; and to contemplate the character and career of such a man is wholesome.

His long and arduous career cannot here be narrated. A bare reference to some prominent points is all that can be given. Colonel Hampton, of the "Hampton Legion," soon became Brigadier-General Hampton, of the cavalry. The horsemen of the Gulf States serving in Virginia were placed under him, and the brigade became a portion of Stuart's command. It soon made its mark. Here are some of the landmarks in the stirring record.

The hard and stubborn stand made at the Catoctin Mountain, when General Lee first invaded Maryland, and where Hampton charged and captured the Federal artillery posted in the suburbs of Frederick City; the rear-guard work as the Southern column hastened on, pursued by McClellan, to Sharpsburg; the stout fighting on the Confederate left there; the raid around McClellan's army in October; the obstinate fighting in front of the gaps of the Blue Ridge as Lee fell back in November to the line of the Rappahannock; the expedition in dead of winter to the Occoquan; the critical and desperate combat on the ninth of June, 1863, at Fleetwood Hill, near Brandy, where Hampton held the right, and Young, of Georgia, the brave of braves, went at the flanking column of the enemy with the sabre, never firing a shot, and swept them from the field; the speedy advance, thereafter, from the Rapidan; the close and bitter struggle when the enemy, with an overpowering force of infantry, cavalry, and artillery, about the twentieth of June, attacked the Southern cavalry near Middleburg, and forced them back step by step beyond Upperville, where in the last wild charge, when the Confederates were nearly broken, Hampton went in with the sabre at the head of his men and saved the command from destruction by his "do or die" fighting; the advance immediately into Pennsylvania, when the long, hard march, like the verses

of Ariosto, was strewed all over with battles; the stubborn attack
at Hanovertown, where Hampton stood like a rock upon the
hills above the place, and the never-ceasing or receding roar
of his artillery told us that on the right flank all was well; the
march thereafter to Carlisle, and back to Gettysburg; the grand
charge there, sabre to sabre, where Hampton was shot through
the body, and nearly cut out of the saddle by a sabre blow upon
the head, which almost proved fatal; the hard conflicts of the
Wilderness, when General Grant came over in May, 1864; the
fighting on the north bank of the Po, and on the left of the army
at Spotsylvania Court-House; the various campaigns against
Sheridan, Kautz, Wilson, and the later cavalry leaders on the
Federal side, when, Stuart having fallen, Hampton commanded
the whole Virginia cavalry; the hot fights at Trevillian's, at
Reanis, at Bellfield, in a hundred places, when, in those expiring
hours of the great conflict, a species of fury seemed to possess
both combatants, and Dinwiddie was the arena of a struggle,
bitter, bloody, desperate beyond all expression; then the fighting
in the Carolinas on the old grounds of the Edisto, the high hills
of the Santee and Congaree, which in 1864 and 1865 sent bul-
letins of battle as before; then the last act of the tragedy, when
Sherman came and Hampton's sabre gleamed in the glare of his
own house at Columbia, and then was sheathed—such were some
of the scenes amid which the tall form of this soldier moved, and
his sword flashed. That stalwart form had everywhere towered
in the van. On the Rappahannock, the Rapidan, the Susquehanna, the Shenandoah, the Po, the North Anna, the James, the
Rowanty, and Hatcher's Run—in Virginia, Maryland, and Pennsylvania—Hampton had fought with the stubborn courage inherited from his Revolutionary sires. Fighting lastly upon the
the soil of his native State, he felt no doubt as Marion and Sumter
did, when Rawdon and Tarleton came and were met sabre to
sabre. In the hot conflicts of 1865, Hampton met the new enemy
as those *preux chevaliers* with their great Virginia comrade,
"Light-Horse Harry" Lee, had met the old in 1781.

But the record of those stubborn fights must be left to another
time and to abler hands. I pass to a few traits of the individual.

## II.

Of this eminent soldier, I will say that, seeing him often in many of those perilous straits which reveal hard fibre or its absence, I always regarded him as a noble type of courage and manhood—a gentleman and soldier "to the finger nails." But that is not enough; generalization and eulogy are unprofitable—truth and minute characterization are better. One personal anecdote of Cæsar would be far more valuable than a hundred common-places—and that is true of others. It is not a "general idea" I am to give; I would paint the portrait, if I can, of the actual man. The individuality of the great South Carolinian was very marked. You saw at a glance the race from which he sprang, and the traits of heart and brain which he brought to the hard contest. He was "whole in himself and due to none." Neither in physical nor mental conformation did he resemble Stuart, the ideal cavalier—Forrest, the rough-rider—or the rest. To compare him for an instant to the famous Stuart—the latter laughed, sang, and rev-elled in youth and enjoyment. Hampton smiled oftener than he laughed, never sang at all that I ever heard, and had the com-posed demeanour of a man of middle age. Stuart loved brilliant colours, gay scenes, and the sparkle of bright eyes. Hampton gave little thought to these things; and his plain gray coat, worn, dingy, and faded, beside the great cavalier's gay "fighting jacket," shining with gold braid, defined the whole difference. I do not say that the dingy coat covered a stouter heart than the brilliant jacket—there never lived a more heroic soul than Stuart —but that in this was shown the individuality of each. The one—Stuart—was young, gay, a West Pointer, and splendid in his merriment, *élan*, and *abandon*. The other, Hampton, a civilian approaching middle age, a planter, not a soldier by profession—a man who embarked in the arduous struggle with the coolness of the statesman, rather than the ardor of the soldier. It was the planter, sword in hand, not the United States officer, that one saw in Hampton—the country gentleman who took up arms be-cause his native soil was invaded, as the race of which he came

had done in the past. That the plain planter, without military
education, became the eminent soldier, is an evidence that "the
strain will show."

Here is an outline of the South Carolinian as he appeared in
July, 1862, when the cavalry were resting after the battles of
the Chickahominy, and he often came to the old shady yard of
Hanover Court-House, to talk with General Stuart under the
trees there. What the eye saw in those days was a personage
of tall stature and "distinguished" appearance. The face was
browned by sun and wind, and half covered by dark side-whis-
kers joining a long moustache of the same hue; the chin bold,
prominent, and bare. The eyes were brown, inclining to black,
and very mild and friendly; the voice low, sonorous, and with a
certain accent of dignity and composure. The frame of the soldier—straight, vigorous, and stalwart, but not too broad for
grace—was encased in a plain gray sack coat of civilian cut, with
the collar turned down; cavalry boots, large and serviceable,
with brass spurs; a brown felt hat, without star or feather; the
rest of the dress plain gray. Imagine this stalwart figure with a
heavy sabre buckled around the waist, and mounted upon a large
and powerful animal of excellent blood and action, but wholly
"unshowy," and a correct idea will be obtained of General Wade
Hampton. Passing from the clothes to the man—what impressed
all who saw him was the attractive union of dignity and simplicity in his bearing—a certain grave and simple courtesy which
indicated the highest breeding. He was evidently an honest
gentleman who disdained all pretence or artifice. It was plain
that he thought nothing of personal decorations or military
show, and never dreamed of "producing an impression" upon
any one. This was revealed by that bearing full of a proud modesty; neither stiff nor insinuating—simple.

After being in his presence for ten minutes, you saw that he
was a man for hard work, and not for display. That plain and
unassuming manner, without pretension, affectation, or "official" coolness, was an index to the character of the individual.
It is easy to tell a gentleman; something betrays that character,

as something betrays the pretender. Refinement, good-breeding, and fealty through all, to honour, were here embodied. The General was as courteous to the humblest private soldier as to the Commander-in-Chief, and you could discover in him no trace whatever of that air of "condescension" and "patronage" which small persons, aiming to be great, sometimes adopt. It was the unforced courtesy of the gentleman, not the hollow politeness of the pretender to that title, which all saw in Hampton. He did not act at all, but lived his character. In his voice, in his bearing, in all that he said and did, the South Carolinian betrayed the man who is too proud not to be simple, natural, and unassuming.

Upon this trait of manner, merely, I may seem to dwell too long. But it is not a trifle. I am trying to delineate a man of whom we Southerners are proud—and this rare grace was his. It reflected clearly the character of the individual—the noble pride, the true courtesy, and the high-bred honour of one who, amid all the jarring stife of an excited epoch, would not suffer his serene equanimity of gentleman to be disturbed; who aimed to do his duty to his country, not rise above his associates; who was no politer to the high than to the low, to the powerful than to the weak; and who respected more the truth and courage beneath the tattered jacket than the stars and wreath on the braided coat. The result of this kindly feeling towards "men of low estate" was marked. An officer long associated with him said to me one day: "I do not believe there ever was a General more beloved by his whole command; and he more than returns it. General Hampton has *a real tenderness*, I do believe, for every soldier who has ever served under him." He was always doing the poorer members of his command some kindness. His hand was open like his heart. Many a brave fellow's family was kept from want by him; and a hundred instances of this liberality are doubtless recorded in the grateful memories of the women and children whom he fought for, and fed too, in those dark days. This munificence was nowhere else recorded. The left hand knew not what the right hand did.

A few words more upon his personal bearing. His composure upon trying occasions, as in every-day life, indicated a self-poised and independent character. He rarely yielded to hearty mirth, but his smile was very friendly and attractive. You could see that he was a person of earnest feelings, and had a good heart. In camp he was a pleasant companion, and those who saw him daily became most attached to him. His staff were devoted to him. I remember the regret experienced by these brave gentlemen when Hampton's assignment to the command of all the cavalry separated them from him. The feeling which they then exhibited left no doubt of the *entente cordiale* between the members of the military family. General Hampton liked to laugh and talk with them around the camp fire; to do them every kindness he could—but that was his weakness towards everybody—and to play chess, draughts, or other games, in the intervals of fighting or work. One of his passions was hunting. This amusement he pursued upon every occasion—over the fields of Spotsylvania, amid the woods of Dinwiddie, and on the rivers of South Carolina. His success was great. Ducks, partridges, squirrels, turkey, and deer, fell before his double-barrel in whatever country he pitched his tents. He knew all the old huntsmen of the regions in which he tarried, delighted to talk with such upon the noble science of venery, and was considered by these dangerous critics a thorough sportsman. They regarded him, it is said, as a comrade not undistinguished; and sent him, in friendly recognition of his merit, presents of venison and other game, which was plentiful along the shores of the Rowanty, or in the backwoods of Dinwiddie. Hampton was holding the right of General Lee's line there, in supreme command of all the Virginia cavalry; but it was not as a hunter of "bluebirds"—so we used to call our Northern friends—that they respected him most. It was as a deer hunter; and I have heard that the hard-fighting cavalier relished very highly their good opinion of him in that character. It is singular that a love for hunting should so often characterize men of elegant scholarship and literary taste. The soldier and huntsman was also a poet, and General Stuart spoke in high praise of his writings. His prose style was forcible and excellent—in letters, reports, and all that he wrote. The admirably written address to the people of South Carolina, which was recently published, will display the justice of this statement. That paper, like all that came from him, was compact, vigorous, lucid, "written in English," and everywhere betrayed the scholar no less than the patriot. It will live when a thousand octavos have disappeared.

### III.

Such was Wade Hampton the man—a gentleman in every fibre of his being. It was impossible to imagine anything coarse or profane in the action or utterance of the man. An oath never soiled his lips. "*Do* bring up that artillery!" or some equivalent exclamation, was his nearest approach to irritation even. Such was the supreme control which this man of character, full of fire, force, and resolution, had over his passions. For, under that simplicity and kindly courtesy, was the largely-moulded nature of one ready to go to the death when honour called. In a single word, it was a powerful organization under complete control which the present writer seemed to recognise in Wade Hampton. Under that sweetness and dignity which made him conspicuous among the first gentlemen of his epoch, was the stubborn spirit of the born soldier.

Little space is left to speak of him in his military character. I preferred to dwell upon Hampton the man, as he appeared to me; for Hampton the General will find many historians. Some traits of the soldier, however, must not be omitted; this character is too eminent to be drawn only in profile. On the field Hampton was noted for his coolness. This never left him. It might almost be called repose, so perfect was it. He was never an excitable man; and as doubt and danger pressed heavier, his equanimity seemed to increase. You could see that this was truly a stubborn spirit. I do not think that anybody who knew him could even imagine Wade Hampton "flurried." His nerve was made of invincible stuff, and his entire absence of all excitability on the field was spoken of by his enemies as a fault. It was said that his coolness amounted to a defect in a cavalry leader; that he wanted

the dash, rush, and impetus which this branch of the service demands. If there was any general truth in this criticism, there was
none in particular instances. Hampton was sufficiently headlong
when I saw him—was one of the most thoroughly successful
commanders imaginable, and certainly seemed to have a natural
turn for going in front of his column with a drawn sabre. What
the French call *élan* is not, however, the greatest merit in a
soldier. Behind the strong arm was the wary brain. Cool and
collected resolution, a comprehensive survey of the whole field,
and the most excellent dispositions for attack or defence—such
were the merits of this soldier. I could never divest myself of the
idea that as a corps commander of infantry he would have figured among the most eminent names of history. With an unclouded brain; a *coup d'œil* as clear as a ray of the sun; invincible
before danger; never flurried, anxious, or despondent; content
to wait; too wary ever to be surprised; looking to great trials of
strength, and to general results—the man possessing these traits
of character was better fitted, I always thought, for the command of troops of all arms—infantry, cavalry, and artillery—
than for one arm alone. But with that arm which he commanded
—cavalry—what splendid results did he achieve. In how many
perilous straits was his tall figure seen in front of the Southern
horsemen, bidding them "come on," not "go on." He was not
only the commander, but the *sabreur* too. Thousands will remember how his gallant figure led the charging column at
Frederick City, at Upperville, at Gettysburg, at Trevillian's, and
in a hundred other fights. Nothing more superb could be imagined than Hampton at such moments. There was no flurry in
the man—but determined resolution. No doubt of the result apparently—no looking for an avenue of retreat. "Sabre to sabre!"
might have been taken as the motto of his banner. In the "heady
fight" he was everywhere seen, amid the clouds of smoke, the
crashing shell, and the whistling balls, fighting like a private
soldier, his long sword doing hard work in the *mêlée*, and carv-
ing its way as did the trenchant weapons of the ancient knights.
This spirit of the thorough cavalier in Hampton is worth dwell-

ing on. Under the braid of the Major-General was the brave soul of the fearless soldier, the "fighting man." It was not a merit in him or in others that they gave up wealth, business, elegance, all the comforts, conveniences, and serene enjoyments of life, to live hard and fight hard; to endure heat, cold, hunger, thirst, exhaustion, and pain, without a murmur; but it was a merit in this brave soldier and gentleman that he did more than his duty, met breast to breast in single combat the best swordsmen of the Federal army, counted his life as no more than a private soldier's, and seemed to ask nothing better than to pour out his heart's blood for the cause in which he fought. This personal heroism —and Hampton had it to a grand extent—attracts the admiration of troops. But there is something better—the power of brain and force of character which wins the confidence of the Commander-in-Chief. When that Commander-in-Chief is called Robert E. Lee, it is something to have secured his high regard and confidence. Hampton had won the respect of Lee, and by that "noblest Roman of them all" his great character and eminent services were fully recognised. These men seemed to understand each other, and to be inspired by the same sentiment— a love of their native land which never failed, and a willingness to spend and be spent to the last drop of their blood in the cause which they had espoused. During General Stuart's life, Hampton was second in command of the Virginia Cavalry; but when that great cavalier fell, he took charge of the whole as ranking-officer. His first blow was that resolute night-attack on Sheridan's force at Mechanicsville, when the enemy were driven in the darkness from their camps, and sprang to horse only in time to avoid the sweeping sabres of the Southerners—giving up from that moment all further attempt to enter Richmond. Then came the long, hard, desperate fighting of the whole year 1864, and the spring of 1865. At Trevillian's, Sheridan was driven back and Charlottesville saved; on the Weldon railroad the Federal cavalry, under Kautz and Wilson, was nearly cut to pieces, and broke in disorder, leaving on the roads their wagons, cannons, ambulances, their dead men and horses; near Bellfield the Federal column sent to destroy the railroad was encountered, stubbornly opposed, and driven back before they could burn the bridge at Hicksford; at Burgess' Mill, near Petersburg, where General Grant made his first great blow with two corps of infantry, at the Southside railroad, Hampton met them in front and flank, fought them all an October day nearly, lost his brave son Preston, dead from a bullet on the field, but in conjunction with Mahone, that hardy fighter, sent the enemy in haste back to their works; thus saving for the time the great war artery of the Southern army. Thenceforward, until he was sent to South Carolina, Hampton held the right of Lee in the woods of Dinwiddie, guarding with his cavalry cordon the line of the Rowanty, and defying all comers. Stout, hardy, composed, smiling, ready to meet any attack—in those last days of the strange year 1864, he seemed to my eyes the *beau ideal* of a soldier. The man appeared to be as firm as a rock, as immovably rooted as one of the gigantic live-oaks of his native country. When I asked him one day if he expected to be attacked soon, he laughed and said: "No; the enemy's cavalry are afraid to show their noses beyond their infantry." Nor did the Federal cavalry ever achieve any results in that region until the ten or fifteen thousand crack cavalry of General Sheridan came to ride over the two thousand men, on starved and broken-down horses, of General Fitz Lee, in April, 1865.

From Virginia, in the dark winter of 1864, Hampton was sent to oppose with his cavalry the advance of General Sherman, and the world knows how desperately he fought there on his *natale solum*. More than ever before it was sabre to sabre, and Hampton was still in front. When the enemy pressed on to Columbia he fell back, fighting from street to street, and so continued fighting until the thunderbolt fell in South Carolina, as it had fallen in Virginia at Appomattox, and the struggle ended. The sword that Hampton sheathed that day was one which no soil of bad faith, cruelty, or dishonour had ever tainted. It was the blade of a brave and irreproachable chevalier, of a man who throughout the most desperate and embittered conflict of all history had kept his ancestral name from every blot, and had proved himself upon a hundred battle-fields the worthy son of the "mighty men of old."

Such, in rough outline, was this brave and kindly soldier and gentleman, as he passed before our eyes in Virginia, "working his work." Seeing him often, in camp, on the field, in bright days, and when the sky was darkest, the present writer looked upon him as a noble spirit, the truthful representative of a great and vigorous race. Brave, just, kindly, courteous, with the tenderness of a woman under that grave exterior; devoted to his principles, for which he fought and would have died; loving his native land with a love "passing the love of woman;" proud, but never haughty; not so much condescending to men of low estate, as giving them—if they were soldiers—the warm right hand of fellowship; merciful, simple-minded; foremost in the fight, but nowhere to be seen in the antechamber of living man; with a hand shut tight upon the sword-hilt, but open as day to "melting charity;" counting his life as nothing at the call of honour; contending with stubborn resolution for the faith that was in him; never cast down, never wavering, never giving back until the torrent bore him away, but fighting to the last with that heroic courage, born in his blood, for the independence of his country. Such was Wade Hampton, of South Carolina. There are those, perhaps, who will malign him in these dark days, when no sun shines. But the light is yonder, behind the cloud and storm; some day it will shine out, and a million rush-lights will not be able to extinguish it. There are others who will call him traitor, and look, perhaps, with pity and contempt upon this page which claims for him a noble place among the illustrious figures shining all along the coasts of history like beacon lights above the storm. Traitor let it be; one hundred years ago there were many in the South, and they fought over the same ground. Had the old Revolution failed, those men would have lived for ever, as Hampton and his associates in the recent conflict will. "Surrender," written at the end of this great history, cannot mar its glory; failure cannot blot its splendour. The name and fame of Hampton will endure as long as loyalty and courage are respected by the human race.

# IV

## ASHBY

### I.

IN THE Valley of Virginia, the glory of two men outshines that of all others; two figures were tallest, best beloved, and today are most bitterly mourned. One was Jackson, the other Ashby. The world knows all about Jackson, but has little knowledge of Ashby. I was reading a stupid book the other day in which he was represented as a guerilla—almost as a robber and highwayman. Ashby a guerilla!—that great, powerful, trained, and consummate fighter of infantry, cavalry, and artillery, in the hardest fought battles of the Valley campaign! Ashby a robber and highwayman!—that soul and perfect mirror of chivalry! It is to drive away these mists of stupid or malignant scribblers that the present writer designs recording here the actual truth of Ashby's character and career. Apart from what he performed, he was a personage to whom attached and still attaches a never-dying interest. His career was all romance—it was as brief, splendid, and evanescent as a dream—but, after all, it was the man Turner Ashby who was the real attraction. It was the man whom the people of the Shenandoah Valley admire, rather than his glorious record. There was something grander than the achievements of this soldier, and that was the soldier himself.

Ashby first attracted attention in the spring of 1862, when Jackson made his great campaign in the Valley, crushing one

after another Banks, Milroy, Shields, Fremont, and their associates. Among the brilliant figures, the hard fighters grouped
around the man of Kernstown and Port Republic at that time,
Ashby was perhaps the most notable and famous. As the great
majority of my readers never saw the man, a personal outline
of him here in the beginning may interest. Even on this soil
there are many thousands who never met that model chevalier
and perfect type of manhood. He lives in all memories and
hearts, but not in all eyes.

What the men of Jackson saw at the head of the Valley cavalry in the spring of 1862, was a man rather below the middle
height, with an active and vigorous frame, clad in plain Confederate gray. His brown felt hat was decorated with a black
feather; his uniform was almost without decorations: his cavalry boots, dusty or splashed with mud, came to the knee; and
around his waist he wore a sash and plain leather belt, holding
pistol and sabre. The face of this man of thirty or a little more,
was noticeable. His complexion was as dark as that of an Arab;
his eyes of a deep rich brown, sparkled under well formed
brows; and two thirds of his face was covered by a huge black
beard and moustache; the latter curling at the ends, the former
reaching to his breast. There was thus in the face of the cavalier
something Moorish and brigandish; but all idea of a melodramatic personage disappeared as you pressed his hand, looked
into his eyes, and spoke to him. The brown eyes, which would
flash superbly in battle, were the softest and most friendly imaginable; the voice, which could thrill his men as it rang like
a clarion in the charge, was the perfection of mild courtesy. He
was as simple and "friendly" as a child in all his words, movements, and the carriage of his person. You could see from his
dress, his firm tread, his open and frank glance, that he was a
thorough soldier—indeed he always "looked like work"—but
under the soldier, as plainly was the gentleman. Such in his plain
costume, with his simple manner and retiring modesty, was
Ashby, whose name and fame, a brave comrade has truly said,
will endure as long as the mountains and valleys which he
defended.

## II.

The achievements of Ashby can be barely touched on here—
history will set them in its purest gold. The pages of the splendid record can only be glanced at now; months of fighting must
here be summed up and dismissed in a few sentences.

To look back to his origin—that always counts for something—
he was the son of a gentleman of Fauquier, and up to 1861 was
only known as a hard rider, a gay companion, and the kindest-
hearted of friends. There was absolutely nothing in the youth's
character, apparently, which could detach him from the great
mass of mediocrities; but under that laughing face, that simple,
unassuming manner, was a soul of fire—the unbending spirit of
the hero, and no less the genius of the born master of the art of
war. When the revolution broke out Ashby got in the saddle,
and spent most of his time therein until he fell. It was at this time
—on the threshold of the war—that I saw him first. I have described his person—his bearing was full of a charming courtesy.
The low, sweet voice made you his friend before you knew it;
and so modest and unassuming was his demeanor that a child
would instinctively have sought his side and confided in him.
The wonder of wonders to me, a few months afterwards, was
that this unknown youth, with the simple smile, and the retiring,
almost shy demeanour, had become the right hand of Jackson,
the terror of the enemy, and had fallen near the bloody ground
of Port Republic, mourned by the whole nation of Virginia.

Virginia was his first and last love. When he went to Harper's
Ferry in April, 1861, with his brother Richard's cavalry company, some one said: "Well, Ashby, what flag are we going
to fight under—the Palmetto, or what?" Ashby took off his hat,
and exhibited a small square of silk upon which was painted the
Virginia shield—the Virgin trampling on the tyrant. "That is
the flag *I* intend to fight under," was his reply; and he accorded
it his paramount fealty to the last. Soon after this incident active
service commenced on the Upper Potomac; and an event occurred which changed Ashby's whole character. His brother

Richard, while on a scout near Romney, with a small detachment, was attacked by a strong party of the enemy, his command dispersed, and as he attempted to leap a "cattle-stop" in
the railroad, his horse fell with him. The enemy rushed upon
him, struck him cruelly with their sabres, and killed him before
he could rise. Ashby came up at the moment, and with eight
men charged them, killing many of them with his own hand.
But his brother was dead—the man whom he had loved more
than his own life; and thereafter he seemed like another man.
Richard Ashby was buried on the banks of the Potomac—his
brother nearly fainted at the grave; then he went back to his
work. "Ashby is now a devoted man," said one who knew him;
and his career seemed to justify the words. He took command
of his company, was soon promoted to the rank of a field officer,
and from that moment he was on the track of the enemy day and
night. Did private vengeance actuate the man, once so kind
and sweet-tempered? I know not; but something from this time
forward seemed to spur him on to unflagging exertion and cease-
less activity. Day and night he was in the saddle. Mounted upon
his fleet white horse, he would often ride, in twenty-four hours,
along seventy miles of front, inspecting his pickets, instructing
his detachments, and watching the enemy's movements at every
point. Here to-day, to-morrow he would be seen nearly a hundred miles distant. The lithe figure on the white horse "came
and went like a dream," said one who knew him at that time.
And when he appeared it was almost always the signal for an
attack, a raid, or a "scout," in which blood would flow.

In the spring of 1862, when Jackson fell back from Winchester, Ashby, then promoted to the rank of Colonel, commanded all his cavalry. He was already famous for his wonderful
activity, his heroic courage, and that utter contempt for danger
which was born in his blood. On the Potomac, near Shepherdstown, he had ridden to the top of a crest, swept by the hot fire
of the enemy's sharpshooters near at hand; and pacing slowly
up and down on his milk-white horse, looked calmly over his
shoulder at his foes, who directed upon him a storm of bullets.
He was now to give a proof more striking still of his fearless

nerve. Jackson slowly retired from Winchester, the cavalry under Ashby bringing up the rear, with the enemy closely pressing them. The long column defiled through the town, and Ashby remained the last, sitting his horse in the middle of Loudoun street as the Federal forces poured in. The solitary horseman, gazing at them with so much nonchalance, was plainly seen by the Federal officers, and two mounted men were detached to make a circuit by the back streets, and cut off his retreat. Ashby either did not see this manœuvre, or paid no attention to it. He waited until the Federal column was nearly upon him, and had opened a hot fire—then he turned his horse, waved his hat around his head, and uttering a cheer of defiance, galloped off. All at once, as he galloped down the street, he saw before him the two cavalrymen sent to cut off and capture him. To a man like Ashby, inwardly chafing at being compelled to retreat, no sight could be more agreeable. Here was an opportunity to vent his spleen; and charging the two mounted men, he was soon upon them. One fell with a bullet through his breast; and, coming opposite the other, Ashby seized him by the throat, dragged him from his saddle, and putting spur to his horse, bore him off. This scene, which some readers may set down for romance, was witnessed by hundreds both of the Confederate and the Federal army.*

During Jackson's retreat Ashby remained in command of the rear, fighting at every step with his cavalry and horse artillery, under Captain Chew. It was dangerous to press such a man. His sharp claws drew blood. As the little column retired sullenly up the valley, fighting off the heavy columns of General Banks, Ashby was in the saddle day and night, and his guns were never silent. The infantry sank to sleep with that thunder in their

---

* Cooke's account of Turner Ashby's withdrawal from Winchester differs widely from that recorded by Ashby's own chaplain, J. B. Avirett, in his book, *The Memoirs of General Turner Ashby and His Compeers.* Avirett, who witnessed the withdrawal, simply says: "Ashby, as quiet as if on dress parade, followed his men down the street, and though followed closely by the enemy, coolly stopped to take a biscuit offered him by a noblehearted lady."—ED.

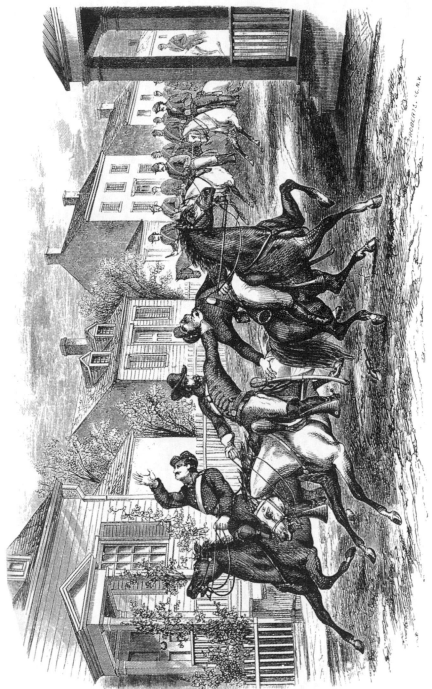

ADVENTURE OF ASHBY AT WINCHESTER.

' Ashby seized him by the throat, dragged him from his saddle, and putting spur to his horse, bore him off.

ears, and the same sound was their reveille at dawn. Weary at last of a proceeding so unproductive, General Banks ceased the pursuit and fell back to Winchester, when Ashby pursued in his turn, and quickly sent intelligence to Jackson, which brought him back to Kernstown. The battle there followed, and Ashby held the turnpike, pressing forward with invincible ardour, flanking the Federal forces, and nearly getting in their rear. When Jackson was forced to retire, he again held the rear; and continued in front of the enemy, eternally skirmishing with them, until Jackson again advanced to attack General Banks at Strasburg and Winchester. It was on a bright May morning that Ashby, moving in front, struck the Federal column of cavalry *in transitu* north of Strasburg, and scattered them like a hurricane. Separated from his command, but bursting with an ardour which defied control, he charged, by himself, about five hundred Federal horsemen retreating in disorder, snatched a guidon from the hands of its bearer, and firing right and left into the column, summoned the men to surrender. Many did so, and the rest galloped on, followed by Ashby, to Winchester, where he threw the guidon, with a laugh, to a friend, who afterwards had it hung up in the Library of the Capitol at Richmond.

### III.

The work of Ashby then began in earnest. The affair with General Banks was only a skirmish—the wars of the giants followed.

Jackson, nearly hemmed in by bitter and determined foes, fell back to escape destruction, and on his track rushed the heavy columns of Shields and Fremont, which, closing in at Strasburg and Front Royal, were now hunting down the lion. It was then and there that Ashby won his fame as a cavalry officer, and attached to every foot of ground over which he fought some deathless tradition. The reader must look elsewhere for a record of those achievements. Space would fail me were I to touch with the pen's point the hundredth part of that splendid career. On every hill, in every valley, at every bridge, Ashby thundered and lightened with his cavalry and artillery. Bitterest of the bitter was the cavalier in those moments; a man sworn to hold his ground or die. He played with death, and dared it everywhere. From every hill came the roar of his guns and the sharp crack of his sharpshooters, but the music, much as he loved it—and he did love it with all his soul—was less sweet to him than the clash of sabres. It was in hand-to-hand fighting that he seemed to take the greatest pleasure. In front of his column, sweeping forward to the charge, Ashby was "happy." Coming to the Shenandoah near Newmarket, he remained behind with a few men to destroy the bridge, and here took place an event which may seem too trifling to be recorded, but which produced a notable effect upon the army. While retreating alone before a squadron of the enemy's cavalry in hot pursuit of him, his celebrated white horse was mortally wounded. Furious at this, Ashby cut the foremost of his assailants out of the saddle with his sabre, and safely reached his command; but the noble charger was staggering under him, and bleeding to death. He dismounted, caressed for an instant, without speaking, the proud neck, and then turned away. The historic steed was led off to his death, his eyes glaring with rage it seemed at the enemy still; and Ashby returned to his work, hastening to meet the fatal bullet which in turn was to strike him. The death of the white horse who had passed unscathed through so many battles, preceded only by a few days that of his rider, whom no ball had ever yet touched. It was on the 4th or 5th of June, just before the battle of Cross Keys, that he ambuscaded and captured Sir Percy Wyndham, commander of Fremont's cavalry advance. Sir Percy had publicly announced his intention to "bag Ashby;" but unwarily advancing upon a small decoy in the road, he found himself suddenly attacked in flank and rear by Ashby in person; and he and his squadron of sixty or seventy men were taken prisoners. That was the last cavalry fight in which the great leader took part. His days were numbered—death had marked him. But to the last he was what he had always been, unresting, fiery, ever on the enemy's track; and he died in harness. It was on the very same evening, I believe, that while commanding the rear-guard of Jackson, he formed the design of flanking and attacking the enemy's infantry, and sent to Jackson for troops. A brave associate, Colonel Bradley Johnson, described him at that moment, when the bolt was about to fall: "He was riding at the head of the column with General Ewell, his black face in a blaze of enthusiasm. Every feature beamed with the joy of the soldier. He was gesticulating and pointing out the country and position to General Ewell. I could imagine what he was saying by the motions of his right arm. I pointed him out to my adjutant—'Look at Ashby! see how he is enjoying himself!' " The moment had come. With the infantry, two regiments sent him by Jackson, he made a rapid detour to the right, passed through a field of waving wheat, and approached a belt of woods upon which the golden sunshine of the calm June evening slept in mellow splendour. In the edge of this wood Colonel Kane, of the Pennsylvania "Bucktails," was drawn up, and soon the crash of musketry resounded from the bushes along a fence on the edge of the forest, where the enemy were posted. Ashby rushed to the assault with the fiery enthusiasm of his blood. Advancing at the head of the Fifty-eighth Virginia in front, while Colonel Johnson with the Marylanders attacked the enemy in flank, he had his horse shot under him, but sprang up, waving his sword, and shouting, "Virginians, charge!" These words were his last. From the enemy's line, now within fifty yards, came a storm of bullets; one pierced his breast, and he fell at the very moment when the Bucktails broke, and were pursued by the victorious Southerners. Amid that triumphant shout the great soul of Ashby passed away. Almost before his men could raise him he was dead. He had fallen as he wished to fall—leading a charge, in full war harness, fighting to the last. Placed on a horse in front of a cavalryman, his body was borne out of the wood, just as the last rays of sunset tipped with fire the foliage of the trees; and as the form of the dead chieftain was borne along the lines of infantry drawn up in column, exclamations broke forth, and the bosoms of men who had advanced without a tremor into the bloodiest gulfs of battle, were shaken by uncontrollable sobs. The dead man had become their *beau-ideal* of a soldier; his courage, fire, dash, and unshrinking nerve had won the hearts of these rough men; and now when they read upon that pale face the stamp of the hand of death, a black pall seemed slowly to descend—the light of the June evening was a mockery. That sunset was the glory which fell on the soldier's brow as he passed away. Never did day light to his death a nobler spirit.


## IV.

Mere animal courage is a common trait. It was not the chief glory of this remarkable man that he cared nothing for peril, daring it with an utter recklessness. Many private soldiers of whom the world never heard did as much. The supremely beautiful trait of Ashby was his modesty, his truth, his pure and knightly honour. His was a nature full of heroism, chivalry, and simplicity; he was not only a great soldier, but a chevalier, inspired by the *prisca fides* of the past. "I was with him," said a brave associate, "when the first blow was struck for the cause which we both had so much at heart, and was with him in his last fight, always knowing him to be beyond all modern men in chivalry, as he was equal to any one in courage. He combined the virtues of Sir Philip Sidney with the dash of Murat. His fame will live in the valley of Virginia, outside of books, as long as its hills and mountains shall endure."

Never was truer comparison than that of Ashby to Murat and Sidney mingled; but the splendid truth and modesty of the great English chevalier predominated in him. The Virginian had the dash and fire of Murat in the charge, nor did the glittering Marshal at the head of the French cuirassiers perform greater deeds of daring. But the pure and spotless soul of Philip Sidney, that "mirror of chivalry," was the true antetype of Ashby's. Faith, honour, truth, modesty, a courtesy which never failed, a loyalty which nothing could affect—these were the great traits which made the young Virginian so beloved and honoured, giving him the noble place he held among the men of his epoch. No man lives who can remember a rude action of his; his spirit seemed to have been moulded to the perfect shape of antique courtesy; and nothing could change the pure gold of his nature. His fault as a soldier was a want of discipline; and it has been said with truth that he resembled rather the chief huntsman of a hunting party than a general—mingling with his men in bivouac or around the camp fire, on a perfect equality. But what he wanted in discipline and military rigour he supplied by the enthusiasm which he aroused in the troops. They adored him, and rated him before all other leaders. His wish was their guide in all things; and upon the field they looked to him as their war-king. The flash of his sabre as it left the scabbard drove every hand to the hilt; the sight of his milk-white horse in front was their signal for "attention," and the low clear tones of Ashby's order, "Follow me!" as he moved to the charge, had more effect upon his men than a hundred bugles.

I pray my Northern reader who does me the honour to peruse this sketch, not to regard these sentences as the mere rhapsody of enthusiasm. They contain the truth of Ashby, and those who served with him will testify to the literal accuracy of the sketch. He was one of those men who appear only at long intervals—a veritable realization of the "hero" of popular fancy. The old days of knighthood seemed to live again as he moved before the eye; the pure faith of the earlier years was reproduced and illustrated in his character and career. The anecdotes which remain of his kindness, his courtesy, and warmth of heart, are trifles to those who knew him, and required no such proofs of his sweetness of temper and character. It is nothing to such that when the Northern ladies about to leave Winchester, came and said, "General Ashby, we have nothing contraband about us—you can search our trunks and our persons;" he replied, "The gentlemen of Virginia do not search ladies' trunks or their persons, madam." He made that reply because he was Ashby. For this man to have been rude, coarse, domineering, and insulting to unprotected ladies—as more than one Federal general at Winchester was—that was simply impossible. He might have said, in the words of the old Ulysses, "They live their lives, I mine."

Such was the private character, simple, beautiful, and "altogether lovely," of this man of fibre so hard and unshrinking; of dash, nerve, obstinacy, and daring never excelled. Behind that

sweet and friendly smile was the stubborn and reckless soul of
the born fighter. Under those brown eyes, as mild and gentle
as a girl's, was a brain of fire—a resolution of invincible strength
which dared to combat every adversary, with whatever odds.
His intellect, outside of his profession, was rather mediocre than
otherwise, and he wrote so badly that few of his productions
are worth preserving. But in the field he was a master mind. His
eye for position was that of the born soldier; and he was obliged
to depend upon that native faculty, for he had never been to
West Point or any other military school. They might have improved him—they could not have made him. God had given him
the capacity to fight troops; and if the dictum of an humble
writer, loving and admiring him alive, and now mourning him,
be regarded as unreliable, take the words of Jackson. That cool,
taciturn, and unexcitable soldier never gave praise which was
undeserved. Jackson knew Ashby as well as one human being
ever knew another; and after the fall of the cavalier he wrote of
him, "As a partisan officer, I never knew his superior. His daring
was proverbial, his powers of endurance almost incredible, his
tone of character heroic, and his sagacity almost intuitive in
divining the purposes and movements of the enemy." The man
who wrote these words—himself daring, enduring, and heroic—
had himself some sagacity in "divining the purposes and movements of the enemy," and could recognise that trait in others.

The writer of this page had the honour to know the dead chief
of the Valley cavalry—to hear the sweet accents of his friendly
voice, and meet the friendly glance of the loyal eyes. It seems
to him now, as he remembers Ashby, that the hand he touched
was that of a veritable child of chivalry. Never did taint of
arrogance or vanity, of rudeness or discourtesy, touch that pure
and beautiful spirit. This man of daring so proverbial, of powers
of endurance so incredible, of character so heroic, and of a
sagacity so unfailing that it drew forth the praise of Jackson,
was as simple as a child, and never seemed to dream that he had
accomplished anything to make him famous. But famous he was,
and is, and will be for ever. The bitter struggle in which he bore
so noble a part has ended; the great flag under which he fought

is furled, and none are now so poor as to do it reverence. But in failure, defeat, and ruin, this great name survives; the cloud is not so black that the pure star of Ashby's fame does not shine out in the darkness. In the memories and hearts of the people of the Valley his glory is as fresh to-day as when he fell. He rises up in memory, as once before the actual eye—the cavalier on his milk-white steed, leading the wild charge, or slowly pacing up and down defiantly, with proud face turned over the shoulder, amid the bullets. Others may forget him—we of the Valley cannot. For us his noble smile still shines as it shone amid those glorious encounters of the days of Jackson, when from every hill-top he hurled defiance upon Banks and Fremont, and in every valley met the heavy columns of the Federal cavalry, sabre to sabre. He is dead, but still lives. That career—brief, fiery, crammed with glorious shocks, with desperate encounters—is a thing of the past, and Ashby has "passed like a dream away." But it is only the bodies of such men that die. All that is noble in them survives. What comes to the mind now when we pronounce the name of Ashby, is that pure devotion to truth and honour which shone in every act of his life; that kind, good heart of his which made all love him; that resolution which he early made, to spend the last drop of his blood for the cause in which he fought; and the daring beyond all words, which drove him on to combat whatever force was in his front. We are proud— leave us that at least—that this good knight came of the honest old Virginia blood. He tried to do his duty; and counted toil, and danger, and hunger, and thirst, and exhaustion, as nothing. He died as he had lived, in harness, and fighting to the last. In an unknown skirmish, of which not even the name is preserved, the fatal bullet came; the wave of death rolled over him, and the august figure disappeared. But that form is not lost in the great gulf of forgotten things. Oblivion cannot hide it, nor time dim the splendour of the good knight's shield. The figure of Ashby, on his milk-white steed, his face in "a blaze of enthusiasm," his drawn sword in his hand—that figure will truly live in the memory and heart of the Virginian as long as the battlements of the Blue Ridge stand, and the Shenandoah flows.

# V

## BEAUREGARD

### I.

THE MOST uniformly fortunate General of the late war was Beauregard. So marked was this circumstance, and so regularly did victory perch upon his standard, that Daniel, the trenchant and hardy critic of the *Examiner*, called him Beauregard *Felix*. Among the Romans that term signified happy, fortunate, favoured of the gods; and what is called "good luck" seemed to follow the Confederate leader to whom it was applied. Often he appeared to be outgeneralled, checkmated, and driven to the "last ditch," but ever some fortunate circumstance intervened to change the whole situation. More than once the fortune of war seemed to go against him, but he always retrieved the day by some surprising movement. In the very beginning of his career, at the first great battle of Manassas, when his left was about to be driven to hopeless rout, his good genius sent thither Evans and Jackson, those stubborn obstacles, and the battle which was nearly lost terminated in a victory.

Of this famous soldier I propose to record some traits rather of a personal than a military character. As elsewhere in this series of sketches, the writer's aim will be to draw the outline of the man rather than the official. History will busy itself with that "official" phase; here it is rather the human being, as he lived and moved, and looked when "off duty," that I am to present. The first great dramatic scene of the war, the attack

on Sumter, the stubborn and victorious combat of Shiloh, the
defence of Charleston against Gilmore, the assault upon Butler
near Bermuda Hundred, and the mighty struggles at Petersburg,
will not enter into this sketch at all. I beg to conduct the reader
back to the summer of the year 1861, and to the plains of Manassas, where I first saw Beauregard. My object is to describe the
personal traits and peculiarities of the great Creole as he then
appeared to the Virginians, among whom he came for the first
time.

He superseded Bonham in command of the forces at Manassas
about the first of June, 1861, and the South Carolinians said one
day, "Old Bory's come!" Soon the Virginia troops had an opportunity of seeing this "Old Bory," who seemed so popular
with the Palmettese. He did not appear with any of the "pride,
pomp, and circumstance of glorious war." No flag was unfurled
before him; no glittering staff officers were seen galloping to
and fro; for some days the very presence of the man of Sumter
was merely rumour. Then the troops began to take notice of
a quiet-looking individual in an old blue uniform coat of the
United States Army, almost undecorated, who, mounted on an
unimposing animal not at all resembling a "war horse," moved
about quite unattended, to inspect the works in process of construction, or select new sites for others. Often this solitary
horseman of the reserved demeanour and unobtrusive air was
seen motionless in the middle of the plains, gazing around him;
or in clear relief against the sky, or looking toward Bull Run,
he peopled the landscape doubtless with imaginary squadrons
in hot conflict. Then another step was taken by the men in making acquaintance with the new commander. The silent horseman would pause as he passed by the camps, and speak to the
sentinels—brifly but not stiffly. When they returned to their
quarters they told how General Beauregard had thus stopped
upon his way, spoken with them familiarly as comrade to comrade, and returned their salute at parting, with his finger to the
rim of his cap. Finally, the troops had "a good look at him."
He reviewed a fine regiment from Tennessee, and all eyes were
fixed upon his soldierly figure with admiration—upon the lithe

and sinewy form, the brunette face and sparkling black eyes, the erect head, the firm seat in the saddle, and the air of command. When this nervous figure passed at a rapid gallop along the line, the keen eyes peering from beneath the Zouave cap, the raw volunteers felt the presence of a *soldier*.

The hard battle of Manassas followed, and as noon approached on that famous twenty-first of July, the Southern army seemed completely flanked—Beauregard outgeneralled. McDowell had turned the Confederate left, and, driving Evans, Bee, and Bartow before him, seized on the Henry-House hill, the key of the whole position. Beauregard was four miles off, awaiting an advance of his right wing and centre on the Federal rear at Centreville, ordered hours before. The order miscarried, and the advance was not made; at near two o'clock the troops were still within the lines of Bull Run, and on the extreme left nothing but the two thousand six hundred and eleven muskets of Jackson, with a few companies of Bee, was interposed between the Southern troops and destruction. About thirty thousand men under General Hunter were advancing upon about three thousand—and to this critical point Beauregard now went at a swift gallop, with General Johnston. The scene which followed was a splendid exhibition of personal magnetism. Bee's men were routed; his ranks broken to pieces; the battalions which had breasted the torrent had been shattered by the weight of the huge wave, and were now scarcely more than a crowd of fugitives. Johnston, with the fiery dash which lay perdu under his grave exterior, caught the colours of an Alabama regiment, calling on the men to follow him; and Beauregard passed along the lines at full gallop, rallying the men amid the terrific fire. If he is ever painted, it should be as he appeared that day; eyes flaming, the sallow face in a blaze of enthusiasm, the drawn sword pointing to the enemy, as with a sonorous voice which rang above the firing, he summoned the men to stand for their firesides, and all they held dear upon earth. Beauregard was the superb leader at that moment, and the cheeks of the gray-haired soldier of to-day must flush sometimes as he recalls that death grapple in which the flash of his sword led the charge.

When not thus filled with hot blood, the face of the great Creole, even amid the heat of battle, was composed, firm, set, and did not exhibit, save in a slight deepening of the dusky tint of the complexion, any unwonted feeling. The man was quiet, silent, and seemed to be waiting calmly. I never saw a smile upon his face until some months after the battle, when President Davis came to review the troops at Fairfax Court-House. That smile was caused by a little incident which may entertain some readers. The present writer was sent one day as aide-de-camp in waiting, to escort the wife and little son of General Stuart from the Court-House to the nearest station on the Orange railroad; when, just as the ambulance reached a point midway between the two points, a company of cavalry made its appearance in front, and the officer commanding requested that the vehicle should draw out of the road to "make way for the President." This was done at once, and soon his Excellency, President Davis, appeared, riding between Stuart and Beauregard—the latter wearing his dress uniform with a Zouave cap, the crown of which was an intensely dazzling circle of scarlet, burning in the sunshine. As soon as young J. E. B. Stuart, a little gentleman who used to call himself General Stuart, Jr., saw his father, he stretched out his arms and exclaimed, "Papa, papa!" in a tone so enthusiastic that it attracted attention, and General Stuart said, "This is my family, Mr. President," Whereupon Mr. Davis stopped, saluted the young lady, patted the boy upon the head, and endeavoured to attract his attention, in which he failed however, as the boy's mind was absorbed in the effort to climb before his father. The scene made everybody laugh, from the grave President to the men of the escort, and among the rest General Beauregard. His laugh was peculiar; the eyes sparkled, the firm muscles slowly moved, and the white teeth came out with a quite startling effect under the heavy black moustache. When the cavalcade passed on he was still smiling.

I pray the reader to pardon this long description of a smile. The strangest of all phenomena is the manner in which trifles cling to the memory.

One more personal recollection of Beauregard as I saw him—

not on review, neither at Manassas, Fairfax, or elsewhere; a stiff official figure in front of the lines, but in private, and this time on the outpost. It was at "Camp Qui-Vive," the headquarters of Stuart, beyond Centreville, and in December, 1861. He came to dine and ride out on the lines to inspect the cavalry pickets; and it is not difficult to recall what manner of man he was—so striking was his appearance. He wore the uniform coat of an officer of the United States Army, dark blue with gilt buttons and a stiff collar. The closely buttoned garment displayed his vigorous chest; from the upper edge protruded a sharp, white, standing collar, and he wore the inseparable Zouave cap, with its straight rim projecting over the eyes.

The face of the soldier speedily drew attention, however, from his dress. The countenance, with its broad brow, firm mouth, covered with a heavy black moustache, and protruding chin, full of courage and resolution, was that of a French Marshal of the Empire to the very life. The iron nerve of the man was indelibly stamped upon his features. It was impossible to doubt the fighting instincts of the individual with that muscular contour of face which seemed to defy opposition. The rest of the physiognomy was gaunt, hard, somewhat melancholy. In the complexion was observable the Southern Creole descent of the soldier; it was brunette, sallow, and the sun and wind had made it resemble bronze. It had the dusky pallor, too, of care and watching—that bloodless hue which the pressure of heavy responsibilities produces in the human face. The position of an army leader is not a bed of roses, and the bloom of youth and health soon fades from the cheeks which are hollowed by the anxieties of command. Such was the appearance of the "Man of Sumter," but I have omitted the most striking feature of his face—the eyes. Large, dark, melancholy, with the lids drooping and somewhat inflamed by long vigils—of a peculiar dreamy expression—those eyes impressed the beholder very strangely. It was the eye of the bloodhound with his fighting instincts asleep, but ready at any moment to be strung for action. It was impossible not to be impressed by this resemblance. Not that there was any ferocity or thirst for blood in that slumbrous glance; but if ever "fight" was plain in any look—obstinate, pertinacious, hard "fight"—it was plain in Beauregard's.

## II.

The outline here drawn of the General's appearance may produce the impression that he was stiff, stern, and unsocial. Such was very far from the fact. On the contrary, the manner of the individual was eminently modest, courteous, and pleasing. This may seem to clash with the bloodhound illustration—but both were true. It would be difficult to imagine a finer air of grave politeness, or a more courtly simplicity than General Beauregard's. Of this the writer took especial note, for at that period a great many very foolish things were written and published in relation to the eminent soldier. It was said that he was frigid, moody, unsocial, rude, repulsing all advances to friendly converse with a military coolness amounting to discourtesy. Stray correspondents of the journals had drawn a curious figure and labelled it "Beauregard"—the figure of a sombre, mysterious, and melodramatic personage, prone to attitudinizing and playing the "distinguished warrior;" fond of wrapping his cloak around him, folding his arms, and turning his back when any one addressed him, as though absorbed in some gigantic scheme upon which his mighty brain was working, in a region far above the dull, cold, every-day earth! Such was the Beauregard of many "intelligent correspondents"—play-actor turned soldier; a sort of Manfred in gray uniform; and lo! here before me was the real man. Instead of a mock hero of tragedy stalking about and muttering, the General appeared to me to be a gentleman of great courtesy and simplicity, who asked nothing better than for some kind friend to amuse him and make him laugh.

For the General laughed; and when he did so, he, strangely enough, seemed to enjoy himself. Standing on the portico of the old house in which Stuart had established his quarters, or partaking of his dinner with mundane satisfaction, he appeared entirely oblivious that he was "Beauregard the Great Tragedian," and joined in the conversation simply and naturally, losing

no opportunity to relax by laughter the weary facial muscles
which had settled into something like grimness and melancholy
from care and meditation. The conversation turned during the
day upon the first battle of Manassas; and when some one mentioned the report in many Northern journals that he, Beauregard, had continued to ride a horse after the animal's head was
carried off by a cannon-ball, the General's moustache curled
and he chuckled in the most untragic manner. "My horse was
killed," he said, "but his head was not carried away. He was
struck by a shell, which exploded at the moment when it passed
under him. A splinter struck my boot, and another cut one
of the arteries in the animal's body. The blood gushed out, and
after going fifty yards he fell dead. I then mounted a prisoner's
horse—there was a map of the country in the saddle pocket—
and I remember it was a small dingy horse with a white face."
Laughter followed the remembrance of the small dingy horse
with the white face; and when one of the company observed
that "General Beauregard had done himself considerable credit
in Missouri," meaning to have said "General Price," the General
burst into a laugh which indicated decided enjoyment of the
mistake.

The incidents here recorded are not to be found in any of
the regular histories; and I doubt if any description will be
found of the manner in which General Beauregard essayed to
assist a young lady bearing a very famous name, to mount her
horse. The lady in question was a very charming person, an
intimate friend of General Stuart; and as she was then upon a
visit to the neighbourhood of Centreville, she was invited by the
gay cavalier to dine with Beauregard, and afterwards ride out
upon the lines under escort. A young aide was sent for Miss ——;
she duly arrived, and dined at the outpost headquarters, and
then the moment came to set out for the lines. Before she had
taken two steps toward her horse, General Beauregard was at
her side, completely distancing the young Prince Polignac, that
brave and smiling youth, afterwards Brigadier-General, but at
this time serving upon Beauregard's staff. To see the grave commander assist the fair young lady to mount her horse was a

pleasing sight, and communicated much innocent enjoyment to the spectators. He brought to the undertaking all the chivalric gallantry and politeness of the French De Beauregards; stooping down with an air of the deepest respect; hollowing his hand to receive her slipper; and looking up to ascertain why she did not take advantage of his offer. Whether it was that the young lady thought it indecorous to make such use of that distinguished hand, or did not need his aid, I know not; she laughed, gracefully vaulted into her saddle, and mounting his own steed, the General gallantly took his place at her side.

These things are recorded in place of the "important events" of Beauregard's career. A narrative of his military operations may be found in the "regular histories," and an estimate of his merits as a commander. Upon this latter point a diversity of opinion exists, owing to the tragic termination of the recent conflict. The secret archives of the Confederate government were destroyed, or remain unpublished. Many questions thus remain unanswered. Was Beauregard fully aware of the enemy's movement against his left at Manassas, and did he disregard it, depending on his great assault at Centreville? Did he, or did he not, counsel an advance upon Washington after the battle—an advance which events now known show to have been perfectly practicable? Were his movements on Corinth, in the West, judicious? Were his operations at Petersburg in accordance with the views of the government? All these questions remain unanswered; for the dispatches containing the solution of the whole were destroyed or are inaccessible to the world. One fact is unfortunately very well known—that there was "no love lost" between the celebrated soldier and the Confederate Executive; and by a portion of the Southern press little praise was accorded him. But he did not need it. The victor of Manassas and Shiloh, the man who clung to Sumter until it was a mass of blackened ruins, will be remembered when partisan rancour and injustice are forgotten. Fame knows her children, and her bugle sounds across the years.

A notable trait in the personal character of Beauregard was his kindly *bonhomie* to the private soldier. In this he resembled the officers of Napoleon, not those of the English Army. He had the French habit of mingling with the men when not upon duty, sharing their pursuits, conversing with them, and lighting his cigar at their camp fires. From this sprang much of his personal popularity, and he thus excited largely that sympathy which rendered him so acceptable to his troops. To a General, nothing is more important than this sympathy. It is a weapon with which the master soldier strikes his hardest blows, and often springs from apparent trifles. Napoleon became the idol of his troops as much by his personal bearing toward them as from his victories. He was the *grand Napoleon*—but he stopped to talk with the men by their fires: he called them *"mes enfans:"* he fixed his dark eyes with magnetic sympathy upon the dying soldier who summoned his last remains of strength to half rise from the earth, extend his arms, and cry, *"Vive l'Empereur!"* He took this personal interest in them—the interest of a comrade—and no one else could rival him in their favour.

Beauregard had certainly secured this personal popularity. He invariably exhibited the utmost kindness, compatible with discipline, toward his men, and they remained true to him—as the Federal troops did to McClellan—through all his reverses, giving him in return for his sympathy and familiarity an immense amount of good feeling and regard. A trifling incident will illustrate this. A private soldier of the "Powhatan troop" —a company of cavalry which served as the General's bodyguard—one day entered Beauregard's apartment, and wishing to write a letter, seated himself, as he supposed, at the desk of one of the clerks for that purpose. Taking a sheet of paper and a pen which lay near, he commenced his letter, and was soon absorbed in it. While thus engaged, he heard a step behind him, turned his head, and saw General Beauregard enter, whereupon he suddenly rose in confusion—for all at once the truth flashed upon him that he was writing at *the General's desk, on the General's paper, and with the General's pen!* Fearing a harsh rebuke for this act of military *lese-majesté*, the trooper stammered out an apology; but no storm came from the General. "Sit down and finish your letter my friend," he said, with a good-humoured smile; "you are very welcome, and can always come in here when you wish to write." It was trifles like this which made the announcement of his removal from the command of the Army of the Potomac run like an electric shock through the camps, which caused a great concourse of soldiers to follow him through Centreville and far upon his road, shouting "Good-by, General!"—"God bless you, General!"

To suppose that this brother-feeling of the soldier for his troops ever led him to relax in discipline, would be a great mistake. In official matters, and wherever "duty" was concerned, he was rigid and immovable, exacted from every man under him the strictest obedience and was wholly inaccessible to any prayer which came in conflict with the good of the public service. When at Centreville, in the fall of 1861, he expected daily an advance of McClellan. One morning a cannoneer from one of the batteries came in person to ask for a leave of absence of ten days to see his dying mother. "I cannot grant any leave," was the reply. "Only for ten days, General," pleaded the soldier. "Not for ten hours!" replied Beauregard; and the interview terminated. Had the moment not been critical he would have given this private soldier the desired leave with the utmost readiness—as he would have commended and promoted him, for the display of skill or gallantry.

That all-important point of rewarding merit in the private soldier was never neglected by Beauregard. An instance was the promotion of a young man in the Loudoun cavalry, whose conspicuous courage and efficiency in reconnoitring and carrying orders at Manassas attracted his attention. At the close of the day the obscure private was summoned to headquarters and informed by Beauregard that he would henceforth rank as a captain of his staff. This gentleman was afterwards Colonel Henry E. Peyton, Inspector-General of the Army of Northern Virginia, one of the bravest and most accomplished officers in the service.

A last incident relating to "Beauregard the Great Tragedian," who was supposed to be playing "Lara," "Manfred," or some other sombre and mysterious character at Manassas, in those far away times. It may add an additional touch to the outline I have aimed to draw. It was in the summer of 1861 that some young ladies of Prince William prepared a handsome nosegay for presentation to the General; and as he had amongst his clerks a gentleman of high culture, the nosegay was entrusted to him for delivery. He consented with reluctance. To present a bunch of flowers to the silent and abstracted commander, whose faculties were burdened by great cares and responsibilities, seemed an incongruity which strangely impressed the ambassador; but there was the nosegay, there were the young ladies, there was his promise, and he nerved himself for the task. Waiting until all intruders had left the General's presence, he timidly knocked at the door of his sanctum, was bidden in a grave voice to enter, and advancing into the apartment, found opposite to him the imposing eye and "brow severe" of General Beauregard, who had never looked more stern. The spectacle very nearly disarmed the ambassador of his presence of mind; but he determined to accomplish is errand in the best manner possible, and accordingly proceeded to address the solemn General in what the newspapers call a "neat little speech." Having finished, he presented the flowers, drew back respectfully, and nerved himself for the result. That result surprisingly differed from his expectations. Beauregard cleared his throat, looked extremely confused, and stammering "Thank you! I am very much obliged!" received the bouquet, blushing as he did so like a girl. Such was the tragedy-hero of those journalists of 1861.

### III.

I have tried to draw an outline of the actual man, not to make a figure of the fancy; to present an accurate likeness of General Beauregard as he appeared to us of Virginia in those first months of the war, not to drape the individual in historic robes, making him an actor or a myth.

He was neither; he was simply a great soldier, and a finished gentleman. Once in his presence, you would not be apt to deny his claim to both of these characters. The nervous figure, the gaunt, French, fighting, brunette countenance, deeply bronzed by sun and wind—these were the marks of the soldier. The grave, high-bred politeness; the ready, courteous smile; the kindly and simple bearing, wholly free from affectation and assumption—these were the characteristics of the *gentilhomme* by birth and habit, by nature as by breeding.

Ten minutes' conversation with the man convinced you that you stood in the presence of one of those men who mould events. The very flash of the dark eyes "dared you to forget."

Nor will the South forget this brave and trusty soldier. His name is cut upon the marble of history in letters too deep to be effaced by the hand of Time, that terrible disintegrator. As long as the words "Manassas" and "Shiloh" strike a chord in the bosoms of men, the name "Beauregard" will also stir the pulses. Those mighty conflicts meet us in the early epoch of the war, grim, bloody, and possessing a tragedy of their own. The soldier who fought those battles confronts us, too, with an individuality of mind and body which cannot be mistaken. Lee is the Virginian, Hood the Texan; Beauregard is the marshal of Napoleon—or at least he looked thus in those early days when the soldiers of Virginia, gathering at Manassas, closely scanned the form and features of their new commander.

From Virginia the great captain went to the West, where, as the world knows, he won new laurels; and to the end he continued to justify his title of "The Fortunate." That is only, however, another name for The Able, The Skilful, The Master of events—not by "luck," but by brains. Good-fortune is an angel who flies from the weak and fearful, but yields herself captive to the resolute soul who clutches her. If any doubted that Beauregard owed his great success to the deepest thought, the most exhausting brain-work, and those sleepless vigils which wear out the life, they had only to look upon him in his latter years to discover the truth. Care, meditation, watching—all the huge responsibility of an army leader—had stamped on the brow of the great Creole their unmistakable impress. The heavy moustache, which had once been as black as the raven's wing, was now grizzled like the beard. In the hair, which before was dark, now shone those silver threads which toil and anxiety weave mercilessly in the locks of their victims. The mouth smiled still, but the muscles had assumed a grimmer tension. The eyes were still brilliant, but more deeply sunken and more slumbrous. In the broad brow, once so smooth, the iron hand of care had ploughed the inexorable furrows.

Beauregard the youthful, daring, and impetuous soldier, had become Beauregard the cautious, thoughtful, self-sacrificing patriot—one of the great props of the mighty edifice then tottering beneath the heavy blows it was receiving in Virginia and the West.

"The self-sacrificing patriot." If any one doubts his claim to that title, it will not be doubted when events now buried in obscurity are known. Beauregard was superb when, in the midst of the dense smoke of Manassas, he shouted in his inspiring voice, "I salute the Eighth Georgia with my hat off! History shall never forget you!" But he was greater still—more noble and more glorious—when after the battle of Corinth he said nothing.

He was silent, and is silent still; but history speaks for him, and will ever speak. He lives in the memories and the hearts of his old soldiers, as in the pages of our annals; and those who followed his flag, who listened to his voice, need no page like this to bring his figure back, as it blazed before their eyes in the far away year '61. They remember him always, and salute him from their hearts—as does the writer of these lines.

Wherever you may be, General—whether in Rome or New Orleans, in the Old World or the New—whether in sickness or in health, in joy or in sorrow—your old soldiers of the Army of Virginia remember you, and wish you long life, health, and happiness, from their heart of hearts.

# VI

## EARLY

### I.

IN THE Virginia Convention of 1860–61, when the great struggle for separation took place, and the hot war of tongues preceded the desperate war of the bayonet, there was a gentleman of resolute courage and military experience who made himself prominent among the opponents of secession. Belonging to the old Whig party, and thinking apparently that the right moment had not yet come, this resolute soldier-politician fought the advocates of the ordinance with unyielding persistence, aiming by his hard-hitting argument, his kindling eloquence, and his parliamentary skill, to give to the action of the Convention that direction which his judgment approved. Many called him a "submissionist," because he opposed secession then; but when the gauntlet was thrown down, this "Whig submissionist" put on a gray coat, took the field, and fought from the beginning to the very end of the war with a courage and persistence surpassed by no Southerner who took part in the conflict. When he was sent to invade Maryland, and afterwards was left by General Lee in command of that "forlorn hope," the little Valley army, if it could be called such, in the winter of 1864–5, he was selected for the work, because it required the brain and courage of the soldier of hard and stubborn fibre. Only since the termination of the war has the world discovered the truth of that great campaign; the desperate character of the situation which Early occupied, and the enormous odds against which he fought.

He entered upon the great arena almost unknown. He had served in the Mexican war, and had there displayed skill and courage; but his position was a subordinate one, and he was better known as a politician than a soldier. In the field he made his mark at once. About four o'clock in the afternoon of the 21st of July, 1861, at Manassas, the Federal forces had been driven by the resolute assault of Jackson and his great associates from the Henry-House hill; but a new and formidable line-of-battle was formed on the high ground beyond, near Dogan's house, and the swarming masses of Federal infantry were thrown forward for a last desperate charge. The object of the Federal commander was to outflank and envelop the Confederate left, and his right wing swayed forward to accomplish that object, when all at once from the woods, which the enemy were aiming to gain, came a galling fire which staggered and drove them back. This fire was delivered by Kirby Smith and Early. So hot was it that it completely checked the Federal charge; and as they wavered, the Southern lines pressed forward with wild cheers. The enemy were forced to give ground. Their ranks broke, and in thirty minutes the grand army was in full retreat across Bull Run. The "Whig Submissionist" had won his spurs in the first great battle of the war. From that time Early was in active service, and did hard work everywhere—in the Peninsula, where he was severely wounded in the hard struggle of Malvern Hill, and then as General Early, at Cedar Mountain, where he met and repulsed a vigorous advance of General Pope's left wing, in the very inception of the battle. If Early had given way there, Ewell's column on the high ground to his right would have been cut off from the main body; but the ground was obstinately held, and victory followed. Advancing northward thereafter, Jackson threw two brigades across at Warrenton Springs, under Early, and these resolutely held their ground in face of an overpowering force. Thenceforward Early continued to add to his reputation as a hard fighter—at Bristoe, the second Manassas, Harper's Ferry, Sharpsburg, Fredericksburg,

Gettysburg, Spotsylvania, Monocacy, and throughout the Valley campaign. During the invasion of Pennsylvania he led General Lee's advance, which reached the Susquehanna and captured York. In Spotsylvania he commanded Hill's corps, and was in the desperate fighting at the time of the assault upon the famous "Horseshoe," and repulsed an attack of Burnside's corps with heavy loss to his opponents. After that hard and bitter struggle the Federal commander gave up all hope of forcing General Lee's lines, and moving by the left flank reached Cold Harbour, where the obstinate struggle recommenced. It was at this moment, when almost overpowered by the great force arrayed against him, that General Lee received intelligence of the advance of General Hunter up the Valley with a considerable army; and it was necessary to detach a commander of ability, vigour, and daring to meet that column. Early was selected, and the result is known. General Hunter advanced, in spite of opposition from the cavalry under General Jones, until he reached the vicinity of Lynchburg; but here he came in collision with his dangerous adversary. A complete defeat of the Federal forces followed, and Hunter's campaign was decided at one blow. He gave ground, retreated, and, with constantly accelerated speed, sought refuge in the western mountains, whence, with a decimated and disheartened army, he hastened towards the Ohio. The great advance up the Valley, from which, as his report shows, General Grant had expected so much, had thus completely failed. The campaign beginning with such high hopes, had terminated in ignominy and disaster. The inhabitants of the region, subjected by General Hunter to the most merciless treatment, saw their powerful oppressor in hopeless retreat; and an advance which threatened to paralyse Lee, and by severing his communications, drive him from Virginia, had been completely defeated. Such was the first evidence given by General Early of his ability as a corps commander, operating without an immediate superior.

He was destined to figure now, however, in scenes more striking and "dramatic" still. General Grant, with about 150,000 men, was pressing General Lee with about 50,000, and forcing him slowly back upon the Confederate capital. Every resource of the Confederacy was strained to meet this terrible assault—the sinews almost broken in the effort. To divert reinforcements from General Grant was a matter of vital importance—a thing of life and death—and Jackson's Valley campaign in 1862 had shown how this could be most effectually done. To menace the Federal capital was evidently the great secret: a moderate force would not probably be able to do more than divert troops from Grant; but this was an object of the first importance, and much might be accomplished by a soldier of decision, energy, and rapidity of movement. Early had been selected for the work, with orders when he left the lowland to "move to the Valley through Swift Run Gap or Brown's Gap, attack Hunter, and then cross the Potomac and threaten Washington." This critical task he now undertook with alacrity, and he accomplished it with very great skill and success.

Not a moment was lost in pushing his column toward Maryland; and such was the rapidity of the march upon Washington, that the capital was placed in imminent danger. In spite of the prostrating heat, the troops made twenty miles a day, and the rumour of this determined advance came to the Federal authorities at the moment when Grant was supposed to be carrying everything before him. To meet the attack of their formidable adversary, the authorities at Washington sent to hurry forward the forces of General Hunter from the Ohio, and a considerable force from General Grant's army was dispatched up the bay to man the fortifications. Early had pressed on, crossed the Potomac, advanced to Frederick City, defeated General Wallace at the Monocacy, and was now in sight of the defences of Washington; the crack of his skirmishers was heard at the "White House" and in the department buildings of the capital. The enormous march, however, had broken down and decimated his army. The five hundred miles of incessant advance, at twenty miles a day, left him only eight thousand infantry, about forty field-pieces, and two thousand badly mounted cavalry—at the moment detached against the railroads northward—with which to assault the powerful works, bristling with cannon, in his front. His position at this moment was certainly critical, and calculated to try the nerves of any but a resolute and daring soldier. He was in the heart of the enemy's country, or at least in sight of their capital city; in his front, according to Mr. Stanton, the Federal Secretary of War, was the Sixth and part of the Eighth and Nineteenth Corps, and General Hunter was hastening from the West to strike his rear and cut him off from his only avenue of retreat across the Potomac. It behoved the Confederate commander under these circumstances to look to his safety; and he was reluctantly compelled to give up his intended assault upon the capital—to abandon the attempt to seize the rich prize apparently in his very grasp. Early, accordingly, broke up his camp, retreated, and, with little molestation, recrossed the Potomac, and stood at bay on the Opequon in the Shenandoah Valley.

Such had been the result of the daring advance upon the Federal capital. The extent of the danger to which Washington was then exposed, still remains a matter of doubt and difference of opinion among the most intelligent persons. It will, no doubt, be accurately defined when the events of the recent struggle come to be closely investigated by the impartial historian of the future, and the truth is sifted from the error. To the world at large, the Federal capital seemed in no little danger on that July morning, when Early's lines were seen advancing to the attack. Northern writers state that, if the assault had been made on the day before, it would have resulted in the capture of the city. But however well or ill-founded this may be, it is safe to say that the primary object of the march had been accomplished when Early retreated and posted himself in the Shenandoah Valley—a standing threat to repeat his audacious enterprise. It was no longer a mere detached column that opposed him, but an army of about 50,000 men. To that extent General Grant had been weakened, and the heavy weight upon General Lee's shoulders lightened.

## II.

These events took place in the summer of 1864, and in the autumn of that year General Early fought his famous battles, and—the world said—sustained his ignominious defeats in the Shenandoah Valley. "Ignominious" was the adjective which expressed the views of nine-tenths of the citizens outside of the immediate region, and probably of one-half the army of Northern Virginia. In the eyes of the world there is a crime for which there is no palliation, and that is failure. There is a criminal to whom all defence is denied—it is the man who fails. No matter what the failure results from, there it is, and no explanations are "in order." Early was defeated in a pitched battle near Winchester, on the 19th of September, and the country, gloomy, despondent, embittered, and clamouring for a victory, broke out into curses almost at the man who had sustained this reverse. It was his bad generalship, they cried; "the troops had no confidence in him;" he was the poorest of soldiers, the veriest sham general—else why, with *his splendid army*, did he allow a second or third-rate general like Sheridan to defeat him? When the defeat at Fisher's Hill followed, and the *fiasco* at Waynesboro' terminated the Valley campaign, people were convinced that General Jubal A. Early was a very great dunce in military matters, had been outgeneralled and outfought by an opponent little, if any, stronger than himself, and the whole campaign was stigmatized as a disgraceful series of blunders, ending in well-merited defeat and disaster.

That was the popular clamour; but it is safe to say that popular clamour is essentially falsehood, because it is based upon passion and ignorance. The truth of that campaign is that Early was "leading a forlorn hope," and that he never fought less than four to one. At Fisher's Hill and Waynesboro', he fought about eight to one. It is not upon General Early's statements in his recent letter from Havana, that the present writer makes the above allegation, but upon the testimony of officers and citizens of the highest character who are unanimous in their statement to the above effect. From the date of the battle of Winchester, or the Opequon, to the present time, it has been persistently declared by the fairest and best informed gentlemen of the surrounding region, who had excellent opportunities to discover the truth, that Early's force in that fight was about eight or ten thousand, and Sheridan's about forty or fifty thousand. General Early states upon his honour—and the world is apt to believe him—that his effective strength in this action was eight thousand five hundred muskets, three battalions of artillery, and less than three thousand cavalry. General Sheridan's force he makes, upon a close calculation, about thirty-five thousand muskets, one of his corps alone numbering, as captured documents showed, twelve thousand men—more than the whole Southern force, infantry, cavalry, and artillery. In the number of guns Sheridan, he says, was, "vastly superior" to him; and official reports captured showed the Federal cavalry "present for duty" two days before the battle, to have numbered ten thousand men.* There

---

* An interesting discussion has taken place in the journals of the day, in reference to the forces of Early and Sheridan at the battle of the Opequon. The latter replied to Early's statement by charging him with falsifying history; and this reply drew forth in turn statements from Southern officers—some sentences from which are quoted:

"I know of my own personal knowledge," wrote an officer in the New Orleans *Picayune*, January 13, 1866, "that General Early's statement is correct, when he states that he had about eight thousand five hundred muskets in the second engagement with General Sheridan. I was a staff officer for four years in the army of Northern Virginia. I was a division staff officer, Second Army Corps, under General Early's command, from the time the Second Corps was detached from the Army of Northern Virginia, June 1864, to the time it was ordered to Petersburg, December, 1864. I was present at the battles of Winchester, Fisher's Hill, and Cedar Creek. I know from the official reports that I myself made, and from actual observation at reviews, drills, inspections in camp, and on the march, the effective strength of every brigade and division of infantry under General Early's command (of the cavalry and artillery I cannot speak so authoritatively), and I can therefore assert that in neither one of these actions above mentioned, did General Early carry nine thousand men (infantry) into the fight."

"*One who served on Early's staff*," writes in the New York *News* of February 10, 1866:

"The writer of this has in his possession the *highest* and most *conclusive* evidence of the truth of Early's statement of his infantry force; and in fact without this proof, it could have been substantially established by the evidence here in Lynchburg of these facts, that fifteen trains of the Virginia and Alexandria Railroad (no one train of a capacity of carrying five hundred men) brought the whole of the Second Corps of the Confederate

Army under division commanders Gordon, Rodes, and Ramseur to this place: that Breckenridge's division, then here, was only about two thousand men: and that these were all of the infantry carried from this place by Early down the Valley after his chase of Hunter. It will thus be perceived that Early's estimate (eight thousand five hundred) was quite full so far; and after the Winchester and Fisher's Hill engagements, his statement that Kershaw's division of two thousand seven hundred then added, did not exceed his previous losses, ought certainly not to be objected to by Sheridan who assails Early's veracity with the assertion that he inflicted on him a loss of twenty-six thousand eight hundred and thirty-one men!"

The *Richmond Times* says: "Of General Early's actual force on the 19th of September, 1864, the day of the battle of Winchester, his first defeat, we can give statistics nearly official, procured from an officer of rank who held a high command during the campaign, and who had every opportunity of knowing. Early's infantry consisted of

| | |
|---|---|
| Gordon's Division | 2,000 |
| Ramseur's Division | 2,000 |
| Rodes' Division | 2,500 |
| Breckenridge's Division | 1,800 |
| Total Infantry | 8,300 |

CAVALRY—FITZ LEE'S DIVISION

| | |
|---|---|
| Wickham's Brigade | 1,000 |
| Lomax's old Brigade | 600 |

LOMAX'S DIVISION

| | |
|---|---|
| McCauseland's Brigade | 800 |
| Johnson's Brigade | 700 |
| Imboden's Brigade | 400 |
| Jackson's Brigade | 300 |
| Total Cavalry | 3,800 |

ARTILLERY

| | |
|---|---|
| Three Battalions Light Artillery | 40 guns |
| One Battalion Horse Artillery | 12 guns |
| Total guns | 52 guns |

About one thousand artillerists.

"This recapitulation embraces all the forces of Early's command. General Sheridan, according to official statements, had under his command over thirty-five thousand muskets, eight thousand sabres, and a proportionate quantity of artillery."

The force of Sheridan is not a matter of dispute: that of Early is defined with sufficient accuracy by the above statements from honourable officers. [J.E.C.]

was thus a terrible disproportion between the Federal and Confederate forces. Greatly outnumbered in artillery; with thirty-five thousand muskets opposed to his eight thousand five hundred; and ten thousand excellently mounted and armed cavalry to his three thousand miserably mounted and equipped horsemen; Early occupied anything but a bed of roses in those days of September, when his little force so defiantly faced the powerful army opposed to it.

Why he was not attacked and driven up the Valley long before the 19th of September, will remain an interesting historical problem. Nothing but the unceasing activity and audacity of the Confederate commander appears to have retarded this consummation. General Hunter seems to have been paralysed, or intimidated by the incessant movements of his wary opponent. From the period of his return to the Valley from Washington, Early had given his adversary no breathing spell. To-day he seemed retreating up the Valley; on the next day he was in Maryland; when he fell back and his adversary followed, a sudden and decisive blow at the head of the pursuing column threw the whole Federal programme into confusion; and grim and defiant, Early faced General Hunter in line of battle, defying him to make an attack.

It will be hard to establish the statement that in these movements, during the summer and autumn of 1864, in the Shenandoah Valley, Early did not carry out in the fullest degree the instructions received from General Lee, and accomplish admirably the objects for which he had been sent to that region. He was placed there as Jackson had been in 1862, to divert a portion of the Federal forces from the great arena of combat in the lowland. By his movements before and after the battle of Kernstown, Jackson, with about four thousand men, kept about twenty-five thousand of the enemy in the Valley. By his movements preceding the battle of Opequon, Early, with eight or ten thousand men, kept between forty and fifty thousand from General Meade's army at Petersburg. That he could meet the Federal force in his front, in a fair pitched battle, was not probably believed by himself or by General Lee. His command was essentially what he calls it, a "forlorn hope"—the hope that it could cope with its opponents being truly forlorn. As long as that opponent was amused, retarded, or kept at arm's length, all was well. When he advanced to attack in earnest, it was doubtless foreseen that the thirty or forty thousand bayonets would drive back the eight or nine thousand. That result followed on the 19th of September, when, Sheridan having superseded Hunter, the attack was made at the Opequon. And yet nothing is better established than the fact that up to the moment when he put his cavalry in motion against the Confederate left, General Sheridan had been virtually defeated. Every assault of his great force of infantry had been repulsed; and nowhere does this more clearly appear than in an account of the action published in *Harper's Magazine*, by a field officer, apparently of one of the Federal regiments. That account is fair, lucid, and records the precise truth, namely, that every advance of the Federal infantry was met and repulsed. Not until the ten thousand cavalry of General Sheridan advanced on the Martinsburg road, attained the Confederate rear, and charged them in flank and rear, was there the least wavering. It is true that from that moment the action was lost. Early's line gave way in confusion; his artillery was fought to the muzzle of the guns, but could do nothing unsupported; and that night the Confederate forces were in full retreat up the Valley.

Such, divested of all gloss and rodomontade, was the battle on the Opequon. It was a clear and unmistakable defeat, but the reader has seen what produced it. Not want of generalship in the Confederate commander. It is gross injustice to him to charge him with the responsibility of that reverse; and no fair mind, North or South, will do so. He was defeated, because the force opposed to him was such as his command could not compete with. By heroic fighting, the little band kept back the swarming forces of the enemy, holding their ground with the nerve of veterans who had fought in a hundred battles; but when the numerous and excellently armed cavalry of the enemy thundered down upon their flank and rear, they gave up the struggle, and yielded the hard fought day.

The second act of this exciting drama was played at Fisher's Hill, three days afterward. Sullenly retiring like a wounded wolf, who snarls and shows his teeth at every step, Early took up a position on the great range of hills above Strasburg, and waited to be attacked. His design was to repulse any assault, and at nightfall retire; but the enemy's large numbers enabling them to turn his flank, they drove him from his position, and he was forced to fall back in disorder, with heavy loss. This result was charged upon the cavalry, but Early's small force could not defend the ground, and the Federals assuredly gained few laurels there. So heavy had been the blow struck by the great force of the enemy three days before, that it is wonderful how the Southern troops could make any stand at all. Early's loss in the battle of the Opequon, in killed, wounded, and "missing" —that terrible item in a defeated and retreating army—was so great, that it is doubtful whether his army, when it stood at bay on Fisher's Hill, numbered four thousand muskets. Such, at least, is the statement of intelligent and veracious officers who took part in the engagement. They are unanimous in declaring that it did not exceed that number. Sheridan's force they declare to have been overpowering, but the Southern troops could and did meet it when the attack was made in front. Not until the great force of the enemy enabled him to turn the left flank of Early and sweep right down his line of works, did the troops give way. Numbers overcame everything.

Early retreated up the Valley, where he continued to present a defiant front to the powerful force of Sheridan, until the middle of October. On the 19th he was again at Cedar Creek, between Strasburg and Winchester, and had struck an almost mortal blow at General Sheridan. The Federal forces were surprised, attacked at the same moment in front and flank, and driven in complete rout from their camps. Unfortunately this great success did not effect substantial results. The enemy, who largely outnumbered Early, especially in their excellent cavalry, re-formed their line under General Wright. Sheridan, who had just arrived, exerted himself to retrieve the bad fortune of the day, and the Confederates were forced to retire in their turn.

General Early's account of this event is interesting: "I went into this fight," he says, "with eight thousand five hundred muskets, about forty pieces of artillery, and about twelve hundred cavalry, as the rest of my cavalry, which was guarding the Luray Valley, did not get up in time, though ordered to move at the same time I moved to the attack. Sheridan's infantry had been recruited fully up to its strength at Winchester, and his cavalry numbered eight thousand seven hundred, as shown by the official reports captured. The main cause why the rout of his army in the morning was not complete, was the fact that my cavalry could not compete with his, and the latter, therefore, remained intact. He claimed all his own guns that had been captured in the morning, and afterward recaptured, as so many guns captured from me, whereas I lost only twenty-three guns; and the loss of these and the wagons which were taken, was mainly owing to the fact that a bridge, on a narrow part of the road between Cedar Creek and Fisher's Hill, broke down, and the guns and wagons, which latter were not numerous, could not be brought off. Pursuit was not made to Mount Jackson, as stated by both Grant and Stanton, but my troops were halted for the night at Fisher's Hill, three miles from Cedar Creek, and the next day moved back to New Market, six miles from Mount Jackson, without any pursuit at all."

Thus terminated the Valley campaign of 1864. In November, Early again advanced nearly to Winchester, but his offer of battle was refused, and he went into winter quarters near Staunton, with the small and exhausted force which remained with him, the second corps having been returned to General Lee. He had then only a handful of cavalry and a "corporal's guard" of infantry. In February, 1865, when the days of the Confederacy were numbered and the end was near, he was to give the *quidnuncs* and his enemies generally one more opportunity of denouncing his bad generalship and utter unfitness for command. In those dark days, when hope was sinking and the public "pulse was low," every reverse enraged the people. The whole country was nervous, excited, irascible, exacting. The people would hear no explanations—they wanted victories. Such was the state of public sentiment when intelligence came from the mountains that Early's "army" had been again attacked, this time near Staunton, and owing to the excessively bad generalship of that officer, had sustained utter and ignominious defeat. How many thousands of men had thus been defeated was not exactly stated; but the public said that it was an "army." It was one thousand infantry and about six pieces of artillery. This force was attacked by two divisions of cavalry, numbering five thousand each—ten thousand in all. Early had not a mounted man, his entire cavalry force, with the rest of his artillery, having been sent off to forage. By the great force of the enemy, Early was driven beyond the mountains, his command hopelessly defeated, and his name was everywhere covered with obloquy and insult. He said nothing, waiting with the equanimity of a brave man for the moment which would enable him to justify himself. He has done it now; and no manly heart will read his noble words without respect for this true patriot and fearless soldier. "Obvious reasons of policy," he says, "prevented any publication of these facts during the war, and it will now be seen that *I was leading a forlorn hope all the time, and the people can appreciate the character of the victories won by Sheridan over me.*"

But this is General Early's account of the campaign, it may be said. It is natural—some persons even now may say—that he should endeavour by "special pleading" to lift from his name the weight of obloquy, and strive to show that he was not deficient in military ability, in courage, skill, and energy. The objection is just; no man is an altogether fair witness in regard to his own character and actions. Somewhere, a fault will be palliated, a merit exaggerated. Fortunately for Early's fame—unfortunately for the theory of his enemies—a document of the most conclusive character exists, and with that paper in his hand, the brave soldier may fearlessly present himself before the bar of history. It is the letter of General Lee, to him, dated March 30, 1865, three days before that "beginning of the end," the evacuation of Petersburg. The clamour against Early had accomplished the object of many of those who raised it. His ability was distrusted; he was regarded as unfit for command; "remove him!" was the cry of the people. Here is General Lee's letter relieving him of his command. It would be an injustice to the good name of Early to suppress a line of it.

"HD. QRS. C. S. ARMIES, March 30, 1865.

"*Lieut.-Gen.* J. A. EARLY, *Franklin C. H., Va.:*

"DEAR SIR: My telegram will have informed you that I deem a change of commanders in your department necessary, but it is due to your zealous and patriotic services that I should explain the reasons that prompted my action. The situation of affairs is such that we can neglect no means calculated to develop the resources we possess to the greatest extent, and make them as efficient as possible. To this end it is essential that we should have the cheerful and hearty support of the people and the full confidence of the soldiers, without which our efforts would be embarrassed, and our means of resistance weakened. I have reluctantly arrived at the conclusion that you cannot command the united and willing co-operation which is so essential to success. Your reverses in the Valley, of which the public and the army judge chiefly by the results, have, I fear, impaired your influence both with the people and the soldiers, and would add greatly to the difficulties which will, under any circumstances, attend our military operations in S. W. Va. While my own confidence in your ability, zeal, and devotion to the cause, is unimpaired, I have nevertheless felt that I could not oppose what seems to be the current of opinion, without injustice to your reputation and injury to the service. I therefore felt constrained to endeavour to find a commander who would be more likely to develop the strength and resources of the country and inspire the soldiers with confidence, and to accomplish this purpose, thought it proper to yield my own opinion, and defer to that of those to whom alone we can look for support. I am sure that you will understand and appreciate my motives, and that no one will be more ready than yourself to acquiesce in any measure which the interests of the country may seem to require, regardless of all personal considerations. Thanking you for the fidelity and energy with which you have always supported my

efforts, and for the courage and devotion you have ever manifested in the service of the country, I am, very respectfully and
truly, your obedient servant,          "R. E. LEE, General."

In defeat, poverty, and exile, this recognition of his merit remains to that brave soldier; and it is enough. There is something
better than the applauses of the multitude—something which
will outweigh in history the clamour of the ignorant or the
hostile; it is this testimony of Robert E. Lee to the "zealous and
patriotic services" of the man to whom it refers; to the "ability,
zeal, devotion, fidelity, energy, and courage" which he had
"ever manifested in the service of the country," leaving the
"confidence" of the Commander-in-Chief in him "unimpaired."

## III.

In concluding this sketch, an attempt will be made to give the
reader some idea of the personal character and appearance of
the brave man who, in his letter from Havana, has made that
calm and decorous appeal to posterity.

General Early, during the war, appeared to be a person of
middle age; was nearly six feet in height; and, in spite of severe
attacks of rheumatism, could undergo great fatigue. His hair
was dark and thin, his eyes bright, his smile ready and expressive,
though somewhat sarcastic. His dress was plain gray, with few
decorations. Long exposure had made his old coat quite dingy.
A wide-brimmed hat overshadowed his sparkling eyes and forehead, browned by sun and wind. In those sparkling eyes could
be read the resolute character of the man, as in his smile was
seen the evidence of that dry, trenchant, often mordant humour,
for which he was famous.

The keen glance drove home the wit or humour, and every
one who ventured upon word-combats with Lieutenant-General
Early sustained "a palpable hit." About some of his utterances
there was a grim effectiveness which it would be hard to excel.
There was a member of the Virginia Convention who had called
him a "submissionist" in that body, but when the war com-

menced, hired a substitute, and remained at home, though healthy and only forty. Early the "submissionist" went into the army, fought hard, and then one day in 1862 met his quondam critic, who said to him, "It was very hard to get you *to go out*" —alluding to Early's course in the Convention on secession. Early's eye flashed, his lip curled. "Yes," he replied, looking at the black broadcloth of his companion, "but it is a d—d sight harder to get you up to the fighting." There was another member of the Convention who had often criticised him, and dwelt upon the importance of "maintaining our rights in the territories at all hazards." This gentleman, being aged, did not go into the army; and one day when Early met him, during the retreat from Manassas, the General said, with his customary wit, "Well, Mr. M——, what do you think about getting our rights in the territories now? It looks like we were going to lose some of our own territory, don't it?" When General Lee's surrender was announced to him, while lying nearly dead in his ambulance, he muttered to his surgeon, "Doctor, I wish there was powder enough in the centre of the earth to blow it to atoms. I would apply the torch with the greatest pleasure. If Gabriel ever means to blow his horn, now is the time for him to do it—no more joyful sound could fall on my ears."

These hits he evidently enjoyed, and he delivered them with the coolness of a swordsman making a mortal lunge. In fact, everything about General Early was bold, straightforward, masculine, and incisive. Combativeness was one of his great traits.

There were many persons in and out of the army who doubted the soundness of his judgment; there were none who ever called in question the tough fibre of his courage. He was universally recognised in the Army of Northern Virginia as one of the hardest fighters of the struggle; and every confidence was felt in him as a combatant, even by his personal enemies. This repute he had won on many fields, from the first Manassas to Winchester; for one of the hardest fights of the war, if it was a defeat, was that affair on the Opequon.

It was not so much good judgment that General Early wanted

in his Valley campaign, as troops. He was "leading a forlorn hope," and forlorn hopes rarely succeed. "He has done as well as any one could," General Lee is reported to have said; and the Commander-in-Chief had better opportunities of forming a correct opinion than others.

Returning to Early the man, what most impressed those who were thrown with him, was that satirical, sometimes cynical humour, and the force and vigour of his conversation. His voice was not pleasing, but his "talk" was excellent. His intellect was evidently strong, combative, aggressive in all domains of thought; his utterance direct, hard-hitting, and telling. He was a forcible speaker; had been successful at the bar; and in the army, as in civil life, made his way by the independent force of his mind and character—by his strong will, sustained energy, and the native vigour of his faculties. Sarcastic and critical, he was criticised in return, as a man of rough address, irascible temperament, and as wholly careless whom he offended. So said his enemies—those who called in question his brains and judgment. What they could not call in question, however, was his "zeal, fidelity, and devotion," or they will not do so to-day. Robert E. Lee has borne his supreme and lasting testimony upon that subject, and the brave and hardy soldier who led that forlorn hope in the Shenandoah Valley, when the hours of a great conflict were numbered, and darkness began to settle like a pall upon the land illustrated by such heroic struggles, by victories so splendid—the brave and hardy Early at last has justice done him, and can claim for himself that, when the day was darkest, when all hearts desponded, he was zealous, faithful, devoted. If the world is not convinced by the testimony of Lee, that this man was devoted to his country, and true as steel to the flag under which he fought—true to it in disaster and defeat as in success and victory—let them read the letter of the exile, signing himself "J. A. Early, Lieut.-Gen. C. S. A."

# VII

## MOSBY

### I.

I WAS reading the other day a work entitled "Jack Mosby, the Guerilla," by a certain "Lieutenant-Colonel ——," of the United States Army. The book is exceedingly sanguinary. Colonel Mosby is therein represented as a tall, powerful, black-bearded, cruel, and remorseless brigand of the Fra Diavolo order, whose chief amusement was to hang up Federal soldiers by their arms, and kindle fires under their feet—for what reason is not explained; and when not thus pleasantly engaged, he is described as cutting down the unfortunate bluecoats with a tremendous sabre, or riddling them with bullets from an extensive assortment of pistols in his belt. He has a sweetheart—for "Lieutenant-Colonel ——" enters into his hero's most private affairs—who makes love to Union officers, and leads them into the toils of the remorseless Mosby. That individual exclaims in moments of excitement, "Confusion!" after the universal fashion of Confederate States officers in the late war; and in order to make the history of his life a full and comprehensive one, the minutest particulars are given of his well known scheme to burn the city of New York—a brilliant idea, exclusively belonging to this celebrated bandit, who is vividly represented in a cheap woodcut as pouring liquid phosphorus on his bed at the Astor House. This biographical work is "profusely illustrated," beautifully bound in a yellow paper cover, and the price is "only ten cents."

It may be said that this is, after all, a species of literature, "so-called," such as no person of character or intelligence ever reads. Such is doubtless the truth in regard to Lieutenant-Colonel ——'s silly performance; but is it equally certain that there are no citizens of the Northern States, both fair-minded and cultivated, who regard Colonel Mosby in some such light as that in which he is here represented? I am afraid the number is considerable. He has been so persistently described as a desperado, such as infests the outskirts of civilization, that some impression must have been made by his traducers. Dr. Johnson said that almost anything could be accomplished by incessantly talking about it; and so many people have reiterated these charges against Colonel Mosby, that a belief in them has, beyond any doubt, fixed itself upon the minds of many fair and candid persons. It is for this class, whose good opinion is worth something, that I propose to state the truth in relation to his character and career. Though in no manner attached to his command, the present writer occupied a position during the late war which enabled him to watch this officer's operations from the commencement almost to the end of the struggle; and what is here set down in relation to him may be relied upon as an honest statement by one who has no object in the world in making it except to record the truth.

Without further preface, it may surprise some of my Northern readers to hear that this man, figuring in the popular eye as a ruffian and low adventurer, was born and bred, and is in character and manners, a gentleman. His family is one of standing and intelligence in Virginia, and he was educated at the University of Virginia, where he studied law. He commenced the practice, married, and would probably have passed through life as a "county court lawyer" had not the war taken place. When Virginia seceded he imitated other young men, and embarked in the struggle as a private in a regiment of cavalry. Here he exhibited courage and activity, and eventually became first-lieutenant and adjutant. When the miserable "reorganization" system of the Confederate States government went into operation in the spring of 1862, and the men were allowed to select

their officers, Mosby—never an easy or indulgent officer—was
thrown out, and again became a private. He returned to the
ranks; but his energy and activity had been frequently exhibited,
and General Stuart, who possessed a remarkable talent for discovering conspicuous military merit of any sort in obscure persons, speedily sent for him, and from that time employed him
as a scout or partisan. It is proper to warn the reader here that
a scout is not a spy. Mosby's duty was to penetrate the region
of country occupied by the Federal forces, either alone or in
command of a small detachment of cavalry; and by hovering in
the woods around the Union camps, interrogating citizens, or
capturing pickets or stragglers, acquire information of the enemy's numbers, position, or designs. If this information could
be obtained without a collision, all the better; but, if necessary,
it was the duty and the habit of the Scouts to attack, or when
attacked, hold their ground as long as possible. In other words,
there was inaugurated in the country occupied by the Federal
forces a regular system of partisan warfare, the object of which
was to harass the invading force, and in every way impair its
efficiency.

It was at this time that I first saw Mosby, and his appearance
was wholly undistinguished. He was thin, wiry, and I should
say about five feet nine or ten inches in height. A slight stoop
in the neck was not ungraceful. The chin was carried well forward; the lips were thin and wore a somewhat satirical smile;
the eyes, under the brown felt hat, were keen, sparkling, and
roved curiously from side to side. He wore a gray uniform, with
no arms but two revolvers in his belt; the sabre was no favourite
with him. His voice was low, and a smile was often on his lips.
He rarely sat still ten minutes. Such was his appearance at that
time. No one would have been struck with anything noticeable
in him except the eyes. These flashed at times in a way which
might have induced the opinion that there was something in
the man, if it only had an opportunity to "come out."

I am not aware that he gained any reputation in the campaign
of 1862. He was considered, however, by General Stuart an
excellent scout and partisan; and the General once related to the

present writer with great glee, the manner in which Mosby had taken nine men, deployed them over several hundred yards, and advanced, firing steadily upon a whole brigade of Federal cavalry, which hastily retired under the impression that the attacking force was heavy. Such things were common with Mosby, who seemed to enjoy them greatly; but in the spring of 1862 the tables were turned upon the partisan. General Stuart sent him from the Chickahominy to carry a confidential message to General Jackson, then in the Valley. He was resting at one of the wayside stations on the Central Railroad while his horse was feeding, when a detachment of Federal cavalry surprised and captured him—making prize also of a private note from Stuart to Jackson, and a copy of Napoleon's "Maxims" accompanying it. Mosby was carried to the Old Capitol, but was soon exchanged; and chancing to discover on his route down the bay that General Burnside was going soon to reinforce General Pope in Culpeper, he hastened on his arrival with that important information to General Lee, who telegraphed it, doubtless, to General Lee, who telegraphed it, doubtless, to General Jackson at Gordonsville. It is probable that the battle of Cedar Run, where General Pope was defeated, was fought by Jackson in consequence of this information.

My object, however, is not to write a biography of Colonel Mosby. It is fortunate that such is not my design; for a career of wonderful activity extending over about three years could not be condensed into a brief paper. I shall speak of but one or two other incidents in his career; and one shall be his surprise of Brigadier-General Stoughton at Fairfax Court-House in the winter of 1862. This affair excited unbounded indignation on the part of many excellent people, though President Lincoln made a jest of it. Let us not see if it was not a legitimate partisan operation. It was in November, I believe, that Mosby received the information leading to his movement.* The Federal forces at that time occupied the region between Fredericksburg and

* Cooke's memory served him badly here. Mosby captured Stoughton in March 1863.—ED.

Alexandria; and as General Stuart's activity and energy were
just causes of solicitude, a strong body of infantry, cavalry, and
artillery, was posted in the neighbourhood of Fairfax Court-
House and Centreville. Colonel Wyndham was in command of
the cavalry, and Acting Brigadier-General Stoughton, a young
officer from West Point, commanded the whole district, with
his headquarters in the small village of Fairfax. Mosby formed
the design of capturing General Stoughton, Colonel Wyndham,
Colonel Johnson, and other officers; and sent scouts to the neighbourhood to ascertain the force there. They brought word that
a strong body of infantry and artillery was at Centreville;
Colonel Wyndham's brigade of cavalry at Germantown, a mile
from Fairfax; and toward the railroad station another brigade
of infantry. Fairfax thus appeared to be inclosed within a cordon
of all arms, rendering it wholly impossible even to approach it.
Those who know the ground, as many of my readers doubtless
do, will easily understand how desperate the undertaking appeared of penetrating to the town, and safely carrying off the
Federal commandant. It was one of those schemes, however,
whose very boldness is apt to cause them to succeed. Men rarely
guard against dangers which they do not dream it possible can
threaten them. Mosby doubtless based his calculations upon this
fact; at any rate he decided upon the movement, and with
twenty-nine men set out one dark and drizzling November night
for the scene of operations. Newspaper writers of the day stated
that the party were dressed in Federal uniforms. This is not true.
There was no sort of advantage in any such precaution. The
party had to steal off with their captures, if any were made, or
cut their way through, and on that black night no uniform was
discernible. Mosby approached Germantown by the Little River
turnpike; but fearing Wyndham's cavalry, obliqued to the right,
and took to the woods skirting the Warrenton road. Centreville
was thus, with its garrison, on his right and rear, Germantown
on his left, and Fairfax, winged with infantry camps, in his
front. It was now raining heavily, and the night was like pitch.
The party advanced by bridle-paths through the woods, thus
avoiding the pickets of the main avenues of approach, and the

incessant patter of the rain drowned the hoof-strokes of the horses. A mile from Fairfax the gleam of tents greeted them in front, and finding the approaches barred in that direction they silently obliqued to the right again, crossed the Warrenton road, and gradually drew near the town on the southern side. Again the woods and the rain served them. Their advance was undiscovered, and at last they were close upon the place. An infantry picket was the only obstacle, but this was soon removed. The sleepy vidette found a pistol at his breast, and the picket was compelled to surrender without firing a shot. The way was then clear, and Mosby entered the town at a gallop. His object was to capture the Federal officers known to be in the place, burn the public stores, and carry off as many horses as possible. His party was accordingly divided for these purposes, and Mosby himself proceeded to General Stoughton's residence. It was afterwards said that a young lady of the place, Miss Ford, had supplied him with information, and now led him personally to the house. This, Colonel Mosby stated to the present writer, was entirely a mistake; he received information neither from Miss Ford nor any one else, except his own scouts. To accompany him, however, in his visit to General Stoughton, he found an orderly at the door, who was taken charge of by one of the men, and then mounted to the general's bedchamber, the occupant of which was fast asleep. At Mosby's unceremonious "Get up, General, and come with me!" the sleeper started erect, and demanded: "Do you know who I am, sir?" apparently indignant at such want of ceremony. "Do you know Mosby, General?" was the reply. "Yes," was the eager response, "have you got the —— rascal?" "No, but he has got you!" And to the startled "What does this mean, sir?" of General Stoughton, Mosby replied, "It means that General Stuart's cavalry are in possession of the Court-House, sir, and that you are my prisoner." This disagreeable state of affairs slowly dawned upon the aroused sleeper, and he soon found himself dressed, mounted, and ready to set out—a prisoner. Several staff officers had also been captured, and a considerable number of horses—Colonels Wyndham and Johnson eluded the search for them. Deciding not to burn the public stores which were in the houses, Mosby then mounted all his prisoners—some thirty-five, I believe, in number, including about half-a-dozen officers—cautiously retraced his steps, passing over the very same ground, and stealing along about down under the muzzles of the guns in the works at Centreville, so close that the sentinel hailed the party, swam Cub Run, struck southward, and at sunrise was safe beyond pursuit.

## II.

The skill and boldness exhibited in the conception and execution of this raid conferred upon Mosby just fame as a partisan officer, and the regular organization of his command commenced. He was made captain, then major, then lieutenant-colonel, and colonel, as his force and his operations increased.

From the solitary scout, or humble partisan, operating with a small squad, he had now grown to be an officer of rank and distinction, entrusted with important duties, and eventually with the guardianship of the whole extent of country north of the Rappahannock and east of the Blue Ridge. The people of the region speak of it, with a laugh, as "Mosby's Confederacy," and the name will probably adhere to it, in the popular mind, for many years to come. Let us pass to these latter days when "Colonel" Mosby gave the Federal forces so much trouble, and aroused so much indignation in Custer, Sheridan, and others, whose men he captured, and whose convoys he so frequently cut off and destroyed. The question of most interest is—Was Colonel Mosby a partisan officer, engaged in a perfectly legitimate warfare, or was he a mere robber? The present writer regards any imputations upon the character of this officer, or upon the nature of the warfare which he carried on, as absurd. If the Confederate States army generally was a mere unlawful combination, and not entitled to be regarded as "belligerent," the case is made out; but there was no officer in that army who occupied a more formally official position than Mosby, or whose operations more perfectly conformed to the rules of civilized warfare. Virginia was invaded by the Federal forces, and large portions of her territory were occupied and laid under contribution. Especially was the country north of the Rappahannock thus exposed. It was a species of border-land which belonged to the party which could hold it; and to protect it from the inroads of the Federal forces, Mosby instituted a regular system of partisan warfare. His headquarters were generally near Upperville, just east of the ridge, and his scouts speedily brought him intelligence of any advance of the Federal cavalry. As soon as he was informed of their approach, he went to meet them, hovered near them, took his moment, and attacked them, his superior skill and knowledge of the country almost uniformly routing the force opposed to him. Another important part of his duty was to cut off and capture or destroy the trains of his adversaries. These things were exceedingly annoying, and made the Federal commanders whose movements were thus crippled quite furious against the author of their embarrassments—but no person with the least knowledge of military affairs will stigmatize the destruction of wagon trains as the work of a brigand. In the same manner the railroads supplying the Federal forces with commissary and other stores were destroyed wherever it could be done. Detached parties out foraging were, if possible, captured. Camps, picket posts, vedette stations, were surprised, when practicable, and prisoners seized upon. To harass, annoy, injure, and in every manner cripple or embarrass the opposing force, was the object of Colonel Mosby, as it has been of partisan officers in all the wars of history. The violent animosity felt toward him was attributable solely to the great skill, vigour, and success of his operations. The present writer has a tolerably full acquaintance with the military record of Colonel Mosby and his command, and he states, in all sincerity, that he can find in it nothing whatever that is "irreguar" or unworthy of an officer and a gentleman. Mosby carried on a legitimate partisan warfare under a regular commission from the President of the Confederate States, and was in command of a regularly organized body of cavalry. He announced clearly his intention of disputing military possession of the country north of the Rappahannock, of harassing, retarding, or crippling any force invading Virginia, and of inflicting as much injury as possible upon his opponents. One single act of seeming cruelty is charged against him, the hanging of seven of Custer's men—but this was in retaliation for seven of his own which had been executed by that officer. This retaliation was in accordance with the rules of warfare in every country, and his superiors disavowed the course of General Custer, and directed such proceedings to cease.

We have expended too much space upon this point. Colonel Mosby can afford to wait to have justice done him. He was respected by Jackson, Stuart, and Lee, and the world will not willingly believe him to have been a bandit.

## III.

What was the appearance and character of the actual individual? What manner of personages were "Mosby and his men," as they really lived, and moved, and had their being in the forests and on the hills of Fauquier, in Virginia, in the years 1863 and 1864? If the reader will accompany me, I will conduct him to this beautiful region swept by the mountain winds, and will introduce him—remember, the date is 1864—to a plain and un-assuming personage clad in gray, with three stars upon his coat-collar, and two pistols in his belt.

He is slender, gaunt, and active in figure; his feet are small, and cased in cavalry boots, with brass spurs; and the revolvers in his belt are worn with an air of "business" which is unmis-takable. The face of this person is tanned, beardless, youthful-looking, and pleasant. He has white and regular teeth, which his habitual smile reveals. His piercing eyes flash out from be-neath his brown hat, with its golden cord, and he reins in his horse with the ease of a practised rider. A plain soldier, low and slight of stature, ready to talk, to laugh, to ride, to oblige you in any way—such was Mosby, in outward appearance. Na-ture had given no sign but the restless, roving, flashing eye, that there was much worth considering beneath. The eye did not convey a false expression. The commonplace exterior of the partisan concealed one of the most active, daring, and penetrating minds of an epoch fruitful in such. Mosby was born to be a partisan leader, and as such was probably greater than any other who took part in the late war. He had by nature all the qualities which make the accomplished ranger; nothing could daunt him; his activity of mind and body—call it, if you choose, restless, eternal love of movement—was something wonderful; and that untiring energy which is the secret of half the great successes of history, drove him incessantly to plan, to scheme, to conceive, and to execute. He could not rest when there was anything to do, and scouted for his amusement, charging pickets *solus* by way of sport. On dark and rainy nights, when other men aim at being comfortably housed, Mosby liked to be moving with a detachment of his men to surprise and attack some Federal camp, or to "run in" some picket, and occasion consternation, if not inflict injury.

The peculiar feature of his command was that the men occupied no stated camp, and, in fact, were never kept together except on an expedition. They were scattered throughout the country, especially among the small farm-houses in the spurs of the Blue Ridge; and here they lived the merriest lives imaginable. They were subjected to none of the hardships and privations of regular soldiers. Their horses were in comfortable stables, or ranged freely over excellent pastures; the men lived with the families, slept in beds, and had nothing to do with "rations" of hard bread and bacon. Milk, butter, and all the household luxuries of peace were at their command; and not until their chief summoned them did they buckle on their arms and get to horse. While they were thus living on the fat of the land, Mosby was perhaps scouting off on his private account, somewhere down toward Manassas, Alexandria, or Leesburg. If his excursions revealed an opening for successful operations, he sent off a well mounted courier, who travelled rapidly to the first nest of rangers; thence a fresh courier carried the summons elsewhere; and in a few hours twenty, thirty, or fifty men, excellently mounted, made their appearance at the prescribed rendezvous. The man who disregarded or evaded the second summons to a raid was summarily dealt with; he received a note for delivery to General Stuart, and on reaching the cavalry headquarters was directed to return to the company in the regular service from which he had been transferred. This seldom happened, however. The men were all anxious to go upon raids, to share the rich spoils, and were prompt at the rendezvous. Once assembled, the rangers fell into column, Mosby said "Come on," and the party set forward upon the appointed task—to surprise some camp, capture an army train, or ambush some detached party of Federal cavalry out on a foraging expedition.

Such a life is attractive to the imagination, and the men came to have a passion for it. But it is a dangerous service. It may with propriety be regarded as a trial of wits between the opposing commanders. The great praise of Mosby was, that his superior skill, activity, and good judgment gave him almost uninterrupted success, and invariably saved him from capture. An attack upon Colonel Cole, of the Maryland cavalry, near Loudon Heights, in the winter of 1863–64, was his only serious failure; and that appears to have resulted from a disobedience of his orders. He had here some valuable officers and men killed. He was several times wounded, but never taken. On the last occasion, in 1864, he was shot through the window of a house in Fauquier, but managed to stagger into a darkened room, tear off his stars, the badges of his rank, and counterfeit a person mortally wounded. His assailants left him dying, as they supposed, without discovering his identity; and when they did discover it and hurried back, he had been removed beyond reach of peril. After his wounds he always reappeared paler and thinner, but more active and untiring than ever. They only seemed to exasperate him, and make him more dangerous to trains, scouting parties, and detached camps than before.

The great secret of his success was undoubtedly his unbounded energy and enterprise. General Stuart came finally to repose unlimited confidence in his resources, and relied implicitly upon him. The writer recalls an instance of this in June, 1863. General Stuart was then near Middleburg, watching the United States army—then about to move toward Pennsylvania —but could get no accurate information from his scouts. Silent, puzzled, and doubtful, the General walked up and down, knitting his brows and reflecting, when the lithe figure of Mosby appeared, and Stuart uttered an exclamation of relief and satisfaction. They were speedily in private consultation, and Mosby only came out again to mount his quick gray mare and set out, in a heavy storm, for the Federal camps. On the next day he returned with information which put the entire cavalry in motion. He had penetrated General Hooker's camps, ascertained everything, and safely returned. This had been done in his gray uniform, with his pistols at his belt—and I believe it was on this occasion that he gave a characteristic evidence of his coolness. He had captured a Federal cavalry-man, and they were riding on together, when suddenly they struck a column of the enemy's cavalry passing. Mosby drew his oil-cloth around him, cocked his pistol, and said to his companion, "If you make any sign or utter a word to have me captured, I will blow your brains out, and trust to the speed of my horse to escape. Keep quiet, and we will ride on without troubling anybody." His prisoner took the hint, believing doubtless that it was better to be a prisoner than a dead man; and after riding along carelessly for some distance, as though he were one of the column, Mosby gradually edged off, and got away safely with his prisoner.

But the subject beguiles us too far. The hundreds of adventures in which Mosby bore his part must be left for that extended record which will some day be made. My chief object in this brief paper has been to anticipate the sanguinary historians of the "Lieutenant-Colonel——" order; to show that Colonel Mosby was no black-browed ruffian, but a plain, unassuming officer of partisans, who gained his widely-extended reputation by that activity and energy which only men of military ability possess. This information in regard to the man is intended, as I have said, for Northern readers of fairness and candour; for that class who would not willingly do injustice even to an adversary. In Virginia, Mosby is perfectly well known, and it would be unnecessary to argue here that the person who enjoyed the respect and confidence of Lee, Stuart, and Jackson, was worthy of it. Mosby was regarded by the people of Virginia in his true light as a man of great courage, decision, and energy, who embarked like others in a revolution whose principles and objects he fully approved. In the hard struggle he fought bravely, exposed his person without stint, and overcame his opponents by superior military ability. To stigmatize him as a ruffian because he was a partisan is to throw obloquy upon the memory of Marion, Sumter, and Harry Lee, of the old Revolution. As long as war lasts, surprise of an enemy will continue to be a part of military tactics; the destruction of his trains, munitions, stores, and communications, a legitimate object of endeavour. This Mosby did with great success, and he had no other object in view. The charge that he fought for plunder is singularly unjust. The writer of this is able to state of his own knowledge that Colonel Mosby rarely appropriated anything to his own use, unless it were arms, a saddle, or a captured horse, when his own was worn out; and to-day, the man who captured millions in stores and money is poorer than when he entered upon the struggle.

This paper, written without the knowledge of Colonel Mosby, who is merely an acquaintance of the writer, and intended as a simple delineation of the man, has, in some manner, assumed the form of an apology for the partisan and his career. He needs none, and can await without fear that verdict of history which the late President of the United States justly declared "could not be avoided." In the pages which chronicle the great struggle of 1862, 1863, and 1864, Colonel Mosby will appear in his true character as the bold partisan, the daring leader of cavalry, the untiring, never-resting adversary of the Federal forces invading Virginia. The burly-ruffian view of him will not bear inspection; and if there are any who cannot erase from their minds this fanciful figure of a cold, coarse, heartless adventurer, I would beg them to dwell for a moment upon a picture which the Richmond correspondent of a Northern journal drew the other day.

On a summer morning a solitary man was seen beside the grave of Stuart, in Hollywood Cemetery, near Richmond. The dew was on the grass, the birds sang overhead, the green hillock at the man's feet was all that remained of the daring leader of the Southern cavalry, who, after all his toils, his battles, and the shocks of desperate encounters, had come here to rest in peace. Beside this unmarked grave the solitary mourner remained long, pondering and remembering. Finally he plucked a wild flower, dropped it upon the grave, and with tears in his eyes, left the place.

This lonely mourner at the grave of Stuart was Mosby.

# VIII

## PELHAM "THE GALLANT"

### I.

ON THE morning of the 17th of March, 1863, Averill's Federal Cavalry, three thousand in the saddle, crossed the Rappahannock at Kelly's Ford, and attacked about eight hundred of General Fitz Lee's command, who faced, without shrinking, these great odds, and fought them stubbornly at every point throughout the entire day.

When the sun set on that tranquil evening—sinking slowly down behind the quiet forest, unstirred by the least breath of wind—the long and desperate struggle was decided. The enemy was retiring, "badly hurt," and General Stuart added in his dispatch: "We are after him. His dead men and horses strew the road."

No harder battle was fought during the entire war. The Southern forces won the day by hard and desperate fighting, in charge after charge; but lost in the struggle some of the most valiant hearts that ever beat. Puller, Harris, and Pelham were among the number—the "gallant Pelham" of the battle of Fredericksburg. He was in the performance of his duty as Chief of Artillery, and was riding towards his General, when a regiment of cavalry swept by him in a charge. He was waving his hat aloft, and cheering them on, when a fragment of shell struck him on the head, mortally wounding him. He lingered until

DEATH OF MAJOR PELHAM, (OF ALA.,) "THE GALLANT."

"He was waving his hat aloft, and cheering them on, when a fragment of shell struck him in the head, mortally wounding him,"

after midnight on the morning of the 18th, when General Stuart telegraphed to Mr. Curry, of Alabama:

"The noble, the chivalric, the gallant Pelham is no more. He was killed in action yesterday. His remains will be sent to you to-day. How much he was beloved, appreciated, and admired, let the tears of agony we have shed, and the gloom of mourning throughout my command, bear witness. His loss is irreparable."

The body of the young officer was sent to Richmond, laid in state in the Capitol of Virginia, and we are told that "some tender hand deposited an evergreen wreath, intertwined with white flowers, upon the case that contained all that was mortal of the fallen hero." His family received the soldier's remains; they were taken to his Southern home; Virginia, the field of his fame, had surrendered him to Alabama, the land of his birth.

"The Major-General commanding," wrote Stuart, in a general order, "approaches with reluctance the painful duty of announcing to the Division its irreparable loss in the death of Major JOHN PELHAM, commanding the Horse Artillery.

"He fell mortally wounded in the battle of Kellysville, March 17th, with the battle-cry on his lips, and the light of victory beaming from his eye.

"To you, his comrades, it is needless to dwell upon what you have so often witnessed—his prowess in action, already proverbial. You well know how, though young in years, a mere stripling in appearance, remarkable for his genuine modesty of deportment, he yet disclosed on the battle-field the conduct of a veteran, and displayed in his handsome person the most imperturbable coolness in danger.

"His eye had glanced over every battle-field of this army, from the first Manassas to the moment of his death, and he was, with a single exception, a brilliant actor in all.

"The memory of 'THE GALLANT PELHAM,' his many virtues, his noble nature and purity of character, is enshrined as a sacred legacy in the hearts of all who knew him.

"His record has been bright and spotless; his career brilliant and successful.

"He fell—the noblest of sacrifices—on the altar of his country, to whose glorious service he had dedicated his life from the beginning of the war."

Thus passed away a noble, lofty soul; thus ended a career, brief, it is true, but among the most arduous, glorious, and splendid of the war. Young, but immortal—a boy in years, but heir to undying fame—he was called away from the scene of his triumphs and glory to a brighter world, where neither wars nor rumours of wars can come, and wounds and pain and suffering are unknown; where

> "Malice domestic, foreign levy, nothing
> Can touch him further!"

## II.

To him who writes these lines, the death of this noble youth has been inexpressibly saddening. It has cast a shadow on the very sunlight; and the world seems, somehow, colder and more dreary since he went away. It was but yesterday almost that he was in his tent, and I looked into his frank, brave eyes, and heard his kind, honest voice.* There is the seat he occupied as we conversed—the bed where he so often slept with me, prolonging his gay talk deep into the night. There are the books he read—the papers which he wrote; at this table he once sat, and here where my own hand rests has rested the hand of the Dead! Every object thus recalls him, even as he lived and moved beside me but a few days ago. His very words seem still echoing in the air, and the dreary camp is full of his presence!

Nor am I the only one whose heart has bled for the young soldier. All who knew him loved him for his gay, sweet temper, as they admired him for his unshrinking courage. I have seen no face over which a sort of shadow did not pass at the announcement, "Pelham is dead!"

"Pelham is dead!" It is only another mode of saying "honour is dead! courage is dead! modesty, kindness, courtesy, the inborn spirit of the true and perfect gentleman, the nerve of the

* Written at "Camp No.—camp," in the spring of 1863. [J.E.C.]

soldier, the gaiety of the good companion, the kindly heart, and the resolute soul—all dead, and never more to revisit us in his person!"

These words are not dictated by a blind partiality or mere personal regard for the brave youth who has fallen in front of the foe, in defence of the sacred liberties of the South. Of his unshrinking nerve and coolness in the hour of peril, the name of "the gallant Pelham," given him by General Lee at Fredericksburg, will bear witness. Of his noble, truthful nature, those who knew him best will speak.

He had made for himself a celebrated name, and he was only twenty-four when he died!

A son of the great State of Alabama, and descended from an old and honourable family there, he had the courage of his race and clime. He chose arms as his profession, and entered West Point, where he graduated just as the war commenced; lost no time in offering his services to the South, and received the appointment of First-Lieutenant in the Confederate States army. Proceeding to Harper's Ferry, when General Johnston was in command there, he was assigned to duty as drill-officer of artillery, and in the battle of Manassas commanded a battery, which he fought with that daring courage which afterwards rendered him so famous. He speedily attracted the attention of the higher Generals of the army, and General J. E. B. Stuart entrusted him with the organization of the battalion of Horse Artillery which he subsequently commanded in nearly every battle of the war upon Virginia soil. Here I knew him first.

From the moment when he took command of that famous corps, a new system of artillery fighting seemed to be inaugurated. The rapidity, the rush, the impetus of the cavalry, were grafted on its more deliberate brother. Not once, but repeatedly, has the Horse Artillery of Pelham given chase at full speed to a flying enemy; and, far in advance of all infantry support, unlimbered and hurled its thunders on the foe. It was ever at the point where the line was weakest; and however headlong the charge of the cavalry, the whirling guns were beside it, all ready for their part. "Trot, march!" had yielded to "gallop!"

with the battalion; it was rushed into position, and put in action with a rush; and in and out among the guns where the bolts fell thickest was the brave young artillerist, cool and self-possessed, but, as one of his officers said the other day, "as gay as a school-boy at a frolic." He loved his profession for its own sake; and often spoke to the officers above alluded to of the "jolly good fights" he would have in the present campaign; but I anticipate my subject.

Once associated with the command of Stuart, he secured the warm regard and unlimited confidence of that General, who employed his services upon every occasion. Thenceforth their fortunes seemed united, like their hearts; and the young man became known as one of the most desperate fighters of the whole army. He was rightly regarded by Jackson and others as pos-sessed of a very extraordinary genius for artillery; and when any movement of unusual importance was designed, Pelham was assigned to the artillery to be employed.

His career was a brief one, but how glorious! How crowded with great events that are history now! Let us glance at it:

When the Southern forces fell back from Manassas in 1861, his batteries had their part in covering the movement, and guard-ing the fords of the Rappahannock. During the campaign of the Peninsula, his Blakely was as a sentinel on post near the enemy; and at the battle of Williamsburg his courage and skill trans-formed raw militia into veterans. In the seven days' battles around Richmond he won fadeless laurels. With one Napoleon, he engaged three heavy batteries, and fought them with a per-tinacity and unfaltering nerve which made the calm face of Jackson glow; and the pressure of that heroic hand, warm and eloquent of unspoken admiration. Soon afterwards, at the "White House," he engaged a gunboat, and driving it away, after a brief but hot encounter, proved how fanciful were the terrors of these "monsters."

His greatest achievements were to come, however; and he hastened to record them on the enduring tablets of history. From the moment when his artillery advanced from the Rappa-hannock, to the time when it returned thither, to the day of Fredericksburg, the path of the young leader was deluged with the blood of battle. At Manassas he rushed his guns into the very columns of the enemy almost; fighting their sharpshooters with canister, amid a hurricane of balls. At Sharpsburg he had command of nearly all the artillery on our left, and directed it with the hand of a master. When the army crossed back into Virginia, he was posted at Shepherdstown, and guarded the ford with an obstinate valour, which spoke in the regular and unceasing reverberation of his deep-mouthed Napoleons, as they roared on, hour after hour, driving back the enemy.

Of the days which succeeded that exciting period, many persons will long hold the memory. It was in an honest old country-house, whither the tide of war bore him for a time, that the noble nature of the young soldier shone forth in all its charms. There, in the old hall on the banks of the Opequon, surrounded by warm hearts who reminded him perhaps of his own beloved ones in far Alabama; there, in the tranquil days of autumn, in that beautiful country, he seemed to pass some of his happiest hours. All were charmed with his kind temper and his sunny disposition; with his refinement, his courtesy, his high breeding, and simplicity. Modest to a fault almost—blushing like a girl at times, and wholly unassuming in his entire deportment—he became a favourite with all around him, and secured that regard of good men and women which is the proof of high traits and fine instincts in its possessor. In the beautiful autumn forests, by the stream with its great sycamores, and under the tall oaks of the lawn, he thus wandered for a time—an exile from his own land of Alabama, but loved, admired, and cherished by warm hearts in this. When he left the haunts of "The Bower," I think he regretted it. But work called him.

The fiat had gone forth from Washington that another "On to Richmond" should be attempted; and where the vultures of war hovered, there was the post of duty for the Horse Artillery. The cavalry crossed the Blue Ridge, and met the advancing column at Aldie—and Pelham was again in his element. Thenceforward, until the banks of the Rappahannock were reached by the cavalry, the batteries of the Horse Artillery disputed every step of ground. The direction of the artillery was left, with unhestitating confidence, by Stuart to the young officer; and those who witnessed, during that arduous movement, the masterly handling of his guns, can tell how this confidence was justified. It was the eye of the great soldier, the hand of the born artillerist, which was evident in his work during those days of struggle. He fell back neither too soon nor too late, and only limbered up his guns to unlimber again in the first position which he reached. Thus fighting every inch of the way from Aldie, round by Paris, and Markham's, he reached the Rappahannock, and posted his artillery at the fords, where he stood and bade the enemy defiance. That page in the history of the war is scarcely known; but those who were present know the obstinacy of the contests, and the nerve and skill which were displayed by the young officer.

That may be unknown, but the work done by Pelham on the great day of Fredericksburg is a part of history now. All know how stubbornly he stood on that day—what laurels encircled his young brow when night at last came. This was the climax of his fame—the event with which his name will be inseparably connected. With one Napoleon gun, he opened the battle on the right, and instantly drew upon himself the fire, at close range, of three or four batteries in front, and a heavy enfilading fire from thirty-pound Parrots across the river. But this moved him little. That Napoleon gun was the same which he had used at the battle of Cold Harbour—it was taken from the enemy at Seven Pines—and, in the hands of the young officer, it had won a fame which must not be tarnished by defeat! Its grim voice must roar, however great the odds; its reverberating defiance must roll over the plain, until the bronze war-dog was silenced. So it roared on steadily with Pelham beside it, blowing up caissons, and continuing to tear the enemy's ranks. General Lee was watching it from the hill above, and exclaimed, with eyes filled with admiration, "It is glorious to see such courage in one so young!" It was glorious indeed to see that one gun, placed in an important position, hold its ground with a firmness so unflinching. Not until his last round of ammunition was shot away did Pelham retire; and then only after a peremptory order sent to him. He afterwards took command of the entire artillery on the right, and fought it until night with a skill and courage which were admirable. He advanced his guns steadily, and at nightfall was thundering on the flank of the retreating enemy, who no longer replied. No answering roar came back from those batteries he had fought with his Napoleon so long; he had triumphed. That triumph was complete, and placed for ever upon record when the great Commander-in-Chief, whom he loved and admired so ardently, gave him the name in his report of "the gallant Pelham."

Supreme tribute to his courage—immortalizing him in history! To be the sole name mentioned beneath the rank of Major-General in all that host of heroes—and mentioned as "the gallant Pelham!"

Thenceforward there was little for him to desire. He had never cared for rank, only longed for glory; and now his name was deathless. It is true that he sometimes said, with modest and noble pride, that he thought it somewhat hard to be considered too young for promotion, when they gave him great commands —as at Sharpsburg and Fredericksburg—and called on him when the hardest work was to be done. But he never desired a mere title he had not won, and did his soldier's duty thoroughly, trusting to time. So noble and important, however, had been his recent services, that promotion was a matter of course. The President said, "I do not need to see any papers about Major Pelham," and had appointed him a Lieutenant-Colonel; and it only awaited the formal confirmation of the Senate, when he fell on the Rappahannock. His fall was a public calamity to the nation, but none to him. It was fit that such a spirit should lay down his great work before the hard life of the world had dimmed the polish of the good knight's spotless shield. He wanted no promotion at the hands of men. He had won, if not worn, the highest honours of the great soldier; and having finished his task, the gentle spirit took its flight, promoted by the tender hand of Death to other honours in a brighter world.

### III.

In this hasty tribute to one whom I knew well, and loved much, it is hard to avoid the appearance of exaggeration. The

character of this young soldier was so eminently noble—his soul
so brave, so true, so free from any taint of what was mean or
sordid or little—that the sober words of truth may be doubted
by some, who will only regard them as that tender and pious
flattery which friendship accords to the dead.

This sentiment will be experienced only by strangers, however. Those who knew him will recognise the true portrait.
His modesty, his gentleness—his bearing almost childlike in its
simplicity—made his society charming. This modesty of deportment was observed by every one, and strangers often referred to
the singular phenomenon in a youth bred in the self-sufficient
atmosphere of West Point, and whose name was already so
famous. He never spoke of himself; you might live with him
for a month, and never know that he had been in a single action.
He never seemed to think that he deserved any applause for his
splendid courage, and was silent upon all subjects connected
with his own actions. In his purse was found folded away,
after his death, a slip from a United States officer, once his
friend, which contained the words, "After long silence, I write.
God bless you, dear Pelham; I am proud of your success." But
he had never even alluded to the paper. Distinguished unmistakably by the affection and admiration of his immediate General—rendered famous by the praise of the Commander-in-Chief
at Fredericksburg—he never exhibited the least trait of self-love,
remaining what he had always been, as modest, unassuming,
and simple as a child.

This and other winning traits come to my mind as I write,
and I could speak at length of all those charming endowments
which endeared him to every one around him. I could dwell on
his nice sense of honour—his devotion to his family—on that
*prisca fides* in his feeling and opinions which made him a great,
true type of the Southern gentleman, attracting the attention and
respect of the most eminent personages of his time. But with
the recollection of those eminent social characteristics comes the
memory always of his long, hard work in the service. I have
often seen him engaged in that work, which gave him his great

fame; and this phase of the young officer's character obtrudes itself, rounding and completing the outline.

With what obstinate and unyielding courage he fought!—with a daring how splendid, how rich in suggestion of the antique days! He entered upon a battle with the coolness and resolution of a great leader trained in a thousand combats, and fought his guns with the fury and *élan* of Murat at the head of his horsemen. No trait of the ground, no movement of the enemy, ever escaped his eagle eye. With an inborn genius for war which West Point had merely developed, and directed in its proper channels, he had the rapid comprehension—intuition almost—which counts for so much in a leader. Where the contest was hottest and the pressure heaviest, there was Pelham with his guns; and the broken lines of infantry, or cavalry giving ground before irresistible numbers, heard their deep voices roaring and saw the ranks of the enemy scattered. Often he waited for no order, took the whole responsibility, and opened his batteries where he saw that they were most needed by the emergencies of the moment. But what he did was always the very best that could be done. He struck at the right moment, and his arm was heavy. To the cavalry, the roar of Pelham's Napoleons was a welcome sound. When the deep-mouthed thunder of those guns was heard, the faintest took heart, and the contest assumed a new phase to all—for that sound had proved on many a field the harbinger of victory.*

Beside those guns was the chosen post of the young artillerist. The *gaudium certaminis* seemed to fill his being at such moments; and, however numerous the batteries which he threw into action, he never remained behind "in command of the whole field." He

* The rumour has obtained a wide circulation that Major Pelham lost one or more of his guns when the cavalry fell back from the mountains. The report is entirely without foundation. *He never lost a gun there or anywhere else.* Though he fought his pieces with such obstinacy that the enemy more than once charged within ten yards of the muzzles of the guns, he always drove them back, and brought his artillery off safely. He asked my friendly offices in making public this statement. I neglected it, but now put the facts on record, in justice to his memory. [J.E.C.]

told me that he considered this his duty, and I know that he never shrank—as he might have done—from performing it. He was ever by the guns which were under the hottest fire, and, when the enemy shifted their fire to other portions of the field, he proceeded thither, riding at full speed, and directed the fresh batteries in person. His men will remember how cheering and inspiring was his presence with them—how his coolness steadied them in the most exciting moments—and his brave, cheerful voice was the herald of success. "He was the bravest human being I ever saw in my life," said one of his officers whom I conversed with recently; and all who have seen him under fire will bear similar testimony. His coolness had something heroic in it. It never deserted him, or was affected by those chances of battle which excite the bravest. He saw guns shattered and dismounted, or men torn to pieces, without exhibiting any signs of emotion. His nature seemed strung and every muscle braced to a pitch which made him rock; and the ghastliest spectacle of blood and death left his soul unmoved—his stern will unbent.

That unbending will had been tested often, and never had failed him yet. At Manassas, Williamsburg, Cold Harbour, Groveton, Oxhill, Sharpsburg, Shepherdstown, Kearneysville, Aldie, Union, Upperville, Markham, Barbee's, Hazel River, and Fredericksburg—at these and many other places he fought his horse artillery, and handled it with heroic coolness. One day when I led him to speak of his career, he counted up something like a hundred actions which he had been in—and in every one he had borne a prominent part. Talk with the associates of the young leader in those hard-fought battles, and they will tell you a hundred instances of his dauntless courage. At Manassas he took position in a place so dangerous that an officer, who had followed him up to that moment, rode away with the declaration that "if Pelham was fool enough to stay there, *he* was *not*." But General Jackson thanked him, as he thanked him at Cold Harbour, when the brave young soldier came back covered with dust from fighting his Napoleon—the light of victory in his eyes. At Markham, while he was fighting the enemy in front, they made a circuit and charged him in the rear; but he turned his guns about, and fought them as before, with his "Napoleon detachment" singing the loud, triumphant *Marseillaise*, as that same Napoleon gun, captured at Seven Pines, and used at Fredericksburg, drove them back. All that whole great movement was a marvel of hard fighting, however, and Pelham was the hero of the stout, close struggle. Any other chief of artillery might have sent his men in at Fredericksburg and elsewhere, leaving the direction of the guns to such officers as the brave Captain Henry; but this did not suit the young chieftain. He must go himself with the one gun sent forward, and beside that piece he remained until it was ordered back—directing his men to lie down, but sitting his own horse, and intent solely upon the movements and designs of the enemy, wholly careless of the "fire of hell" hurled against him. It was glorious, indeed, as General Lee declared, to see such heroism in the boyish artillerist; and well might General Jackson speak of him in terms of "exaggerated compliment," and ask General Stuart "if he had *another Pelham*, to give him to *him*." On that great day, the young son of Alabama covered himself with glory—but no one who knew him felt any surprise at it. Those who had seen him at work upon other fields knew the dauntless resolution of his brave young soul—the tough and stern fibre of his courage. That hard fibre could bear any strain upon it and remain unmoved.

In all those hard combats, no ball or shell ever struck him. The glance of the blue eyes seemed to conquer Danger, and render Death powerless. He seemed to bear a charmed life, and to pass amid showers of bullets without peril or fear of the result. It was not from the enemy's artillery alone that he ran the greatest danger in battle. He was never content to remain at his guns if they were silent. His mind was full of the contest, pondering its chances, as though he had command of the whole army himself; he never rested in his exertions to penetrate the designs of the enemy. Upon such occasions he was the mark at which the sharpshooters directed their most dangerous fire; but they never struck him. The balls passed to the right or left, or overhead—his hour had not yet come.

It came at last in that hard fight upon the Rappahannock, and the famous youth lies low at last. He fell "with the battle-cry on his lips, and the light of victory beaming from his eye." In the words of the general order which his beloved commander issued, "His record had been bright and spotless; his career brilliant and successful; he fell the noblest of sacrifices on the altar of his country."

The theme grows beneath the pen which at first attempted a slight sketch only, and my paper is growing too long. A few words more will complete the outline of this eminent young soldier.

The name of Pelham will remain connected for ever with great events; but it will live perennial, too, in many hearts who mourn bitterly his untimely end. All who knew him loved him; I believe that no human being disliked him. His character was so frank, and open, and beautiful—his bearing so modest and unassuming—that he conciliated all hearts, and made every one who met him his friend. His passions were strong; and when he was aroused fire darted from the flint, but this was seldom. During all my acquaintance with him—and that acquaintance dated back to the atumn of 1861—I never had a word addressed to me that was unfriendly, and never saw him angry but twice. "Poor boy!" said Stuart one day, "he was angry with me *once*," and the speaker had known him longer than I had. He had rare self-control, and I think that this sprang in a great measure from a religious sense of duty. He would sit and read his Bible with close attention; and, though he never made a profession of his religious convictions, it is certain that these convictions shaped his conduct. The thought of death never seemed to cross his mind, however; and he once told me that he had never felt as if he was destined to be killed in the war. Alas! the brief proverb is the comment: "Man proposes, God disposes."

Thus, modest, brave, loving, and beloved—the famous soldier, the charming companion—he passed away from the friends who cherished him, leaving a void which none other can fill. Alabama lent him to Virginia for a time; but, alas! the pale face smiles no more as he returns to her. As many mourn his early death here, where his glory was won, as in the southern land from which he came. To these—the wide circle who loved him for his great qualities, and his kind, good heart—his loss is irreparable, as it is to the whole South. The "breed of noble minds" like his is not numerous, and when such forms disappear the gap is hard to fill—the struggle more arduous than before. But the memory of this great young soldier still remains with us, his name is immortal in history as in many hearts which throbbed at his death!

Poor colourless phrases!—faded flowers I try to strew on the grave of this noble soul! But the loss is too recent, and the wound has not yet healed. The heart still bleeds as the pen traces the dull words on the page.

> "Mourn for him! Let him be regarded
> As the most noble corse that ever herald
> Did follow to his urn!"

Strange words!—it may be said—for a boy little more than twenty! Exaggerated estimate of his loss!

No, the words are not strange; the loss is not exaggerated—for the name of this youth was John Pelham.

# IX

## FARLEY "THE SCOUT"

### I.

IN THE old "Confederate Army of the Potomac," and then in the "Army of Northern Virginia," there was a man so notable for daring, skill, and efficiency as a partisan, that all who valued those great qualities honoured him as their chiefest exemplar. He was known among the soldiers as "Farley, the Scout," but that term did not express him fully. He was not only a scout, but a partisan leader; an officer of excellent judgment and magnificent dash; a soldier born, who took to the work with all the skill and readiness of one who engages in that occupation for which, by Providence, he is especially designed.

He served from the beginning of the war to the hard battle of Fleetwood, in Culpeper, fought on the 9th of June, 1863. There he fell, his leg shattered by a fragment of shell, and the brave true soul went to rejoin its Maker.

One of the chiefest spites of fate is that oblivion which submerges the greatest names and events. The design of this brief paper is to put upon record some particulars of the career of a brave soldier—so that, in that "aftertime" which sums up the work and glory of the men of this epoch, his name shall not be lost to memory.

Farley was born at Laurens village, South Carolina, on the 19th of December, 1835. He was descended, in a direct line, from the "Douglas" of Scotland, and his father, who was born on the Roanoke river, in Charlotte county, Virginia, was one of the most accomplished gentlemen of his time. He emigrated to South Carolina at the age of twenty-one, married, and commenced there the practice of law. To the son, the issue of this marriage, he gave the name of William Downs Farley, after his father-in-law, Colonel William F. Downs, a distinguished lawyer, member of the Legislature, and an officer of the war of 1812. The father of this Colonel Downs was Major Jonathan Downs, a patriot of '76; his mother, a daughter of Captain Louis Saxon, also distinguished in our first great struggle; thus our young partisan of 1863 had fighting blood in his veins, and, in plunging into the contest, only followed the traditions of his race.

From earliest childhood he betrayed the instincts of the man of genius. Those who recollect him then, declare that his nature seemed composed of two mingled elements—the one gentle and reflective, the other ardent and enthusiastic. Passionately fond of Shakspeare and the elder poets, he loved to wander away into the woods, and, stretched beneath some great oak, pass hour after hour in dreamy musing; but if, at such times, he heard the cry of the hounds and the shouts of his companions, his dreams were dissipated, and throwing aside his volume, he would join in the chase with headlong ardour.

At the age of seventeen, he made, in company with a friend, the tour of the Northern States, and then was sent to the University of Virginia, where his education was completed. The summer vacation gave him an opportunity of making a pedestrian excursion through Virginia; and thus, having enlarged his mind by study and travel through the North and a portion of the South, he returned to South Carolina. Here he occupied himself in rendering assistance to his father, who had become an invalid, and, we believe, commenced the practice of the law. His love of roving, however, did not desert him, and his father's business required repeated journeys into the interior of the State. The scenery of the mountains proved a deep and lasting source of joy to him, and, standing on the summits of the great ranges, he has been seen to remain in such rapt contemplation of the landscape that he could scarcely be aroused and brought back to the real world. These expeditions undoubtedly fostered in the youthful South Carolinian that ardent love of everything connected with his native State which, with his craving for wild adventure, constituted the controlling elements of his being.

"He had now attained," a friend writes, "the pride and maturity of manhood. There were few handsomer or more prepossessing men." As a young man said, after the battle of Culpeper, in speaking of the loss of Farley and Hampton, "two of the handsomest men in our State have fallen." His figure was of medium height, elegantly formed, graceful, well knit, and, from habitual exercise in the gymnasium, possessing a remarkable degree of strength and activity. His hair was dark brown; his eyebrows and lashes were so dark, and so shaded the dark grey eyes beneath as to give them the appearance of blackness. His manner was generally quiet, polished, and elegant; but let him be aroused by some topic which awoke his enthusiasm (secession and the Yankees, for instance), and he suddenly stood transformed before you; and in the flashing eye and changing cheek you beheld the dashing "Hero of the Potomac!"

"His moral character," says the same authority, "was pure and noble—'Sans peur et sans reproche.' It is a well known fact among his friends and associates that ardent spirits of any kind had never passed his lips until the first battle of Manassas, when, being sick with measles, he fought until almost fainting, and accepted a draught from the canteen of a friend. This was the *first* and *last* drink he ever took.

"His father, whose last hours he watched with untiring care and attention, died just before the opening of the war. Captain Farley had, from an early age, taken great interest in the political affairs of the country; he was a warm advocate of State Rights, and now entered into the spirit of secession with eagerness and enthusiasm. He was very instrumental in bringing about a unanimity of opinion on this subject in his own district.

"He made frequent visits to Charleston, with the hope of being in the scene of action should an attack be made on the city; and was greatly chagrined that the battle of Sumter was fought during a short absence, and he only reached the city on the day following. He was the first man in his district to fly to the defence of Virginia, whose sacred soil he loved with a devotion only inferior to that which he bore his own State. He joined Gregg's regiment, in which he served three months, and on the disbanding of which he became an independent fighter."

From this time commences that career of personal adventure and romantic exploits which made him so famous. Shouldering his rifle—now riding, then on foot—he proceeded to the far out-posts nearest to the enemy, and was indefatigable in penetrating their lines, harassing detached parties, and gaining information for Generals Bonham and Beauregard. Falling back with the army from Fairfax, he fought—though so sick that he could scarcely stand—in the first battle of Manassas, and then entered permanently upon the life of the scout, speedily attracting to himself the unconcealed admiration of the whole army. To note the outlines even of his performances at that time, would require thrice the space we have at our disposal. He seemed omnipresent on every portion of the lines; and if any daring deed was under-taken—any expedition which was to puzzle, harass, or surprise the enemy—Farley was sure to be there. With three men he took and held Upton's Hill, directly in face of the enemy; on num-berless occasions he surprised the enemy's pickets; and with three others, waylaid and attacked a column of several hundred cav-alry led by Colonel (afterwards General) Bayard, whose horse he killed, slightly wounding the rider. This audacious attack was made some ten or fifteen miles beyond the Southern lines, and nothing but a love of the most desperate adventure could have led to it. Farley ambushed the enemy, concealing his little band of three men in some pines; and although they might easily have remained *perdus* until the column passed, and so escaped, Farley determined to attack, and did attack—firing first upon Bayard, and nearly stampeding his whole regiment. After a desperate encounter he and his little party were all captured or killed, and Farley was taken to the Old Capitol in Washington, where he remained some time in captivity. General Bayard mentioned this affair afterwards in an interview with General Stuart, and spoke in warm terms of the courage which led Farley to undertake so desperate an adventure. Released from prison, Farley hastened back to his old "stamping ground" around Centreville, reaching that place in the winter of 1861. He speedily received the most flattering proposals from some eminent officers who were going to the South-west; but chancing to meet General Stuart, that officer took violent possession of him, and thenceforth kept him near his person as volunteer aide-de-camp. With this arrangement Farley soon became greatly pleased. He had already seen Stuart at work, and that love of adventure and contempt of danger—the coolness, self-possession, and mastery of the situation, however perilous—which characterized both, proved a lasting bond of union between them.

## II.

Thenceforth, Farley was satisfied. His position was one which suited his peculiar views and habits admirably. Untrammelled by special duties—never tied down to the routine of command, or the commonplace round of camp duty—free as the wind to go or come whenever and wheresoever he pleased, all the instincts of his peculiar organization had "ample room and verge enough" for their development; and his splendid native traits had the fullest swing and opportunity of display. It was in vain that General Stuart, estimating at their full value his capacity for command, repeatedly offered him position. He did not want any commission, he said; his place suited him perfectly, and he believed he could do more service to the cause as scout and partisan than as a regular line-officer. He had not entered the army, he often declared to me, for place or position; promotion was not his object; to do as much injury as possible to the enemy was his sole, controlling sentiment, and he was satisfied to be where he was.

His devotion to the cause was indeed profound and almost passionate. He never rested in his exertions, and seemed to feel as if the success of the struggle depended entirely on his own exertions. A friend once said to him: "If, as in ancient Roman days, an immense gulf should miraculously open, and an oracle should declare that the honour and peace of the country could only be maintained by one of her youths throwing himself into it, do you believe you could do it?" He looked serious, and answered earnestly and with emphasis, *"I believe I could."*

Thus permanently attached as volunteer aide to General Stuart, Farley thereafter took part in all the movements of the cavalry. He was with them in that hot falling back from Centreville, in March, 1862; in the combats of the Peninsula, where, at Williamsburg, he led a regiment of infantry in the assault; in the battles of Cold Harbour and Malvern Hill, at the second Manassas, Sharpsburg, Fredericksburg, and the scores of minor engagements which marked almost every day upon the outposts. He missed the battle of Chancellorsville, greatly to his regret, having gone home, after an absence of two years, to witness the bombardment of Charleston and see his family.

It was soon after his return in May that the fatal moment came which deprived the service of this eminent partisan. At the desperately contested battle of Fleetwood, in Culpeper county, on the 9th of June, 1863, he was sent by General Stuart to carry a message to Colonel Butler, of the 2d South Carolina cavalry. He had just delivered his message, and was sitting upon his horse by the Colonel, when a shell, which also wounded Butler, struck him upon the right knee and tore his leg in two at the joint. He fell from the saddle and was borne to an ambulance, where surgical assistance was promptly rendered. His wound was, however, mortal, and all saw that he was dying.

At his own request the torn and bleeding member, with the cavalry boot still on, was put in the ambulance, and he was borne from the field. His strength slowly declined, but his consciousness remained. Meeting one whom he knew, he called him by name, and murmured, "I am almost gone." He lingered but a few hours, and at twilight of that day the writer of these lines looked on him in his shroud—the pale, cold features calm and tranquil in their final sleep.

He was clad in his new uniform coat, and looked every inch a soldier taking his last rest. He had delivered this coat to a lady of Culpeper, and said, "*If anything befalls me, wrap me in this and send me to my mother.*"

Such was the end of the famous partisan. His death left a void which it seemed impossible to fill. His extraordinary career had become fully known, and a writer some months before his death gave utterance to the sentiment of every one when he wrote: "The story—the plain, unvarnished story—of his career since the war began is like a tale of old romance. Such abnegation of self! Office and money both spurned, because they seemed to stand in the way of his duty. What thrilling incidents! What strength and courage! and what wonderful escapes! No wonder, as he rides by, we so often hear it exclaimed, 'There goes the famous scout, Farley! The army has no braver man, no purer patriot!' "

We put on record here the following passage from the letter of a lady in Culpeper to his mother, giving, as it does, an outline of the man, and bearing testimony in its simple words, warm from a woman's heart, to the affection which was felt for him:

"MY DEAR MADAM—I want you to know how we in Virginia admired, appreciated, and loved your son. Had he been *her own*, Virginia could not have loved him more; certainly she could not *owe* him more—so long and so bravely had he fought upon her soil. He was particularly well known in this unfortunate part of the State, which has been, sometimes for months, over-run by our foes. Many families will miss his coming, so daring was he, and so much depended on by General Stuart. He scouted a great deal alone in the enemy's lines, and was often the bearer of letters and messages from loved ones long unheard from. Often, when we have been cut off from all communication from our own people, he has been the first to come as the enemy were leaving, often galloping up when they were scarcely out of sight—always inspiring us with fresh hope and courage, his cheerful presence itself seeming to us a prophecy of good.

"On Tuesday night, just one week before the battle in which he fell, he came here, about one o'clock at night. We were surprised and alarmed to see him, as a large party of the enemy had passed our very doors only a few hours before. When my aunt opened the door she found him sitting on the steps, his head resting on his hands, as if tired and sleepy. We asked him if he did not know the Yankees were near. 'Oh, yes,' he replied; 'they have been chasing me, and compelled me to lengthen my ride considerably.' He came in, but said, 'I cannot rest with you long, as I must be riding all night.' We gave him some bread, honey and milk, which we knew he loved. He said he had been fasting since morning. 'Ah,' said he, 'this is just what I want.' He buckled on his pistols again before sitting down, and said laughingly to me, 'Lock the doors and listen well, for I'll never surrender.' We stood in the porch when he left, and watched him walk off briskly (he had come on foot, having left his horse in the woods). We hated to see him go out in the dark and rainy night-time; but *he* went cheerfully, so willing was he to encounter danger, to endure hardships, 'to spend and be spent' in his country's service."

To "spend and be spent" in the cause of the South was truly this brave spirit's chief delight. These are not idle words, but the truth, in relation to him. The writer of this page was long and intimately associated with him; and so far from presenting an exaggerated picture of him, the incidents and extracts above given do him only partial justice. I never saw a braver man, nor one more modest. He had a peculiar refinement of feeling and bearing which stamped him a *gentleman* to the utmost fibre of his being. This delicacy of temperament was most notable; and it would be difficult to describe the remarkable union of the most daring courage and the sweetest simplicity of demeanour in the young partisan. Greater simplicity and modesty were never seen in human bearing; and so endearing were these traits of his character, that ladies and children—those infallible critics— were uniformly charmed with him. One of the latter wrote:

"His death has been a great sorrow to us. He was with us frequently the week before the battle, and won our entire hearts by his many noble qualities, and his superiority to all around him. He talked much about his family; he loved them with entire devotion. He read to us some of your poems, and repeated one of his own. I close my eyes, and memory brings back to me the thrilling tones of that dear voice, which, though heard no more on earth, has added to the melody of heaven."

His manner was the perfection of good-breeding, and you saw that the famous partisan, whose exploits were the theme of every tongue, had not been raised, like others of his class, amid rude associates and scenes, but with gently nurtured women, and surrounded by the sweet amenities of home. His voice was a peculiar one—very low and distinct in its tones; and these subdued inflections often produced upon the listener the impression that it was a habit acquired in scouting, when to speak above a murmur is dangerous. The low, clear words were habitually accompanied by a bright smile, and the young man was a favourite with all—so cordial was his bearing, so unassuming his whole demeanour. His personal appearance has already been described, but it may interest some of his friends in the far South to know how he appeared when "at work." He dressed uniformly in a plain suit of gray, wearing a jacket, and over this a dark blue overcoat, with a belt, holding his pistol, tightly drawn around his waist. In his hat he wore the black cavalry feather; and his boots were of that handsome pattern which is worn by Federal officers, with patent-leather tops and ornamental thread-work. None of his equipments cost him or the Confederate States a single dollar. They were all captured—either from sutlers' wagons or the enemies he had slain with his own hand. I never knew him to purchase any portion of his own or his horse's accoutrements —saddle, bridle, halter, sabre, pistols, belt, carbine, spurs, were all captured from the enemy. His horses were in the same category, and he rarely kept the same riding-horse long. They were with great regularity shot under him; and he mounted the first he found running riderless, or from which his pistol hurled one of the enemy.

### III.

I have spoken of his modest, almost shy demeanour. All this disappeared in action. His coolness remained unaffected, but he evidently felt himself in his proper element, and entitled to direct others. At such moments his suggestions were boldly made, and not seldom resulted in the rout of the enemy. The cavalry once in motion, the quiet, modest gentleman was meta-morphosed into the fiery partisan. He would lead a charge with the reckless daring of Murat, and cheer on the men, with con-tagious ardour, amid the most furious storm of balls.

His disregard of personal exposure was supreme, and the idea that he was surrounded by peril never occurred to him. He has repeatedly told the present writer, with that simplicity and sin-cerity which produce conviction, that in action he was wholly unconscious of the balls and shells flying and bursting around him—that his interest in the general result was so strong as to cause him to lose sight of them. Those who knew him did not venture to doubt the assertion.

He delighted in the wild charge, the clash of meeting squad-rons, and the roar of artillery. All these martial sights and sounds ministered to the passionate ardour of that temperament which made him most at home where balls were whistling, and the air oppressive with the odour of battle. But, I think, he even pre-ferred the life of the scout—the long and noiseless hunt for his foe—the exercise of those faculties, by means of which an enemy is surprised and destroyed—the single combat with sabre and pistol, often far off in the silence of the woods, where a dead body half concealed amid the grass is all that remains to tell the tale of some hand-to-hand encounter. The number of such con-tests through which Farley had passed would seem incredible to those who did not know him, and thus comprehend how the naked truth of his career beggared romance. He rarely spoke of these affairs, and never, unless to certain persons, and under peculiar circumstances. He had a great horror of appearing to boast of his own exploits, and so greatly feared securing the reputation of colouring his adventures that he seldom alluded to them, even. Fortunately for his memory, many persons wit-nessed his most desperate encounters, and still live to testify to the reckless daring of the young partisan. With these his event-ful career will long remain the subject of fireside tales; and in the coming days of peace, when years have silvered the hair of his contemporaries, old men will tell their grand-children of his strange adventures and those noble traits which made his name so famous.

To the world at large, he will always thus appear—as the daring partisan and adventurous scout—as one who risked his life in a hundred hot encounters, and in all those bloody scenes never quailed or shrank before a foe, however powerful or dangerous. But to those who lived with him—heard his low, friendly voice, and saw every day his bright kindly smile—he appears in a different character. To such the loss we have sustained is deeper— it seems irreparable. It was the good fortune of the writer of these lines to thus see the brave young man—to be beside him in the field; and, at home, to share his confidence and friendship. Riding through the summer forests, or wandering on across the fields of broom-straw, near Fredericksburg—better still, beside the good log-fire of winter—we talked of a thousand things, and I saw what a wealth of kindness, chivalry, and honour he possessed—how beautifully the elements were mixed in his character. Brave and true—simple and kind—he passed away; and among those eminent natures which the writer encountered in the late struggle, few are remembered with such admiration and affection as this noble son of Carolina.

The best conclusion of this brief and inadequate sketch will be the mention made of the brave partisan in General Stuart's report of the battle of Fleetwood. It is as follows:

"Captain W. D. Farley, of South Carolina, a volunteer aide on my staff, was mortally wounded by the same shell which wounded Colonel Butler, and displayed even in death, the same loftiness of bearing and fortitude which characterized him through life. He had served, without emolument, long, faithfully, and always with distinction. No nobler champion has fallen. May his spirit abide with us."

# X

## HARDEMAN STUART

THE YOUNG CAPTAIN OF THE SIGNAL CORPS

### I.

I NEVER knew a braver or lovelier spirit than Hardeman Stuart's. When the wave of war rolled over his young head and swept him away, one of the truest gentlemen of the South disappeared.

The old Greek dogma that the favourites of the gods die early, had in him another illustration. His figure moved before the eyes of those who loved him for a moment only; his brave gay voice was heard; his bright smile shone—then he flitted from the great arena like some youthful actor, who has played his allotted part, and is seen no more.

It was not necessary to know him long to love him. He was with his Virginia comrades for a brief space only, but he soon won every heart. His kindness, his courage, his high-bred courtesy and delightful gaiety, made him the most charming of companions. Every one loved him. Indeed, to know him was to love him; and since his death even strangers have spoken of him in terms of the warmest affection, so deeply had he impressed all who saw him.

He was scarce twenty-one when he died, and in the flush of youth and joy and hope. He was a native of the great State of Mississippi, where hearts are warm and tempers impulsive. The bright sun of the farthest South seemed to have fired his blood; and on the battle-field he fought with the gallantry and nerve, the vigour and *élan* of one of Napoleon's young heroes of the *grand armée*.

His laughing face looked out on the world with an exquisite frankness; the lips were mobile, joyous, and expressive; the large, honest eyes met your own with smiles in their blue depths, which spoke the real character of the youth. I was first attracted toward the youthful stranger by the dash and nerve of his behaviour on the field. It was in the battle of Cold Harbour, where he served as a volunteer upon the staff of General Stuart. He was the model of an aide-de-camp that day, and was specially .nentioned in the general's official report for the valuable services which he rendered. I saw him frequently on this occasion, and was struck with his great gallantry. Nothing could exceed the gay ardour of his bearing, the joyous abandon with which he threw himself into the contest, his ardent and complete performance of all duties assigned to him. He courted danger with a boyish gaiety which shone in his dancing eyes and on his smiling lips, and seemed to covet opportunities of exposing himself to the heaviest fire, in the thickest portion of the fight. No bullet touched him, however; the shot and shell, bursting and plunging everywhere, seemed determined to avoid him and do him no harm. He came out of the battle gay, laughing, and unharmed as he had entered it. At the "White House," afterward, he went with Pelham in that boyish frolic, the chase of the gunboats, and then we rode back "all a summer's day" to the banks of the Chickahominy, conversing. The delightful gaiety of the boy made the long, hot miles of sandy highway slip away unseen; and here I first obtained an insight into the character of the noble young Mississippian, before a stranger, but to be to me from that moment a valued friend.

His gallantry during the battle had attracted attention, and he now secured, through his cousin, General Stuart, the commission of captain in the signal corps. He performed the duties of his rank with alacrity, and I had frequent opportunities of seeing and conversing with him. As I have said, to know him was to love him. There was so much candour and sincerity in his character, such a light-hearted gaiety and sweetness of temper, that he became a favourite even with those who saw with difficulty any merit in their brother men, and repelled all sentiments of liking for their fellow-creatures. Even the surly melted, and grew smiling as his cheerful voice saluted them, and I think the sourest of curmudgeons would have done him a favour without being solicited. His voice had a special charm in its tones. It was what the French call *caressante*. In the accent and intonation of every word which he uttered it was impossible not to discern the goodness of his heart. Distress had never yet laid its heavy hand upon him, and he seemed as free from all knowledge or suspicion of human bitterness or meanness. He looked into the face of the world with a smile full of friendly regard, and the hard, cold world relaxed in its scowl, and smiled back kindly in response. Suspicion or misanthropy never appeared to have visited him; and living, as it were, in an atmosphere of joy and hope and youthful gaiety, he made all around him gay, and had the whole world for his friends.

The brief season of respite from hostilities which followed the battles around Richmond soon came to an end. General Stuart broke up his headquarters in the old grassy yard of Hanover Court-house; his bugle sounded to horse; and the cavalry advanced to place itself on the right of the army about to give battle to Pope on the Rapidan. Here Hardeman Stuart left us, in performance of his duties as signal officer——and I never saw him again but for a single moment. That meeting was on the field of Manassas, when the opposing lines were about to grapple; when the Southern army, hungry, weary, and travel-worn, but undaunted, was about to enter upon the decisive conflict with its old adversary.

Going back in memory to that time, I recall with melancholy interest the little trifling details of this my last meeting and "last greeting" with Hardeman Stuart. I was riding, about noon, to the front of Longstreet's line in search of General Stuart. Under a tree, immediately in rear of his front line, General Longstreet had just dismounted, and was taking off a brown linen overall, the face of the "old war horse" composed, good-natured, but "full of fight." Learning from him that General Stuart was "just on the right of his line," I rode in that direction along the front of the infantry drawn up for battle; the men kneeling on the left knee; the bayonets bristling above; finger on trigger; eyes fixed intently on the crest in front over which the advancing enemy were about to appear.

I went on, and in crossing a fallow of considerable extent, passed one of those small wooden houses which dot the region around Manassas. Often as I beheld such spectacles, this melancholy mansion attracted my attention. It was torn and dismantled—the huge besom of war seemed to have swept over it, sparing its very existence only from a sense of its insignificance. In the broken-down porch were some frightened young women, and crowds of soldiers had straggled up to cool their parched lips from a well in the yard.

There were swarms of these crowding around the nearly exhausted well, and others basked in the sun with a careless air, which indicated natures callous to the coming battle.

All this was taken in at a single glance, and I was galloping on, when suddenly I heard a voice which uttered my name.

I drew up and turned around. As I did so, a form detached itself from the rest, came running toward me with the gay exclamation, "How d'ye, Captain!" and I recognised Hardeman Stuart.

But what a change! He had always been the neatest person imaginable in his dress and appearance. His brown hair had always been carefully parted and brushed, his boots as polished as assiduous rubbing could make them, and his new uniform coat, with its gay new braid, had been almost too nice and unwrinkled for a soldier.

His appearance was in vivid contrast with all this. He was coatless, unwashed, his boots covered with dust and his clothes had the dingy look of the real soldier, who is so often compelled to lie upon the ground, and to sleep in his apparel. His hair was unbrushed, and hung disordered around his face, and the gallant young captain of the Signal Corps had the appearance of a sapper and miner.

But the face was unchanged—that was the same; gay, ardent, joyous, as he held out his hand, and grasped mine with the same old friendly manner. The young captain was the image of martial energy and abandon. The bright smile broke forth from his face like sunshine, and his cheerful voice as he greeted me was full of the old kindly music.

He was evidently overjoyed to see a familiar face among all the strange ones around him, where the eye met only alien glances; to press a friendly hand where none seemed ready to stretch forth and greet him.

I can see the bright face now, as he turned it up and smiled; hear the voice with its tones of boyish music as he related his misfortunes. He had posted himself upon a ridge with his detachment, and from his station was signalling the movements of the enemy, when a strong force surprised him, and compelled him to retire precipitately.

So sudden was the attack that he was very nearly captured. His horse had been tied near; the young officer's uniform coat, which he had taken off, from the heat of the weather, strapped behind the saddle—and there was no time to mount. He escaped in the woods with his men minus horse and coat; but seemed to regard the whole affair as an excellent jest, and only the ordinary "fortune of war."

His gay laughter followed the narrative, and I remember the ardent light of the blue eyes looking out from the tangled curls of the brave boy.

"Well, Hardeman, you have had bad luck," I said, "but get another horse and come on."

"I intend to; tell the General I'll soon be there."

"Yes."

"Good-bye."

I shook the brave hand and rode on. I was never more to touch it.

I have scarcely the heart to continue my narrative and relate the sequel. Something affects the throat as you think of these dead comrades whose hands you have clasped, whose voices you have heard. Some of the sunshine left the world when they went, and life grows dull.

Poor Hardeman! But how can I call him *poor*? Rich, rather, beyond the wealth of kingdoms; for he died in the bloom of youth, before sorrow touched him, fighting for his native land.

He did not succeed in procuring a horse, which is always difficult just before a battle; and his brave young soul revolted from inaction at that moment. He must take his part in the action, in one capacity if not in another; if not as captain, then as private; and this resolution was speedily carried out. Procuring a musket and cartridge-box—old friends of his before his promotion—he sought for his old Mississippi company, entered its ranks, charged with them, and fell, shot through the heart.

He died where he fell, and sleeps in the weird path of Manassas. God rest his soul!

Such was the fate of Hardeman Stuart—an event which brought the tears to many eyes, albeit unused to the melting mood—and here my sketch might end. I will add, however, a somewhat curious incident which occurred a day or two after the battle.

General Stuart followed the enemy on Sunday, and coming up with his rear at the bridge over Cub Run, had a slight artillery engagement, and took many prisoners. The bridge was destroyed and the cavalry turned to the left, and making a circuit came into the Little River turnpike, at the mouth of the Frying Pan road. Proceeding down the turnpike in the direction of Germantown, a squadron captured a company of the enemy's cavalry; and advancing further to a small tavern on the roadside, took prisoners another company who were feeding their horses in fancied security at the place.

This cavalry formed a portion of that which had operated in the battles around Groveton; and in possession of one of the men was found Hardeman Stuart's coat, captured with his horse and accoutrements on the mountain.

There was no trouble at all in identifying the coat. In the breast pocket was his captain's commission.

# XI

## JENNINGS WISE

CAPTAIN OF "THE BLUES"

### I.

I FOUND in an old portfolio, the other day, the following slip from a Norfolk paper of the year 1862:

"The Confederate steamer Arrow arrived here this morning, from Currituck, having communicated with a steamer sent down to Roanoke Island under a flag of truce. She brought up the bodies of Captain O. J. Wise, Lieutenant William Selden, and Captain Coles. Captain Wise was pierced by three balls, and Lieutenant Selden was shot through the head. The Yankees who saw Captain Wise during the fierce and unequal contest, declare that he displayed a gallantry and valour never surpassed. Alas, that he has fallen in a contest so unequal! But who has fallen more honourably, more nobly? Young Selden, too, died at his gun, while gallantly fighting the enemy that had gathered in so superior numbers upon our shores.

"Last night, when the steamer arrived at Currituck, General Wise directed that the coffin containing the remains of his son be opened. Then, I learn from those who were present, a scene transpired that words cannot describe. The old hero bent over the body of his son, on whose pale face the full moon threw its light, kissed the cold brow many times, and exclaimed, in an agony of emotion: 'Oh, my brave boy, you have died for me, you have died for me.' "

What an epitaph!

147

The gray-haired father, forgetting the past and the future, losing sight, for the moment, of the war and all other things—bending and weeping over the dead body of the son who "had displayed a gallantry and valour never surpassed"—giving his heart's blood to the cause he loved—the annals of tragedy contain no spectacle more touching!

Of the remarkable young man who thus poured forth his blood, and passed away, before the age of thirty, in defence of his native soil, I propose to give a few personal recollections. It is hard that a noble soul should go from the haunts of the living, to be remembered only by the small circle of loving friends who knew and appreciated him. And though I shall not attempt anything in the shape of a memoir of young Jennings Wise, my few words may not prove uninteresting to those who watched, from a distance, his meteoric career, and perhaps admired his brave spirit, while ignorance of his real character led them to misunderstand him.

Jennings Wise!

How many memories that name recalls!—memories of gentleness and chivalry, and lofty honour, to those who knew him truly—of fancied arrogance and haughty pride, and bloody instincts, to those who accepted common rumour for their estimate of him. For there were many rumours of this description afloat—and it must be acknowledged that there was some excuse for the misconception. He had little of the spirit of conciliation if he believed a man to be his foe; managed early to arouse bitter enmities; and continued to defy his opponents without deigning to explain his character or his motives. Before he was better understood—when the mists were only beginning to clear away, and show his virtues of devotion, and patriotism, and kindness—death called him.

Born in Virginia, and going in his early manhood to Europe, as Secretary of Legation, he there perfected himself in riding, fencing, and all manly exercises; studying political science, and training himself, consciously or unconsciously, for the arena upon which he was to enter soon after his return. He came to Virginia at a time when the atmosphere was stifling with the heat of contending factions in politics, and becoming the chief editor of the Richmond *Enquirer*, plunged into the struggle with all the ardour of a young and ambitious soldier who essays to test the use of those arms he has been long burnishing for battle. He did not lack for opponents, for a great contest was raging, and the minds of men were red-hot with the mighty issues of the time. He had scarce thrown down the glove when many hands were extended to take it up. Then commenced a strife on the political arena, in which the opponents fought each other with bitter and passionate vehemence. What the pen wrote, the pistol, unhappily, was too often called upon to support; and the young politician was ere long engaged in more than one duel, which achieved for him a widely-extended notoriety and a venomous party hatred. Of these quarrels I do not design to speak. It is no part of my purpose to inquire who was to blame or who was faultless; and I would not move the ashes resting now upon the details of those unhappy affairs, under which the fire perhaps still smoulders, full of old enmities. That he was carried away by passion often, is unfortunately too true; but he had no love for conflict, and publicly declared his aversion to "private war." Unhappily the minds of his political opponents were too profoundly swayed by the passions of the epoch to give him credit for these declarations. They were not listened to, and the young politician became the mark of extreme political hatred. The sins of passion and the heated arena were regarded as the coolly planned and deliberately designed crimes of a moral monster, who had never felt the emotion of pity or love for his brother man. Intelligent and honourable persons believed that all the young man's instincts were cruel; that his hatreds were capricious and implacable; that his nature was that of the tiger, thirsting for blood; his conscience paralysed or warped by a terrible moral disease. His splendid oratory, his trenchant pen, the dash and courage of his nature, were allowed; but these were his only "good gifts;" he was, they said, the Ishmael of the modern world.

All this he knew, and he continued his career, trusting to time. He fought for secession; joined the First Virginia Regiment, and served at Charlestown, in the John Brown raid. Then war came in due time. He was elected captain of the Blues—the oldest volunteer company in Virginia—took the leadership from the first, as one born to command, and fought and fell at that bloody Roanoke fight, at the head of his company, and cheering on his men.

His body was brought back to Richmond, laid in the capitol, and buried, in presence of a great concourse of mourners, in Hollywood Cemetery. That was the end of the brief young life—death in defence of his native land, and a grave in the beloved soil, by the side of the great river, and the ashes of Monroe, brought thither by himself and his associates.

Then came a revulsion. His character was better understood; his faults were forgotten; his virtues recognised. Even his old opponents hastened to express their sympathy and admiration. It was remembered that more than once he had refused to return his adversary's fire; that championship of one whom he loved more than life had inflamed his enmity—no merely selfish considerations. His sweetness of temper and kindness were recalled by many, and the eyes which had been bent upon him with horror or hatred, shed tears beside the young soldier's grave.

Oh, tardy justice of good men! Oh, laurel-wreath upon the coffin!—soft words spoken in the dull, cold ear of death! This soul of chivalry and honour—this gentle, kindly, simple heart—had been branded as the enemy of his species—as a haughty, soulless, pitiless monster!

In speaking of this young Virginian, I wish to espouse no personal or party quarrel—to arouse none of those enmities which sleep now—to open no old wounds, and to fan into flame none of the heart-burnings of the past. Those who contended with him most bitterly have long ago forgotten their feud. Many shed tears for the noble youth when he fell, and speak of him now as one of those great Virginians whom it is the pride of our soil to have produced. They know him better now, and understand that this man was no hater of his species—no Ishmael of civilization, cold and haughty and implacable—but a beautiful and noble nature, attuned to every honourable impulse, and only embittered temporarily by party passion. Dying, he has suffered change; and there is a beauty in the pale, cold face, which it never possessed while living. Traits never suspected come out now, when Death has stamped the countenance with his melancholy seal; and love and pity have quite banished the old scorn and hatred. The green grass on his grave has covered all enmity, and the love of friends has taken the place of the bitterness of foes.

Among those friends who knew and loved him living, I count myself. To know him thus was speedily to love him—for his traits and instincts were so conspicuously noble and endearing, that he irresistibly attracted the affection of all who were thrown in familiar contact with him. How gentle, modest, and unassuming these inner instincts of his heart were, those who knew him in his private life will bear witness. They will tell you of his honest and truthful nature; his unpretending simplicity; his chivalric impulses, and nobility of feeling. Indeed, you would have said that the Creator had breathed into this clay the loveliest traits of humanity, and raised up in the prosaic nineteenth century a "good knight" of old days, to show the loveliness of honour.

This was one side of the young man's character, only. With these softer traits were mingled some of the hardiest endowments of strong manhood. No man was ever braver. Indeed, his nerve had in it something antique and splendid, as of the elder days of chivalry, when neither monster nor magician, giant nor winged dragon, could make the heart of the good knight quail, or move him from his steadfast purpose. What in other men was the courage of habit, or training, or calculation of forces, was in him that of native endowment and birthright. To match himself, if need be, against any odds, however overwhelming, and breast all opposition with a stubborn, dauntless front, was to act as his character dictated, and to follow his temperament. The sentiment of fear, I believe, never entered his breast; if it did, it never stayed there long enough for him to make its acquaintance. He would have led the charge of the English cavalry at Balaklava with the nerve and dash of Hotspur, glorying in the roar of the enemy's artillery, and resolute to take their guns or die. At Thermopylæ, he would have stood beside Leonidas, and fought and died without the shudder of a nerve. In battle at the head of his men, his coolness and resolution were invincible. The grim front of war possessed no terrors for him, and he advanced into the gulf of battle with the calmness of a holiday soldier on parade.

## II.

He was early in the lists as the advocate of resistance to the North, and fought its opponents with persistent vehemence. To "wait" was to sign the death-warrant of the State, he declared. "God save the liberties of this brave old Commonwealth!" if this was the course defined for her. What he preached he practised. He sounded the onset, and the lines once in motion, he took his place in the great army. At first as a private, with musket on shoulder; eager, active, untiring; inspiring all with his own brave spirit. Then, when his acknowledged capacity for leadership placed him at the head of a command, he took the post as his of right, and led his men as all who knew him expected. How he led them on that disastrous day at Roanoke—with what heroic nerve, and splendid gallantry, in the face of the deadliest fire— let his old comrades in arms declare. There, in the front of battle, he fell—giving his life without a single regret to the cause he loved.

It was the phase of character, indicated above, which the outer world chiefly considered, and estimated him by. Yet this was by no means his most attractive phase. The dauntless nerve, the stubborn and indomitable will, revealed themselves on certain occasions only—the social virtues of the individual were seen every day. It would be difficult to imagine a human being more modest, kindly, and simple. His modesty amounted almost to shyness; and it was doubtless this species of reserve which led many to regard him as cold, and destitute of feeling. Let it not be understood, however, that he was subject to *mauvaise honte* —the diffidence of one who distrusts his own powers, and shrinks from collision with other minds. His peculiarity was rather the reverse, as his perfect self-possession and control of every faculty in public speaking indicated. Self-reliance, rather than self-distrust, marked the character of his intellect—boldness to undertake, and unshrinking courage to execute. But in this there was no arrogance—no *hauteur*. In the combat he would contend with all his powers, and shrink from no odds: but the contest once over, the hot blood cool, the old modesty returned, and the kindly, gentle smile. The indulgence of his affections was evidently one of his chief happinesses. He was fond of children, and delighted to play with them, sharing their gambols and amusements with the *bonhomie* and abandon of a boy. In such scenes, the vehement young politician no doubt took refuge from the strife of the public arena, where so many hot passions met and clashed, and found in the playful antics of children the antidote to the scorns and hatreds of those grown-up children— men. It was in the society of the eminent Virginian, his father, however, that he seemed to experience his greatest happiness; and his devotion to him was the controlling sentiment of his being. If this sentiment impelled him to a partisanship too violent at times, the fault will not be regarded as a mean or ignoble one, nor detract in any measure from the character here attributed to him, of the kindest and simplest of gentlemen.

The intellect which accompanied this courageous spirit and kindly heart was eminently vigorous and original. It was rather that of the actor than the thinker—rather, ready, acute, inventive and fruitful in resources—quick to move and to strike, in debate or reasoning with the pen—than deliberate, philosophic, or reflective. It wanted the breadth and depth which result from study and meditation, but as a sharp and tempered weapon to accomplish direct tangible results, it was exceedingly forcible and effective. As a writer in the larger acceptation of the term, he was not conspicuously endowed; but his style as a journalist was fluent, eloquent, and when his nature was strongly moved, full of power and the fire of invective. Some of his editorial writings deserve to be collected, and preserved in a permanent form, as among the most forcible expositions of the great prin-

ciples involved in the struggle which absorbed the energies of
the South.

His most notable gift was unquestionably that of oratory. He
possessed native endowments which entitled him to very high
rank as a public speaker. In the columns of a daily journal his
powers were always more or less cramped, and did not assert
their full strength, but on "the stump" he was in his own element. Here all the faculties of his intellect and nature had full
swing, and "ample room and verge enough" for their exercise.
The spectator saw at a glance that the young man with the thin
slight figure and quiet manner, was a born orator. His first words
justified the opinion, and stamped him as one born to move, to
sway, to direct the thoughts and the actions of men. The crowd
—that unfailing critic of a public speaker's ability—always received him with acclamations, and hailed his appearance on the
rostrum with loud applause. They felt that, youth as he was,
and as yet untrained in the arts of the orator, he was a match
for the oldest opponents, and they were content to leave the
advocacy of great principles, at momentous crises, in the hands
of this young man—to accept and rely on him as their champion.

He did not disappoint their expectations ever. A born politician, and thrilling with the great party issues before the country,
he entered the arena with the bold and self-possessed demeanour
of one in his chosen element, and equal to the occasion. Political
history—the careers of public men—the principles underlying
the American frame of government—all were thoroughly familiar to him, and his knowledge was available at a moment's
notice. His speeches were skilful combinations of philosophic
reasoning anad hard-hitting illustrations. In the employment of
invective, his handling was that of a master; and when his scorn
of some unworthy action or character was fully aroused, his delivery of the scathing sarcasm or the passionate defiance was
inexpressibly vehement and bitter. Those who have seen the
flashing eye and the scornful lip of the young orator at such
times, will not readily forget them, or wonder at the wild excitement of the crowd as they listened to these outbursts. Even
the cool intellects of old men were taken captive with the rest,

and I think all who heard the youthful speaker, came away with the impression that time and training only were needed, to make him one of the most famous orators of the old Commonwealth which has produced so many giants.

With the termination of his speeches disappeared all the passion, vehemence, and ardour of the man. The handkerchief passed over the damp brow, seemed to wipe away all excitement; and the fiery gladiator, swaying all minds by his fierce invective, or his vivid reasoning, subsided into the quiet, almost shy young man. The old modesty and simplicity of demeanour returned, and the forces of the vigorous intellect returned to rest, until some other occasion should call them into exercise.

I could add many things relating to this eminent young man in his personal and private character, but the subject may not interest the general reader as much as it does him who writes. Perhaps, too, they are better kept for other years, when time shall have extinguished the few heart-burnings that remain, and obliterated the scars of old contests. I have thought it right, however, to put thus much concerning him on record without shaping my discourse to please either friend or foe. Foes, I believe, he has no longer. Even those who most bitterly opposed him while living, now acknowledge his great qualities, and lament his untimely end.

If enmity exist toward him in any heart, however, no answering defiance comes back. The weapon of the good knight will never more be drawn—he has fought his last battle and yielded up his soul. He sleeps now quietly, after all the turmoils of life—after heart-burnings and triumphs, and loves and hatreds—sleeps in the bosom of the land he loved, and toiled, and thought, and fought, and died for. His is not the least worthy heart which has poured out its blood for Virginia and the South; and in the pages of our annals, among the names of our dead heroes who surrendered youth, and coming fame, and friends, and home, and life for their native land—surrendered them without a murmur or a single regret—among these great souls the Genius of History must inscribe the name of Jennings Wise.

PART 2

# IN THE CAVALRY

"STUART'S RIDE AROUND McCLELLAN.

The gay chase continued until we reached the Tottapotamoi."

# INTRODUCTION

THE infantry and the artillery of an army live and move and have their being in a sphere widely different from that of the cavalry.

The first named arms of the service perform the "heavy work" in the great pitched battles. When armies face each other, and the moment has come for a final trial of strength, it is the infantry and artillery to which a commander looks. When the sun rises on one of these days of history, the foot-soldier or the cannoneer feels that all his energies will be required. If he falls he falls; but if the enemy's bullets spare him, he can look for rest on the morrow—for a great pitched battle decides everything. The column may advance or retire, but it seldom fights very heavily thereafter. The weather, too, counts greatly for or against active service with the artillery or infantry—the winter is fatal. Then the wheels of the guns sink in the slushy soil; wagons cannot move with rations; and thus conquered by the rain and snow, the cannoneers and musket-bearers settle down in their comfortable camps, build their log-cabins, or their arbours of boughs; and days, and weeks, and months pass by in perfect quiet, until the spring sun dries the roads, and the thunder of artillery and musketry again roars across the fields of May or June.

Thus the gunners and footmen bear the brunt in the great

battles, to retire thereafter to camp and rest. Their ranks may be decimated, but those who survive enjoy something like repose. They build their chimneys, broil their meat, smoke their pipes, and lounge, and laugh, and sing around the camp-fire, with "none to make them afraid."

The life of the cavalry is different. They do not perform the hard work in the conflicts of armies, where the improved fire-arms of modern times would speedily destroy their horses—and horses were beyond the value of gold, almost, to the South in the recent war—nor are the losses of the cavalry in any one engagement as great as those of the infantry. But the work performed by the mounted men of an army is incessant. They fight throughout the year—in winter as in summer—when the ground is a quagmire, as when it is firm. They cannot rest, from the very nature of things, for they are the "eyes and ears" of an army. Their duty is to watch—and to watch, the cavalier must be in the saddle with carbine ready. He must watch by night as well as day; for night is the season of surprises, and to guard the army against surprise is the chief duty of the cavalry. Seeing the long column falling slowly back on days of conclusive battle, the infantry are apt to sneer, and think, if they do not say— and they *say* it often—"*We* do the hard fighting, the cavalry the fancy work!" or, "Here comes the cavalry, going to the rear— a fight is on hand!" They forget, however, one thing—that while the infantry has been resting in camp, with regular rations and sound sleep, the cavalry have been day and night in the saddle, without rations at all, watching and fighting all along the front. Let justice be done to all; and it is not the noble infantry or artillery of the late army of Northern Virginia who will be guilty of injustice to their brethren of the cavalry, who, under Stuart, Ashby, Hampton, and the Lees, did that long, hard work, leaving Virginia, Maryland, and Pennsylvania strewed with their dead bodies.

But a comparison of the relative value of the different arms was not the writer's purpose. His aim was to point out the contrast which exists in the mere mode of living. The foot-soldier is confined to his camp for the greater portion of the time, and sameness rather than variety, common-place rather than inci-dent, marks his days. In the cavalry this does not exist. As there is no rest for the cavalry-man, so there is no dull routine—no "every day the same." His life is full of movement, variety, in-cident, and adventure; he is ever in the saddle, and fighting, either as a unit of the long drawn column, advancing or retiring with the army, or in scouts and skirmishes—the theatre of his work shifts quietly as do the scenes of a drama on the stage. All that makes the hard and brutal trade of war endurable seems to gather around him, wreathing with brilliant flowers the keen edge of the sabre.

The bugle sounding "Boots and saddles!" and then "To horse!" replaces the drum. "To horse and away!" is the cavalry motto. Once in the saddle and moving, his life of quick transi-tions, odd experiences, and perilous or grotesque adventures, begins in earnest. There is a "glorious uncertainty" about his movements which is not without a singular charm. He is not so much a common soldier, as a gay knight-errant, knowing not where he may lay his head at the end of his day's journey—cer-tain only that it will not be beneath the shelter of a tent, nor with any regular ration upon which to stay his hunger. The infantry and artillery have wagons and rations; and theoretically the cavalry have also—but only in theory. They are never "up"—these dilatory wagons—and as to tents, those are a luxury of which the cavalry-man seldom even dreams. The blanket behind his saddle is his tent; he lies down by the bivouac fire supperless often; neither quarter-master nor commissary favours him; and when he "forages" for food, he is denounced as a "straggler."

But the cavalry-man accepts philosophically the uncompli-mentary opinion entertained of him, in view of the certain charms of his existence. He is the child of adventure, roaming the fields and forests, and revelling in his freedom. He knows whence he comes, but not whither the winds will waft him. He is never at rest; never certain what the next hour, nay, the coming moment, will bring forth. At any instant may come a surprise, an attack, the bang of carbines, the clash of sabres—and then, pursuit or retreat, defeat or victory. If he falls, he falls; if he survives, he sleeps serenely, wrapped up in his blanket, the root of a tree or a saddle for a pillow, overhead "the canopy," all studded with the fires of night, and dreams of scenes and faces far away.

Such a life is ever fresh, and possesses never-ending attractions. To-day an exhausting march and a heavy fight—to-morrow rest, and stories, and jests, and laughter; one day a feast of the rarest—the next a famine of the sorest. To ride on, hour after hour, through the gloom of night, until the frame is weary unto death, and the cavalry-man totters in the saddle for very exhaustion and sleeplessness—that is not pleasant. But then sleep is magical when he halts at last; food is ambrosial when he broils his chance slice of bacon on the end of a stick in the blaze of the camp-fire!

To the cavalry-man belongs the fresh life of the forest—the wandering existence which brings back the days of old romance. Do you wish to form some conception of the life of that model cavalry-man and gentleman, Don Quixote? To do so, you have only to "join the cavalry." Like the Don, your cavalry-man goes through the land in search of adventures, and finds many. He penetrates retired localities—odd, unknown nooks—meeting with curious characters and out-of-the-way experiences, which would make the fortune of a romance writer. Here, far away from the rushing world and the clash of arms, he finds bright faces, and is welcomed by "heaven's last best gift"—for woman is ever the guardian angel of the soldier. She smiles upon him when he is gloomy; feeds him when he is hungry; and it is often the musical laughter of a girl which the cavalry-man hears as he rides on musing—not the rattle of his miserable sabre! Thus romance, sentiment, and poetry meet him everywhere. And is he fond of the grotesque? That meets him, too, in a thousand places. Of the pathetic? Ah! that salutes him often on the fierce arena of war! Thus, living a fresh life, full of vivid emotions, he passes his days and nights, till the fatal bullet comes—laughing, fighting, feasting, starving, to the end.

His life is better than a collegiate education, for it teaches him the mysteries of human nature. He does not pass his days amid social circles, marked by respectable uniformity and maddening common-place, but is thrown in contact with every species of "moving accident," every variety of the human species; scouts, "guerillas," secret agents, prisoners, night-hawks, spies, friends in blue coats, enemies in gray—all that the highways and the byways, the fields, the forests, and the day and the night contain, pass before the eyes of the cavalry-man. He sees the adventurous life of the ranger and partisan, hears the ring of the sabre, the crack of sharpshooters, the roar of cannon, and the shouts of the squadrons as they charge. His is the existence of the rover: the sudden peril, the narrow escape, and the fun and frolic of the bivouac. When he summons his recollections, it is not so much the "great events" of war as its pictures and incidents of which he discourses. He revives its romantic scenes and gay adventures, only—remembering its smiles, sighs, laughter, tears, its gloom or sunlight, as it actually lowered or shone. The writer of this eulogy has carried a musket, albeit he never did hard work with it; has served in the artillery, and loves it, as he honours the great arm which thundered upon every battle-field, and held the rear, all along the Valley, against Sheridan, and fired the last gun of the war at Appomatox. It is simply not possible that he could utter a word against those heroes of the infantry and artillery whom he is proud to call his comrades; but he remembers with most interest and pleasure the gay days when he "followed the feather" of Stuart, that *fleur des chevaliers.* In the saddle, near that good knight of the nineteenth century, war became a splendid drama, rather than mere bloody work; a great stage, whereon the scenes were ever shifting, and the "exits" were all made to the sound of the bugle! That sound was stirring; and recalling now his various experiences, the writer of this page hears the ring of the bugle, not the roll of the drum; remembers the life of the cavalry rather than that of the infantry or the artillery.

Some of these memories are here recorded. The narratives are necessarily egotistical in appearance, since the writer was compelled to speak of what he saw in person, not by others' eyes, to give any value to his recollections. The reader is solicited, however, to regard this circumstance as unavoidable, and further to believe that a fondness for making himself conspicuous is not a trait of the writer's character. For the rest, the pictures he has drawn are accurate, as far as his ability has enabled him to present figures and events in their real colours. If the record is dull, it is the dulness of truth, not the stupidity of a bad romance.

# I

## STUART'S "RIDE AROUND MCCLELLAN"

### IN JUNE, 1862

### I.

WHO that went with Stuart on his famous "Ride around Mc-Clellan" in the summer of 1862, just before the bloody battles of the Chickahominy, will ever forget the fun, the frolic, the romance—and the peril too—of that fine journey? Thinking of the gay ride now, when a century seems to have swept between that epoch and the present, I recall every particular, live over every emotion. Once more I hear the ringing laugh of Stuart, and see the keen flash of the blue eyes under the black feather of the prince of cavaliers!

If the reader will follow me he shall see what took place on this rapid ride, witness some incidents of this first and king of raids. The record will be that of an eye-witness, and the personal prominence of the writer must be excused as inseparable from the narrative. I need not dwell upon the "situation" in June, 1862. All the world knows that, at that time, McClellan had advanced with his magnificent army of 156,000 men, to the banks of the Chickahominy, and pushing across, had fought on the last day of May the bloody but indecisive battle of the Seven Pines. On the right it was a Confederate, on the left a Federal success; and General McClellan drew back, marshalled his great lines, darkening both the northern and southern banks of the Chickahominy, and prepared for a more decisive blow at the Confederate capital, whose spires were in sight. Before him, however, lay the Southern army, commanded now by Lee, who had succeeded Johnston, wounded in the fight of "Seven Pines." The moment was favourable for a heavy attack by Lee. Jackson had just driven before him the combined forces of Shields and Fremont, and on the bloody field of Port Republic ended the great campaign of the Valley at one blow. The veterans of his command could now be concentrated on the banks of the Chickahominy against McClellan; a combined advance of the forces under Lee and Jackson might save the capital. But how should the attack be made? In council of war, General Stuart told me he proposed an assault upon General McClellan's left wing from the direction of James River, to cut him off from that base. But this suggestion was not adopted; the defences were regarded as too strong. It was considered a better plan to attack the Federal army on the north bank of the Chickahominy, drive it from its works, and try the issue in the fields around Cold Harbour. The great point was to ascertain if this was practicable, and especially to find what defences, if any, the enemy had to guard the approach to their right wing. If these were slight, the attack could be made with fair prospects of success. Jackson could sweep around while Lee assailed the lines near Mechanicsville; then one combined assault would probably defeat the Federal force. To find the character of the enemy's works beyond the stream—his positions and movements—General Stuart was directed to take a portion of his cavalry, advance as far as Old Church, if practicable, and then be guided by circumstances. Such were the orders with which Stuart set out about moonrise on the night, I think, of June 12, upon this dangerous expedition.

As the young cavalier mounted his horse on that moonlight night he was a gallant figure to look at. The gray coat buttoned to the chin; the light French sabre balanced by the pistol in its black holster; the cavalry boots above the knee, and the brown hat with its black plume floating above the bearded features, the brilliant eyes, and the huge moustache, which curled with laughter at the slightest provocation—these made Stuart the perfect picture of a gay cavalier, and the spirited horse he rode seemed to feel that he carried one whose motto was to "do or die." I chanced to be his sole companion as he galloped over the broad field near his headquarters, and the glance of the blue eyes of Stuart at that moment was as brilliant as the lightning itself.

Catching up with his column of about 1500 horsemen, and two pieces of horse-artillery under Colonels William H. F. Lee, Fitz Lee, and Will. T. Martin, of Mississippi—cavalier as brave as ever drew sabre—Stuart pushed on northward as if going to join Jackson, and reaching the vicinity of Taylorsville, near Hanover Junction, went that night into bivouac. He embraced the opportunity, after midnight, of riding with Colonel W. H. F. Lee to "Hickory Hill," the residence of Colonel Williams Wickham—afterward General Wickham—who had been recently wounded and paroled. Here he went to sleep in his chair after talking with Colonel Wickham, narrowly escaped capture from the enemy rear, and returning before daylight, advanced with his column straight upon Hanover Court-House. Have you ever visited this picturesque spot, reader? We looked upon it on that day of June—upon its old brick court-house, where Patrick Henry made his famous speech against the parsons, its ancient tavern, its modest roofs, the whole surrounded by the fertile fields waving with golden grain—all this we looked at with unusual interest. For in this little bird's nest, lost as it were in a sea of rippling wheat and waving foliage, some "Yankee cavalry" had taken up their abode; their horses stood ready saddled in the street, and this dark mass we now gazed at furtively from behind a wooden knoll, in rear of which Stuart's column was drawn up ready to move at the word. Before he gave the signal, the General dispatched Colonel Fitz Lee round to the right, to flank and cut off the party. But all at once the scouts in front were descried by the enemy; shots resounded; and seeing that his presence was discovered, Stuart gave the word, and swept at a thundering gallop down the hill. The startled "blue birds," as we used to call our Northern friends, did not wait; the squadron on picket at the court-house, numbering some one hundred and fifty men, hastily got to horse— then presto! they disappear in a dense cloud of dust from which

echo some parting salutes from their carbines. Stuart pressed
on rapidly, took the road to Old Church, and near a place called
Hawes' Shop, in a thickly wooded spot, was suddenly charged
himself. It did not amount to much, and seemed rather an attempt at reconnoissance. A Federal officer at the head of a detachment came on at full gallop, very nearly ran into the head
of our column, and then seeing the dense mass of gray coats,
fired his pistol, wheeled short about, and went back at full speed,
with his detachment.

Stuart had given, in his ringing voice, the order: "Form fours!
draw sabre! charge!" and now the Confederate people pursued
at headlong speed, uttering shouts and yells sufficiently loud to
awaken the seven sleepers! The men were evidently exhilarated
by the chase, the enemy just keeping near enough to make an
occasional shot practicable. A considerable number of the Federal cavalrymen were overtaken and captured, and these proved
to belong to the company in which Colonel Fitz Lee had formerly been a lieutenant. I could not refrain from laughter at
the pleasure which "Colonel Fitz"—whose motto should be
"*toujours gai*"—seemed to take in inquiring after his old cronies.
"Was Brown alive? where was Jones? and was Robinson sergeant still?" Colonel Fitz never stopped until he found out
everything. The prisoners laughed as they recognised him. Altogether, reader, the interview was the most friendly imaginable.

The gay chase continued until we reached the Tottapotamoi,
a sluggish stream, dragging its muddy waters slowly between
rush-clad banks, beneath drooping trees; and this was crossed
by a small rustic bridge. The line of the stream was entirely
undefended by works; the enemy's right wing was unprotected;
Stuart had accomplished the object of his expedition, and afterward piloted Jackson over this very same road. But to continue
the narrative of his movements. The picket at the bridge had
been quickly driven in, and disappeared at a gallop, and on the
high ground beyond, Colonel W. H. F. Lee, who had taken
the front, encountered the enemy. The force appeared to be
about a regiment, and they were drawn up in line of battle in

the fields to receive our attack. It came without delay. Placing himself at the head of his horsemen, Colonel Lee swept forward at the *pas de charge*, and with shouts the two lines came together. The shock was heavy, and the enemy—a portion of the old United States Regulars, commanded by Captain Royal—stood their ground bravely, meeting the attack with the sabre. Swords clashed, pistols and carbines banged, yells, shouts, cheers resounded; then the Federal line was seen to give back, and take to headlong flight. They were pursued with ardour, and the men were wild with this—to many of them—their first fight. But soon after all joy disappeared from their faces, at sight of a spectacle which greeted them. Captain Latanè, of the Essex cavalry, had been mortally wounded in the charge, and as the men of his company saw him lying bloody before them, many a bearded face was wet with tears. The scene at his grave afterward became the subject of Mr. Washington's picture, "The Burial of Latanè;" and in his general order after the expedition, Stuart called upon his command to take for their watchword in the future "*Avenge Latanè!*" Captain Royal, the Federal commandant, had also been badly wounded, and many of his force killed. I remember passing a Dutch cavalryman who was writhing with a bullet through the breast, and biting and tearing up the ground. He called for water, and I directed a servant at a house near by to bring him some. The last I saw of him, a destitute cavalryman was taking off his spurs as he was dying. War is a hard trade.

Fitz Lee immediately pressed on and burst into the camp near Old Church, where large supplies of boots, pistols, liquors, and other commodities were found. These were speedily appropriated by the men, and the tents were set on fire amid loud shouts. The spectacle was animating; but a report having got abroad that one of the tents contained powder, the vincinity thereof was evacuated in almost less than no time. We were now at Old Church, where Stuart was to be guided in his further movements by circumstances. I looked at him; he was evidently reflecting. In a moment he turned round to me and said: "Tell Fitz Lee to come along, I'm going to move on with my column." These words terminated my doubt, and I understood in an instant that the General had decided on the bold and hazardous plan of passing entirely round McClellan's army.

"I think the quicker we move now the better," I said, with a laugh.

"Right," was Stuart's reply; "tell the column to move on at a trot."

So at a rapid trot the column moved.

## II.

The gayest portion of the raid now began. From this moment it was neck or nothing, do or die. We had one chance of escape against ten of capture or destruction.

Stuart had decided upon his course with that rapidity, good judgment, and decision, which were the real secrets of his splendid efficiency as a leader of cavalry, in which capacity I believe that he has never been surpassed, either in the late war or any other. He was now in the very heart of the enemy's citadel, with their enormous masses upon every side. He had driven in their advanced force, passed within sight of the white tents of General McClellan's headquarters, burned their camps, and ascertained all that he wished. How was he to return? He could not cross the Pamunkey, and make a circuit back; he had no pontoons. He could not return over the route by which he had advanced. As events afterward showed, the alarm had been given, and an overpowering force of infantry, cavalry, and artillery had been rapidly moved in that direction to intercept the daring raider. Capture stared him in the face, on both of these routes—across the Pamunkey, or back as he came; he must find some other loophole of escape.

Such was the dangerous posture of affairs, and such was the important problem which Stuart decided in five minutes. He determined to make the complete circuit of McClellan's army; and crossing the Chickahominy below Long Bridge, re-enter the Confederate lines from Charles City. If on his way he encountered cavalry he intended to fight it; if a heavy force of infantry barred his way he would elude, or cut a path through it;

if driven to the wall and debarred from escape he did not mean
to surrender. A few days afterward I said to him:

"That was a tight place at the river, General. If the enemy
had come down on us, you would have been compelled to have
surrendered."

"No," was his reply; "one other course was left."

"What was that?"

"To *die game*."

And I know that such was his intention. When a commander
means to die game rather than surrender he is a dangerous
adversary.

From Old Church onward it was *terra incognita*. What force
of the enemy barred the road was a question of the utmost
interest, but adventure of some description might be safely
counted on. In about twenty-four hours I, for one, expected
either to be laughing with my friends within the Southern lines,
or dead, or captured. Which of these three results would follow,
seemed largely to depend upon the "chapter of accidents." At
a steady trot now, with drawn sabres and carbines ready, the
cavalry, followed by the horse-artillery, which was not used during the whole expedition, approached Tunstall's Station on the
York River railroad, the enemy's direct line of communication
with his base of supplies at the "White House."

Everywhere the ride was crowded with incident. The scouting and flanking parties constantly picked up stragglers, and
overhauled unsuspecting wagons filled with the most tempting
stores. In this manner a wagon, stocked with champagne and
every variety of wines, belonging to a General of the Federal
army, fell a prey to the thirsty gray-backs. Still they pressed on.
Every moment an attack was expected in front or rear. Colonel
Will. T. Martin commander the latter. "Tell Colonel Martin,"
Stuart said to me, "to have his artillery ready, and look out for
an attack at any moment." I had delivered the message and was
riding to the front again, when suddenly a loud cry arose of
"Yankees in the rear!" Every sabre flashed, fours were formed,
the men wheeled about, when all at once a stunning roar of
laughter ran along the line; it was a *canard*. The column moved

up again with its flanking parties well out. The men composing the latter were, many of them, from the region, and for the first time for months saw their mothers and sisters. These went quite wild at sight of their sons and brothers. They laughed and cried, and on the appearance of the long gray column instead of the familiar blue coats of the Federal cavalry, they clapped their hands and fell into ecstasies of delight. One young lady was seen to throw her arms around a brother she had not before met for a long time, bursting into alternate sobs and laughter.

The column was now skirting the Pamunkey, and a detachment hurried off to seize and burn two or three transports lying in the river. Soon a dense cloud rose from them, the flames soared up, and the column pushed on. Everywhere were seen the traces of flight—for the alarm of "hornets in the hive" was given. Wagons had turned over, and were abandoned—from others the excellent army stores had been hastily thrown. This writer got a fine red blanket, and an excellent pair of cavalry pantaloons, for which he still owes the United States. Other things lay about in tempting array, but we were approaching Tunstall's, where the column would doubtless make a charge; and to load down a weary horse was injudicious. The advance guard was now in sight of the railroad. There was no question about the affair before us. The column must cut through, whatever force guarded the railroad; to reach the lower Chickahominy the guard here must be overpowered. Now was the time to use the artillery, and every effort was made to hurry it forward. But alas! it had got into a tremendous mudhole, and the wheels were buried to the axle. The horses were lashed, and jumped, almost breaking the traces; the drivers swore; the harness cracked—but the guns did not move. "Gat! Lieutenant," said a sergeant of Dutch origin to the brave Lieutenant McGregor, "it can't be done. But just put that keg on the gun, Lieutenant," pointing, as he spoke, to a keg of whiskey in an ambulance, the spoil of the Federal camp, "and tell the men they can have it if they only pull through!" McGregor laughed, and the keg was quickly perched on the gun. Then took place an exhibition of herculean muscularity which would have delighted Guy Livingston. With eyes fixed ardently upon the keg, the powerful cannoneers waded into the mudhole up to their knees, seized the wheels of gun and caisson loaded down with ammunition, and just simply lifted the whole out, and put them on firm ground. The piece whirled on—the keg had been dismounted—the cannoneers revelled in the spoils they had earned.

Tunstall's was now nearly in sight, and that good fellow Captain Frayser, afterward Stuart's signal officer, came back and reported one or two companies of infantry at the railroad. Their commander had politely beckoned to him as he reconnoitred, exclaiming in wheedling accents, full of Teutonic blandishment, "Koom yay!" But this cordial invitation was disregarded! Frayser galloped back and reported, and the ringing voice of Stuart ordered "Form platoons! draw sabre! charge!" At the word the sabres flashed, a thundering shout arose, and sweeping on in column of platoons, the gray people fell upon their blue adversaries, gobbling them up, almost without a shot. It was here that my friend Major F———— got the hideous little wooden pipe he used to smoke afterward. He had been smoking a meerschaum when the order to charge was given; and in the rush of the horsemen, dropped and lost it. He now wished to smoke, and seeing that the captain of the Federal infantry had just filled his pipe, leaned down from the saddle, and politely requested him to surrender it.

"I want to smoke!" growled the Federal captain.

"So do I," retorted Major F——.

"This pipe is my property," said the captain.

"Oh! what a mistake!" responded the major politely, as he gently took the small affair and inserted it between his lips. Anything more hideous than the carved head upon it I never saw.

The men swarmed upon the railroad. Quick axes were applied to the telegraph poles, which crashed down, and Redmond Burke went in command of a detachment to burn a small bridge on the railroad near. Suddenly in the midst of the tumult was heard the shrill whistle of a train coming from the direction of the Chickahominy. Stuart quickly drew up his men in a line on the side of the road, and he had no sooner done so than the train came slowly round a wooded bend, and bore down. When within two hundred yards it was ordered to halt, but the command was not obeyed. The engineer crowded on all steam; the train rushed on, and then a thundering volley was opened upon the "flats" containing officers and men. The engineer was shot by Captain Farley, of Stuart's staff, and a number of the soldiers were wounded. The rest threw themselves upon their faces; the train rushed headlong by like some frightened monster bent upon escape, and in an instant it had disappeared.

Stuart then reflected for a single moment. The question was, should he go back and attack the White House, where enormous stores were piled up? It was tempting, and he afterwards told me he could scarcely resist it. But a considerable force of infantry was posted there; the firing had doubtless given them the alarm; and the attempt was too hazardous. The best thing for that gray column was to set their faces toward home, and "keep moving," well closed up both day and night, for the lower Chickahominy. So Stuart pushed on. Beyond the railroad appeared a world of wagons, loaded with grain and coffee—standing in the road abandoned. Quick work was made of them. They were all set on fire, and their contents destroyed. From the horse-trough of one I rescued a small volume bearing on the fly-leaf the name of a young lady of Williamsburg. I think it was a volume of poems—poetic wagon-drivers!

These wagons were only the "vaunt couriers"—the advance guard—of the main body. In a field beyond the stream thirty acres were covered with them. They were all burned. The roar of the soaring flames was like the sound of a forest on fire. How they roared and crackled! The sky overhead, when night had descended, was bloody-looking in the glare.

Meanwhile the main column had moved on, and I was riding after it, when I heard the voice of Stuart in the darkness exclaiming with strange agitation:

"Who is here?"

"I am," I answered; and as he recognised my voice he exclaimed:

"Good! where is Rooney Lee?"

"I think he has moved on, General."

"Do you *know* it?" came in the same agitated tone.

"No, but I believe it."

"Will you *swear to it*? I must know! He may take the wrong road, and the column will get separated!"

"I will ascertain if he is in front."

"Well, do so; but take care—you will be captured!"

I told the General I would "gallop on for ever till I found him," but I had not gone two hundred yards in the darkness when hoof-strokes in front were heard, and I ordered:

"Halt! who goes there?"

"Courier, from Colonel William Lee."

"Is he in front?"

"About a mile, sir."

"Good!" exclaimed the voice of Stuart, who had galloped up; and I never heard in human accents such an expression of relief. If the reader of this has ever commanded cavalry, moving at night in an enemy's country, he will understand why Stuart drew that long, deep breath, and uttered that brief word, "Good!" Once separated from the main column and lost— good-by then to Colonel Lee!

Pushing on by large hospitals which were not interfered with, we reached at midnight the three or four houses known as Talleysville; and here a halt was ordered to rest men and horses, and permit the artillery to come up. This pause was fatal to a sutler's store from which the owners had fled. It was remorselessly ransacked and the edibles consumed. This historian ate in succession figs, beef-tongue, pickle, candy, tomato catsup, preserves, lemons, cakes, sausages, molasses, crackers and canned meats. In presence of these attractive commodities the spirits of many rose. Those who in the morning had made me laugh by saying "General Stuart is going to get his command destroyed— this movement is mad," now regarded Stuart as the first of men; the raid as a feat of splendour and judicious daring which could not fail in terminating successfully. Such is the difference in the views of the military machine, unfed and fed.

## III.

In an hour the column moved again. Meanwhile a little incident
had happened which still makes me laugh. There was a lady
living some miles off in the enemy's line whom I wished to visit,
but I could not obtain the General's consent. "It is certain capture," he said; "send her a note by some citizen, say Dr. H——;
he lives near here." This I determined to do, and set off at a
gallop through the moonlight for the house, some half a mile
distant, looking out for the scouting parties which were probably prowling on our flanks. Reaching the lonely house, outside
the pickets, I dismounted, knocked at the front door, then the
back, but received no answer. All at once, however, a dark figure
was seen gliding beneath the trees, and this figure cautiously
approached. I recognised the Doctor, and called to him whereupon he quickly approached, and said, "I thought you were a
Yankee!" and greeting me cordially, led the way into the house.
Here I wrote my note and entrusted it to him for delivery—
taking one from him to his wife, within our lines. In half an
hour I rode away, but before doing so asked for some water,
which was brought from the well by a sleepy, sullen, and insolent negro. This incident was fruitful of woes to Dr. H——! A
month or two afterwards I met him looking as thin and white
as a ghost.

"What is the matter?" I said.

"The matter is," he replied, with a melancholy laugh, "that I
have been starving for three weeks in Fortress Monroe on your
account. Do you remember that servant who brought you the
water that night on Stuart's raid?"

"Perfectly."

"Well, the very next day he went over to the Yankee picket
and told them that I had entertained Confederate officers, and
given you all information which enabled you to get off safely.
In consequence I was arrested, carried to Old Point, and am
just out!"

I rejoined the column at Talleysville just as it began to move on the road to Forge Bridge. The highway lay before us, white in the unclouded splendour of the moon. The critical moment was yet to come. Our safety was to turn apparently on a throw of the dice, rattled in the hand of Chance. The exhaustion of the march now began to tell on the men. Whole companies went to sleep in the saddle, and Stuart himself was no exception. He had thrown one knee over the pommel of his saddle, folded his arms, dropped the bridle, and—chin on breast, his plumed hat drooping over his forehead—was sound asleep. His sure-footed horse moved steadily, but the form of the General tottered from side to side, and for miles I held him erect by the arm. The column thus moved on during the remainder of the night, the wary advance guard encountering no enemies and giving no alarm. At the first streak of dawn the Chickahominy was in sight, and Stuart was spurring forward *to the ford*.

It was impassable! The heavy rains had so swollen the waters that the crossing was utterly impracticable! Here we were within a few miles of McClellan's army, with an enraged enemy rushing on our track to make us rue the day we had "circumvented" them, and inflicted on them such injury and insult; here we were with a swollen and impassable stream directly in our front—the angry waters roaring around the half-submerged trunks of the trees—and expecting every instant to hear the crack of carbines from the rear-guard indicating the enemy's approach! The "situation" was not pleasing. I certainly thought that the enemy would be upon us in about an hour, and death or capture would be the sure alternative. This view was general. I found that cool and resolute officer, Colonel William H. F. Lee, on the river's bank. He had just attempted to swim the river, and nearly drowned his horse among the tangled roots and snags. I said to him:

"What do you think of the situation, Colonel?"

"Well, Captain," was the reply, in the speaker's habitual tone of cheerful courtesy, "I think we are caught."

The men evidently shared this sentiment. The scene upon the river's bank was curious, and under other circumstances would have been laughable. The men lay about in every attitude, half-overcome with sleep, but holding their bridles, and ready to mount at the first alarm. Others sat their horses asleep, with drooping shoulders. Some gnawed crackers; others ate figs, or smoked, or yawned. Things looked "blue," and that colour was figuratively spread over every countenance. When this writer assumed a gay expression of countenance, laughed, and told the men it was "all right," they looked at him as sane men regard a lunatic! The general conviction evidently was that "all right" was the very last phrase by which to describe the situation.

There was only one man who never desponded, or bated one "jot or tittle of the heart of hope." That was Stuart. I had never been with him in a tight place before, but from that moment I felt convinced that he was one of those men who rise under pressure. He was aroused, strung for the hard struggle before him, and resolute to do or die; but he was not excited. All I noticed in his bearing to attract attention was a peculiar fashion of twisting his beard, certain proof with him of surrounding peril. Otherwise he was cool and looked dangerous. He said a few words to Colonel Lee, found the ford impassable, and then ordering his column to move on, galloped down the stream to a spot where an old bridge had formerly stood. Reaching this point, a strong rear-guard was thrown out, the artillery placed in position, and Stuart set to work vigorously to rebuild the bridge, determined to bring out his guns or die trying.

The bridge had been destroyed, but the stone abutments remained some thirty or forty feet only apart, for the river here ran deep and narrow between steep banks. Between these stone sentinels, facing each other, was an "aching void" which it was necessary to fill. Stuart gave his personal superintendence to the work, he and his staff labouring with the men. A skiff was procured; this was affixed by a rope to a tree, in the mid-current just above the abutments, and thus a movable pier was secured in the middle of the stream. An old barn was then hastily torn to pieces and robbed of its timbers; these were stretched down to the boat, and up to the opposite abutment, and a foot-bridge was thus ready. Large numbers of the men immediately unsaddled their horses, took their equipments over, and then returning, drove or rode their horses into the stream, and swam them over. In this manner a considerable number crossed; but the process was much too slow. There, besides, was the artillery, which Stuart had no intention of leaving. A regular bridge must be built without a moment's delay, and to this work Stuart now applied himself with ardour.

Heavier blows resounded from the old barn; huge timbers approached, borne on brawny shoulders, and descending into the boat anchored in the middle of the stream, the men lifted them across. They were just long enough; the ends rested on the abutments, and immediately thick planks were hurried forward and laid crosswise, forming a secure footway for the cavalry and artillery horses. Standing in the boat beneath, Stuart worked with the men, and as the planks thundered down, and the bridge steadily advanced, the gay voice of the General was heard humming a song. He was singing carelessly, although at every instant an overpowering force of the enemy was looked for, and a heavy attack upon the disordered cavalry.

At last the bridge was finished; the artillery crossed amid hurrahs from the men, and then Stuart slowly moved his cavalry across the shaky footway. A little beyond was another arm of the river, which was, however, fordable, as I ascertained and reported to the General; the water just deep enough to swim a small horse; and through this, as through the interminable sloughs of the swamp beyond, the head of the column moved. The prisoners, who were numerous, had been marched over in advance of everything, and these were now mounted on mules, of which several hundred had been cut from the captured wagons and brought along. They were started under an escort across the ford, and into the swamp beyond. Here, mounted often two on a mule, they had a disagreeable time; the mules constantly falling in the treacherous mud-holes, and rolling their riders in the ooze. When a third swamp appeared before them, one of the Federal prisoners exclaimed, with tremendous indignation, "How many d—d *Chicken*-hominies are there, I wonder, in this infernal country!"

The rear-guard, under Colonel W. H. F. Lee, had meanwhile

moved down steadily from the high ground, and defiled across
the bridge. The hoofs clattered on the hasty structure, the head
of the column was turned toward the ford beyond, the last
squadron had just passed, and the bridge was being destroyed,
when shots resounded on the opposite bank of the stream, and
Colonel Rush thundered down with his "lancers" to the bank.
He was exactly ten minutes too late. Stuart was over with his
artillery, and the swollen stream barred the way, even if Colonel
Rush thought it prudent to "knock up against" the one thousand
five hundred crack cavalry of Stuart. His men banged away at
Colonel Lee, and a parting salute whizzed through the trees as
the gray column slowly disappeared.

A lady of New Kent afterwards told me that Colonel Rush
stopped at her house on his return, looking weary, broken down,
and out of humour. When she asked him if he had "caught
Stuart," he replied, "No, he has gone in at the back door. I only
saw his rear-guard as it passed the swamp."


## IV.

Stuart had thus eluded his pursuers, and was over the Chickahominy in the hospitable county of Charles City. The gentlemen of the county, we afterwards heard, had been electrified by
the rumour that "Stuart was down at the river trying to get
across," and had built a hasty bridge for us lower down. We
were over, however, and reaching Mr. C——'s, the General
and his staff lay down on a carpet spread on the grass in the
June sunshine, and went to sleep. This was Sunday. I had not
slept since Friday night, except by snatches in the saddle, and
in going on to Richmond afterwards fell asleep every few minutes on horseback.

Two hours of slumber, however, made Stuart as fresh as a
lark; and having eaten Mr. C—— very nearly out of house and
home, we pushed on all day. At night the column stopped, and
I thought the General would stop too; but he said, "I am going
to Richmond to-night; would you like to ride with me?" I was
obliged to decline; my horse was worn out. Stuart set out by

himself, rode all night, and before daylight had passed over the thirty miles. An hour afterwards General Lee and the President knew the result of his expedition. The cavalry returned on the same day, moving slowly in front of the gunboats, which fired upon them; but no harm was done. Richmond was reached; and amid an ovation from delighted friends we all went to sleep.

Such was Stuart's ride around McClellan's army in those summer days of 1862. The men who went with him look back to it as the most romantic and adventurous incident of the war. It was not indeed so much a military expedition as a raid of romance—a "scout" of Stuart's with fifteen hundred horsemen! It was the conception of a bold and brilliant mind, and the execution was as fearless. "That was the most dangerous of all my expeditions," the General said to me long afterwards; "if I had not succeeded in crossing the Chickahominy, I would have been ruined, as there was no way of getting out." The Emperor Napoleon, a good soldier, took this view of it; when tracing out on the map Stuart's route from Taylorsville by Old Church to the lower Chickahominy, he characterized the movement as that of a cavalry officer of the first distinction. This criticism was only just, and the raid will live in history for three reasons:

1. It taught the enemy "the trick," and showed them the meaning of the words "cavalry raid." What General Kilpatrick, Sheridan, and others afterwards effected, was the work of the pupil following the master.

2. It was on a magnificent arena, to which the eyes of the whole world were attracted at the time; and,

3. In consequence of the information which Stuart furnished, Gen. Lee, a fortnight afterwards, attacked and defeated General McClellan.

These circumstances give a very great interest to all the incidents of the movement. I hope the reader has not been wearied by my minute record of them. To the old soldiers of Stuart there is a melancholy pleasure in recalling the gay scenes amid which he moved, the exploits which he performed, the hard work he did. He is gone; but even in memory it is something to again follow his feather.

# II

## STUART ON THE OUTPOST

A SCENE AT "CAMP QUI VIVE"

### I.

SOMETIMES, in dreams as it were, the present writer—like many others, doubtless—goes back in memory across the gulf of years to 1861, recalling its great scenes and personages, and living once more in that epoch full of such varied and passionate emotions. Manassas! Centreville! Fairfax! Vienna!—what memories do those names excite in the hearts of the old soldiers of Beauregard! That country, now so desolate, was then a virgin land, untouched by the foot of war. The hosts who were to trample it still lingered upon the banks of the Potomac; and the wildest fancy could not have prefigured its fate. It was a smiling country, full of joy and beauty—the domain of "ancient peace;" and of special attraction were the little villages, sleeping like Centreville in the hollow of green hills, or perched like Fairfax on the summit of picturesque uplands. These were old Virginia hamlets, full of recollections; here the feet of Mason and Washington had trod, and here had grown up generation after generation ignorant of war. Peace reigned supreme; the whole landscape was the picture of repose; the villages, amid the foliage of their elms or oaks, slept like birds that have nestled down to rest amid the grass and blossoms of the green spring fields.

Look first upon that picture, then on this!—the picture of a region blasted by the hot breath of war. Where now was the joy of the past? where the lovely land once smiling in fresh beauty, and the charm of peaceful years? All the flowers and sunshine had disappeared. The springing grasses, the budding forests, the happy dwellings—all had vanished. Over the smiling fields the hoofs of cavalry had trampled; the woods had been cut down to furnish fuel for the camp fires; the fences had preceded them; the crops and forage had been gleaned for the horses of the troopers. The wheels of artillery and army trains had worn the roads into ruts and quagmires; opposing columns had advanced or retreated over every foot of ground, leaving their traces everywhere; those furrows over which the broomstraw waved in the winter wind, or the spring flowers nodded in the airs of May, were ploughed by cannon-balls.

The war-dogs had bayed here, and torn to pieces house and field and forest. The villages were the forlorn ghosts of themselves, and seemed to look at you out of those vacant eyes, their open windows, with a sort of dumb despair. They were the eloquent monuments of the horrors of war—the veritable "abodes of owls." Had a raven croaked from the dead trees riven by cannon-balls, or a wolf growled at you from the deserted houses, you would have felt not the least astonishment. As you passed through those villages, once so smiling, the tramp of the cavalry horses, or the rumbling wheels of the artillery, made the echoes resound; and a few heads were thrust from the paneless windows. Then they disappeared; silence settled down again, and the melancholy hamlet gave place to the more melancholy fields. Here all was waste and desolate; no woods, no fences, no human face; only torn-down and dismantled houses, riddled with bullets, or charred by the torch of war. The land seemed doomed, and to rest under a curse. That Federal vedette yonder, as we advance, is the only living object we behold, and even he disappears like a phantom. Can this, you murmur, be the laughing land of yesterday, the abode of peace, and happiness, and joy? Can this be Fairfax, where the fields of wheat once rolled their golden waves in the summer wind, and the smiling houses held out arms of welcome? Look, it has become a veritable Golgotha—the "place of skulls"—a sombre Jehoshaphat full of dead men's bones!

I remember all that, and shall ever remember it; but in contrast with these scenes of ruin and desolation, come back a thousand memories, gay, joyous, and instinct with mirth. The hard trade of war is not all tragedy; let us laugh, friends, when we can; there are smiles as well as tears, comedy as well as tragedy, in the great and exciting drama. You don't weep much when the sword is in the hand. You fight hard; and if you do not fall, you laugh, and even dance, perhaps—if you can get some music—by the camp fire. It is a scene of this description which I wish to describe to-day. This morning it came back to my memory in such vivid colours that I thought, if I could paint it, some of my readers would be interested. It took place in autumn of the gay years 1861, when Johnston and Beauregard were holding the lines of Centreville against McClellan; and when Stuart, that pearl of cavaliers, was in command of the front, which he guarded with his cavalry. In their camps at Centreville, the infantry and artillery of the army quietly enjoyed the bad weather which forbade all military movements; but the cavalry, that "eye and ear" of an army, were still in face of the enemy, and had constant skirmishes below Fairfax, out toward Vienna, and along the front near the little hamlet of Annandale.

How well I remember all those scenes! and I think if I had space I could tell some interesting stories of that obstinate *petite-guerre* of picket fighting—how the gray and blue coats fought for the ripe fruit in an orchard just between them, all a winter's afternoon; how Farley waylaid, with three men, the whole column of General Bayard, and attacked it; and how a brave boy fell one day in a fight of pickets, and was brought back dead, wrapped in the brilliant oil-cloth which his sister took from her piano and had sent to him to sleep upon.

But these recollections would not interest you as they interest me. They fade, and I come back to my immediate subject—a visit to General "Jeb Stuart" at his headquarters, near Fairfax Court-House, where, in this December of 1861, I saw the gay cavalier and his queer surroundings.

Stuart was already famous from his raids against General Patterson in the Valley. He had harassed that commander so persistently—driving in his pickets, getting in rear of his camps, and cutting off his foraging parties—that Johnston said of him: "He is worse than a *yellow-jacket*—they no sooner brush him off than he lights back again." Indefatigable in reconnoissance, sleepless in vigilance, possessed of a physical strength which defied fatigue and enabled him to pass whole days and nights in the saddle, Stuart became the evil genius of the invading column; and long afterwards, when transferred to the West, General Johnston wrote to him: "How can I eat, sleep, or rest in peace, without you upon the outpost!" From the Valley he came to Manassas, charged the Zouaves there, and then was made a Brigadier-General and put in command of the cavalry of the army which held the front toward Alexandria. It is at this time, December, 1861, that I present him to the reader.

Go back with me to that remote period, and you shall have no fancy sketch, or "dignified" picture of a General commanding, but the actual portrait of the famous General "Jeb Stuart" in the midst of his military household.

## II.

I found the cavalry headquarters at an old house known as Mellen's, but officially as "Camp Qui Vive," between Centreville and Fairfax Court-House.

It was a day of December; the sun shone brightly, the frosty airs cut the cheek. The house was bare and bleak; everything about it "looked like work." Horses were picketed to the fences and trees, couriers went and came with jingling spurs and clanking sabres, and the bugle sounded the gay "stable-call." Before the door, the red battle-flag, just adopted, ripples in the wind; and not far from it you see the grim muzzle of a Blakely gun, for Stuart is devoted to artillery, and fights it whenever he can. You may regard that gun as a somewhat unusual feature of a cavalry camp upon the outpost, but the sentinel placed over it to guard it is still queerer. It is nothing less than an enormous raccoon—black, wary, with snarling teeth, and eyes full of "fight!" Look at him for a moment as you pass. He is tied by a rope around his neck to the trail by the lunettes, and roosts serenely on the pintal-hook. When he stretches his rope he can run over the rings for the trail handspike and the prolonge, to the cascabel and brass base, for the pendulum hausse. His natural line of sight, however, is between the spokes of the limber-wheels, and he has a box to go in when he is tired.

The sentinel is evidently aware of his duty, for he snaps at everybody. You will find, when General Stuart comes out laughing to show him to you, that his owner regards him as the pearl of sentinels, the paragon of "coons."

It was sunset as I entered, and amid a gay group I saw the young General of cavalry. Fancy a man of low stature and athletic form, with an enormous brown beard; a huge moustache, ready to curl with laughter; a broad and lofty forehead; an eye, blue, brilliant, and penetrating as that of the eagle. This figure was clad in a gray cavalry uniform, top-boots with small bright spurs; and on a chair lay his sabre and pistol, beside the brown felt hat looped up and adorned with a black feather.

In this man who wrote away busily at his desk, or, throwing one leg carelessly over the arm of his chair, turned to utter some jest or break out in some snatch of song, you could discern enormous physical strength—a vigour of constitution which made him a veritable war-machine. This person, it was plain, cared nothing for the exhausting work which breaks down other men; could live in the saddle, and was ever ready for a march, a raid, a charge—anything. Young—he was then but twenty-seven—ardent, ambitious, gay, jovial, of immense unbounded animal spirits, with that clear, blue eye whose glance defies all peril, a seat in the saddle, and a hand for the rein and the sabre unsurpassed, Stuart was truly a splendid machine in magnificent order, and plainly asked nothing better than to "clash against his foe" and either fall or conquer. All this was evident in the man before me, with that bronzed cheek, athletic figure, and eye ready to fill full with laughter, or flash at the thought of battle. In Stuart I saw a cavalier whom Rupert would have made his bosom friend, and counted on to charge the pikes of the Ironsides, and "die for King Charles" without a murmur.

Gayest of the gay was Stuart's greeting, and in five minutes he had started up, put on his hat, and was showing me his Blakely gun, then a recent acquisition. His satisfaction at the ferocious snarling of his "coon" was immense; the incorruptible fidelity of that black sentinel plainly charmed him, and he made the place echo with his laughter.

I was truly sorry to hear afterwards that this animal, so trusted and admired—who had at last become like a member of the staff—betrayed a low dissatisfaction at short rations, and gnawing in two the rope which confined him, actually deserted, and was never more seen!

As night fell we reëntered the house; a table was brought into the bare room for supper; and then to my astonishment—enter two ladies! I thought the house entirely unoccupied except by the gay cavalier and his "following;" but here was a delegation from the fairer half of humanity. Who were they? How did they come there? How did that little flower of seventeen, with the rosy cheeks and the soft, blue eyes, come to bloom on this hot surface of war, amid the rattle of spurs and sabres?

All these questions were speedily answered by General Stuart. The beautiful girl of seventeen, and her grim, irate companion, an elderly lady, were "prisoners of war!" On the preceding evening they had—after making vain applications for a pass—attempted to "flank the pickets" of Stuart, and steal through his lines to Alexandria. Now, as General McClellan was sojourning with a large escort near that place, and would doubtless be glad to ascertain a number of things in relation to Beauregard, Stuart had refused the pass. When the fugitives attempted to elude his pickets they were caught, forwarded to headquarters, and there they were.

The young lady was smiling, the elder frowning terribly. The one evidently admired the gallant Stuart, with his bright, blue eye and floating plume, regarding the whole affair as a romantic adventure, to be enjoyed, not regretted; the other as plainly resented the liberty taken with her movements, and was determined to preserve a grim, forbidding, and hostile attitude—that of the martyr overwhelmed, but defiant to the last. I saw all this at a glance, and then I understood as plainly, in a very few moments, that General Stuart had determined to charm away, if

possible, the evil spirit of hostility in the hearts of his fair prisoners, and reconcile them to their fate.

He lost no time in this hospitable work. It was delightful,
and laughable too, to watch him. Never did gallant cavalier
demean himself with more profound and respectful courtesy,
with which, however, was mingled that easy off-hand fun which
never left Stuart. In the first advance he had been repulsed. The
ladies had been up-stairs when I arrived, and the General had
sent up his compliments: "Would they come down to supper?" The reply was, "No, I thank you; we are not hungry."
Whereupon that politest of Marylanders, Captain Tiernan Brien,
A.A.G., was dispatched—assault number two—and, under the
effect of his blandishments, the fair enemy gave way. They
appeared, the young lady blushing and smiling; the elder stern
and stormy. Stuart received them, as I have said, with charming courtesy and frankness; compelled them to take part in his
supper, and then, although, as very soon appeared, he had a
great deal of work to do, did not suffer them to depart to their
room.

They were not to be allowed to mope there all the winter
evening. Music, dance, and song were to while away the hours
—so Stuart sent for three members of his military household,
and they soon appeared. All were black. The first was an accomplished performer on the guitar; the second gifted with the
faculty of producing in his throat the exactest imitation of every
bird of the forest; and the third was a mighty master of the back-
step, viz. an old Virginia "breakdown."

Upon their appearance the "performances commenced!"


## III.

Behold the scene now, reader, as I looked at it, on that evening
of December in 1861. We are in a bleak room, with no furniture
but a desk, a chair, and a camp couch. At the desk sits Stuart,
writing away with immense rapidity, and stopping now and
then to hum a song. On the couch, near the fire, are the ladies—
the younger smiling, the elder frowning. Around stand the staff,

and at the door are the laughing faces of couriers, who look on and listen. In front of them stand the sable musicians, and the great performer of the breakdown—ebon-hued, dilapidated in costume, awaiting orders, and approaching the performance with serious and unmistakable satisfaction.

Stuart calls out from his desk, without turning his head, and the process of charming away the evil spirit commences. The guitar is played by the General's body-servant Bob, a young mulatto of dandified appearance—the air, indeed, of a lady killer —and an obvious confidence in his own abilities to delight, if not instruct and improve, his audience. Bob laboriously tunes his instrument; gazes thoughtfully at the ceiling, as he absently "picks upon the string;" and then commences singing the popular air, "Listen to the Mocking-Bird." He is accompanied in the chorus by the sable ventriloquist, who imitates all the feathered tribe in his throat; and lo! as you listen, the room seems full of mocking-birds; the air is alive with the gay carol of robins, larks, jay-birds, orioles; the eyes of the ventriloquist roll rapturously like balls of snow against a wall of charcoal, and the guitar keeps up its harmonious accompaniment.

The young lady listens and her eyes dance. Her cheeks grow more rosy, her smiles brighter; even her elderly companion relaxes somewhat from her rigidly hostile expression, and pays attention to the music. The "Mocking-Bird" ends, and is succeeded by the plaintive "Alabama! Alabama!"—the guitar still thrumming, the ventriloquist still accompanying the music with his bird-notes. Other songs succeed, and then General Stuart turns round with a laugh and calls for a breakdown. Thereupon the dilapidated African, who has up to this time remained motionless, advances into the arena, dropping his hat first at the door. Bob strikes up a jig upon his guitar, the ventriloquist claps, and the great performer of the breakdown commences his evolutions, first upon the heel-tap, then upon the toe. His antics are grand and indescribable. He leaps, he whirls, he twists and untwists his legs until the crowd at the door grows wild with admiration. The guitar continues to roar and Stuart's laughter mingles with it; the ventriloquist not only claps with ardour,

but also imitates his favourite songsters. The dancer's eyes roll
gorgeously, his steps grow more rapid, he executes unheard-of
figures. Finally a frenzy seems to seize him; the mirth grows
fast and furious; the young lady laughs outright and seems about
to clap her hands. Even the elder relaxes into an unmistakable
smile; and as the dancer disappears with a bound through the
door, the guitar stops playing, and Stuart's laughter rings out
gay and jovial, the grim lips open and she says:

"You rebels *do* seem to enjoy yourselves!"

These were the exact words of the lady, reader, and I think I
can recall a few words of General Stuart, too. He had been
busily engaged with his official papers all this time, at his desk—
for he never permitted pleasure to interfere with business—and
the gay scene going on in the apartment did not seem to disturb
him in the least degree. Indeed, upon this, as upon many other
occasions, I could see that music of any description aroused his
mind, and was an assistance to him—the banjo, singing, anything
—and by its aid now he had hurried through his work. Thereupon he rose, and approached the ladies, with gay smiles and
inquiries, if they were amused:

"They had heard his musicians; would the ladies now like to
see something which might interest them?"

Irresistible appeal to that sentiment which is said to be the
weakness of the fair sex—curiosity!

"They would like very much to see what the General spoke
of;" and thereupon Stuart pointed to a coat and waistcoat hanging upon a nail on the wall over their heads. The clothes were
torn by a bullet and bloody.

The young lady looked, and her smiles all disappeared.

"What is that, General?" said the elder.

"It is the coat and waistcoat of a poor boy of my command,
madam," replied Stuart, "who was shot and killed on picket the
other day—young Chichester, from just below Fairfax Court-
House. He was a brave fellow, and I am keeping these clothes
to send to his mother."

"Poor boy!" from the young lady; and from the elder a look
of unmistakable sympathy.

Stuart then gave an account of the fight; and his voice, as he spoke of the death of the boy, was no longer gay—it was serious, feeling, and had in it something delightfully kind and sweet. Under that gay exterior of the young cavalier there was a warm and earnest heart—as beneath the stern eye of the man was all the tenderness of a woman. It was plain to me on that evening, and plainer afterwards when a thorough acquaintance with the great leader made me fully cognizant of his real character. There was something more charming even than the gaiety of Stuart— it was the low, sad tone in which he spoke of some dead friend, the tear in the bright blue eye which dimmed its fire at the thought of some face that was gone.

## IV.

So, between mirth and pathos—between the rattling guitar and the bloody coat of the dead boy—the ladies were fairly con- quered. When Stuart gallantly accompanied them to the door, and bowed as they retired, the elderly lady smiled, and I think the younger gave him a glance full of thanks and admiration.

But stern duty required still that the fair fugitives should be further cabined and confined. Stuart could not release them; he must send them to Centreville, by standing order from General Johnston, and thither they were accordingly dispatched on the next morning after breakfast. The General had at his head- quarters—procured where, I know not—an old carriage. To this two horses were harnessed; a son of Erin from the couriers was detailed as a driver, and the general requested me to accompany the ladies and conduct them to General Johnston.

Then he exhibited his gallantry after the military fashion. The ladies had entered the carriage; the pretty blushing face of the young damsel of seventeen was seen at the window, her little white hand hung out of the carriage. Stuart took it and pressed it warmly to his lips—a slight exclamation, a hand withdrawn hastily, and a little laugh, as the young lady's face disappeared— and the carriage moved on. I mounted and got ready to follow; but first I turned to Stuart, who was standing with the bright

December sunshine on his laughing face, looking after the carriage.

"General," I said, "will you answer me one or two questions
before I leave you?"

"Well, ask them—I'll try."

"Why did you put yourself out so much, when you were so
busy last night, and get up that frolic?"

"Don't you understand?" was his laughing reply. "When
those ladies arrived they were mad enough with me to bite my
head off, and I determined to put them in good humour before
they left me. Well, I have done it; they are my good friends
at this moment."

"You are right; now for my other question. I saw you kiss
that pretty little hand of the young lady as it lay in the carriage
window; why didn't you kiss that of the elder, too?"

Stuart approached my horse, and leaning his arm upon the
mane, said in low tones, as though he was afraid of being overheard:

"Would you like me to tell you?"

"Yes," was my reply.

"The old lady's hand had a glove upon it!" was his confidential whisper; and this was followed by a real explosion, in which
the gay cavalier seemed to find vent for all the pent-up laughter
which had been struggling in him since the preceding evening.

I accompanied the ladies to Centreville, and they did not utter
a single unfriendly word upon the way in relation to Stuart.
Indeed, the young lady seemed altogether charmed with the
whole adventure, and appeared to have warmly welcomed the
incident which gave her a sight of that black plume, those brilliant, laughing eyes. If this page should meet her eye, will she
pardon me if I say: "Fair flower of seventeen, you may have
drawn your hand away that day, and thought the kiss imprinted
on it a liberty; but do not regret it now, for those lips belonged
to the 'flower of cavaliers,' and to-day they are cold in death!"

I have made this little sketch of Stuart at "Camp Qui Vive"
for those who like the undress picture of a famous man, rather
than the historic bust—cold, still, and lifeless. Have you not

seen, reader, there upon the outpost as you followed me, the gay face of Stuart; heard his laughter as he called for the "Mocking Bird;" and listened to his sad tones as he pointed to the bloody coat, and told of the brave boys shot on picket? If you cannot see those figures and hear the accents, it is the fault of the writer, and perhaps his merriment is not gay. Always those long-dead scenes came to him with a sort of dreamy sadness— the mirth is mournful, and the laughter dies away.

No more at "Camp Qui Vive," or any other camp, will the laugh of Stuart ring out joyous and free. He is gone—but lives still here upon the soil of Virginia, and will live for ever!

# III

## ONE OF STUART'S ESCAPES

### I.

I NEVER pass the little village of Verdiersville, on the road from Orange Court-House to Chancellorsville, without casting a glance upon a small house—the first upon the right as you enter the hamlet from the west.

There is nothing remarkable in the appearance of this house; and unless some especial circumstance directed to it your attention, you would pass it by completely without notice. A small wooden mansion, such as every village contains; a modest, rather dilapidated porch; a contracted yard in front, and an ordinary fence of narrow palings, through which a narrow gate gives access to the road—there is the whole. Now why should this most commonplace and uninteresting of objects cause the present writer, whenever he passes it, and however weary he may be, to turn his horse's head in the direction of the little gate, pause on his way, and remain for some moments gazing in silence at the dilapidated porch, the tumble-down fence, and the narrow gateway, yawning now wide open, gateless? Because the sight of this house recalls a scene of which it was the theatre about three years ago—that is to say in August, 1862. It was here that Stuart had one of those narrow escapes which were by no means unusual in his adventurous career, and which will make his life, when time has mellowed the events of this epoch, the chosen subject of those writers dealing in the romance of war.

Ah! those "romances of the war!" The trifling species will

come first, in which the Southern leaders will be made to talk an incredible gibberish, and figure in the most tremendous adventures. We shall then see, my dear reader, the august form of Lee, dressed in that splendid new uniform which he always wore, riding that swift Arabian, blazing with his golden caparison, and exclaiming, "Behold yonder battery, my men! Charge on it! Sweep the foeman from your path!" The gay and elegant form of Stonewall Jackson will be seen as he leads his cavalry, and swears in the charge; Stuart will give his cautious counsel to fall back; and we shall have, in the yellow-covered pamphlets, a truthful picture of the war. But then will come the better order of things, when writers like Walter Scott will conscientiously collect the real facts, and make some new "Waverley" or "Legend of Montrose." For these, and not for the former class, I propose to set down here an incident in the life of the great commander of the Southern cavalry, of which he told me all the particulars, for I was not present.

It was about the middle of August, 1862, and Jackson, after deciding the fate of the day at Cold Harbour, and defeating General Pope at Cedar Mountain, was about to make his great advance upon Manassas with the remainder of the army. In all such movements Stuart's cavalry took its place upon the flanks, and no sooner had the movement begun, than, leaving his headquarters in the grassy yard of the old Hanover Court-House where Patrick Henry made his famous speech against the parsons, Stuart hastened to put his column in motion for the lower waters of the Rapidan.

Such was the situation of affairs when the little incident I propose to relate took place. Fitz Lee's brigade was ordered to move by way of Verdiersville to Raccoon Ford, and take position on Jackson's right; and General Stuart hastened forward, attended only by a portion of his staff, toward Verdiersville, where he expected to be speedily joined by "General Fitz."

Stuart reached the little hamlet on the evening, I believe, of the 16th of August, and selecting the small house which I have described for his temporary headquarters, awaited the approach of his column.

Half an hour, an hour passed, and nothing was heard of the expected cavalry. General Stuart's position was by no means a safe one, as the event showed. He was ten miles distant from any succour in case of an attack. The country around Verdiersville was known to be full of prowling detachments of Federal cavalry; and the daring cavalier, upon whose skill and energy so much depended at that crisis, might be quietly picked up by some scouting party of the enemy, and carried as a rich prize to General Pope. Stuart was, however, well accustomed throughout his adventurous career to take such risks; they even seemed to possess an irresistible charm to him, and he prepared to spend the night, if necessary, in this exposed spot. He accordingly tied his horse to the fence, the bridle having been taken from his mouth to allow the animal to feed, spread his gray riding-cape upon the porch of the little house, and prepared to go to sleep. First, however, he called Major Fitz Hugh, of his staff, and sent him back about a mile down the road to look out for General Fitz Lee. The major was to go to the mouth of the Richmond and Antioch Church road, await General Fitz's arrival, and communicate further orders. Having arranged this, Stuart lay down with his staff and they all went to sleep.

Let us now accompany Major Fitz Hugh, an old (though still youthful and alert) cavalryman—used to scouting, reconnoitring, and dealing generally with Federal cavalry. The major took a courier with him, and riding down the road about a mile in the direction of Chancellorsville, soon reached the mouth of the Antioch Church road—a branch of that most devious, puzzling, bewildering of all highways, the famed "Catharpin road." Major Fitz Hugh found at his stopping-place an old deserted house, and as this house was a very good "picket post" from which to observe the road by which General Fitz Lee must come, the major came to a halt at the old rattle-trap—forlornest of abandoned wayside inns—and there established his headquarters. An hour, two hours passed—there was no sign of General Fitz; and the major, who had ridden far and was weary, tied his handsome sorrel near, directed the courier to keep a sharp look-out, and, entering the house, lay down on the floor to take a short nap.

Such resolutions, under such circumstances, generally end in a good night's sleep. About daylight Major Fitz Hugh was awakened by a noise of hoofs on the road without, and, rising, he went to meet *General Fitz Lee*. The first circumstance which induced him to change his views of the "situation" was the sight of a swarm of *blue-coated* cavalrymen around the house, one of whom had untied and was leading off in triumph his glossy sorrel! A dozen others, who had arrived too late to secure the prize, were uttering imprecations on their luck.

A glance took in the whole scene—Major Fitz Hugh found himself surrounded by Federal cavalry, and a party soon burst into the house, and, with pistols at his breast, ordered him to surrender. The major was furious at this *contretemps*, and glanced around for his weapons. He clutched his pistol and cocked it; but his wrist was immediately seized, and an attempt made to wrench the weapon from his grasp. The major retorted by twisting his hand, and firing one or two barrels, but without result. They then rushed upon him, threw him down; his arms were wrested from him in a trice, and he was conducted to the commanding officer of the force, at the head of his column without.

The officer was a colonel, and asked Major Fitz Hugh a great number of questions. He was evidently lost. The major declined replying to any of them, and now his fears were painfully excited for General Stuart. If the column should take the direction of Verdiersville there was every reason to fear that the General would be surprised and captured. Meanwhile Major Fitz Hugh had taken a seat upon a fence, and as the column began to move he was ordered to get up and walk. This he declined doing, and the altercation was still proceeding, when an officer passed and the major complained of having his horse taken from him. "I am accustomed to ride, not to walk," he said; and this view of the subject seemed to impress the Federal officer, who, either from courtesy or to secure a mounted guide, had his horse brought and returned to him for the nonce. The major mounted and rode to the front amid "There goes the rebel major!" "Ain't he a fine dressed fellow?" "Don't he ride proud?" sounds soothing and pleasant to the captured major, who was dressed in a fine new roundabout with full gold braid.

But his thoughts suddenly became far from pleasant. The head of the cavalry column had turned *toward Verdiersville*, only a mile distant, and General Stuart's danger was imminent. The courier had also been captured; no warning of his peril could be got to the General; and worse than all, he would doubtless take the column for that of General Fitz Lee, which was to come by this very road, and thus be thrown completely off his guard. A more terrible *contretemps* could not have occurred than the Major's capture, and he saw no earthly means of giving the alarm. He was riding beside the colonel commanding, who had sent for him, and was thus forced to witness, without taking part in it, the scene about to be enacted.

## II.

Let us return now to the small party asleep on the porch of the house in Verdiersville.

They did not awake until day, when Stuart was aroused by the noise of hoofs upon the road, and concluding that General Fitz Lee had arrived, rose from the floor of the porch, and, without his hat, walked to the little gate. The column was not yet discernible clearly in the gray of morning; but in some manner Stuart's suspicions were excited. To assure himself of the truth, he requested Captain Mosby and Lieutenant Gibson, who were with him, to ride forward and see what command was approaching.

The reception which the two envoys met with, speedily decided the whole question. They had scarcely approached within pistol-shot of the head of the column, when they were fired upon, and a detachment spurred forward from the cavalry, calling upon them to halt, and firing upon them as they retreated. They were rapidly pursued, and in a few moments the Federal

cavalry had thundered down upon the house, in front of which
General Stuart was standing.

The General had to act promptly. There was no force within
many miles of him; nothing wherewith to make resistance; flight
or instant capture were the alternatives, and even flight seemed
impossible. The Federal horsemen had rushed at full gallop
upon the house; the horses of the General and staff were unbridled, and the only means of exit from the yard seemed to be
the narrow gate in front, scarcely wide enough for a mounted
man to pass, and right in face of the enemy. In addition to this,
the little party had just been aroused; the General had even left
his hat and cape upon the floor of the porch, so complete was
the feeling of security; and when Mosby was fired on, he was
standing bare-headed at the gate.

What followed all took place in an instant. The General and
his party leaped on their horses, some of which had been hastily
bridled, and sought for means of escape. One of the staff officers
darted through the narrow gate with his bridle-reins hanging
down beneath his horse's feet, and disappeared up the road followed by a shower of balls. The rest took the fence. Stuart,
bare-headed, and without his cape, which still lay on the porch,
threw himself upon his unbridled horse, seized the halter, and
digging his spurs into his sides, cleared the palings, and galloped
off amid a hot fire. He went on until he reached a clump of
woods near the house, when he stopped to reconnoitre.

The enemy did not at once follow, and from his point of observation the General had the mortification of witnessing the
capture of his hat and cape. The Federal cavalrymen dashed up
to the porch and seized these articles, which they bore off in
triumph—raising the brown hat, looped up with a golden star,
and decorated with its floating black feather, upon the points
of their sabres, and laughing at the escapade which they had
thus occasioned.

Major Fitz Hugh, at the head of the main column, and beside
the Federal Colonel, witnessed all, and burst into laughter and
sobs, such was his joy at the escape of his General. This attracted
the attention of the Federal officer, who said:

"Major, who was that party?"

"That have escaped?"

"Yes."

The Major looked again and saw that, on his fleet "Skylark," Stuart was entirely safe by this time, and unable to contain his triumph, exclaimed:

"Do you really wish to know who that was, Colonel?"

"I do."

"Well, it was General Stuart and his staff!"

"General Stuart!" exclaimed the officer; "was that *General Stuart?*"

"Yes, and he has escaped!" cried the overjoyed Major.

"A squadron there!" shouted the Colonel in great excitement; "pursue that party at once! Fire on them! It is General Stuart!"

The squadron rushed forward at the word upon the track of the fugitives to secure their splendid prize; but their advance did not afford the General much uneasiness. Long experience had told him that the Federal cavalry did not like woods, and he knew that they would not venture far for fear of a surprise. This idea was soon shown to be well founded. The Federal squadron made a very hot pursuit of the party until they came to the woods; they then contented themselves with firing and advancing very cautiously. Soon even this ceased, and they rapidly returned to Verdiersville, from which place the whole column hastily departed in the direction of the Rapidan. The Colonel carried off Major Fitz Hugh to serve as a guide, for he had lost his way, and stumbled thus upon Verdiersville. If you wish to laugh, my dear reader, go and see Major Fitz Hugh, and ask him what topographical information he gave the Federal commandant. It very nearly caused the capture of his command; but he got back safe to Pope's army, and took our friend, the Major, with him.

Such was Stuart's narrow escape at Verdiersville. He succeeded in eluding them, but he lost his riding cape and hat, which the enemy had seized upon, and this rankled in the mind of the General, prompting him to take his revenge at the earliest practicable moment.

STUART'S ESCAPE FROM THE FEDERAL CAVALRY.

"Stuart threw himself upon his unbridled horse, seized the halter, and digging his spurs into his sides, cleared the pailings, and galloped off amid a hot fire."

That moment soon came. Just one week afterwards, when General Lee had pressed on to the Rappahannock, and General Pope had hastily retired before him, Stuart made an expedition to the enemy's rear, and struck the Orange and Alexandria Railroad at Catlett's.

It was one dark and stormy night that the attack was made—the column plunging forward at full speed, through ditches and ravines, without light enough to see their hands before them; and by a singular chance Stuart came on Pope's headquarters, which was at Catlett's. The Federal commander fled with his staff, and Stuart captured all his official papers containing the fullest information of his strength, position, and designs. Those papers were transmitted to General Lee, and probably determined him to send Jackson to Pope's rear.

In addition to the papers Stuart made a capture which was personally soothing to his feelings. In his flight, General Pope left his coat behind! and when the leader of the Southern cavalry, so recently despoiled of his cape and hat, left Catlett's, he bore off with him the dress uniform coat of the Federal commander, who had prophetically announced to his troops upon taking command, that "disaster and shame lurked in the rear."

The account was thus balanced. Catlett's had avenged Verdiersville!

And so, my dear reader, you know why I always glance at that little house in the village as I pass. The dilapidated porch is still there, where Stuart slept, and the fence which he leaped still stands, as he pointed it out to me one day, when we rode by, describing with gay laughter his adventure. All these inanimate objects remain, but the noble figure which is associated with the place will never more be seen in the flesh—the good knight has been unseated by a stronger arm than that of man. He passed unscathed through this and a thousand other perils; but at last came the fatal bullet. At the Yellow Tavern he fell in front of his line, cheering on his men to the last, and on a beautiful slope of Hollywood Cemetery, above the city which he died defending, he "sleeps well."

Thus passed away the "flower of cavaliers," the pearl of chivalry. Dying, he did not leave his peer.

# IV

## A Glimpse of Colonel "Jeb Stuart"

THIS sketch, may it please the reader, will not contain any "historic events." Not a single piece of artillery will roar in it—not a single volley of musketry will sound—no life will be lost from the very beginning to the end of it. It aims only to draw a familiar outline of a famous personage as he worked his work in the early months of the war, and the muse of comedy, not tragedy, will hold the pen. For that brutal thing called war contains much of comedy; the warp and woof of the fabric is of strangely mingled threads—blood and merriment, tears and laughter follow each other, and are mixed in a manner quite bewildering! To-day it is the bright side of the tapestry I look at—my aim is to sketch some little trifling scenes "upon the outpost."

To do so, it will be necessary to go back to the early years of the late war, and to its first arena, the country between Manassas and the Potomac. Let us, therefore, leave the present year, 1866, of which many persons are weary, and return to 1861, of which many never grow tired talking—1861, with its joy, its laughter, its inexperience, and its confiding simplicity, when everybody thought that the big battle on the shores of Bull's Run had terminated the war at one blow.

At that time the present writer was attached to Beauregard's or Johnson's "Army of the Potomac," and had gone with the advance force of the army, after Manassas, to the little village of Vienna—General Bonham commanding the detachment of a brigade or so. Here we duly waited for an enemy who did not come; watched his mysterious balloons hovering above the trees, and regularly "turned out" whenever one picket (gray) fired into another (gray).

This was tiresome, and one day in August I mounted my horse and set forward toward Fairfax Court-House, intent on visiting that gay cavalry man, Colonel "Jeb Stuart," who had been put in command of the front toward Annandale. A pleasant ride through the summer woods brought me to the picturesque little village; and at a small mansion about a mile east of the town, I came upon the cavalry headquarters.

The last time I had seen the gay young Colonel he was stretched upon his red blanket under a great oak by the roadside, holding audience with a group of country people around him— honest folks who came to ascertain by what unheard-of cruelty they were prevented from passing through his pickets to their homes. The laughing, bantering air of the young commandant of the outpost that day had amused me much. I well remembered now his keen eye, and curling moustache, and cavalry humour—thus it was a good companion whom I was about to visit, not a stiff and silent personage, weighed down with "official business." Whether this anticipation was realized or not, the reader will discover.

The little house in which Colonel Jeb Stuart had taken up his residence, was embowered in foliage. I approached it through a whole squadron of horses, picketed to the boughs; and in front of the portico a new blood-red battle flag, with its blue St. Andrew's cross and white stars, rippled in the wind. Bugles sounded, spurs clashed, sabres rattled, as couriers or officers, scouts or escorts of prisoners came and went; huge-bearded cavalrymen awaited orders, or the reply to dispatches—and from within came song and laughter from the young commander. Let me sketch him as he then appeared—the man who was to become so famous as the chief of cavalry of General Lee's army; who was to inaugurate with the hand of a master, a whole new system of cavalry tactics—to invent the raid which his opponents were to imitate with such good results—and to fall, after a hundred hot fights in which no bullet ever touched him, near the scene of his first great "ride" around the army of McClellan.

As he rose to meet me, I took in at a glance every detail of his appearance. His low athletic figure was clad in an old blue undress coat of the United States Army, brown velveteen pantaloons worn white by rubbing against the saddle, high cavalry boots with small brass spurs, a gray waistcoat, and carelessly tied cravat. On the table at his side lay a Zouave cap, covered with a white havelock—an article then very popular—and beside this two huge yellow leathern gauntlets, reaching nearly to the elbow, lay ready for use. Around his waist, Stuart wore a black leather belt, from which depended on the right a holster containing his revolver, and on the left a light, keen sabre, of French pattern, with a basket hilt. The figure thus was that of a man "every inch a soldier," and the face was in keeping with the rest. The broad and lofty forehead—one of the finest I have ever seen—was bronzed by sun and wind; the eyes were clear, piercing, and of an intense and dazzling blue; the nose prominent, with large and mobile nostrils; and the mouth was completely covered by a heavy brown moustache, which swept down and mingled with a huge beard of the same tint, reaching to his breast. Such was the figure of the young commandant, as he appeared that day, in the midst of the ring of bugles and the clatter of arms, there in the centre of his web upon the outpost. It was the soldier ready for work at any instant; prepared to mount at the sound of the trumpet, and lead his squadrons in person, like the hardy, gallant man-at-arms he was.

After friendly greetings and dinner on the lid of a camp-chest, where that gay and good companion, Captain Tiernan Brien, did the honours, as second in command, Stuart proposed that we should ride into Fairfax Court-House and see a lady prisoner of his there. When this announcement of a "lady prisoner" drew forth some expressions of astonishment, he explained with a laugh that the lady in question had been captured a few days before in suspicious proximity to the Confederate lines, which she appeared to be reconnoitring; and that she was a friend of the "other faction" was proved by the circumstance that when captured she was riding a Federal Colonel's horse, with army saddle, holsters, and equipments complete. While on a little re-connoissance, all by herself, in this guise she had fallen into Stuart's net; had been conducted to his headquarters; assigned by him to the care of a lady resident at the Court-House, until he received orders in relation to her from the army headquarters —and this lady we were now about to visit.

We set out for the village, Stuart riding his favourite "Sky-lark,"—that good sorrel which had carried him through all the scouting of the Valley, and was captured afterwards near Sharpsburg. This horse was of extraordinary toughness, and I remember one day his master said to me, "Ride as hard as you choose, you can't tire Skylark." On this occasion the good steed was in full feather; and as I am not composing a majestic historic narrative, it will be permitted me to note that his equipments were a plain "McClellan tree," upon which a red blanket was confined by a gaily coloured surcingle: a bridle with single head-stall, light curb-bit, and single rein. Mounted upon his sorrel, Stuart was thoroughly the cavalry-man, and he went on at a rapid gallop, humming a song as he rode.

We found the lady-prisoner at a hospitable house of the vil-lage, and there was little in her appearance or manner to in-dicate the "poor captive," nor did she exhibit any "freezing terrour," as the romance writers say, at sight of the young *militaire*. At that time some amusing opinions of the Southerners were prevalent at the North. The "rebels" were looked upon pretty much as monsters of a weird and horrible character—a sort of "anthropophagi," Cyclops-eyed, and with heads that "did grow beneath their shoulders." Short rations, it was popu-larly supposed, compelled them to devour the bodies of their enemies; and to fall into their bloody clutch was worse than death. This view of the subject, however, plainly did not possess the captive here. Her fears, if she had ever had any of the terrible gray people, were quite dissipated; and she received us with a nonchalant smile, and great indifference.

I shall not give the fair dame's name, nor even venture to describe her person, or conjecture her age—further than to say that her face was handsome and laughing, her age about twenty-five or thirty.

The scene which followed was a little comedy, whose gay particulars it is easier to recall than to describe. It was a veritable crossing of swords on the arena of Wit, and I am not sure that the lady did not get the better of it. Her tone of *badinage* was even more than a match for the gay young officer's—and of *badinage* he was a master—but he was doubtless restrained on the occasion by that perfect good-breeding and courtesy which uniformly marked his demeanour to the sex, and his fair adversary had him at a disadvantage. She certainly allowed her wit and humour to flash like a Damascus blade; and, with a gay laugh, denounced the rebels as perfect wretches for coercing her movements. Why, she would like to know, was she ever arrested? She had only ridden out on a short pleasure excursion from Alexandria, and now demanded to be permitted to return thither. "Why was she riding a Federal officer's horse?" Why, simply because he was one of her friends. If the Colonel would "please" let her return through his pickets she would not tell anybody anything—upon her word!

"The Colonel" in question was smiling—probably at the idea of allowing anything on two feet to pass "through his pickets" to the enemy. But the impossibility of permitting this was not the burden of his reply. With that odd "laughter of the eye" always visible in him when thoroughly amused, he opposed the lady's return, on the ground that he would miss her society. This he could not think of, and it was not friendly in her to contemplate leaving him for ever so soon after making his acquaintance! Then she was losing other pleasant things. There was Richmond—she would see all the sights of the Confederate capital; then an agreeable trip by way of Old Point would restore her to her friends.

Reply of the lady extremely vivacious: She did not wish to see the Confederate capital!—she wished to go back to Alexandria!—straight! She was not anxious to get away from *him*, for he had treated her with the very greatest courtesy, and she should always regard him as her friend. But she wanted to go back to Alexandria, through the pickets—straight!

That the statement of her friendly regard for the young Colonel was unaffected, the fair captive afterwards proved. When in due course of time she was sent by orders from army headquarters to Richmond, and thence *via* Old Point to Washington, she wrote and published an account of her adventures, in which she denounced the Confederate officials everywhere, including those at the centre of Rebeldom, as ruffians, monsters, and tyrants of the deepest dye, but excepted from this sweeping characterization the youthful Colonel of cavalry, who was the author of all her woes. So far from complaining of him, she extolled his kindness, courtesy, and uniform care of her comfort, declaring that he was "the noblest gentleman she had ever known." There was indeed about Colonel Jeb Stuart, as about Major-General Stuart, a smiling air of courtesy and gallantry, which made friends for him among the fair sex, even when they were enemies; and Bayard himself could not have exhibited toward them more respect and consideration than he did uniformly. He must have had serious doubts in regard to the errand of his fair prisoner, so near the Confederate lines, but he treated her with the greatest consideration; and when he left her, the bow he made was as low as to the finest "lady in the land."

It is possible that the worthy reader may not find as much entertainment in perusing the foregoing sketch as I do in recalling the scene to memory. That faculty of memory is a curious one, and very prone to gather up, like Autolycus, the "unconsidered trifles" of life. Every trivial incident of the times I write of comes back now—how Stuart's gay laugh came as he closed the door, and how he caught up a drum which the enemy had left behind them in the yard of the mansion, sprang to the saddle, and set off at a run through the streets of the village, causing the eyes of the inhabitants to open with astonishment at the spectacle of Colonel Stuart running a race, with a drum before him, singing lustily a camp song as he rode. In a number of octavo volumes the reader will find an account of the great career of Major-General Stuart—this was Colonel Jeb Stuart on the outpost.

And now if the worthy reader is in that idle, unexacting mood so dear to chroniclers, I beg he will listen while I speak of another "trifling incident" occurring on the same day, which had a rather amusing result. In return for the introduction accorded me to the captive, I offered to make the young Colonel acquainted with a charming friend of my own, whom I had known before his arrival at the place; and as he acquiesced with ready pleasure, we proceeded to a house in the village, where Colonel Stuart was duly presented to Miss ——.* The officer and the young lady very soon thereafter became close friends, for she was passionately Southern—and a few words will present succinctly the result.

In the winter of 1862, Colonel Mosby made a raid into Fairfax, entered the Court-House at night, and captured General Stoughton and his staff—bringing out the prisoners and a number of fine horses safely. This exploit of the partisan greatly enraged the Federal authorities; and Miss ——, having been denounced by Union residents as Mosby's "private friend" and pilot on the occasion—which Colonel Mosby assured me was an entire error—she was arrested, her trunks searched, and the prisoner and her papers conveyed to Washington. Here she was examined on the charge of complicity in Mosby's raid; but nothing appeared against her, and she was in a fair way to be released, when all at once a terrible proof of her guilt was discovered. Among the papers taken from the young lady's trunk was found

* Cooke, with characteristic carelessness, forgets that he has already revealed the name of the young lady identified here only as Miss ——. He gave it on page 107. She was Miss Antonia J. Ford. After her release from the Old Capitol Prison, she married a young Union major who was the founder of a hotel that has played an important part in Washington politics ever since the Civil War. His name was Joseph C. Willard. Until her death in 1871, this former friend of prominent Confederate officers, who had also acted as a spy, presided as hostess in the world-famed Willard Hotel. Cooke, who may have been in love with the pretty young Confederate sympathizer, made her into a character in one of his novels. She appears as Violet Grafton in *Surry of Eagle's Nest* (1866).—ED.

the following document. This was the "damning record" which left no further doubt of her guilt.

I print the paper *verbatim et literatim*, suppressing only the full name of the lady:

"*To all Whom it May Concern:*

"Know Ye, That reposing special confidence in the patriotism, fidelity, and ability of Antonia J. ——, I, James E. B. Stuart, by virtue of the power vested in me as Brigadier-General of the Provisional Army of the Confederate States of America, do hereby appoint and commission her my *honorary Aide-de-Camp*, to rank as such from this date. She will be obeyed, respected, and admired by all true lovers of a noble nature.

"Given under my hand and seal at the Headquarters Cavalry Brigade, at Camp Beverly, the 7th October, A. D. 1861, and the first year of our independence.

"J. E. B. Stuart.

"By the General:
    "L. Tiernan Brien, A. A. G."

Such was the fatal document discovered in Miss ——'s trunk, the terrible proof of her treason! The poor girl was committed to the Old Capitol Prison as a secret *commissioned* emissary of the Confederate States Government, was kept for several months, and when she was released and sent South to Richmond, where I saw her, she was as thin and white as a ghost—the mere shadow of her former self.

All that cruelty had resulted from a jest—from the harmless pleasantry of a brave soldier in those bright October days of 1861!

# V

## A DESERTER

OF ALL human faculties, surely the most curious is the memory. Capricious, whimsical, illogical, acting ever in accordance with its own wild will, it loses so many "important events" to retain the veriest trifles in its deathless clutch! Ask a soldier who has fought all day long in some world-losing battle, what he remembers most vividly, and he will tell you that he has well-nigh forgotten the most desperate charges, but recalls with perfect distinctness the joy he experienced in swallowing a mouthful of water from the canteen on the body of a dead enemy.

A trifling incident of the second battle of Manassas remains in my memory more vividly than the hardest fighting of the whole day, and I never recall the incident in question without thinking, too, of De Quincey's singular paper, "A Vision of Sudden Death." The reader is probably familiar with the article to which I refer—a very curious one, and not the least admirable of those strange leaves, full of thought and fancy, which the "Opium Eater" scattered among the readers of the last generation. He was riding on the roof of a stage-coach, when the vehicle commenced the descent of a very steep hill. Soon it began moving with mad velocity, the horses became unmanageable, and it was obvious that if it came in collision with anything, either it or the object which it struck would be dashed in pieces. All at once, there appeared in front, on the narrow road, a light carriage, in which were seated a young man and a girl. They either did not realize their danger, or were powerless to avoid it; and on swept the heavy stage, with its load of passengers, its piled-up baggage, and its maddened horses—rushing straight down on the frail vehicle with which it soon came in collision. It was at the moment when the light little affair was dashed to pieces, the stage rolling with a wild crash over the boy and girl, that De Quincey saw in their awestruck faces that singular expression which he has described by the phrase, "A Vision of Sudden Death."

It requires some courage to intrude upon the literary domain of that great master, the "Opium Eater," and the comparison will prove dangerous; but a reader here and there may be interested in a *vision of sudden death* which I myself once saw in a human eye. On the occasion in question, a young, weak-minded, and timid person was instantaneously confronted, without premonition or suspicion of his danger, with the abrupt prospect of an ignominious death; and I think the great English writer would have considered my incident more stirring than his own.

It was on the morning of August 31, 1862, on the Warrenton road, in a little skirt of pines, near Cub Run bridge, between Manassas and Centreville. General Pope, who previously had "only seen the backs of his enemies," had been cut to pieces. The battle-ground which had witnessed the defeat of Scott and McDowell on the 21st of July, 1861, had now again been swept by the bloody besom of war; and the Federal forces were once more in full retreat upon Washington. The infantry of the Southern army were starved, broken down, utterly exhausted, when they went into that battle, but they carried everything before them; and the enemy had disappeared, thundering with their artillery to cover their retreat. The rest of the work must be done by the cavalry; and to the work in question the great cavalier Stuart addressed himself with the energy, dash, and vigour of his character. The scene, as we went on, was curious. Pushing across the battle-field—we had slept at "Fairview," the *Conrad House* on the maps—we saw upon every side the reeking traces of the bloody conflict; and as the column went on across

Bull Run, following the enemy on their main line of retreat over the road from Stonebridge to Centreville, the evidences of "demoralization" and defeat crowded still more vividly upon the eye. Guns, haversacks, oil-cloths, knapsacks, abandoned cannon and broken-down wagons and ambulances,—all the *debris* of an army, defeated and hastening to find shelter behind its works— attracted the attention now, as in July, 1861, when the first "On to Richmond" was so unfortunate. Prisoners were picked up on all sides as the cavalry pushed on; their horses, if they were mounted, were taken possession of; their sabres, guns, and pistols appropriated with the ease and rapidity of long practice; and the prisoners were sent in long strings under one or two mounted men, as a guard, to the rear.

As we approached Cub Run bridge, over which the rear-guard of the Federal army had just retired, we found by the roadside a small wooden house used as a temporary hospital. It was full of dead and wounded; and I remember that the "Hospital steward" who attended the Federal wounded was an imposing personage. Portly, bland, "dignified," elegantly dressed, he was as splendid as a major-general; nay, far more so than any *gray* major-general of the present writer's acquaintance. Our tall and finely-clad friend yielded up his surplus ambulances with graceful ease, asked for further orders; and when soon his own friends from across Cub Run began to shell the place, philosophically took his stand behind the frail mansion and "awaited further developments" with the air of a man who was resigned to the fortunes of war. Philosophic steward of the portly person! if you see this page it will bring back to you that lively scene when the present writer conversed with you and found you so composed and "equal to the occasion," even amid the shell and bullets!

But I am expending too much attention upon my friend the surgeon, who "held the position" there with such philosophic coolness. The cavalry, headed by General Stuart, pushed on, and we were now nearly at Cub Run bridge. The main body of the enemy had reached Centreville during the preceding night, and we could see their white tents in the distance; but a strong rear-guard of cavalry and artillery had been left near the bridge, and as we now advanced, mounted skirmishers from the Federal side forded the stream, and very gallantly came to meet us. On our side, sharpshooters were promptly deployed—then came the bang of carbines—then Stuart's Horse Artillery galloped up, under Pelham, and a "rear-guard affair" began. Stuart formed his column for a charge, and had just begun to move, when the Federal skirmishers were seen retiring; a dense smoke arose from Cub Run bridge, and suddenly the enemy's artillery on a knoll beyond opened their grim mouths. The first shot they fired was admirable. It fell plump into a squadron of cavalry—between the files as they were ranged side by side in column of twos—and although it burst into a hundred pieces, did not wound man or horse. The Horse Artillery under Pelham replied to the fire of the opposing guns; an animated artillery duel commenced, and the ordinary routine began.

## II.

There is a French proverb which declares that although you may know when you set out on a journey, you do not know when you will arrive. Those who journey through the fine land of memory are, of all travellers, the most ignorant upon that score, and are apt to become the most unconscionable vagarists. Memory refuses to recall one scene or incident without recalling also a hundred others which preceded or followed it. "You people," said John Randolph to a gentleman of an extensive clan, with which the eccentric orator was always at war, "you people all take up each other's quarrels. You are worse than a pile of fish-hooks. If I try to grasp one, I raise the whole bunch." To end my preface, and come to my little incident. I was sitting on my horse near General Stuart, who had put in the skirmishers, and was now superintending the fire of his artillery, when a cavalry-man rode up and reported that they had just captured a deserter.

"Where is he?" was Stuart's brief interrogatory.

"Coming yonder, General."

"How do you know he is a deserter?"

"One of my company knew him when he joined our army."

"Where is he from?"

"—— county."

And the man mentioned the name of a county of Western Virginia.

"What is his name?"

"M——."

(I suppress the full name. Some mother's or sister's heart might be wounded.)

"Bring him up," said Stuart coldly, with a lowering glance from the blue eyes under the brown hat and black feather. As he spoke, two or three mounted men rode up with the prisoner.

I can see him at this moment with the mind's eye, as I saw him then with the material eye. He was a young man, apparently eighteen or nineteen years of age, and wore the blue uniform, tipped with red, of a private in the United States Artillery. The singular fact was that he appeared completely at his ease. He seemed to be wholly unconscious of the critical position which he occupied; and as he approached, I observed that he returned the dark glance of Stuart with the air of a man who says, "What do you find in my appearance to make you fix your eyes upon me so intently!" In another moment he was in Stuart's presence, and calmly, quietly, without the faintest exhibition of embarrassment, or any emotion whatever, waited to be addressed.

Stuart's words were curtest of the curt.

"Is this the man?" he said.

"Yes, General," replied one of the escort.

"You say he is a deserter?"

"Yes, sir; I knew him in —— county, when he joined Captain ——s' company; and there is no sort of doubt about it, General, as he acknowledges that he is the same person."

"Acknowledges it!"

"Yes, sir; acknowledges that he is M——, from that county; and that after joining the South he deserted."

Stuart flashed a quick glance at the prisoner, and seemed at a loss to understand what fatuity had induced him to testify against himself—thereby sealing his fate. His gaze—clear, fiery, menacing—was returned by the youth with apathetic calmness. Not a muscle of his countenance moved, and I now had an opportunity to look at him more attentively. He was even younger than I at first thought him—indeed, a mere boy. His complexion was fair; his hair flaxen and curling; his eyes blue, mild, and as soft in their expression as a girl's. Their expression, as they met the lowering glances of Stuart, was almost confiding. I could not suppress a sigh—so painful was the thought that this youth would probably be lying soon with a bullet through his heart.

A kinder-hearted person than General Stuart never lived; but in all that appertained to his profession and duty as a soldier, he was inexorable. Desertion, in his estimation, was one of the deadliest crimes of which a human being could be guilty; and his course was plain—his resolution immovable.

"What is your name?" said the General coldly, with a lowering brow.

"M——, sir," was the response, in a mild and pleasing voice, in which it was impossible to discern the least trace of emotion.

"Where are you from?"

"I belonged to the battery that was firing at you, over yonder, sir."

The voice had not changed. A calmer tone I never heard.

"Where were you born?" continued Stuart, as coldly as before.

"In ——, Virginia, sir."

"Did you belong to the Southern army at any time?"

"Yes, sir."

The coolness of the speaker was incredible. Stuart could only look at him for a moment in silence, so astonishing was this equanimity at a time when his life and death were in the balance. Not a tone of the voice, a movement of the muscles, or a tremor of the lip indicated consciousness of his danger. The eye never quailed, the colour in his cheek never faded. The prisoner acknowledged that he was a deserter from the Southern army with the simplicity, candour, and calmness of one who saw in that fact nothing extraordinary, or calculated in any manner to affect his destiny unpleasantly. Stuart's eye flashed; he could not understand such apathy; but in war there is little time to investigate psychological phenomena.

"So you were in our ranks, and you went over to the enemy?" he said with a sort of growl.

"Yes, sir," was the calm reply.

"You were a private in that battery yonder?"

"Yes, sir."

Stuart turned to an officer, and pointing to a tall pine near, said in brief tones:

"Hang him on that tree!"

It was then that a change—sudden, awful, horrible—came over the face of the prisoner; at that moment I read in the distended eyeballs the "vision of sudden death." The youth became ghastly pale; and the eyes, before so vacant and apathetic, were all at once injected with blood, and full of piteous fright. I saw in an instant that the boy had not for a single moment realized the terrible danger of his position; and that the words "Hang him on that tree!" had burst upon him with the sudden and appalling force of a thunderbolt. I have seen human countenances express every phase of agony; seen the writhing of the mortally wounded as their life-blood welled out, and the horror of the death-struggle fixed on the cold upturned faces of the dead; but never have I witnessed an expression more terrible and agonizing than that which passed over the face of the boy-deserter, as he thus heard his sentence. He had evidently regarded himself as a mere prisoner of war; and now he was condemned to death! He had looked forward, doubtless, to mere imprisonment at Richmond until regularly exchanged, when "hang him on that tree!" burst upon his ears like the voice of some avenging Nemesis.

Terrible, piteous, sickening, was the expression of the boy's face. He seemed to feel already the rope around his neck; he choked; when he spoke his voice sounded like the death-rattle. An instant of horror-struck silence; a gasp or two as if the words were trying to force their way against some obstacle in his throat; then the sound came. His tones were not loud, impassioned, energetic, not even animated. A sick terror seemed to have frozen him; when he spoke it was in a sort of moan.

"I didn't know," he muttered in low, husky tones. "I never

meant—when I went over to Maryland—to fight against the South. They made me; I had nothing to eat—I told them I was a Southerner—and so help me God I never fired a shot. I was with the wagons. Oh! General, spare me; I never——"

There the voice died out; and as pale as a corpse, trembling in every limb—a spectacle of helpless terror which no words can describe, the boy awaited his doom.

Stuart had listened in silence, his gaze riveted upon the speaker; his hand grasping his heavy beard; motionless amid the shell which were bursting around him. For an instant he seemed to hesitate—life and death were poised in the balances. Then with a cold look at the trembling deserter, he said to the men:

"Take him back to General Lee, and report the circumstances."

With these words he turned and galloped off; the deserter was saved, at least for the moment.

I do not know his ultimate fate; but if he saw General Lee in person, and told his tale, I think he was spared. That great and merciful spirit inflicted the death-penalty only when he could not avoid it.

Since that day I have never seen the face of the boy—nor even expect to see it. But I shall never forget that "vision of sudden death" in his distended eyes, as Stuart's cold voice ordered, "Hang him on that tree."

# VI

## A Young Virginian and His Spurs

### I.

THERE is a young gentleman in Virginia bearing a name so illustrious that, if I were to give it, the most ardent opponents of the "F. F. V.'s" would take a certain historic interest in what I am going to relate. When I say that he is called Lieutenant W——, you cannot possibly guess his name. But to the curious incident with which I propose to amuse those readers who take an interest in the veritable occurrences of the great struggle just terminated.

On the ninth day of June, 1863, there took place at Fleetwood Hill, near Brandy Station, in Culpeper, the greatest and most desperate cavalry conflict of the war. Nearly twenty-five thousand horsemen fought there "all a summer's day"—as when Earl Percy met the Douglas in the glades of Chevy Chase—and the combat was of unexampled fury. General Stuart, commanding all the cavalry of General Lee's army, had held a grand review some days before, in the extensive fields below the Court-House, and a mimic battle had taken place, preceding the real one. The horse artillery, posted on a hill, fired blank cartridges as the cavalry charged the guns; the columns swept by a great pole, from which the white Confederate flag waved proudly in the wind. General Lee, with his grizzled beard and old gray riding-cape, looked on, the centre of all eyes; bands played, the artillery roared, the charging squadrons shook the ground, and from the great crowd assembled to witness the imposing spectacle shone the variegated dresses and bright eyes of beautiful women, rejoicing in the heyday of the grand review.

But that roar of artillery in the mimic battle reached other ears than those for which it was intended. There were some friends of ours upon the opposite shore of the Rappahannock who took even greater interest in the movements of General Lee than the fair daughters of Virginia. The thunder of the artillery was heard by them, and they at once conceived a burning curiosity to know what all this firing meant. So, one bright morning about dawn, they came across the river, about seventeen thousand in number, to see what "Old Uncle Robert" was about. Thereupon followed the hard fight of Fleetwood Hill.

A description of this long and desperate struggle is no portion of the present subject. The Federal forces advanced in front, on the right flank, on the left flank—everywhere. The battle was thus fought, so to speak, "from the centre outwards." What the eye saw as Stuart rapidly fell back from the river and concentrated his cavalry for the defense of Fleetwood Hill, between him and Brandy, was a great and imposing spectacle of squadrons charging in every portion of the field—men falling, cut out of the saddle with the sabre; artillery roaring, carbines cracking —a perfect hurly-burly of conflict.

Some day, perhaps, the present historian may give a page to this hard battle, and speak of its "moving accidents;" of the manner in which the cannoneers of the horse-artillery met and repulsed a charge upon their guns with clubs and sponge-staffs; how that gallant spirit, P. M. B. Young, of Georgia, met the heavy flanking column attacking from the side of Stevensburg, and swept it back with the sabre; how the brave William H. F. Lee received the charge upon the left and fell in front of his squadrons at the moment when the Federal forces broke; and how Stuart, on fire with the heat of battle, was everywhere the soul and guiding spirit of the desperate struggle.

At four in the evening the assault had been repulsed, and the Federal cavalry were in hasty retreat across the river again. Many prisoners remained in the hands of the Confederates, but they had also lost not a few; for the fight had been so "mixed up," and so many small detachments of the Southern cavalry had been cut off and surrounded in the *mêlée*, that the captures were considerable.

## II.

Among those who were thus cut off and captured in this wild struggle made up of dust, smoke, blood, and uproar, was Lieutenant W——. His horse had mired in the swampy ground near the Barbour House, and he was incontinently gobbled up by his friends in the blue coats, and marched to the rear, that is to say, across the Rappahannock. Lieutenant W—— was an excellent specimen of those brave youths of the Valley who gathered around Jackson in the early months of the war, and in the hot fights of the great campaign against Banks and Fremont had borne himself with courage and distinction. Wounded and captured at Kernstown—I think it was—he had been exchanged, secured a transfer to the cavalry, and was now again a prisoner.

He was conducted across the Rappahannock with the Confederate prisoners captured during the day, and soon found himself minus horse, pistol, and sabre—all of which had, of course, been taken from him—in front of a bonfire on the north bank of the river. Around this fire a crowd of Federal cavalry-men were now assembled, discussing the events of the day, and many of them entered into conversation with the prisoners, their late adversaries. Lieutenant W—— was standing by the fire, no doubt reflecting upon the curious "ups and downs" of that curious trade called war, when all at once something familiar in the voice of a young officer of the Federal force, who was not far from him, attracted his attention. Looking at the officer closely, he recognised in him an old friend of his who had formerly resided in Baltimore; and going up to him, the young Virginian made himself known.

He was greeted with the utmost pleasure, and the youths shook hands, laughing like boys at the odd meeting. If I were a novelist instead of an historian, my dear reader, I would here insert a lengthy dialogue between the friends; but not having been present, I can only give you the bare outline of W——'s adventure. From talk about old scenes, and things of the past, the conversation glided to the present, and the young Virginian's unlucky situation. Relying upon their former friendship, the latter at once broached the subject of his escape.

"I wish I could help you," was the reply; "but I see no sort of chance of your getting away, W——."

"I think I can get off in the dark."

"Perhaps; but crossing the river is the difficulty. The bridge is picketed."

The young Virginian, nevertheless, determined to make the attempt. From that moment he kept a close watch on the movements of his captors. Having eaten their supper, they now addressed themselves to the task of counting, assorting, and taking down the names of their prisoners. The latter were drawn up in a line near the fire, and a Federal officer went along the line, entering their names and regiments in his memorandum-book. Lieutenant W—— was near the head of the line, and having given his name and regiment—the Twelfth Virginia Cavalry— saw the officer pass on. I have called him *Lieutenant W——*, but the young man was at that time a private; and at the announcement of his historic name the Federal soldiers began to laugh, one of them saying "The Old Dominion must be hard up when her aristocracy have to go in the ranks and wear a jacket like that!" And he pointed to W——'s old, discoloured cavalry jacket.

The young man was, however, not thinking of the jokes of his captors; he was watching his opportunity to glide out of the line. It soon came. The Federal soldiers were not looking at him; the recording officer had passed around the fire, the light of which thus shone for an instant in his eyes and dazzled him, and Lieutenant W—— saw his opportunity. The space outside of the firelight was as gloomy as Eblis, and in a moment he had stepped from his place, and was lost in the darkness. He glided behind a tent, ran a few steps, and then paused to listen.

Had his movement been observed? Would they go over the

count again, to verify the record? Then one man would be found missing; he would be at once pursued, recaptured, and rewarded for his attempt to escape by painful or ignominious punishment. He listened with all his ears; held his breath, and soon found that he was not missed. The officer did not suspect the *ruse* which had been played upon him; and the prisoners were marched off under guard. Lieutenant W—— saw them disappear with profound satisfaction, and then all his energies were bent to the hard task of getting out of the Federal camp and crossing the river. The prospect looked sufficiently dispiriting. He was in the centre of a city of tents, where he could not stir a step without attracting attention; and even if he succeeded in escaping the vigilance of the men and the quarter-guard, the broad and deep current of the Rappahannock lay still in his path—the single bridge heavily picketed. The young man did not lose heart for a single moment, however, and, like a good soldier, determined to "take the chances."

The first thing was to conceal his identity from the men around the fires. He accordingly took off his gray jacket, and rolling it up, put it under his arm. His pantaloons were blue, and his hat was of an indefinable colour, which might be either Confederate or Federal. In his bosom, between his shirt and naked breast, he concealed his spurs, which he had unbuckled and hidden when he was captured. Having thus prepared himself, Lieutenant W—— walked boldly on, and lounged carelessly by the fires. One of the men asked him what regiment he belonged to, as if they observed something unfamiliar in his demeanour; but his ready reply, giving the name of some Federal regiment, entirely disarmed suspicion. So much cavalry had taken part in the fight, and had been so much scattered, that W—— was set down for one of the many stragglers; and walking by the fires, and the quarter-guard, who stared at, but did not challenge him, he gained the bank of the Rappahannock.

He had thus succeeded in his second attempt; but obstacle number three threatened to be more serious. The river before him was broad, deep, black, and cold. The bridge near by was guarded; he heard the sentinel pacing to and fro, and a second at

the further extremity. What was to be done? Kill the sentinel
by suddenly attacking and seizing his weapon? That, under
other circumstances, might have been done; but there was the
other sentinel, who would at once give the alarm; then recapture, and a "latter end worse than the first." This plan was thus
out of the question. But one hope presented itself. The fugitive
could not swim the river; but if by any means he could climb
up to the floor of the bridge *inside* of the sentinel, he might, perhaps, crawl along without being discovered, "flank" the sentinel
beyond, and so get back to his friends. Young, lithe, and determined, Lieutenant W—— speedily made a reconnoissance of the
abutments of the bridge to ascertain the possibility of executing
his project. To his great satisfaction he discovered a pipe running from a tank above to the water below—for this was the
Orange and Alexandria Railroad bridge; and the rivets securing
the pipe to the masonry afforded him an excellent foothold
in climbing. Gliding beneath the sentinel in the darkness, he
crept into the shadow, grasped the pipe, and, with hands and
knees, climbed foot by foot up the abutment, until he reached
the edge of the floor-way. His hands were torn and his knees
lacerated, but he had taken another step toward liberty.

What now remained to be done was to crawl along the narrow
edge of the parapet, under shadow of a species of low railing,
and crossing the bridge, pass around the other sentinel in some
manner, and escape. This, however, was the most doubtful, as it
was certainly the most dangerous portion of the adventure.
The bridge was very lofty, the ledge narrow, slippery, and unprotected for he must move outside of the railing for fear of discovery; a single false step would precipitate him into the river
beneath. Even if this danger were avoided, there was the sentinel beyond, and a picket, doubtless, beyond the sentinel. Lieutenant W—— was revolving in his mind these various circumstances, and had begun to take a rather discouraging view of
things, when his attention was attracted by the sound of steps
coming from the direction of the Federal camp. A detachment
of dismounted men were evidently approaching the bridge, and
in a few moments the voice of the sentinel was heard giving the

challenge. "Relief," was the reply; and then came, "Advance
relief!" which was immediately followed by the appearance of
the relief-guard. The new sentinel was relieved from his post,
and took his place among the guard, one of whom was posted,
and the detachment was heard tramping across the bridge to relieve in the same manner the other sentinels. As they came on,
tramp! tramp! like the statue of the commander in "Don Gio-
vanni," the young Virginian conceived an idea as bold as it was
original. It was difficult to crawl along the narrow ledge without falling into the black gulf below, and it was questionable
whether any friendly water-pipe would enable him to "flank"
the sentinel at the opposite extremity of the bridge. Why not
"fall in" in the darkness with the unsuspecting detachment, pass
*through* the guard beyond, and then take the chances of making
his escape? His resolution was at once taken; and as the guard
came opposite his place of concealment behind the low wood-
work of the railing, he crouched lower, waited until they had
passed, and then quietly stepping over a railing, fell in behind.
The movement had been undiscovered; he was now advancing
with measured step to "assist," as the French say, at relieving the
"Old Guard" on the bridges—himself an honorary member of
the relief.

His *ruse* was crowned with complete success. He passed with
the detachment undiscovered to a point beyond the bridge; and
then stepping from the ranks—a manœuvre which the pitch darkness rendered by no means difficult—he concealed himself until the unsuspecting Federals disappeared. He then crawled on
his hands and knees, crouching close to the ground by another
picket which he saw upon the road, and reaching a point where
he believed himself beyond range, rose to his feet and commenced moving. All at once he saw before him another picket-
fire; and not knowing whether it was that of friends or enemies,
he again crouched down and slowly approached the fire, crawl-
ing upon his chest along the surface of the ground.

He had succeeded too well up to this time to risk anything;
and he accordingly continued to "snake along" toward the fire,
in order to discover, before making himself known, whether the

ground around it were friends or enemies. In this slow and cautious manner he approached until he was within ten yards of it; where, hidden behind a stump, he attentively reconnoitred. The result was indecisive. He could not possibly succeed in discovering whether the pickets were Federal or Confederate; and in relating his adventure afterwards, Lieutenant W—— declared that his heart now throbbed with greater anxiety than at any other time during the whole affair. He continued for some time thus crouching behind the stump, and his doubt was painful and protracted. At last it came to an end; he breathed freely again. One of the men rose from the ground, yawned, and said: "I don't believe there will be a Yankee on this side of the river by the morning."

Whereupon Lieutenant W—— rose up, approached the fire, and with a laugh, made himself known, to the profound astonishment and confusion of the sleepy pickets, who had thus received a practical illustration of the ease with which an enemy might approach and send a bullet through their hearts. They, however, received Lieutenant W—— with military hospitality, gave him a portion of their rations, divided their blankets; and overcome with fatigue, he lay down and slept until daylight. Before sunrise he was at General Stuart's headquarters, and was relating his curious adventure, to the huge amusement of the laughing cavalier. He was without horse, arms, or other clothes than those which he wore; but he was free, and he had his spurs, carried throughout against his naked breast.

Such was the adventure of Lieutenant W——, and such the means he used in making his escape. The narrative may appear romantic, but I assure the reader that it is literally true.

# VII

## To Gettysburg and Back Again

### I.

"Ho! for the Valley!"

This was the somewhat dramatic exclamation of Major-General J. E. B. Stuart, about the 24th of June, 1863, as he got into the saddle at the little village of Rector's Cross-Roads, between Middleburg and Upperville, and turned his horse's head westward toward the Blue Ridge mountains.

If the worthy reader will return in memory to that epoch, and recall the route which the gay cavalier speedily directed his column over, the words above quoted will appear somewhat mysterious. "The situation" at the moment may be described in a very few words; for the full record, see the "historian of the future." After the crushing defeat of Chancellorsville, General Hooker cut behind him the pontoons covered with pine boughs, to deaden the noise of his artillery wheels in crossing, and took up a strong position on the northern bank of the Rappahannock to repulse the expected onslaught of his great adversary, Lee. No such attack, however, was intended. Lee preferred to manœuvre his opponent out of Virginia—it was the more bloodless proceeding—and very soon the soldiers of the army understood that "Lee was moving."

A grand review of the cavalry was ordered, near Culpeper Court-House, and General Fitz Lee politely sent an invitation to General Hood to attend it, and "bring any of his friends." A day or two afterwards, Hood appeared with his great division, announcing that these were all "his friends," and he thought he would bring them along. The review duly took place east of the Court-House. The squadrons of cavalry charged—General Stuart and his staff in front; cannon thundered in mimic conflict; the sun shone; bright eyes flashed; and beneath the Confederate banner, rippling on its lofty pole, the Commander-in-Chief sat his iron-gray, looking on. Festivities at the Court-House followed; the youngsters of the army had a gay dance with the young ladies from the country round; and almost in the midst of the revelry, as at Brussels on the night of Waterloo, the thunder of artillery was heard from the direction of Fleetwood Hill, near Brandy. In fact, Stuart had been assailed there by the *élite* of the Federal infantry and cavalry, under some of their ablest commanders—the object of the enemy being to ascertain, by reconnoissance in force, what all the hubbub of the review signified—and throughout the long June day, they threw themselves, with desperate gallantry, against the Southern horse—no infantry on our side taking part in the action. Colonel Williams was killed; Captain Farley, of Stuart's staff, was killed; Captain White, of the staff, too, was wounded; Colonel Butler was wounded; General W. H. F. Lee was shot down at the head of his charging column; and Stuart himself was more than once completely surrounded. For three hours the battle was "touch and go;" but thanks to the daring charges of Young and Lee, the enemy were driven; they slowly and sullenly retired, leaving the ground strewed with their dead, and at nightfall were again beyond the Rappahannock.

The trumpet of battle had thus been sounded; action followed. Lee put his columns in motion for Pennsylvania; Stuart advanced with his cavalry to hold the country east of the Blue Ridge, and guard the passes as the long column moved through; and then commenced a war of the giants between the opposing horse of the Federal and Confederate armies. It was a matter of grave importance that Hooker should undo the designs of Lee; and mighty efforts were made to burst through the cavalry cordon, and strike the flank of the moving army. Stuart was, however, in the way. On all the roads was his omnipresent cav-

alry, under the daring Hampton, Fitz Lee, the gay and gallant
cavalier, and others as resolute. Everywhere the advance of the
enemy's cavalry was met and driven back, until about the twentieth of June. Then a conclusive trial of strength took place. A
grand reconnoitring force, composed of a division of infantry
under General Birney, I believe, and several divisions of cavalry, with full supports of artillery, was pushed forward from
Aldie; Stuart was assailed simultaneously along about fifteen
miles of front; and in spite of his most strenuous efforts, he was
forced slowly to fall back toward the Ridge. This was one of
the most stubborn conflicts of the war; and on every hill, from
the summit of every knoll, Stuart fought with artillery, cavalry,
and dismounted sharpshooters, doggedly struggling to hold his
ground. The attempt was vain. Behind the heavy lines of Federal skirmishers advanced their dense columns of cavalry; behind
the cavalry were seen the bristling bayonets of their infantry;
from the right, the left, and the front, thundered their excellently served artillery. Stuart was pushed from hill to hill, the
enemy came on mile after mile, and at Upperville a great disaster
seemed imminent. The Federal forces closed in on front and
flanks, made a desperate attack with the sabre, and the result
seemed about to be decided. Stuart was in the very hottest of
the press, sword in hand, determined evidently to repulse the
enemy or die, and his black feather was the mark of a hundred
pistol-balls—his rich uniform clearly indicating his rank to the
Federal troopers almost in contact with him. This was the depressing situation of affairs—the centre driven, and the column
on the Bloomfield road falling rapidly back on the left, thus
exposing the main body to imminent danger of being cut off,
when the *Deus ex machinâ* appeared in the person of Wade
Hampton. That good cavalier saw the crisis, formed his column
under the heavy fire, and taking command in person, went at
them with the sabre, scarcely firing a shot. The result was that
the Federal line was swept back, the *élite* of the charging force
put *hors du combat* by the edge of the sabre, and the Southern
column fell back toward Paris, in the mouth of Ashby's Gap,
without further difficulty.

The enemy had accomplished their object, and they had not accomplished it. Stuart was forced to retire, but they had not succeeded in penetrating to the Ridge. No doubt the presence of infantry there was discovered or suspected, but otherwise the great reconnoissance was unproductive of substantial results.

On the same night they retired. Stuart followed them at dawn with his whole force; and by mid-day he was in possession of Middleburg, several miles in advance of his position on the day before.

Such was the quick work of these two days.

## II.

It was about three days after these events that Stuart sprang with a gay laugh to saddle, turned his horse's head *westward*, and uttered that exclamation:

"Ho! for the Valley!"

Now, if the reader will permit, I beg to descend from the lofty heights of historic summary to the level champaign of my personal observations and adventures. From the heights alluded to, you see a long distance, and distinguish the "important events" in grand outline; but in the level you are greeted by more of the *colouring* of what occurs. In this paper I design recording some scenes and incidents as they passed before my own eyes, rather than to sum up *facts* in "official" form. A memoir rather than a history is intended; and as a human being can only remember what he has seen and felt, the present writer —even at the risk of being charged with egotism—is going to confine himself, as closely as possible, to his own adventures and *impressions de voyage*.

"Ho for the Valley!" was a truly delightful exclamation to me. Bright eyes of various colours shone there by the Shenandoah and Opequon; there were some voices whose music I had not heard for a long time. The prospect now of seeing the eyes, and hearing the voices, banished every other thought, even the remembrance of that heavy misfortune of having had my military satchel, with all I possessed in the way of a wardrobe, cap-

tured by the enemy a few days before when they drove us from
the Cross-Roads. There could certainly be no doubt about the
General's meaning. He had turned his horse toward the Ridge.
"Ho! for the Valley!" indicated his intended line of march;
he, like myself, was going to see his good friends all in that
land of lands along the Shenandoah.

Alas! and whenever the pithy word is employed by a writer,
the reader knows what he has to expect. General Stuart had
scarcely got out of sight of the village, carolling a gay song as
he rode, when the disconsolate staff-officer beside him observed
a movement of the General's left rein; his horse cleared a fence;
and ten minutes afterwards he was riding rapidly *eastward*, in
a direction precisely opposite to the Blue Ridge. The General
had practised a little *ruse* to blind the eyes of the Cross-Roads
villagers—was doubling on the track; he was going after General Hooker, then in the vicinity of Manassas, and thence—
whither?

We bivouacked by the roadside under some pines that night,
advanced before dawn, drove a detachment of the enemy from
Glasscock's Gap, in the Bull Run mountain, and pushed on to
cut off any force which lingered in the gorge of Thoroughfare
Gap. When cavalry undertake to cut off infantry, the process
is exciting, but not uniformly remunerative. It was the rear of
Hancock's corps which we struck not far from Haymarket;
there, passing rapidly toward Manassas, about eight hundred
yards off, were the long lines of wagons and artillery; and behind these came on the dense blue masses of infantry, the sunshine lighting up their burnished bayonets.

Stuart hastened forward his artillery; it opened instantly upon
the infantry, and the first shot crashed into a caisson, making
the horses rear and run; the infantry line bending backward
as though the projectile had struck it. This "good shot" highly
delighted the General, who turned round laughing, and called
attention to the accuracy of the fire. The individual addressed
laughed in response, but replied, "Look out, though; they are
going to enfilade you from that hill on the right, General." "Oh!
I reckon not," responded the General; but he had scarcely

spoken when a puff of white smoke rose from the wooded knoll in question, and a shot screamed by, just grazing the top of one of our caissons near the guns. This was followed by another and another; the enemy were seen hastily forming line, and advancing sharpshooters; whereupon Stuart ordered back his guns, and dismounted cavalry to meet them.

A running fight; enemy merely holding their flank intact; soon the line had passed on and disappeared; the cavalry saw vanish safely all those tantalizing wagons filled with good, rich forage, and who knew what beside. Stuart meanwhile had sent off Mosby, with a party of picked men, to reconnoitre, and was sleeping with his head upon an officer's breast—to the very extreme discomfort of that personage, whose profound respect for his sleepy military superior prevented him from changing his position.

With night came rain, and the General and his staff were invited to the handsome mansion of Dr. ——, near Bucklands, where all slept under cover but Stuart. Everywhere he insisted on faring like his men; and I well remember the direction given to his body-servant a few days before, to spread his blankets under a tree on a black and stormy night with the rain descending in torrents—the house in which he had established his headquarters being only twenty paces from the tree. On this night at Bucklands he repeated the ceremony, but a gay supper preceded it.

That supper is one of the pleasant memories the present writer has of the late war. How the good companions laughed and devoured the viands of the hospitable host! How the beautiful girls of the family stood with mock submission, servant-wise, behind the chairs, and waited on the guests with their sweetest smiles, until that reversal of all the laws of the universe became a perfect comedy, and ended in an *éclat* of laughter! General and staff waited in turn on the waiters; and when the tired troopers fell asleep on the floor of the portico, it is certain that a number of bright eyes shone in their dreams. Such is the occasional comedy which lights up the tragedy of war.

The bugle sounded; we got into the saddle again; the columns moved; and that evening we had passed around Manassas, where Hooker's rear force still lingered, and were approaching Fairfax Station through the great deserted camps near Wolf Run Shoals. The advance pushed on through the wild and desolate locality, swarming with abandoned cabins and army *débris*; and soon we had reached the station, which is not far from the Court-House.

Here took place a little incident, known afterwards among the present writer's friends as the "Cherry-Pie Breakfast." A brief notice of this historic occurrence may entertain the reader. Three members of the staff and a young courier left the column to seek a blacksmith, whose services were needed; and the house of this worthy was found about half a mile east of the station. He was a friend of the gray, prompt and courteous, and soon was busy at the hoofs of the horses; his good wife meanwhile getting breakfast for the party. It was speedily served, and consisted of every delicacy—bread of all descriptions, fresh butter, yellow cream, sweetmeats, real coffee, then an extreme luxury, and some cherry pies, which caused the wandering staff officers to break forth into exclamations of rapture. A heavy attack was made upon all, and our "bluebird" friends themselves, fond as they are said to be of the edible, could not have surpassed the devotion exhibited toward the cherry pies. At the end of the repast one of the party, in the enthusiasm of the moment, piled up several pieces of the pie, drew out his purse, and determined to carry off the whole for future consumption; whereat a friendly contest occurred between himself and the excellent dame, who could not be induced to receive pay from any member of the party for her entertainment. "She had never charged a Confederate soldier a cent, and never meant to."

All this was peaceful and pleasing; but all at once there was a stir in the yard, and without securing the pie, we went out. Lo! a gentleman in a blue coat and mounted was seen rapidly approaching below the house, followed by others.

"Look out!" said Major V——; "there are the Yankees!"

"They are running by—they won't stop. What are you going to do?" I said.

"I am going to put the bridle on my horse!"

And the Major bridled up and mounted rapidly.

"Well, I am going to wait to have the shoes put on mine."

Idle and absurd intent! Even as I spoke, the party scattered, Major V—— galloping to the right, Major Mc—— to the left, with the courier. A single glance revealed the "situation." Another party of blue-coats were rushing at full gallop toward the house from above. Shot suddenly resounded. "Hi! hi! halt!" followed; and I had just time to mount and pass at full speed across the front of the party, pursued by more shots and "hi-hi's!" Admire, reader, the spectacle of the stampeded staff officers! My friend in front resembled the worthy Gilpin, with a pistol holster for the jug—his horse's tail "floating free," and every nail in the hind shoes of the animal visible as he darted headlong toward the protecting woods! We plunged through a swamp, jumped fences and fallen trees, and reaching the forest-cover, penetrated a thicket, and stopped to listen. The shouts died away; no sound of hoofs came, and doubling back, we came again to the station to find the meaning of everything. Stuart had been quietly waiting there for his column, with the bridle out of his horse's mouth, in order that the animal might champ some "Yankee oats," when all at once a scouting-party had come at full gallop from the direction of the Court-House. Before he was aware of their approach, they were nearly upon him; he had just had time to escape by seizing the halter and digging the spurs into his horse.

Then the scouting party, finding the size of the hornets' nest into which they had leaped, turned their horses' heads eastward, bore down on the blacksmith's whither we had gone, interrupted the "cherry-pie breakfast," and vanished toward Sanxter's, chasing Major V—— until he came up with Munford. When our probable capture was announced to General Stuart, and a squadron requested for our recovery, I am sorry to say that the General responded with a laugh, "Oh! they are too intelligent to be caught!" and when the incident of the abandonment of the cherry-pie was related to Stuart, he enjoyed it in a remarkable degree!

Do you remember still, my dear companions, that good cherry-pie breakfast, the chase which followed, and the laughter of Stuart? That was a jovial trip we made across the border in the good year 1863; and the days and nights were full of incident and adventure. Do you find the present year, 1866, as "gay and happy" as its predecessor? I do not.

## III.

Our mishap above related was truly unfortunate. It gave the advance-guard the start, and when we reached Fairfax Court-House, they had rifled the public store-houses and sutlers' shops of their entire contents.

It was impossible to forbear from laughing at the spectacle which the cavalry column presented. Every man had on a white straw hat, and a pair of snowy cotton gloves. Every trooper carried before him upon the pommel of his saddle a bale of smoking tobacco, or a drum of figs; every hand grasped a pile of ginger-cakes, which were rapidly disappearing. But hospitality to the rear-guard was the order of the day. We did not suffer. The mishaps of my comrades and myself had in some manner become known, and we were greeted with shouts of laughter, but with soldierly generosity too. Every hand proffered a straw hat of the most elegant pattern, or a pair of gloves as white as the driven snow. Every comrade held out his figs, pressed on his cakes, or begged us to try his smoking tobacco—which I am compelled to say was truly detestable.

Such was the gay scene at Fairfax Court-House when Stuart entered the place.

The cavalry did not stop long. Soon the column was again moving steadily towards the Potomac, intelligence having arrived that General Hooker's main body had passed that river at Leesburg. What would Stuart do—what route would he now follow? There were few persons, if any, in the entire command, who could reply to that question. Cross at Leesburg? To merely follow up Hooker while Hooker followed up Lee, was very unlike Stuart. Strike across for the Blue Ridge, and cross at

Shepherdstown? That would lose an immense amount of invaluable time and horse-flesh. Cross below Leesburg? That seemed impossible with the artillery, and difficult even for cavalry. The river was broad, deep, with a rocky and uneven bed; and so confident were the enemy of the impossibility of our crossing there, that not a picket watched the stream.

Stuart's design was soon developed. We reached at nightfall an elevation not far from the Great Falls—the spot laid down on the maps at Matildaville, or near it—Stuart riding with staff and advance guard far in front. The latter pushed on—the rest stopping—when all at once shots came from the front, and Stuart called out cheerily to the staff: "Look out! Here they come! Give it to them with pistols!" The bang of carbines followed: a squadron hastened to the front, and opened fire; and in the midst of it Stuart said, "Tell Hampton—you can follow his trail —that Chambliss is up, and Fitz Lee coming." The "trail" was plain in the moonlight; I followed it; and reaching the Potomac just above the Falls, found Hampton *crossing.*

The spectacle was picturesque. The broad river glittered in the moon, and on the bright surface was seen the long, wavering line of dark figures, moving "in single file;" the water washing to and fro across the backs of the horses, which kept their feet with difficulty. The hardest portion of the task was crossing the cannon of the horse-artillery. It seemed impossible to get the limbers and caissons over without wetting, and so destroying the ammunition; but the ready brain of Stuart found an expedient. The boxes were quickly unpacked; every cavalry-man took charge of a shell, case, or solid shot with the fixed cartridge; and thus held well aloft, the precious freight was carried over dry. Once on the other side, the shell-bearers deposited the ammunition on the beach; it was repacked in the caissons, which had been dragged by the plunging horses over the rocky bed in safety; the guns followed; the artillery was over!

At Hanovertown, in Pennsylvania, two or three days afterwards, the cavalry did not by any means regret the trouble they had been put to in carrying over that ammunition "dry shod." Breathed thundered with it from the heights, and with shell after shell broke the heavy line advancing to the assault. Never was thunder sweeter and more musical! But I anticipate.

The river was crossed; also the Chesapeake and Ohio canal, by a narrow bridge; and the cavalry halted for brief rest—the General and staff receiving open-handed hospitality from Mr. —— and his family; those guardian angels of the soldier, the ladies, staying up all night to wait upon the weary gray-backs, and give them food.

The column moved at dawn toward the "undiscovered land" of Star-and-Stripe-dom, in a northern direction, toward Rockville. It was not long before we came on the blue people. "Bang! bang! bang!" indicated that the advance guard was charging a picket; the shots ended; we pushed on, passing some dead or wounded forms, bleeding by the grassy roadside; and the town of Rockville came in sight. The present writer pushed on after the advance guard, which had galloped through, and riding *solus* along a handsome street, came suddenly upon a spectacle which was truly pleasing. This was a seminary for young ladies, with open windows, open doors—and doors and windows were full and running over with the fairest specimens of the gentler sex that eye ever beheld. It was Sunday, and the beautiful girls in their fresh gaily coloured dresses, low necks, bare arms, and wildernesses of braids and curls, were "off duty" for the moment, and burning with enthusiasm to welcome the Southerner; for Rockville, in radical parlance, was a "vile secesh hole." Every eye flashed, every voice exclaimed; every rosy lip laughed; every fair hand waved a handkerchief or a sheet of music (smuggled) with crossed Confederate flags upon the cover. The whole façade of the building was a tulip-bed of brilliant colours, more brilliant eyes, and joy and welcome!

Pardon, friend, if you are of the "other faction," this little burst of enthusiasm, as I remember Rockville on that gay June morning. Pleasant it is in the dull hours of to-day to recall that scene; and the bright eyes flash once more, the laughter again sounds!

As the present historian drew near, riding as aforesaid, ahead of his commander, a beautiful girl of about sixteen rushed forth from the portico, pirouetting and clapping her hands in an ecstasy at the sight of the gray uniform, exclaiming, "Oh! here is one of General Stuart's Aides!" and finished by pulling some hair from the mane of my calm and philosophic old war-horse, on the expressly stated ground that he was "a Secession horse!" Then General Stuart approached with his column—gay, laughing, his blue eyes under the black feather full of the joy of the soldier; and a wild welcome greeted him. The scene was one which beggars description, and it remains in my memory to-day as clearly as though cut deep in "monumental alabaster." Sweet faces, with the beautiful welcoming eyes, and smiling lips! an ex-rebel—he who writes this page—takes off his hat and bows low to you, saluting you as the pearls of loveliness and goodness!

## IV.

Stuart did not tarry. In war there is little time for gallant words, and news had just reached us from the front which moved the column on like the sound of the bugle.

This news was, that while we approached Rockville from the south, a mighty train of nearly two hundred wagons—new, fresh-painted, drawn each by six sleek mules, as became the "Reserve Forage Train" of the Department at Washington—had in like manner approached from the east, intent on collecting forage. The rumour of the dread vicinity of the graybacks had come to them, however, blown on the wind; the column of wagons had instantly "counter-marched" in the opposite direction; they were now thundering at full gallop back toward Washington, pursued by the advance guard.

Stuart's face flushed at the thought of capturing this splendid prize; and shouting to a squadron to follow him, and the main column to push on, he went at a swift gallop on the track of the fleeing wagons.

Soon we came up with them, and then commenced an indescribably grotesque scene. The immense train was seen covering the road for miles. Every team in full gallop, every wagon whirling onward, rebounding from rocks, and darting into the air,—one crashing against another "with the noise of thunder"—here one overturned, and lying with wheels upward, the mules struggling and kicking in the harness; then one toppling over a steep bank, and falling with a loud crash: others burning, others still dashing for shelter to the woods,—the drivers cursing, yelling, lashing, blaspheming, howling amid the bang of carbines, the clatter of hoofs, and cries of "Halt! halt! halt!"

Stuart burst into laughter, and turning round, exclaimed: "Did you ever see anything like that in all your life!" And I certainly never had. The grotesque ruled; the mules seemed wilder than the drivers. They had been cut by the score from the over-turned wagons, and now ran in every direction, kicking up at every step, sending their shrill cries upon the air, and presenting a spectacle so ludicrous that a huge burst of "Olympian laughter" echoed from end to end of the turnpike.

Soon they were all stopped, captured, and driven to the rear by the aforesaid cursing drivers, now sullen, or laughing like the captors. All but those overturned. These were set on fire, and soon there rose for miles along the road the red glare of flames, and the dense smoke of the burning vehicles. They had been pursued within sight of Washington, and I saw, I believe, the dome of the capitol. That spectacle was exciting—and General Stuart thought of pushing on to make a demonstration against the defences. This, however, was given up; and between the flames of the burning wagons we pushed back to Rockville, through which the long line of captured vehicles, with their sleek, rosetted mules, six to each, had already defiled, amid the shouts of the inhabitants. Those thus "saved" were about one hundred in number.

The column moved, and about ten that night reached Brook-ville, where the atmosphere seemed Southern, like that of Rock-ville, for a bevy of beautiful girls thronged forth with baskets of cakes, and bread and meat, and huge pitchers of ice-water—penetrating fearlessly the press of trampling hoofs and minister-ing to the necessities of the rebels with undisguised satisfaction. If the fair girl living in the handsome mansion below Mr. Hamilton's, remembers still to whom she insisted upon presenting nine cups of coffee with every delicacy, the rebel in question begs to assure her of his continued gratitude for her kindness. At Brookville some hundreds of prisoners—the greater part captured by General Wickham in a boat at the Potomac—were paroled and started for Washington, as an act of humanity.

At one o'clock in the morning Stuart mounted and moved on, speedily falling asleep in the saddle, and tottering from side to side. In this he was not alone; and I remember the laughable spectacle of Major M——, sitting grave, erect, and motionless upon his horse in front of a country store by the roadside, to which the animal had made his way and halted. The Major seemed to be waiting—for somebody, or something—meanwhile he was snoring. Moving steadily on, the column approached Westminster, and here Fitz Lee, who was in advance, found the enemy drawn up in the street awaiting him. A charge quickly followed, carbines banged, and the enemy gave way—but we left behind, lying dead by the roadside, Lieutenants Murray and Gibson, two of our best officers, shot dead in the skirmish. The enemy were pursued at full gallop through the town, to their camp on the heights to the west; the camp was taken with all its contents—and the bugles of Fitz Lee, sounding on the wind from the breezy upland, told that he had driven the Federal cavalry before him. Westminster was ours.

Stuart took possession, but was not greeted with much cordiality. Friends, and warm ones, met us, but they had a "hacked" demeanour, and many of them spoke under their breath. Westminster was evidently "Union," but some families warmly welcomed us—others scowled. The net results of the capture of the place were—one old dismounted gun of the "Quaker" order on a hill near the cavalry camp aforesaid, and a United States flag taken from the vault of the Court-House, with the names of the ladies who had made it worked across each star. What became of this I do not know. We left the town that night, bivouacked in the rain by the roadside, pushed on at dawn, and were soon in Pennsylvania, where details were immediately sent out to seize horses. These, as I saw them pass in great numbers, were large, fat, sleek, and apparently excellent. I was not long, however, in discovering that they were worthless as riding-horses; one of the thin, wiry, rawboned Virginia horses, half the weight of these Conestogas, would wear out a dozen. One had "blood," the other had not—and blood will tell.

We were enemies here, but woman, the angelic, still suc-coured us; woman, without shoes or stockings often, and speak-ing Dutch, but no less hospitable. One of them presented me with coffee, bread spread with "apple-butter"—and smiles. I don't think the Mynheers found the gray people very fierce and bloody. The horses were appropriated; but beyond that nothing—the very necks of the chickens went unwrung.

The column was in high glee thus far, and the men were rapidly receiving "remounts." No enemy approached—your old soldier never very bitterly laments that circumstance; but all at once as we approached Hanovertown, we stirred up the hornets. Chambliss—that brave soul who afterwards fell heroically fight-ing in Charles City—at the head of the Ninth Virginia drove in their pickets; and he had just swept on down the heights toward the town, whose steeples shone before us nestling beneath the mountain, when Stuart in person rode up rapidly.

"Well, General," I said, "Chambliss has driven them, and is going right on."

"Good!" was Stuart's reply. "Tell him to push on and occupy the town, but not to pursue them too far."

These words were impressed upon my memory by the sequel, which laughably but very disagreeably reversed the General's expectations. Hastening down the declivity with the order for Chambliss, I found him advancing rapidly in column of fours to charge the enemy, who were drawn up in the outskirts of the town. Before he could issue the order it was rendered somewhat nugatory by the blue people in front. We had supposed their force to be small, but it was now seen to be heavy. They swarmed everywhere, right, left, and front; rapidly formed line of battle, and delivering a sharp volley at short range in the faces of the Confederates, made a gallant and headlong charge.

The result made it unnecessary to warn the men not to "pursue too far." They met the charge sabre to sabre; a hot conflict ensued, but the enemy pressing on with unbroken front in heavy force, the Ninth fell back in good order to the higher ground in their rear, keeping off the assailants at the edge of the sabre. The road over which they made this "retrograde" was narrow, and the *mêlée* of trampling hoofs, shouts, and sabre-cuts, was more exciting than amusing. Men fell all around before the fire of the excellent Spencer rifles of the enemy; and while gallantly rallying the men, Captain John Lee was shot through the arm. To add to the disagreeable character of the situation, I now observed General Stuart in person, and unattended, coming across the field to the right at full gallop, pursued by a detachment of cavalry who fired on him as they came, and as I reached his side his face was stormy, his voice irate.

"Have the artillery put in position yonder on the road; tell it to open!" was his brief order.

And in a few minutes it was hurried forward, and opened fire. Returning to the field in which I had left the General, I found him the second time "falling back" before a hotter pursuit than the first. The Federal cavalry-men, about a company, were nigh upon him as he galloped across the field; shots whistled; orders to halt resounded; but it may be understood that it was inconvenient to comply. We went on headlong, leaped a tremendous ravine with the enemy almost in contact, and following a friendly lane where the rails were down, reached the slope where the artillery had just opened its thunders.

This checked the enemy's further advance, and Hampton having opened on the right, things settled down somewhat. We had evidently waked up a real hornets' nest, however. Long columns of blue cavalry were seen defiling down the mountain, and advancing to the front, and a heavy force was observed closing in on the left. All at once the edge of the town swarmed with blue figures; a heavy line was seen advancing, and soon this line pushed on with cheers, to charge the artillery on the heights.

Breathed replied by opening upon them with shell and canister. The first shell burst in the line; the second near the first; and the third made it waver. A more rapid fire succeeded; everything depended upon these few moments, and then the line was seen slowly retiring. At the same instant intelligence came that the force on the left was Fitz Lee, who had come in on that flank; and the continuous thunder of Hampton on the right showed plainly that in that direction all was well. This advance of the Federal sharpshooters was one of the finest sights I ever beheld; and at one moment I thought Breathed's guns would never leave that field of tall rye where they were vomiting fire and smoke—under the command of this gallant Major at least. Whether this historian also would succeed in retiring without capture seemed equally doubtful, as he had mounted a huge Conestoga—fat, sleek, elephantine, and unwieldy—a philosophic animal who stood unmoved by the cannon, never blinking at the discharges, and appeared superior to all the excitements of the moment. Breathed's fire, however, repulsed the charge; and as night drew on, Stuart set his column in motion—the wagons in the centre—toward Jefferson. One ludicrous scene at that moment I perfectly remember. A fat Dutchman who had been lounging about, and reconnoitring the strength, etc., of the Confederate force, was regarded as too well informed to be left behind with the enemy; and this worthy was accordingly requested to "come along" on the back of a huge Conestoga. This request he treated with calm disregard, when a cavalry-man made a tremendous blow at him, which caused him to mount in hot haste, with only a halter to guide his elephant. He had no sooner done so than the Conestoga ran off, descended the slope at full speed, bounded elephant-wise over an enormous ditch— and it was only by clinging close with knees and hands that the Dutchman kept his seat. Altogether, the spectacle was one to tickle the ribs of death. The last I saw of the captive, he was in the very centre of the cavalry column, which was moving at a trot, and he was swept on with it; passing away for ever from the eyes of this historian, who knows not what became of him thereafter.

The sun began to decline now, and we rode, rode, rode—the

long train of wagons strung out to infinity, it seemed. At dark the little village of Jefferson was reached—of which metropolis I recall but one souvenir. This was a pretty Dutch girl, who seemed not at all hostile to the gray people, and who willingly prepared me an excellent supper of hot bread, milk, coffee, and eggs fried temptingly with bacon. She could not speak English —she could only look amiable, smile, and murmur unintelligible words in an unknown language. I am sorry to say, that I do not recall the supper with a satisfaction as unalloyed. I was sent by the General to pass somebody through his pickets, and on my return discovered that I was the victim of a cruel misfortune. The young hostess had placed my supper on a table in a small apartment, in which a side door opened on the street; through this some felonious personage had entered—hot bread, milk, coffee, eggs, and ham, had vanished down some hungry cavalry- man's throat.

Mounting despondingly, I followed the column, which had again begun to move, and soon reached the village of New Salem.

## V.

It was nearly midnight when we arrived at this small village; and, to continue my own personal recollections, the village tav- ern appeared to present a favourable opportunity to redeem my misfortune at Jefferson.

It was proposed, accordingly, to the General that he should stop there and procure some coffee, of which he was very fond —and as he acceded to this cheerfully, I applied to the burly landlord, who responded encouragingly. In a quarter of an hour the coffee was ready; also some excellent ale; also some bread and the inseparable "apple butter," or "spreading," as the Penn- sylvanians call this edible. When General Stuart had emptied his coffee-cup—which always put the stout cavalier in a gay humour —he laughed, mounted his horse, and said to me:

"By the by, suppose you stay here until Hampton comes along; I am going on with Fitz Lee. Tell Hampton to move on steadily on the road to Dover, and show him the way."

With these words, the General rode away on the track of General Fitz Lee, and the present writer was left *solus*, to "hold the position alone" at Salem. This position, it speedily appeared, was not wholly desirable. The advance division under Lee had pushed on several miles ahead—there was not a single cavalryman beside myself in Salem—and Hampton was several miles behind. To add to the charms of the "situation," there were a number of extremely cut-throat looking individuals of the "other faction" lounging about the porch, eyeing the lonely Confederate askance, and calculating apparently the chance of "suppressing" him without danger—and the individual in this disagreeable situation was nearly dead for want of sleep.

There appeared, however, to be very little real hostility—such as I imagine would have been exhibited by the inhabitants of a Southern village had an officer of the U. S. army been left behind under similar circumstances. Doubtless the hangers-on were impressed with the conviction that in case the wandering staff-officer did not rejoin his command, General Stuart would return to look for him, torch in hand, when the village of New Salem would make its exit in a bonfire. The portly landlord, especially, appeared to be a real philosopher; and when asked the meaning of a distant noise, replied with a laugh, "Some of your people tearing up the railroad, I guess!"

In spite of the worthy's strong coffee and the unpleasing expression of eye in the crowd around, I was just dropping asleep in my chair on the porch, when the clatter of hoofs resounded, and the voice of General Hampton was heard in the darkness, asking if there .was any one there to direct him. This sound aroused me, and in a few moments I was riding with the brave cavalier at the head of his column toward Dover. Toward dawn General Hampton halted, and I asked if he was going to stop.

"Yes, for a little while—I am perishing for sleep."

And with these words the General proceeded to a haystack near the road, pulled down some of the hay, wrapped himself in his cape, and in a few minutes was fast asleep—his companion exactly imitating him.

At daylight we reached the straggling little village of Dover, where more prisoners were paroled; thence proceeded through a fine country towards Carlisle; at Dillstown procured dinner from the landlord of the principal tavern, a philosophic Mr. Miller, whose walls were covered with pictures of black trotters in skeleton conveyances, making rapid time; and at night reached Carlisle, which General Stuart immediately summoned to surrender by flag of truce.

The reply to this was a flat refusal from General Smith; and soon a Whitworth gun in the town opened, and the Southern guns replied. This continued for an hour or two, when the U. S. barracks were fired, and the light fell magnificently upon the spires of the city, presenting an exquisite spectacle.

Meanwhile, the men were falling asleep around the guns, and the present writer slept very soundly within ten feet of a battery hotly firing. Major R—— leaned against a fence within a few paces of a howitzer in process of rapid discharge, and in that upright position "forgot his troubles." The best example, however, was one which General Stuart mentioned. He saw a man climb a fence, put one leg over, and in that position drop asleep!

Any further assault upon Carlisle was stopped by a very simple circumstance. General Lee sent for the cavalry. He had recalled Early from York; moved with his main column east of the South Mountain, toward the village of Gettysburg; and Stuart was wanted. In fact, during the afternoon of our advance to Carlisle—the first of July—the artillery fire of the "first day's fight" was heard, and referring to Lloyd's map, I supposed it to be at Gettysburg, a place of which I had no knowledge. How unexpected was the concentration of the great opposing forces there, will appear from General Stuart's reply, "I reckon not," when the firing was spoken of as "near Gettysburg." No one then anticipated a battle there—Generals Lee and Meade almost as little as the rest.

In spite of the broken-down condition of his command, Stuart moved at once—and whole columns went to sleep in the saddle. Pennsylvania had so far proved to us a veritable "Land of Drowsy-head!"

This night march was the most severe I ever experienced. The long succession of sleepless nights had prostrated the strongest, and General Stuart and his staff moving without escort on the Willstown road, passed over mile after mile asleep in the saddle. At dawn, the General dismounted in a clump of trees by the roadside; said, "I am going to sleep two hours;" and wrapping himself in his cape simply leaned against a tree and was immediately asleep. Everybody imitated him, and I was awakened by the voice of one of the couriers, who informed me that "the General was gone." Such was the fact—Stuart had risen punctually at the end of the two hours, stretched himself, mounted, and ridden on *solus*, a wandering Major-General in the heart of Pennsylvania! In the afternoon the cavalry were at Gettysburg.


## VI.

General Stuart arrived with his cavalry on the evening of the "second day's fight" at Gettysburg, and took position on the left of Ewell, whose command composed the left wing of the army.

All Stuart's energies were now bent to acquire an accurate idea of the ground, and hold the left against the enemy's horse, who were active and enterprising. In reconnoitring their position on the railroad, he was suddenly fired upon at close quarters —the bullets passing in dangerous proximity—and having thus satisfied himself of the enemy's whereabouts, the General returned to his impromptu headquarters, namely a tree on the side of the Heidelburg road, about a mile from the town. Meanwhile we had learned the particulars of the two hard fights—A. P. Hill's on the evening of the first of July; and Longstreet's on the second, when he made that desperate flank attack on the enemy's left at Round Top. It is easy to see, now, that this assault was the turning point of the tremendous struggle. For thirty minutes the issue hung suspended in the balances, and there is some truth in the rhetorical flourish of a Northern verse writer, to the effect that "the century reeled," when Longstreet paused on the brow of the hill. Had he gained possession of the Round Top, General Meade's line would have been taken in flank and reverse; he would doubtless have been forced to fall back to another position; this would have been undertaken under the fire of the Southern cannon and muskets; and once in motion it is doubtful if the U. S. army could have been brought up to a new struggle. If not, Baltimore and Washington would speedily have been occupied by the Southern forces—the result of which would probably have been peace.

But this is a long digression from the cavalry operations. The "third day" dawned; Stuart took post with his cavalry on the extreme right and rear of the Federal forces—and the thunder opened. We could only hear the battle, not see it. The Federal cavalry kept us quite busy. It was handled here with skill and gallantry—the heavy lines were seen to form, the officers galloping up and down; three measured cheers were given by the men, apparently by formal military order, they were so regular; then the bugle sounded, and the blue horsemen came on shaking the ground with their trampling hoofs. The struggle was bitter and determined, but brief. For a moment the air was full of flashing sabres and pistol smoke, and a wild uproar deafened the ears; then the Federal horse gave back, pursued by their opponents. We lost many good men, however; among the rest, General Hampton was shot in the side, and nearly cut out of the saddle by a sabre stroke. Ten minutes before I had conversed with the noble South Carolinian, and he was full of life, strength, and animation. Now he was slowly being borne to the rear in his ambulance, bleeding from his dangerous wounds. General Stuart had a narrow escape in this charge, his pistol hung in his holster, and as he was trying to draw it, he received the fire of barrel after barrel from a Federal cavalryman within ten paces of him, but fortunately sustained no injury.

Having failed in this charge the enemy did not attempt another; the lines remained facing each other, and skirmishing, while the long thunder of the artillery beyond, indicated the hotter struggle of Cemetery Hill. Pickett's Virginians, we afterwards knew, were making their "wild charge" at that moment: advancing into that gulf of fire from which so few were to return; Kemper was being shot down; Armistead was falling as he leaped his horse over the Federal breastworks—the fate of Gettysburg was being decided.

Night settled down, and still ignorant of the result, Stuart rode along the whole front where the sharpshooters were still firing. In the yard of a house there was a dead man lying, I remember, in a curious position—as men killed in battle often do—and another blue sharpshooter, who had been summoned to advance and surrender, was staggering up with his face all bloody. Such are the trifles which cling to the memory.

Returning through the darkness towards the Heidelburg road, an amusing discussion took place upon a somewhat interesting point.

"General," said one of the staff, "we are travelling in the wrong direction—this road will lead you straight into the enemy's lines."

"No," was Stuart's reply, "look at the stars."

"Well, yonder is the North Star."

"You are certainly mistaken."

"I am sure I am not."

"And I am sure you are! However, we can easily decide."

And the General drew from his pocket a small portable compass which he had carried with him on the prairies of the West, when in the U. S. army. The compass overthrew the General, and vindicated the good judgment of the staff officer. Laughter followed; the direction of march was changed; a wide ditch leaped; and we gained the Heidelburg road—the staff pushing on intent on sleep, a single courier being left with the General. The sequel was amusing. The General went to sleep in the saddle: the courier rode on: and the General's horse not recognising headquarters in the dark, quietly walked on by, and nearly carried Major-General Stuart into the cavalry pickets of the enemy.

These minute details will, I fear, prove less interesting to the reader than to him who recalls them. The length of the narrative dictates, for the future, a more rapid summary. The third day's fight decided the event of Gettysburg, and General Lee fell back toward the Potomac, not very hotly pursued. Nothing is more erroneous than the idea that the Southern army was "demoralized" by the result of the bloody actions of these three memorable days. Their nerve was unshaken, their confidence in Lee and themselves unimpaired. Longstreet said truly that he desired nothing better than for General Meade to attack his position—that his men would have given the Federal troops a reception such as *they* had given Pickett. The stubborn resolution of the Army of Northern Virginia was thus unbroken—but the game was played for the time. The army was moving back, slow and defiant, to the Potomac.

The cavalry protected its flanks and rear, fighting in the passes of South Mountain, and holding obstinately the ridge in front of Boonsboro, while General Lee formed his line to cover the crossing at Falling Waters and Williamsport. Here, near Boonsboro, Stuart did some of his hardest fighting, and successfully held his ground, crowning every knoll with the guns of his horse artillery. When the infantry was in position, the cavalry retired, and took position on the flanks—the two armies faced each other, and a battle seemed imminent—when one morning General Meade discovered that General Lee was on the south bank of the Potomac.

It is said that the Federal commander designed attacking Lee that day, against the opinion of his officers. What would have been the result? That is a difficult question. A humble soldier of the Southern army may, however, be permitted to say that *a rout* of the army of Northern Virginia, under Lee, never seemed to him possible. Nor was it ever routed. It was *starved*, and it surrendered.

General Lee was thus over with his army, where provisions and ammunition were obtainable; and the opposing forces rested. Then General Meade advanced, his great adversary made a corresponding movement, and about the first of August the cavalry were once more posted in Culpeper.

In about six weeks they had marched many hundreds of miles; fought a number of battles; lost about *one-third* of their force by death in action, or disabling wounds; and were again on the war-harried banks of the Rappahannock.

## VII.

A few words will terminate this sketch of the summer campaign of 1863.

Of this great ride with the cavalry through Pennsylvania, the present writer has preserved recollections rather amusing and grotesque, than sad or tragic. The anxiety expressed by a fat lady of Dutch origin, to secure a blue postage stamp with the head of President Davis upon it, a gentleman whom she evidently expected to find endued with horns and tail *en Diable*; the manner in which an exceedingly pretty damsel in a town through which the army was retreating, turned her back upon the writer, as he smiled respectfully upon catching her eye; turned her back, tossed her head, and "looked daggers;" the air of hauteur and outraged feeling with which another refused to lend a coffee-pot, not even melting at the offender's low bow, and "I will not insist, madam"—these return to memory and make the recollection of those times more amusing than disagreeable. We were sore then, but time obliterates pain, and heals nearly every wound. There were harsh emotions, painful scenes, and bitter hostility; but there were some of the amenities of war too; among which I recall the obliging manner in which Major P——, of the United States cavalry, enabled me to gratify some lady friends in Virginia.

The Major was brought in to the headquarters—or bivouac, rather—in a grassy yard near Hagerstown, during the absence of General Stuart, and whilst the present writer was in command. I found him very much of a gentleman; laughed at his description of the manner in which he was captured—"Your men snapped a carbine at me, and then 'halted' me!"—and simply took his parole not to attempt escape, after which we lay down and slept on the grass, the major sharing my blankets. On the next morning we were perfectly intimate; and hearing me express a wish to secure some "greenbacks" for the purchase of small articles in Hagerstown, where Confederate money would not pass, the major politely pulled out his purse, declaring that he would exchange dollar for dollar "as he only wished to have enough of money to buy cigars in Richmond." The comedy of the scene which ensued lay in the mutual anxiety of Major P—— and the present writer, lest each should wrong the other. Each was afraid he would get the advantage of his companion, and the polite speeches delivered on the occasion were truly admirable. An equitable arrangement was finally made. I came into possession of about forty dollars in Federal money, and with this bought out nearly the whole stock of lace, ribands, and handkerchiefs of a milliner's store, to the extreme but suppressed amusement of the young lady behind the counter, who disinterestedly gave her advice in the selection. With this big bundle on the pommel of his saddle, the present writer made his exit from the State of Maryland!

Such, in rapid and discursive outline, was the march of the cavalry "to Gettysburg and back again," in that last year but one of the great civil war. Scores of miles were passed over, while the weary cavalry-man who writes this, slept in the saddle. So, it is no wonder Pennsylvania appears to him to-day like a land seen in a dream! Gettysburg was, however, a rough waking, and over that far locality where the fate of the struggle was decided, a lurid cloud seems to hang, its edges steeped in blood. "Gettysburg! Gettysburg!" That murmur comes to the lips of many whose dear ones sleep their last sleep under the sod there; but this souvenir is sad. Let me remember rather the gay laugh of Stuart; the voices of Fitz Lee, Hampton, and their noble comrades; the fun, the frolic, and the adventure of the long journey, when so much mirth lit up the dark horizon of war.

It is a hard and brutal business, the trade of war; but the odd, grotesque, and bizarre mix everywhere with the tears and the blood. All were mingled in this heavy work of the bustling year 1863.

# VIII

## FROM THE RAPIDAN TO FRYING-PAN

### IN OCTOBER, 1863

### I.

GENERAL MEADE's retreat from Culpeper, in October, 1863, was one of the liveliest episodes of the late war. This officer was not unpopular in the Southern army. Few depredations were laid to his charge, and he was generally regarded as a fair and honorable opponent. There was evidently no rhodomontade about him, and few trumpets were blown in his honour; but General Lee is said to have declared that he had given him as much trouble as any Federal general of the war. Of his status as a soldier, let history speak. The present sketch will show, I think, that no general ever better understood the difficult art of coolly retiring without loss, and promptly advancing to his former position at the right moment. As in other sketches, the writer will aim rather to present such details and incidents as convey a clear idea of the actual occurrence, then to indulge in historical generalization. Often the least trifling of things are "trifles."

In October, 1863, General Meade's army was around Culpeper Court-House, with the advance at Mitchell's Station, on the Orange road, and General Lee faced him on the south bank of the Rapidan. One day there came from our signal-station, on Clarke's Mountain, the message: "General Meade's head-quarters are at Wallack's, and Pleasanton's at *Cumberland, Georgia*." General Fitz Lee thereupon sent to General Stuart, after the jocose fashion of "General Fitz," to ask why Pleasanton had been sent to *"Cumberland, Georgia."* The message should have been *Cumberland George's*—the house, that is to say, of the Rev. Mr. George, in the suburbs of Culpeper Court-House.

Every day, at that time, the whistle of the "Yankee cars," as we used to call them, was heard a few miles off, at Mitchell's Station; and as General Meade was plainly going to advance, it was obvious that he was going to fall back. It was at this time, early in October, that "for reasons best known to himself," General Lee determined upon a movement through Madison, along the base of the Blue Ridge, to flank General Meade's right, cut him off from Manassas, and bring on a general engagement between the two armies. The plan was a simple one. Ewell and A. P. Hill were to move out with their corps from the works on the Rapidan, and marching up that stream, cross into Madison, leaving Fitz Lee's cavalry division to occupy their places in the abandoned works, and repulse any assault. Once across the Upper Rapidan, Ewell and Hill would move toward Madison Court-House with the rest of Stuart's cavalry on their right flank, to mask the movement; and, thence pushing on to the Rappahannock, make for Warrenton, somewhere near which point it was probable that they would strike General Meade's column on its retreat. Then a decisive trial of strength in a pitched battle.

The cavalry, by common consent of the army, "did the work" on this movement—the infantry having few opportunities to become engaged—and I shall ask the reader to follow "Stuart and his horsemen."

I think it was the morning of the 10th of October when, moving on the right of the long column of Ewell and Hill then streaming toward Madison Court-House, Stuart came on the exterior picket of the enemy—their advance force of cavalry, infantry, and artillery, being near the little village of James City. The picket on a little stream was driven in, and pushing on to Thoroughfare Mountain (not to be confounded with that near Manassas), we ran into a regiment of infantry which had hastily formed line of battle at the noise of the firing. Gordon, that gallant North Carolinian, at once became hotly engaged; but there was no time to stop long. Stuart took Young's brigade—he had but two—and, making a detour to the left, charged straight down upon the enemy's right flank. Cheers, yells, carbines cracking—and the infantry broke and scattered in the mountains, dropping large numbers of the newest, brightest, and handsomest muskets ever handled. The force was declared by prisoners to have numbered two hundred and fifty, of whom about twenty were taken. Stuart now pushed on without stopping, and speedily became engaged with the main force of Federal cavalry at James City. This force was commanded by General Kilpatrick, we afterwards discovered, and this gentleman had been enjoying himself greatly. There was a race-course near the town where races were held, General Kilpatrick having, it is said, a favorite mare called "Lively" which he used to run against a blood horse in his artillery called the "Battery Horse." What became of the "Battery Horse" this historian cannot say; but—to anticipate events—the fate of "Lively" can be stated. Later in the fall, the general was running "Lively" near Manassas, when she flew the track, and two men were sent after her. Neither "Lively" nor the men ever returned. In fact, some of "Mosby's people" had been unseen spectators of the race from the adjoining woods, and these gentry took charge both of the mare and the men sent after her. "I really must have that mare," General Stuart said, when he heard the incident, but her captors retained her.

I am anticipating. General Kilpatrick was in command at James City, and, drawing up his cavalry on the high ground beyond, prepared to receive Stuart's attack. None was made. It was not a part of the programme. Stuart's orders were to keep the enemy off the infantry flanks, and this could best be accomplished by remaining quiet. So, every demonstration was made; lines of sharpshooters were advanced, our artillery opened, and —no attack was made. Thus the hours passed on. Shells raced across the little valley. Carbines cracked. An outside spectator would have said that the opponents were afraid of each other. The truth was that General Stuart was playing his own game, and his adversary did not understand it. At last, even the firing ceased. Fronting each other in line of battle, the opponents waited in silence for some movement. The stillness was, however, broken suddenly by an incident, amusing, but by no means agreeable, at least from our point of view. General Stuart was lying down, surrounded by his staff and escort, with his flag floating on the top of the hill, when, behind a fringe of woods, near the Federal cavalry drawn up in long line of battle on the opposite plateau, was seen a puff of white smoke. A roar followed, then the whistle of a shell, and this polite visitor fell and burst in the very midst of the group. It was a percussion shell, and exploded as it struck, tearing up a deep hole and vanishing, without injuring a single individual. As the present writer was covered with the dirt where he lay, and found by inspection that it had been a "line shot," striking within three or four feet of his head, the incident was highly pleasing. The shell was followed by others, but no harm was done by them, and it is not necessary to say that the friendly group, with the flag floating so temptingly above it, deployed to the right and left, laughing, and not displeased at the result of the first "good shot."

At night the Federal cavalry were still there, and Stuart still remained quiet. His headquarters that night were at Mr. H——'s where that brave spirit, General Gordon, of the cavalry, came to see him. It is a melancholy pleasure to recall the gallant face of Gordon, now that he is dead; to remember his charming smile, his gay humour; the elegant little speech which he made as he gallantly presented a nosegay to the fair Miss H——, bowing low as he did so amid friendly laughter. When he fell he left behind him no braver soldier or kindlier gentleman.

## II.

At dawn Stuart was again in the saddle, pressing forward upon the retiring enemy.

Ewell and Hill had moved unseen to their position on the Sperryville road, thanks to the stand of Stuart at James City; and now, for the first time, the enemy seemed to understand the nature of the blow about to be struck. General Meade had put his army in motion toward the Rappahannock; and, as the advance force in our front retired, Stuart pressed them closely. It is hard to say whether this great soldier was better in falling back or in advancing. When he retired he was the soul of stubborn obstinacy. When he advanced he was all fire, dash, and impetus. He was now following up a retreating enemy, and he did not allow the grass to grow under his feet.

Below Griffinsburg the rear-guard of the Federal cavalry was attacked and driven; and Stuart was pushing on, when the presence of a Federal infantry regiment in the woods to his right was announced. To this he paid no attention, but drove on, firing upon their cavalry, and soon the good judgment of this was shown. The infantry regiment heard the firing, feared being cut off, and double-quicked toward the rear. They reached the fields on Stone House Mountain as quickly as Stuart, moving parallel to his column, and suddenly their line appeared. I have rarely seen General Stuart more excited. It was a rich prize, that regiment, and it appeared in his grasp! But, unfortunately, his column was not "up." He was leading a mere advance guard, and that was scattered. Every available staff-officer and courier was hurried back for the cavalry, and the "Jefferson Company," Lieutenant Baylor, got up first, and charged straight at the flank of the infantry. They were suddenly halted, formed line of battle, and the bright muskets fell to a level like a single weapon. The cavalry company received the fire at thirty yards, but pressed on, and would doubtless have ridden over the infantry, now scattering in great disorder, but for an impassable ditch. Before they could make a detour to avoid it, the Federal infantry had scattered, "every man for himself," in the woods, dropping guns, knapsacks, and blankets.

The huge camps at Stone House Mountain, as afterwards around Culpeper Court-House, were a sort of "Arabian Nights" of wonder to the gray people. The troops had fixed themselves in the most admirable manner to defy the coming winter. Excellent stone chimneys, of every form; cabins, stoves, tables, magazines, books, wine and rum-bottles (empty), oil-cloths, coats, shoes, arms—everything was scattered about. *Harpers' Magazine* seemed to be a favourite; and full files of papers might have been collected in the deserted cabins. From this abode of the *dolce far niente* the rude hand of war, in the shape of Stuart's cavalry, had pushed them.

Stuart continued to press the enemy toward the Court-House; and there their cavalry had made a stand. As to the infantry, it was nowhere visible in the immense camps around the place—those camps which contained, like the first, only rubbish. Not a wagon, ambulance, or piece of artillery, I believe, was captured. General Meade had swept clean. There were even very few empty boxes.

On "Cumberland George's" hill, the Federal artillery fought hard for a time, inflicting some loss; but Gordon was sent round by the Rixeyville Road to the left; Stuart advanced in front; and the enemy fell back toward Brandy. The reader will remember that General Fitz Lee had been left on the Lower Rapidan to repulse any assault in that direction, and the expected assault had been made. I think it was General Buford who attacked him; but the attack was unsuccessful, and as the enemy fell back Fitz Lee pressed forward on the track of the retreating column toward Brandy. We now heard the thunder of his guns upon the right as he pushed on toward the Rappahannock, and everything seemed to be concentrating in the neighbourhood of Fleetwood Hill, the scene of the sanguinary conflict of the 9th of June preceding. There the great struggle, in fact, took place—Stuart pressing the main column on their line of retreat from above, General Fitz Lee pushing as vigorously after the strong force which had fallen back from the Rappahannock. As it is not the design of the writer to attempt any "battle pictures" in this discursive sketch, he omits a detailed account of the hard fight which followed. It was among the heaviest of the war, and for a time nothing was seen but dust, smoke, and confused masses reeling to and fro; nothing was heard but shouts, cheers, yells, and orders, mixed with the quick bang of carbines and the clash of sabres—above all, and the continuous thunder of the artillery. It was as "mixed up" as any fight of the war, and at one time General Stuart, with Colonel Peyton, of General Lee's staff, and one or two other officers, found him-

self cut off by the enemy. He got out, joined his column to
Fitz Lee's, and charging the Federal forces, cavalry and infantry
—the latter being drawn up on Fleetwood Hill—pressed them
back to the Rappahannock, which they hastened to cross. General Meade has thus retreated from Culpeper, but it was the
"cleanest" retreat on record, as far as the present writer's observation extended. He imitated it in December at Mine Run.

General Lee had meanwhile advanced with his infantry toward Warrenton Springs, still aiming to cut General Meade off
from Manassas. On the next day commenced the trial of skill
between the two commanders. General Meade's cavalry had
been so rudely hustled by Stuart, and the cordon placed by the
latter along the Rappahannock was so effective, that the Federal
commander was absolutely in the dark as to his great adversary's
position and designs. On the afternoon of this—next—day, therefore, a Federal force consisting of a corps of infantry and two
brigades of cavalry, was moved across the Rappahannock where
the Orange railway crosses it, and this force pushed straight toward the Court-House. The design was evidently to ascertain
if General Lee was in that vicinity, and the column rapidly
advanced. Near Brandy it encountered what seemed to be
Stuart's entire cavalry. At various openings in the woods the
*heads of different columns* were seen, calmly awaiting an attack, and the Federal infantry and cavalry speedily formed
line of battle, prepared for vigorous engagement. They would
scarcely have given themselves so much trouble if they had
known that the entire force in their front consisted of about
*one hundred and eighty men*, with one gun under Colonel
Rosser, as a sort of grand picket guard. He had arranged detachments of eight or ten men as above indicated, at openings
in the woods, to produce the impression of several heavy columns; and it was not until they attacked him that they discovered the ruse. The attack once made, all further concealment was impossible. Rosser's one hundred and eighty men, and
single piece of artillery, were rapidly driven back by the enemy;
and his gun was now roaring from the high ground just below
the Court-House, when the clatter of hoofs was heard upon

the streets of the village. It was the gay and gallant P. M. B. Young, of Georgia, who had been left with his brigade near James City, and now came to Rosser's assistance. Young passed through the Court-House at a trot, hastened to the scene of action, and, dismounting his entire brigade, deployed them as sharpshooters, and made a sudden and determined attack upon the enemy. This vigorous movement seems to have completely deceived them. Night was now falling; they could not make out the numbers or character of Young's force; and an attack as bold as his must surely proceed from a heavy force of infantry! Was General Lee still at the place, with one of his *corps d'armée?* If this idea entered the minds of the enemy, it must have been encouraged by Young's next move. He had held his ground without flinching; and now, as night descended, he ordered camp fires to be built along two miles of front, and bringing up his splendid brass band, played the "Bonnie Blue Flag" and "Dixie" with defiant animation. This ruse seemed to decide the matter; the Federal commander made no further effort to advance; and in the morning there was not a Federal soldier on the south bank of the Rappahannock. Their corps of infantry and two brigades of cavalry had "fallen back in good order:" and the laughing Young remained master of the situation.

Stuart had pushed on, meanwhile, toward Warrenton Springs, and just as the fight above described commenced, a gallant affair took place above. The enemy were attacked in the town of Jeffersonton, and after a hot fight forced back to Warrenton Springs, where the Jefferson Company again distinguished itself. The attempt was made to charge over the bridge, in face of the enemy's fire. In the middle of the structure the column suddenly recoiled, and retreated. The cause of this movement was soon discovered. Several of the planks had been torn up in the flooring of the bridge, and to cross was impossible. The Jefferson Company, however, did not abandon their work. They galloped to the ford, Stuart placed himself at their head, and, in the face of a heavy and determined fire from a double line of Federal sharpshooters, they charged across. The Federal force gave way before them, and crossing his whole column Stuart pushed on upon the track of the enemy toward Warrenton, followed by the infantry, who had witnessed the feats of their cavalry brethren with all the satisfaction of "outside spectators."

In Jeffersonton and at Warrenton Springs many brave fellows had fallen, and sad scenes were presented. Lieutenant Chew had fought from house to house in the first named place, and in a mansion of the village this gallant officer lay dying, with a bullet through his breast. At Mr. M——'s, near the river, young Marshall, of Fauquier, a descendant of the Chief Justice, was lying on a table, covered with a sheet—dead, with a huge, bloody hole in the centre of his pale forehead; while in a bed opposite lay a wounded Federal officer. In the fields around were dead men, dead horses, and abandoned arms.

The army pushed on to Warrenton, the cavalry still in advance, and on the evening of the next day Stuart rapidly advanced with his column to reconnoitre toward Catlett's Station, the scene of his great raid in August, 1862, when he captured General Pope's coat and official papers. The incident which followed was one of the most curious of the war.

### III.

Stuart had just passed Auburn, when General Gordon, commanding the rear of his column, sent him word that a heavy force of the enemy's infantry had closed in behind him, completely cutting him off from General Lee. As at the same moment an army corps of Federal infantry was discovered moving across his front, General Stuart awoke to the unpleasant consciousness that his little force of cavalry was securely hemmed in between overpowering masses of the enemy, who, as soon as they discovered the presence of the audacious interlopers, would unquestionably attack and cut them to pieces.

The "situation" was now in the highest degree critical. In fact, Stuart had managed to get his command inclosed between the two retreating columns of General Meade—infantry, cavalry, and artillery—and these columns, as they moved across his front and rear, were converging toward Bristoe, near Manassas. The only hope of safety lay in complete concealment of his presence, and General Stuart issued the most stringent orders to his troops that no noise of any description should be made during the night. There was little necessity to impress this upon the command. Within a few hundred yards of them, in front and in rear, were moving the huge columns of the enemy; the feet of the infantry shuffling, the hoofs of the cavalry clattering, the artillery wheels and chains rolling and jingling, and above the whole the stifled hum of an army on the march. The men sat motionless and silent in the saddle, listening, throughout the long hours of the night. No man spoke; no sound was heard from human lips as the little force remained *perdu* in the darkness. But the "dumb animals" were not equally intelligent, and more than once some thoughtless horse neighed or some indiscreet donkey in the artillery uttered his discordant notes. In the noise of the Federal retreat these sounds, however, were not observed, and thus the night wore on and daylight came.

The first glimmer showed General Stuart that the Federal forces had nearly all passed. In fact the rear force had halted within a few hundred yards of his position and were cooking their breakfasts. Now was his opportunity, not only to extricate himself, but to take vengeance for the long hours of anxiety and peril. Picked men had been sent during the night to pass through the advancing column and announce the critical position of affairs to General Lee, and Stuart had suggested a vigorous infantry attack upon the enemy's left flank while he attacked their right. Not hearing from General Lee, he took the initiative. At dawn he put his artillery in position, drew up his cavalry, and opened a thundering fire upon the Federal troops; knocking over their coffee-pots, and scattering them in wild confusion. They rallied, however, and made a vigorous attack— a severe though brief engagement following—but Stuart repulsed this assault, slowly fell back, and soon his little command was extricated from its peril. Altogether this was a curious affair. It was not attractive, however "romantic." One of the bravest infantry officers of the army, who accompanied the expedition as an amateur, declared, laughing, that he was "done with the cavalry—the infantry was enough for him thereafter."

Meanwhile General Lee was pressing the retiring enemy toward Bristoe; Stuart on the right, and General Fitz Lee moving on their left, through New Baltimore. There was some fatal blunder, however, in the execution of General Lee's orders, or else some obstacle which could not be overcome. General Meade pushed on and crossed Broad Run, making with his main body for Manassas. When the Southern advance force reached Bristoe they found the main Federal army gone. A strong force, however, remained, and this was drawn up behind a long railroad embankment serving admirably as a breastwork. The men had only to lie down upon the slope, rest their muskets on the track of the railroad, and sweep the open field in their front with a shower of balls if the Confederates attacked. The attack was made—straight across open ground, down a slope, right on the embankment. The consequence was that Cooke's brigade, which was ordered to make the attempt, was nearly annihilated, the General falling among the first at the head of his troops: and, advancing against the line to his left, the enemy captured, I believe, nine pieces of artillery. After this exploit they quietly retired across Broad Run, and rejoined the main column. A worse managed affair than that fight at Bristoe did not take place during the war. "Well, well, General," Lee is reported to have said to the officer who essayed to explain the occurrence, "bury these poor men, and let us say no more about it." General Meade was behind Bull Run fortifying.

Thus terminated General Lee's vigorous attempt to bring on a pitched battle with Meade. That was his design, as it was General Meade's design in coming over to Mine Run in the succeeding December. Both schemes failed. From the high ground beyond Bristoe, Lee, surrounded by his generals, reconnoitered the retiring rear-guard of the enemy, and issued his orders for the army to retrace its steps to the Rappahannock. The cavalry had not, however, finished their work. The fine October weather was admirable for active movement, and Stuart pushed straight on to Manassas, harassing the Federal forces as they crossed Bull Run. At Blackburn's Ford, General Fitz Lee had a brisk engagement, which drove the Federal cavalry across;

and, near Yates's Ford, General Stuart charged over a barricade at the head of his horsemen, scattered the Federal sharpshooters, and drove to and across the stream their cavalry and artillery.

An odd incident marked this occasion. It was about dusk when the enemy began to retire from our front, their artillery roaring on the right, but taking position after position, each nearer Bull Run. General Stuart was within about four hundred yards of the Federal guns, in the edge of the woods, surrounded by his staff, escort, etc., one of whom had just taken up a dead man before him to carry off. At this moment, among the figures moving to and fro, one—apparently a member of the staff or escort—was seen quietly riding out into the field, as if to gain a better view of the Federal artillery. "Who is that?" said General Stuart, pointing to the figure, indistinct in the dusk. "One of the couriers," some one replied. "No!" returned Stuart, "halt him!" Two men immediately galloped after the suspected individual, who was easily, carelessly, and quietly edging off; and he speedily returned between them. Behold! he wore under his oilcloth a blue coat! "What do you belong to?" asked Stuart. "The First Maine, sir," responded the other with great *nonchalance*. In fact, the "gentleman from Maine" had got mixed up with us when the column went over the barricade; and, wrapped in his oilcloth, had listened to the remarks of Stuart and his staff, until he thought he could get away. The quick eye of General Stuart, however, penetrated his disguise, and he was a prisoner.

It was now night, and operations were over for the day. The retreat had been admirably managed. General Meade had carried off everything. We did not capture a wagon wheel. All was beyond Bull Run. The present writer here records his own capture, viz. one oilcloth, one feed of oats, found in the road, and one copy of *Harper's Magazine*, full of charming pictures of rebels, running, or being annihilated, in every portion of the country. On the next morning, Stuart left Fitz Lee in front of Bull Run, to oppose any advance of the Federal cavalry there, and, taking Hampton's division, set out through a torrent of rain to make a flank movement against General Meade's right beyond the Little River Turnpike. He had intended to cross at Sudley Ford, but coming upon the Federal cavalry near Groveton, a fight ensued, and the column could not cross there without having the movement unmasked. Stuart accordingly turned to the left; made a detour through Gainsville; and advancing, amid a violent storm, bivouacked that night beyond the Little Catharpin. The General on this day kept his entire staff and surroundings in great good-humour, by his songs and laughter, which only seemed to grow more jovial as the storm became more violent. I hope the reader will not regard this statement as "unworthy of the dignity of history." Fortunately I am not writing history; only a poor little sketch of a passage in the life of a very great man; and it has seemed to me that all concerning him is interesting. Pardon! august muse of history, that dealest in protocols and treaties! We pass on.

The weather was charming, as on the next morning the column advanced toward "Frying-Pan Church," and the troopers subsisted delightfully upon chinquepins, chestnuts, persimmons, and wild grapes. Reaching a magnificent apple-tree, weighed down with fruit as red as carnations, the men, with the fullest permission from the hospitable owner, threw themselves upon it, and soon the whole was stripped, the soldiers going on their way rejoicing. Never have I seen more splendid weather than those October days, or more beautiful tints in the foliage. Pity that the natural red of the birch and dogwood was not enough without blood! Stuart advanced rapidly, and near Frying-Pan Church came upon and at once attacked the Second corps of Federal infantry. A long line of sharpshooters was formed, which advanced on foot in line of battle. The artillery roared, and at first the Federal troops gave ground. The aspect of affairs speedily changed, however, and a strong Federal force, advancing in order of battle, made it necessary for Stuart to withdraw. This was done at once, with great deliberation, and at the "Recall" of the bugle the skirmishers slowly moved back and gained the woods. A spectacle which aroused the good-humoured laughter of those who witnessed it, was a staff officer carrying off in his arms a young lady of about fourteen from a house which the enemy were about to have within their lines. This was done at the suggestion of the General; and although the bullets were flying and the officers' horse was "dancing upon all four feet," the young lady declared herself "not afraid," and did not change colour at the bullets. If this meets the fair girl's eye she is informed that the officer has still the gray who came near unseating her as he jumped the fence, and that his rider has not forgotten the smiling little face, but remembers it with admiration and pleasure!

## IV.

That night General Stuart was moving steadily back by the same route which he had pursued in advancing, and on the next day he had reached the vicinity of Bucklands.

The army had fallen back, tearing up the road, and General Stuart now prepared to follow, the campaign having come to an end. He was not, however, to be permitted to fall back without molestation, and his command was to be present at the "Buckland Races." This comic episode will be briefly described, and the event related just as it occurred, without embellishment or exaggeration. General Kilpatrick, commanding the Federal cavalry, had been very much outraged, it would appear, at the hasty manner in which Stuart had compelled him to evacuate Culpeper; and he now felt an ardent desire, before the campaign ended, to give the great cavalier a "Roland for his Oliver." With about 3,000 cavalry he accordingly crossed Bull Run, following upon Stuart's track as the latter fell back; and soon he had reached the little village of Bucklands, not far from New Baltimore.

Stuart had disappeared; but these disappearances of Stuart, like those of Jackson, were always dangerous. In fact, a ruse was about to be practised upon General Kilpatrick, who was known to want caution, and this ruse was of the simplest description. Stuart had arranged that he should retire before Kilpatrick as he advanced, until the Federal column was beyond Bucklands—then Fitz Lee, who had fallen back from Manassas on the line of the Orange Railroad, would have an opportunity to fall upon the enemy's flank and rear. The sound of Fitz Lee's guns would be the signal for Stuart to face about and attack; Kilpatrick would thus be assailed in front and flank at the same instant, and the result would probably be satisfactory. This plan was carried out exactly as Stuart had arranged. General Kilpatrick reached Bucklands, and is said to have stated while dining at a house there that "he would not press Stuart so hard, but he (Stuart) had boasted of driving him (Kilpatrick) out of Culpeper, and he was going to give him no rest." It is said that General Kilpatrick had scarcely uttered this threat when the roar of artillery was heard upon his left flank, and this was speedily reëchoed by similar sounds in his front. In fact, General Fitz Lee had carried out his half of the programme, and Stuart hastened to do the rest. At the sound of General Lee's artillery Stuart faced about, formed his command in three columns, and charged straight upon the enemy's front, while General Fitz Lee fell upon his flanks. The consequence was a complete rout of the Federal cavalry, who scattered in every direction, throwing down their arms as they fled, and the flight of many, it is said, was not checked until they reached Alexandria. General Custer's headquarter wagons and papers were captured—as happened, I believe, to the same officer twice subsequently—and the pursuing force, under Kilpatrick, gave Stuart no more trouble as he fell back. This engagement afforded huge enjoyment to the Southern cavalry, as it was almost bloodless and resembled a species of trap into which their opponents fell. Nothing amuses troops more than this latter circumstance, and the affair continues to be known among the disbanded troopers of Stuart, as the "Buckland Races."

This engagement ended the campaign as far as the cavalry were concerned, and it was the movements of this arm that I proposed to outline. These were uniformly successful, while those of the infantry, from what appeared to be some fatality, were regularly unsuccessful. While the cavalry drove their opponents before them at Stone House Mountain, Culpeper Court-House, Brandy, Warrenton Springs, Bull Run, and Bucklands, the infantry failed to arrest the enemy at Auburn; were repulsed at Bristoe with the loss of several guns; and now, on the Rappahannock, was to occur that ugly affair at the railroad bridge, in which two brigades of General Lee's army were surprised, overpowered, and captured almost to a man. Such is the curiously mingled "warp and woof" of war. It was the *Army of Northern Virginia*, led by Ewell and Hill, with General Lee commanding in person, which sustained these losses, and failed in the object which the great soldier declared he had in view— to cut off and fight a pitched battle with General Meade. The movements of this latter commander entitled him to high praise, and he exhibited throughout the brief campaign a vigour and acumen which only belong to the thorough soldier.

Such is an outline of some incidents in this rapid campaign; this hasty movement backward and forward on the great chessboard of war. The discursive sketch here laid before the reader may convey some idea of the occurrences as they actually took place. From the "official reports" the grave Muse of History will sum up the results, generalizing upon the importance or non-importance of the events. This page aims at no generalization at all, but simply to show how Stuart and Fitz Lee, with their brave comrades, did the work assigned to them in those bright October days of 1863.

# IX

## MAJOR R——'S LITTLE PRIVATE SCOUT

NOTHING is more curious than the manner in which a sudden and unexpected attack imposes upon the recipients thereof; and it is safe to say that none but the best troops, trained and disciplined to stand firm under all contingencies, can be counted on in such moments of emergency.

The following incident will prove the truth of this assertion. It is not related "for the greater glory" of the Southern arms, so much as to present a curious illustration of the effect upon the human mind of a sudden surprise.

A word first of the doughty *sabreur* who figured as hero on the occasion, my friend, Major R——, of the C. S. A.

The Major is stout, rosy, of a portly figure, and from his appearance you would not take him for a very active or dangerous personage. But he is both. No man delights more in movement, adventure, and combat. No man sits a horse with more of the true cavalry ease. You may see from the manner in which he handles his sabre that he is master of that weapon; and in the charge he is a perfect thunderbolt. He fingers his pistol and makes the barrels revolve with admirable grace; his salute with the sabre is simply perfection; his air, as he listens to an order from his superior officer, says plainly, "All I wish is to know what you want me to do, General—if it can be done it will be done." This air does not deceive. It is well known to the Major's friends that his motto is, "Neck or nothing." At Mine Run, when General Meade confronted the Southern lines, the worthy said to me, "A soldier's duty is to obey his orders; and if General Stuart told me to charge the Yankee army by myself, I would do it. *He* would be responsible."

It will be seen from the above sketch of the gallant Major, that he is a thorough soldier. In fact he loves his profession, and is not satisfied with performing routine duty. He is fond of volunteering on forlorn hopes, and in desperate emergencies— when he cannot get at the blue-coats for any length of time—he pines.

This mood came to him in the fall of 1862. Quiet had reigned along the lines so long, that he grew melancholy. His appetite did not fail, as far as his friends could perceive, but something obviously rested on his mind. He was rusting, and was conscious of the process. "Why don't they come out and fight?" the Major seemed to ask with his calm, sad eyes. They were in Virginia for the purpose of "crushing the rebellion,"—why didn't they set about the work?

These questions meeting with no satisfactory response, Major R—— determined himself to take the initiative, and see if he could not bring on a little fight, all on his private account. He would thus relieve his bosom of the perilous stuff which preyed upon his heart. It had, indeed, become absolutely necessary to his peace of mind to come into collision with his friends across the way, and he set about devising the best plan for arriving at his object.

The Southern cavalry to which the Major was attached, at that time occupied the county of Culpeper, and picketed along the Rappahannock. So did the enemy's horsemen, and the Federal pickets were stationed on the southern bank at every ford. This was the case at Warrenton Springs, where a bridge, afterwards destroyed, spanned the Rappahannock; and at this point Major R—— determined to bring on the little affair which had become so necessary to his happiness. He intended to combine pleasure with business by visiting some young ladies at a hospitable mansion not far from the bridge; and having thus laid out his programme he proceeded to execute it, and "all alone by himself" attack the picket guard of some twenty of the enemy.

Behold the Major now in warlike panoply—that is to say, in fine gray dress coat with burnished buttons (for the eyes of Venus after the conflict with Mars); pistol carefully loaded, in holster on his right side; and sabre in excellent order, jingling against his top boots. It was a saying of the worthy, that he "generally kept his arms in good order," and on this occasion nothing was left to be desired. His pistol revolved at the touch, with a clear ringing click; and you could see your face in his sabre blade. Thus accoutred, and mounted on a good, active horse, he set off from Hazel river, and making a detour around Jeffersonton, came to an elevation in rear of Mr. ——'s house, where he stopped to reconnoitre.

The Federal picket—of nineteen men, as he afterwards discovered—was at the bridge; and in the yard of the mansion were two videttes, with their horses tied to the trees under which they were lying. Whether he could succeed in "driving in" the whole picket was problematical, but the videttes were pretty sure game. He would either run them off or capture them.

With the Major execution followed conception rapidly. Pushing boldly over the crest from behind which he had made his reconnoissance, he charged across the field at a thundering gallop, whirling his burnished sabre around his head, yelling in a manner that was truly awful; and shouting as he rode to a supposititious squadron:

"Charge! charge! cut down every man!"

So portentous was the reverberating shout of onset from the lips of the Major, that the videttes started to their feet, and clutched the bridles of their horses instantly. As the warlike figure, surrounded by the brilliant lightning of the flashing sabre, swept on, the videttes probably saw at least a squadron of "Rebel cavalry" in the dust which rose behind; and hastily mounting, darted away, pursued by the triumphant Major, whose yells were now more tremendous than ever.

Across the broad field, past the house, on toward the bridge, galloped the furious assailant, bent on striking terror to the enemy's hearts, and successfully completing his adventure. Before him fled the frightened videttes—their movements accelerated by several balls, which issued from the Major's pistol, and whistled by their ears. On toward the bridge, and into the midst of the picket fled the videttes; and as the Major's shouts, and vociferous orders to his cavalry to charge, and let no one escape, resounded nearer, the pickets, too, mounted in hot haste, and clattered across the bridge, pursued by the Major's pistol shots.

In vain did the officer in charge of the picket-post shout to his men:

"Halt! halt! Shoot down the rascal! Shoot him down, I say! There's only one of them!"

His voice was unheard or his order unheeded. The picket was composed of stuff less soldierly than their officer, and would not obey him. Before their vivid imaginations rose at least a squadron of Confederate cavalry, sweeping on to ride over them, sword in hand.

The result was that Major R—— in ten minutes had possession of the bridge, and sat his horse defiantly in the middle of it. He then amused himself by sending a few parting shots after the demoralized picket, and having performed this agreeable duty rode back to the house of Mr. ——, laughing low in his peculiar way; his breast completely lightened of the oppressive weight which had so long weighed upon it.

At Mr. ——'s he met with a triumphant reception; was greeted with a perfect ovation. The young ladies of the mansion were crazy almost with delight at the manner in which they had been delivered from the presence of their enemies; and when the hero of the occasion made his appearance they met him as women only can meet their deliverers—with smiles such as shine rarely for the poor "civilian." After all it is something to be a soldier. The trade is hard, but the feminine eye has a peculiar brightness when it rests on the sons of Mars!—of Mars, proverbially the favourite of Venus!

The Major was an old soldier, and in no hurry to depart. He counted on the extent of the "scare" he had given the enemy,

and quietly enjoyed himself in the charming society of his host-
esses. He had once more become "excellent company." The
smile had returned to his lips, the light to his eyes. That melancholy which had made his friends uneasy had quite disappeared,
and the Major was "himself again"—that is to say, the gayest
and most delightful of companions.

When, rising slowly and carelessly, he bade his friendly entertainers good-bye, he was again happy. He came back to
camp, smiling, amiable, the soul of sweetness and cheerfulness.
I saw him. He was absolutely radiant. His eloquent eye beamed
brightly; his countenance was charming; his movements energetic and elastic; the fullest satisfaction was apparent in every
lineament of his face. His gay and friendly smile seemed to say,
"I went at nineteen of them; ran them off; held the bridge against
them; had an excellent supper, a delightful talk—I am happy!"

Such was the gay little comedy which I heard from the family
of Mr. ——, as I sat upon his porch and conversed with them
one day. The narrative is precisely true in every particular, and
has always impressed me as a curious illustration of the effect of
"surprises" upon troops—of the enormous power exerted by the
human imagination.

# X

## A Dash at Aldie

### I.

IN CARELESSLY looking over an old portfolio yesterday—October 31, 1866—I found among other curious records of the war a rude, discoloured scrap of paper, written in pencil, and bearing date October 31, 1862.

Four years, day for day, had passed, since those pencil marks were traced. Four years! not a long time, you may say, in the life of man. But longest of long years—most snail-like in their movement—most terrible for that delay which makes the stoutest heart grow sick, were those four twelvemonths between October, 1862, and October, 1866. The larger portion of the period was spent in hoping—the rest of it in despairing.

But I wander from the subject of this sketch. The paper found in my portfolio contained the following words, written, as I have said, in pencil:

"Mountsville, October 31, 1862.

"I hereby bind myself, on my word of honour, not to take up arms against the Confederate States, or in any manner give aid and comfort to the Federal cause, until I am regularly exchanged.

"L. —. GOVE,
Captain ——."

I read this paper, and then went back and read it over again. A careless observer would have seen in it only a simple and very hastily written parole. Read at one instant, it would have been forgotten in the next—a veritable leaf of autumn, dry and worthless.

For me it contained much more than was written on it. I did not throw it aside. I read it over a third time, and it made a dolorous impression on my heart. For that paper, written by myself four years ago, and signed by a dying man whose hand staggered as it traversed the sheet, leaving the name of the writer almost illegible, his full official rank unrecorded—that paper brought back to my memory a day near Aldie, when it was my sorrowful duty to parole a brother human being *in articulo mortis.*

"A brother human being, do you say? He was only a Yankee!" some one may object. No—he was my brother, and yours, reader, whether you wore blue or gray. Did you wear the gray, then? So did I. Did you hate the invaders of Virginia? So did I. You may have been able to see this enemy die in agony, and not pity him. I was not. And the proof is, that the sight of the paper which his faint hand touched as he drew his last breath, has struck me wofully, and blotted out a part of the autumn sunshine yonder on the mountains.

I have nothing to reproach myself with—the reader shall judge of that—but this poor rough scrap of paper with its tremulous signature moves me all the same.


II.


It was in the last days of October, 1862. McClellan had followed Lee to Sharpsburg; fought him there; refitted his army; recrossed the Potomac, and was rapidly advancing toward Warrenton, where the fatal fiat from Washington was to meet him, "Off with his head! So much for Buckingham."

But in these last days of October the wind had not yet wafted to him the decree of the civilians. He was pressing on in admirable order, and Lee had promptly broken up his camps upon the Opequon to cross the Blue Ridge at Chester's Gap, and interpose himself between McClellan and the Rapidan.

The infantry moved; the cavalry followed, or rather marched to guard the flank.

Stuart crossed the Shenandoah at Castleman's; the column moved through Snicker's Gap; then from the eastern slopes of the Blue Ridge were seen the long trains of McClellan in the distance, winding toward Middleburg and Aldie.

In front of these trains we knew very well that we would find the Federal cavalry under that able soldier, General Bayard, if he did not find us. For we had trains also, and it was more than probable that Bayard would strike at them through the passes of the Ridge. To prevent him from so doing it seemed most advisable to carry the war into Africa by a blow at *him*, and Stuart moved on without pausing toward Bloomfield. This village was passed; we reached the little hamlet of Union, where the people told us, with what truth I know not, that a party of the enemy had just ridden through, firing right and left upon citizens and children; then pushing on, in the splendid autumn sunshine, the brigade—Fitz Lee's, commanded by the gallant Wickham—reached the vicinity of Mountsville.

Stuart was riding gaily at the head of his horsemen, when Wickham galloped up from the advance guard, and announced that a heavy picket force was camped at Mountsville, visible through the lofty trees upon its hill.

"Charge it!" was the General's reply; and pushing on, he was there almost as soon as the advance guard.

They dashed upon the camp, or bivouac rather, with shouts; bang! bang! bang! from the carbines told that the blue and gray people had come into collision: and then the cheers of the Southerners indicated that they were driving in the picket force upon the main body.

In a moment we had reached the spot, and in a field were the hastily abandoned accoutrements of the Federal cavalry. Saddles, blankets, oil-cloths, carbines, sabres, and coats were scattered everywhere. Upon the ground, a bright red object glittered in the sunshine—it was the flag, or guidon of the enemy, abandoned like the rest. The Federal picket force, consisting of the First Rhode Island Cavalry, between seventy-five and one hundred in number, had disappeared as a handful of dry leaves disappear, swept away by the wind.

The Southerners pursued with shouts and carbine shots—but officers and men, bending from the saddle, caught upon the points of their sabres, as they passed at full speed, those precious "quartermaster stores," blankets, oil-cloths, so scarce in the poverty-stricken Confederacy. The present writer was almost destitute on the last day of October—on the first day of November he was rich. His cavalier outfit had been reinforced by an excellent regulation blanket, heavy and double: and a superb india-rubber poncho, on which was inscribed the name "Lougee." If the original owner of that fine military cloak survives, I beg to express my hope that he did not suffer, in the winter nights of 1862, for want of it.

The Federal camp had vanished, as I have said, as though carried away by the wind. The carbine shots were heard receding still toward Aldie—prisoners began to come back toward the rear. The name of another member of the First Rhode Island I can give. A young attaché of General Stuart's staff had captured a stout animal, and while leading him, was suddenly saluted by the words, "There is Brown's horse!" from a Federal prisoner passing. Brown's horse travelled afterwards extensively, and visited the low country of North Carolina. Most erratic of lives for men and animals is the military life. You know whence you come, not at all whither you go!

These trifles have diverted me from the main subject of the present sketch. I approach that subject with reluctance, for the picture to be drawn is a sad one. It is nothing to record the gay or comic incidents of other times—to let the pen glide, directed by the memory, when the lips are smiling and the heart is gay. To record the sad events, however, the blood, the tears—believe me, that is different.

I was pushing on, when a groan from the roadside drew my eyes in that direction. I looked and saw a man lying on his back, writhing to and fro, upon the grass. Some cavalrymen had stopped, and were looking at him curiously.

"Who is that?" I asked.

"The Yankee captain, sir," replied one of the men.

"The Captain commanding the picket?"

"Yes, sir; when his men ran, he mounted his horse to keep from being captured. The horse was unbridled—the Captain could not guide him with the halter, and he ran away. Then one of our men rode up close and shot him—the horse jumped the fence and threw him—he looks like he was dying."

"Poor fellow! but I suppose he is only wounded. Look after him."

And I went on to catch up with General Stuart, who had ridden on in advance.

Two hundred yards from the spot I found him sitting on his horse in the road and waiting for his column.

"General," I said, "do you know that the officer commanding the picket was shot?"

"No; where is he?"

"He is lying yonder in the corner of the fence, badly wounded."

Stuart looked in the direction of the wounded man.

"This ought to be attended to," he said. "I do not like to leave him there, but I must go on. I wish you would see to this— Dr. Mount is at Mountsville, tell him to have the officer carried there, and to look to his wound. But first take his parole. He is a prisoner."

The General then rode on, and I hastened back to the suffering officer.

The spectacle was a piteous one. He was lying in a corner of the fence, writhing and groaning. From his lips came incessantly those pathetic words which the suffering utter more than all others—"Oh! my God! my God!"

I dismounted, and bent over him.

"Are you in very great pain?"

"Oh! my God!"

"Where are you wounded?"

"Oh! my God! my God!"

I could see no blood, and yet this human being was evidently stretched upon the rack. What he required was a physician; and mounting my horse I galloped to Mountsville, only a few hundred yards distant, where I saw and gave the General's message to Dr. Mount. The doctor promptly answered that he would send immediately for the sufferer, and dress his wound; and having received this assurance, I returned to the spot where he lay.

"Do you suffer as much now?" I asked.

A groan was the reply.

"You will be taken care of—a surgeon is coming."

But I could not attract his attention. Then all at once I remembered the general's order. I was to parole this man—that order must be obeyed, unless I thought him dying or sure to die. It was my duty as a soldier to observe the directions which I had received.

I looked at the sufferer; could see no blood; thought "this wound may be only very painful;" and, taking from my military satchel a scrap of paper, wrote with a pencil the parole which I have copied in the beginning of this paper.

Then kneeling down beside the officer, I placed the pencil in his hand, read the parole, and he attached his name to it, without objection—exhibiting, as he did so, many evidences of suffering, but none of approaching death.

Fifteen minutes afterwards a vehicle was brought, and Captain Gove, of the First Rhode Island Cavalry, was conveyed, in charge of a surgeon, to Mountsville.


                                    III.


Here the writer had intended to terminate his sketch—attaching to it the title, "Paroled in Articulo Mortis." But in so determining he did not take into consideration the curious faculty of memory—that faculty which slumbers, and seems dead often, but none the less lives; which, once set in motion, travels far. Two or three recollections of that period, and allied to the subject, have come back—among them the attack on Aldie; the ovation which awaited us at Middleburg; and the curious manner in which the heavy silver watch and chain of the wounded officer—taken from his body by an officer of the staff—was afterwards restored to his family.

A word of each incident in its turn.

The force at Mountsville was one of the *antennæ* of that dangerous foe, General Bayard. Touched, it recoiled—but behind it were the veritable claws. At Aldie, Bayard was posted with artillery, and a cavalry force which we estimated from the accounts of prisoners—some seventy in number—at about 5000.

Stuart had only the brigade of Fitz Lee, about 1000 men, but once in motion the "Flower of Cavaliers" always followed the Scriptural precept to forget those things which were behind, and press on to those which were before. His column, therefore, moved on steadily; and before I had finished paroling Captain Gove, was nearly out of sight.

Nothing now detained me, and pushing on at full gallop, I came up with Stuart on the high hill west of Aldie. All along the road were dead and wounded men—one of the former was lying in a pool of blood pierced through from breast to back by a sabre thrust.

Fifty yards further, the long column was stationary on the road which wound up the hill—stationary, but agitated, restless. From the front came carbine shots.

On the summit of the hill, relieved against the sky, was the form of Stuart, with floating plume, drawn sword, and animated gesture. His horse was rearing; his sabre, as he whirled it around his head, flashed like lightning in the October sun. No officer was with him—he had distanced all. I never saw him more impatient.

"Go to the head of the column, and make it charge!" was his order—an order so unlike this *preux chevalier*, who generally took the front himself, that I would not record it, did I not recall the exact words—"tell them to charge right in!"

A storm of bullets hissed around the speaker; his horse was dancing the polka on his hind feet.

Before I had reached the head of the column, going at a run,

Stuart was there too. Then the cause of the halt was seen. The enemy had dismounted a double line of marksmen—if they were not infantry—and those adventurous cavaliers who had pushed on into the hornets' hive, Aldie, had fallen back, pursued by balls. At the same moment the Federal artillery was seen coming into position at a rapid gallop on the opposite hill.

Stuart threw one fiery glance in that direction, flashed a second towards the front, and said briefly:

"Tell Wickham to form on the hill, and bring up Pelham at a gallop!"

The order was delivered to Wickham; then I went to hurry Pelham. I found him advancing, alone, at a walk, riding a huge artillery horse, his knees drawn up by the short stirrups.

"The pieces are coming at a gallop," was his smiling answer; "anything going on?"

"The General is going to fall back to the hill, and needs the guns."

"All right; they'll be there."

And soon the roll of wheels, and the heavy beat of artillery horses' hoofs, was heard. A cloud of dust rose behind. The pieces approached at a gallop, and ascending the hill, came into position, flanked by cavalry. Then they opened, and at the third shot the Federal artillery changed its position. I always thought they must have known when Pelham was opposed to them. In the Southern army there was no greater artillerist than this boy.

Stuart was now upon the hill, where he had drawn up his line to meet Bayard's charge. He had scarcely made his dispositions, however, when a mounted man approached him at full gallop, from the side of Mountsville, that is to say, his rear, and delivered a message.

The face of the General flushed, and he threw a rapid glance in that direction. He had received intelligence that a heavy force of the enemy was closing in upon his rear from the side of Leesburgh. With Bayard's 5000 in front, and that column in rear, the little brigade seemed to be caught in a veritable hornets' nest.

But to extricate himself without difficulty from every species of "tight place," seemed to be a peculiar faculty of Stuart's. He gave an order to Wickham; the cavalry moved slowly back, with the enemy's shell bursting above them. Pelham limbered up coolly; the column headed to the left; a friendly by-road, grassy, skirted with trees and unperceived by the enemy, presented itself; and in fifteen minutes the whole Southern force was out of Bayard's clutch, moving steadily across to Middleburg. Stuart was out of the trap.

At Middleburg, that charming little town, dropped amid the smiling fields of Loudoun, the General and his followers were received in a manner which I wish I could describe; but it was indescribable. The whole hamlet seemed to have been attacked by a sudden fit of joyous insanity. Men, women, and children, ran from the houses, shouting, laughing, cheering—crazy, it appeared, for joy, at sight of the gray horsemen. Six hours before they were in the "enemy's country," and the streets had been traversed by long columns of blue cavalry. Now the same streets resounded to the hoofstrokes of Stuart's men, clad in no precise uniform, it might be—real nondescripts—but certainly there was not a single "blue-bird" among them, unless he was a prisoner.

It was this spectacle of gray nondescripts which aroused the general enthusiasm. As Stuart advanced, superb and smiling, with his brilliant blue eyes, his ebon plume, his crimson scarf, and his rattling sabre, in front of his men, the town, as I have said, grew wild. His hand was grasped by twenty persons; bright eyes greeted him; beautiful lips saluted him. Believe me, reader, it was something to be a soldier of the C. S. A., when the name of that soldier was Stuart, Jackson, Gordon, or Rodes. Fair hands covered them with flowers, cut off their coat-buttons, and caressed the necks of the horses which they rode. Better still than that, pure hearts offered prayers for them; when they fell, the brightest eyes were wet with tears.

Most striking of all scenes of that pageant of rejoicing at Middleburg, was the ovation in front of a school of young girls. The house had poured out, as from a cornucopia, a great crowd of damsels, resembling, in their variegated dresses, a veritable collection of roses, tulips, and carnations. They were ready there, these living flowers, to greet their favourite, when he appeared; and no sooner did his column come in sight in the suburbs than a wind seemed to agitate the roses, tulips, and carnations; a murmur rose—"He is coming!"

Then at sight of the floating plume the tempest of welcome culminated. Beautiful eyes flashed, fair cheeks flushed, red lips were wreathed with smiles; on every side were heard from the young maidens, fairly dancing for joy, exclamations of rapturous delight.

As he came opposite the spot Stuart halted, and taking his hat off, saluted profoundly. But that was not enough. They had not assembled there to receive a mere bow. In an instant his hand was seized; he was submerged in the wave of flowers; for once, the cavalier who had often said to me, "I never mean to surrender," was fairly captured. Nor did he seem to regret it. He returned good for evil, and appeared to be actuated by the precept which commands us to love our enemies. Those enemies pressed around him; overwhelmed him with their thanks; grasped his hands, and allowed the brave soldier's lip, as he bent from the saddle, to touch the fresh roses of their cheeks.

Do you blame them? I do not. Do you say that they were too "forward?" Believe me, your judgment is harsh. This soldier was a pure-hearted Christian gentleman, who had fought for those children, and meant to die for them soon. Was it wrong to greet him thus, as he passed, amid the storm? and does any young lady, who kissed him, regret it? Do not be afraid, mademoiselle, should you read this page. The lip which touched your cheek that day never trembled when its owner was fighting, or going to fall, for you. That hand which you pressed was a brave and honest Virginian's. That heart which your greeting made beat faster and more proudly, was one which never shrank before the sternest tests of manhood; for it beat in the breast of the greatest and noblest of our Southern cavaliers!

When Stuart lay down in his bivouac that night, wrapping his red blanket around him by the glimmering camp fire, I think he must have fallen asleep with a smile on his lips, and that the hand of night led him to the land of Pleasant Dreams!

## IV.

A few words will end the present sketch. They will refer to the manner in which the watch and chain of Captain Gove were returned.

In the year 1863, the cavalry headquarters were at "Camp Pelham," near Culpeper Court-house.

The selection of that title for his camp by Stuart, will indicate little to the world at large. To those familiar with his peculiarities it will be different. Stuart named his various headquarters after some friend recently dead. "Camp Pelham" indicated that this young immortal had finished his career.

Pelham, in fact, was dead. At Manassas, Williamsburg, Cold Harbour, Groveton, Sharpsburg, Fredericksburg, and a hundred other battles, he had opposed his breast to the storm, but no bullet had ever struck him. In the hard and bitter struggle of Kelly's Ford, with Averill, in March, 1863, he had fallen. The whole South mourned him—dead thus at twenty-four. Stuart wept for him, and named his new quarters "Camp Pelham."

To-day, in this autumn of 1866, the landscape must be dreary there; the red flag floats no more, and Pelham lives only in memory. But that is enough. There are some human beings who, once encountered, "dare you to forget."

To terminate my sketch. In those days of 1863, I had long forgotten Mountsville, the little fight there, and Captain Gove—for the months of war are long—when one evening at "Camp Pelham" I saw approach a small party of cavalrymen escorting a Federal prisoner. This was so common an occurrence that it attracted no attention. The loungers simply turned their heads; the men dismounted; the orderly announced the fact to the General, and the Federal prisoner, who was an officer, disappeared behind the flap of General Stuart's tent.

Half an hour afterwards the General came out with the prisoner, a short, thick-set man, and approaching the fire in front of my tent, introduced him to me as Captain Stone, of the United States Army. Then, drawing me aside, the General said:

"I wish you would make Captain Stone's time pass as agreeably as possible. We ought to treat him well. In fording a stream near Warrenton, after his capture, he saved the life of Colonel Payne. The Colonel was wearing a heavy overcoat with a long cape, when his horse stumbled in the water, threw him, and as the heavy cape confined his arms, he would have been drowned but for the prisoner, who jumped into the water and saved him. You see we ought to treat him like a friend, rather than as a prisoner," added the General smiling, "and I wish you would give him a seat and make yourself agreeable generally!"

I saluted, returned the General's laugh, and made a profound bow to Captain Stone as I offered him the only camp stool which I possessed. Then we began to talk in a manner perfectly friendly.

This conversation lasted for half an hour. Then General Stuart, who had finished his evening's task at his desk, approached, in company with several members of the staff, and everybody began to converse. The comments of Captain Stone upon his capture and his captors, were entirely amicable. He had been "taken in charge" with perfect politeness; and his personal effects had been religiously respected. In proof of this statement he drew out his watch, and commended it as a timepiece of most admirable performance.

"It is not better than mine, I think, Captain," said a member of the staff, with a smile; and he drew from his breast pocket a large silver watch of the most approved pattern.

"That seems to be an excellent timepiece," was the response of the Federal prisoner. "Where did you purchase it?"

"It was captured; or rather I took it from a Federal officer who was dying, to preserve it—intending if I ever had an opportunity to return it to some member of his family."

Stuart took the watch and looked at it.

"I remember this watch," he said; "it belonged to Captain Gove, who was killed in the skirmish at Mountsville."

"Captain Gove, of the First Rhode Island, was it, General?" asked the prisoner.

"The same, Captain."

"I know his people very well."

"Then," returned Stuart, handing him the watch, "you will be able to return this to his family."

So when Captain Stone left Camp Pelham on the next morning, he took away with him the watch, which the family of the unfortunate Captain Gove no doubt preserve as a memorial of him.

This little incident has occupied an amount of space disproportioned, it may be thought, to its importance. But memory will have no master. The sight of the paper which that dying man at Mountsville affixed his name to, aroused all these recollections. Unwritten, they haunted the writer's mind; recorded, they are banished. The past takes them. There they sleep again, with a thousand others, gay or sorrowful, brilliant or lugubrious, for of this changeful warp and woof is war.

# XI

## JACKSON'S DEATH-WOUND

### I.

THERE is an event of the late war, the details of which are known only to a few persons; and yet it is no exaggeration to say that many thousands would feel an interest in the particulars. I mean the death of Jackson. The minute circumstances attending it have never been published, and they are here recorded as matter of historical as well as personal interest.

A few words will describe the situation of affairs when this tragic scene took place. The spring of 1862* saw a large Federal army assembled on the north bank of the Rappahannock, and on the first of May, General Hooker, its commander, had crossed, and firmly established himself at Chancellorsville. General Lee's forces were opposite Fredericksburg chiefly, a small body of infantry only watching the upper fords. This latter was compelled to fall back before General Hooker's army of about one hundred and fifty thousand men, and Lee hastened by forced marches from Fredericksburg toward Chancellorsville, with a force of about thirty thousand men—Longstreet being absent at Suffolk—to check the further advance of the enemy. This was on May 1st, and the Confederate advance force under

* This is either a typographical error or a prime example of Cooke's carelessness about dates. The battle of Chancellorsville, of course, took place in the spring of 1863. Jackson was wounded on May 2 and died at Guinea Station on May 10.—ED.

Jackson, on the same evening, attacked General Hooker's intrenchments facing toward Fredericksburg. They were found
impregnable, the dense thickets having been converted into
abattis, and every avenue of approach defended with artillery.
General Lee therefore directed the assault to cease, and consulted with his corps commanders as to further operations. Jackson suggested a rapid movement around the Federal front, and
a determined attack upon the right flank of General Hooker,
west of Chancellorsville. The ground on his left and in his front
gave such enormous advantages to the Federal troops that an
assault there was impossible, and the result of the consultation
was the adoption of Jackson's suggestion to attack the enemy's
right. Every preparation was made that night, and on the morning of May second, Jackson set out with Hill's, Rodes's, and
Colston's divisions, in all about twenty-two thousand men, to
accomplish his undertaking.

Chancellorsville was a single brick house of large dimensions,
situated on the plank-road from Fredericksburg to Orange, and
all around it were the thickets of the country known as the
Wilderness. In this tangled undergrowth the Federal works had
been thrown up, and such was the denseness of the woods that
a column moving a mile or two to the south was not apt to be
seen. Jackson calculated upon this, but fortune seemed against
him. At the Catherine Furnace, a mile or two from the Federal
line, his march was discovered, and a hot attack was made on
his rear-guard as he moved past. All seemed now discovered,
but, strange to say, such was not the fact. The Federal officers saw him plainly, but the winding road which he pursued
chanced here to bend toward the south, and it was afterward
discovered that General Hooker supposed him to be *in full retreat upon Richmond.* Such at least was the statement of Federal
officers. Jackson repulsed the attack upon his rear, continued
his march, and striking into what is called the Brock Road,
turned the head of his column northward, and rapidly advanced
around General Hooker's right flank. A cavalry force under
General Stuart had moved in front and on the flanks of the
column, driving off scouting parties and other too inquisitive

wayfarers; and on reaching the junction of the Orange and Germanna roads a heavy Federal picket was forced to retire. General Fitz Lee then informed Jackson that from a hill near at hand he could obtain a view of the Federal works, and proceeding thither, Jackson reconnoitred. This reconnoissance showed him that he was not far enough to the left, and he said briefly to an aide, "Tell my column to cross that road," pointing to the plank-road. His object was to reach the "old turnpike," which ran straight down into the Federal right flank. It was reached at about five in the evening, and without a moment's delay Jackson formed his line of battle for an attack. Rodes's division moved in front, supported at an interval of two hundred yards by Colston's, and behind these A. P. Hill's division marched in column like the artillery, on account of the almost impenetrable character of the thickets on each side of the road.

Jackson's assault was sudden and terrible. It struck the Eleventh corps, commanded on this occasion by General Howard, and, completely surprised, they retreated in confusion upon the heavy works around Chancellorsville. Rodes and Colston followed them, took possession of the breastworks across the road, and a little after eight o'clock the Confederate troops were within less than a mile of Chancellorsville, preparing for a new and more determined attack. Jackson's plan was worthy of being the last military project conceived by that resolute and enterprising intellect. He designed putting his entire force into action, extending his left, and placing that wing between General Hooker and the Rappahannock. Then, unless the Federal commander could cut his way through, his army would be captured or destroyed. Jackson commenced the execution of this plan with vigour, and an obvious determination to strain every nerve, and incur every hazard to accomplish so decisive a success. Rodes and Colston were directed to retire a short distance, and re-form their lines, now greatly mingled, and Hill was ordered to move to the front and take their places. On fire with his great design, Jackson then rode forward in front of the troops toward Chancellorsville, and here and then the bullet struck him which was to terminate his career.

The details which follow are given on the authority of Jackson's staff officers, and one or two others who witnessed all that occurred. In relation to the most tragic portion of the scene, there remained, as will be seen, but a single witness.

Jackson had ridden forward on the turnpike to reconnoitre, and ascertain, if possible, in spite of the darkness of the night, the position of the Federal lines. The moon shone, but it was struggling with a bank of clouds, and afforded but a dim light. From the gloomy thickets on each side of the turnpike, looking more weird and sombre in the half light, came the melancholy notes of the whippoorwill. "I think there must have been ten thousand," said General Stuart afterwards. Such was the scene amid which the events now about to be narrated took place.

Jackson had advanced with some members of his staff, considerably beyond the building known as "Melzi Chancellor's," about a mile from Chancellorsville, and had reached a point nearly opposite an old dismantled house in the woods near the road, whose shell-torn roof may still be seen, when he reined in his horse, and remaining perfectly quiet and motionless, listened intently for any indications of a movement in the Federal lines. They were scarcely two hundred yards in front of him, and seeing the danger to which he exposed himself one of his staff officers said, "General, don't you think this is the wrong place for you?" He replied quickly, almost impatiently, "The danger is all over! the enemy is routed—go back and tell A. P. Hill to press right on!" The officer obeyed, but had scarcely disappeared when a sudden volley was fired from the Confederate infantry in Jackson's rear, and on the right of the road—evidently directed upon him and his escort. The origin of this fire has never been discovered, and after Jackson's death there was little disposition to investigate an occurrence which occasioned bitter distress to all who by any possibility could have taken part in it. It is probable, however, that some movement of the Federal skirmishers had provoked the fire; if this is an error, the troops fired deliberately upon Jackson and his party, under the impression that they were a body of Federal cavalry reconnoitring. It is said that the men had orders to open upon any object in front, "especially upon cavalry;" and the absence of pickets or advance force of any kind on the Confederate side explains the rest. The enemy were almost in contact with them; the Federal artillery, fully commanding the position of the troops, was expected to open every moment; and the men were just in that excited condition which induces troops to fire at any and every object they see.

Whatever may have been the origin of this volley, it came, and many of the staff and escort were shot, and fell from their horses. Jackson wheeled to the left and galloped into the woods to get out of range of the bullets; but he had not gone twenty steps beyond the edge of the turnpike, in the thicket, when one of his brigades drawn up within thirty yards of him fired a volley in their turn, kneeling on the right knee, as the flash of the guns showed, as though prepared to "guard against cavalry." By this fire Jackson was wounded in three places. He received one ball in his left arm, two inches below the shoulder-joint, shattering the bone and severing the chief artery; a second passed through the same arm between the elbow and the wrist, making its exit through the palm of the hand; and a third ball entered the palm of his right hand, about the middle, and passing through broke two of the bones. At the moment when he was struck, he was holding his rein in his left hand, and his right was raised either in the singular gesture habitual to him, at times of excitement, or to protect his face from the boughs of the trees. His left hand immediately dropped at his side, and his horse, no longer controlled by the rein, and frightened at the firing, wheeled suddenly and ran from the fire in the direction of the Federal lines. Jackson's helpless condition now exposed him to a distressing accident. His horse darted violently between two trees, from one of which a horizontal bough extended, at about the height of his head, to the other; and as he passed between the trees, this bough struck him in the face, tore off his cap, and threw him violently back on his horse. The blow was so violent as nearly to unseat him, but it did not do so, and rising erect again, he caught the bridle with the broken and bleeding fingers of his right hand, and succeeded in turning his horse

DEATH WOUND OF STONEWALL JACKSON.

"He was then carried to the side of the road, and laid under a tree." His last words were, "Let us cross over the river and rest under the shade."

back into the turnpike. Here Captain Wilbourn, of his staff, succeeded in catching the reins and checking the animal, who was almost frantic from terror, at the moment when, from loss of blood and exhaustion, Jackson was about to fall from the saddle.

The scene at this time was gloomy and depressing. Horses mad with fright at the close firing were seen running in every direction, some of them riderless, others defying control; and in the wood lay many wounded and dying men. Jackson's whole party, except Captain Wilbourn and a member of the signal corps, had been killed, wounded, or dispersed. The man riding just behind Jackson had had his horse killed; a courier near was wounded and his horse ran into the Federal lines; Lieutenant Morrison, aide-de-camp, threw himself from the saddle, and his horse fell dead a moment afterwards; Captain Howard was wounded and carried by his horse into the Federal camps; Captain Leigh had his horse shot under him; Captain Forbes was killed; and Captain Boswell, Jackson's chief engineer, was shot through the heart, and his dead body carried by his frightened horse into the lines of the enemy near at hand.

## II.

Such was the fatal result of this causeless fire. It had ceased as suddenly as it began, and the position in the road which Jackson now occupied was the same from which he had been driven. Captain Wilbourn, who with Mr. Wynn, of the signal corps, was all that was left of the party, notices a singular circumstance which attracted his attention at this moment. The turnpike was utterly deserted with the exception of himself, his companion, and Jackson; but in the skirting of thicket on the left he observed some one sitting on his horse, by the side of the road, and coolly looking on, motionless and silent. The unknown individual was clad in a dark dress which strongly resembled the Federal uniform; but it seemed impossible that one of the enemy could have penetrated to that spot without being discovered, and what followed seemed to prove that he belonged to the

Confederates. Captain Wilbourn directed him to "ride up there and see what troops those were"—the men who had fired on Jackson—when the stranger slowly rode in the direction pointed out, but never returned. Who this silent personage was, is left to conjecture.

Captain Wilbourn, who was standing by Jackson, now said, "They certainly must be our troops," to which the General assented with a nod of the head, but said nothing. He was looking up the road toward his lines with apparent astonishment, and continued for some time to look in that direction as if unable to realize that he could have been fired upon and wounded by his own men. His wound was bleeding profusely, the blood streaming down so as to fill his gauntlets, and it was necessary to secure assistance promptly. Captain Wilbourn asked him if he was much injured, and urged him to make an effort to move his fingers, as his ability to do this would prove that his arm was not broken. He endeavoured to do so, looking down at his hand during the attempt, but speedily gave it up, announcing that his arm was broken. An effort which his companion made to straighten it caused him great pain, and murmuring, "You had better take me down," he leaned forward and fell into Captain Wilbourn's arms. He was so much exhausted by loss of blood that he was unable to take his feet out of the stirrups, and this was done by Mr. Wynn. He was then carried to the side of the road and laid under a small tree, where Captain Wilbourn supported his head while his companion went for a surgeon and ambulance to carry him to the rear, receiving strict instructions, however, not to mention the occurrence to any one but Dr. McGuire, or other surgeon. Captain Wilbourn then made an examination of the General's wounds. Removing his fieldglasses and haversack, which latter contained some paper and envelopes for dispatches, and two religious tracts, he put these on his own person for safety, and with a small pen-knife proceeded to cut away the sleeves of the india-rubber overall, dresscoat, and two shirts, from the bleeding arm.

While this duty was being performed, General Hill rode up with his staff, and dismounting beside the general expressed his great regret at the accident. To the question whether his wound was painful, Jackson replied, "Very painful," and added that "his arm was broken." General Hill pulled off his gauntlets, which were full of blood, and his sabre and belt were also removed. He then seemed easier, and having swallowed a mouthful of whiskey, which was held to his lips, appeared much refreshed. It seemed impossible to move him without making his wounds bleed afresh, but it was absolutely necessary to do so, as the enemy were not more than a hundred and fifty yards distant, and might advance at any moment—and all at once a proof was given of the dangerous position which he occupied. Captain Adams, of General Hill's staff, had ridden ten or fifteen yards ahead of the group, and was now heard calling out, "Halt! surrender! fire on them if they don't surrender!" At the next moment he came up with two Federal skirmishers who had at once surrendered, with an air of astonishment, declaring that they were not aware they were in the Confederate lines.

General Hill had drawn his pistol and mounted his horse; and he now returned to take command of his line and advance, promising Jackson to keep his accident from the knowledge of the troops, for which the general thanked him. He had scarcely gone when Lieutenant Morrison, who had come up, reported the Federal line advancing rapidly, and then within about a hundred yards of the spot, and exclaimed: "Let us take the General up in our arms and carry him off." But Jackson said faintly, "No, if you can help me up, I can walk." He was accordingly lifted up and placed upon his feet, when the Federal batteries in front opened with great violence, and Captain Leigh, who had just arrived with a litter, had his horse killed under him by a shell. He leaped to the ground, near Jackson, and the latter leaning his right arm on Captain Leigh's shoulder, slowly dragged himself along toward the Confederate lines, the blood from his wounded arm flowing profusely over Captain Leigh's uniform.

Hill's lines were now in motion to meet the coming attack, and as the men passed Jackson, they saw from the number and rank of his escort that he must be a superior officer. "Who is that—who have you there?" was asked, to which the reply was,

"Oh! it's only a friend of ours who is wounded." These inquiries became at last so frequent that Jackson said to his escort: "When asked, just say it is a Confederate officer."

It was with the utmost difficulty that the curiosity of the troops was evaded. They seemed to suspect something, and would go around the horses which were led along on each side of the General to conceal him, to see if they could discover who it was. At last one of them caught a glimpse of the general, who had lost his cap, as we have seen, in the woods, and was walking bareheaded in the moonlight—and suddenly the man exclaimed "in the most pitiful tone," says an eye-witness: "Great God! that is General Jackson!" An evasive reply was made, implying that this was a mistake, and the man looked from the speaker to Jackson with a bewildered air, but passed on without further comment. All this occurred before Jackson had been able to drag himself more than twenty steps; but Captain Leigh had the litter at hand, and his strength being completely exhausted, the General was placed upon it, and borne toward the rear.

The litter was carried by two officers and two men, the rest of the escort walking beside it and leading the horses. They had scarcely begun to move, however, when the Federal artillery opened a furious fire upon the turnpike from the works in front of Chancellorsville, and a hurricane of shell and canister swept the road. What the eye then saw was a secene of disordered troops, riderless horses, and utter confusion. The intended advance of the Confederates had doubtless been discovered, and the Federal fire was directed along the road over which they would move. By this fire Generals Hill and Pender, with several of their staff, were wounded, and one of the men carrying the litter was shot through both arms and dropped his burden. His companion did likewise, hastily flying from the dangerous locality, and but for Captain Leigh, who caught the handle of the litter, it would have fallen to the ground. Lieutenant Smith had been leading his own and the General's horse, but the animals now broke away, in uncontrollable terror, and the rest of the party scattered to find shelter. Under these circumstances the litter was lowered by Captain Leigh and Lieutenant Smith into the road, and those officers lay down by it to protect themselves, in some degree, from the heavy fire of artillery which swept the turnpike and "struck millions of sparks from the flinty stones of the roadside." Jackson raised himself upon his elbow and attempted to get up, but Lieutenant Smith threw his arm across his breast and compelled him to desist. They lay in this manner for some minutes without moving, the hurricane still sweeping over them. "So far as I could see," wrote one of the officers, "men and horses were struggling with a most terrible death." The road was, otherwise, deserted. Jackson and his two officers were the sole living occupants of the spot.

The fire of canister soon relaxed, though that of shot and shell continued; and Jackson rose to his feet. Leaning on the shoulders of the party who had rejoined him, he turned aside from the road, which was again filling with infantry, and struck into the woods—one of the officers following with the litter. Here he moved with difficulty among the troops who were lying down in line of battle, and the party encountered General Pender, who had just been slightly wounded. He asked who it was that was wounded, and the reply was, "A Confederate officer." General Pender, however, recognised Jackson, and exclaimed: "Ah! General, I am sorry to see you have been wounded. The lines here are so much broken that I fear we will have to fall back." These words seemed to affect Jackson strongly. He raised his head, and said with a flash of the eye, "You must hold your ground, General Pender! you must hold your ground, sir!" This was the last order Jackson ever gave upon the field.

### III.

The General's strength was now completely exhausted, and he asked to be permitted to lie down upon the ground. But to this the officers would not consent. The hot fire of artillery which still continued, and the expected advance of the Federal infantry, made it necessary to move on, and the litter was again put in requisition. The General, now nearly fainting, was laid upon it, and some litter-bearers having been procured, the whole party continued to move through the tangled woods, toward Melzi Chancellor's.

So dense was the undergrowth, and the ground so difficult, that their progress was very slow. An accident now occasioned Jackson untold agony. One of the men caught his foot in a vine, and stumbling, let go the handle of the litter, which fell heavily to the ground. Jackson fell upon his left shoulder, where the bone had been shattered, and his agony must have been extreme. "For the first time," says one of the party, "he groaned, and that most piteously." He was quickly raised, however, and a beam of moonlight passing through the foliage overhead, revealed his pale face, closed eyes, and bleeding breast. Those around him thought that he was dying. What a death for such a man! All around him was the tangled wood, only half illumined by the struggling moonbeams; above him burst the shells of the enemy, exploding, says an officer, "like showers of falling stars," and in the pauses came the melancholy notes of the whippoorwills, borne on the night air. In this strange wilderness, the man of Port Republic and Manassas, who had led so many desperate charges, seemed about to close his eyes and die in the night.

But such was not to be the result then. When asked by one of the officers whether he was much hurt, he opened his eyes and said quietly without further exhibition of pain, "No, my friend, don't trouble yourself about me." The litter was then raised upon the shoulders of the men, the party continued their way, and reaching an ambulance near Melzi Chancellor's placed the wounded General in it. He was then borne to the field hospital at Wilderness Run, some five miles distant.

Here he lay throughout the next day, Sunday, listening to the thunder of the artillery and the long roll of the musketry from Chancellorsville, where Stuart, who had succeeded him in command, was pressing General Hooker back toward the Rappahannock. His soul must have thrilled at that sound, long so familiar, but he could take no part in the conflict. Lying faint and pale, in a tent in rear of the "Wilderness Tavern," he seemed to be perfectly resigned, and submitted to the painful probing of his wounds with soldierly patience. It was obviously necessary to amputate the arm, and one of his surgeons asked, "If we find amputation necessary, General, shall it be done at once?" to which he replied with alacrity, "Yes, certainly, Dr. McGuire, do for me whatever you think right." The arm was then taken off, and he slept soundly after the operation, and on waking, began to converse about the battle. "If I had not been wounded," he said, "or had had one hour more of daylight, I would have cut off the enemy from the road to United States ford; we would have had them entirely surrounded, and they would have been obliged to surrender or cut their way out; they had no other alternative. My troops may sometimes fail in driving an enemy from a position, but the enemy always fails to drive my men from a position." It was about this time that we received the following letter from General Lee: "I have just received your note informing me that you were wounded. I cannot express my regret at the occurrence. Could I have directed events I should have chosen for the good of the country to have been disabled in your stead. I congratulate you upon the victory which is due to your skill and energy."

The remaining details of Jackson's illness and death are known. He was removed to Guinney's Depot, on the Richmond and Fredericksburg Railroad, where he gradually sank, pneumonia having attacked him. When told that his men on Sunday had advanced upon the enemy shouting "Charge, and remember Jackson!" he exclaimed, "It was just like them! it was just like them! They are a noble body of men! The men who live through this war," he added, "will be proud to say 'I was one of the Stonewall brigade' to their children." Looking soon afterwards at the stump of his arm, he said, "Many people would regard this as a great misfortune. I regard it as one of the great blessings of my life." He subsequently said, "I consider these wounds a blessing; they were given me for some good and wise purpose, and I would not part with them if I could."

His wife was now with him, and when she announced to him, weeping, his approaching death, he replied with perfect calmness, "Very good, very good; it is all right." These were nearly his last words. He soon afterwards became delirious, and was heard to mutter "Order A. P. Hill to prepare for action!—Pass the infantry to the front!—Tell Major Hawks to send forward provisions for the men!" Then his martial ardor disappeared, a smile diffused itself over his pale features, and he murmured: "Let us cross over the river and rest under the shade of the trees!" It was the river of death he was about to pass; and soon after uttering these words, he expired.

Such were the circumstances attending the death-wound of Jackson. I have detailed them with the conciseness—but the accuracy, too—of a *procès-verbal*. The bare statement is all that is necessary—comment may be spared the reader.

The character and career of the man who thus passed from the arena of his glory, are the property of history.

# XII

## FACETIAE OF THE CAMP

SOUVENIRS OF A C. S. OFFICER

### I.

NOTHING is more tiresome than a "Collection of Anecdotes;" nothing more wearying than the task of gathering them from the four winds.

In the memory of every human being, however, linger many "trifling incidents" which he is loth to have completely disappear from the sum of things. Unrecorded they are forgotten—recorded they live. They may not be "important," but they are characteristic. They were witnessed by the narrator; hence he writes or tells them with an interest infinitely greater than he feels in repeating what he has read, or has heard passing from mouth to mouth. For him the personages live, the localities exist; the real surroundings frame the picture, however valueless it may appear. If therefore, worthy reader, the following *trivia* seem dull to you, it is because you did not "know the parties," as the writer did. Turn the page if they weary you—but perhaps you will laugh. They are "trifles," it is true; but then life is half made up of trifles—is it not?

General Fitz Lee, one day in the fall of 1863, sent a courier up from the Lower Rappahannock, to ask General Stuart why General Pleasanton of the U. S. Army "had been sent to Georgia?"—a dispatch by signal from corps headquarters having communicated that intelligence.

Grand tableau when the affair was explained!

General Stuart had signalled: "Meade's Headquarters are at Wallack's, and Pleasanton's at *Cumberland George's*"—names of persons residing near Culpeper Court-house.

The signal flags had said: "Meade's headquarters are at Wallack's, and Pleasanton's at *Cumberland Georgia!*"

## II.

In November, 1863, Lieutenant —— was in an old deserted mansion near Culpeper Court-house, with some prisoners confined in the upper rooms; the enemy not being far distant. While waiting, a blaze shot up from a fire which some soldiers had kindled near, and threw the shadow of the Lieutenant on the wall. Thinking the shadow was a human being he called out:

"Halt! there!"

No reply from the intruder.

"Answer, or I fire!"

The same silence—when the Lieutenant drew a pistol from his belt. The shadow did the same. The pistol was levelled: the opposing weapon performed the same manœuvre. The Lieutenant thereupon was about to draw trigger, when one of his men called out:

"Why law! Lieutenant, it ain't nothin' but your own shadow!"

Immense enjoyment in camp, of this historic occurrence. Colonel ——, our gay visitor, drew a sketch of the scene, appending to it the words:

> "Now by the Apostle Paul: shadows to-night
> Have struck more terror to the soul of——
> Than could the substance of ten thousand soldiers
> Armed all in proof and led by shallow Buford!"

## III.

Captain F—— was the best of good fellows, and the most amiable of signal officers. He was visiting his signal posts near Culpeper one day, when an infantry-man, clad in a "butternut" costume lounged up, and looked on with the deepest interest while the man on duty was "flopping" away right and left with his flag. Butternut continued to gaze with ardour upon the movements of the signal-man's flag; then he suddenly drawled out in a tone of affectionate interest:

"I sa-a-y, str-a-nger! Are the fli-ies a pestering of you?"

## IV.

In 1863 the enemy caught an old countryman near Madison Court-house, and informed him that he must do one of two things—either take the oath of allegiance to the United States Government or prepare to be *buried alive*. He declined taking the oath, when his captors deliberately proceeded in his presence to dig a grave, and when it was finished they led him to it, and said:

"Will you take the oath?"

"No!" responded the prisoner.

"You had better!"

"I won't!"

"If you don't take that oath you'll be buried alive in that grave, in the next five minutes!"

The old fellow approached nearer, looked with attention at the pit yawning before him, and then turning round with his hands in his pockets replied calmly:

"Well, go on with your d—d old funeral!"

Laughter from the blue-birds, and release of the prisoner as, in the fullest acceptation of the phrase, a "hard case."

## V.

General Order to Inspector-General V——, from Corps Head-quarters:—

"Cry aloud—spare not—show my people their transgressions!"

## VI.

General —— made a true cavalier's speech, one evening at our camp on the Rapidan. He had ridden to headquarters on his beautiful mare "Nelly Gray," whom he had had ever since the first battle of Manassas, and had thus become warmly attached to. When he went to mount again, he found the mare wince under him, and after riding a few yards, discovered she was lame, and limped painfully.

Thereupon the General dismounted, examined the hoof, rose erect again, and uttering a deep sigh exclaimed:

"Poor Nelly! I wish they could fix it some way, so as *you* could ride *me* home!"

That ought to find a place in the biography of the brave officer who uttered it.

## VII.

While I was in the Valley in 1863, I heard an incident which was enough to "tickle the ribs of Death," and for its truth I can vouch. A body of the enemy's cavalry had advanced to the vicinity of Millwood, and two or three men left the column to go and "forage," that is, take by the strong hand what they wanted for supper, from the first house. Very soon they came in sight of a cabin in the woods, and cautiously approaching— for the Confederate scouts were supposed to be everywhere —knocked at the low door.

A negro woman came at the summons, exhibiting very great terror at the sight of the blue coats—and the following colloquy ensued:

"We want some supper."

"Yes, sir."

"But, first, is there anybody here?"

"No, sir."

"Are you sure?"

"Oh! they ain't nobody here but me—'cept—"

"Except who?"

"Only Colonel Mosby, sir."

"Colonel Mosby!!!" exclaimed the speaker, with at least three exclamation points in his accent, and getting hastily into the saddle.

"Are you joking?" he added. "You better not. Is *Colonel Mosby* here?"

"Ye—s, sir," stammered the woman in great terror; and at the same moment a low noise like that produced by the footstep of a man was heard within.

No sooner did they hear this than the men turned their horses' heads, hurried off, and, rejoining their command, reported that Colonel Mosby, the celebrated partisan and "guerilla," was alone in a house in the woods—to which house they could easily conduct a party for his capture.

The information was promptly conveyed to the officer in command, and as promptly acted upon. A detachment was immediately ordered to mount, and, led by the guides, they advanced straight towards the house, which they soon saw rise before them.

It was then necessary to act with caution. Colonel Mosby was well known to be an officer of desperate courage, and it was certain that before permitting himself to be captured he would make a resolute resistance. This was to be counted on, both from the soldierly nerve of the individual and from the fact that he was regarded by many of his enemies as a "bushwhacker" and outlaw, and might be hanged to the first tree, if captured, not treated as a prisoner of war. From this resulted the conviction that the celebrated partisan would sell his life dearly; and the party bent upon his capture omitted no precautions in advancing to attack the wild animal in his lair.

An advance-guard was thrown forward; carbineers were dismounted, and directed to make a circuit and approach the house, from front, flanks, and rear; and having thus made his dispositions, the officer in command pushed up at the head of his men to the house, at the door of which he gave a thundering knock.

No sooner had the trembling negro woman laid her hand on the latch to reply to this summons, than the force burst in, cocked pistols in hand, ready to capture Mosby.

He was not visible. In fact there was no other human being in the cabin except a negro baby, lying in a cradle, and sucking its thumb.

"Where is Mosby?" thundered the officer.

"Oh! there he is!" was the trembling reply of the woman.

"Where?"

"There, sir!"

And the woman pointed to the cradle.

"What do you mean?"

"Oh, sir! I don't mean—I didn't mean nothin'! I call him 'Mosby,' sir—'Colonel Mosby,' sir—that's his name, sir!"

And awaiting her doom, she stood trembling before the intruders. Those personages looked from the woman to the baby, sucking away at his thumb; scowled, growled, took another look; saw that the woman told the truth; and then a roar of laughter followed, which continued until they had mounted and were out of sight.

It is said that this incident was not mentioned by the men upon their return; they only reported Mosby "not found." I have mentioned it, however, and I vouch for it. The mother of "Colonel Mosby," Black and Jr., was a servant of the hospitable mansion in which I tarried; the family declared the incident exactly true; and the hero of the affair, the black baby, namely, is still living. Lastly, I know the woman, she is very worthless, but all are.

## VIII.

There was down in Stafford, during the war, a youthful negro of six or eight years of age, who excited the admiration of everybody by his passionate devotion to the Confederacy, and the "big words" which he used. In fact, his vocabulary was made up of what Mr. Thackeray calls "the longest and handsomest words in the dictionary."

Still he could be terse, pointed, epigrammatic, and hard-cutting in speech. Of these statements two illustrations are given.

1. When an artillery fight took place near the mansion which had the honour of sheltering him, the young African was observed to pause, assume an attitude of extreme attention, remove his hat, scratch his head, and listen. Then turning to his master, he said with dignity, "Hear that artillery, sir. Those are, beyond a doubt, the guns of Stonewall Jackson."

2. Second illustration. A Federal officer of high rank and character, a bitter Democrat and opponent of the negro-loving party, with an extreme disgust, indeed, for the whole black race; this gentleman visited the house where the young Crichton lived, and taking a seat in the parlour, began conversing with the ladies.

While so doing he was startled by a voice at his elbow, and a vigorous clap upon the back of his splendid uniform. Turning quickly in extreme wrath at this disrespect, he saw the grinning face of young ebony behind him; and from the lips of the youth issued the loud and friendly address:

"Hallo, Yank! Do you belong to Mr. Lincoln? You are fighting for me—ain't you?"

The officer recoiled in disgust, looked daggers, and brushing his uniform, as though it had been contaminated, growled to the lady of the house:

"*You* taught him this, madam!"

## IX.

In June, 1863, General Lee was going to set out for Gettysburg. To mask the movement of his infantry from the Lower Rappahannock, a cavalry review was ordered, on the plains of Culpeper.

That gay and gallant commander, General Fitz Lee, thereupon, sent word to General Hood to "come and see the review, and bring any of his people"—meaning probably his staff and headquarters.

On the second day the gray masses of Hood's entire division emerged, with glittering bayonets, from the woods in the direction of the Rapidan.

"You invited me *and my people*," said Hood, shaking hands with General Fitz, "and you see I have brought them!"

Laughter followed, and General Fitz Lee said:

"Well, don't let them halloo, 'Here's your mule!' at the review."

"If they do we will charge you!" interrupted General Wade Hampton, laughing.

For all that the graybacks of Hood, who duly attended the review, did not suppress their opinions of the cavalry. As the horsemen charged by the tall flag under which General R. E. Lee sat his horse looking at them, a weather-beaten Texan of Hood's "Old Brigade" turned round to a comrade and muttered:

"Wouldn't we clean *them* out, if Old Hood would only let us loose on 'em!"

The infantry never could forgive their cavalry brethren the possession of horses—while they had to walk.


## X.

General W—— gave me, one day, a good anecdote of Cedar Run. He was then Colonel of artillery, and when the Confederates' left wing was thrown into disorder, strenuously exerted himself to induce the stragglers to return to the fight. This was not an easy task—the troops were demoralized for the moment by the suddenness of the attack.

In consequence, the Colonel had small success; and this enraged him. When enraged the Colonel swore, and when he swore he did so with extraordinary vehemence and eloquence. On this occasion he surpassed all his previous performances, uttering a volley of oaths sufficient to make a good Christian's hair rise up.

He had just grasped the collar of a straggler, who would not stop at his order, and was discharging at him a perfect torrent of curses, when, chancing to turn his head, he saw close behind him no less a personage than the oath-hating and sternly-pious General Stonewall Jackson.

Jackson's aversion to profanity was proverbial in the army. It was known to excite his extreme displeasure. Colonel W—— therefore stopped abruptly, hung his head, and awaited in silence the stern rebuke of his superior.

It came in these words, uttered in the mildest tone:

"That's right, Colonel—get 'em up!"

## XI.

Another anecdote of Jackson—but this one, I fear, has crept into print. Some readers, however, may not have seen it.

After Port Republic, the General was riding along the line when he heard the following colloquy between two soldiers of the Stonewall Brigade.

"Curse the Yankees! I wish they were in hell, every one of them!"

"I don't."

"Why don't you?"

"Because if they were, Old Jack would be following 'em up close, with the old Stonewall Brigade in front!"

Jackson's face writhed into a grin; from his lips a low laugh issued; but he rode on in silence, making no comment.

## XII.

General C—— was proverbial for his stubborn courage and bulldog obstinacy in a fight. In every battle his brigade was torn to pieces—for he would never leave the ground until he was hurled back from it, crushed and bleeding.

The views of such a man on the subject of military courage are worth knowing. He gave them to me briefly one day, on the battle-field.

Here is the statement of General C——.

"The man who says that he likes to go into an infantry charge, such as there was at Spotsylvania—is a liar!"

## PART 3

# OUTLINES FROM THE OUTPOST

# I

# A SCOUT ACROSS THE RAPPAHANNOCK

My friend, Lieutenant T——, is a *beau garçon*. He is tall, comely, about nineteen, and calls a very illustrious personage "Cousin Robert." He wears a hat with a wide rim, and an ebon feather "floating free" as becomes a cavalry officer; around his waist a black leather belt holds his pistol; huge horseman's boots reach above his knees, and afford him in his lesiure moments a very great resource in pulling them up.

Many idle hours have afflicted my friend lately in consequence of the cessation of hostilities. He has spent his time chiefly in whittling sticks, which proves an unfailing, though not exciting resource to him. While whittling he talks, and he is a gay and delightful companion; relating his adventures with a charming nonchalance, and laughing "in the pauses." Though still young, he has had numerous experiences of a stirring character. In Maryland, just before the battle of Sharpsburg, he was taken prisoner, and had a private interview with General McClellan, who had known some of his relations, and sent for him. The General, he declares, was a very pleasant personage, and very much of a gentleman; easy, bland, smiling; and asked "how many brigades of cavalry Stuart had." Whereto my friend replied evasively, when the General added, laughing:

"Oh, I merely asked to satisfy my private curiosity—not to extract information."

"Of course, General."

"I have heard he had *four* brigades."

"If you have heard that, of course it must be so, General."
Laughter from General McClellan, and friendly termination of
the interview. The General, he says, was "quite a gentleman,"
and ordered him to be released on his parole to return to and
remain in the county of Fauquier until he was exchanged. Returned there; and was still at home when—McClellan's head having fallen—Burnside came along, when he was arrested as a suspicious character, and taken before the new commander, Burnside, portly, polite, not at all stern—rather good-humoured.
T—— gave an account of himself, and was released and sent
back to his home in Fauquier. Here he remained until a scouting
party of his friends came in, when he had himself captured and
returned to the army. He did not make this return journey on
foot. He was mounted, as became a cavalier—but on a white
mule. This white mule was not, however, a portion of his patri-
monial property of a movable character. He procured it from
a Northern friend in the following manner: he was wearily
walking along the road, and saw a "blue-bird" approach him,
mounted on the mule in question. He was unarmed, but so was
my friend—and the Lieutenant immediately, in a voice of thunder, ordered him to get down and surrender. The blue-bird
obeyed, and the Lieutenant mounted—magnanimously permitting his prisoner to go free, inasmuch as he had no means of
securing him. Having paroled him formally, he made haste out
of the line.

Such is the young Lieutenant who, having nothing to do,
whittles sticks.

He has a comrade whose name is Lieutenant H——. This
young gentleman is of about the same age, and his countenance
is comely and smooth. His manners are unusually soft and mild,
and he spends all his leisure in reading. He is familiar with
Shakespeare, and quotes that great bard, going through all the
attitudes, and astonishing the bystanders. Having mounted my
horse some days since to visit a young lady, I was suddenly
startled by the appearance of Lieutenant H——, who, leaning
one hand on my knee, struck an attitude, and broke forth, "Tell

her she's the sun, and I the moon! Arise, fair sun, and shine upon my night!" Having entrusted me with this commission, my friend returned in silence to his literary pursuits. The Lieutenant is so mild and comely of face, that he has been declared to be "like a girl." But he is a man, and a dangerous one, when after the blue-coats. He is devoted to these, and pays them his respects upon all occasions. He is fond of reading, but greatly prefers fighting. Happily married, and keeping house with his helpmate, in camp, he is still impatient at the *idlesse* of the times. Like his friend, Lieutenant T——, he is longing for some movement, and sustains the dull days with difficulty.

If the characters of my two friends are sufficiently indicated by the above sketch, the reader will comprehend with what pleasure they obtained permission in December last (1862) to go on a romantic little scout into the lines of the enemy, beyond the Rappahannock. Burnside was then getting ready to cross at Fredericksburg, and his cavalry scouted daily along the north bank of the river, up and down—so the commission of entering King George was an exciting one, promising no little adventure.

But to procure information of the enemy's designs was only a part of their orders—the most agreeable portion remains behind. They were directed not only to spy out the land, and the position of the foe, but also to escort a young lady, then in King George county, through the enemy's lines into our own. As the reader will imagine, this was far from disagreeable to the chivalric young officers; and they made their preparations with alacrity.

Leaving their swords behind, as calculated to impede their movements when they entered the enemy's country, as they must do, on foot, they took only pistol and carbine, and set out for a point down the river.

The place which they chose for crossing was Port Royal, that lovely little village which nestles down prettily, like a bird, in the green fields—and here, leaving their horses at the house of a friend, they were taken across in a canoe, by a sympathizing boatman, and landed on the northern bank.

From that moment it was necessary to bring into play all the keenness and ready faculties of the woodman and the scout.

They were armed, as I have said, with pistol and carbine; but these were of little use against the enemy, who, if encountered at all, would outnumber and overpower them. Their only hopes of success lay in eluding such scouting parties as they came across, and "snaking it" to their destination and back again.

Soon after leaving the river their adventures commenced. Avoiding the roads, and making their way through the woods, they came all at once upon a large Federal camp, and passed so near it that they could hear the words uttered by the soldiers, but fortunately the darkness of the night prevented them from being seen. Leaving the camp to the right, they continued their way, walking all night, and giving a wide berth to such picket fires as they saw glimmering near their route. They thus reached in safety the house of a lady whom one of the party knew, and where they were certain of food and rest. These were now greatly needed by the young adventurers. Their tramp had been exciting and prolonged, over very rough ground—they had not tasted food since the preceding day—and the whole night had been spent upon the road, or rather in the woods, without rest or sleep.

Reaching the hospitable mansion about daybreak, they aroused the lady, and informed her, in a few words, of their object. "Up went the hushed amaze of hand and eye," as the English laureate says; but the worthy dame acted quickly. Without stopping to parley she admitted them, closed the door, and had an excellent breakfast prepared at once. Having done full honour to the meal, the young men, worn out with fatigue and want of sleep, went to bed, and slept several hours, quite oblivious of the fact that they were far within the lines of the enemy, and subject at any moment to be "caught napping."

Rising at last, the first thing which they did was to look around for something more to eat! It was ready on the table, awaiting them, and they attacked the substantial viands as if they had not eaten before for a month. Some excellent cider accompanied the solids—and this, it appeared, was a present from a young lady who, living close by, had been informed of their presence, and thus manifested her sympathy.

As they rose from the table, the young lady in question entered the dining-room; and looking very attentively at Lieutenant T——, said, smiling:

"I have your picture, sir!"

The young man was naturally astonished at the announcement, as he had certainly never seen the young girl before; and said, with a laugh, that she must be mistaken.

"No, indeed I am not," was the smiling reply; "are you not Lieutenant T——?"

"Yes, madam."

"As I thought."

And the explanation followed. The young lady had a cousin who had gone to school with Lieutenant T——, and the two had become great friends. When they parted, they had recourse to a friendly means of remembering each other, very common with young men—they had their daguerreotypes taken together, both in the same picture, and each took one. The young lady's cousin had presented his own to her; and thus as soon as she saw Lieutenant T——, she recognised the original of the friend of whom her cousin had often spoken.

This romantic little incident was far from putting the young adventurers in a bad humour with their enterprise. They tarried at the house of the hospitable dame long enough to become excellent friends with the pretty maiden, and to procure all the information which the laides could give them. Then, as soon as the shades of evening drew on, they took up the line of march again toward their destination—passing more Federal camps, but running the gauntlet successfully between them all —and arriving safely.

Disappointment awaited them here. The fair lady whom they came to carry off to the "happy land of Dixie," was not ready to return with them. For some reason—doubtless a good one, which I may have heard, but have now forgotten—she determined to remain where she was; and the young men, having secured valuable information of the number and positions of the enemy, set out on their return.

They succeeded, after many adventures, in reaching the vicinity of the river again. To recross was the great difficulty—for there was no longer a sympathizing friend near at hand with a boat. In addition to this, the banks were at this point thoroughly picketed, and they were in danger of being stopped by a musket-ball if they even secured a canoe.

The attempt to cross was necessary to be made, however. It was now night, and if they were detained on the north bank of the Rappahannock until the next day, they would be in imminent danger of capture.

They accordingly set to work. Necessity, the benign mother of invention, pointed out two logs, lying in a sort of marsh, on the edge of the stream; and these logs the young men proceeded to lash together. Having no cords of any description, they used their suspenders, and finally succeeded in launching the impromptu raft upon the stream.

As it floated off, they found all at once that they were moving into view of a sentinel posted upon the rising ground beyond the swampy bottom; and every moment expected to be challenged—the challenge to be succeeded by the whizzing of balls.

The enterprise terminated for the moment, differently, however. The raft had been constructed without very profound science; the suspenders gave way; and Lieutenant T—— found himself astraddle one log, and Lieutenant H—— the other.

Grand tableau!—and the aforesaid "happy land of Dixie" as far off as ever!

They were forced to return to the northern bank, which they succeeded in doing with difficulty, and "as wet as drowned rats." It was necessary to scout along the stream, to find if possible some better means of crossing. This river is difficult to pass —General Burnside was, at the same moment, engaged in the same task which absorbed the energies of the gay youths.

Ascending the bank, and flanking the picket, they plunged into the wood, and struck down the river.

They were not to be so fortunate as before.

Seeing no picket-fires for a long way ahead, they ventured into the road—but were suddenly startled by the tramp of cavalry coming toward them from below.

They leaped the ditch and brushwood fence, and were about to scud across the field, when the troop was upon them, and discovered the moving figures in the dim starlight.

"Halt!" came from the officer in command, as he drew up; and seeing that their further progress would be arrested by a shower of carbine balls, the young men threw themselves upon the ground close beside the brush fence, trusting to the darkness to hide them.

"I certainly saw men there," said the officer.

"I don't think it was anything but cows," said another voice.

"Send a man to see."

And a trooper pushed across into the field, and rode up to the truants, who, finding themselves discovered, put the best face upon the matter.

They were conducted to the officer in command, who said: "Who are you?"

"Third Indiana Cavalry," responded Lieutenant T——, promptly.

"What are you doing here, away from your regiment?"

"We were left behind, sick, sir," was the reply, "and sent on our horses with the baggage. We are now looking for the camp."

This was uttered in the most plausible manner imaginable, and as the darkness hid the young man's Confederate uniform, there was nothing suspicious about him to the eyes of the officer. The two youths seemed to be what they represented themselves—stragglers or sick, trying to rejoin their companies— and no doubts appeared to rest upon the Federal Captain's mind.

He reprimanded them for dodging about, and proceeded on his way—taking the precaution, however, of a good officer, of leaving a mounted man in charge of them, with orders to conduct them to the camp of the regiment to which he belonged, about half a mile distant, and report to the Colonel.

The troop was soon out of sight, and the cavalry-man and his prisoners proceeded slowly in the same direction; their conductor holding a cocked pistol in his right hand.

The young men exchanged glances. Now or never was their opportunity. In fact, something more than loss of liberty was involved in their capture. They had represented themselves as members of the Third Indiana Cavalry; were within the Federal lines; they were clearly reducible under the head of *spies;* and in that character would have a short shrift and a stout rope for their pains.

The camp was near, the time short, action was necessary.

To action they accordingly proceeded.

Lieutenant H——, as I have said, is young; has an engagingly girlish expression of countenance, and his voice is as bland and kindly as possible.

"You have a good horse, there, my friend," said Lieutenant H—— mildly, and with an innocent smile.

"Yes, *sir,*" was the reply; "as good a horse as ever was foaled in the State of York."

"What stock is he?" continued Lieutenant H——, softly; and he laid his hand on the rein as he spoke.

Before the cavalry-man could reply, Lieutenant H—— made a sudden clutch at the pistol which the trooper held; missed it, and found the muzzle instantly thrust into his face.

It was quickly discharged, and again, and again; but strange to say, not a single ball took effect.

Lieutenant H—— retreated, and the trooper turned round and rode at Lieutenant T——, who was armed with a carbine which he had borrowed from me for the expedition.

As the trooper rode at him, he raised the weapon, took aim, and fired. In narrating this portion of his adventures, the Lieutenant says:

"I don't know whether I killed him, but he gurgled in his throat, his horse whirled round and ran, and fifty yards off, he fell from the saddle."

To continue my narrative. The situation of the youths was more critical than ever after the "suppression" of the trooper. The company of cavalry were not far off; the firing had certainly been heard, and a detachment would speedily be sent back to inquire what had occasioned it, even if the riderless horse did not announce fully all that had taken place. No time was to be lost, and the adventurous youths leaped the brush fence, ran across the field, and took shelter in a pine thicket, through which they continued to advance as before, down the river.

They did not observe any signs of pursuit, and after a weary march, reached the vicinity of Port Conway.

One more incident occurred.

Toward daylight they found themselves near a country house on the river bank. Half dead for want of food, for they had eaten nothing since the forenoon of the preceding day, they ventured to approach the building, and knocked at the door.

No reply came; no evidence that the place was inhabited. They knocked again, and this time were more successful.

An upper window of the house was raised, the head of a lady in *coiffure de nuit* thrust out, and a voice asked—

"Who is there?"

"Friends," returned Lieutenant T——, at a venture; "we are worn out with hunger and fatigue, and want a little bread and rest."

"The old story!" returned the voice; "I am tired of you stragglers."

"Stragglers!"

"Yes; there are thousands of you going about and plundering people. You can't come in!"

And the head made a motion to retire.

My friend, Lieutenant T——, is an intelligent youth. He understands readily, and an instant sufficed to make him comprehend that he and his friend were refused admittance because they were regarged as *Yankees*. There were no other "stragglers" in that region; it was plain how the land lay in regard to the fair lady's sentiments, and the result of these quick reflections was the reply:

"We are not Yankees, we are Confederates!"

At these words the head all at once returned to the framework of the window.

"Confederates!" exclaimed the head; "you are trying to deceive me."

"Indeed we are not!"

"What are you doing over here?"

"We came across on a scout, and are now going back. We were captured by a party of cavalry, but got away from them, and are pushing down the river to find a place to cross."

"Are you telling me the truth?"

"Indeed we are."

"What is your name?"

"Lieutenant T—— T——."

"What is the name of your home?"

"Kinloch."

"What is your father's name?"

The young man gave it.

"Your mother's name?"

He gave that, also.

"You are my cousin!" said the lady, completely satisfied; "wait and I will come down and let you in."

Who will doubt about the clans of Virginia after that!

The good lady, who was really a relative of Lieutenant T——, admitted them, gave them a warm welcome, and a hot breakfast; had her best beds prepared for them; and as before, they proved mighty trenchermen; after which they proceeded to sleep like the seven champions of Christendom.

On the same afternoon they succeeded in procuring a canoe, bade their good hostess farewell, and crossed the river, just in time to hear the roar of the cannon at Fredericksburg. These events had passed between the tenth and thirteenth days of December.

I have used no colours of fancy in narrating the adventure; my sketch is a simple statement of facts, which I hope will amuse some of my readers.

Lieutenant T—— related the incidents of the trip with cheerful laughter, and wound up by saying, as he sat by the blazing fire in my tent:

"I tell you, I am glad to get back here, Captain!"

# II

## How I Was Arrested

### I.

I WAS sitting in my tent one day in the year 1863, idly gazing over a newspaper, when my eye fell upon the following paragraph:

"*Killed on the Blackwater.*—We learn that Captain Edelin, of the old First Maryland Regiment, but who recently joined the Confederate forces in North Carolina, was killed a few days since in a skirmish on the Blackwater."

I laid down the paper containing this announcement, and speedily found myself indulging in reverie.

"Thus fall," I murmured, "from the rolls of mortality the names we have known, uttered, been familiar with! The beings with whom we are thrown, whose hands we touch, whose voices we hear, who smile or frown as the spirit moves them, are to-morrow beyond the stars. They are extinguished like the fitful and wandering fires of evening—like those will-o'-wisps which dance for an hour around the fields and then disappear in the gathering darkness!"

This "Captain Edelin, of the old First Maryland Regiment," I had chanced to know. It was but a moment—his face passed before me like a dream, never more to return; but reading that paragraph announcing his death recalled him to me clearly as I saw and talked with him one night on the outpost, long ago.

Captain Edelin once arrested me at my own request.

Let me recall in detail, the incidents which led to this acquaintance with him.

It was, I think, in December, 1861.

I was at that time Volunteer A. D. C. to General Stuart of the cavalry, and was travelling from Leesburg to his headquarters, which were on the Warrenton road, between Fairfax and Centreville.

I travelled in a light one-horse vehicle, an unusual mode of conveyance for a soldier, but adopted for the convenience it afforded me in transporting my blankets, clothes, sword, and other personal effects, which would certainly have sunk a horseman fathoms deep in the terrible mud of the region, there to remain like the petrified Roman sentinel dug out from Pompeii.

The vehicle in question was drawn by a stout horse, who was driven by a cheerful young African; and achieving an ultimate triumph over the Gum Spring road, we debouched into the Little River turnpike, and came past the "Double Toll-gate" to the Frying Pan road.

Here the first picket halted me. But the Lieutenant of the picket took an intelligent view of things, and suffered me to continue the road to Centreville.

Toward that place, accordingly, I proceeded, over the before-mentioned "Frying Pan," which, like the "Charles City road" below Richmond, means anything you choose.

Night had fully set in by the time I reached Meacham's, a mile from Centreville; and I then remembered for the first time that general orders forbade the entrance of carriages of any description into the camp.

This general order, in its special application to myself, was disagreeable. In fact, it was wanton cruelty, and for the following good reasons.

1. I was tired and hungry.

2. That was my route to the headquarters I sought.

3. By any other road I should arrive too late for supper.

This reasoning appeared conclusive, but there was the inexorable order; and some method of flanking Centreville must be devised.

The method presented itself in a road branching off to the left, which I immediately turned into. A small house presented itself, and inquiring the way, I was informed by a cheerful-looking matron that the road in question was the very one which "led to the turnpike."

Never did Delphic oracle make a more truthful or a falser announcement. It was the *Warrenton* turnpike which I desired to reach by flanking Centreville, and cutting off the angle—and lo! with a cheerful heart, I was journeying, as will be seen, toward other regions!

The vehicle proceeded on its way without further pause, merrily gliding along the forest road between dusky pine thickets, the heart of the wandering soldier inspired by the vision of an early supper.

The evening was mild for December—the heavens studded with stars. Now that I had found the road, and would soon arrive, the landscape became picturesque and attractive.

Lonely cavalrymen appeared and disappeared; scrutinizing eyes reconnoitred the suspicious vehicle as it passed; noises of stamping horses were heard in the depths of the thicket. But accustomed to these sights and sounds, the adventurous traveller in search of lodging and supper did not disquiet himself.

Mile after mile was thus traversed. Still the interminable road through the pines stretched on and on. Its terminus seemed as distant as the crack of doom.

Most mysterious of mysteries! The Warrenton turnpike did not appear, though I knew it was but a mile or two through to it. Where was it? Had it disappeared under the influence of some enchantment? Had I *dreamed* that I knew the country thoroughly, from having camped there so long, and had I never in reality visited it? It so appeared; I was certainly travelling over a road which I had never before traversed.

One resource remained—philosophy. To that I betook myself. When a traveller of philosophic temperament finds that he has lost his way, he is apt to argue the matter with cheerful logic as follows:

1. The road I am following must lead somewhere.

2. At that "somewhere," which I am sure eventually to reach, I shall find some person who will have the politeness to inform me in what part of the globe I am.

Having recourse to this mode of reasoning, I proceeded through the pines with a cheerful spirit, entered a large field through which the road ran, and at the opposite extremity "stumbled on a stationary voice."

This voice uttered the familiar

"Halt! Who goes there?"

"Friend without the countersign."

"Advance, friend!"

I jumped out and walked to the voice, which remained stationary.

"I am going to General Stuart's headquarters. Came from Leesburg and have no countersign. This is a picket?"

"Yes."

"Where is the officer of the picket?"

"At the fire yonder. I will go with you."

"Then you are not the sentinel?"

"No; the serjeant."

And the serjeant and myself walked amicably towards the picket fire, which was burning under a large tree, just on the side of *the turnpike.*

The turnpike! Alas!

But, as the novelists say, "let us not anticipate."


## II.

At the picket fire I found half-a-dozen men, neatly dressed in Confederate gray.

"Which is the officer of the picket?" I said to the Serjeant.

"The small man—Captain Edelin."

As he spoke Captain Edelin advanced to the foreground of the picture, and the ruddy firelight gave me, at a glance, an idea of the worthy.

He was about five feet six inches high, with a supple figure—legs bent like those of a man who rides much—and a keen pair of eyes, which roved restlessly. His boots reached to the knee; an enormous sword clattered against them as he walked. The worthy Captain Edelin was no bad representative of Captain D'Artagnan, the hero of Dumas' "Three Guardsmen."

When the Captain fixed his eyes upon me, he seemed to aim at reading me through. When he questioned me he evidently scrutinized my words carefully, and weighed each one.

Such a precaution was not unreasonable. The period was critical, the time "dangerous." Our generals entertained well grounded fears that the enemy designed a flank movement on Centreville, up this very road, either to attack Johnston and Beauregard's left, or to cut off Evans at Leesburg, and destroy him before succour could reach him. I was personally cognizant of the fact that General Evans suspected such an attack, from conversation with him in Leesburg, and was not surprised to find, as I soon did, that the road over which the enemy must advance to assail him was heavily picketed all along its extent in the direction of Fairfax.

If this "situation" be comprehended by the reader, he will not fail to understand why the Captain scrutinized me closely. I was a stranger to him, had passed through the Confederate lines, and was now far to the front. If I was in the Federal service I had learned many things which would interest General McClellan. Spies took precautions in accommodating their dress and entire appearance to the role they were to play; and why might I not be a friend of his Excellency President Lincoln, wearing a Confederate uniform for the convenience of travelling?

So Captain Edelin scanned me with great attention, his eyes trying to plunge to the bottom of my breast, and drag forth some imaginary plot against the cause.

Being an old soldier of some months' standing, and experiencing the pangs of hunger, I rapidly came to the point. Something like the following dialogue passed between us:

"Captain Edelin, officer of the picket?" I inquired.

"Yes, sir," returned the worthy, with a look which said, as plainly as any words, "Who are you?"

I responded to the mute appeal:

"I am Aide to General Stuart, and in search of his head-quarters. I have no countersign. I left Leesburg this morning, and to-night lost my way. What road is that yonder?"

"The Little River turnpike."

"The Little River turnpike?"

"Yes."

Then it all flashed on my bewildered brain! I had missed the road which cut off the angle at Centreville, had taken a wrong one in the dark, and been travelling *between* the two turnpikes towards Fairfax, until chance brought me out upon the Little River road, not far from "Chantilly."

I stood for a moment looking at the Captain with stupification and then began to laugh.

"Good!" I said. "I should like particularly to know how I got here. I thought I knew the country thoroughly, and that this was the Warrenton road."

"Which way did you come?" asked the Captain, suspiciously.

"By the Frying Pan road. I intended to take the short cut to the left of Centreville."

"You have come three or four miles out of the way."

"I see I have—pleasant. Well, it won't take me much longer than daylight to arrive, I suppose, at this rate."

The Captain seemed to relish this cheerful view of the sub-ject, and the ghost of a smile wandered over his face.

"How far is it to General Stuart's headquarters?" I asked; "and which road do I take?"

"That just what I can't tell you."

"Well, there's no difficulty about going on, I suppose? Here are my papers; look at them."

And I handed them to him. He read them by the firelight, and returning them said:

"That's all right, Captain, but—sorry—orders—unless you have the countersign——"

"The countersign! But you are going to give me that?"

The Captain shook his head.

"Hang it, Captain, you don't mean to say you have the heart to keep me here all night?"

"Orders must be obeyed——"

"Why, you are not really going to take possession of me? I don't mind it for myself, as I have my blankets, and you will give me some supper; but there's my horse without a mouthful since morning."

"That's bad; but——"

"You don't know me; I understand you. These papers, my uniform, all may be got up for the occasion; still——"

"That's a fact; and you know orders are orders. On duty—can't know anybody; and I'd like to see the man that can catch Edelin asleep. My boys are just about the best trained fellows you ever saw, and can see in the dark."

"I have no doubt of it, Captain."

"Just about the best company to be found."

"I believe you."

This cheerful acquiescence seemed to please the worthy.

"We're on picket here, and a mouse couldn't get through."

"Exactly; and I wouldn't mind staying with you the least if I had some supper."

"Sorry you didn't come a little sooner; I could have given you some."

"See what I've missed; and after travelling all day, one gets as hungry as a hawk. I'm afraid General Stuart's supper will be eat up to the last mouthful."

This seemed to affect the Captain. He had supped; I, his brother soldier, had not.

"I'll tell you what," he said, "I'll pass you through my picket, but you can't get on to-night. Major Wheat's pickets are every ten yards along the turnpike, and it would take you all night to work your way."

"Cheerful."

"The best thing is to stay here."

"I'd much rather get on."

"But I can't even tell you the road to turn off on. I have no one to send."

As he spoke an idea struck me.

"What regiment is yours, Captain?" I asked.

"The First Maryland—as fine a regiment—"

"Who's your Colonel?"

"Bradley Johnson."

"Well, arrest me, and take me to him."

The Captain laughed.

"That *would* be best," he said. "The Colonel's headquarters are in a small house just across the field. I'll go with you."

So we set out, the huge sword of the worthy clattering against his tall boots as he strode along. On the way he related at considerable length the exploits of his Maryland boys, and renewed his assurances of sympathy with my supperless condition—lamenting the disappearance of his own.

In fact, I may say with modest pride that I had conquered the worthy captain. Eloquence had reaped its reward—had had its "perfect work." From frigid, the Captain had become lukewarm; from lukewarm, quite a pleasant glow had diffused itself through his conversation. Then his accents had become even friendly: he had offered me a part of his Barmeside supper, and proposed to pass me through his picket.

I remember very well his short figure as it moved beside me; his gasconades *à la* D'Artagnan; and his huge sabre, bobbing as he walked. The end of it trailed upon the ground—so short was the Captain's stature, so mighty the length of his weapon.

He strode on rapidly, talking away; and we soon approached a small house in the middle of the large field, through whose window a light shone.

In this house Colonel Bradley Johnson had established his headquarters.

### III.

The Captain knocked; was bidden to enter, and went in—I following.

"A prisoner, Colonel," said the Captain.

"Ah!" said Colonel Bradley Johnson, who was lying on his camp bed.

"At my own request, Colonel."

And pulling off one of a huge pair of gauntlets, I stuck a paper at him.

Colonel Johnson—than whom no braver soldier or more delightful companion exists—glanced at the document, then at me, and made me a bow.

"All right. From Leesburg, Captain?"

"Yes, sir."

"Any news?"

"None at all. All quiet."

"Are you going to General Stuart's headquarters to-night?"

"If I can find the road."

"I really don't know it. I know where it is, but——"

"It will be necessary to send me, I suppose, Colonel?"

"Necessary?"

"I am a prisoner, you know, and I think General Stuart is in command of the outpost."

The Colonel began to laugh.

"That's true," he said.

And turning 'round, he uttered the word—

"Courier."

Now "courier" was evidently the designation of a gentleman who at that moment was stretching himself luxuriously in one corner of the room, drawing over his head a large white blanket, with the air of a man who has finished his day's work, and is about to retire to peaceful and virtuous slumber.

From several slight indications, it was obvious that the courier had just returned after carrying a dispatch, and that he experienced to its fullest extent the grateful sensation of having performed all the duty that could be expected of him, and regarded himself as legally and equitably entitled to at least six hours sleep, in the fond embrace of his white blanket.

Alas for the mutability of mundane things!—the unstable character of all human calculations!

Even as he dismounted, and took off his saddle for the night, Fate, in the person of the present writer, was on his track. As he lay down, and wrapped himself luxuriously in that white blanket, drawing a long breath, and extending his limbs with Epicurean languor, the aforesaid Fate tapped him on the shoulder, and bade him rise.

"Courier!"

And the head rose suddenly.

"Saddle up, and go with this gentleman to General Stuart's headquarters."

A deep sigh—almost a groan—a slowly rising figure rolling up a white blanket, and this most unfortunate of couriers disappeared, no doubt maligning the whole generation of wandering aides-de-camp, and wishing that they had never been born.

With a friendly good-night to Colonel Johnson, whose hard work in the field since that time has made his name familiar to every one, and honourable to his State, I returned in company with Edelin to the picket fire.

The courier disconsolately followed.

On the way I had further talk with Captain Edelin, and I found him a jovial companion.

When I left him, we shook hands, and that is the first time and the last time I ever saw "Captain Edelin of the old First Maryland Regiment." It was Monsieur D'Artagnan come to life, as I have said; and I remembered very well the figure of the Captain when I read that paragraph announcing his death.

He was a Baltimorean, and I have heard that his company was made up in the following manner:

When the disturbances took place in Baltimore, in April, 1861, the leaders of the Southern party busied themselves in organizing the crowds into something like a military body, and for that purpose divided them into companies, aligning them where they stood.

A company of about one hundred men was thus formed, and the person who had counted it off said:

"Who will command this company?"

Two men stepped forward.

"I can drill them," said the first.

"I have been through the Mexican war. I can fight them," said the other.

The command was given to the latter, and this was Edelin. When the war commenced, he marched his company out, and joined the Southern army.

Poor Edelin! He did not know he was arresting his historian that night on the outpost!

## IV.

A few words will terminate my account of "How I was arrested." I have spoken of the courier supplied me by Colonel Johnson, and this worthy certainly turned out the most remarkable of guides. After leaving Captain Edelin's picket, I proceeded along the turnpike toward Germantown—continuing thus to follow, as I have said, the very road I had travelled over when the first picket stopped me at the mouth of the "Frying Pan."

I had gone round two sides of a triangle and was quietly advancing as I might have done over the same route!

There was this disagreeable difference, however, that the night was now dark; that the pickets were numerous and on the alert; that neither I nor the courier knew the precise point to turn off; and that Wheat's "Tigers," then on picket, had an eccentric idea that everybody stirring late at night, at such a time, was a *Yankee*, and to be fired upon instantly. This had occurred more than once—they had shot at couriers—and as they had no fires you never knew when a picket was near.

This was interesting, but not agreeable. To have a friendly "Tiger" regret the mistake and be sorry for killing you is something, but not affecting seriously the general result.

Such appeared to be the view taken by my friend the courier. He was in a tremendous state of excitement. I was not composed myself; but my disquiet was connected with the idea of supper, which I feared would be over. A day's fasting had made me ravenous, and I hurried my driver constantly.

This proceeding filled my friend the courier with dire forebodings. He several times rode back from his place some fifty yards in advance to beg me pathetically to drive slower—he could not hear the challenge if I drove so fast, and "they would shoot!" This view I treated with scorn, and the result was, that my guide was nearly beside himself with terror.

He besought me to be prudent; but as his idea of prudence

was to walk slowly along listening with outstretched neck and eager ears for the challenge of the pickets from the shadow of the huge trees, and to shout out the countersign immediately upon being halted, with a stentorian voice which could be heard half a mile; as his further views connected with the proprieties of the occasion seemed to impel him to hold long and confidential conversations with the "Tigers," to the effect that he and I were, in the fullest sense of the term, "all right;" that I was Aide to General Stuart; that I had come that day from Leesburg; that I had lost my way; that I was not a suspicious character; that *he* was in charge of me—as this method of proceeding, I say, seemed to constitute the *prudence* which he urged upon me so eloquently, I treated his remonstrances and arguments with rude and hungry disregard.

Instead of waiting quietly while he palavered with the sentinels, I broke the dialogue by the rough and impolite words to the sentinel:

"Do you know the road which leads in to General Stuart's headquarters?"

"No, sir."

"Drive on!"

And again the vehicle rolled merrily along, producing a terrible rattle as it went, and filling with dismay the affrighted courier, who, I think, gave himself up for lost.

But I am dwelling at too great length upon my "guide, philosopher, and friend," the courier, and these subsequent details of my journey. I have told how I was arrested—a few words will end my sketch.

We soon reached the "Ox Hill Road," and here *some* information was obtained.

A friendly and intelligent "Tiger," with a strong Irish brogue, declared that this was the route, and I proceeded over a horrible road into the woods.

A mile brought me to camp fires and troops asleep—no answer greeted my shout, and, getting out of the carriage, I went through a sort of abattis of felled trees, and stirred up a sleeper wrapped to the nose in his blanket.

"Which is the road to General Stuart's headquarters?" I asked.

"Don't know, sir."

And the head disappeared under the blanket.

"What regiment is this?"

The nose re-appeared.

"Tigers."

Then the blanket was wrapped around the peaceful Tiger, who almost instantly began to snore.

A little further the road forked, and I took that one which led toward a glimmering light. That light reached, my troubles ended. It was the headquarters of Major Wheat, who poured out his brave blood, in June, 1862, on the Chickahominy, and I speedily received full directions. Ere long I reachd Mellen's, my destination, in time for supper, as well as a hearty welcome from the best of friends and generals.

So ends my story, gentle reader. It cannot be called a "thrilling narrative," but is true, which is something after all in these "costermonger times."

At least, this is precisely "How I was arrested."

# III

## Mosby's Raid into Fairfax

### I.

Among the daring partisans of the war, few have rendered such valuable services to the cause as Captain John S. Mosby.

His exploits would furnish material for a volume which would resemble rather a romance than a true statement of actual occurrences. He has been the chief actor in so many raids, encounters, and adventures, that his memoirs, if he committed them to paper, would be regarded as the efforts of fancy. Fortunately, there is very little fancy about "official reports," which deal with naked facts and figures, and those reports of these occurrences are on record.

It is only necessary to glance at the Captain to understand that he was cut out for a partisan leader. His figure is slight, muscular, supple, and vigorous; his eye is keen, penetrating, ever on the alert; he wears his sabre and pistol with the air of a man who sleeps with them buckled around his waist; and handles them habitually, almost unconsciously. The Captain is a determined man in a charge, dangerous on a scout, hard to outwit, and prone to "turn up" suddenly where he is least expected, and bang away with pistol and carbine.

His knowledge of the enemy's character is extensive and profound; his devices to deceive them are rarely unsuccessful. Take in proof of this a trifling occurrence some time since, in the neighbourhood of Warrenton. The enemy's cavalry, in strong

334

force, occupied a position in front of the command which Captain Mosby accompanied. Neither side had advanced, and, in the lull which took place, the Captain performed the following amusing little comedy: taking eight or ten men, he deployed them as skirmishers in front of an entire brigade of the enemy, and at a given signal from him, they advanced steadily, firing their carbines as they did so, without further intermission than the time necessarily spent in reloading. This manœuvre was executed with such spirit and apparent design to attack in force that the enemy were completely taken in. As the sharpshooters advanced, led on gallantly by the Captain, who galloped about cheering his imaginary squadrons, the enemy were seized with a sudden panic, wavered, and gave way, thus presenting the comic spectacle of an entire brigade retiring before a party of eight or ten sharpshooters.

This is only one of a thousand affairs in which Captain Mosby has figured, proving himself possessed of the genius of a true partisan. If I could here relate these adventurous occurrences, the reader would soon comprehend how steady the Captain's nerve is, how ready his resources in an emergency, and how daring his conception and execution. For the present, I must content myself with one recent adventure, prefacing it with a statement which will probably throw some light upon the motives of the chief actor, and the feelings which impelled him to undertake the expedition.

In the summer of 1862, Captain Mosby was sent from Hanover Court-House on a mission to General Jackson, who was then on the Upper Rapidan. He was the bearer of an oral communication, and as the route was dangerous, had no papers about him except a brief note to serve as a voucher for his identity and reliability. With this note, the Captain proceeded on his journey, and stopping at Beaver Dam Station on the Virginia Central Railroad, to rest and feed his horse, was, while quietly sitting on the platform at the depot, surprised and bagged by a detachment of the enemy's cavalry.

Now, to be caught thus napping, in an unguarded moment, was gall and wormwood to the brave Captain. He had deceived and outwitted the enemy so often, and had escaped from their clutches so regularly up to that time, that to find himself surprised thus filled him with internal rage. From that moment his sentiments toward them increased in intensity. They had been all along decidedly unfriendly—they were now bitter. They took him away with them, searched him, appropriated his credentials, published them as an item of interest in the Northern papers, and immured the partisan in the Old Capitol.

In due course of time he was exchanged. He returned with a handsome new satchel and an increased affection for his friends across the way. He laughed at his misfortunes, but set down the account to the credit of the enemy, to be settled at a more convenient opportunity.

Since that time the Captain has been regularly engaged in squaring his account. He has gone to work with a thorough air of business. Under an energy and perseverance so systematic and undeviating the account has been gradually reduced, item by item.

On the night of Sunday, the eighth of March, 1863, it may fairly be considered that the account was discharged. To come to the narrative of the event alluded to, and which it is the design of this paper to describe:

Previous to the eighth of March Captain Mosby had put himself to much trouble to discover, the strength and positions of the enemy in Fairfax county, with the design of making a raid in that direction, if circumstances permitted. The information brought to him was as follows: On the Little River turnpike at Germantown, a mile or two distant from Fairfax, were three regiments of the enemy's cavalry, commanded by Colonel Wyndham, Acting Brigadier-General, with his headquarters at the Court-House. Within a few hundred yards of the town were two infantry regiments. In the vicinity of Fairfax Station, about two miles off, an infantry brigade was encamped. And at Centreville there was another infantry brigade, with cavalry and artillery.

Thus the way to Fairfax Court-House, the point which the Captain desired to reach, seemed completely blocked up with troops of all arms—infantry, artillery, and cavalry. If he at-tempted to approach by the Little River turnpike, Colonel Wyndham's troopers would meet him full in front. If he tried the route by the Warrenton turnpike, a brigade of infantry, with cavalry to pursue and artillery to thunder at him, was first to be defeated. If he glided in along the railroad, the brigade at Fairfax Station was in his track.

The "situation" would have appeared desperate to almost any one, however adventurous, but danger and adventure had at-tractions for Captain Mosby. If the peril was great and the prob-ability of success slender, all the greater would be the glory if he succeeded. And the temptation was great. At Fairfax Court-House, the general headquarters of that portion of the army, Brigadier-General Stoughton and other officers of high rank were then known to be, and if these could be captured, great would be his triumph.

In spite of the enormous obstacles which presented themselves in his path, Captain Mosby determined to undertake no less an enterprise than entering the town, seizing the officers in their beds, destroying the huge quantities of public stores, and bear-ing off his prisoners in triumph.

## II.

The night of Sunday, March 8th, was chosen as favorable to the expedition. The weather was terrible—the night as dark as pitch—and it was raining steadily. With a detachment of twenty-nine men Captain Mosby set out on his raid.

He made his approach from the direction of Aldie. Proceed-ing down the Little River turnpike, the main route from the Court-House to the mountains, he reached a point within about three miles of Chantilly. Here, turning to the right, he crossed the Frying Pan road about half-way between Centreville and the turnpike, keeping in the woods, and leaving Centreville well to the right. He was now advancing in the triangle which is made by the Little River and Warrenton turnpikes and the Frying Pan road. Those who are familiar with the country there will easily understand the object of this proceeding. By thus cutting through the triangle, Captain Mosby avoided all pickets, scouting parties, and the enemy generally, who would only keep a lookout for intruders on the main roads.

Advancing in this manner through the woods, pierced with devious and uncertain paths only, which the dense darkness scarcely enabled them to follow, the partisan and his little band finally struck into the Warrenton road, between Centreville and Fairfax, at a point about midway between the two places. One danger had thus been successfully avoided—a challenge from parties of cavalry on the Little River road, or discovery by the force posted at Centreville. That place was now in their rear— they had "snaked" around it and its warders; but the perils of the enterprise had scarcely commenced. Fairfax Court-House was still about four miles distant, and it was girdled with cavalry and infantry. Every approach was guarded, and the attempt to enter the place seemed desperate, but the Captain determined to essay it.

Advancing resolutely, he came within a mile and a half of the place, when he found the way barred by a heavy force. Directly in his path were the infantry camps of which he had been notified, and all advance was checked in that direction. The Captain did not waver in his purpose, however. Making a detour to the right, and leaving the enemy's camp far to his left, he struck into the road leading from Fairfax southward to the railroad.

This avenue was guarded like the rest, but by a picket only; and the Captain knew thoroughly how to deal with these. Before the sleepy and unsuspicious pickets were aware of their danger, they found pistols presented at their heads, with the option of surrender or death presented to them. They surrendered immediately, were taken in charge, and without further ceremony Captain Mosby and his band entered the town.

From that moment the utmost silence, energy, and rapidity of action were requisite. The Captain had designed reaching the Court-House at midnight, but had been delayed two hours by mistaking his road in the pitch darkness. It was now two o'clock in the morning; and an hour and a half, at the very utmost, was left him to finish his business and escape before daylight. If morning found him anywhere in that vicinity he knew that his retreat would be cut off, and the whole party killed or captured —and this would have spoiled the whole affair. He accordingly made his dispositions rapidly, enjoined complete silence, and set to work in earnest. The small band was divided into detachments, with special duties assigned to each. Two or three of these detachments were sent to the public stables which the fine horses of the General and his staff officers occupied, with instructions to carry them off without noise. Another party was sent to Colonel Wyndham's headquarters to take him prisoner. Another to Colonel Johnson's, with similar orders.

Taking six men with him, Captain Mosby, who proceeded upon sure information, went straight to the headquarters of Brigadier-General Stoughton.

The Captain entered his chamber without much ceremony, and found him asleep in bed.

Making his way toward the bed, in the dark, the partisan shook him suddenly by the shoulder.

"What is that?" growled the General.

"Get up quick, I want you," responded the Captain.

"Do you know who I am?" cried the Brigadier, sitting up in bed, with a scowl. "I will have you arrested, sir!"

"Do you know who *I* am?" retorted the Captain, shortly.

"Who are you?"

"Did you ever hear of Mosby?"

"Yes! Tell me, have you caught the —— rascal!"

"No, but he has caught you!"

And the Captain chuckled.

"What does all this mean, sir!" cried the furious officer.

"It means, sir," the Captain replied, "that Stuart's cavalry are in possession of this place, and you are my prisoner. Get up and come along, or you are a dead man!"

Bitter as was this order, the General was compelled to obey, and the partisan mounted him, and placed him under guard. His staff and escort were captured without difficulty, but two of the former, owing to the darkness and confusion, subsequently made their escape.

Meanwhile the other detachments were at work. They entered the stables, and led out fifty-eight very fine horses, with their accoutrements, all belonging to officers, and took a number of prisoners. Hundreds of horses were left, for fear of encumbering the retreat.

The other parties were less successful. Colonel Wyndham had gone down to Washington on the preceding day; but his A. A. General and Aide-de-camp were made prisoners. Colonel Johnson having received notice of the presence of the party, succeeded in making his escape.

It was now about half-past three in the morning, and it behoved Captain Mosby, unless he relished being killed or captured, to effect his retreat. Time was barely left him to get out of the lines of the enemy before daylight, and none was to be lost.

He had intended to destroy the valuable quartermaster, commissary, and sutler's stores in the place, but these were found to be in the houses, which it would have been necessary to burn; and even had the proceeding been advisable, time was wanting. The band was encumbered by three times as many horses and prisoners as it numered men, and day was approaching. The captain accordingly made his dispositions rapidly for retiring.

The prisoners, thirty-five in number, were as follows:

Brig.-Gen. E. H. Stoughton.

Baron R. Wordener, an Austrian, and Aide-de-camp to Col. Wyndham.

Capt. A. Barker, 5th New York Cavalry.

Col. Wyndham's A. A. General.

Thirty prisoners, chiefly of the 18th Pennsylvania and 1st Ohio Cavalry, and the telegraph operator at the place.

These were placed upon the captured horses, and the band set out in silence on their return.

Captain Mosby took the same road which had conducted him into the Court-House: that which led to Fairfax Station. But this was only to deceive the enemy as to his line of retreat, if they attempted pursuit. He soon turned off, and pursued the same road which he had followed in advancing, coming out on the Warrenton turnpike, about a mile and a half from the town. This time, finding no guards on the main road, he continued to follow the turnpike until he came to the belt of woods which crosses the road about half a mile from Centreville. At this point of the march, one of the prisoners, Captain Barker, no doubt counting on aid from the garrison, made a desperate effort to effect his escape. He broke from his guards, dashed out of the ranks, and tried hard to reach the fort. He was stopped, however, by a shot from one of the party, and returned again, yielding himself a prisoner.

Again turning to the right, the Captain proceeded on his way, passing directly beneath the frowning fortifications. He passed so near them that he distinctly saw the bristling muzzles of the cannon in the embrasures, and was challenged by the sentinel on the redoubt. Making no reply he pushed on rapidly, for the day was dawning, and no time was to be lost; passed within a hundred yards of the infantry pickets without molestation, swam Cub Run, and again came out on the Warrenton turnpike at Groveton.

He had passed through all his enemies, flanked Centreville, was on the open road to the South: he was safe!

# IV

## MY FRIEND LIEUTENANT BUMPO

YESTERDAY I received a letter from my friend Lieutenant N. Bumpo, Artillery Corps, P. A. C. S.* To-day I have been thinking of the career of this young gentleman from the outset of the war.

"Representative men" are profitable subjects for reflection. They embody in their single persons, the characteristics of whole classes.

Bumpo is a representative man.

He represents the Virginia youth who would not stay at home, in spite of every attempt to induce him to do so; who, shouldering his musket, marched away to the wars; who has put his life upon the hazard of the die a thousand times, and intends to go on doing so to the end.

I propose to draw an outline of Lieutenant Bumpo. The sketch shall be accurate; so accurate that he will be handed down to future generations—even as he lived and moved during the years of the great revolution. His grandchildren shall thus know all about their at present prospective grandpa—and all his descendants shall honour him. His portrait over the mantelpiece shall

* This chapter was probably based on the army career of Cooke's nephew, Nathaniel, the son of his elder brother, Philip Pendleton Cooke. This young nephew is often referred to by Cooke as "Nat" or "my boy."—ED.

be admiringly indicated, *uno digito*. The antique cut of his uniform shall excite laughter. Bumpo will live in every heart and memory!

He is now seventeen and a half. Tall for his age; gay, smiling; fond of smoking, laughing, and "fun" generally. I have said that he is an officer of the Artillery Corps, at present—but he has been in the infantry and the cavalry.

He was born in the Valley of Virginia, and spent his youth in warring on partridges. His aim thus early became unerring. When the war broke out it found him a boy of some fifteen and a half—loving all mankind, except the sons of the famous "Pilgrim Fathers." Upon this subject Bumpo absorbed the views of his ancestors.

April, 1861, arrived duly. Bumpo was in the ranks with a rifle. Much remonstrance and entreaty saluted this proceeding, but Private Bumpo, of the "—— Rifles," remained obstinate.

"Young?" Why he was FIFTEEN!

"The seed corn should be kept?" But suppose there was no Southern soil to plant it in?

"A mere boy?"—Boy!!!

And Private Bumpo stalked off with his rifle on his shoulder—outraged as Coriolanus, who, after having "fluttered the Volsces in Corioli," was greeted with the same opprobrious epithet.

Obstinacy is not a praiseworthy sentiment in youth, but I think that young Bumpo was right. He would have died of chagrin at home, with his comrades in the service; or his pride and spirit of *haute noblesse* would have all departed. It was better to run the risk of being killed.

So Bumpo marched.

He marched to Harper's Ferry—and thenceforth "Forward—march!" was the motto of his youthful existence.

Hungry?—"Forward, march!"

Cold?—"Forward, march!"

Tired?—"Forward, march!"

Bumpo continued thenceforth to march. When not marching he was fighting.

The officer who commanded his brigade was a certain Colonel Jackson, afterwards known popularly as "Old Stonewall." This officer could not bear Yankees, and this tallied exactly with Private Bumpo's views. He deeply sympathized with the sentiments of his illustrious leader, and loaded and fired with astonishing rapidity and animation. At "Falling Water" he "fought and fell back." Thereafter he marched back and forth, and was on the Potomac often. A slight historic anecdote remains of this period in the Bumpo annals. He was on picket near the river bank with a friend of ours, when suddenly an old woman, of hag-like, Macbeth-witch appearance, came in view on the opposite bank, gesticulating violently to hidden observers that yonder were the Rebels! The friend of our youth, in a jocose spirit, fired, as he said, ahead of the old hag to frighten her—or behind, to put a ball through her flying skirts—but Bumpo upbraided him with his bloody real intentions. We regret to say, however, that he afterwards retired behind a tree and indulged in smothered laughter as the Macbeth-witch disappeared with floating robes toward her den.

From the Valley, Private Bumpo proceeded rapidly to Manassas, where he took part in the thickest of the fight, and was bruised by a fragment of shell. Here he killed his first man. His cousin, Carey ——, fell at his side, and Bumpo saw the soldier who shot him, not fifty yards off. He levelled his rifle, and put a ball through his breast. He went down, and Bumpo says with laughter, "I killed him!"

He was starved like all of us at Manassas, and returning to the Valley continued to have short rations. He fought through all the great campaigns there, and wore out many pairs of shoes in the ranks of the Foot Cavalry. At Kernstown he had just fired his gun, and as he exclaimed "By George! I got him that time!" received a ball which tore his coat-sleeve to pieces, and numbed his wrist considerably. He regards himself as fortunate, however, and says Kernstown was as hot as any fight he has seen. Thereafter, more marching. He had been back to the Fairfax country, where I saw him two or three times—and now traversed the Valley again. The Rommey march, he says, was a hard one; no blankets, no rations, no fire, but a plenty of snow. I saw him on his return at Winchester, and compared notes. The weather was bad, but Bumpo's spirits good. He had held on to his musket, remaining a high private in the rear rank.

Some of these days he will tell his grandchildren, if he lives, all about the days when he followed Commissary Banks about, and revelled in the contents of his wagons. Altogether they had a jovial time, in spite of snow and hunger and weariness.

The days hurried on, and Port Republic was fought. Private Bumpo continued to carry his musket about. He had now seen a good deal of Virginia—knew the Valley by heart—was acquainted with the very trees and wayside stones upon the highways. Riding with me since, he has recalled many tender memories of these objects. Under that tree there, he lay down to rest in the shade on a hot July day. On that stone he sat, overcome with weariness, one afternoon of snowy December. There's the road we fell back on! Yonder is the hollow where we advanced! Consequent conclusion on the part of Private Bumpo that he has graduated in the geography of that portion of his native State.

The lowland invited him to visit its sandy roads, after Cross Keys. The stones of the Valley were exchanged for the swampy soil of the Chickahominy.

On the morning of the battle of Cold Harbour, I saw a brigade in the pine woods as I passed, and inquiring what one it was, found it was Bumpo's. I found the brave youth in charming spirits as ever; and surrounded by his good comrades, lying on the pine-tags, he told me many things in brief words.

Bumpo, like his brave companions, had the air of the true soldier—cheerful, prone to jest, and ready for the fray. He was clad in gray, or rather brown, for the sun had scorched his good old uniform to a dingy hue—and the bright eyes of the young gentleman looked at you from beneath an old drab-coloured hat. Bumpo, I think, had an irrational admiration for that hat, and, I remember, liked his black "Yankee" haversack. I had a fine new, shiny one which I had purchased, at only fifteen times its original cost, from a magnanimous shop-keeper of Richmond; and this I offered to Bumpo. But he refused it—clinging to his plainer and better one, but slenderly stocked with crackers.

Suddenly the drum rolled. Bumpo shouldered his musket.

"Fall in!"

And the brigade was on its march again.

Poor Colonel A——! I pressed your hand that day, for "the first time and the last time!" Your face was kind and smiling as you told me you would always be glad to see me at your camp—but four hours afterwards it was cold in death. The fatal ball had pierced your breast, and your heart's blood dyed that hard-fought field with its crimson.

Such are the experiences of a soldier.

The battle was already raging—the brigade rapidly approached. They arrived in time—the order passed along the line—the corps of General Jackson went in with colours flying.

"Yesterday was the most terrific fire of musketry I ever heard."

Such were the words of General Jackson an hour past midnight.

On that succeeding morning, I set out to find Corporal Bumpo —for to this rank he had been promoted. I met General Jackson on the way, his men cheering the hero, and ascertaining from him the whereabouts of the brigade, proceeded thither.

Corporal Bumpo smiling and hungry—a cheerful sight. He was occupied in stocking his old haversack with biscuits—excellent ones. They had been sent to an officer of the command, but he was killed; and his comrades divided them. Corporal Bumpo had charged, with his company, at sundown, near the enemy's battery, on their extreme right. A piece of shell had bruised him, and a ball cut a breast button of his coat in two. The under side remained, with the name of the manufacturer still legibly stamped thereon. Magnanimous foes! They never interfere with "business." That button was an "advertising medium"—and even in the heat of battle they respected it.

Corporal Bumpo ought to have preserved that jacket as a memorial of other days, for the honours of age. But its faded appearance caused him to throw it away, part company with a good old friend. What matter if it was discoloured, Bumpo? It had sheltered you for many months. You had lain down in it on the pine-tags of the valley and the lowlands, in the days of July, and the nights of January; on the grass and in the snow; with a gay heart or a sad one, beating under it. I do not recognise you, Corporal, in this wanton act—for do not all the members of the family adhere to old friends? The jacket may have been sun-embrowned, but so is the face of an old comrade. Lastly, it was not more brown than that historic coat which the immortal Jackson wore—whereof the buttons have been taken off by fairy hands instead of bullets.

After Cold Harbour, Corporal Bumpo began marching again as usual. Tramping through the Chickahominy low-grounds, he came with his company to Malvern Hill, and was treated once more to that symphony—an old tune now—the roar of cannon. The swamp air had made him deadly sick—him, the mountain born—and, he says, he could scarcely stand up, and was about to get into an ambulance. But well men were doing so, and the soul of Bumpo revolted from the deed. He gripped his musket with obstinate clutch, and stayed where he was—shooting as often as possible. We chatted about the battle when I rode to see him, in front of the gunboats, in Charles City; and, though "poorly," the Corporal was gay and smiling. He had got something to eat, and his spirits had consequently risen.

"Fall in!" came as we were talking, and Bumpo marched.

Soon thereafter, I met the Corporal in the city of Richmond, whither he had come on leave. I was passing through the Capitol Square, when a friendly voice hailed me, and behold! up hastened Bumpo! He was jacketless, but gay; possessor of a single shirt, but superior to all the weaknesses of an absurd civilization. We went to dine with some elegant lady friends, and I offered the Corporal a black coat. He tried it on, surveyed himself in the glass, and, taking it off, said, with cheerful *naiveté*, that he believed he would "go so." I applauded this soldierly decision, and I know the fair dames liked the young soldier all the better for it. I think they regarded his military "undress" as more becoming than the finest broadcloth. The balls of the enemy had respected that costume, and the lovely girls with the brave, true hearts, seemed to think that they ought to, too.

I linger too long in these by-ways of the Corporeal biography, but remember that I write for the gay youth's grandchildren. They will not listen coldly to these little familiar details.

From Richmond the Corporal marched northward again. This time he was destined to traverse new regions. The Rapidan invited him, and he proceeded thither, and, as usual, got into a battle immediately. He says the enemy pressed hard at Cedar mountain, but when Jackson appeared in front, they broke and fled. The Corporal followed, and marched after them through Culpeper; through the Rappahannock too; and to Manassas. A hard fight there; two hard fights; and then with swollen and bleeding feet, Bumpo succumbed to fate, and sought that haven of rest for the weary soldier—a wagon not until he had his surgeon's certificate, however; and with this in his pocket, the Corporal went home to rest a while.

I think this tremendous tramp from Winchester to Manassas, by way of Richmond, caused Corporal Bumpo to reflect. His feet were swollen, and his mind absorbed. He determined to try the cavalry. Succeeding, with difficulty, in procuring a transfer, he entered a company of the Cavalry Division under Major-General Stuart, whose dashing habits suited him; and no sooner had he done so than his habitual luck attended him. On the second day he was in a very pretty little charge near Aldie. The Corporal—now private again—got ahead of his companions, captured a good horse, and supplied himself, without cost to the Confederate States, with a light, sharp, well balanced sabre. Chancing to be in his vicinity I can testify to the gay ardour with which the ex-Corporal went after his old adversaries, no longer on foot, and even faster than at the familiar "double quick."

His captured horse was a good one; his sabre excellent. It has drawn blood, as the following historic anecdote will show. The ex-Corporal was travelling through Culpeper with two mounted servants. He and his retinue were hungry; they could purchase no food whatever. At every house short supplies—none to be vended—very sorry, but could not furnish dinner. The hour for that meal passed. Supper-time came. At many houses supper was demanded, with like unsuccess. Then the soul of Bumpo grew enraged—hunger rendered him lawless, inexorable. He saw a pig on the road by a large and fine looking house; poor people living beside the road disclaimed ownership, and declined selling. Impressment was necessary—and Bumpo, with a single blow of his sabre, slaughtered the unoffending shoat. Replacing his sword with dignity in its scabbard, he indicated the prostrate animal with military brevity of point, and rode on, apparently in deep reflection. The retinue followed with a pig which they had found recently killed, upon the road—and bivouacking for the night in the next woods he reached, with the aid of some bread in his servants' haversacks, Bumpo made an excellent supper.

This incident he related to me with immoral exultation. It is known in the family as the "Engagement in Culpeper."

Bumpo was greatly pleased with the cavalry, and learned fast. He displayed an unerring instinct for discovering fields of new corn for horse feed; was a great hand at fence rails for the bivouac fire; and indulged in other improper proceedings which indicated the old soldier, and free ranger of the fields and forests. The "fortunes of war" gave me frequent opportunities of enjoying the society of Bumpo at this time. We rode together many scores of miles, with Augustus Cæsar, a coloured friend, behind; and lived the merriest life imaginable.

Worthy Lieutenant of the C. S. Artillery, do you ever recall those sunshiny days? Don't you remember how we laughed and jested as we rode; how we talked the long hours away so often; and related to each other a thousand stories? How we bivouacked by night, and halted to rest by day, making excellent fires, and once kindling the dry leaves into a conflagration which we thought would bring over the enemy? Have you forgotten that pleasant little mansion in the woods, where a blazing fire and real coffee awaited us—where I purchased "Consuelo," and you, "The Monk's Revenge?" You were Bumpo "by looks" and Bumpo "by character" that day, my friend, for you feasted as though a famine were at hand! Then the supper at Rudishill's, and the breakfast at Siegel's old head-quarters. The march by night, and the apparition of Rednose, emissary of Bluebaker! Those days were rather gay—in spite of wind and snow—were they not, Lieutenant Bumpo? You live easier now, perhaps, but when do you see tableaux like Rednose in your journey? Rednose, superior to the Thane of Cawdor, in-asmuch as *he* was "not feared!"

The Lieutenant will have to explain the above mysterious allusion to his grand-children. I think he will laugh as he does so, and that a small chirping chorus will join in.

The young soldier soon left the cavalry. He went to see a kinsman, was elected lieutenant of artillery in a battery which he had never seen, and on report of his merits only, and returned with his certificate of election in his pocket. The old luck at-tended him. In a fortnight or so he was in the battle of Fred-ericksburg, where he kept up a thundering fire upon the enemy —roaring at them all day with the utmost glee; and now he has gone with his battery, in command of a section, with plenty of brave cannoneers to work the pieces, to the low grounds of North Carolina.

Such is the career of Bumpo, a brave and kindly youth, which the letter received yesterday made me ponder upon.

Some portions of the epistle are characteristic:

"Last night I killed a shoat which kept eating my corn; and made our two Toms scald it and cut it up, and this morning we had a piece of it for breakfast. We call the other Tom 'Long Tom,' and Thomas 'Augustus Cæsar!'"

Bumpo! Bumpo! at your old tricks, I see. Shoat has always been your weakness, you know, from the period of the famous "Engagement in Culpeper," where you slew one of these inof-fensive animals. But here, I confess, there are extenuating cir-cumstances. For a shoat to eat the corn of a lieutenant of a battery, is a crime of the deepest and darkest dye, and in this case that swift retribution which visited the deed, was consistent with both law and equity.

The natural historian will be interested in the announcement that he had killed a good many robins, but none were good, as they live altogether on a kind of berry called gall-berry, which makes them bitter." "Bears, deers, coons, and opossum" there are; but the Lieutenant has killed none.

"The weather," he adds, "is as warm here as any day in May in the valley. We are on a sort of island, bounded by *dense swamp on each side, and a river before and behind, with the bridges washed away.* We are throwing up fortifications, but I don't think we will ever need them, *as it is almost impossible for the Yankees to find us here.*"

Admire the impregnable position in which Lieutenant Bumpo with two pieces of artillery, "commanding in the field," awaits the approach of his old friends. Dense swamps on his flanks, and rivers without bridges in his front and rear, across which, unless they come with pontoons, he can blaze away at them to advantage! That he is certain to perform that ceremony if he can, all who know him will cheerfully testify. If he falls it will be beside his gun, like a soldier, and "dead on the field of honour" shall be the young Virginian's epitaph.

But I do not believe he will fall. The supreme Ruler of all things will guard the young soldier who has so faithfully performed his duty to the land of his birth.

"I think," he adds in his letter before me, "if luck does not turn against us, we shall be recognised very soon. I don't care how soon, but I am no more tired of it than I was twelve months ago."

Is not that the ring of the genuine metal? The stuff out of which the good soldier is made? He is no more tired of it than he was a year ago, and will cheerfully fight it out to the end. Not "tired of it" when so many are "tired of it." When such numbers would be willing to compromise the quarrel—to abandon the journey through the wilderness to Canaan—and return a-hungered to the fleshpots of Egypt!

Such, in rapid outline, is the military career of my friend. I said in the beginning that he was a "representative man." Is he not? I think that he represents a great and noble race to the life—the true-hearted youths of the South. They have come up from every State and neighbourhood; from the banks of the Potomac and the borders of the Gulf. They laid down the school-book to take up the musket. They forgot that they were young, and remembered only that their soil was invaded.

They were born in all classes of the social body. The humble child of toil stood beside the young heir of an ancient line, and they lived and fared alike. One sentiment inspired them in common, and made them brethren—love for their country and hatred of her enemies. Their faces were beardless, but the stubborn resolution of full manhood dwelt in every bosom. They fought beside their elders, and no worse, often better. No hardships made them quail. They were cheerful and high-spirited, marching to battle with a gay and chivalric courage, which was beautiful and inspiring to behold.

When they survived the bloody contest they laughed gaily, like children, around the camp fire at night. When they fell they died bravely, like true sons of the South.

I have seen them lying dead upon many battle-fields; with bosoms torn and bloody, but faces composed and tranquil. Fate had done her worst, and the young lives had ended; but not vainly has this precious blood been poured out on the land. From that sacred soil shall spring up courage, honour, love of country, knightly faith, and truth—glory, above all, for the noble land, whose very children fought and died for her!

So ends my outline sketch of the good companion of many hours.

Send him back soon, O Carolina, to his motherland Virginia, smiling, hearty, "gay and happy," as he left her borders!

*Ainsi soit-il!*

# V

## CORPORAL SHABRACH

Camp Quattlebum Rifles, Army of Northern Virginia,
December 10, 1863.

WHEN I left home, my dear boys, I promised to write to you whenever an opportunity occurred, and give you some of my views and opinions.

I have an opportunity to-morrow to send you this; and as the characters of great men are valuable guides to growing boys who are shaping their own, I will take this occasion to tell you something about the famous Commander of the Army of Northern Virginia, General Lee.

I will first describe his appearance; for I have always observed that when we know how a great man looks, we take far more interest in his sayings and doings, for we have an accurate idea of the sort of person who is talking or acting. I remember reading once that Cæsar, the celebrated Roman General, was a dandy in his youth—a sort of "fine gentleman" about Rome; and had lost all his hair, which he regretted greatly, and tried to conceal with the laurel crown he wore. Also, that when he conquered Gaul he was thin and pale, had frequent fainting fits, and yet was so resolute and determined that while he was riding on horseback, over mountains and through rivers, he would dictate dispatches to as many as seven secretaries at a time, who were carried in litters at his side. I also remember reading how the Em-

353

peror Napoleon looked, and all about his old gray overcoat, his cocked hat, his habit of taking snuff from his waistcoat pocket, and his dark eyes, set in the swarthy face, and looking at you so keenly as he spoke to you. I was greatly helped, too, in my idea of General Washington—whom General Lee, to my thinking, greatly resembles—by finding that he was tall, muscular, and carried his head erect, repulsing with a simple look all meddling or impertinence, and impressing upon all around him, by his grave and noble manner, a conviction of the lofty elements of his soul. Knowing these facts about Cæsar, Napoleon, and Washington, I noticed that I had a much better understanding of their careers, and indeed seemed to see them when they performed any celebrated action which was related in their biographies.

General Lee is now so justly famous that, although posterity will be sure to find out all about him, my grandchildren (if I have any) will be glad to hear how he appeared to the eyes of Corporal Shabrach, their grandfather, one of the humble soldiers of his army.

I have seen the General frequently, and he once spoke to me, so I can describe him accurately. He has passed middle age, and his hair is of an iron gray. He wears a beard and moustache, which are also gray, and give him a highly venerable appearance. He has been, and still is, an unusually handsome man, and would attract attention in a crowd from his face alone. Exposure to sun and wind has made his complexion of a ruddy, healthy tint, and from beneath his black felt hat a pair of eyes look at you with a clear, honest intentness, which gives you thorough confidence both in the ability and truthfulness of their owner. I have always observed that you can tell the character of a man by his eyes, and I would be willing to stake my farm and all I am worth upon the statement that there never was a person with such eyes as General Lee's who was not an honest man. As to his stature, it is tall, and his body is well knit. You would say he was strong and could bear much fatigue, without being heavy or robust. His bearing is erect, and when his head bends forward, as it sometimes does, it appears to stoop under the weight of some

great scheme he is concocting. His dress is very simple, consisting generally of an old gray coat, dark-blue pantaloons, a riding
cape of the same colour; boots worn outside, and a black hat.
Sometimes a large dark overcoat is worn over all. He seldom
carries a sword. He rides fine horses, and is my model of an old
Virginia Cavalier, who would rather be torn to pieces by shell
and canister than give up any of his rights.

If I was asked to describe General Lee's ordinary appearance
and attitude, either in the saddle, in front of the line-of-battle,
or standing with his field-glass in his hand, reconnoitring the
enemy keenly from beneath the gray eyebrows, I should say,
in words I have met with in some book, that his attitude was
one of *supreme invincible repose.* Here you see a man whom
no anxieties can flurry, no reverses dismay. I have seen him thus
a dozen times, on important occasions; and that, if nothing else,
convinces me that he is, in the foundations of his character, a
very great man. No man in public affairs now, to my thinking
at least, is so fine a representative and so truthful a type of the
great Virginia race of old times.

As to his character, everybody has had an opportunity of
forming an opinion upon the subject—at least of his *military*
character. Some persons, I know—Captain Quattlebum for instance, who is a man of no great brains himself, however, con-
fidentially speaking—say that Lee is not a great general, and
compares him to Napoleon, who, they say, won greater victories, and followed them up to better results. Such comparisons,
to my thinking, are foolish. I am no great scholar, but I have
read enough about Napoleon's times to know that they were
very different from General Lee's. He, I mean Napoleon, was
at the head of a French army, completely disciplined, and bent
on "glory." They wanted their general to fight on every occasion, and win more "glory." If he didn't go on winning "glory"
he was not the man for them. The consequence was that Napoleon, who was quite as fond of "glory" as his men, fought
battles whenever he could get at the enemy, and as his armies
were thoroughly disciplined, with splendid equipments, and
plenty of provisions and ammunition, he was able to follow up

his successes, as he did at Marengo and Austerlitz, and get the full benefit of them. Lee is in a very different situation from Napoleon. This is an army of volunteers, who did not come into the field to gain "glory," but to keep the Yankees from coming further South. They have no disposition to rebel and get rid of General Lee if he does not feed them on a dish of "glory" every few weeks. They are not as well organized as they ought to be, and are badly equipped, provisioned, and ammunitioned.

With such an army it is unreasonable to expect General Lee to fight as often and as desperately as Napoleon did, or to follow up his victories. He takes the view, I suppose, that he is Commander-in-Chief of the Confederate States in the field; that "glory" is a secondary matter; that worrying out the enemy is the best tactics for us, with our smaller number and superior material; and that no risks ought to be run with our army, which, once destroyed by an unlucky step, could not be replaced. Altogether, for the reasons stated above, I think General Lee is a better soldier for the place he occupies than Napoleon would be.

I can look back to many occasions where I think a different course from that which he pursued would have been better, but I do not, on that account, mean to say that he was wrong. I think he was right. My dear boys, there is no man so wise as he who explains what ought to have been done, *after the event*. It is like the progress of science. A child, in the year 1864, knows ten thousand things that the wisest philosopher of 1764 knew nothing about. So a boy may be able to understand that this or that would have been better, from what he now knows, when our wisest generals, from want of information at the time, could not. It is a solemn thing to be in command of an army which cannot be renewed, if once destroyed; especially when that army is the only breakwater against the torrent attempting to sweep us away .

I have, on all occasions, expressed these opinions of General Lee, and I intend to go on expressing them, with many others like them, and if anybody thinks I do so from interested motives they are welcome to their opinion. It is not likely that the Com-

mander-in-Chief will ever know whether Fifth Corporal Shabrach likes or dislikes him—whether he admires him, or the
contrary. I am glad of that. I consider myself just as good as
General Lee as long as I am honest and a good soldier, doing
my duty to the country in the upright, brave, and independent
attitude of a free Virginian; and let me tell you that the General
would be the first to acknowledge it. My dear boys, there is nobody so simple and unassuming as a gentleman, and I tell you
again that General Lee is not only a gentleman, but a great man,
and Corporal Shabrach takes off his hat and salutes him, whether
noticed by the General or not. It is his duty to salute him, and
he performs that duty without expecting to be promoted to
Fourth Corporal for it.

I will therefore say of General Lee that, to my thinking, his
character bears the most striking and surprising resemblance
to that of General Washington. When I say this, you will know
my opinion of him, for I have always taught my boys to revere
the name of the Father of his Country. In saying this about General Lee, I do not mean any empty compliment. It is very easy
to talk about a "second Washington" without meaning much,
but I mean what I say. I read Marshall's Life of the General
some years since, and I remember taking notice of the fact that
Washington appeared to be the tallest and strongest of all the
great men around him. I did not see that he excelled *each one*
of them in *every particular*. On the contrary, there was Patrick
Henry; he could make a better speech. There was Jefferson; he
could write a better "State paper." And there was Alexander
Hamilton, who was a much better hand at figures, and the
hocus-pocus of currency and "finance." (I wish we had him
now, if we could make him a *States' Rights* man.) But Washington, to my thinking, was a much greater man than Henry, or
Jefferson, or Hamilton. He was *wiser*. In the balance and har-
mony of his faculties he excelled them all, and when it came to
his *moral* nature they were nowhere at all! In reading his life,
I remember thinking that he was the *fairest* man I ever heard
of. His very soul seemed to revolt against injustice to the mean-
est creature that crawled; and he appeared to be too proud to

use the power he wielded to crush those who had made him
their enemy by their own wrong-doing. Although he was a man
of violent temper, he had it under perfect control, and he seems
to have gone through life with the view of having carved on
his tombstone: "Here lies a man who never did intentional injustice to a human creature." Now anybody that knows General Lee knows that this is just like *him*. For my part, I am just
as sure as I can be of anything, that if one of his Major-Generals
tried to oppress the humble Fifth Corporal Shabrach, he would
put the Major-General under arrest, and make him answer for
his despotism. If you will look at the way General Washington
fought, also, you will find a great resemblance to General Lee's
tactics. The enemy had then, as now, to be worried out—to be
evaded by falling back when the ammunition or rations gave
out—to be harassed by partisans, and defeated at one point to
balance their success at another. The account current was cast
up at the end of each year, the balance struck, and preparations
made to open a new account for the next year, and the next!

That's the way we are fighting this war, and that is General
Lee's plan, I think, as it was Washington's.

All this army has pretty much the same opinion of General
Lee that I have, and is glad that it is commanded by one whom
it both respects and loves. There is not doubt about the General's
popularity with the army, and its confidence in him. The men
call him "Uncle Robert," and are proud of his notice. I told you
that he once spoke to your father, who is nothing but Fifth
Corporal, and you will be proud when I tell you that little
Willie's letter, the first he ever wrote me, was the cause. I was
sitting on a stump by the roadside reading it with a delight that
showed itself, I suppose, in my countenance, when, hearing
horses' hoofs near me, I raised my head and saw General Lee, in
his old riding-cape, with several members of his staff. I rose
quickly to my feet and made the military salute—two fingers to
the hat—when what was my surprise to see the General stop
with all his staff. His hand went to his hat in return for my
salute, and looking at me with his clear eyes, he said in a grave,
friendly voice:

"I suppose that is a letter from your wife, is it not, my friend?"

It was a proud moment for Corporal Shabrach, I assure you, my children, to be called "my friend" by old Uncle Robert. But somehow, he didn't make me feel as if he was *condescending*. It was just as if he had said: "Shabrach, my friend, we are both good patriots, fighting for our country, and because I am Commander-in-Chief that is no reason why I should not respect an honest Fifth Corporal, and take an interest in him and his domestic matters." His voice seemed to say all that, and thinking he was in no hurry that morning, I replied:

"No, General; I have no wife now, although I have had two in my time, the last one having been a great trial to me, owing to her temper, which was a hard thing to stand."

The General smiled at this, and said with a sort of grave humour that made his eyes twinkle:

"Well, my friend, you appear to be too well advanced in life to have a sweetheart, although" (I saw him look at the chevrons on my sleeve) "all the Corporals I ever knew have been gallant."

"It is not from a sweetheart, General," I replied; "after Mrs. Shabrach the Second died, I determined to remain unmarried. My little boy, Willie, wrote it; he is only six years old, but is anxious to grow up and be one of General Lee's soldiers."

"That is a brave boy," returned the General; "but I hope the war will not last so long. You must give him my love, and tell him to fight for his country if he is ever called upon. Good day, my friend."

And saluting me, the General rode on. He often stops to speak to the soldiers in that way; and I mention this little incident, my children, to show you how kindly he is in his temper, and how much he loves a quiet joke, with all his grave air, and the anxieties that must rest on him as Commander-in-Chief of the army.

I have always despised people that looked up with a mean worship to great men, but I see nothing wrong or unmanly in regarding with a sort of veneration—a mixture of affection and respect—this noble old cavalier, who seems to have stepped out of the past into the present, to show us what sort of men Virginia can still produce. As for myself, I never look at him without thinking: "It is good for you to be alive to let the youths of 1863 see what their fathers and grandfathers were in the great old days." The sight of the erect form, the iron-gray hair and beard, the honest eyes, and the stately figure, takes me back to the days when Washington, and Randolph, and Pendleton, used to figure on the stage, and which my father told me all about in my youth. Long may the old hero live to lead us, and let no base hand ever dare to sully the glories of our well beloved General—the "noblest Roman of them all," the pink of chivalry and honour. May health and happiness attend him!

Your affectionate father,

SOLOMON SHABRACH,

5th Corporal, Army Northern Virginia.

## II. HIS DESCRIPTION OF THE PASSPORT OFFICE

Camp Quattlebum Rifles, A. N. V.,

January 25, 1864.

When you come out of Richmond, my dear boys, you have to get a passport. As you have never yet travelled from home, I will explain what a passport is. It is a paper (always brown) which is signed by somebody or his clerk, and which induces a melancholy-looking soldier at the cars, with a musket and fixed bayonet, to let you go back from the horrors of Richmond to the delights of camp.

As without this brown paper (for unless the paper is brown the passport is not good) you cannot get back home—that is to camp, the soldier's home—there is, of course, a great crowd of applicants always at the office where the papers are delivered. I was recently in Richmond, having been sent there on business connected with the Quartermaster's Department of our regiment, and I will describe for your instruction the passport office, and the way you get a passport.

I thought at first I would not need one, because my orders were approved by several high officers, and last by Major Taylor, Adjutant-General of the army, "by command of General

Lee," and nobody had demanded any other evidence of my right to travel before I reached Richmond. "Uncle Robert" will not allow his provost-marshals at Orange or Gordonsville to deny his sign-manual, and I was under the mistaken impression that I could enjoy the luxury of taking back a lot of shoes and blankets to the Quattlebum Rifles, without getting a permit on brown paper from some Major or Captain in Richmond. I accordingly went to the cars, and on presenting my orders to the melancholy young man with the musket and bayonet, posted there, found his musket drop across the door. When I asked him what that meant, he shook his head and said I had "no passport." I called his attention again to my orders, but he remained immovable, muttering in a dreary sort of way, "You must get a passport."

"Why, here are the names of a Brigadier and Major-General."

"You must get a passport."

"Here is Major Taylor's signature, *by command of General Lee.*"

"You must get a passport."

"From whom?"

"Captain ——," I forget who, "at the passport office."

This appeared to be such a good joke that I began to laugh, at which the sentinel looked very much astonished, and evidently had his doubts of my sanity. I went back and at once looked up the "passport office." I found that it was in a long wooden building, on a broad street, in the upper part of the city, and when I reached the place I found a large crowd assembled at the door. This door was about two feet wide, and one at a time only could enter—the way being barred by a fierce-looking sentinel who kept his musket with fixed bayonet. I observed that everything was "fixed bayonet" in Richmond, directly across the door. This ferocious individual let in one at a time, and as each one entered the crowd behind him, which was as tightly packed together as a parcel of herrings in a barrel, surged forward with a sort of rush, only to be driven back by the sentinel, who scowled at them pretty much as a farmer does at a parcel of lazy negroes who have neglected their work and incurred the penalty of the lash. As fast as the passports were granted, those who got them passed out at another door; a second sentinel, with musket and fixed bayonet also, bade defiance to the crowd.

Well, after working my way through the mass, and remaining jammed in it for over an hour, my turn came, and with a slow and reluctant motion, the sentinel, who had been eyeing me for some time with a sullen and insolent look, raised his musket and allowed me to enter. His eye continued to be fixed on me, as if I had come to pick some one's pocket, but I did not heed him, my curiosity being too much excited by the scene before me. A row of applicants were separated from a row of clerks in black coats, by a tall railing with a sort of counter on top, and the clerks were *bullying* the applicants. That is the only word I can use to describe it. I am not mistaken about this. Here were very respectable looking citizens, officers of the army, fine looking private soldiers, and all were being *bullied*. "Why do they bully people at the passport office?" you will probably ask, boys. I don't know, but I have always observed that small "official" people always treat the world at large with a sort of air of defiance, as if "outsiders" had no right to be coming there to demand anything of them; and the strange thing is, that everybody submits to it as a matter of course.

Well, there were a large number of persons who wanted passports, and only a few clerks were ready to wait on them. A considerable number of well dressed young men who would make excellent privates—they were so stout and well fed—sat around the warm stove reading newspapers and chatting. I wondered that they did not help, but was afterwards informed that this was not "their hour," and they had nothing to do with the establishment until "their hour" arrived.

At last my turn came round, and I presented my orders to a clerk, who looked first at the paper, then at me, pretty much as a cashier in a bank would do if he suspected that a draft presented to him was a forgery. Then the official again studied the paper, and said in the tone of a Lieutenant-General commanding:

"What is your name?"

"It is on my orders," I said.

"I asked your name," snapped the official.

"Solomon Shabrach."

"What rank?"

"Fifth Corporal."

"What regiment?"

"Quattlebum Rifles."

"Hum! don't know any such regiment. What army?"

"General Lee's."

"What did you visit Richmond for?"

"On public business."

"I asked you what you came to Richmond for!" growled the clerk, with the air of a man who is going to say next, "Sentinel, arrest this man, and bear him off to the deepest dungeon of Castle Thunder."

"My friend," I said mildly, for I am growing too old to have my temper ruffled by every youngster, "the paper you hold in your hand is my orders, endorsed by my various military superiors. That paper will show you that I am Corporal Shabrach, of the Quattlebum Rifles, — Virginia regiment, ——'s brigade, ——'s division, ——'s corps, Army of Northern Virginia. You will also see from it that I am in Richmond to take charge of Quartermaster's stores, and return with them to camp 'without unnecessary delay.' I have obtained the stores, which are shoes and blankets, and I want to obey my order and take them to the company. If you are unwilling to give me the necessary passport to do so, give me back my orders, and I will go to General Winder, who is the commanding officer here, I believe, and ask him if there is any objection to my returning with my shoes and blankets to the army."

At the name of General Winder a growl ran along the table, and in about a minute I had my passport handed me without further discussion. It was a permit to go to Orange Courthouse, Corporal Shabrach binding himself on honour not to communicate any intelligence (for publication) which, if known to the enemy, would be prejudicial to the Confederate States;

also signing an oath on the back of the paper, by which he further solemnly swore that he would yield true faith and allegiance to the aforesaid Confederate States. This was on brown paper—and I then knew that I could get out of Richmond without trouble. The sentinel at the other door raised his musket, scowled at me, and let me pass; and at the cars, the melancholy sentinel there, too, did likewise. I observed that he read my pass upside down, with deep attention; but I think he relied upon the fact that the paper was brown, as a conclusive proof of its genuineness.

I have thus described, my dear boys, the manner in which you procure a passport in Richmond. Why is the public thus annoyed? I really can't tell you. Everybody has to get one; and even if Mrs. Shabrach (the second) was alive she would have to sign that oath of true allegiance if she wanted to get on the cars. I shall only add that I think the clerk who put her under cross-examination would soon grow tired of the ceremony. Her tongue was not a pleasant one; but she is now at rest.

I must now say good-by, my dear boys.

Your affectionate father,<br>
SOLOMON SHABRACH,<br>
Fifth Corporal.

# VI

## THE BAND OF THE "FIRST VIRGINIA"

THAT band in the Pines again! It is always playing, and intruding on my reveries as I sit here in my tent, after work, and muse. Did I say intruding? A word both discourteous and unjust; for the music brings me pleasant thoughts and memories. May you live a thousand years, O brave musicians, and the unborn generations listen to your grand crescendos and sad cadences!

That music brings back some I heard many years ago, on the Capitol square, in Richmond. From a platform rising between the Capitol and City-Hall this music played, and it was listened to by youth and maiden, under the great moon, with rapture. O summer nights! O happy hours of years long gone into the dust! Will you ever come back—never? And something like a ghostly echo answered, "never!" That band is hushed; the musicians have departed; the instruments are hung up in the halls of oblivion; but still it plays in memory these good old tunes of "Far Away in Tennessee," "The Corn Top's Ripe," and "The Dear Virginia Bride." O flitting figures in the moonlight of old years, return! Ring, clarionet, though the drooping foliage of the elms, and drum, roar on! The summer night comes back, and the fairy face, like an exile's dream of home in a foreign land.

But that band is not still; the musicians are not dead; they

365

live to-day, and blow away as before, for they roll the drum and sound the bugle for the First Virginia Regiment of the Army of Northern Virginia. I heard them afterwards, on two occasions, when the music was charming, and the recollection of the scenes amid which it sounded interests me. The second time I heard the brave musicians was at Fairfax Court-house, in 1861 —or was it in 1761? A century seems to have rolled away since then.

In 1761 the present writer must have been a youth, and appears to remember that a fair face was beside him on that moonlit portico at Fairfax, while the band of the First Virginia played the "Mocking Bird," from the camp across the mills. The scene is clear in memory to-day, as then to the material eye: the moonlight sleeping on the roofs of the village; the distant woods, dimly seen on the horizon; the musing figure in the shadow; and the music making the air magical with melody, to die away in the balmy breeze of the summer night. To-day the Federal forces occupy the village, and their bands play "Yankee Doodle," or "The Star-Spangled Banner." No more does the good old band of the First Virginia play there, telling you to listen to the "Mocking Bird," and Colonel Wyndham's bugles ring in place of Stuart's!

The third occasion when the performance of this band impressed me was in August, 1861, when through the camps at Centreville ran a rumour, blown upon the wind, which rumour taking to itself a voice, said—

"The Prince is coming!"

All at once there appeared upon the summit of the hill, west of Centreville, a common hack, which stopped not far from where I was standing, and around this vehicle there gathered in a few moments quite a crowd of idlers and sightseers. Then the door was opened; from the carriage descended three or four persons, and these gentlemen walked out on the hill from which a view of the battle-field of Manassas in the distance was obtained.

One of these gentlemen was Prince Jerome Bonaparte, all knew; but which was the Prince? Half-a-dozen officers in foreign uniform had ridden with the carriage, and one of these officers was so splendidly clad that he seemed to be the personage in question.

"I suppose that is the Prince," I said to a friend beside me.

"No, you are mistaken."

"Which is, then?"

"Look around in the crowd, and see if you cannot tell him from the family likeness."

Following this suggestion, my gaze all at once was arrested by a plainly clad person in the midst of the cortège—a farmer apparently, for he wore a brown linen coat and common straw hat, with nothing whatever to indicate the soldier or dignitary in his appearance. But his dress disappeared from view and was speedily forgotten; the face absorbed attention from the first moment; that face was the most startling reproduction of Napoleon's—the first Emperor's. There was no possibility of making a mistake in this—every one who was familiar with the portraits of Napoleon recognised the prince at a glance. He was taller and more portly than the "Man of Destiny;" but the family resemblance in feature and expression was absolutely perfect. I needed no one to say "This is a Bonaparte." The blood of the Corsican was there for all to recognise; this was a branch of that tree whose boughs had nearly overspread a continent.

Soon afterwards the forces then at Centreville were drawn up for review—the infantry ranged across the valley east and west; the artillery and cavalry disposed on the flanks of the brigades. Thus formed in line of battle, the forces were reviewed by the French Prince, by whose side rode Beauregard. Then the cortège stopped; an aide left it at full gallop—soon the order which he carried was understood by all. The First Virginia regiment was seen in motion, and advancing; reaching the centre of the field, it went through all the evolutions of infantry for the Prince's inspection; and while the movements were going on, the band of the regiment—that same old band!—played the "Mocking Bird," and all the well known tunes, impressing itself upon the memory of everybody present, as an inseparable "feature" of the occasion!

It was not Napoleon I. who reviewed the forces of Beauregard at Centreville; but it was a human being astonishingly like him. And if Prince Jerome ever sees this page, and is led to recall what he looked upon that day, I think he will remember the band of the First Virginia, playing the "Mocking Bird" and the "Happy Land of Dixie."

Fairfax, Centreville, Leesburg! Seldom does the present writer recall the first two names without remembering the third; and here it was—at Leesburg—that a band of the enemy's made a profound impression upon his nerves. The band in question performed across the Potomac, and belonged to the forces under General Banks, who had not yet encountered the terrible Stonewall Jackson, or even met with that disastrous repulse at Ball's Bluff. He was camped opposite Leesburg, and from the hill which we occupied could be heard the orders of the Federal officers at drill, together with the roar of their brass band playing "Yankee Doodle" or "Hail Columbia." To the patriotic heart those airs may be inspiring, but it cannot be said with truth that they possess a high degree of sweetness or melody. So it happened that after listening for some weeks from the grassy slope above "Big Spring" to this band, the present writer grew desperate, and was filled with an unchristian desire to slay the musicians, and so end their performances. Columbia was hailed at morning, noon, and night; Yankee Doodle became a real personage and walked through one's dreams—those horrible brass instruments became a thorn in the flesh, a torture to the soul, an inexpressible jar and discord.

So, something like joy filled the heart of this writer when the order came to march to a point lower down the river. The column moved; the point was reached; the tents were pitched—then suddenly came "the unkindest cut of all." The very same band struck up across the river, playing "Hail Columbia" with energy, in apparent honour of our presence opposite. When we had moved, it had moved; when we halted, it halted—there was the wretched invention of Satan playing away as before with enormous ardour, and evidently rejoicing in its power over us. The musicians played at every guard-mounting and drill;

the drums rolled at tattoo and reveillé; the bugles rang clearly through the air of evening; and the friends of General Banks seemed to be having the jolliest time imaginable. That miserable band continued to play its "patriotic airs" until everybody grew completely accustomed to it. It was even made useful by the sergeant of a company, I heard. He had no watch, and economically used the tattoo and reveillé of the enemy's drums to regulate his roll-call, and "lights out."

I thought to speak only of the good old band of the First Virginia; but have spoken too of its rival over the Potomac. A word still of the band in the pine wood yonder, which plays, and plays, with splendid and rejoiceful ardour. It is loud, inspiring, moving, but it is not gay; and I ask myself the question, Why? Alas! it is the ear that listens, not the music, which makes mirthful or the reverse these animated strains. The years bring many changes, and we—alas! we change *cum illis*! Once on a time the sound of music was like laughter; now it seems to sigh. Does it sigh for the good companions gone, or only for lost youth, with the flower of the pea, and the roses that will never bloom more? O martial music, in your cadences are many memories—and memory is not always gay and mirthful! So, cease your long-drawn, splendid battle anthem!—play, instead, some "passionate ballad, gallant and gay"—or better still, an old Virginia reel, such as the soldiers of the army used to hear before they lived in tents. Unlike the great Luria, we long to see some "women in the camp"—or if not in person, at least in imagination!

Has some spirit of the air flashed to the brave musicians what I wish? Do they feel as I do? The gayest reel of all the reels since time was born, comes dancing on the wind, and every thought but mirth is banished. Gay reel, play on! Bright carnival of the years that have flown, come back—come back, with the smiling lips and the rose-red cheeks, with the braided hair and the glimmer of mischievous eyes!

# VII

## THE "OLD STONEWALL BRIGADE"

IN EVERY army there is a *Corps d'Élite* which bears the heaviest brunt of battle, and carries off the chief glories of the conflict. In the forces of Cæsar it was the "Tenth Legion" which that "foremost man of all this world" took personal command of, and led into action, when the moment for the last struggle came. In the royal troops of Louis XIV., fighting against Marlborough, it was the *Garde Français* who were called upon when "do or die" was the word, and men were needed who with hats off would call on their enemies to deliver the first fire, and then close in, resolved to conquer or leave their dead bodies on the field. In the *Grand Armée* of Napoleon it was the *Vieux Garde* which the Emperor depended upon to retrieve the fortunes of the most desperate conflicts, and carry forward the Imperial Eagles to victory.

In the Army of Northern Virginia there is a corps, which, without prejudice to their noble commander, may be said to represent the Tenth Legion of Cæsar, the French Guard of Louis, and the Old Guard of Napoleon. This is the Old Stonewall Brigade of Jackson.

*The Old Stonewall Brigade!* What a host of thoughts, memories, and emotions, do those simple words incite! The very mention of the famous band is like the bugle note that sounds "to arms!" These veterans have fought and bled and conquered on

370

so many battle-fields that memory grows weary almost of recalling their achievements. Gathering around Jackson in the old
days of 1861, when Patterson confronted Johnston in the Valley
of the Shenandoah—when Stuart was a simple Colonel, and
Ashby only a Captain—they held in check an enemy twenty
times their number, and were moulded by their great commander into that Spartan phalanx which no Federal bayonet
could break. They were boys and old men; the heirs of ancient
names, who had lived in luxury from childhood, and the humblest of the unlettered sons of toil; students and ploughmen, rosy-
cheeked urchins and grizzled seniors, old and young, rich and
poor; but all were comrades, trained, united, fighting for a common end, and looking with supreme confidence to the man in
the dingy gray uniform, with the keen eyes glittering under
the yellow gray cap, who at Manassas was to win for himself
and them that immortal name of "Stonewall," cut now with a
pen of iron on the imperishable shaft of history.

It was the Shenandoah Valley which more than all other
regions gave the corps its distinctive character and material; that
lovely land which these boys fought over so often afterwards,
charging upon many battle-fields with that fire and resolution
which come only to the hearts of men fighting within sight of
their homes. Jackson called to them; they came from around
Winchester, and Millwood, and Charlestown; from valley and
mountain; they fell into line, their leader took command, and
then commenced their long career of toil and glory; their wonderful marches over thousands of miles; their incessant combats
against odds that seemed overpowering; their contempt of all
that makes the soldier faint-hearted, of snow and rain, and cold
and heat, and hunger and thirst, and marching that wears down
the strongest frames, making the most determined energies yield.
Many dropped by the way, but few failed Jackson. The soul of
their leader seemed to have entered every breast; and thus in
thorough *rapport* with that will of iron, they seemed to have
discovered the secret of achieving impossibilities. To meet the
enemy was to drive him before them, it seemed—so obstinately
did the eagles of victory continue to perch upon the old battle

flag. The men of the Old Stonewall Brigade marched on, and fought, and triumphed, like war machines which felt no need of rest, food, or sleep. On the advance to Romney they marched —many of them without shoes—over roads so slippery with ice that men were falling and guns going off all along the line, and at night lay down without blankets or food upon the snow, to be up and moving again at dawn. When Shields and Fremont were closing in on Jackson's rear, they marched in one day from Harper's Ferry to Strasburg, nearly fifty miles. On the advance in August, 1862, to the Second Manassas, they passed over nearly forty miles, almost without a moment's rest; and as Jackson rode along the line which was still moving on "briskly and without stragglers," no orders could prevent them from bursting forth into tumultuous cheers at the sight of him. He had marched them nearly to death, to reach a position where they were to sustain the whole weight of Pope's army hurled against them—they were weary unto death, and staggering—but they made the forests of Fauquier resound with that electric shout which said, "We are ready!"

Such has been the work of the Old Brigade—not their *glory*; that is scarcely here alluded to—but their hard, unknown *toil* to carry out their chief's orders. "March!" has been the order of their going. The very rapidity of their marches separates them from all soldier comforts—often from their very blankets, however cold the weather; and any other troops but these and their Southern comrades would long since have mutinied, and demanded bread and rest. But the shadow of disaffection never flitted over forehead in that command. Whatever discontent may be felt at times at the want of attention on the part of subordinate officers to their necessities, the "long roll" has only to be beaten—they have only to see the man in the old faded uniform appear, and hunger, cold, fatigue, are forgotten. The Old Brigade is ready—"Here!" is the answer to the roll-call, all along the line: and though the eye is dull from want of food and rest, the arm is strong and the bayonet is sharp and bright.

That leader in the faded uniform is their idol. Anecdote, song, story—in all he is sung or celebrated. The verses professing to

have been "found upon the body of a serjeant of the Old Stonewall Brigade at Winchester," are known to all—the picture
they contain of the men around the camp fire—the Shenandoah
flowing near, the "burly Blue Ridge" echoing to their strains—
and the appearance of the "Blue Light Elder" calling on his men
to pray with him:

> "Strangle the fool that dares to scoff!
>  Attention! 'tis his way
> Appealing from his native sod
> *In formâ pauperis* to God,
> 'Lay bare thine arm, stretch forth thy rod!
>  Amen!'—that's Stonewall's way."

Here is the rough music of the singer as he proceeds with his
strain, and recalls the hard conflict of the second Manassas, when
Longstreet was at Thoroughfare, Jackson at Groveton:

> "He's in the saddle now! Fall in!
>  Steady—the whole Brigade!
> Hill's at the ford, cut off! We'll win
>  His way out—ball and blade.
> What matter if our shoes are worn!
> What matter if our feet are torn!
> 'Quick-step—we're with him before dawn!'
>  That's 'Stonewall Jackson's way.'

> "The sun's bright lances rout the mists
>  Of morning, and, by George,
> There's Longstreet struggling in the lists,
>  Hemmed in an ugly gorge.
> Pope and his Yankees whipped before—
> 'Bay'net and Grape!' hear Stonewall roar,
> 'Charge, Stuart! Pay off Ashby's score!'
>  That's 'Stonewall Jackson's way!' "

Lastly, hear how the singer at the camp fire, in sight of the
firs of the Blue Ridge and the waters of the Shenandoah, indulges
in a wild outburst in honour of his chief:

"Ah, maiden! wait and watch and yearn
    For news of Stonewall's band;
Ah, widow! read, with eyes that burn,
    That ring upon thy hand!
Ah, wife! sew on, pray on, hope on:
Thy life shall not be all forlorn—
*The foe had better ne'er been born*
*Than get in Stonewall's way!*"

These words may sound extravagant, but defeat has met the enemy so persistently wherever Jackson has delivered battle at the head of the Old Brigade and their brave comrades, that the song is not so unreasonable as it may appear. And here let me beg that those "brave comrades" of the Old Brigade will not suppose that I am oblivious of their own glory, their undying courage, and that fame they have won, greater than Greek or Roman. They fought as the men I am writing of, did—with a nerve as splendid, and a patriotism as pure and unfaltering as ever characterized human beings. It is only that I am speaking now of my comrades of the Shenandoah Valley, who fought and fell beneath the good old flag, and thinking of those dear dead ones, and the corps in which they won their deathless names, I am led to speak of them and it only.

Of these, and the Old Brigade, I am never weary thinking, writing, or telling: of the campaigns of the Valley; the great flank movement on the Chickahominy; the advance upon Manassas in the rear of Pope; the stern, hard combat on the left wing of the army at the battle of Sharpsburg; all their toils, their sufferings, their glories. Their path has been strewed all over with battles; incredible have been the marches of the "Foot Cavalry;" incessant their conflicts. Death has mowed down whole ranks of them; the thinned line tells the story of their losses; but the war-worn veterans still confront the enemy. The comrades of those noble souls who have thus poured out their hearts' blood, hold their memory sacred. They laughed with them in the peaceful years of boyhood, by the Shenandoah, in the fields around Millwood, in Jefferson, or amid the Alleghanies; then they fought beside them, in Virginia, in Maryland, wherever the flag was borne; they loved them, mourn them, every name is written on their hearts, whether officer or private, and is ineffaceable. Their own time may come, to-day or to-morrow; but they feel, one and all, that if they fall they will give their hearts' blood to a noble cause, and that if they survive, the memory of past toils and glories will be sweet.

Those survivors may be pardoned if they tell their children, when the war is ended, that they fought under Jackson, in the "Old Stonewall Brigade." They may be pardoned even if they boast of their exploits, their wonderful marches, their constant and desperate combats, the skill and nerve which snatched victory from the jaws of defeat, and, even when they were retiring before overwhelming numbers, made it truly better that the foe had "ne'er been born" than meet their bayonet charge.

In speaking of this veteran legion, "praise is virtue." Their history is blazoned all over with glory. They are "happy names, beloved children"—the favourites of fame, if not of fortune. In their dingy uniforms, lying stretched beneath the pines, or by the roadside, they are the mark of many eyes which see them not, the absorbing thought in the breast of beauty, and the idols of the popular heart. In line before the enemy, with their bristling bayonets, they are the life-guard of their dear old mother, Virginia.

The heart that does not thrill at sight of the worn veterans, is cold indeed. To him who writes, they present a spectacle noble and heroic; and their old tattered, ball-pierced flag is the sacred ensign of liberty.

Their history and all about them is familiar to me. I have seen them going into action—after fighting four battles in five days—with the regularity and well dressed front of holiday soldiers on parade. There was no straggling, no lagging; every man stood to his work, and advanced with the steady tramp of the true soldier. The ranks were thin, and the faces travel-worn; but the old flag floated in the winds of the Potomac as defiantly as on the banks of the Shenandoah. That bullet-torn ensign might have been written all over, on both sides, with the names of battles, and the list have then been incomplete. Manassas, Winchester, Kernstown, Front Royal, Port Republic, Cold Harbour, Malvern Hill, Slaughter Mountain, Bristow Station, Groveton—Ox Hill, Sharpsburg, Fredericksburg, were to follow. And these were but the larger names upon the roll of their glory. The numberless engagements of minor character are omitted; but in these I have mentioned they appear to the world, and sufficiently vindicate their claim to the title of heroes.

I seemed to see those names upon their flag as the old brigade advanced that day, and my whole heart went to greet them, as it had gone forth to meet and greet the brave youth whom I spoke to just before the battle, by the roadside, where he lay faint and weak but resolute and smiling.*

Whatever be the issue of the conflict, these brave spirits will be honoured, and held dear by all who love real truth and worth and courage. Wherever they sleep—amid the Alleghaneys, or by the Potomac, in the fields of Maryland, or the valleys and lowlands of Virginia—they are holy. Those I knew the best and loved most of all, sleep now or will slumber soon beneath the weeping willow of the Old Chapel graveyard in the Valley. There let them rest amid tears, but laurel-crowned. They sleep, but are not dead, for they are immortal.

* The brave Lieutenant Robert Randolph. *"Requiescat in pace!"* [J. E. C.]

# VIII

## ANNALS OF THE "THIRD"

### I.

SAD but pleasing are the memories of the past! Gay and grotesque as well as sorrowful and sombre, are the recollections of the "old soldiers" who, in the months of 1861, marched to the rolling drum of Beauregard!

At that time the present writer was a Sergeant of Artillery, to which high rank he had been promoted from the position of private: and the remembrance of those days when he was uniformly spoken to as "Sergeant" is by no means unpleasing. The contrary is the fact. In those "callow days" the war was a mere frolic—the dark hours were yet unborn, when all the sky was over-shadowed, the land full of desolation—in the radiant sunshine of the moment it was the amusing and grotesque phase of the situation that impressed us, not the tragic.

The post of Sergeant may not be regarded as a very lofty one, compared with that of field or general officers, but it has its advantages and its dignity. The Sergeant of Artillery is "Chief of Piece"—that is to say, he commands a gun, and gun-detachment: and from the peculiar organization of the artillery, his rank assimilates itself to that of Captain in an infantry regiment. He supervises his gun, his detachment, his horse picket, and is responsible for all. He is treated by the officer in command with due consideration and respect. A horse is supplied to him. He is, to all intents and purposes, a commissioned officer.

But the purpose of the writer is not to compose an essay upon
military rank. From the Sergeant let us pass to the detachment
which he commanded. They were a gay and jovial set—those
young gentlemen of the "Third Detachment"—for they were
for the most part youths of gentle nurture and liberal education, who had volunteered at the first note of the bugle. They
fought hard to the end of the war, but in camp they were not
energetic. Guard duty and horse-grooming were abominable in
their eyes; and the only pursuits to which I ever saw them apply
themselves with activity and energy were visiting young ladies,
and smoking pipes. From this it may be understood that they
were bad material for "common soldiers," in the European acceptation of the term; and their "Chief" was accustomed to
appeal rather to their sense of propriety than the fear of military
punishment. The appeal was perfectly successful. When off
duty, he magnanimously permitted them to do what they chose;
signed all their passports without looking at them; and found
them the most orderly and manageable of soldiers. They obeyed
his orders when on duty, with energy and precision: were ready
with the gun at any alarm before all the rest, the commanding
officer was once pleased to say; and treated their Chief with a
kindness and consideration mingled, which he still remembers
with true pleasure.

The battery was known as the "Revolutionary Ducks." This
sobriquet requires explanation, and that explanation is here
given. When John Brown, the celebrated Harper's Ferry "Martyr," made his onslaught, everything throughout Virginia was
in commotion. It was said that the "Martyr" and his band were
only the advance guard of an army coming from Ohio. At this
intelligence the battery—then being organized in Richmond by
the brave George W. Randolph, afterwards General, and Secretary of War—rushed quickly to arms: that is, to some old
muskets in the armory, their artillery armament not having been
obtained as yet. Then commanded by the General to be, they
set out joyously for Harper's Ferry, intent on heading off the
army from Ohio. In due time they landed from the boat in
Washington, were greeted by a curious and laughing crowd,

and from the crowd was heard a voice exclaiming, "Here's your Revolutionary Ducks!" The person who had uttered this severe criticism of the ununiformed and somewhat travel-worn warriors was soon discovered to be an irreverent hackman; but the nick-name made the youthful soldiers laugh—they accepted it. They were thenceforth known to all their friends and acquaintances as the "Revolutionary Ducks."

The *Revolutionnaires* marched to Manassas at the end of May, 1861, and a few days after their arrival one of the South Carolinians camped there, asked me if I had "seen the little General," meaning General Beauregard, who had just assumed command. The little General visited the battery, and soon dispatched it with his advance-force under Bonham to Fairfax Court-House, where it remained camped on a grassy slope until the middle of July, when it came away with unseemly haste. In fact, a column of about fifty-five thousand blue-coats were after it; and the "Third Detachment," with their gun, had a narrow escape. They were posted, *solus*, near the village of Germantown, with the trees cut down, four hundred and thirty yards by measurement, in front to afford range for the fire. Here they awaited with cheerfulness the advance of the small Federal force, until a horseman galloped up with, "Gentlemen! the enemy are upon you," which was speedily followed by the appearance of blue uniforms in the wood in front. The infantry supports were already double-quicking to the rear. The odds of fifty-five thousand against twenty-five was too great for the "Third;" and they accordingly limbered to the rear, retiring with more haste than dignity. A friend had seen the huge blue column passing from Flint Hill toward Germantown, and had exclaimed with tragic pathos that the present historian was "gone." He was truly "gone" when the enemy arrived—gone from that redoubt and destined to be hungry and outflanked at Centreville.

The *Revolutionnaires* had but an insignificant part in the great battle of Manassas. The "little General" intended them to bear the brunt, and placed them in the centre at Mitchell's Ford. From this position they saw the splendid spectacle of the Federal Cavalry dividing right and left to unmask the artillery which speedily opened hotly—but beyond this shelling they were not assailed. Caissons blew up all around, and trees crashed down; but the blue infantry did not charge the breastworks. Then Beauregard resolved to advance himself with the Revolutionnaires and Bonham straight on Centreville, and sent the order —but it never arrived. Thus the "Third" was cheated of the glory which they would have won in this great movement; and despite the shells which burst for four days in the trenches, they are not entitled to inscribe "Manassas" on their flag.

Two days after the battle they were ordered to advance with General Bonham to Vienna. All obeyed but the "Third," which being seized with a violent desire to go to Alexandria instead of Vienna, gave the rest the slip, joined Colonel Jeb Stuart's column of cavalry and infantry, going toward Fairfax, and never stopped until they reached that village, wherein they had made a number of most charming friends. They made their reëntrance amid waving handkerchiefs from the friends alluded to, and cheering joyously—but were speedily desired to explain their presence in the column of Colonel Stuart, who thus found himself in command of a surplus gun, of which he knew nothing. The present writer at once repaired to the Colonel's headquarters, which consisted of a red blanket spread under an oak, explained the wishes of the "Third," and begged permission to accompany him to Washington. The young Colonel smiled: he was evidently pleased. We should go, he declared—he required artillery, and would have it. The "Chief" received this reply with extreme satisfaction; put his gun in battery to rake the approach from Annandale; and was just retiring to his blanket, with the luxury of a good conscience, when an order came from General Bonham to repair with the gun, before morning, to Vienna! The General ranked the Colonel: more still, the gun was a part of the General's command. With heavy hearts the "Third" set out through the darkness for the village to which they were ordered.

As the writer is not composing a log-book of his voyages through those early seas, he will only say that at Vienna the *Revolutionnaires* saw for the first time the enemy's balloons hovering above the woods; turned out more than once, with ardour, when Bonham's pickets fired into Stuart's; and smoked their pipes with an assiduity that was worthy of high commendation. Soon the order came to move; they hung their knapsacks with energy upon the guns, for the horses to pull, and thus returned to Centreville, where they were ordered to join the hard-fighting Colonel Evans at Leesburg.

At the name of Leesburg, every heart of the "Noble Third" still beating, will beat faster. Leesburg! Paradise of the youth-full warrior! dear still to the heart of him who writes, and to all his brave companions! Land of excellent edibles, and beautiful maidens! of eggs and romance, of good dinners and lovely faces! No sooner had the ardent cannoneers reached camp, and pitched their tents, than they hastened into Leesburg to "spy out the land." The reconnoissance was eminently satisfactory. The report brought back by the scouts thus thrown forward, represented the place as occupied in force by an enemy of the most attractive description—and from that time to the period of their abrupt departure, the brave young artillerists were engaged in continuous skirmishes with their fair faces, not seldom to their own discomfiture.

When the "Third" with another detachment went to camp at Big Spring, in a beautiful grove, they applied themselves to the military duties above specified with astonishing ardor. The number of horses which required shoeing at the blacksmith's in town was incredible; and such was their anxiety to rush to combat, that the young soldiers surreptitiously knocked shoes from the horses' feet, to be "ordered to the front," toward the foe.

The *Revolutionnaires* had a little skirmish about this time with the Federal force at White's Ferry, and the "Third" had the satisfaction of setting a house or barn on fire with shell, and bursting others in the midst of a blue regiment. These exploits were performed with a loss of one man only, wounded by sharpshooters; the "Third" having dodged the rest of the enemy's bullets with entire success. They were highly pleased with the result of the combat, and soon afterwards were called to new fields of glory. This time the locality was at Loudoun Heights, opposite Harper's Ferry; and having dragged their gun up the rugged mountain road with great difficulty, they opened from the summit at the moment when the brave Ashby charged. The result was cheering. Ashby sent word that the shells were falling among his own troops, but directed the fire to proceed— it was admirable: and thus encouraged, the "Third" continued at their post until the enemy's batteries on Maryland Heights had gotten our range, and their rifle shell began to tear the ground near by. Concluding that the distance was too great to render a reply necessary, the "Third" came away soon after this—but the order to retire had been previously given, and the piece did not move off at a faster gait than a rapid trot—it might have been a gallop.

This little affair was in October, and on our return to Leesburg the enemy were preparing to cross and attack us. General Evans put on the road to Edwards' Ferry all the guns, with the exception of the "Third," which was sent with the Eighth Virginia regiment to repel an assault from General McCall, who was approaching Goose Creek, on our right, with a Division, and twelve pieces of artillery. The "Third" undertook this with alacrity, and remained in position at the "Burnt Bridge" with ardour, hoping that the enemy would have the temerity to approach. He did not do so, and at mid-day General Evans sent down for the regiment and the gun, and ordered them at "double-quick" and "trot-march" to the vicinity of Ball's Bluff. The regiment—the Eighth Virginia—was ordered to "drive the enemy from those woods," and the "Third" was directed to open fire, "when the Eighth fell back." Owing to the circumstance that the Eighth never fell back, this order was not carried out, and the *Revolutionnaires* in general had no part in one of the most desperate and gallant battles of the whole war. For the second time they were held in reserve, in a great combat, and they chafed at it: but the enemy in Leesburg remained to be conquered, and after the battle, they immediately commenced attending to the deficiency of horseshoes as before.

These raids upon the territory of the foe were now made from their camp at "Fort Evans," on the hill. Fort Evans was on the top of a commanding eminence. Looking northward, you beheld the winding Potomac, and on the upland beyond, were seen the tents of the enemy, and their watch-fires at night—their tattoo and reveille being heard distinctly, and affording an economical measurement of time to their foes. East, south, and west, was a beautiful country of field, and forest, and meadow, and hill—and Leesburg rose with its white houses and spires, in the midst of it, about a mile away.

Thus the *Revolutionnaires* had around them all the elements of comfort. An enemy to reconnoitre through spy-glasses, across the river, and another enemy in the town to keep up a brisk assault upon. Many "solitary horsemen" were seen at sunset and other hours, dotting the road which led to the borough;—and these returned in various moods, as "the day" had been adverse or triumphal for them. They delivered battle with astonishing regularity, and looked after the shoeing of the artillery horses with an efficiency which reflected the highest credit on the corps.

In the performance of this duty the "Third" was not behind its companions—indeed took the lead. To smoke pipes and attack the enemy in Leesburg were the chosen occupations of the "Third." To dress in full costume for battle—with white collar, and dress uniform—seemed indeed the chief happiness of these ardent young warriors: and then they lost no time in advancing upon the foe. When circumstances compelled them to remain inactive at Fort Evans for a day or days, they grew melancholy and depressed. Their pipes still sent up white clouds of smoke—but the ashes were strewed upon their heads.

"Fort Evans" was not an inspiring locality. The view was superb; but the wind always blowing there, nearly removed the hair from the head, and the mud was of incredible depth and tenacity. In addition to this, Fort Evans got all the rain and snow. But these were provided against. A distinguished trait of the *Revolutionnaires* was a strong propensity for making themselves comfortable; and they soon discovered that, in winter at least, tents were vanity and vexation of body. From the realization of the want, there was only a step to the resolution to supply it. They cut down trees, and hauled the logs; tore down deserted houses, and brought away the plank; carried off old stoves, and war-worn tables, and then set to work. A log hut rose suddenly—the abode of the "Brigand of the Cliff," who was a most excellent companion and uncommonly jovial for a bandit —many plank cabins were grouped near it, stoves were set up, log chimneys built, and the bold *Revolutionnaires* were in winter quarters.

Fort Evans was in process of construction anew, under the supervision of General D. H. Hill—and the workmen were encouraged by the presence and approval of the "Third" and their companions. They rarely failed to visit it several times a day; and generously instructed General Hill's engineer how to lay it out without charge. They did not mind the deep mud, and perseveringly remained for hours, looking on while the infantry "detail" worked. Personne, one of the "Third," superintended the filling and revetting—and it was whispered around that the General had assured him that "This work would remain to speak of him." At this the worthy Personne is said to have smiled as only he could smile. He no doubt does so still.

In these virtuous and useful occupations—mingled with much smoking, and close attention to horseshoes—the hours and days sped away, there near Leesburg, in the fall and winter of the good year 1861. Posted on the far Potomac there, to guard the frontier, the "Third" and their companions had a large amount of time upon their hands which it was necessary to dispose of. Sometimes the enemy opposite amused them—as when they ran a gun down to the river, and in a spirit of careless enjoyment, knocked a hole with a round shot in the gable end of the abode of the "Brigand of the Cliff." But these lively moments were the exception. The days generally passed by without incident; and when debarred from visiting Leesburg, the *Revolutionnaires* visited each other.

Among gentlemen so well-bred as themselves there was no neglect of the amenities of life. You never entered a cabin, but the owner rose and offered you the best seat. You never got up to depart, but you were feelingly interrogated as to the occasion of your "hurry," and exhorted to remain. If boxes came from home, their contents were magnanimously distributed; when anybody got leave of absence, which was exceedingly seldom, his *return* was greeted with acclamations—perhaps because the transaction was a good precedent. Lounging was the habitual amusement, except when they aroused themselves to contend with the enemy—at Leesburg. The town was their favourite arena for combat. They delighted to visit, and early established a dining acquaintance there—selecting those houses where, between the courses, they could gaze into fair eyes, and "tempt their fate." When they returned after these expeditions in search of horseshoes, they revelled in descriptions of ham and turkey and dessert—making ration-beef tougher, and camp flat-cake more like lead than ever. On the main street of Leesburg, near Pickett's tavern, the "Third" especially congregated. They wore the snowiest shirt bosoms, the bluest gray jackets, and the reddest cuffs imaginable. Thus armed to the teeth, and clad for war and conquest, they would separate in search of young ladies, and return at evening with the most glowing accounts of their adventures.

## II.

A glance at the headquarters of the "Third," and a brief notice of one of those worthies, may prove of interest to the descendants of these doubty *Revolutionnaires*.

They dwelt in three or four cabins of considerable size, constructed of plank—the middle and largest one being the headquarters of their commander. These cabins were warmed by old stoves, obtained on the Rob Roy principle from deserted houses; and were fitted up with berths, popularly known as "bunks," filled with straw. The space above the cornice afforded an excellent shelf for clothes, which were then economically washed whenever it rained—but the great feature of the headquarter mansion was the crevice at the summit of the roof. This permitted the smoke to escape without difficulty, and on windy nights when others were suffering, ventilated the

apartment superbly. Nor did the advantages stop there. The
crevice was no mere crack, but an honest opening; and when a
snow-storm came on, the snow entered without difficulty, driving downward, and enveloping the sleepers in its close white
mantle. As the warmth which snow communicates to a sleeper
is well known, this circumstance will be duly appreciated.

From the headquarters let us pass to the inhabitants. The
"Third," as I have said, were a gay and social set, and possessed
of many peculiarities, which their "Chief," sitting apart with a
borrowed volume (from Leesburg) in his hand, was accustomed
to watch with a covert smile. A marked feature of the young
warriors was their devotion to the habit of eating. Rations were
ample and excellent then, but they did not satisfy the youths.
They foraged persistently: brought back eggs, butter, pies,
every delicacy; and these they as persistently consumed. They
always ate butter all day long, toasting slices of bread upon the
roaring stove with a perseverance that was truly admirable. The
announcement of dinner by the polite mulatto who officiated
as cook, was uniformly received with rapture; and the appearance of a "box from home" supplied the fortunate possessor with
the largest and most affectionate circle of visiting friends.

Among the "characters" of the detachment, Corporal Personne, my gunner—he who superintended the construction of
the breastworks—occupied a prominent place. He was tall and
gaunt, with a portentous moustache; had the imposing air of a
Field-Marshal on parade, and a fund of odd humour that was
inexhaustible. To hear Personne laugh was to experience an
irresistible desire to do likewise; to listen while he talked was
better than to attend a theatrical performance. Personne rarely
relaxed into that commonplace deportment which characterizes
the great mass of dull humanity. He could not have been dull
even if he had tried, and his very melancholy was humorous.
In his tone of voice and hearing he was *sui generis*—"whole in
himself and due to none." All his utterances were solemn and
impressive; his air deeply serious—when he laughed he seemed
to do so under protest. He generally went away after laughing;
no doubt to mourn over his levity in private. One of Personne's

peculiarities was a very great fondness for cant phrases, and odd turns of expression. These afforded him undisguised delight, and he handled them with the air of a master. He was never known to ask for smoking tobacco in any other words than, "Produce the damnèd invention!" which he uttered with a truly terific scowl, and an accent of wrath which was calculated to strike terrour to the stoutest heart. A form of logic in which he evidently reposed the fullest faith was, "An ought's an ought— a figure's a figure—therefore you owe me a dollar and a half;" and another mysterious phrase, "Speak to me, Gimlet," was a fund of unending enjoyment to him. His comparison of distance was, "As far as a blue-winged pigeon can fly in six months;" his measure of cold was, "Cold enough to freeze the brass ears on a tin monkey;" his favourite oath, "Now, by the gods who dwell on high Olympus!" and his desire for a furlough was uniformly urged upon the ground that he wished to "go home and see his first wife's relations."

Personne was thus the victim of a depraved taste for slang, but he was a scholar and a gentleman—a travelled man and a very elegant writer. When the war broke out he was residing in New York; but at the call of Virginia, his native State, he had left all the delights of Broadway and the opera; abandoned bright waist-coats, gay neckties, and fine boots, to put on the regulation gray, and go campaigning with the *Revolutionnaires*. The contrast was great, but Personne did not grumble; he adapted himself to his new sphere with the air of a philosopher. It was only at long intervals that he spoke of his travels—only occasionally that he broke forth with some opera air heard at the Academy of Music, and now hummed with great taste and delicacy. He sup-plied the stage action to these musical airs, but his powers in that department were defective. The performance, it is sufficient to say, would have done honour to a—windmill.

To witness Personne in the character of "Sergeant of the Guard" was a superb spectacle. The stern and resolute air with which he marshalled his guard; the hoarse and solemn tones in which he called the roll; the fierce determination with which he took command, and marched them to their post, was enough to

"tickle the ribs of death." Once having posted them, Personne
returned as solemnly to his quarters, from which soon afterwards
would be heard his low guttural laugh. The great tableau, however, was Personne in Leesburg, mounted. He was a study at such
moments, and attracted general attention. He sat sternly erect
upon his horse, never indulged in a smile even, and had the air of
a Field-Marshal at the head of an army. It was only when he entered the presence of the ladies that his brows unbent, his features relaxed. With these he was a very great favourite, and he
cultivated their regard in a manner which exhibited a profound
knowledge of human nature. A proof of this assertion is here
given. One day Personne, with a friend of his, went forth on a
foraging expedition, rations running low, and appetite rising.
But the neighbourhood had been ransacked by a whole brigade,
and by what device could they operate upon the female heart?
Personne found the device he wished, and proceeded to execute
it, having first drilled his friend in the part assigned him. Before
them was a modest mansion; through the window were seen the
faces of young ladies; the friends entered the yard, bowed politely, and lay down upon the grass. Then the following dialogue
took place in the hearing of the ladies:

PERSONNE, *carelessly.*—"A charming day, my friend; hum—
what were you saying?"

FRIEND, *with deference.*—"I was saying, Mr. Personne, that
the remarkable feature in the present war is the rank and character of the men who have embarked in it—on the Southern side—
as privates. Take yourself, for instance. You belong to one of
the first families of Mississippi; you have three or four planta-
tions: you are worth very nearly half a million of dollars—and
here you are, serving in the ranks as a private soldier."

PERSONNE, *with an air of careless grandeur.*—"No matter! no
matter! The cause is everything. My estates must take care of
themselves for the present, and I expect to live hard and fight
hard, and starve—as we are doing to-day, my friend. When the
war is over, things will be different. I intend to enjoy myself, to
live in luxury—above all, to marry some charming creature—and
I am now looking out for one to suit me. I do not ask riches, my

friend; a plain country girl would please me best—one who is warm-hearted and kind to the soldier!'"

A few moments afterwards a smiling face appeared at the door; a pair of female lips said, "Walk in, gentlemen;" and starting from a deep reverie into which he had fallen, Personne rose, bowed, and accepted the invitation, bowing low again as he entered, with his lofty air of Field-Marshal. Is it necessary to continue the narrative, to say that Personne and his friend nearly produced a famine, and when they retired had their haversacks filled with every delicacy? It was only when well beyond ear-shot that he laughed his low laugh, and exclaimed with solemn earnestness, "Now by the gods that dwell on high Olmpus!—we are in luck to-day!"

Such was Personne, the pride of the "Third," the object of the admiring affection and regard of all the *Revolutionnaires!* The writer designed drawing more than one additional portrait of odd characters in his old detachment, but the figure of Personne has pushed all others from the canvas—the brush moves in the air. That canvas, it may be, perchance, is already too extensive; not every one will find in these familiar recollections of the "Third" that interest which the writer does; and terrible is the crime of producing yawns! Do you think you never wearied anybody, my dear reader, with your recollections? Do you fancy that *your* past amuses others as it amuses you? But, for fear this mass of logic will rebound upon the head of him who sets it in motion, the "Annals of the Third" are here concluded.

As he closes up those Annals, and sets forward on his way, the writer waves his hat in friendly farewell, salutes each one, and calls out, "Good-by, Personne!—good-by, warriors of the 'Noble Third!'—all health and happiness attend you in the coming years!—and never call your old commander anything but 'Sergeant!'"

# IX

## BLUNDERBUS ON PICKET

SCENE.—*Banks of the Rappahannock, in the winter of 1862–3; a camp-fire blazing under an oak, and Captain Blunderbus conversing with a Staff Officer on inspection duty—the picket stationed near, and opposite the enemy.*

BLUNDERBUS *loquitur.*—"This is pleasant—picketing always is. Uncommonly dark, however—the night black but comely, and that frosty moon yonder trying to shine, and dance on the ripples of the river! Don't you think it would look better if you saw it from the porch at home, with Mary or Fanny by your side?

"Picturesque, but not warm. Pile on the rails, my boy; never mind the expense. The Confederacy pays—or don't pay—for all the fences; and nothing warms the feet, expands the soul, and makes the spirits cheerful like a good rail-fire. I was reading in an old paper, the other day, some poetry-writing which they said was found on the body of one of Stonewall's sergeants at Winchester—a song he called 'Jackson's Way.' He tells his comrades to 'pile on the rails,' and says,

> " 'No matter if the canteen fails,
>     We'll make a roaring light!'

Sensible—and speaking of canteens, is there anything in yours, my boy? Nothing. Such is fate!

"I was born unlucky, and always will be so. Now a drop of brandy would not have been bad to-night; or say a mouthful of whiskey, or a little apple or peach-brandy, gin, madeira, sherry, claret, or even bottled porter, crab-cider or champagne! Any of these would have communicated a charm to existence, which—wanting them—it lacks.

"But let us be content with what we have, and accept all fortunes as they come! If ever you hear people say that Blunderbus is a mere trooper, old fellow—that he cares for nothing but eating and drinking, and sleeping—just tell 'em you heard him express that fine sentiment, and they will think better of him. You see I'm a philosopher, like yourself, and I don't let trifles get the better of me. The soul superior to misfortune is a noble spectacle, and warms the heart of the beholder like generous wine. I wish I had some.

"I think, however, I prefer this water. Now that I observe it, it is excellent—with a body to it, a flavour, a sweetness, and stimulating effect which I never noticed before. And then our fire! Just look at it! You're an old hand at rails, I'll be willing to bet—for you fix 'em on the fire with the art of a master. What a glorious sight to see! How it warms the soul!

"I observe that the Yankee pickets over yonder have a miserable fire—made of green wood, doubtless, and smouldering. I was looking at them just now through my glass, and I am glad to say one of the blue-coats was slapping his arms violently against his breast to keep up the circulation. Pleasant; for if anything can increase the comfort of a fire like this, it is the consciousness that our friends over the way are shivering by one that won't burn.

"I believe I will smoke. Nothing assists intellectual conversation like a pipe. Help yourself. You will find that pouch—Yankee plunder from Manassas last August—full of the real article, and the best you ever smoked. It is real, pure Lynchburg—brown, free from stems, and perfumed with the native aroma of the weed. Smoke, guest of mine! That brand is warranted to drive off all blue-devils—to wrap the soul in Elysian dreams of real Java coffee, English boots, French wines, and no blockade. There are men, I am told, who don't smoke. I pity 'em! How do they sustain existence, or talk or think? All real philosophers use the magical weed; and I always thought Raleigh, when I used to read about him, the most sensible man of his time, because he smoked. I have no doubt Shakespeare carried a pipe about, and wrote his plays with it in his mouth.

"I'll trouble you to hand me that chunk when you are done with it. Thank you. Now the summit glows; the mysterious depths are illumined. All right; I am lit.

"This is soothing; all care departs when you smoke a good pipe. Existence assumes a smiling and bright aspect; all things are rose-coloured. I find my spirits rising, my sympathies expanding, even until they embrace the whole Yankee nation. This is an excellent root I am leaning my back against—I never knew a rocking-chair more agreeable. Our fire is magnificent; and observe the picturesque effect of the enemy's blaze reflected in the stream!

"The enemy! Who knows if that is fair? Perhaps that good fellow over there, who was slapping his arms, I am sorry to say, just now, by way of restoring the circulation and keeping himself warm, came here to fight us against his will! Honest fellows! who blames them? They are unfortunate, and I sympathize with them. I observe that the fire over yonder, which our friends have kindled, burns feebly, and doubtless is fed with green wood. We could spare them a few rails, eh? But then to communicate with them is against orders.

"I believe they come down here from pure curiosity, and rather like to be taken prisoner. But it takes a good deal to feed them. We want all our provisions. Often I have been nearly starved, and I assure you starving is a disagreeable process. I have tried it several times, and I can tell you where I first experienced the sensation in full force. At Manassas, in July, 1861.

"I was in the artillery then, and had command of a gun, which gun was attached to a battery, which battery was a part of General Bonham's brigade. Now General Bonham commanded the advance force of Beauregard's army, and was stationed at the village of Fairfax. Well, we had a gay time at Fairfax in those early months of the war, playing at soldiering, and laughing at the enemy for not advancing. The red cuffs of the artillery, the yellow of the cavalry, and the blue of the infantry, were all popular in the eyes of the village beauties, and rarely did any-thing of a melancholy character interfere with our pleasures. Sometimes a cavalry-man would be shot on picket—as we may be to-night, old fellow; and I remember once a noble boy of the 'Black Horse,' or Radford's regiment, was brought back dead, wrapped in an oil-cloth which his sister had taken from her piano and given him to sleep on. Poor thing! she must have cried when she heard of that; but there has been a good deal of crying during the present war.

"Kick that rail-end up. It makes me melancholy to see a fire dying down. Well, we had a pleasant time in the small village of Fairfax, until one July day my gun was ordered to a breast-work not far off, and I heard that the 'Grand Army' was coming. Now I was thinking about the Commissary department when I heard this news, for we had had nothing to eat for a day nearly; but I went to work, finishing the embrasure for my piece. Bags marked 'The Confederate States' were filled with sand and piled up skilfully; trees obstructing the range were chopped down rapidly; and then, stepping off the ground from the earthwork to the woods from which the enemy would issue, I had the pleasure of perceiving that the foe would be compelled to pass over at least four hundred and thirty yards before reaching me with the bayonet. Now in four hundred and thirty yards you can fire, before an enemy gets up to you, about one round of solid shot, and two rounds of canister—say three of canister. I depended, therefore, upon three rounds of canister to drive back the Grand Army, and undertook it with alarcrity. I con-tinued hungry, however, and grew hungrier as night fell, on the 16th July.

"At daylight I was waked by guns in front, and found myself hungrier than ever. At sunrise a gentleman on a white horse passed by at a gallop, with the cheerful words: 'Gentlemen, the enemy are upon you!' and the cannoners were ranged at the gun, with the infantry support disposed upon the flanks. All was ready, the piece loaded, the lanyard-hook passed through the ring of the primer, and the sharpshooters of the enemy had appeared on the edge of the woods, when they sent us an order to retire. We accordingly retired, and continued to retire until we reached Centreville, halting on the hill there. We were posted in battery there, and lay down—very hungry. A cracker I had borrowed did not allay hunger; and had a dozen Yankees been drawn up between me and a hot supper, I should have charged them with the spirit of Winkelried, when he swept the Austrian spears in his embrace, and 'made a gap for liberty.'

"We did not fight there, however; we were only carrying out General Beauregard's plan for drawing on the enemy to Bull Run, where he was ready for them. At midnight we limbered up, the infantry and cavalry began to move, blue and red signal rockets were thrown up, and the little army slowly retired before the enemy, reaching the southern flank of Bull Run at daylight. The Federals were close upon our heels, and about ten o'clock commenced the first fight there, the 'battle of the 18th.'

"Now when I arrived at Bull Run, I was hungry enough to eat a wolf. I lay down on the wet ground, and thought of various appetizing bills of fare. Visions of roast beef, coffee, juleps, and other Elysian things rose before my starving eyes; and the first guns of the enemy, crashing their round shot through the trees overhead, scarcely attracted my attention. I grew hungrier and hungrier—things had grown to a desperate pitch, when—beautiful even in the eyes of memory!—an African appeared from our wagons in the rear with hot coffee, and broiled bacon, and flat-cake, yet hot from the oven! At the same moment a friend, who had stolen off to the wagons, made an imperceptible gesture, and indicating his tin canteen, gave me an inquiring look. In the service this pantomime always expresses a willingness to drink your health and pass the bottle. I so understand it—and retiring from the crowd, swallowed a mouthful of the liquid. It was excellent whiskey, and my faintness from hunger and exhaustion made the effect magical. New life and strength filled my frame—and turning round, I was saluted by an excellent breakfast held out to me by the venerable old African cook!

"Ye gods! how that breakfast tasted! The animal from which that ham was cut must surely have been fattened on ambrosia; and the hot, black coffee was a tin cup full of nectar in disguise! When I had finished that meal I was a man again. I had been in a dangerous mood before—my patriotism had cooled, my convictions were shaken. I had doubted of the Republic, and thought the Confederacy in the wrong, perhaps. But now all was changed. From that moment I was a true Southerner again, and my opinions had the genuine ring of the true Southern metal. I went into the battle with a joyous soul—burning with love of my native land, and resolved to conquer or die!

"I wish I could get at that bill of fare to-night. Hunger sours the temper—men grow unamiable under it. Hand me that carbine—it is not more than four hundred yards to the picket across yonder, and I'll bet you I can put a bullet through that bluebird nodding over the fire. Against orders, do you say? Well, so it is; but my fingers are itching to get at that carbine.

"I'll trouble you to stick my pipe in the hot ashes by you, my friend. I am fixed here so comfortably with my back against this tree, that I hate the idea of getting up. You see I get lazy when I begin to smoke, old fellow; and I think about so many things, that I don't like to break my reflections by moving. I have seen a good deal in this war, and I wish I was a writer to set it down on paper. You see if I don't, I am certain to forget everything, unless I live to eighty—and then when the youngsters, grandchildren, and all that (if I have any, which I doubt), gather around me, with mouths open, I will be certain to make myself out a tremendous warrior, which will be a lie; for Blunderbus is only an old Captain of Cavalry, good at few things but picketing. Besides, all the real colours of the war would be lost, things would be twisted and ruined; if I could set 'em down now in a book, the world would know exactly how the truth was. Oh, that Blunderbus was an author!

"I have my doubts about the figure we will cut when the black-coats, who don't see the war, commence writing about us. Just think what a mess they will make, old fellow! They will be worse than Yankee Cavalry slashing right and left—much ink will be shed, but will the thing be history? I doubt it. You see, the books will be too elegant and dignified; war is a rough, bloody trade, but they will gild it over like a looking-glass frame. I shouldn't wonder if they made me, Blunderbus, the old bear, a perfect 'carpet knight'—all airs, and graces, and attractions. If they do, they will write a tremendous lie, old fellow! The way to paint me is rough, dirty, bearded, and hungry, and always growling at the Yankees. Especially hungry—the fact is, I am really wolfish to-night; and I see that blue rascal over yonder gnawing his rations and raising a black bottle to his lips; Wretch! —the thing is intolerable; give me the carbine—I'll stop him!— cursed order that keeps me from stopping his amusement—the villain! Who can keep his temper under trials like this, Sergeant?"

SERGEANT OF PICKETS *advancing.*—"Here, Captain."

BLUNDERBUSS, *scowling.*—"Are all the men present? Call the roll—if any are missing——"

(*The Sergeant calls the roll and returns to the fire.*)

SERGEANT.—"All present but Tim Tickler, Captain."

BLUNDERBUS, *enraged.*—"Where is Tickler—the wretched Tickler?"

TICKLER, *hastening up.*—"Here, Captain—present, Captain."

BLUNDERBUS, *wrathful.*—"So you are absent at roll-call! So you shirk your duty on picket! Sergeant, put this man tomorrow in a barrel shirt; on the next offence, buck him! What are you standing there for, villain?"

TICKLER, *producing a canteen.*—"I don't bear malice, I don't, Captain. I just went to the house yonder, thinking the night was cold—for a few minutes only, Captain, being just relieved from post—to get a little bit to eat, and a drop of drink. Prime apple-jack, Captain; taste it, barrel shirt or no."

(TICKLER *extends the canteen, which Blunderbus takes, offers his friend, and drinks from.*)

TICKLER, *offering ham and bread.*—"And here's a little prog, Captain."

BLUNDERBUS, *calling to the Sergeant, who retires with*

*Tickler.*—"Remit Private Tickler's punishment, Sergeant; under the circumstances he is excusable."

STAFF OFFICER.—"Ha, ha!"

BLUNDERBUS, *smiling.*—"You may laugh, my friend; but applejack like that is no laughing matter. What expands the soul like meat, bread, and drink? Do you think me capable of punishing that honest fellow? Never! My feelings are too amiable. I could hug the whole world at the present moment, even the Yanks yonder. Poor fellows! I fear their fire is dying down, and they will freeze; suppose we call across and invite them to come and warm by our fire? They are not such bad fellows after all, my dear friend; and Blunderbus will answer for their peaceful propensities. Nothing could tempt them to fire upon us—they are enemies alone from the *force of circumstances!*"

(*A stick rolls from the fire, and the carbine lying near is discharged. The enemy start to arms, and a shower of bullets whistles round, one from a long-range Spencer rifle striking Blunderbus on the buckle of his sword belt, and knocking him literally heels over head.*)

BLUNDERBUS, *rising in a tremendous rage.*—"Attention! fire on 'em! Exterminate 'em! Give it to the rascals hot and heavy, boys! Go it! Fire! (*Bang! bang! bang!*) Pour it into 'em! Another round! That's the thing! I saw one fall! Hoop! give 'em another, boys! Hand me a carbine!"

STAFF OFFICER, *from his post behind the oak.*—"Ha! ha! You are a philosopher, my dear Blunderbus, and a real peace missionary—but the '*force of circumstances*' alters cases, eh?"

BLUNDERBUS, *sardonically.*—"I rather think it does."

(*Staff Officer mounts, and continues his rounds, the fire having ceased, leaving Blnuderbus swearing and rubbing the spot where he was struck.*)

STAFF OFFICER, *moving on.*—"Good-night!"

BLUNDERBUS, *in the distance.*—"Good-night! Curse 'em."

# X

## ADVENTURES OF DARRELL

### I. HOW HE TOOK UPTON'S HILL

CAPTAIN DARRELL comes to see me sometimes; and as we are old companions in arms, we have a good many things to talk about.

The Captain is a pleasant associate; mild in his manners, and apparently much too amiable to hurt a fly. He is a terrible man after the enemy, however, and exhibits in partisan warfare the faculties of a great genius. His caution, his skill, his "combinations," are masterly;—his *élan* in a charge or a skirmish is superb. Then only is the worthy Captain in his native element, and he rises to the height of the occasion without effort or difficulty.

I am going to give some of his experiences in the service—to record some of his scouts and performances. Every hero should have his portrait first drawn, however;—here is the Captain's:

He is not yet thirty, and is of medium height and thickness. His frame is strongly knit, and his arm muscular. His countenance is a pleasant one; his expression mild; black hair, black moustache, black eyebrows, black eyes. He wears a dark surtout, cavalry boots, and a hat with a black feather. Around his waist he carries habitually a pistol belt with a revolver in it. In the field he adds a carbine or short rifle, and a sabre. His pistol and sabre were once the enemy's property—they are the spoil of his bow and spear.

I am going to let the Captain speak for himself. He is not given

398

to talk about his experiences without provocation, and the reader must carefully guard against the injustice of supposing him a trumpeter of his own performances. He is wholly ignorant of the fact that I am writing about him; and all that I shall record was drawn from him by adroit prompting and questions. Averse to talk at first, and to make himself the centre of attention among my visitors, he soon grew animated, and his ordinary somewhat listless demeanor was replaced by ardour and enthusiasm.

I had asked how many of the enemy he had killed in his career.

"I don't know," he replied, "I never counted them—a good many."

"A dozen?"

"Oh, yes. I can remember six officers. I never counted the men."

"Where did you kill your first officer?"

The Captain reflected—musing.

"Let me see," he said; "yes, at Upton's Hill, just by Upton's house."

"Tell me all about it?"

The Captain smiled, and yawned.

"Well," he said, "it was in the fall of '61, I think, or it might have been late summer."

And leaning back, clasping his hands around his knees, he thus commenced. I give the narrative, as I design giving others, as nearly as possible in the words of the Captain:

"It was in the fall of that year, I think, when General Stuart was below Fairfax, and the enemy occupied Munson's, Upton's, Hall's, and Mason's Hills. Our troops were at Falls Church, about two miles from Upton's Hill, and the enemy had pickets all along in front. I was then scouting around on my own responsibility, and used to go from one place to another, and get a shot at them whenever I could. The First South Carolina boys had often told me that I would get killed or wounded, and be taken and hung as a bushwhacker or spy; but I was not afraid, as I had determined never to be taken alive.

"At the time I speak of, we used to send three or four companies down to Falls Church on picket, to stay some days, and then they would be relieved by other companies. As I knew the whole country—every road and picket-post—the officers used to come to me and get me to go with them, and show them the neighbourhood. General Longstreet, whose brigade was then in front, gave me a letter, which was my credential, and I posted all the pickets at the right places regularly.

"One day it occurred to me that I could take and hold Upton's Hill, if I had the right sort of men; and I offered, if they would give me a detail, to attempt it. Major Skinner, of the First Virginia, was officer of the day, and he agreed; and Captain Simpson, of the Seventeenth Virginia, offered me as many men as I required. I thought I would only take a small scouting party first, however, and I picked out four men whom I knew. My intention was to creep up, make a sudden rush on the picket on Upton's Hill, and capture it, and hold the hill until the enemy advanced; if I was not reinforced I would retire again. Well, I got the men, all good fellows for that sort of work, and we set out about nine o'clock at night on our expedition. The night was very dark, and you could not see the road before you; but I knew every foot of the ground, and had no difficulty on that score. We stopped at a house on the way, where we found two negroes; but they could give me no information, and I pushed on in silence toward Upton's house, where the Yankee picket was always stationed.

"Just in front of the house there is a tree, you may have noticed, which we could see easily from Taylor's Hill, where our picket was—about eight hundred yards off—and the men used to fire at each other, though I never did, as it was too far. Now I knew that if the enemy occupied the hill that night, their picket would be at this tree; and I accordingly made a circuit and crept up toward it, to reconnoitre, leaving the men a short distance behind. I got near the tree, which I could see indistinctly, but observed nothing in the shape of a picket. To find if any was really there, I picked up a stone to throw at a fence; for I knew if there were any Yankees there, that as soon as they heard it strike, they would jump up and exclaim, 'Hello! didn't you hear something, Tom, or Dick! What was that?' They would naturally be startled, and would in some manner betray their presence.

"Well, I threw the stone, and it struck the fence, bouncing off and making a tremendous noise. There was no reply; the silence remained entirely unbroken, and I was satisfied that there was no picket at that particular spot, at least. I therefore advanced boldly, and reached the tree, making a signal to the men to come up. The enemy had evidently been at the spot only a short time before. There were the remains of a picket fire, and a quantity of green corn lying about, taken from the field before the house, which was about two hundred yards off, and on the tree was hanging a canteen. I took it and put it on, and then cautiously approached the house, supposing that the Yankee pickets had gone in to sleep. Upton was then in the Yankee Congress, and his house was vacant, and I supposed the enemy used it as a place of shelter.

"I walked noiselessly around the house, but could see no sign of any one. I thought I would try the same game as before, and found a stone, which I threw against the side of the house. Bang! it went, but no one replied; and I was then pretty sure that I had everything in my own hands. We knocked at the door, and a sleepy voice said something—probably a negro's—but we could not get in, though we tried to prise the door open.

"I had thus got possession of the hill, and the next thing was to hold it. I reflected for a moment, and then sent two of the men back to Captain Simpson, with a message to the effect that I had obtained possession of the place without resistance, and that if he would send me fifteen men, I would stay there, engaging the enemy if they tried to recapture it. The men started off, but lost their way in the darkness—they were some of those town boys not used to scouting—and only one arrived at last; the other went away round the whole line of the enemy, but got back safely next day.

"I was thus left with only two men; and one of these I posted as a vedette at the house, while I returned with the other, whose name was Jackson, to the tree by the gate, where the picket fire had been.

"It was now near day, and I began to be very anxious for the appearance of the fifteen men. The messengers had had abundance of time to go and return, but no men! I knew the programme of the enemy now perfectly well. They were very nervous at that time, and were always afraid of being 'cut off,' as they called it, and every night would leave their place on the hill, retiring to the woods down in the rear to prevent being 'cut off' by scouting parties in the dark. When day returned, they would resume their position at the picket tree.

"I knew, therefore, that everything depended upon getting my reinforcement promptly, or it would be too late. I could not hold the hill with one man against them all, and I didn't like the thought of slinking off as I came, and making nothing by the expedition. So I listened anxiously for sounds from the direction of Falls Church, expecting every moment to hear the footsteps of the men. I could hear nothing, however, and for the reason I have given—that my messenger arrived so late. Capt. Simpson, as he told me afterwards, promptly ordered out the detail I asked for; but they did not arrive in time.

"All this time I was listening attentively in the opposite direction, too. I knew that if *my* men did not come, the enemy *would* at the first streak of daylight, and I did not wish to be caught. I determined to 'fire and fall back,' if I could not fight them—and the night was so still that I could hear the slightest sound made by a man before he approached me. My plan had been all arranged, counting on the arrival of the fifteen men, and it was to place them in a cut of the road near the house—and as the enemy came up, make the men rest their guns on the bank, and pour a sudden fire into the flank of the column. I knew this would rout them completely—and everything was arranged to carry out the plan—but, as I said, the men did not come. If I held the hill I would have to do so with *two* instead of *fifteen*.

"Everything turned out as I expected. Just at the first blush of day, while everything was yet hazy and indistinct, I heard the enemy—tramp! tramp! tramp!—coming up the hill. The man watching the house was two hundred yards off; and Jackson and myself were, as I have said, at the gate near the tree, hid in the tall corn. He was armed with a Minié musket, and I had the same weapon, with a six-shooter besides.

"I leaned on the fence, crouching down and listening. The tramp of the Yankees came nearer, and, in the dim light, I could see a company of them, with an officer at their head, approaching. When they were about ten yards off, and I could make them out perfectly distinct, I whispered, 'Now, Jackson!' and, resting my gun on the fence, I took deliberate aim at the officer, and fired, striking him in the breast. I then dropped my gun, and poured into them the fire of all the barrels of my revolver, killing a Sergeant, and wounding three men.

"Although badly wounded, the Lieutenant in command stood gallantly, and shouted to the men, who had for the most part broken, and were running:

" 'Halt there! Fire on the scoundrels! Halt, I say! Fire on them!'

"Some of them turned, and I heard the click of the locks as the guns were cocked.

" 'Look out, Jackson!' I whispered, and I crouched down behind the fence. At the same moment a hot volley came tearing through the tall corn, and cutting the blades over our heads. I knew it would not do to let them discover that there were only two men in front; so, having no more loads in my pistol, I thundered out as though addressing a company who had fired without orders:

" 'Steady, men! steady there, I tell you! Hold your fire! Steady! Dress to the right!'

"This completely took them in, and made them believe that they were ambushed by a large force. In spite of all the Lieutenant could do, they broke and ran down the hill, leaving one man—the Sergeant—dead behind them.

"The Lieutenant was carried off by some of the men, and taken to a house not far from the spot. I was there soon afterwards, and they told me he was shot in the left breast, just above the heart, and died of the wound.

"That was the first officer I ever killed, and the whole of the story.

"Knowing that the enemy would soon return with a heavy force to dislodge me, and that nothing was to be gained by remaining there longer without reinforcements, I called to the man at the house, and took up the line of march back to Falls Church.

"If they had sent me the men, I could have held the hill; but, as I told you, the messengers I sent got lost."

## II. His Recollections of Manassas and the "Gamest Yankee"

I have continued to extract from Captain Darrell, at various times, accounts of his life and adventures. A day or two since we were talking about the earlier scenes of the war, and the half-forgotten incidents which occurred before our eyes at the time. To my surprise, I found that we had often been near each other—that he had slept once by the battery to which I was attached; and that, doubtless, I had seen, without noticing him, however. The memories of the Captain were not without interest; and following my theory that the traits and details of this period should be collected now, I proceed to let the Captain relate his adventures:

"I was in Bonham's command at Manassas before Beauregard came there, and my regiment went along toward Centreville on the very day the Federals took possession of Alexandria. We stayed at Centreville some time, and then advanced to Fairfax. Here I commenced scouting around, and kept at it until the enemy made their advance on the 16th of July. They came in heavy columns on the Flint Hill road, and Bonham fell back quietly with only a few shots from his artillery. The men were all in the breastworks, hot for a fight, which they all expected; but they were marched out and back on the road to Centreville.

"I was out on the road to the left of Germantown with a companion when their column appeared, and we were cut off. We struck into the woods, made a circuit, and came out again on a high hill above Germantown, on the turnpike, from which we could see them rushing into Fairfax. They seemed to overflow in a minute, and we could hear their yells as they entered—thinking the whole Rebel army had fled before them. They were soon at Germantown, and burned most of the houses, hurrying on in pursuit of Bonham toward Centreville. I thought it best to get away from there as soon as possible, so I went on through the woods, and arrived at Centreville about the time you all ran your guns up on the hill there, to cover the retreat. There I saw General Bonham, whom I knew very well, and I told him I believed I would go out and scout around, to try and find what the enemy were about. He said he would be glad if I would do so, and I started off toward the Frying Pan road, and heard them moving in every direction. I tramped around for a long time, to try and make something out; but finding I could not, I returned to Centreville. The army was gone and the enemy were pressing in just as I arrived. I thought I was certainly gone; but I avoided them in the dark, and pushed on toward Bull Run.

"I reached the high land just above the stream in an hour or two, and remember meeting Captain, now Lieutenant-Colonel Langhorne, whose company was on the side of the road, a part of the rear-guard. I entered into conversation with him, and he asked me to what command I was attached. I told him I was an independent, scouting around on my own responsibility; and he invited me to stay with him. So, after eating some of his supper, I laid down on his blankets and went to sleep.

"I woke early, and went on toward Bull Run. As I was going along, I saw a man on horseback ride across the field, and remember looking at him and taking him for one of our own men. I was stooping and picking blackberries at the time, and took no particular notice of him, or I might have killed him, and got his horse and accoutrements, which I needed very much at the time. I allowed him to pass me; and when he got near the small house on the hill, he called out to three or four soldiers posted there:

"Where is General McDowell?'

" 'General *who?*' was the reply.

" 'General McDowell!' he repeated. 'Make haste! I am looking for him!'

" 'Halt! halt!' came from the soldiers, who caught up and cocked their guns. The Yankee saw his mistake too late. He wheeled his horse round, and dug the spurs into him, but at that minute our men fired on him, and he fell to the ground, dead.

"He proved to be General McDowell's quartermaster—I heard his name, but forget it now. He had seven hundred and sixty-odd dollars on his person, I was told.

"After that I went on toward Blackburn's Ford, and found our men drawn up there in line of battle on the south bank. Soon after I got over General Longstreet rode down, smoking a cigar, and I heard the enemy coming.

" 'Who will volunteer to go across and observe their movements?' asked Longstreet.

" 'I will, General,' said Captain Marye, of Alexandria.

" 'Go on, then, Captain,' said Longstreet. 'Hurrah for the Alexandria Guards!'

" 'The Alexandria *Rifles*, General,' said Captain Marye, turning round, and bowing.

" 'Hurrah for the Rifles, then!' said Longstreet; and Marye advanced across the Run with his company.

"It was soon after this, I think, that the artillery fight commenced between our batteries and those of the Federals. Ours were in the plain there, on the slope of a little rising ground, and the enemy's were near the house, on the other side, with all the position on us. Our batteries were fought beautifully, and I remember how exicted we all were, watching the shells passing over us—we could see them. When some of our horses were killed we all felt deeply for the artillery; but it was pushed forward, and got out of range for the moment. The Yankees soon fell back, and we stayed there, waiting for them to renew the attack. The men were terribly excited, and fired at everything over the Run, whether it was an enemy or not. Some fresh regiments came down, and they were sitting with their guns up, expecting every minute to begin, and eager for the enemy to approach. They would fire in the air, or at anything they saw; and sometimes whole companies would rise up, and blaze away right into the opposite bank.

"This made me mad. I was as sick as I could be, with the measles breaking out all over me, and was going about with my face red and swollen, my shirt-bosom open, and my head feeling curiously. The men noticed me as I was rambling around, and semed anxious to know who I was. I mixed with them, but said nothing until they began to throw away their ammunition, firing into the wood; when I halloed at them, and told them to stop that.

" 'There are no Yankees there,' I shouted to them; 'don't be wasting your cartridges in that way, men!'

"But they took no notice of me, except one or two, who asked me where I was from. I told them I was from South Carolina, and then they went on firing. The thing looked so ridiculous to me that I began to laugh, and just at that moment a whole company blazed away into the pines across the run. I jumped up, clapped my hands, and shouted enthusiastically:

" 'That was a *glorious* volley, men!—perfectly *glorious! You* are the boys! and that fire would have killed *at least three thousand* Yankees—if there were any within three or four miles of you!'

"They laughed at this, and just as they stopped a shell came from the enemy and cut off the top of a large tree under which I was standing. It crashed down, and a big limb struck me on the side of the head and knocked me over. Another piece, I heard, broke the back of a man in one of the companies. When they saw me knocked down they all laughed worse than ever, and shouted out:

" 'Look out, South Carolina! Take care of yourself!'

"I thought I would move on. After that I got so sick that I could not keep up, so I went along toward Mitchell's Ford above, and fell in with some friends of General Bonham's staff. His headquarters were just in rear of our batteries there, and they pitched me a small tent—the only one put up—and I lay down, not minding the heavy cannonading, I was so sick. I stayed

408 WEARING OF THE GRAY

there until the 21st, when I could stand it no longer, and determined to get up and strike for the battle-field on our left. I went in that direction and fell in with a young counsin of mine, Edward Farley, who had come down from the University of Virginia to see the fun. We went together, and I got on the field just when Evans, and Bee, and Bartow were fighting to the left of the Stone bridge. I was so weak that I could hardly stand up; and my cousin advised me to take a drink of whiskey, as he had some along with him. I did not wish to do so at first, but he persuaded me that it would be best for me; and I poured out a tin cup half full of the whiskey and swallowed it. I had never taken a drink before in my life—and I have never taken one since. I was so weak and exhausted, and my stomach was so empty, that it made me as tight as anything! I went charging around, half out of my senses, and tried to make the men stand to the work. They were falling back, however, when all at once Beauregard came galloping up, and rode up and down the line, making the men a speech, and urging them not to give up their firesides and altars to the foe. They answered with shouts all along the line, and soon afterwards charged, and drove the enemy back toward Sudley. After that the battle was a rout. Our cavalry came down. at a gallop, and the enemy took to flight.

"I staggered on after them, and saw them running. I ran on too, firing at them, until I got nearly to Centreville. I was then obliged to stop and sit down, with my back to a tree, on the roadside, as I was too sick and weak to proceed. The effect of the liquor had worn off, and I remained there half dozing, until I heard cavalry coming along. It was Captain Powell's cavalry, from Alexandria—one of the first companies organized—and as they swept by me at a gallop, I shouted:

" 'Go it, boys! Give it to 'em.'

"They passed on, and as soon as I was strong enough I got up, and went towards a house near by, to get something to eat. They did not want to let me in, but I had my pistol, and told them that I was sick, and could go no further, and I intended to come in whether or no. I accordingly entered, and among a crowd there found Edward, who had been separated from me in the battle, and followed on as I had.

"I lay down on a sofa, and sent out for something to eat, which I soon got. I then went to sleep, and when I woke next morning was a great deal better. I left the house, took the road to Fairfax, and never stopped until I got to the Chain Bridge, on the Potomac, where I proposed to Captain Powell to cross and capture the pickets on the other side. That's all I saw of the battle of Manassas."

I shall conclude my article with one other adventure of the worthy Captain. We had been discussing the highly interesting subject of saddles, the merits of the "McClellan," the desirability of a good one of that pattern, and the criminal negligence of those who had passed by whole piles of them and never secured one, when the Captain said he had a very fine one which had "belonged to the *gamest* Yankee he ever saw." There was something in that phrase which I have quoted, strongly suggestive of some *belle aventure*, and I therefore made an assault upon the Captain to compel him to relate the incident.

He did so, as usual, after repeated urgings; and here is the narrative as nearly as possible in the words of the narrator:

"I got the saddle when we were advancing after the battle of Cedar Run, last August. I went with a part of the command to which I was attached, down the road which leads from Culpeper to Kelley's Ford, on the Rappahannock. Just before you get to the river there are two gates, within a short distance of each other, which you have to pass through. There is a fence on the right side of the road, and another gate in that, opening into a field. On the left there is no fence—open field and a high hill.

"Well, I took two men and went scouting down that way, and came to the first gate. I opened it, and rode through, but before the men could follow it shut to. All at once I saw in front of me three Yankees on foot—two privates and a sergeant, as I soon found. The sergeant was carrying a bucket.

"As soon as I saw them I called to them to surrender.

" 'Throw down your arms!' I called out, pointing my pistol at them ,'or you are dead men!'

"The privates threw down their muskets, but the sergeant drew a pistol and was about to fire on me, when I covered him with my pistol, and said:

"Now, you just fire, you scoundrel, and I'll kill you!'

"He hesitated for a moment, but finally lowered his pistol, and said he would not have surrendered to one man if I had not taken him *at a disadvantage*. I turned over the prisoners, and went on. As I moved on, Mosby and Hardeman Stuart came by, and pushed on to the high hill on the left, to reconnoitre. I had not gone far before I saw three Yankee cavalry in the field to the right, riding straight down towards us, evidently intending to pass through the gate in the fence. I had my two men with me, and as I wanted to overpower the Yankees, I beckoned to Mosby and Hardeman, who were in sight, and they came riding down. We then opened the gate, and all five of us pushed towards the three Yankees, who, instead of running, as I expected, drew up in line to receive our charge—the rascals! We galloped at them, and they held their fire until we got within five yards of them, when bang! bang! bang! went their revolvers at us. We replied, and in a minute were right in the middle of them with the sabre, ordering them to surrender.

"They obeyed, and I thought the fight was over, when suddenly one of the scoundrels put his pistol right in my face and fired—so close that the powder burned my ear; here is the mark still. As he fired he dashed off, and two of our men pushed to cut him off from the gate. I was mad enough, as you may understand; and I rode at him, full speed. When he saw himself thus surrounded, he lowered his sabre which he had drawn, and called out that he would surrender. I rode up to him, and shook my fist at him, gritting my teeth.

" '*You* scoundrel!' I exclaimed. '*You* black-hearted villain! to fire on me after surrendering! I am almost tempted to blow your brains out with my pistol!'

"He made no reply; and telling the men to take charge of him I turned to ride back. I had not gone ten steps before I heard a sudden cry behind me, and looking hastily round, I saw one of the men falling from the saddle, with one arm thrown up, as if to ward off a blow. He had tried to do so, but failed. The infernal scoundrel of a Yankee had, after surrender, suddenly cut the man over the head with his sabre, and running against the other, nearly knocked him from his horse!

"Instead of running, the rascal then turned his attention to me, and made a wipe at me as his horse darted by, which just grazed my head. He might perhaps have got off if he had tried, then; but he came at me again, riding right down with his sabre ready.

"I saw my chance, then, and just as he was driving at me, I levelled my pistol and fired. The ball struck him just under the left ear, and passed entirely through his head.

"He fell from his saddle, and I caught his horse, which was a very fine one. That was the gamest Yankee I ever fought with, and his saddle was a first-rate one—a bran new 'McClellan;' and if you want one I will give it to you, as I have as many as I want."

So terminated the Captain's story of the "gamest Yankee." It may interest those who like the clash of sabres and the crack of fire-arms—on paper.

### III. How he was Captured

Among the most interesting narratives which I extracted, by adroit urging, from my friend Captain Darrell, was that of the hard fight which he had at Langly, and his capture. Let me here again, in justice to the Captain, guard the reader from supposing that these relations were volunteered by the hero of them. Such was by no means the case. It was only after skilful manœuvring and repeated urging that the worthy was induced—with many preliminary protests, accompanied by a determined twisting of his mustache—to enter on the subject of his adventures.

This explanation is due to him. Nothing is more perilous than what is called egotism. When a man sits down to narrate his own performances, or when he relates them orally to a circle of listeners, the instinctive feeling of the reader or the listener is prone to be one of doubt. Human nature is so curiously constituted that whatever even *appears* egotistical is offensive; and the revenge which men take for being silenced or eclipsed, is to question the truth of what the egotist utters. So sure is this proclivity to underrate what throws us into the shadow, that

Bulwer, in one of those books in which he shows so much keen observation of the world, makes the company rejoice when a profound talker has left the room, and think far more highly of Mr. Pelham, the exquisite, who only said, "Good!" and "Very true!" as *others* talked. If Captain Paul Jones talked for two hours steadily, all about his adventures, he would have many persons to declare him a bore, and doubt whether he ever fought the *Serapis*. If Marion spoke of swamp-encounters all through an evening, there would be many to question whether he ever mounted steel. Such is human nature.

The reader will please observe, therefore, that Captain Darrell did not volunteer these statements. Instead of being an egotist, and an incessant talker, he is really the most retiring and silent of men. You may be with him for a month, and during the whole of that time he will not once refer to any event of his experience. He will talk with you quietly, upon this or that subject, but never about his own exploits. I cannot too often repeat, in justice to the Captain, that the narratives here given were extracted from him by the process of direct interrogation. Having the present highly praiseworthy end in view—that of putting upon record some singular chapters of the war—I attacked him, and drew forth his recollections, as water is drawn from a well, by working at the windlass. The adventures came out in reply to my questions, and solely to gratify an evident curiosity to hear them. If I give them to the reader, he will act with great ingratitude in attributing either egotism or *gasconade* to the worthy Captain.

With these few words of caution to the reader, I proceed to let the Captain tell how he was captured.

"It is a long story," he said, "but you have managed to set me talking, and I suppose I may as well go on. My capture was an accident—it ought never to have occurred. The way of it was this:

"It took place about November, 1861; and at that time I was scouting around, trying to find some opening to 'go in.' When one place got too hot for me, I went to another. I would work around for some time, up by Dranesville; then near Vienna and

HOW DARREL WAS CAPTURED.

Falls Church; and then by Annandale, down to Occoquon. The South Carolina boys—you know I came on with them—used to tell me that I would certainly get caught; that I was too rash and reckless; and they would not go with me any more. But that was unjust. That has been said of me a hundred times; but there is no man more cautious than I am.

"I had a scout on hand, and I got a man to go with me, whose name was Carper. Also Frank Decaradeux, First Lieutenant of Company G, 7th South Carolina—a noble fellow, who was killed at Charleston in the fight lately. At Dranesville we got another named Coleman, who is dead, too, I believe, poor fellow—and set out on the scout.

"The enemy were then at Langly, with their pickets in front, and we heard that they were going to make an expedition toward Dranesville, where we had a picket post. Our intention was to waylay the party, whatever its strength, and attack it from the woods on the side of the road; then, during the confusion, to make our escape in the thicket, if necessary. I was at that time in first-rate spirits—hot for a fight—and I knew I could depend upon my companions, especially Frank Decaradeux. So we set out toward Langly, and when within a mile or so of their pickets, took post in the woods where the road suddenly descended between high banks, and gave us an excellent opportunity to ambush them as they approached.

"Well, we waited there two or three hours, and there was no sign of an enemy. Then as night had come we concluded to give it up for that day, and go across to a house which I knew of, and get supper and lodging. We went there accordingly, and had a good supper, telling the old man to have us a hot cup of coffee at daylight, when we were going to try again. Soon after day we left him in high spirits, and made for the main road again. We had just come near, in the field, when I saw the head of a column of Federal Cavalry, coming from the direction of Dranesville. They had passed us in the night! At Dranesville they had caught our pickets—Whitton and Hildebrand—and about thirteen citizens, whom they were now carrying back to Langly.

"My first thought was to get to the big pines where we had been on the evening before; but this was impossible. The enemy were so close upon us that if we started to run they would certainly see us—and the pines were more than half a mile off. The only thing I thought of was to take advantage of a rise in the ground, cross the road, and get in some pine bushes—short second growth about as high as a man—where I determined to open fire upon them. We accordingly ran across as hard as we could, and passing by a small house, a Mrs. Follen's, got in the bushes. The enemy were coming on quickly and we held a council of war.

" 'I'll tell you what, boys, it won't do for us to let them get by without doing them some damage. They have been up there robbing and plundering, and I for one intend to fire into them, and die if necessary. But we can get off. They will think we are a heavy force sent to ambush them; and in the confusion we can get into the big pines below, where they never can catch us.'

"Decaradeux said he would stand by me, and the others did too, at last—but they looked very pale. We looked carefully to our arms and saw that all was right. We had guns, or carbines, except Decaradeux, who carried a short revolving rifle, which had got clogged up with the spermaceti on the cartridges. He worked at it, and got it in order, however, and said he was ready.

"The cavalry had now got within twenty yards of us, and at the head of the column rode General Bayard, then Colonel, with some staff officers: the prisoners were in the rear. As they came within ten or fifteen yards I arose and said, 'Now, boys!' and we gave them a volley which threw them into tremendous confusion. Whitton told me afterwards that the men trembled in their very boots, and turned their horses to run—thinking they were ambushed by the rebel army. Bayard shouted, 'Steady! steady, men!' and pushed forward—he was a brave fellow—and I was ready for him. As he got within five yards of me I fired and tore his coat skirt all to pieces—killing his horse, which fell upon him. As he fell, some of the officers whose horses had run on by, to the front, came galloping back; and seeing one in uniform with straps, I fired and shot him through the body, killing him.

"We might have got off in the confusion had it not been for Mrs. Follen, who cried, 'Oh! they are only four men!' Poor thing, I suppose she was frightened. The enemy, as soon as they heard this, rallied, and threw dismounted men into the bushes after us; it seemed to me that they were down and in the pines in one minute. Frank Decaradeux had been shot through the right hand, and Coleman through the side. No time was to be lost, and we made a break for the big pines, where I expected to be able to escape. We could not reach them—the flankers coming in and cutting us off—and soon found that we were surrounded. I got separated from the rest, and was running around trying to find an opening to escape, but they were all around me. I could hear their howls as they closed in.

" '*Here's* the First Pennsylvania! Bully for us, boys! We are the boys! We'll give 'em h—l!'

"It was like a pack of wolves. I had fired all my loads, and stopped under a sapling to reload. I remember my feelings at that moment perfectly. I never was so miserable in all my life before. I had that feeling of desperation which you can imagine a dog has when he is run into a corner, and glares up and snaps at you. My hand did not tremble a particle, however, as I was loading my revolver. I had a small flask, and I put in the proper amount of powder and rammed the balls home, and then got up from the ground. Half-a-dozen of the enemy were closing right around me, and as soon as they saw me they fired, and I returned it. I could not find an opening to get out—I was surrounded upon every side, and I didn't know what to do. Every moment they were popping at me, only a few yards off, as I doubled about, and I had eight balls in my clothes and the cape of my coat, and one in my cap. At last I got into an open space, towards the road, and saw a gap in the fence which one cavalryman was watching.

" 'Now is my chance,' I thought.

"And I made a rush straight at him. I had kept one load in my pistol, and if I killed him, as I thought I could easily, I could get his horse and then good-by to them! As I ran towards him he raised his carbine and fired at me, but I did not mind that. I was up to him in a minute, and put my pistol straight at his breast and shot him out of the saddle. He fell, and I was just about to catch the rein, when—I scarcely remember, but Hildebrand told me, the cavalrymen rode me down, one of the men striking me across the head with the barrel of his carbine. But I think the hoof of the horse must have struck me as he jumped over me—my left side was all bruised and bloody.

"When I came to my senses I was lying on my face, and the first words I heard were, I remember perfectly:

" 'Dead as hell, by ——!'

"I raised my head a little, and finding I was not dead, they collared me, and made me stand up, hustling me about from side to side, and jabbering in every language. I got tired of being held in this way, and clutched a carbine from one of them, intending to club it, and hit right and left, but they got it away from me. I remember there was one fellow with a cocked pistol who seemed anxious to get at me, and the officers around were laughing, and saying, 'Let the Italian get at him! he'll finish him!'

" 'Put me out in that field with a pistol,' I said, 'and your Italian or any can try me!'

"They only laughed at this, and hustled me about, as they did poor Frank Decaradeux and Coleman, whom they had caught. Carper got off. Decaradeux had lost his hat, like myself, and had an oilcloth wrapped over his head, which made his pale cheeks and black eyes like a girl's. They laughed at this resemblance, and said, pointing at me:

" 'Who is that fellow there, with his hand in the breast of his coat? He looks like he didn't care what the price of tobacco was!'

"I had gotten *dignified*, however, and made no answer; and soon after an officer rode up, and said:

" 'Captain Darrell, I am sorry to see you in this predicament. Captain McKewn of General McCall's staff. I remember having the pleasure of your acquaintance at the University of Virginia.'

"I bowed, and he asked me what had become of my cap. I told him I had unfortunately lost it, but I observed one of the men riding around with it. He went off and got me a fine new one, and soon afterwards the fellow who wore my cap—it was a red one—came prancing around.

" 'Hey!' he said to me, 'you see I've got your cap, you d—d rebel!'

" 'Yes,' I replied, 'but you are only getting back your own property. I got that from a Brooklyn Fire Zouave, and you are entitled to it, I suppose. I killed the owner.'

"This was really the case. In the charge made by Colonel Fitz Lee, near Annandale, a short time before, I had lost my hat in running the enemy, and came nearly up with two of them who had jumped the fence and were scudding through the pines. I threw myself from the saddle over the fence, and aiming at one of the Yankees, shot him through the breast. I called to the other to surrender, but he turned round and levelled his carbine at me, not more than ten steps off. I had no load in my pistol, and would have been a dead man, had it not been for one of my friends in the road, who fired on the Yankee just as he took aim at me. The ball passed just over my shoulder, and struck him in the face, and he fell. I took off his pistol-belt and pistol; and as I had no hat, picked up his red cap and wore it. This was the same cap which the fellow prancing round had on.

"When we came near Langly, the General, McCall, came out with his division, and I heard him say, that he had heard the firing, and thought Bayard had been ambushed by the whole rebel army.

" 'It was worth your while, general,' I said, 'to bring out your division to capture *four men*.'

" 'Who is this?' asked General McCall.

" 'Captain Darrell, one of the prisoners, General,' said an officer.

"The general ordered me to be brought to him, and asked me who I was. I told him and he said:

" 'You are from the Confederate army, are you not, Captain?' "

" 'Yes, sir,' I replied.

" 'What is their force in front of us?'

" 'General McCall,' I said, 'you ought to know that that is not a proper question to ask me; and that it would be highly improper for me to give you any information upon the subject. I am a soldier, sir, and know my duty too well for that.'

"He laughed and said no more; and then Colonel Bayard came up, and talked with me a short time; he was not wounded. He only asked what command I belonged to and then rode on.

"That evening we were put in a wagon, and carried to Washington—Decaradeux and myself. I don't know what became of Coleman. Here we were put in the third story of the Old Capitol, and I soon understood that they were trying to make out that I was a spy, and hang me as such. When they asked me my name, I told them Captain Darrell, of General Bonham's Staff, as General Bonham, who was an old acquaintance of mine, had often urged me to accept a commission in the C. S. A., to protect me if I was captured. He told me he could easily procure one for me, as at that time they were making appointments every day; but I replied that I would rather remain free, as they might put me off in some fort somewhere, when I would never lay eyes on a Yankee. He then told me to consider myself his volunteer aide, on his staff; and accordingly I reported myself as such, and was so published in the morning papers.

"I was constantly scheming how to escape while in prison, but had crowds of inquisitive visitors coming in on me at all times, and pestering me to death. One day a big pompous army surgeon came in and flourished around, with

" 'Well, Captain—hem!—you young fellows have got yourselves into a bad scrape—hem!'

" 'Not that I am aware of, sir,' I replied coolly. 'How so?'

" 'Why, you came inside of our lines by night, and waylaid our troops, against all the usages of civilized warfare, sir.'

" 'I was on a scout, like General Bayard,' I returned.

" 'A scout, sir!' he exclaimed, growing red in the face; 'we were on no *scout*, sir! we were on a *reconnoissance*, sir, with a force of one thousand cavalry, sir!'

" 'Well, I was on a *reconnoissance*, too, with a force of four infantry men. You came out to *reconnoitre* us, and we *recon-noitred* you. The *reconnoitring* parties happened to meet on the road, and *my* reconnoitring party got the better of *yours*.'

"This seemed to make him furious. He swelled, and swaggered, and puffed, like a big turkey-gobbler, and tried to frown me down, but it was not successful.

" 'Well, sir,' he said, 'if you did get the better of us, you at least are our prisoner, sir; and there are grave charges against you, sir—*very* grave charges, sir!'

"I began to get mad, and asked him what he meant by that.

" 'I mean, sir,' he said, raising his voice and swelling out his breast, 'that you have shot a *doctor*, sir!—yes, sir; a DOCTOR, sir!'

" 'What doctor? Where did I shoot a doctor?'

" 'On the road, sir! He was a doctor, sir; the officer you killed, sir! a non-combatant, without arms, in the performance of his official duties, sir!'

" 'Oh! a doctor was he!' I said, 'a doctor! Well, you doctors ought to take care how you ride along at the head of columns of cavalry in our country, and put yourselves in the way of balls, in uniform, with straps on your shoulder. It is dangerous.'

" 'He was a *doctor*, sir; I say! a non-combatant! a DOCTOR, sir; and you murdered him! yes, murdered him, sir!'

" 'Look here, sir,' I said; 'this is my room and if you can't behave yourself in it, I wish you to leave it. I wish to have no more of your talk!'

" 'Oh, well, sir! very well, sir!'

"And the doctor swaggered out. The next who came was a Major, a little smiling finicky fellow, who was oily and polite in his manner, and seemed uncommonly friendly.

" 'This is an unfortunate affair, Captain,' he began in a sympathizing tone.

" 'Not very,' I said.

" 'I fear it is. You see, you were taken inside of our lines, and it is probable you will be treated as a spy.'

" 'I reckon not, sir.'

" 'Why, so I hear, at least. Do you often enter our lines, Captain?'

" 'I have done so, frequently.'

" 'In citizen's dress, Captain?' he inquired, smiling; and then I saw what he was after, and was on my guard.

" 'No,' I replied, 'I come with my arms to make a military reconnoissance.'

" 'Do your officers enter our lines in this way often, Captain?'

" 'Well,' I said, 'tolerably often. Colonel Fitz Lee made a reconnoissance or scout, as you please, down beyond Annandale, the other day, with a squadron of cavalry; and General Jeb Stuart is particularly fond of such expeditions—indulging in them frequently.'

He tried to make me commit myself in several other ways, but finding he could not succeed, got up and left. After that I told the sentinel at my door not to admit any more of them—which, however, I lost by, as they would not allow my friends to come and see me, or any of the delicacies they sent to reach me. They permitted me to walk in the yard, however, but forbade the prisoners to exchange any words or signs with those confined above. One day I saw some ladies at an upper window of the prison, who waved their handkerchiefs to me, and I took off my hat to them. The sentinel told me it was against orders, but I replied that in the South gentlemen always returned the salutation of ladies—and I didn't mind him. One of the ladies then dropped a little secession flag, made of riband; and I picked it up and put it in my hat. The sentinel ordered me to take it out, but I refused; and told him to call his Sergeant. The Sergeant came, and I told him to call the officer of the guard. I was going on through the officer of the guard, and the officer of the day, up to the Provost-Marshal; but the officer of the guard was an old Lieutenant, who said, 'Oh, everybody knows his politics. There is no harm in letting him wear a riband in his hat.' So I continued to wear it.

"One of the ladies was Mrs. Greenough,* and she had a little

* "Mrs. Greenough" is Rose O'Neal Greenow, the Confederate spy who was sent to the Old Capitol Prison in January 1862 for giving information to Beauregard about Union troop movements before the First Battle of Bull Run (First Manassas).—ED.

daughter of about twelve or thirteen, who used to run about the prison and visit all the rooms, as the sentinel would not stop such a mere child. She and myself became great friends, and one day she brought me some flowers from her mother, and whispered—for a guard was always present—that I would find a note in them. I found the note, and after that carried on quite a correspondence. I would make her a present of an apple, which I had cut and hollowed out—putting a note in it, and then sticking it together again. As the crowd were going down to dinner one day, I slipped up instead of down, and went into Mrs. Greenough's room, and had a long talk with her and another lady who was with her; getting back again without discovery.

"I was always thinking of plans to escape, however, and three schemes suggested themselves. Either to bribe the sentinel in the back yard not to see us—or stab the sentinels at the outer and inner door—or drop out of the front window by blankets torn in strips, just as the sentry walked off on his beat, taking the chances of his fire when he discovered us. I had two associates in these plans, a prisoner named Conner, and Lieutenant Harry Stewart. They preferred the first, while I liked the last best. Our plan was to escape to Baltimore, where some friends were fitting out secretly a tug with guns on it, to run down the bay, and attack Burnside's transports. This played exactly into my hand— to cut and slash, and blaze away at them—and I was so anxious to undertake the expedition, instead of being sent down tamely, with a white flag and all that sort of thing, to be exchanged at Fortress Monroe, that when they told me I would be regarded as prisoner of war and soon released, I did not give up my plan of escaping. It was all stopped, though, by Major Wood's coming into my and Decaradeux's room, and telling us he suspected something, and had put Conner and Harry Stewart into solitary confinement.

"Before I could arrange any new plan Decaradeux and myself were exchanged, and I was free again. It was well I didn't adopt Harry Stewart's plan. After a while he was allowed to go back to his room, and having bribed the two sentinels in the back yard, he attempted with Conner to escape one night. Just as he raised the window to get out, one of the sentinels said, 'There is the d——d rascal—fire on him!' The man fired, and shot him through the heart. I don't know what became of Conner.

"When I got to Richmond, I set off for Centreville to get my trunk, intending to go out and join some friends in the Southwest; but General Stuart met me there; gave me a fine horse; and told me if I would stay with him, he would show me some sport.

"I accepted his offer; and have been with him ever since."

### IV. Incidents of the Peninsula

Having given me the history of his adventures at Langly and in Washington, Captain Darrell yawned, and persisted in changing the subject. It was evident that he had made up his mind not to talk any more at that time upon military matters; and we accordingly passed to other topics.

He was here again yesterday, however, and I immediately attacked him on the subject of his adventures.

He shook his head.

"You are making me talk too much about myself," said the Captain, "and I will get up the reputation of a boaster. One of the greatest dangers with hunters, partisans, and scouts, is the temptation to exaggerate, and tell 'good stories.' All that I say is true, and scouting with me is no more than hunting—as if it were after bear or deer—and I speak of it as such. But I don't wish to be thought a boaster."

It was some time before I could eradicate from the Captain's mind the impression that his histories were listened to with sentiments of cynical doubt. He yielded very gradually—thawing very slowly before the warmth of my assurances; but at last I succeeded in quieting his scruples, and getting him in a talkative humour. One thing led to another; this incident brought forth that; and finally the Captain was persuaded to give me the following story of his adventures at Williamsburg.

As before, I give the narrative almost exactly in the words of the speaker. It was as follows:

"I might as well commence at the beginning. On the retreat from Yorktown, last spring, when our army was falling back to the Chickahominy, I was with General Stuart, and the cavalry were retiring by the Telegraph and Williamsburg roads, covering our rear. These two roads make a sort of triangle; like the two sides of the letter V, the point of the V being down the Peninsula. The Williamsburg road was the left side of the V —look at these two straws—and the Telegraph road the other. There were two by-roads running through the triangle and connecting the main roads. If you have a clear idea of this, you will understand what took place easily.

"The cavalry were falling back in two columns upon the Telegraph and Williamsburg roads, General Stuart being in command of the force on the latter. He was anxious to keep up thorough communications with the other column, however, and as I was familiar with every part of that country, he sent me with Captain Conner, of the Jeff. Davis Legion, who was ordered to cut across with a party, leave pickets at openings, and see that the cavalry on the Telegraph road fell back regularly in good order—parallel with the other column, and neither too fast nor too slow. Well, I proceeded with Captain Conner along the sort of bridle path which was the lowest down of the two which I have mentioned, as connecting the main roads, keeping a keen look-out for the enemy, who, I was pretty sure, were all around us. The pines were too thick to see much, however—you know what sort of a country it is—and we went on rather blindly. About half way we met a countryman who was leading a cow by the horns, and he told us that a party of the enemy's cavalry had just passed along the other cross road above toward the Williamsburg road.

"It occurred to me at once that our men on the Telegraph road had fallen back more rapidly than the other column, and unmasked the mouth of the upper cross road, which the enemy had then struck into, intending to get into the Williamsburg

road and cut the General off. I stated my opinion to Captain
Conner, but he seemed to think differently. The cavalry which
the countryman had seen could not possibly be any but our
own, he said. I stuck to it, however, that they were probably
the enemy's; and as the countryman told us they were then
drawn up on the cross road, I offered to go and reconnoitre.
Captain Conner said he would go with me, and we started off at
a gallop through the pines toward the spot where the man said
they were.

"When I got within fifty yards I could see a party of cavalry
drawn up, as the countryman stated, and I was sure they were
Yankees. Captain Conner still adhered to his opinion, however,
that they were a part of our own force, and I told him I would
dismount, creep up, and determine the matter. He agreed; and
I got off my horse, threw the bridle over a stump, and crept
through the pine brush until I was within fifteen feet of them.
I saw the blue pantaloons and jackets plainly, and knew they
were Federals; so I crept back toward my horse. At the same
moment—it all occurred in a twinkling—I heard, 'Halt! halt! halt!
halt! bang! bang! bang!' in front, and saw Captain Conner, who
had pushed on, certain that they were Confederates, taken prisoner by the enemy. I had mounted, and the first thing I knew I
was in the midst of them—carried by my horse, who became un-
governable—and I saw that my best chance would be to make
straight for the Williamsburg road, which was not far, and if
I got out, inform the General that a party was lying in wait for
him. I ran through them, followed by bang! bang! bang! from
their carbines, and drove ahead into the Williamsburg road—
right plump against a column of the enemy's cavalry, drawn up
to charge the General, when he came near enough. My horse
ran right against a Yankee's, who wiped at me with his sabre—
for they all had their sabres drawn—and just missed me. I was
going so fast though that I passed straight through the column,
and seeing that the other side of the road was lined with heavy
undergrowth, I jumped off my horse and ran in, leaving my
horse to the Yankees.

"They banged away at me as I went in, but only a few had

their carbines ready, and they did not come near me. They could not follow me, as the pines were too thick for any horseman to enter. My object now was to get back to the General and tell him of the attempt to cut him off. I thought I would reconnoitre, however, first, and ascertain their force, so I crept up to the edge of the bushes, and looked out. As I did so, I saw them moving backwards and forwards, greatly excited, with 'Here they are!' 'Look out!' but soon afterwards they fell back, apparently look-ing for a better position. The next thing I saw was Colonel Goode, of the Third Cavalry, coming up the road, and I ran out and met him, telling him what I knew, and stating that they were going to charge him. He drew his men up on the right of the road so as to let the Yankees charge by, and slash into them; and as I had no horse I got into the bushes just in advance of the head of the column, intending to shoot the commander of the Federal cavalry as soon as I could see him well. I had my carbine and pistol, which I had hung on to through all, and soon I heard the enemy coming, shouting and yelling, right down on Colonel Goode.

"As they came within about fifteen yards, I levelled my car-bine at the officer in front, and pulled trigger; but the cursed thing snapped. I had been skirmishing all day, and it had got dirty. I fired my pistol into them, however, and the Federal Cavalry halted, both sides sitting in the saddle and banging away with carbines. Our men had the better of it, though, as the Yankees had their sabres drawn, and we got the first fire on them, killing several of them, I saw in the road afterwards. I wounded three or four myself, and was still popping at them when they concluded to give it up, and go back. They turned round, and I ran out, looking for a good horse, as several were running about without riders. I got a good one, but found he was wounded, and just then I saw a splendid black stallion, who took my eye wonderfully. I tried to catch him—walking up and holloing 'woe!' to him—but whenever I got near, he trotted off, and I missed him. I determined not to give it up, however—and I kept following and trying to catch him until I was at least a mile and a half back toward Williamsburg. I caught him at last, mounted him, and started back toward the scene of the skirmish. I remember feeling in fine spirits, and looking down at my splendid stallion, who was full of fire and spirit—a big black fellow, the very horse I wanted—admiring his neck and action. I was still examining him, with my head down, as we went on at full speed toward the spot where I expected to find Colonel Goode, when suddenly I heard a quick 'Halt! halt! halt!' 'Here's one of 'em!' in front; and a carbine ball whizzed by me. I looked up, and there was the enemy in the road instead of Colonel Goode, who had fallen back. They had got reinforcements, and brought up artillery to plant in the road—and I had run right into them!

"There was only one thing for me to do, and that was to get away from there as fast as possible. I accordingly wheeled round and went back over the same road I had come, followed by a dozen men, shouting 'halt! halt! halt!' and firing at me. I leaned over on my horse, and could hear the balls whizzing by me every second—I afterwards found the accoutrements, especially the thick bundle behind the saddle, full of bullet holes. I would have got away from them, but all at once my horse threw up his head—a ball had passed clean through it. He still kept on, however,—horses will go long with that sort of wound—but another bullet struck him right behind my leg, on the left side, and I felt him staggering. The party saw this, and set up a whoop, which was rather too near. I saw that they would catch me, if I depended on my horse, so I threw myself off and ran down a little path in the bushes, by the side of the road, and did not stop until I was well concealed. They fired at me and around several times, but as they were afraid of coming on our infantry, they gave it up, and rode away.

"As soon as they were gone I came out of the bushes, and went to my horse. He had fallen in the road, and I took from him several articles strapped to the saddle, and left him to die.

"I knew now that the General would retire by the Beach road, the only one left, and I determined to strike across and join him, trusting to luck to get a horse somewhere. I accordingly set out in that direction, trusting to my skill to flank the enemy's pickets,

which I knew I could do, and get through. My only fear was
that I would be shot by our own pickets, as it was now getting
dusk. I went on, through the woods and fields, avoiding the
enemy's fires whenever I saw them, and approaching our lines.
I had got very nearly through, when suddenly I came upon three
cavalrymen in the middle of the road, near a little bridge I had
to pass. I was sure they were Yankees, so I cocked my pistol,
and walked up to them boldly, saying in a loud commonplace
tone—

" 'Hem!—ah!—what company do you belong to, men?'

" 'Company A, sir.'

"This was not sufficient. Company A might be a *Yankee* company. So I said,

" 'What regiment?'

" 'The Fourth.'

"This was no more definite than the other.

" 'Ah!' I said, 'ahem—the Fourth, eh? Fourth New York, I
suppose?'

" 'No—the Fourth Virginia,' replied one of the men. I never
was more relieved in my life, and told them how things stood,
and which way to look out. I went on through the awful mud,
and when I had gone some distance met a regiment of Confederate infantry coming down, with an officer on horseback at
their head, who was very much out of humour.

" 'Where is the post?' he was saying. 'I don't believe it is this
way, and we must have come in the wrong direction. Where is
the regiment to be relieved?'

"I recognised General Pryor, and said:

" 'I can tell you, General.'

" 'Hello! who's that!' he replied, looking through the dark,
'how did you know me?'

" 'By your voice. I remember meeting you at the Commercial
Convention in Knoxville, to which I was a delegate—and making
your acquaintance.'

" 'What is your name, sir?'

"I told him, and added,

" 'The regiment you are looking for is down in the fortifications, in that direction; and though it will be going back, I will act as your guide.'

"So I went with him, and finding some friends in the Nineteenth Mississippi, commanded by Colonel Mott, a friend of mine, I lay down, and went to sleep.

"On the next morning, I was still talking with my friends of the Nineteenth, when chancing to look toward the front, I saw a line of men advancing through the brushwood, who, I was certain, were Yankees. It was drizzling, and no attack was expected, though we knew that the enemy was right in our front; and when I told the Lieutenant, in command of the company I was with, that the men in front were certainly Yankees, he did not believe it.

" 'They can't be,' he said; 'they are a party of our own men who have been out on a scout toward the enemy, and are coming in.'

"As he was speaking, the line came on steadily, and I saw distinctly the blue pantaloons, and oil-cloth capes thrown over their heads as a protection from the rain. I knew from this that it was the enemy, as none of our men had capes; and I jumped up, crying to the men:

" 'They are Yankees! Fire, men! They are right on you!'

" 'Hold your fire!' shouted the Lieutenant, 'don't shoot your friends! It is some of the Seventh Alabama from our left.'

" 'There are no troops on our left!' I replied, 'the Seventh Alabama is on the right, and those people are Yankees! Fire, men!'

"And I ran out pointing at them where they were advancing, within twenty yards, in the pines.

" 'Don't fire, I say!' shouted the Lieutenant to his men, 'they are friends!'

"Well, *I'll* take the responsibility, as far as I am concerned!' I said; and levelling my carbine I took aim, and saw one of the men fall. As soon as I shot, the whole party stopped suddenly, as though they were astonished.

" 'Fire!' I cried to the Mississippians, 'give it to 'em, boys!' Charge!'

"And I blazed away with my pistol as I ran toward them.

They did not wait for the expected charge—it turned out to be only a company—and broke and ran. I followed, and came to the man I had shot, who was dying. His gun was lying by him, and I seized it, and fired on them as they were running; but finding no one following me, I concluded I had better go back. When I got to the fortification I found Colonel Mott there, attracted by the firing; and showed him the gun I had brought back, telling him that they were Yankees.

" 'Certainly they were,' he replied, 'and the Lieutenant in command ought to have known that there were none of our troops on the left.'

"As I had nothing to do, I proposed to the Colonel that if he would give me half-a-dozen men I would go and scout in front, and bring him any information I could procure of the enemy's movements. He agreed to this, and called for volunteers. A dozen men stepped out, but I told him I did not want more than six; and with these, I went along in the track of the party of Yankees. I remember one of them was named Bryant, a first-rate man, and he stuck to me all day, though he was wounded; but he would not leave me.

"Well, I followed the party, marching the men in single file, and looking out every moment for the Yankees. I came on their trail at last, and thought I could hear the hum of their voices just over a knoll in front of me. The woods there have hollows in them, and you can get very close to a party of men without knowing it if they are in one of them. There was a hollow of this sort just before me, and the hill sloped up in such a way, that you could get right on them and not be perceived. I crept up the side of the hill, going from tree to tree, looking and listening. I could not see anybody, but I was sure I heard the hum of voices not far off; and I determined to reconnoitre and ascertain who the party were. I accordingly went cautiously up the hill, to peep over, leaving my men behind.

"Just as I got near the top I heard the tramp of feet, and could see the heads of the men coming up the hill. The officer in command was walking in front, and before I knew it he was right on me, within three yards.

" 'Dress up to the right!' he cried quickly to his men.

" 'Dress up, yourself, sir!' I shouted to him, suddenly.

"And as I spoke, I levelled my carbine at his breast, fired, and shot him through the body. Before the enemy had recovered from their surprise, I shouted back, as if I was speaking to my company:

" 'Charge 'em, men! Fire on 'em! Char-r-r-rge!'

"And I set the example by firing my pistol as fast as I could at their heads, which was all I could see above the hill. They fired a volley at me, but their position was too unfavourable, and the bullets went whizzing high up in the trees. My men came up promptly, and we all took trees and commenced skirmishing with them, neither side advancing, but keeping up a scattering fire all the time.

"The captain, when I had shot him, sat down on the ground, and remained there leaning his shoulder against the trunk of a tree. The tree I had dodged behind was not far off, and we carried on a conversation for some time; I suppose about half an hour. I asked him why he had come down to the South, and he said he wished now that he had stayed at home. He said a good many things, but I don't remember them now. His name was a singular one; he told me what it was, and I've got it somewhere; his company was the 47th Sharpshooters, New York.

"I had shot away all my ammunition, and I got up and went to him, asking him for his pistol. He took hold of the belt, and tried to unbuckle it, but was too weak.

" 'It's no use,' he said, 'I can't undo it, and you had better go back. You will just make them shoot both of us.'

"He did not look as if he was shot; I could see no marks of a wound; but soon after I had gone back to my tree, he raised his shoulder from the trunk which he was leaning against, sat upright, and then fell upon his back, dead.

"About this time there was a general advance of our line upon the enemy, all along; and the company of sharpshooters fell back, firing as they went. Our troops came along, and charged their main line, which was posted behind a fence, some distance in front; and here Colonel Mott was killed as he was leading the charge. I went along with them, but had first gotten the dead officer's sword. As soon as our men advanced, and the enemy went away, I came from behind the tree where I had been sitting down firing, and approached the body. He was lying on his back, with his eyes open—dead from my bullet, which had passed through his breast. I had no sword, having left mine behind that morning; so I unbuckled his belt, and drew it from under his body, and buckled it around my own waist. It had a good pistol and cap-pouch, besides the sword, on it—I have the sword still.

"That was a hot day," concluded the Captain; "this was where Tom —— got wounded. He came up to a Federal officer, a finely dressed fellow, and ordered him to surrender. He obeyed, but made no motion to yield his arms. Tom said:

" 'Give up your arms, sir!'

"The officer handed over his sword which he held in his hand; but did not seem to remember the pistol in his belt.

" 'Give me your pistol!' exclaimed Tom, with a scowl at him.

" 'I have surrendered my sword,' was the reply, 'spare me the disgrace, sir, of giving up my pistol also to a *private*!'

"He had surrendered his *sword*, but wished to spare himself the mortification of handing over his pistol! Tom put his bayonet at him, and he soon surrendered his pistol.

"Soon afterwards Tom had a duel at ten yards distance, with a Yankee. They loaded and fired twenty times without hitting each other, until Tom made a good shot and bored him through the breast. He dropped his musket, threw up his hands and fell back. Tom was very soon wounded, however, and was firing still when Colonel Baldwin came along with a led horse, and, as he knew him, put him on it. He was going to the rear when he saw General A. P. Hill, sitting by a stump, smoking; and as the young man was an acquaintance, he asked him what was the matter. He informed him that he was wounded; and the General took off his cravat, and tied it around his leg, above the wound. Tom then rode on into Williamsburg.

"That was my great fighting day, and some time or other I will tell you all about it. I had command of two or three regiments, and never had more fun in my life."

# XI

## LONGBOW'S HORSE

### I.

MY FRIEND, Captain Longbow, is a very different personage from Captain Darrell. The latter is brave, honest, simple, and candid. He relates only what really occurred, and never unless you overcome his repugnance to such narratives: he is modest, retiring—the model of an officer and a gentleman.

Longbow is a striking contrast, I am sorry to say, to all this. He is a tremendous warrior—according to his own account; he has performed prodigies—if you can only believe him; more moving accidents and hair-breadth escapes have happened to him than to any other soldier in the service—if they have only happened. The element of confidence is thus wanting in the listener when Longbow discourses, and you are puzzled how much to believe, how much to disbelieve. But then the worthy is often amusing. He has some of the art of the *raconteur*, and makes his histories or stories, his real events or his fibs, to a certain degree amusing. I am always at a loss to determine how much of Longbow's narratives to believe; but they generally make me laugh. It is certain that he mingles truth with them, for many incidents related by him, in the course of his narratives, are known to me as real circumstances; and thus there ever remains upon the mind, when this worthy has ceased speaking, an impression that although the narrative is fabulous, portions of it are true.

These prefatory words are intended to introduce the following account of Longbow's adventures in the Valley, when General Johnston was opposed to General Patterson there, in the
summer of 1861, just before the battle of Manassas. Some of
the incidents related I know to be true; others, it is proper that
I should warn the reader, I regard as purely romantic. The manner in which Longbow professed to have obtained his "blood
bay" I believe to be imaginary; the untimely end to which the
animal came may not, doubtless is not, of historical verity, but
it is certain that an officer did kill his horse under the circumstances narrated. Thus the mind is left in a state of bewilderment
as to how much is true and how much is false in the worthy's
story; and perhaps the safest proceeding would be to set down
the whole as an "historical romance."

I have thought it best to convey this caution to the reader,
lest the narrative here given might cast discredit upon the other
papers in these "Outlines," which contain, with the exception
of "Corporal Shabrach" and "Blunderbus," events and details of
strict historical accuracy.

I have never told you, said Longbow, of the curious adventures which I met with in the Valley in 1861, and how I got
my fine blood bay, and lost him. I was then a private, but had
just been detailed as volunteer aide to Colonel Jackson—he was
not "General" or "Stonewall" yet—and had reported a few days
before the engagement at Falling Waters.

I need not inform you of the state of affairs at that time, further than to say that while Beauregard watched the enemy in
front of Washington, with his headquarters at Manassas, Johnston held the Valley against Patterson, with *his* headquarters at
Winchester. Well, it was late in June, I think, when intelligence
came that General Patterson was about to cross the Potomac at
Williamsport, and Colonel Jackson was sent forward with the
First Brigade, as it was then called, to support Stuart's cavalry,
and feel the enemy, but not bring on a general engagement. This,
the Colonel proceeded to do with alacrity, and he had soon advanced north of Martinsburg, and camped near the little village

of Hainesville—Stuart continuing in front watching the enemy on the river.

This was the state of things, when suddenly one morning we were aroused by the intelligence that Patterson had crossed his army; and Jackson immediately got his brigade under arms, intending to advance and attack him. He determined, however, to move forward first, with one regiment and a single gun—and this he did, the regiment being the Fifth Virginia, Colonel Harper, with one piece from Pendleton's battery.

I will not stop here to describe the short and gallant fight near Falling Water, in which Jackson met the enemy with the same obstinacy which afterwards gave him his name of "Stonewall." Their great force, however, rendered it impossible for him to hold his ground with one regiment of less than four hundred men, and finding that he was being outflanked, he gave the order for his line to fall back, which was done in perfect order. It was at this moment that Colonel Jackson pointed out a cloud of dust to me on the left, and said:

"That is cavalry. They are moving to attack my left flank. Where is Stuart? Can you find him?"

"I think so, Colonel."

"Well, present my compliments to him, and tell him that the enemy's cavalry will probably attack him. Lose no time, Captain."

I obeyed at once, and passing across the line of fire, as the men fell back fighting, entered a clump of woods, and took a narrow road, which led in the direction I wished.

My fortune was bad. I had scarcely galloped a quarter of a mile when I ran full tilt into a column of Federal cavalry, and suddenly heard their unceremonious "halt!"

Wheeling round, I dug the spurs into my horse, and darted into the woods, but I was too late. A volley came from the column; my horse suddenly staggered, and advancing a few steps, fell under me. A bullet had penetrated his body behind my knee, and I had scarcely time to extricate myself, when I was surrounded. I was forced to surrender, and did so to a gray-haired officer who came up a moment afterwards.

He saluted me, and seeing my rank from my uniform, said:

"I hope you are not hurt, Captain?"

"No, sir," I said angrily; "and if my horse had not fallen, you would never have captured me."

The old officer smiled.

"When you are as old a soldier as I am, sir," he replied, "you will not suffer these accidents to move you so much. Are you a line or staff officer?"

"A staff officer."

"Who commands yonder?"

"The ranking officer."

Another smile came to his face.

"I see you are prudent. Well, sir, I will not annoy you. Take this officer to the rear," he added to a subaltern; "treat him well, but guard him carefully."

The column continued its advance, and I was conducted to the rear. I heard the firing gradually recede toward Martinsburg, and knew that Jackson must be still falling back. Skirmishing on the right of the column I moved with, indicated the presence of Stuart; but this too gradually receded, and soon word was passed along the line that the Colonel had received intelligence of the Confederates having retreated. This announcement was greeted with a cheer by the men, and the column continued to advance, but soon halted.

That night I bivouacked by a camp fire, and on the next morning was conducted into Martinsburg, which the enemy had occupied in force.

I was on foot, and of course had been deprived of my arms.

I was placed in a house under guard, with some other Confederate prisoners, and could only learn from the Federal Corporal that our forces had fallen back, south of the town, losing "a tremendous amount of stores, wagons, tents, commissary and quartermaster stores, and all they had." I laughed, in spite of myself, at this magniloquent statement, knowing in what "light marching order" Jackson had been, and resolved philosophically to await the progress of events.

The day thus passed, and on the next morning I was aroused

from my bed upon the floor by a thundering salvo of artillery. I started up joyfully, fully convinced that Jackson was attacking the town, when the Corporal came in, and cried:

"Hurrah for the glorious Fourth!"

"Fourth what?" I said.

"Why, Fourth of July!"

"Oh, that is the cause of the firing, is it?" I growled; "then I'll finish my nap."

And I again lay down. Soon afterwards a breakfast of "hard tack," pork, and coffee, was supplied to the prisoners, and I had just finished my meal when I was informed that General Patterson had sent for me. Fifteen minutes afterwards I was conducted through the streets, swarming with blue-coats, galloping cavalry, and wagons, to a fine mansion in the southern suburbs of the town, where the commanding General had established his headquarters—Colonel Falkner's.

Here all was life and bustle; splendidly caparisoned horses, held by orderlies, were pawing the turf of the ornamented grounds; other orderlies were going and coming; and the impression produced upon my mind was, that the orderly was an established institution. At the door was a sentinel with a musket, and having passed this Cerberus, my guard conducted me to an apartment on the left, where I was received by a staff officer, whose scowling hauteur was exceedingly offensive.

"Who are you?" he growled, looking at me in the most insolent manner.

"Who are you?" was my response, in a tone equally friendly.

"I will have no insolence," was his enraged reply. "Are you the prisoner sent for by the General?"

"I am, sir," was my reply; "and I shall ascertain from General Patterson whether it is by his order that an officer of the Confederate States Army is subjected to your rudeness and insults."

He must have been a poor creature; for as soon as he found that I would not endure his brow-beating he became polite, and went to announce my arrival.

I was left alone in the ante-room with an officer, who wrote so busily at his desk that he seemed not to have even been aware of any one's presence; and this busy gentleman I afterwards discovered was General Patterson's Adjutant-General.

## II.

I waited for half an hour, when I was informed that General Patterson was ready to see me. I found him seated at a table covered with papers, which stood in the middle of a large apartment filled with elegant furniture, and ornamented with a fine Brussels carpet. On the mantel-piece a marble clock ticked; in Gothic bookcases were long rows of richly bound volumes; the Federal commander had evidently selected his headquarters with an eye to comfort and convenience.

He was a person of good figure and agreeable countenance; and wore the full-dress uniform of a Major-General of the U. S. Army. As I entered he rose, advanced a step, and offered me his hand.

"I am glad to make your acquaintance, Captain," he said; then he added with a smile, "I doubt, however, if you are equally pleased at making mine."

"Delighted, General, I assure you," was my reply, "though the incident to which I am indebted for this honour was rather rough."

"What was that?"

"My horse was shot and fell with me."

"That is a pity, and the thing was unfortunate. But war is altogether a rough business. I am disposed to agree with Franklin, Captain, that 'there never was a good war, or a bad peace.' But we will not discuss this vexed question—you are Captain Longbow, I believe."

"Yes, sir."

"Of Colonel Jackson's command?"

"Of the command which engaged you the day before yesterday."

General Patterson smiled.

"I see you are reticent, and it is a good habit in a soldier. But I know that Colonel Jackson commanded, and from his boldness in opposing me with so small a force, he must be a man of nerve and ability."

"He has that reputation, General."

"Do you know General Johnston?"

"Yes, sir."

"I am afraid of his retreats. General Scott declares that one of them is equal to a victory."

I assented with a bow.

"Colonel Stuart, commanding your cavalry, I do not know," continued the General, "but I am afraid he gobbled up one of my companies of infantry just before the late fight. That makes the number of prisoners taken considerably in your favour. The company was commanded, however, only by a Second Lieutenant, and as I have you, Captain," he added with a smile, "the odds are not so great."

The General's courtesy and good-humour began to put me in the same mood, and I said:

"How long are you going to keep me, General? not long, I hope."

"Not a day after I can have an exchange."

"That may, however, be for a long time."

"Possibly, but you shall be well treated, Captain."

"I have no doubt of that, General, but you know the proverb, or what ought to be a proverb—'to the exile honey itself is bitter.' Well, it is the same with prisoners."

"You shall not be confined. I will take your parole, and you can then have the freedom of the town of Martinsburg. Winchester, too, if you wish."

"I am very much obliged to you, especially for Winchester, General—but I cannot accept."

"Why not?"

"Because I am going to try to escape."

The General began to laugh.

"You will find it impossible," he replied; "even if you eluded the sentinel you could not get through my lines. The pickets would stop you."

"General," I said, "you are really so very courteous, and our interview is so completely divested of all formality, that I am tempted to presume upon it."

"In what manner?"

"By offering to make you a bet."

"A bet! Well, what is it?" said the General, laughing.

"This. My horse was killed, and as we poor Confederates are not over rich, I will lay you a horse and equipments that I make my escape."

The General greeted this proposal with evident enjoyment.

"In what time?" he asked.

"Before you reach Richmond."

He made a humorous grimace.

"Richmond is a long way off, Captain—let the limit be the 1st day of August, and I will agree."

"Very well, General; I will pay my bet if I lose; and if I win, you will send me my horse through the lines."

"Most assuredly."

At this moment an orderly brought in a dispatch, which the General read with attention.

"From the front," he said. "Jackson is at Darkesville, Captain, and is preparing to make a stand there."

"And you will attack, I suppose, in a day or two, General?"

These words were greeted with a quick glance, to which I responded innocently:

"As I have no chance to escape in that time, you could reply without an indiscretion, could you not, General?"

"Caution is never amiss, my dear Captain," he replied; "I pay you a compliment in imitating your own reticence. But here is another dispatch. Excuse me while I read it."

The contents of the paper seemed to be important; for the General turned to his table, and began to write busily. His back was turned to me, and seeing a newspaper lying in the ante-chamber, I rose and went to procure it.

"You are not leaving me, Captain?" the General called out, without turning round.

"Is it forbidden to go into the ante-room, General?"

"Not at all—you can't escape, as my sentinel is too good a soldier to permit an officer in Confederate uniform to pass!"

And he went on writing.

His words operated upon my mind like a challenge; and at the same moment my eye fell upon two objects, the sight of which thrilled through every nerve. These objects were simply a light linen overall lying upon a chair, and on a table the tall blue hat of the Adjutant-General, encircled with its golden cord. At the same instant a shrill neigh attracted my attention to the grounds without; and looking through the window, I saw an orderly holding a magnificent horse, from which an officer had just descended.

In one instant I had formed an audacious resolution; and sitting down at a table upon which were pen, ink, and paper, I wrote:

"Captain Longbow presents his compliments to General Patterson, and informs him that he is about to make an attempt to win the bet just made. There is an excellent horse now at the door, which has only to be secured in case Captain Longbow can pass the sentinel—when his escape will not be difficult in spite of the pickets.

"Headquarters of General Patterson, July 4, 1861."

I had just placed this note in an envelope, and directed it to "Major-General Patterson, com'd'g, etc.," when the Adjutant-General turned his head, and said courteously:

"Are you writing a letter, Captain?"

"Yes, sir," I said.

"To send through the lines, I suppose. If you give me your word of honour that it contains only private matter, and nothing contraband, I will forward it unread by the first flag of truce."

I paused a moment, and then made up my mind.

"It is not to go through the lines," I said; "it is addressed to General Patterson."

"Ah!" said the officer.

"Yes, sir. It refers to a subject upon which the General and myself were conversing when we were interrupted. I do not wish to trouble him further at present, as he seems busy; but if you will have the goodness to hand it to him this evening or to-morrow, I will be greatly indebted to you."

"I will do so with pleasure, Captain," said this most courteous of enemies; and taking the note, he placed it in one of the pigeon-holes of his desk.

At the same moment the officer who had dismounted from the fine horse was introduced, and soon afterwards my pulse leaped. The voice of General Patterson was heard calling his Adjutant-General; and that officer hastened to the inner room, closing the door after him.

## III.

I did not lose an instant. Seizing the light linen overall, I put it on and buttoned it up to the chin, as though to guard my uni-form from the dust; and throwing my brown felt hat under the table, placed upon my head the high-crowned blue one, with its golden cord and tassel. I then opened the outer door; negligently returned the salute of the sentinel, who came to a "present" with his musket at sight of my cord and tassel; and walked out to the gate, which was set in a low hedge, above which appeared the head of the splendid animal I had determined to "capture."

Every instant now counted. My ruse might at any moment be discovered; for on the Adjutant-General's return to his room, he must observe my absence. It was necessary to act rapidly, and with decision.

Strolling with a careless air to the spot where the orderly stood, holding his own and the officer's bridle, I patted the horse on the neck, and said:

"That is a fine animal."

"Yes, sir," replied the orderly, touching his hat *to the Adju-tant-General's hat;* "the Colonel paid six hundred dollars for him only last week."

"Excellent equipments, too," and I raised the flap of one of the holsters, which contained a pair of silver-mounted pistols.

In an instant I had drawn one of the weapons, cocked it, and placed it at the orderly's head.

"I am a Confederate prisoner, determined to escape or die," I said. "If you move I will blow your brains out. Wait until I get a fair start, and then tell your Colonel I took his horse by force!"

With one bound I was in the saddle, and turning the horse's head to the fence on the south of the house, cleared it, and set out at full speed for a wood near by. As I did so, I saw a sudden tumult, and crowds running about at the house, among whom I recognised the Adjutant-General.

"Good-by, Major," I called out; "I will send your hat and coat by flag of truce!"

And in a moment I had gained the clump of woods, and was out of sight.

My captured horse was an animal of superb action, and I soon found that I must make him show his points. As I looked over my shoulder, I saw a company of cavalry—evidently the body-guard of the General, whose horses always remained saddled—leave the town, and follow furiously upon my track.

Between these and the pickets which would certainly bar my passage, I seemed to stand little chance; but it was worth the trial, and I went on at full speed, keeping as much as possible in the woods. Stopping for nothing in the shape of a fence, I made straight across the country, and gradually seemed distancing my pursuers. What words, however, can describe my mortification when, issuing from a dense covert, I found they had followed by a parallel road, and were on my very heels! I heard the tramp of their horses, and the quick shout they gave as they caught sight of me.

Then commenced on the narrow wood road what is called a "stern chase" at sea. It was a question of the speed of our horses; but I found, unfortunately, that my pursuers were as well mounted as myself. They were steadily gaining on me, when I ran straight into a regiment of infantry, who had pitched their small tents *de l'arbre*, under the trees. The quarter-guard, however, made no effort to stop me, and I shot past the camp, but in four hundred yards came in sight of the cavalry pickets.

It was now "neck or nothing." I had to ride through or over every obstacle in my way, or surrender. The picket consisted of about a company of cavalry, every man standing by his horse; and as I approached, the officer came out, evidently supposing that I brought him some important message.

The officer staggered back, nearly knocked down by my horse; and I passed on, followed by a quick volley which did not harm me. I knew now that if once I could pass the external pickets, my escape would be certain; and all at once I came on them. The picket consisted of four or five mounted men; and as I approached, the vidette in the middle of the road ordered me to halt, presenting his carbine. I drew my revolver and fired, and at the same moment he discharged his carbine, but missed me.

I do not know whether I struck him or not. I went past him, and did not look back to see. Suddenly the whole picket fired, and the bullets hissed close to me; but not one touched me or my horse, and I was free! In ten minutes I was out of sight, and in five minutes more saw the Confederate pickets in front of me.

They received me rather roughly. The vidette fired on me and then ran, and I followed him. A hundred yards further I drove in the whole external picket, which retired firing.

The first person I saw near the "Big Spring" was Colonel Stuart, with his cavalry drawn up in line of battle. As soon as he recognised me he burst into laughter, and cried: "Ho, ho! here's Longbow in a Yankee uniform!"

"Exactly, Colonel."

"Where are you from?"

"Martinsburg—driving in your pickets on the way."

"No wonder," laughed Stuart. "Your appearance is enough to frighten a whole brigade. I hope my pickets fired on you before they ran."

"Furiously, Colonel, as the enemy were doing behind."

"But how did you escape? I was truly sorry to hear from Jackson that you had ridden to look for me, and never turned up afterwards."

I briefly related my adventures, and offered my horse, hat, and pistols in proof. Stuart listened, laughing heartily, and when I had finished, said:

"So all that firing was only a Fourth of July salute! I thought so, but never take anything on trust; so I've been ready all the morning, and thought when the picket fired that you were the enemy."

Soon afterwards I parted from this great soldier; and riding on, found Jackson at Darkesville, to whom I reported, receiving his congratulations upon my escape.

But I must hasten on and tell you about my horse.

## IV.

A few days afterwards I was at General Johnston's headquarters, and ascertaining that he was about to send a flag through the lines, thought it a good opportunity to return the Adjutant-General's hat and coat. I therefore rolled up these articles, and wrote a note to accompany them, thanking the Major for the use of them, and begging him to excuse the little liberty I had taken in appropriating them.

I went with the flag; and when the business of the interview was transacted, gave the hat, coat, and note, to the Federal officer who met us, and who was a gentleman of good-sense and breeding. He laughed when I explained how I had procured the articles, and informed me that he had already heard the story.

"I even heard there was a bet between you and General Patterson," he said. "Is that the fact, Captain? and what was the amount?"

"It was not money, but a horse and equipments, which the General has lost."

"Then he will certainly pay, and he has some very fine horses."

"I am afraid he has forgotten me."

"On the contrary, he has remembered you, Captain," said the officer, smiling; and at a sign from him a mounted man led forward a beautiful bay, splendidly equipped, which every member of the party had been looking at and admiring.

"The General requested me to send this horse to you, Captain," said the officer; "but as you are present, I deliver him in person. He is a splendid animal, and I only hope I shall soon have the pleasure of capturing you, and getting him into my own possession."

Everybody began to laugh, and admire my horse. I mounted and put him at a fence, which he went over like a deer.

"Thank the General for me, Major; his horse is excellent," I said.

"I will do so with pleasure; this is really the poetry of war!"

And saluting each other, the two parties separated.

I have thus told you how I got my fine blood bay. He was a magnificent animal. I will next proceed to inform you how I lost him.

Two days afterwards I was riding out with Colonel Jackson, when General Johnston, wholly unattended, met him, and the two officers rode on, in earnest conversation, pointing as they did so to the various hills and knolls which afforded good positions for troops. I had fallen back some distance to allow them to converse without reserve, when all at once I saw General Johnston turn and look at me; then Jackson beckoned to me. I rode up and saluted the General, who gravely returned the bow, and said:

"Captain, I have determined to send you to Manassas with a dispatch to General Beauregard, which I wish delivered at once. The dispatch will be ready in two hours from this time, and I would like to have you set off at once. Can you do so?"

"Yes, sir," I replied; "this moment, if necessary."

"Very good; ride back with me to headquarters, and I will give you a message also."

I followed the General back to Darkesville, waited an hour, and then was sent for, and received the dispatch and instructions. On the same night I set out on my bay horse, and by morning was at General Beauregard's headquarters, and had delivered the dispatch. An hour afterwards I was sound asleep.

I was waked by the clatter of hoofs, and rising, found couriers going and coming.

"What is the matter?" I asked of an orderly.

"The Yankees are coming," he replied, "and they are already near Fairfax Court-house."

I immediately hurried to General Beauregard, and found him about to mount and ride out on the lines. At sight of me, he exclaimed—

"Good! I was just about to send for you, Captain. The enemy are upon us, and I wish General Johnston to know that if he desires to help me, now is the time."

"I will carry the message, General."

"Will your horse hold out?"

"Yes, sir."

"Well, tell General Johnston the condition of things here. A very large force of the enemy are within a few miles of me, and are still advancing. Say to the General simply this—that if he wishes to help me, now is the time."

With these words General Beauregard saluted me, and rode on. I immediately called for my horse, mounted, and set off at a rapid gallop for the Valley.

General Patterson's present was now destined to be subjected to a hard trial. I had already ridden him nearly fifty miles within the last twenty-four hours, and was about to pass over the very same ground almost without allowing him any rest.

I galloped on toward Thoroughfare. My bay moved splendidly, and did not seem at all fatigued. He was moving with head up, and pulling at the rein.

"Good! my gallant bay!" I said; "if you go on at that rate we'll soon be there!"

I had not counted on the heat of the July weather, however; and when I got near Salem my bay began to flag a little. I pushed him with the spur, and hurried on. Near Paris he began to wheeze; but I pushed on, using the spur freely, and drove him up the mountain road, and along the gap to the river. This we forded, and in the midst of the terrible heat I hurried on over the turnpike.

My bay had begun to pant and stagger at times; but there was no time to think of his condition. I had undertaken to deliver

General Beauregard's message; and I must do so, on horseback or on foot, without loss of time. I dug the spur into my panting animal and rushed on.

At Millwood some citizens gathered in the middle of the street to ask the news. I continued the gallop without stopping, and in an hour approached Winchester, where Johnston had established his general headquarters.

Beyond the Opequon my bay staggered, blood rushed from his nostrils, and his eyes glared; as I neared the town the spur scarcely raised him; from his chest issued a hollow groan.

All at once an officer, followed by some couriers, appeared at a turn of the road, and I recognised General Johnston.

In an instant I was at his side, and had delivered my message.

"Very good!" exclaimed the General; "and I am greatly obliged by your promptness; but look at your horse, Captain—he is dying!"

At the same instant my bay fell, and rolled over.

"You are wrong, General," I said, as I sprang up; "he is dead!"

In fact he was then gasping in the death agony, and in ten minutes he was dead.

"Pity you should lose so fine an animal, Captain," said the General.

"Easy come, easy go, General. I got him from General Patterson—I believe Colonel Jackson told you how."

"Ah! that is the horse? Well, sir, I will give you one of my own in place of him, for he has enabled you to bring me information, upon the receipt of which the result of the battle at Manassas depended."

"I wonder if General Patterson contemplated such a thing, General, when he sent me the horse."

"Doubtful!" replied Johnston, with his calm, grim smile; and saluting me, he rode away rapidly.

Six hours afterwards his army was in motion for Manassas, where the advance arrived on the night of the 20th of July. On the next day Jackson's brigade held the enemy in check, and Kirby Smith ended the fight by his assault upon their right.

Jackson and Smith belonged to the Army of the Shenandoah, and this will show you that without that army the battle would have been lost.

*I* brought that army, my dear friend, by means of General Patterson's bay horse!

Such was the narrative of Captain Longbow, and I would like to know how much of it is true. The incident of the hard ride, and the death of the Captain's horse especially, puzzles me. That incident is veracious, as I have once before said; but a serious question arises as to whether Longbow bore that message! I have a dim recollection that my friend Colonel Surry told me once that *he* had been sent to Beauregard; had killed *his* horse; and the high character of the Colonel renders it impossible to doubt any statement which he makes. I expect him on a visit soon, as he intends to make a little scout, he tells me, to Fauquier to see a young lady—a Miss Beverley—there, and doubtless will call by; then I shall ask him what are the real facts of this affair.

Meanwhile my friend Longbow is entitled to be heard; and I have even taken the trouble to set down his narrative for the amusement of the friend to whom it will be sent. If Colonel Surry ever composes his memoirs, as I believe is his intention, the real truth on this important point will be recorded. Until then—*Vive Longbow!*

# XII

## ROSLYN AND THE WHITE HOUSE

### BEFORE AND AFTER

*"Quantum mutatus ab illo!"* That is an exclamation which rises to the lips of many persons on many occasions in time of war.

In 1860, there stood on the left bank of the Chickahominy, in the county of New Kent, an honest old mansion, with which the writer of this page was intimately acquainted. Houses take the character of those who build them, and this one was Virginian, and un-"citified." In place of flues to warm the apartments, there were big fires of logs. In place of gas to light the nights, candles, or the old-fashioned "astral" lamps. On the white walls there were no highly coloured landscape paintings, but a number of family portraits. There was about the old mansion a cheerful and attractive air of home and welcome, and in the great fireplaces had crackled the yule clogs of many merry Christmases. The stables were large enough to accommodate the horses of half a hundred guests. The old garden contained a mint patch which had supplied that plant for the morning juleps of many generations. Here a number of worthy old planters had evidently lived their lives, and passed away, never dreaming that the torch of war would flame in their borders.

The drawing-room was the most cheerful of apartments; and the walls were nearly covered with portraits. From the bright or faded canvas looked down beautiful dames, with waists just beneath their arms, great piles of curls, and long lace veils; and

449

fronting these were gentlemen with queer blue coats, brass buttons, snowy ruffles, hair brushed back, and English side-whis-
kers. The child in the oval frame above the mantel-piece—with
the golden curls, and the little hand on the head of her pet dog—
could look at her father and mother, grandfather, grandmother,
and great-grandmother, almost without turning her head. Four
generations looked down from the walls of the old mansion;
about it was an indefinable but pervading air of *home*.

Of the happy faces which lit up this honest old mansion when
I saw it first, I need not speak. Let me give a few words, however,
to a young man who was often there—one of my friends. He
was then in the bloom of youth, and enjoyed the spring-days of
his life. Under the tall old trees, in the bright parlour full of
sunshine, or beneath the shadow of the pine-wood near, he
mused, and dreamed, and passed the idle hours of his "early
prime." He was there at Roslyn in the sweetest season of the
year; in spring, when the grass was green, and the peach-blossom
red, and the bloom of the apple-tree as white as the driven snow;
in summer, "when the days were long" and all the sky a magical
domain of piled-up clouds upon a sea of blue; and in the
autumn, when the airs were dreamy and memorial—the woods
a spectacle from faëry-land, with their purple, gold, and orange,
fading slow. Amid these old familiar scenes, the youth I write
of wandered and enjoyed himself. War had not come with its
harsh experiences and hard realities—its sobs and sighs, its anxieties and hatreds—its desolated homes, and vacant chairs, and
broken hearts. Peace and youth made every object bright; and
wandering beneath the pines, dreaming his dreams, the young
man passed many sunny hours, and passed them, I think, ra-
tionally. His reveries brought him no money, but they were
innocent. He had "never a penny to spare," but was rich in
fancy; few sublunary funds, but a heavy balance to his credit in
the Bank of Cloudland; no house to call his own, but a number
of fine chateaux, where he entered as a welcome guest, nay, as
their lord! Those brave chateaux stood in a country unsurpassed,
and those who have lived there say no air is purer, no sky more
bright. War does not come there, nor the hum of trade; grief

and care fly away; sorrow is unknown; the doors of these old chateaux are closed against all that carries that most terrible of maladies, the Heartache.

They were *Chateaux en Espagne*, you will say, good reader; and truly they were built in that fine land. Do you know a better? I do not.

Many years have passed since the youth I speak of wandered amid these happy scenes; but I know that the dead years rise like phantoms often before his eyes, and hover vague and fitful above the waves of that oblivion which cannot submerge them. While memory lives they will be traced upon her tablets, deeper and more durable than records cut on "monumental alabaster." The rose, the violet, and the hyacinth have passed, but their magical odour is still floating in the air—not a tint of the sky, a murmur of the pines, or a song of the birds heard long ago, but lives for ever in his memory!

But I wander from my subject, which is Roslyn "before and after." The reader has had a glimpse of the old house as it appeared in the past; where is it, and what is it now?

That question will be answered by a description of my last visit to the well-known locality. It was a day or two after the battle of Cold Harbour, and I was going with a few companions toward the White House, whither the cavalry had preceded us. I thought I knew the road; I was sure of being upon it; but I did not recognise a single locality. War had reversed the whole physiognomy of the country. The traces of huge camps were visible on the once smiling fields; the pretty winding road, once so smooth, was all furrowed into ruts and mud-holes; the trees were hewn down; the wayside houses dismantled; the hot breath of war had passed over the smiling land and blasted it, effacing all its beauty. With that beauty, every landmark had also disappeared. I travelled over the worn-out road, my horse stumbling and plunging. Never had I before visited, I could have made oath, this portion of Virginia!

All at once we came—I and the "merry comrades" who accompanied me—in sight of a great waste, desolate-looking field, of a clump of towering trees, and a mansion which the retreating enemy had just burned to the ground. There were no fences around this field; the roads were obliterated, deep ruts marking where army wagons had chosen the more level ground of the meadow, or had "doubled" in retiring; no landmarks were distinguishable. I recognised nothing—and yet something familiar in the appearance of the landscape struck me, and all at once the thought flashed on me, "I know this place! I know those peach-trees by the garden-fence! the lawn, the stables, the great elms! —this is Roslyn!"

It was truly Roslyn, or rather the ghost of it. What a spectacle. The fair fields were trodden to a quagmire; the fences had been swept away; of the good old mansion, once the abode of joy and laughter, of home comfort and hospitality, there remained only a pile of smoking bricks, and two lugubrious, melancholy chimneys which towered aloft like phantoms!

I heard afterwards the house's history. First, it had been taken as the headquarters of one of the Federal generals; then it was used as a hospital. Why it was burned I know not; whether to destroy, in accordance with McClellan's order, all medical and other stores which could not be removed, or from wanton barbarity, it is impossible to say. I only know that it was entirely destroyed, and that when I arrived, the old spot was the picture of desolation. Some hospital tents still stood in the yard with their comfortable beds; and many articles of value were scattered about—among others, an exquisitely mounted pistol, all silver and gilding, which a boy had picked up and wished me to purchase. I did not look at him, and scarcely saw the idle loungers of the vicinity who strolled about with apathetic faces. It was the past and present of Roslyn that occupied my mind— the recollection of the bright scenes of other years, set suddenly and brutally against this dark picture of ruin. There were the tall old trees, under which I used to wander; there was the wicker seat where I passed so many tranquil hours of reverie in the long, still afternoons, when the sun sank slowly to the western woods; there was the sandy road; the dim old pine-wood; the flower-garden—every object which surrounded me in the glad hours of youth—but Roslyn itself, the sunny old mansion, where the weeks and months had passed so joyously, where was Roslyn? That smouldering heap of *débris*, and those towering, ghost-like chimneys, replied. From the shattered elms, and the trodden flowers, the genius of the place seemed to look out, sombre and hopeless. From the pine-trees reaching out yearning arms toward the ruin, seemed to come a murmur, "Roslyn! Roslyn!"

In war you have little time for musing. Duty calls, and the blast of the bugle jars upon the reveries of the dreamer, summoning him again to action. I had no time to dream over the faded glories, the dead splendour of Roslyn; those "merry comrades" whereof I spoke called to me, as did the friends of the melancholy hero visitor to Locksley Hall, and I was soon *en route* again for the White House.

This was McClellan's great depôt of stores on the Pamunkey, which he had abandoned when deciding upon the James river line of retreat—"change of base," if you prefer the phrase, reader —and to the White House General Stuart had hurried to prevent if possible the destruction of the stores. He was too late. The officer in charge of the great depôt had applied the torch to all, and retreated; and when the cavalry arrived, nothing was visible but a black-hulled gunboat which slunk away down the stream, chased by the shots of the Horse Artillery under Pelham. Behind them they left fire and destruction; a scene in which a species of barbaric and disgusting splendour seemed to culminate.

Strange moment for my first visit to the White House! to a spot which I had seen often in fancy, but never before with the mortal eye. For this place was one of those historic localities where the forms and voices of the "mighty men of old" appeared still to linger. Here young Colonel Washington, after that bloody march of Braddock, had paused on his journey to Williamsburg to accept the hospitalities of John Parke Custis. Here he had spent hour after hour conversing with the fair young widow who was to become Mrs. Washington, while his astonished body-servant held the bridle for him to mount; here he had been married; here were spent many happy days of a great life—a century at least before the spot saluted my gaze!

In this old locality some of the noblest and fairest forms that eye ever beheld had lived their lives in the dead years. Here gay voices had echoed, bright eyes had shone; here a sort of masquerade of ruffles and silk stockings, furbelows and flounces, and lace and embroidery, and powder and diamonds, was played still in the eyes of fancy! The White House had been to the present writer an honest old Virginia mansion of colonial days, full of warm hearts, and kindness and hospitality, where bright eyes outshone "the gloss of satin and glimmer of pearls;" where the winding river flowed amid blooming fields, beneath lofty trees, and the suns of earlier years shone down on Washington and his bride.

Again, as at the White House—*quantum mutatus ab illo!*

Let me outline the objects that met my view as I galloped up the avenue, between the great trees which had seen pass beneath them the chariots of other generations. The house, like Roslyn, was a ruin still smouldering. No traces of it were left but overthrown walls, bricks calcined and shattered, and charred timbers still sending up lurid smoke. The grounds were the picture of desolation; the flower-beds, once carefully tended by fair hands, had been trampled beneath the feet of Federal soldiery; the trees were twisted or champed by the cavalry horses; and the fences had been long since torn up and burned. The mansion was gone; it had passed like a dream away. The earth upon which the feet of Washington had trodden so often was a waste; the house which stood upon the site of that former one in which he was married, had been swept away by the hot breath of war.

On each side of the avenue were the beds of an extensive field hospital. The enemy had carried off the large "hospital tents;" but the long rows of excellent beds, carefully protected from the damp of the earth by plank floors, had not been removed. Here were the general headquarters of disease; the camp of the sick, the dying, and the dead. The arrangements were admirable. The alleys between the tents were wide; the beds of the best quality, with ornamental coverlids, brought probably by friends; and everywhere lay about, in admired disorder, books, pamphlets, magazines, journals, with which the sick had doubt-

less wiled away the tedious hours. Many Bibles and Testaments
were lying on the ground; and Harper's "Monthly" and "Week-
ly" were seen in great numbers, their open pages exhibiting
terrific engravings of the destruction of rebels, and the triumph
of their "faction." Here were newspapers fixing exactly the date
of General McClellan's entrance into Richmond; with leading
editorials so horrible in their threatenings, that the writers must
have composed them in the most comfortable sanctums, far
away from the brutal and disturbing clash of arms. For the rest,
there was a chaos of vials, medicines, boxes, half-burnt lemons;
and hundreds of empty bottles, bearing the labels, "Chateau
Margot," "Lafitte," "Clicquot," "Bordeaux," and many others—
the very sight of which *spolia* of M.S. nearly drove the hungry
and thirsty Confederates to madness!

It was a sombre and frightful spot. Infection and contagion
seemed to dwell there—for who could tell what diseases had
afflicted the occupants of these beds? No article was touched
by the troops; fine coloured blankets, variegated shirts, ornamental caps, and handkerchiefs, and shawls, remained undisturbed. One object, however, tempted me; and, dismounting, I
picked it up. It was a little black lace veil, lying upon one of the
beds, and evidently had belonged to a woman. I looked at it,
musing, and asking myself whether it had belonged to wife, sister, or daughter—and I pitied her. This girl or woman, I thought,
had probably no hatred in her heart towards us; if *she* had been
consulted, there would have been no war; her child, or her
husband, or her brother, would have stayed at home with her,
leaving his "Southern brethren" in peace. Women are best
after all; and, doubtless, they of the North would even yet end
this "cruel war" if they could; would shatter the sword, break
the musket to pieces, and sink the rifled cannon a thousand
fathoms deep in the waters of the Atlantic! If the women of the
North could have their way, I think they would call to those
who remain alive to return to them,—would heal their broken
hearts, and joyfully bid the "erring sisters" go in peace—furling
the battle-flag for ever. This daughter, or sister, or wife, may
have been one of these angels; perhaps she did not see that she had

dropped her lace veil—she was crying, poor thing! . . . .

A curious subject for reverie—a lace veil picked up in an enemy's camp; but such are the vagaries of the human mind. It
seemed strange to me there,—that delicate woman's veil, in the
Plague City, on the hot arena of war.

Passing the hospital and the ruined mansion, I hastened to the
locality of the camp; and here the whole wild scene burst on
the eye. I cannot describe it. Stench, glare, insufferable heat,
and dense, foul, lurid smoke—there was the "general impression." A city had been laid out here, and this was now in
flames. Jews, pedlers, hucksters, and army followers of every
description, had thronged here; had worked like beavers, hammering up long rows of "shanties" and sutlers' shops; had covered the plain with a cloud of tents; and every steamer from
New York had brought something to spread upon the impro-
vised counters of the rising city. Moses and Levi and Abraham
had rushed in with their highly superior stock of goods, going
off at an enormous sacrifice; Jonathan and Slick had supplied
the best quality of wooden hams and nutmegs; Daüerflinger and
Sauerkraut had brought the best malt liquors and lager, with
brandy and whiskey and gin under the rose. In a few weeks a
metropolis of sutlerdom had thus sprung up like a mushroom;
and a whole host of pedlers and hucksters had scratched and
burrowed, and made themselves nests like Norway rats;—the
very place smelled of them.

The rats had thus gone far in building their capital of Rat-
dom; but those cruel terriors, the Confederates, had discovered
them, given chase, and scattered them to the four winds, to return no more! Their own friends struck them the heaviest
blow. The officer commanding at the White House had
promptly obeyed the orders sent him, and the nascent city was
set fire to without mercy. When the Confederates arrived, the
long rows of sutlers' stores, the sheds on the wharf, the great
piles of army-stores, the surplus guns, pistols, sabres, and the
engine on the railroad, were wrapt in roaring flames. From
this great pile of fire rose a black and suffocating smoke, drift-
ing far away across the smiling landscape of June. Destruction,

like some Spirit of Evil, sat enthroned on the spot, and his red
bloodshot eye seemed to glare through the lurid cloud.

The heat was frightful, but I rode on into the midst of the
disgusting or comic scenes—advancing over the ashes of the
main bulk of the stores which had been burned before our arrival. In this great chaos were the remnants of all imaginable
things which a great army needs for its comfort or luxury in the
field. Barrels of pork and flour; huge masses of fresh beef; boxes
of hard bread and cakes; hogsheads of sugar and molasses; bags
of coffee and beans, and all conceivable "army stores"—had been
piled up here in a great mass nearly a quarter of a mile long, and
set on fire in many places. The remains of the stores were still
burning, and emitted a most disgusting odour; next came the row
of sutlers' shops, among which the advance guard of the cavalry
had scattered themselves in search of edibles. These were found
in profusion, from barrels of excellent hams, and crackers and
cakes, to the luxuries so costly in the Confederate capital, of
candy and comfits, lemons and oranges, bottles of Jamaica ginger, and preserved fruits. There was no little interest in a walk
through that *débris* of sutlerdom. You knocked in the head of a
barrel, entirely ignorant whether hard bread or candy, pork or
preserved strawberries, would greet your curious eyes. The
box which you dashed to pieces with an axe might contain fine
shoes and elastic socks, or excellent combs and hair-brushes, or
snowy shirt bosoms and delicate paper collars, penknives,
pickles, portmonnaies, or perfumes. All these things were found,
of the last New York fashion, abandoned by the sutler rats, no
doubt with inexpressible anguish. The men helped themselves
freely to everything which they took a fancy to, and revelled for
that day in a plenty which repaid them for all their hardships.

One amusing example of the wholesale destruction was furnished by the barrels of fresh eggs set on fire. But they were
only half burned. The salt in which they had been packed
resisted the fire; and the result was that the eggs were only
roasted. They could not have been prepared more excellently
for the visitors; and every taste was gratified. Some were charred
and roasted hard, others less than the first, others again were

only heated through. You could take your choice without difficulty; nothing more was necessary than to take them from their
beds of salt; and a pinch of that salt, which was excellent, made
them palatable. Crackers were at hand; jars of preserved fruits
of all descriptions. There were strawberries and figs and dates
for dessert; and whole boxes of tobacco, if you wished to
smoke after your meal. The greatèst luxury of all was iced
lemonade. The day was terribly hot, and the men, like their
horses, were panting with the combined heat of the weather and
the great conflagration. Under such circumstances, the reader
may understand that it was far from unpleasant to discover a
cool spring beneath the bank; to take water and ice and lemons
and Jamaica ginger, and make a drink for the gods!

Of this pandemonium of strange sights and sounds and smells
—of comic or tragic, amusing or disgusting details—I shall mention but one other subject; one, however, which excited in me,
I remember, at the time a very curious interest. This was a tent
filled with coffins, and a dead body ready *embalmed* for trans-
portation to the North. In front of the tent stood an oblong
pine box, and in this box was a coffin, so richly ornamented that
it attracted the attention of all who approached. It was apparently of rosewood, with massive silver handles, curiously carved
or moulded, and the interior was lined with rich white satin,
with a fringed pillow, covered with the same material to sustain
the head of the corpse. Above the tents occupied by this mor-
tuary artist, was a long strip of canvas stretched between two
upright poles, and this bore the inscription in large black letters:

"EMBALMING THE DEAD!
NEW AMERICAN PROCESS.
BY ORDER OF THE SECRETARY OF WAR"

This strange locality, as I and my comrades approached it,
"gave us pause." All these paraphernalia of this grave struck
us with profound astonishment, and the force of novelty. Our
poor Confederate dead we buried in pine boxes, or in none; often
a long trench received them, wrapped only in their old tattered
uniforms or threadbare blankets; and lo! here was quite another

mode of preparing men for their last rest; quite a superiour conveyance for them, in which they might make their journey to
the other world! That rich and glossy rosewood; that soft-
fringed pillow; those silver handles, and the opening in the lid,
where through fine plate-glass the face of the corpse might be
seen!—strange flattery of the dead—the dead who was no longer
to crumble to dust, and go the way of humanity, but was to be
embalmed by the new American process, in accordance with the
"order" of the Secretary of War! In the streets of a city that
spectacle would, no doubt, have appeared quite commonplace
and unsuggestive; but here, amid the insufferable heat, the
strangling smoke, and the horrible stench, that dead body, the
coffin, and the embalmers' whole surroundings, had in them I
know not what of the repulsive and disgusting. Here the hideous
scene had reached its climax—Death reigned by the side of
Destruction.

Such was the scene at the White House on that June day of
1862; in this black cloud went down the star of the enemy's
greatest soldier, McClellan. A great triumph for the Confederates followed that furious clash of arms on the Chickahominy;
but alas! when the smoke rolled away, the whole extent of the
waste and desolation which had come upon the land was revealed; where peace, and joy, and plenty had once been, all was
now ruin. The enemy were lighted on their way, as they retreated through the marshes of Charles City, by the burning
houses to which they had applied the torch.

Of two of these houses I have spoken, because they chanced
to attract my attention; and I have tried to convey the emotions which the spectacle excited. It was useless and barbarous
to burn these private dwelling-houses; the wanton indulgence of
spite and hatred on the part of a defeated enemy, who destroys
in order to destroy. But let that pass.

Since that time I have never revisited Roslyn or the White
House.

# XIII

## ON THE WING

THE days of "Camp No-Camp" are numbered. The cannon begin to move—the bugle calls—the hours of idleness and "outlines" are a thing of the past.

Whither will the winds of war now waft us? That is a hard question to reply to; for a marked peculiarity of the Southern military theory is mystery. General Monck, of the time of Charles II, was so reticent, I have heard, that when any one said, "Good-morning, General," he reflected for twelve hours, and then replied, "Good-evening;" which caused every one to wonder at the accuracy of the response. That is an excellent example to be followed by officers; and thus—being ignorant—I carefully conceal the route we are about to take.

But we go, that is certain; and it is not without a feeling of regret that I leave this old familiar spot, where so many pleasant hours have passed away with song and laughter. As I gaze around, I fall into a reverie, and murmur.

Strange that I ever thought the spot dull and commonplace. It is really charming; and memory I know will make it still more attractive. There is that music in the pines again—the band of the brigade, camped yonder in the green thicket. I heard that band more than one thousand times, I suppose; strange that I thought it annoying, when it is evidently a band of unusual excellence. It plays all day long, and the regiments are eternally cheering. Do you hear that echoing shout? You would think they were about to charge the enemy; but it is only an old hare that has jumped up, and the whole brigade is hot upon the trail, with uproar and excitement. If there is no old hare, it is a stray horse—a tall woman riding behind a short man—a big negro mounted on a small mule—anything whatever. The troops must cheer and make a noise; and the band must play.

Exquisite music! How could I ever think it a little excessive in quantity, and deficient in quality? "We are going! we are going!! we are going!!!" I imagine it says—the refrain of music, surging to me from the pine woods. And as the brave musicians are about to leave me, they appear to excel all their brethren. "That strain again!" and I hear the brigade cheering. They are Georgians—children of the sun, "with whom revenge is virtue." Brave fellows, they have got the order to move, and hail it with delight; for all the wood is burned, and they are going to fresher fields and forests, and a fight, perhaps.

Farewell, familiar band in the pines! I have spent some happy moments listening to your loud, triumphant strains; some moments filled with sadness, too, as I thought of all those good companions gone into the dust—for music penetrates the heart, and stirs the fount of memory; does it not, good reader? As I listened to that band, I often saw the old familiar faces; and the never-to-be-forgotten forms of loved friends came back. They looked at me with their kindly eyes; they "struck a sudden hand in mine," and once again I heard their voices echoing in the present, as they echoed in the happy days before!

So, sweet memorial music, floating with a wild, triumphant ardour in the wind, farewell!

Farewell, brave comrades cheering from the pines!

All health and happiness attend you!

In addition to the brass band above referred to, my days have been alive here with the ringing strains of the bugle. The tattoo, reveille, and stable-call have echoed through the pine woods, making cheerful music in the short, dull days, and the winter nights. It is singular how far you can hear a bugle-note. That one is victor over space, and sends its martial peal through the forest

for miles around. There is something in this species of music unlike all others. It sounds the call to combat always to my ears;
and speaks of charging squadrons, and the clash of sabres,
mingled with the sharp ring of the carbine. But what I hear now
is only the stable-call. They have set it to music; and I once
heard the daughter of a cavalry officer play it on the piano—a
gay little waltz, and merry enough to set the feet of maidens and
young men in motion. As there are no maidens in these fields of
war—at least none in camp—we cannot dance to it.

The bugle takes its place among the old familiar sounds, which
have not been sufficiently attended to and appreciated. All these
winter days, it has been but a call to rise or go to rest: now it is
eloquent with poetry and battle! So, blow old bugle! Sound the
tattoo, and the reveille, and stable-call, to your heart's content!
No "purple glens" are here to ring through, or to "set replying"
—but the echoes in the pines are "dying, dying, dying," with a
martial melody and sweetness, and a splendid ardour, which are
better than the weird sound of the "horns of elf-land faintly
blowing!"

There is our banjo too—could I think of neglecting that great
instrument in my list of "sights and sounds?" It plays "O Johnny
Booker, help this Nigger," "Wake up in the Morning," "The
Old Gray Hoss," "Come Back, Stephen," "Hard Times and
Worse a-comin," "Sweet Evelina," and a number of other songs.
It is a good banjo. I hear it at present playing "Dixie" with a
fervour worthy of that great national anthem. It is a "Yankee"
instrument, captured and presented to the minstrel who now
wields it, by admiring friends! But—*proh pudor!*—it plays Southern ditties only, and refuses obstinately to celebrate the glories
of the "Happy Land of Lincoln." I have heard the songs of our
minstrel which he plays on his banjo, something like a thousand
times—but they always make me laugh. They ring so gaily in
the airs of evening that all sombre thoughts are banished—and, if
sometimes I am tempted to exclaim, "There is that old banjo
rattling again!" I always relent, and repent me of my disrespect
toward the good old friend; and go and listen and laugh at the
woes of Booker, or the colloquy with Stephen—above all, at the

"Old Gray Hoss," noblest of melodies, and now adopted as the national air of all the dwellers in Camp No-Camp!

Good-by, jolly old Yankee banjo! Rattle on gaily, and play all the old tunes! It is singular how new and delightful they are—what a world of mirth they contain.

All around the woods are deserted and lonely. I say "the woods," but there are scarcely any left; they have fallen before the ringing axes of the troops.

Your soldier is a foe to wood-lands. Did you ever see a division, after a long and dreary march through rain, and mud, and mire, halt at evening and advance to attack a forest? They carry it at the point of the bayonet, and cheer as they "close in." A moment ago, and the weary column lagged, and dragged its slow length along like a wounded snake—painfully toiling on without talk or laughter. Now a party of children seem to have scattered through the woods. Songs, shouts, and jests resound; the axes are ringing against a hundred trunks, huge monarchs of the forest crash down, roaring in their fall, and fires spring up everywhere like magic.

The bivouac-fire is the soldier's delight. It warms his limbs and cheers his spirit, dries his wet clothes, cooks his rations, and dispels all his gloomy thoughts.

The gay groups pass the jest and sing their songs, and tell their stories. Then they sleep; and sleep is so pleasant after a long tramp—the luxury of the gods!

War teaches many valuable lessons never learned in peace.

O Sybarite, tossing on your couch of down and grumbling at the rose leaf which destroys your slumber! O good Lucullus, searching for an appetite, though all the dainties of the earth are on your table—shoulder a musket and tramp all day without rest or food, and you will learn this truth—that the greatest of luxuries are bread and water and sleep!

I have said that the woods around camp are deserted and lonely. Not long since they were filled with troops. But the troops are gone.

Before the onslaught of the regiments and brigades the forest disappeared—vanished and floated off in smoke. For miles you can see through long vistas once impenetrably closed. Many traces remain of the army which has moved. Riding out the other day I came suddenly, in a hollow of the hills, on a deserted camp. The soldiers had built the most excellent log cabins, with enormous chimneys, and stout roofs held down by cross-poles well secured; but just as they were finished, they were forced to leave them. One curious structure I remember observing especially. It was a large log chimney on the side of the declivity, with "flankers" of timber. In the hillside the original genius who had planned this retreat had dug a sort of cave, piled dirt on the timber roof, and made his retreat bomb-proof! He evidently designed retiring from the world to this comfortable retreat, extending his feet toward his blazing fire, and sleeping or reflecting without thought of the enemy's artillery.

One and all, these "winter quarters" were deserted, and I thought as I looked at them of those excellent houses which our forces left near Centreville and Manassas in March, 1862.

Dreary, bare, lonely, melancholy—such is the landscape around me.

That bugle! It sounds "to horse!"

Camp No-Camp goes, and becomes a thing of the Past!

The band, the bugle, the banjo, sound no more—at least in this portion of the world. I leave with a sigh that excellent stable for my horse: I cast a last lingering look upon the good log chimney which I have mused by so often, pondering idly on the future or the past.

Farewell chimney, that does not smoke; and stable, which a new log floor has just perfected! Farewell pine-trees and mud, and dreams and reveries, and recollections—at least here!

Strike the tent, O African of the scriptural name! Put my traps in the wagon—strap my blanket behind the saddle—give me my sabre and pistol, and hold my stirrup!

You will oblige me particularly if you will tell me where I am going, friend.

There is the bugle, and the colours are unrolled.

"Forward!"

And so we depart.

PART 4

# SCOUT LIFE

# I

## THE SCOUTS

ON THE borders of Scotland, in the good old times, there was a "Debatable land"—bone of contention between Pict and Anglo-Saxon. In Virginia, lately, there was a similar region, the subject of dispute between Federal and Southron. In Scotland, the men-at-arms and barons fought along the banks of the Tweed; in Virginia, "Mosby's men" and their blue opponents contended on the banks of the Rappahannock. Our "Debatable land" was, in fact, all that fine and beautiful country lying between the Potomac and the last-named river, over which the opposing armies of the North and the South alternately advanced and retired.

This land was the home of the scout; the chosen field of the ranger and the partisan. Mosby was king there: and his liegemen lived as jovial lives as did the followers of Robin Hood in Sherwood Forest, in the old days of Merry England.

But the romantic lives of Mosby and his men will not be touched on here. The subject would become enthralling were it to be more than alluded to—the pen would drag the hand into a sketch, and not a short one, of that splendid ranger-life amid the Fauquier forests, the heart of "Mosby's Confederacy." Not to-day can I delineate the lithe, keen partisan, with his roving glance, his thin curling lip, his loose swaying belt containing the brace of pistols ready loaded and capped. Some abler hand must draw the chief of rangers, and relate his exploits—the design of the present writer is to record some adventures of "scout life," which differs in many points from that of the regular partisan, though not wholly.

The scout proper is "commanding in the field," with no one near to give him orders. He goes and comes at will, having that about him which all pickets obey. He is "on detached service;" and having procured certain information, reports to the officer who has sent him, without intermediate ceremony. Operating within the enemy's lines at all times, he depends for success and safety on the quickness of his eye and hand—and his reliance on these is great. He is silent in his movements, low-toned in his speech, abstemious in his habits, and as untiring on the track of the enemy as the Cuban blood-hound on the trail of the fugitive. He sleeps rarely in houses, preferring the woods; and always slumbers "with one eye open," on the look out for his enemy.

The scout has a thorough knowledge of the country, and is even acquainted with "every hog path." He travels in the woods; and often in crossing a sandy highway dismounts, and backs his horse across the road, to mislead the enemy, on the watch for "guerillas," as to the direction of his march. He thus "flanks" their pickets, penetrates to their camps, reconnoitres their number and position, and strives to pick up some straggler whom he can pump for information. Thus lurking and prowling around the enemy's camps, by night and day, the scout never relaxes his exertions until he discovers what he wishes. That discovery once made—of the strength, situation, and probable designs of the enemy—the stealthy emissary "snakes" back as he came; mounts his trusty steed in the depth of the wood; and first listening attentively, sets out on his return with his supply of valuable information.

If he cannot "flank" the enemy's pickets, he charges them. If he cannot glide through, he fights through. If he meets a straggling enemy or enemies not in too great number, he puts his pistol to his or their heads, and brings him or them along—pleasantly chatting with them as he goes along, but keeping his eye and his pistol muzzle upon them.

When he relates his adventures, he does so with a laugh—noting the humorous side of things. Indeed his life seems chiefly attractive to him from that very humorous phase, and he jests about his perils with a gay light spirit which is one of the greatest charms of his society. He has extricated himself from deadly peril safely, "fooled" his foe, and is chatting after the occurrence with his friends by the camp fire. Could anything be more satisfactory? So the scout plays over the comedy for your entertainment; relates every incident in a spirit of dry humour; rolls up in his blanket by the fire when he is tired; and, before daylight, has disappeared on another expedition.

Thus toiling, watching, and fighting, enduring hardship, risking liberty and life hourly, the scout passes his life. He is not a paid spy—not a spy at all, for he goes uniformed and armed, and the work is his reward. The trump of fame will never sound for him. If he falls, it will be in the depths of some forest, where his bones will moulder away undiscovered; if he survives, he will return to obscurity as a rain-drop sinks into the ocean and is seen no more.

That will be his fate; but while he is alive, he lives. He loves his vocation, and gives to the cause what he possesses—a piercing eye, a ready hand, and a daring soul. For his services, often invaluable, and his risk of life night and day, he receives—when he can get it—eleven dollars a month; and with this, or with nothing, he is perfectly content. What he asks is simply the liberty to rove; to hunt the enemy after the fashion most agreeable to him; to have himself killed, if the killing must take place, in single combat, with the pistol, rather than in line of battle with the musket.

It results from this that the life of the scout is apt to be crowded with adventure, contrast, and all that is picturesque. Here to-day, away to-morrow; closeted with the commanding general, while an orderly keeps off all intruders, and then disappearing like a shadow on some secret mission; passing the most obdurate pickets with a single word; silently appearing in the houses of friends far behind the enemy's lines; reconnoitring their camps, picking up stragglers, attacking them alone or in company with others, upon all occasions—such are some of the phases which the scout exhibits, such some of the occupations of his stirring existence.

A few of these adventurous incidents are here recorded just as I heard them from an accomplished scout of General Stuart. They will be found sufficiently "romantic," but I believe them to be exactly true.

As such, they possess a value which no mere fiction could.

# II

## HUNTED DOWN

### I.

AMONG the numerous scouts employed by General Stuart, none was braver or more intelligent than a young man named Frank S——. Innumerable were his adventures, almost incredible his hair-breadth escapes and his reckless, dare-devil exploits. The annals of fiction contain nothing more curious and moving than some of his experiences; and in this and the succeeding sketch I propose to indicate the species of daily life which S—— lived during the late war.

A few words, first, of the scout himself. He certainly was a ranger born. Passionately devoted to his dangerous calling, and following it from predilection, not from any hope of reward, or spurred on by ambition of distinction, he was never so happy as when beating up the quarters of the enemy, and throwing them into confusion by some sudden attack. He was not an officer, and never moved a finger to secure a commission; all he asked was permission to mount his horse, wander off and seek the neighbourhood of the enemy's camps, in search of incident and adventure. On such occasions he preferred to be alone, to follow his appointed work without assistance, depending only upon his own strong arm and trusty weapons. He cared little for society, though no one seemed more amiable; I never saw a brighter or more friendly smile than his. That smile did not deceive; there was no deceit of any sort in S——. He loved his

471

friends, but he loved his calling better still. It might have been said of him that man delighted him not, nor woman either. His "chief delight" was to penetrate the dense woods of Fauquier, assail the enemy wherever he found an opening, and inflict upon them all the injury in his power. In the eyes of the scout those enemies were wolves, and he hunted them. This sketch will demonstrate the fact that now and then they returned the compliment.

In person S—— was suited to his calling; stout but active; a good hand with pistol and sabre; quick of eye; and with nerves which no peril could shake. Soldiers generally prefer broad daylight and an open country to operate; S—— liked a forest where no moon shone; whose soft earth gave back no sound when the hoofs of his horse fell upon it; and where even in the gloomy silence of midnight he could approach a vidette undiscovered. When he found it necessary to penetrate the hostile lines, and could not elude the watchful guardians of the night, his habit was to brace himself in his stirrups, draw his pistol, and to the quick, "Halt! who goes there?" shout, "Form fours! draw sabres! charge!" to an imaginary squadron behind him, and pass on with loud yells, firing his pistol as he advanced. The result was, generally, that the picket fired wildly at him, and then fled before the tremendous onslaught of "rebel cavalry," whereupon the adventurous scout passed through at a thundering gallop, drove the picket before him, and adroitly slipping, at the opportune moment, into some by-path of the woods, was "within the lines." When the enemy made a stand at the next rising ground to receive the expected charge, none came. When they returned to look for S——, he had disappeared.

But to come to the incident I design narrating.

It was in November, 1863, when the Federal army lay around Culpeper Court-House and Mitchell's Station, that S—— was sent on a scout to ascertain the number, position, and movements of the Federal forces. Taking with him two companions, he crossed the upper Rapidan, passed the Confederate cavalry pickets, and carefully worked his way toward Mitchell's Station. General Meade had pushed forward his lines to this point a few days before—or rather established large camps there—and this fact, visible from Clark's mountain, made it desirable to ascertain, if possible, his designs. This was S——'s mission.

In due time the small party reached the vicinity of the station, and it now became necessary to prosecute the remainder of the journey on foot. They accordingly dismounted, and leaving their horses in a thick copse, "snaked" in the direction of a large Federal camp near at hand, taking advantage of every cover. In this manner they came close upon the camp, and were rewarded with a sight of acres of canvas. Lazy-looking infantry were strolling about, quarter-guards walking their posts, and officers in gay uniforms went to and fro, saluted by the sentinels with a "present" as they passed. The size of the encampments enabled S—— to form a tolerably accurate estimate of the amount of force which General Meade had concentrated at this point; and having passed the whole day thus moving cautiously around the spot, thereby discovering all which a mere reconnoissance could reveal, the scout began to look for stragglers, from whom, as his prisoners, he might derive more accurate information still. The love of rambling is inherent in soldiers of every nation; and the prospect of butter and eggs, resulting from a foraging expedition to the neighbouring farms, was well known to be irresistible with the Federal troops. To pick up these wandering foragers, if they were not in too great numbers, was the object of S——. His method on such occasions was to come upon the individual or the party unawares, silently present the muzzle of his pistol, and "take them in charge." Once his prisoners, all was friendly and peaceful, and all the information possible was extracted.

After a fatiguing day, S—— and his party lay down in the woods near the Federal camp, to snatch an hour's sleep before proceeding to their nocturnal work. But on this occasion, Fate had determined to play them a sorry trick. The "stragglers" whom they designed hunting and entrapping during the hours of darkness were to "turn up" in a fashion and at a moment neither expected nor desired. The woful adventures which befell the scout and his companions I now proceed to relate.

S—— had selected for his bivouac a retired spot where the encircling woods gave excellent promise of concealment, and the covert was so dense as to set him completely at his ease. Through the thick brushwood no glimmer of firelight could be seen; and the scouts ventured to kindle a fire, which the chill November night rendered far from unacceptable. By the carefully shaded blaze they warmed their benumbed fingers, ate their supplies of hard bread and bacon, and spread their blankets for a brief sleep. S—— took off his shoes; laid his hat at his head; and having picked up somewhere a certain "Life of Stonewall Jackson," recently published in Richmond, now drew it from his haversack, and read a few passages by the firelight. Although he did not inform me of the fact, this volume must have produced a soothing effect upon his feelings, for in a short time his eyelids drooped, the volume fell from his hands, and he sank to slumber. His companions were already snoring by his side.

They slept longer than they designed doing—in fact throughout the entire night. The weather, which had been lowering at nightfall, became gradually more threatening; and soon an imperceptible drizzle began, just sufficient to wet the blankets of the sleepers, but not to chill and awake them. They slept on serenely; and now as day drew near, the hostile Fate approached. It came in the shape of a squad of infantry soldiers, armed with muskets, from the adjoining camp; and this party, on their way to forage for butter, eggs, poultry, and other desirable components of a military breakfast, had stumbled on the slumbering scouts.

The first intimation which S—— had of the danger which menaced him was, he declared, an instinctive feeling that some dangerous foe was near; and this even before he woke. He was not long, however, to remain in doubt, or be compelled to question his instincts. He opened his eyes to find the blanket suddenly drawn away from his face, and to hear a harsh and sarcastic voice exclaim: "How are you, Johnny Reb? Come, get up, and we will give you more comfortable accommodations than out here in the rain!"

S—— was wide-awake in an instant, and through his half-closed lids reconnoitred, counting his opponents. They were six in number, all armed and ready. The situation looked ugly. With his companions wide-awake and on the alert there might have been some ground for hope; but they were slumbering like the Seven Sleepers, and in utter unconsciousness of danger. As to S—— himself, he was in their very grasp, and practically disarmed; for it was obvious that at the first movement which he made to draw his pistol from the holster around his waist, the six muskets, cocked and pointing at his breast, would be discharged as one piece, and his body riddled with bullets.

The situation was depressing. S—— and his companions were in a veritable trap. The least movement which he made would at once put an end to him, if six balls through the body could do so; and it was obviously necessary to surrender at once or betake himself to strategy. The first was out of the question, for S—— had made up his mind never to surrender, had indeed sworn a solemn oath not to do so under any circumstances; the second alternative remained. A *ruse* had already suggested itself to his quick and daring mind; and this he now proceeded instantly to carry out. To the sneering address of his opponent bidding him get up, he made no immediate reply, but again closed his eyes, pulled the blanket up again over his shoulders, and turning his back, muttered in a sleepy voice: "Oh! go away, and let me sleep, will you!"

This reply highly tickled his adversaries; and so much did they relish the evident impression of the "Johnny Reb" that he was among his own comrades in the Confederate camp, that they shook all over in the excess of their mirth. S—— was a dangerous man, however, to jest with; and no doubt believed in the proverb which declares that "they laugh best who laugh last." While his opponents were thus indulging their merriment, and highly enjoying the surprise and mortification he would feel when awake to the real nature of his situation, S—— was busy executing the plan which he had determined upon. Pulling his blanket still further over his head, he drew a long labouring breath, turned as men do languidly in slumber, and cautiously moved his hand beneath the blanket toward the pistol in his belt. The hand slowly stole downwards under the cover, approached the weapon, and then he had grasped the handle. A second careless movement extracted the pistol from the holster; his finger was on the hammer—without noise the weapon was cocked.

The scout was just in time. The squad had finished their laugh, enjoyed their little comedy sufficiently, and now designed bringing the affair to an end. The leader accordingly stooped down and dragged away the blanket—when a shot followed, with the muzzle of the pistol upon his breast, and he fell forward dead, covering S—— with his blood. The scene which followed was brief. The rest of the squad levelled their muskets at the scout, and fired with the muzzles nearly touching him, but he was wounded by none. The body of their companion lying across him received the larger portion of the balls; and S—— rose to his feet, armed with his deadly revolver, which still contained four charges. These he fired in succession rapidly, but with good aim, and two of the five remaining men were wounded. The three others, finding their guns discharged, dropped them, and hastily ran toward the Federal camp.

S——'s companions had been aroused by the firing, but were of no assistance to him. One disgracefully fled into the woods without firing a shot, and the other had committed the fatal fault of allowing his arms to become wetted by the rain. When he attempted to fire his pistol the cap snapped, and none of the barrels could be discharged.

This proved, however, of no great importance. S—— had repulsed the whole party for the moment, and did not need assistance. What remained for them now was a rapid retreat from the dangerous locality. The sudden firing, and the men running in, had alarmed the Federal camp, and a large party were seen approaching rapidly to take vengeance for the blood of their comrades. S—— accordingly hastened to retire, and disappeared with his companion just as the enemy rushed upon the area near the bivouac fire. In this sudden "change of base," stores of some value to him were necessarily abandoned. In fact he was compelled to leave his horse, hat, shoes, blanket, and "Life of Jackson"—to fly bareheaded and in his stocking feet. Even thus lightened of all superfluous weight, it was doubtful if he could escape; for the shouts which now resounded as he ran showed that the enemy were pursuing him hotly, with the evident determination of running him "to earth" and destroying him.

In a few moments it became plain to S—— that he was to be "hunted down." In fact, the encounter at the bivouac—resulting so disastrously to the assailants—had profoundly enraged their friends, and a large detachment speedily scattered, blocking up every avenue by which the scout could escape. In the distance cavalry could be seen preparing to cut him off from the mountain, and before S—— had gone half a mile he awoke to the unpleasant consciousness that he was surrounded. Stealing along, a solitary figure—for his companion had gone another way—he peered warily from his covert, seeking a loop-hole of escape; but wherever he turned the paths were picketed, and the chances of escape seemed hopeless indeed.

Under circumstances so discouraging, an ordinary man would have lost "heart of hope." But S—— was not an ordinary man. His perilous situation only developed the strong manhood of his character.

He surveyed his position at a glance, and estimated the chances. It seemed that nothing but his own quick eye and knowledge of woodcraft could save him; if he was caught, there appeared to be small likelihood of his escaping death. He had penetrated the Federal lines, reconnoitred their encampments, slain their foraging parties; and although this was done in full Confederate uniform, with arms at his side, as a legitimate partisan operation, S—— had little doubts of the light in which his enemies would insist upon regarding him. He felt that he would probably be treated as a "guerilla," if not as a spy, and shot without benefit of clergy. For this reason he did not intend to surrender. He proposed to escape if he could; if he could not, he would sell his life as dearly as possible.

One conviction is apt to result very powerfully from scout life—that few situations are so greatly hopeless that skill and nerve will not extricate their possessor. S—— had these qualities in great perfection, and now brought all his courage and *finesse* to bear upon the contest for life and death. His enemies were on every side following the trail of their game, and with videttes posted at every point around, were beating the covert for the prey.

S—— had, however, been hunted before, and his brave heart did not recoil from the struggle. Running silently with bare head and shoeless feet through the woods, he paused from time to time to listen to the shouts of his pursuers, and it soon became obvious that they were rapidly approaching upon every side. However fleet of foot he might be, and whatever might be his accomplishments in woodcraft, the probabilities of escape grew more and more doubtful. As he doubled, and turned, and circled, like a hunted wolf, the enemy every instant drew nearer, and soon their detached parties were nearly upon him. It was evident that they knew the country perfectly; and such was their success in intercepting his retreat, that he very soon found himself completely hemmed in, and his enemies in every direction cutting off his escape. The parties gradually closed in upon him on every side, and in a few minutes more, unless he could discover some place of concealment, he must inevitably fall into their hands, when a bullet or a cord would terminate the hunt and his career on earth at the same time.

This conviction induced S——, whose nerve had never faltered, to seek on every side for some hiding-place. But the result was discouraging. The woods were open—without undergrowth —and every moment was now precious. S—— redoubled his speed, and darting through the wood, suddenly found himself in a small open field, in the middle of which rose a clump of pines, one of which had recently fallen. In the bushy top of this fallen tree he now concealed himself, panting from his long run, and listening to the sound of his approaching foes closing in on every side. To fight and die seemed his only resource; and reloading his pistol, he grimly waited for the moment which should find him at bay, in the presence of his enemies.

He did not wait long. A few minutes only had elapsed when a party of three or four Federals entered the little area, and approached the clump of pines. They passed close to the scout, looking everywhere for traces of him; but he crouched down, held his breath, and they seemed about to prosecute their search in some other direction. S—— was indeed congratulating himself upon his safety, when, raising his head, he caught the eye of one of the enemy, who had lingered behind the rest, fixed steadily upon him. He was discovered; and starting to his feet, was greeted with the shout, "Here he is!" which was instantly echoed by a hundred voices.

S—— now saw that his life hung upon a thread. Unless he could force his way through the cordon hemming him in, he was lost. He was unwilling to waste the loads in his pistols before the final struggle took place—the last desperate struggle which was to terminate all. But that conflict now seemed about to take place.

For a single instant the scout and his foes stood looking at each other, and neither made any movement to fire. In presence of this desperate man, the enemy seemed averse to the encounter, and waited for their comrades to come up. This short pause gave the scout the opportunity to decide upon his course. If he could only secure a short "start,"—if he were only mounted! His feet were bruised and sore, his strength greatly diminished by the close, hot chase. Oh! for a horse to charge them and break through, as he felt he could though they were forty deep! As the thought flashed through his mind, his eyes fell on a mule which was grazing in the field not far from him. To dart to the animal and throw himself upon its back was the work of an instant; and in the midst of furious outcries and hastily fired shots he dug his heels into the sides of the frightened animal, and commenced his race for life.

Behold S—— now, mounted on his mule, with bare head and shoeless feet, grasping the mane of the animal with one hand, holding his pistol in the other, and driving onward like some grotesque figure of the German ballads! Such was the speed to which he forced the animal, that he would probably have distanced his pursuers had not the perversity of the brute defeated all his calculations. The mule had no sooner recovered from his first fright at finding himself so unceremoniously mounted, than he made violent attempts by "roaching" his back, and kicking up, to unseat his rider. S—— was an excellent horseman, and might have defied the kicking-up portion of the performance, despite the fact that he was riding without saddle or bridle; but no horsemanship could counteract the detestable roaching of the animal's spine. At the fifth or sixth kick-up, accompanied by a movement which made the mule resemble an angry cat in outline, the scout was landed on *terra firma*, amid the shouts of his enemies, who rushed toward him, firing as they came.

They reached the spot, uttering outcries and curses; but their obstinate foe had once more eluded them. The scout had risen quickly, darted into the woods, and the chase again commenced with more ardour than at first.

S—— now put forth all his remaining strength to distance the enemy, following more hotly than ever on his track. Panting and worn out almost, half resolving a hundred times to turn and fight and die, he still kept on, the shouts of his enemies in his very ears. He was growing desperate, and had become nearly exhausted. A burning thirst raged in his throat; and although the enemy were on his very heels, he could not resist the temptation, as he reached a little meadow through which ran a limpid stream, to pause and quench his thirst. Throwing himself upon his knees on the margin of the brook, he stooped and swallowed one refreshing draught of the cool water, and then rising up, found from the shouts of his pursuers that they were at last upon him—all further hope from flight of no avail. A last desperate expedient suggested itself—concealment in the undergrowth which skirted the stream; and throwing himself at full length amid the bushes, not far from the spot where he had knelt down, he hastily drew the undergrowth around him and awaited the struggle.

He had scarcely disappeared from view when his enemies reached the spot. He heard their footsteps; their cries resounded; and suddenly the voice of one of them exclaimed:

"Here's the scoundrel's knee-print in the sand where he drank just now! He ain't far off!"

This cry was the signal for all the detached parties to converge toward the spot; and very soon the field was full of them. The scout heard them deploying in every direction to guard all the outlets, preparatory to a rigid search of every species of covert in which a fugitive could conceal himself. The green meadow was dotted with clumps of bushes, which grew in thicker luxuriance along the little watercourse; and in some of these hiding-places it was obvious to the enemy that their victim lay hidden. The prey was at last hunted down; had taken to earth; and it was now only necessary to beat the undergrowth with efficient diligence in order to flush the dangerous game.

The hunters proceeded to their task with energy and excellent method. No portion of the ground was neglected, and their attention was especially directed to the bushes along the stream.

Lying on his back in the dense jungle, with a cocked pistol in each hand, his finger on the trigger, the scout listened with ears rendered preternaturally acute to the cries and exclamations of his enemies, who moved up and down the watercourse, and on every hand searching every foot of ground for their prey. S—— had not wasted a moment in deciding upon his plan of action if discovered. He was exhausted, and could no longer fly; and to be taken prisoner was not an alternative. He would fight as long as he could stand; give his enemies the full benefit of the ten barrels of his revolvers at close range; grapple with them breast to breast; and if he could not fight his way out—die.

Such was his plan; and he listened to the footsteps around him with that firm nerve which the brave man summons to his aid when face to face with death.

The moment had now come which was to decide his fate. The pursuers had searched every portion of the field without success, and now returned to the point from which they had set forth, subjecting the covert to a second and more rigid inspection. Their feet were heard trampling amid the undergrowth; they stopped to put aside the bushes, and peer into every nook. S—— heard their very breathing, and cast an eye upon his pistols to see that he had neglected nothing; that every tube was capped, every barrel loaded, and both weapons cocked.

All was right, and he experienced the fierce joy of the man who feels that at least he need not die without dragging down more than one enemy in his fall.

The steps were at his side; oaths and exclamations echoed in his very ears. One of the hostile party determined to leave no inch of the ground unexplored, and bent down, plunging his glances into the very bushes over the scout's head.

S—— grasped his pistols with a firmer clutch, strung his nerves for instant contest, and prepared to rise suddenly to his feet, lay the curious individual before him dead with a pistol bullet through the heart, and throw himself like a tiger at bay into the midst of his enemies.

The bushes were thrust aside; an oath resounded within three feet of him; he had covered the heart of his enemy with the muzzle of his right-hand pistol crossed over his breast—when the autumn foliage swayed back to its place, an exclamation of disappointment followed, and the footsteps retreated from his hiding-place.

The scout drew a long breath. He was saved.

All day long he lay hidden, hearing more than one sound which proved that his enemies were still hovering near; but they had given up the search in despair. At night he quietly rose, and found that the coast was clear. Proceeding cautiously to reconnoitre, he discovered that the ground around his hiding-place was only partially guarded, and had little difficulty in escaping. Eluding such parties as were still prowling around, he flanked the Federal pickets, travelled all night, and before daylight was safe within the Southern lines.

Such was the narrative of S——, related to me in my tent on the Rapidan. To suspect exaggeration or inaccuracy in the narrator would be to do a brave and truthful soldier great injustice; and I have recorded this true incident as a veritable illustration of the curious "scout-life" of the war.

# III

## HOW S— OVERHEARD HIS DEATH-WARRANT

### I.

In "Hunted Down," I have attempted to give some idea of scout life on the Rappahannock during the late war. Another narrative of the same description may interest those readers who relish wild adventure; and the present incident will be found more curious than the former. It befell the same personage, S——, one of General Stuart's scouts, and I again beg to warn the worthy reader against regarding these relations as fanciful. Imagination has nothing to do with this one; if it possesses no other merit, I am sure it does possess that of truth. It was told me by the brave man whom it concerns, and I never knew him to boast or exaggerate.

The incident took place during the summer of 1863, in the country beyond the Rappahannock, not far from the foot of the Blue Ridge. This region—the county of Fauquier—was the true Paradise of the scout. On its winding and unfrequented roads, and amid its rolling hills and mountain spurs, the scout and ranger wandered at will, bidding defiance to all comers. The thick woods enabled him to approach unseen until almost in contact with the Federal parties or their encampments; and if pursued, he had only to leap the nearest stone wall, rush under a crest of a hill, and disappear like a shadow, or one of those phantoms of diablerie which vanish in the recesses of the earth. For secret operations of every description, no country in the world is more favourable; and the present writer has journeyed by roads and across fords in the immediate vicinity of hostile forces, by which a column of ten thousand men might have moved with no more difficulty than a solitary horseman. No prying eyes followed the scout upon his way; the extensive uplands were pasture ground for grazing great herds of cattle. The traveller went on, mile after mile, unespied by any one, and in presence only of tall forests and azure mountains.

In Fauquier, S—— had many friends whom he was fond of visiting on his adventurous excursions; but unfortunately he had also a number of enemies in the persons of Federal soldiers. Detached bodies of the enemy had pitched their tents in the region, and the Federal cavalry scouted the main roads, greatly harassing the inhabitants. To harass their parties in return was the work of the ranger; and scarce a day passed without some collision in the extensive fields or the forest glades, in which, on one side or both, blood would flow.

Among the Federal forces, S—— had achieved a high reputation as a scout and a partisan; and had also aroused in his enemies a profound hatred. His daring reconnoissances, secret scouts, and audacious attacks on foraging parties, had made them pass a lively time—and great was the joy of a Federal Colonel commanding pickets on the upper Rappahannock when he received intelligence one day in this summer of 1863 that the well known S—— was alone at a house not far from camp, where his capture would be easy.

S—— was, in fact, at the house indicated, without the least suspicion that his presence had been discovered. He had been sent upon a scout in that region, and finding himself in the neighbourhood of the family with whom he had long been on terms of intimacy, embraced the occasion to visit them and rest for a few hours before proceeding upon his way. On the evening when the events about to be related occurred, he was seated in the parlour, conversing with one of the young ladies of the family, and perfectly at his ease both in body and mind. His horse—an excellent one, captured a few days before from the enemy—was in the stable, enjoying a plentiful supply of corn;

he had himself just partaken of a most inviting supper, to which bright eyes and smiles had communicated an additional attraction; and he was now sitting on the sofa, engaged in conversation, not dreaming of the existence of an enemy within a thousand miles. Let it not be supposed, however, that S—— was disarmed either of his caution or his weapons. His eye wandered unconsciously, from pure habit, every few moments toward the door, and around his waist was still buckled the well-worn belt containing his pistols. These never left his person day or night as long as he was in the vicinity of his enemies.

Such was the comfortable and peaceful "interiour" which the mansion presented when the incident I purpose to relate took place. S—— was tranquilly enjoying himself in the society of his kind hostess, and laughing with the light-hearted carelessness of a boy who finds a "spirit of mirth" in everything, when suddenly his quick ear caught the clatter of hoofs upon the road without, and rising, he went to the window to reconnoitre. A glance told him that the new-comers were the enemy; and the crack through which he looked was sufficiently large to enable him to see that they consisted of a detachment of Federal cavalry, who now rapidly approached the house. With such rapidity did they advance, that before S—— could move they had reached the very door; and no sooner had they done so, than at a brief order from the officer commanding, several men detached themselves from the troop, hurried to the rear of the house, and in an instant every avenue of escape was effectually cut off.

S—— was now fairly entrapped. It was obvious that in some manner the enemy had gained intelligence of his presence at the house, and sent out a detachment for his capture or destruction. The scout required no better proof of this than the systematic manner in which they went to work to surround the house, as though perfectly sure of their game, and the business-like method of proceeding generally on the part of the men and officers. To meet this sudden and dangerous advance of his foes, S—— saw that he must act with rapidity. Skill and decision would alone save him, if anything could; and in a few rapid words he explained the state of affairs. He informed his entertainers that he was the game for whom they were hunting; he had heard that a price was set upon his head; if there was no means of leaving the house or concealing himself, he did not mean to surrender; he would not be taken alive, but would fight his way through the whole party and make his escape, or die defending himself.

Such was the tenor of the brief address made by S—— to his fair entertainers; but they informed him in quick words that he need not despair, they would conceal him; and then the brave hearts set to work. One ran to the window and demanded who was without; another closed the door in rear, the front door being already shut; and while these movements were in progress S—— was hurried up the staircase by one of the young ladies, who was to show him his hiding-place. Before he had reached the head of the staircase a novel proof was given by the Federal cavalry of the terror which they attached to his name. A sudden explosion from without shook the windows; six or eight carbine-balls pierced the front door, passed through and whistled around the ladies; and a loud shout was heard, followed by heavy shoulders thrust against the door. It was afterwards discovered that the rattle of the door-latch in the wind had occasioned the volley; the noise was supposed to be that made by S—— as he was about to rush out upon them!

The scout had, meanwhile, been conducted by his fair guide to his hiding-place, which was in a garret entirely destitute of furniture, with bare walls, and apparently without any imaginable facility for enabling a man to escape the prying eyes of the "party of observation." Here, nevertheless, S—— was concealed; and his hiding-place was excellent, from its very simplicity. The garret had no ceiling; and the joists were even unboarded; but upon them were stretched two or three loose planks. The young lady hurriedly pointed to these. S—— understood in an instant; and, swinging himself up, he reached the joist, lay down at full length upon one of the planks next to the caves, and found himself completely protected from observation, unless the search for him was so minute as to leave no corner unexplored.

Having assisted the scout to ensconce himself in his hiding place, the young lady hastened down from the garret, and descended the main staircase, just as the Federal soldiers burst open the front door and swarmed into the passage. From the plank beneath the eaves, as the door of the garret had been left open, S—— informed me he heard every word of the following colloquy:

"Where is the guerilla we are after?" exclaimed the officer in command, sternly addressing the lady of the house.

"What guerilla?" she asked.

"S——."

·"He was here, but is gone."

"That is untrue, and I am not to be trifled with!" was the irate reply. "I shall search this house—but first read the orders to the men!" he added, addressing a non-commissioned officer of the troop.

This command was obeyed by a sergeant, holding an official paper in his hand; and S—— had the satisfaction of hearing read aloud a paper which recited his various exploits, commented upon his character in terms far from flattering, declared him a bushwhacker and guerilla, and ordered him to be put to death wherever he was found—the men being expressly forbidden to take him prisoner. This order was from Colonel ——, commanding the neighbouring force, and S—— heard every word of it. He was to be pistoled or sabred. No hope of mercy—no surrender taken. Death to him!

Peril unnerves the coward, but arouses a fierce pride and courage in the breast of the brave, to dare all, and fight to the death. S—— was made of the stuff which does not cower before danger, but enables a man to look the King of Terrours in the face without the shudder of a nerve. He was armed as usual with two pistols carefully loaded and capped—for he never neglected his arms—and before he was taken, or rather killed, he hoped to lay low more than one of his assailants. This was his calculation; but the scout was still a long way from regarding his fate as sealed, his death as certain. He had an obstinate faculty of hoping, and took the brightest view of his critical situation.

He might not be discovered; or if discovered, he was in a position to fight to an advantage which would make the issue of the struggle exceedingly doubtful. He intended to spring to the door, shoot the one or two men who would probably penetrate to the garret, and hurl them down the staircase—and then placing himself at the head of the stairs, sheltered from bullets by a projection of the wood-work, defy them to ascend. "They never *could* have got me out of there," said S—— with a laugh, "unless they had burned the house, or brought *a piece of artillery to shell me out*. I had two pistols, and could have held my ground against the whole of them all day."

But not to digress from the actual *res gestæ* of the occasion, the search for S—— speedily commenced. First the parlour and dining-room were subjected to a rigid examination, and finding there no traces of the scout, the men scattered themselves over the house, ransacking every apartment, and compelling the young ladies to throw open the most private recesses of their chambers. They looked under beds, into closets, and behind dresses hanging up in the wardrobes, in vain search for the game. Sabres were thrust into beds, to pierce and immolate the dangerous wild animal if he were lying *perdu* between the mattresses; and the points of the weapons did not spare the female clothing depending from pegs in the closets. The scout might be straightened up against the wall, behind those white garments in closet or wardrobe; but an assiduous search failed to discover him, and soon no portion of the whole esablishment remained unexplored but the garret. To this the party now directed their attention.

"What room is up there?" was the curt question of one of the men to the young lady who stood near him.

"A garret," was the reply.

"He may be up there—show me the way!"

"You see the way—I do not wish to go up there; the dust will soil my dress."

A growl greeted these quiet words, and the trooper turned to a black servant-girl who had been made to go around with the party in their search, holding a lighted candle.

"You go before, and show us the way," said the trooper. The girl laughed, declared that nobody was up there; but on hearing the order repeated, ascended the stairs, followed by the man.

S—— had listened attentively and lost nothing; the architecture of the house enabling him to catch the least sound without difficulty. After the protracted search in the rooms beneath, during which his hiding-place had not been approached, he began to hope that the danger was over. This hope, however, was found to be illusory, and he prepared for the crisis.

The steps of the servant-girl were heard ascending, followed by the tramp of the trooper, whose heavy sabre rattled against the stairs as he moved. Then a long streak of light ran over the garret floor; and cautiously thrusting out his head from his hiding-place, S—— saw the head of the girl and her companion, as step by step they mounted to the apartment. The girl held up her dress with affected horror of the dust; and when she had reached a position from which a full stream of light could be directed into the room, she paused, and with a low laugh called her companion's attention to the fact that there was nothing whatever in the garret.

This, however, did not satisfy him, and he insisted upon making a thorough search. The girl was obliged to obey his order, and in a moment they were both standing in the room.

## II.

S—— measured the man before, or rather beneath him, through a crevice in the plank, and calculated where he could shoot him to the best advantage. This resource seemed all that was left. Discovery appeared inevitable. The scout was lying upon a single plank, directly over the head of his enemy, and it was only necessary, apparently, for the latter to possess ordinary eyesight to discover him. This was the scout's conviction, as he now cautiously moved his finger to the trigger of the pistol, which he had drawn and cocked, in expectation of the coming struggle. He would certainly be discovered in ten seconds, and then for an exhibition of his prowess as a Confederate soldier and scout, which should either extricate him from his peril, or force his very enemies to respect the courage of the man they overwhelmed and put to death! His plan, as I have said, was simple. He would throw himself upon this man, shoot him through the heart, hurl the body upon the heads of those below, and then hold his position against the whole party at the pistol's muzzle. It was improbable that the Federal troopers could be induced to mount the narrow stairway, at the head of which stood at bay a desperate and determined man, armed with a revolver in each hand. It would be certain death to them; he must either be burned out or shelled out with artillery! That either of these courses, however, would be resorted to, appeared improbable; they would place a guard around the house, and either starve or attempt to dislodge him in some other manner. But then he would gain time; now if time were only gained, the scout had so much confidence in his own resources that he believed himself safe.

To return to the scene actually occurring: the Federal trooper gazed around the garret for some hidden nook or cranny wherein a rebel could be stowed away. Some empty boxes attracted his attention, but an examination of them resulted in nothing. Then, all at once, the eyes of the man were directed toward the spot where the scout was concealed.

S—— gave himself up for lost; his finger was on the trigger, and he was about to forestall his enemy by sending a ball through his brain, when suddenly he drew a long breath, removed his finger from the trigger, and flattened himself almost to nonentity on his plank. The girl had adopted an excellent *ruse*, and as simple as it was excellent. Whilst conversing carelessly with the man, she had moved *directly beneath* S——, in consequence of which movement the candle threw the shadow of the plank on which he lay *directly upward*. Thus the person of the scout, prone on the plank, was wholly hidden from view. In vain did the man move from side to side, evidently suspecting something, and order the girl to hold the light in such a manner as to illuminate the dusky recess beneath the rafters. She readily did so, but so adroitly that at every movement the shadow was made still to conceal the scout; and ere long this comedy, in the issue of which the life of a man was involved, came to an end. Satisfied that the garret contained no one, the man retired, and the clank of his sabre on the staircase as he descended gradually receded from the hearing of S——. He was saved.

The Federal troopers remained at the house some time longer, their officer exhibiting the utmost anger and disappointment at the result of the expedition; but they finally departed, warning the lady of the mansion that if she harboured "guerillas" thereafter, her house would be burned. Leaving videttes behind, the officer then departed with his detachment.

This was the signal for S—— to descend, which he did at once. A brief reconnoissance through the window revealed the dark figures posted at stated intervals around the house— but these only made him laugh. He did not fear them, and had only one regret—the impossibility of getting his horse off. The attempt would reveal his presence, involve the family in danger, and might fail. He accordingly resolved to retire on foot. This was at once and successfully accomplished. S—— bade his kind friends farewell, stole out of the back door, glided along the garden fence, beneath the shadow of the trees, and gained the wood near by without being challenged.

In an hour he was safe from all pursuit, at a friend's, on one of the spurs of the Blue Ridge. Soon afterwards he was relating this narrative to the present writer, near Orange.

I was interested in it, and thought that the reader might share this interest. He knows, at least, how S—— overheard his death-warrant.

# IV

## How S— Captured
## a Federal Colonel's Hat

ANOTHER adventure of S——, the scout, will be here narrated.
He related it to me in my tent near Orange more than a year
ago; but the incidents come back, as do many things in memory—
living, breathing, real, as it were, in the sunshine of to-day; not
as mere shapes and recollections of the past.

In the summer of the good year 1863, S—— went with two
or three companions on a little scout toward Warrenton.

Do you know the pretty town of Warrenton, good reader?
'Tis a delightful little place, full of elegant mansions, charming
people, and situated in a lovely country. Nowhere are the eyes
of youthful maidens bluer—*au revoir bien-tôt*, sweet stars of my
memory!—nowhere are truer hearts, or more open hands. Here
Farley, the famous partisan—one of the friends I loved—used to
scout at will, and when chased by his foes, rein up his horse on
the suburbs, and humorously fire in their faces as they darted
in pursuit of him; laughing quietly with that low musical laugh
of his, as his good horse ("Yankee property" once) bore him
away. Here a friend of mine afterwards—but whither am I
wandering? See the force of habit, and the inveterate propensity
to *rove* even on paper; the result of life in the cavalry! I forget
that another branch of the service now claims my thoughts—
that the blanket wrapped in its "Yankee oil-cloth" is rarely
strapped behind my saddle as in the good old days when, fol-

lowing one illustrious for ever, I knew not whither I was going,
where I would stop, or what greenwood tree would shelter me.
Look! the red battle-flag is floating in the wind; the column
moves; will we sleep in Virginia, Maryland, or Pennsylvania?
We knew not, for the cavalry are your true rovers of the greenwood; so I, who once was a cavalry-man, rove still, even on
paper.

I perceive I am growing dull. To return to S—— and his little
scout near Warrenton in 1863. I cannot fail to interest then,
you see, my dear reader; for there is a certain species of human
interest in the adventures of those who deal in

> "bloody noses, and crack'd crowns,
>    And pass them current too,"

which everybody experiences; and the relation of these sanguinary adventures demands very little "style." You tell your
plain story as plainly as possible; and behold! you secure the
luxury of luxuries, a satisfied reader.

S—— had, as I have said, two or three companions with him;
and having slept in the woods near Warrenton, the party proceeded toward Catlett's in search of adventures. There were
plenty of Federal camps there, and in the neighbourhood; and
our scout promised himself much amusement. Behold them then,
full of the spirit of fun, and intent on celebrating the day by an
exciting hunt which should result in the running down, and killing or capturing of some of the blue people.

They reached the vicinity of the railroad without adventures,
and then proceeded carefully to reconnoitre for the camps
known to be in that vicinity. This search was soon rewarded.
Reaching the summit of a hill, where some trees concealed
them, but the view was unobscured, they perceived in the valley
beneath two extensive camps, one on the right, the other on the
left; the Federal soldiers lounging about in careless security.

Here was S——'s game plain before him, and waiting as it
were to be trapped. Stragglers from Federal camps—adventurous
explorers of the surrounding country in search of butter, eggs,
or fowls—these were the favourite victims of the scout; for

from such he often obtained valuable information, excellent horses and equipments, and the finest patterns of revolvers; all "articles in his line." To lie in wait for stragglers or others was thus a very safe game; but on this occasion S—— had loftier views. He had two or three men with him, tried and trusty comrades; and with an army of this size, he felt himself able to operate in the open field; making up by dash and audacity what he lacked in numbers.

Having thus arrived at the conclusion that he could effect something important, the scout waited for his opportunity, and this opportunity soon came.

All at once a *cortège* of cavalry was seen advancing along the road in the valley from one camp in the direction of the other; apparently the escort of some officer of distinction. The party numbered at least twenty, and the ground was unfavourable for a surprise; but S—— was unable to resist the temptation to attack them, and at least throw them and their camps into confusion—your true scout and hunter of bluebirds never experiencing greater pleasure than when he can alone, or with two or three companions, frighten and startle "to arms" a whole brigade or regiment of his enemies. S—— accordingly stole down the hill, as much under cover as possible, until he reached the side of the road over which the officer and his escort were approaching—then in a few words he explained his design to the others, and awaited.

The Federal officer came on in profound security, no doubt considering himself as safe as though at home in his own country; when suddenly, with a yell that rang through the hills, S—— and his party darted from their place of concealment, and charged full tilt upon the frightened escort, firing on them as they charged.

The escort did not await the shock. Believing themselves waylaid by "Rebel cavalry," and doomed to certain destruction if they remained, they turned their horses' heads and broke in disorder, flying back to the camp from which they came, pursued by S——'s men.

Their commander, a Colonel, acted with more courage. S—— had shot him through the arm, inflicting a dangerous wound; but he attempted to draw his pistol and resist, calling all the time to his cowardly escort to stand. S—— immediately closed in with him and attempted to kill him, but in this he failed. The Colonel's horse set off at full speed in the direction of the camp, toward which his rider had been going, and, turning his own horse, S—— followed, yelling and firing his pistol as he went.

The chase was exciting; the situation altogether singular. The camp of a whole brigade was directly in front, not four hundred yards distant, and S—— was on the heels of the Colonel, who was already on the outskirts of the encampment. The men ran from their tents in astonishment and dismay at the firing, persuaded that a whole regiment of Confederate cavalry was charging; and still the Colonel, like John Gilpin of old, ran his race—not for "a thousand pounds," but for a more valuable stake, his life.

S—— did not relax his gait or cease pursuit. Now they were in the very camp; the Colonel still dashes on, and the scout still follows on his track, firing as he goes. The Colonel gesticulates violently, and shouts to the men:

"Shoot the d——d rascal! shoot him! There's only one of them!"

S—— laughs and bangs away still with his revolver.

The Colonel is in a frenzy of rage; his frightened horse shies; the Colonel's hat drops, but the owner cannot stop to regain it.

S—— throws himself from the saddle, picks up the hat, and again mounts, laughing.

But by this time the game was growing too dangerous. The men had recovered from their astonishment and were running to their guns. S—— had no desire to receive a volley of musketry; and, waving the captured hat with one hand, fired his last barrel with the other at the Colonel, and then retreated at a gallop, followed by a number of musket-balls, at which, however, he only laughed.

He soon rejoined his men, who had pursued the escort into

the other camp; and then, as the whole place was buzzing like a nest of hornets, they quietly disappeared and were soon lost in the extensive woods, where pursuit was impossible.

What S—— did with his hat I am unable to say; but, doubtless, the heart of some "high Confederate" was charmed by the offering, for mighty is the market price of all that comes through the blockade.

If not thus disposed of, the trophy lies somewhere hidden among the *opima spolia* of S——, to be shown some day as a memorial of that gay adventure in the summer forests of Fauquier.

# V

## How S—— Carried Off
## a Federal Field-Officer

I HAVE not yet done with S——, the scout. Still another adventure of his comes back to my memory, and this also shall proceed to be narrated.

The chosen field for the operations of the scout fraternity was, as I have said, the county of Fauquier—not only because the enemy frequented habitually that region, but from its great adaptability to partisan manœuvres. Behold now, in this bloody year 1863, our friend the scout making a little excursion into the Chinquepin Territory in search of information, adventure, spoils —whatever is calculated to charm the heart of the free ranger of the woods. Mounted on a good fresh horse, with pistols at side, and a good stout heart to back the ready hand, the scout joyfully set forth all alone on his journey, trusting to Providence to guide him, and to his own skill and courage for the result.

The country swarmed with the enemy; and to find out all about them, their strength, position, and probable designs, was the main object of S—— in going on his scout. If, however, any opportunity of striking a blow presented itself, he intended to avail himself of the "opening." As will be seen, such opportunity did present itself, and was promptly improved.

The scout reached, without adventures, the vicinity of Warrenton, and was riding through a thick body of woods, when all at once, on turning a bend in the winding bridle-path, he came suddenly upon a Federal Colonel, followed by two order-lies. The undergrowth was so thick, and the earth so soft, that he was entirely unaware of the vicinity of his foes, until the horses' heads were almost touching.

For a moment the opponents gazed upon each other motion-less and in silence. The Colonel and his escort seemed to have a dim impression that the silent man before them was *a foe*, and S—— soon gave them good reason for becoming confirmed in this opinion. His hand darted to his pistol, but for some moments he was unable to draw it. The Colonel was busy doing the same; and, meanwhile, something like the following dialogue took place between the opponents:

Colonel, *excitedly*.—"You are a guerilla?"

Scout, *sternly*.—"Yes, I am."

Colonel.—"What do you want?"

Scout.—"You."

And with these words S—— banged away with his pistol, missing his aim, but causing the two orderlies to beat a sudden and complete retreat. The Colonel fired his pistol, and then turned his horse's head to retreat, but S—— was too quick for him. In an instant he was beside his man, and ordered him to drop his pistol and surrender. This command was doggedly obeyed; but S—— had no sooner achieved his object than he saw himself threatened with a new danger.

Horses' hoofs were heard upon the road behind him; and look-ing through an opening in the trees, he saw a party of Federal cavalry, who had no doubt been attracted by the report of his pistol, and were now approaching the spot at a rapid gallop, evidently bent on ascertaining the cause of the firing.

Not a moment was to be lost. S—— saw his prize about to be snatched from him, and was called upon to act with rapidity and resolution. Cocking his pistol, which he held in his right hand, he ordered his prisoner to refrain from any outcry on peril of instant death; and then seizing the Colonel's bridle in his left hand, he put spur to his horse and set off at a tremen-dous gallop—the prisoner's horse galloping beside his own.

Thus commenced the race for life. The pursuers had evidently described him and comprehended his intention, for they uttered loud shouts, calling on him to stop or they would fire.

The scout laughed his grim laugh. It was probable that such a threat would influence him! He had long cultivated a contempt for bullets issuing from carbines levelled by cavalry; and if the coolest and most experienced marksmen, firing from a rest, had menaced him, the effect would have been the same with him. Even if his soul had not scouted the thought, *surrender* was out of the question; and, instead of slackening his gait, he put spurs to his horse, flying even faster, and carrying along with him the Colonel, whose bridle was still grasped in his inexorable hand.

The pursuers howled with rage and followed like wolves upon his track. Every moment they seemed gaining on him, and the Colonel's countenance began to indicate a lively anticipation of rescue. But to aid his friends seemed hopeless. S—— had him completely in his power. Whenever he turned his eyes toward the scout as they sped on, the grim muzzle of a pistol met his view; and the expression of the scout's countenance but too plainly proved that he would hesitate at nothing. If anything was certain, this was, that S—— had determined to bring him out of the lines a prisoner, or leave him dead; and the Colonel, like an intelligent man, did not venture to raise his hand, or make any open efforts to assist his friends and effect his release.

The pursuers still thundered on the track of the scout and his prisoner; and the two horsemen continued to fly at headlong speed. They passed out of the woods across an open space, and into the woods again. All trace of a road, except a narrow bridle-path, was now lost, and the trunks of the trees grew so close together that it was difficult for the pursuers to follow them except in single file. This it was soon obvious they were doing, for the shouts were again close upon the track of the fugitives; and the near approach of his friends induced the prisoner to undertake a *ruse* on his own part, to assist them in their exertions.

This he proceeded to do as follows. The wood, as I have said, was very dense, and the trees so close together as to make it difficult for S—— and his companion to pass along the narrow bridle-path abreast between the trunks. On this circumstance the

Colonel based his hopes of delaying the flight of himself and
S——, and thus giving time to his friends to come up.

They were passing at this moment through a very narrow
space; there was scarce room for more than a single horse; and
on the side of the Colonel, that is, the left side, a stout tree-trunk
made it necessary to incline his horse's head to the right, and
draw in his knee well to the saddle, to avoid scaping against the
trunk in passing. It was the Colonel's object now to pass to the
*left* of this tree; and then force S——, as he passed on the *right*
of it, to loose his hold of the prisoner's bridle, who might then
suddenly check his horse, wheel round, and so escape.

No sooner was this *ruse* determined on than it was attempted.
By violently turning his horse's head to the left, and digging
his right heel into the animal's flanks, the Federal officer endeavoured to interpose the tree between them, and so accomplish
his purpose; but S—— was too quick for him. The scout was not
one to be outgeneralled by so simple and transparent a device.
No sooner had the Colonel jerked his bridle to the left, than the
scout counteracted his plan by still more violently jerking it
toward himself, and forcing the animal to dart by *between* himself and the tree, instead of upon the opposite side.

The consequence was, that the Colonel's knee crashed against
the trunk; his foot was dragged out of the stirrup, and his boot
nearly torn from his leg, which was painfully bruised and
lacerated.

He had no sooner regained his seat in the saddle than the low
tones of S——, supported by a levelled pistol, were heard warning him that a repetition of that manœuvre, or any attempt to
escape whatever, would be followed by his instant death.

Having communicated this warning with an accent of voice
that satisfied the listener that the speaker was ready, and even
desirous to carry out his threat, S—— again darted on, still followed by the Federal cavalry.

No further effort was made by the prisoner to escape, and the
pursuers began gradually to relax the ardour of the chase; but all
at once a new danger presented itself. Directly in front of them
was a large camp; and to S——'s rapid questions, the Colonel

replied that the camp before them was *his own*. Realize now, reader, the full comedy of the "situation." S—— was charging at a thundering gallop the camp of a full Federal regiment, with scores of the men lounging about the opening of the tents; and by his side, a prisoner, was the Colonel of the regiment, charging, somewhat unwillingly, with his captor! This is not the fancy of a romance-writer, inventing the odd contrasts of comedy for the amusement of his readers, but an occurrence which really took place just as is here stated.

The scout was, however, equal to the occasion. Not only did he unhesitatingly charge *upon* the camp, but *through* it. No other course was left; but even if the choice had been possible, this—the boldest—was the safest. It was necessary to take the enemy completely by surprise; and having informed his prisoner that at the first outcry which he made, a pistol bullet would be sent through his heart, he dug the spur into his horse's side, dragged his companion on, and before the thoughtless loungers of the camp realized the truth, had darted through unopposed, and was racing with his prisoner far beyond pursuit.

Once in the woods again, S—— was comparatively safe. There was no cavalry near, and the slow infantry could not follow the rough rider and his captive. To the latter S—— now coolly turned, and demanded his name and regiment. The reply was a sullen refusal to give the required information, and the scout saw that "coercion" was absolutely necessary to attain his object. He accordingly crossed the pistol which he held in his right hand in front of his breast, covered the prisoner's heart, and said politely:

"Colonel, I asked you your name, and the number and State of your regiment."

"I refused to give it."

"If you do not, I will kill you."

This response admitted of no reply. The officer looked at his captor, saw that he was quite in earnest, and replied:

"My name is Colonel——, and my regiment is the—— Pennsylvania."

"All right, Colonel; I see we understand each other. Now I

wish you would tell me anything you know that will interest me."

And laughing in his low fashion, the scout rode on with his prisoner, whose good-humour gradually began to return. To explain this, it may be conjectured that S—— had not upon this occasion encountered a very desperate son of Mars, but a philosopher who contemplated the probabilities of an early exchange, and submitted gracefully to his fate. In an hour the scout and his prisoner had become quite sociable.

"That was a daring act of yours," said the Colonel, "and you have got out of this thing well."

"I rather think so, Colonel."

"I ought to have been more on my guard. Well done—yes, very well done; especially going through my camp!"

It will be seen that the two had grown quite friendly, and this amicable understanding continued uninterrupted. S—— had long since returned to the black leather holster that impolite instrument first directed at his companion's breast, and they rode on together in the friendliest manner imaginable, still keeping in the woods.

Night thus surprised them; and no house being visible, a proceeding took place which will seem to display the *entente cordiale* between S—— and his companion. They were both sleepy; they determined to bivouac; and the scout simply took his prisoner's parole not to attempt escape. Five minutes afterwards they were sleeping side by side.

Rising at daylight, they proceeded on their way, and in a few hours S—— was within the Confederate lines with his prisoner.

# VI

## An Adventure with the "Bluebirds"

S—— is a scout who has had many very curious adventures, as the narratives already laid before the reader will serve to show. He is not a "man of peace," nor is his life a tranquil one. While you, my dear quiet citizen, have been sleeping in your comfortable bed, with the curtains drawn and the firelight shining on Brussels carpeting and mahogany furniture, or luxuriously stretching out your slippered feet toward the fender in the breakfast-room, as you glance over the morning papers before going to your cent. per cent. employments down town; while you have been thus agreeably engaged, not knowing what it is to wear a soiled shirt or miss a meal, or suffer from cold or fatigue, S—— has been in the saddle, hungry, weary, exposed to rain and snow and storm, hunting Bluebirds.

Bluebird hunting is not a remunerative employment in a pecuniary point of view, but it has its attractions. You don't realize a hundred per cent. profit, and you run some risk; but the blood flows faster and much more gloriously through the veins than in trade, to say nothing of the "fuller life" it communicates to all the faculties. But this is not denied. I proceed to give a brief account of a recent scout which S—— made into the Federal lines:

One fine summer day in 1863 he took four men, made his way unperceived across the Rappahannock, and soon reached the neighbourhood of Warrenton. Leaving that place to his left, he struck out with his party for the railroad, and coming near a Federal camp, placed his four men in ambush, and taking a position on the road, awaited the appearance of some prey. He had not waited long when a stray Federal cavalry-man came along, and seeing S—— dressed in a blue overcoat and Federal accoutrements generally, had no fear of him. His confiding simplicity was his ruin. When he had come within a few yards S—— "put his pistol on him," in military parlance, and took him prisoner, calling one of his men from the woods to take charge of him. The captive had scarcely been conducted into the underwood when two others appeared, coming from the same direction, and S—— determined to capture these also. He called to the man who had taken charge of the prisoner; but that worthy was too busy rifling the unfortunate bluebird, and did not hear. S—— then resolved to capture the two new cavalry-men by himself. He accordingly advanced toward them, when suddenly another came out of the woods and joined them, making three. He still designed attacking them, when another appeared, making four; and as these now approached S—— they suddenly drew their pistols, and levelling them, ordered him to surrender. He was within five feet of them, holding his pistol in his hand, and said coolly:

"What do you mean?"

"We mean," said the men, "that you are a guerilla, and you are our prisoner."

"I am no guerilla," was the reply.

"What do you belong to?"

"The First New Jersey."

"Who comamnds it?"

"Major Janaway."

"Right. Who commands the brigade?"

"Colonel Taylor."

"Right again. Where is it stationed?"

"In the edge of Warrenton."

"Yes. Who commands the division?"

"Look here," said S——, who was thoroughly acquainted

with every part of his *rôle*, "I am tired of your asking me so many questions; but I will answer. The First New Jersey is in Taylor's brigade, Gregg's division, and Pleasanton commands the whole. I belong to the regiment, and am no guerilla."

"He's all right, boys," said one of the men; "let him go."

"No," said another; "I saw him capture one of our men ten minutes ago."

"You are mistaken," said S——.

"You are a guerilla!" exclaimed the man.

"And how do I know *you* are not guerillas?" said S——; "you have on blue coats, but let me see your pantaloons."

They raised their coat-skirts and showed their blue regulation pantaloons.

"Now show yours," they said.

S—— had foreseen this, and readily exhibited his own, which were those of a Federal officer.

"He's one of our officers, boys," said the former spokesman.

"Yes, I am," said S——, "and I'll report you all for this conduct."

"None of your talk," said the incredulous cavalry-man. "I *know* you are a guerilla, and you've got to go with us."

"Very well," returned S——; "the picket post is just down the road. I'll take you there and convince you."

"All right," was the reply; and they ranged themselves, two on each side, with drawn pistols, and all rode back.

S—— now saw that it was neck or nothing. If he was conducted to the picket he knew that his real character would be discovered, his fate to be a stout rope and a short shrift, and that his body would soon be dangling from a tree as a warning to all spies. He accordingly watched his chance, and suddenly crossing his pistol over his breast, shot the man on his left through the back; a second shot wounded a horse on his right; and all four shot at him so close that their pistols nearly touched him. Strange to say, not a ball struck him.

He then turned his horse and dashed back until he was opposite the point where his men were concealed, when he wheeled round, and they all stopped suddenly. S—— coolly crossed his leg over the pommel of his saddle, covered them with his pistol, and said:

"Now come on, you cowardly rascals! Charge me if you dare! I'm certain of two of you."

They remained consulting hurriedly within fifteen steps of him for some minutes, and then turned round and rode back. They had not gone fifty yards, however, when shame seemed to overcome them; and whirling round, the three who were unwounded charged him, firing as they came with their pistols. S—— charged forward to meet them, emptying his barrels in quick succession; and the whole party turned their horses and fled down the road, S—— pursuing them with shouts, and firing upon them until they had reached their picket post.

Such was S——'s curious adventure. There is no reason to doubt it. Every army contains brave men and faint hearts. S—— seems to have encountered the latter.

PART 5

# LATTER DAYS

# I

## ON THE ROAD TO PETERSBURG

NOTES OF AN OFFICER OF THE C. S. A.

### I.

So JUNE wears on in this good or bad year 1864, and our friend General Grant is leaving Cold Harbour for a "new base," I think.

He has had a hard time of it since he crossed the Rapidan, and we also; fighting in the Wilderness, (I came near "going under" there); fighting at Spotsylvania Court-House (*our* Po is more famous now than the classic stream of Virgil); fighting on the North Anna, a maiden who stretched her arms between the fierce combatants and commanded the peace; fighting on the slopes of Hanover, when that Indian girl, the Tottapotamoi, did the same; and then fighting here, how fiercely! on the famous ground of old Cold Harbour, where the thunder of the guns has seemed to many like an echo of those guns of McClellan, which made such a racket hereabouts in June, 1862, just two years since!

A good many things have happened since that period, but we remain more faithful to our first loves than the blue people. *Then* the Federal commander-in-chief was called McClellan— now he is called Grant. The leader of the South was then called Lee, and Lee is his name to-day. But each seems to have a constant, never-faltering attachment for the "good old place," Cold Harbour, just as they appear to have for the blooming *parterres* of the beautiful and smiling Manassas! The little affair near Stone

509

Bridge, in July, 1861, was not sufficient; again in August, 1862, the blue and gray lovers of the historic locality must hug each other in the dear old place! "Malbrook s'en va-t en guerre," to the old tune on the old ground!

The game is played here for the present, however. Every assault upon the Confederate lines has been repulsed with heavy loss, and Grant has evidently abandoned any further attempt to storm them; he is moving toward James river. The fighting has been heavy, incessant, deadly. Wind, rain, sunshine, heat, cold, nothing has stopped it. But the Southern lines have stood intact; so the war goes elsewhere. It is escorted on its way, as usual, with a salute.

This morning a decided racket is going on. Boom! boom! whiz-z-z-z! pow-w-w-w! there is a shell which has burst near me. Won't our friends across the way permit an inoffensive Confederate to smoke his pipe in peace, without disturbance from these disgusting visitors? I have just dined on an infinitesimal ration, and am smoking peaceably when my reverie is thus invaded. That shell, which in bursting has raised a little cloud of dust, might have hurt me; it *has* interrupted me. Why do they fire so high, and why at *me?* I am not a general.. My flag is not up. I am not even fighting to-day. I am smoking, and indulging no sort of spite against anybody. I am thinking of some scenes and faces an enormous distance from this spot, and am, in every sense of the words, "off duty." It is pleasure, not duty, which enthralls me. Recreation, not work, is my programme for the nonce. Respect, my friends, the rights of a neutral and non-combatant!

The cannonade continues. They are having a hot artillery skirmish yonder, but I go on smoking without much excitement thereat, being used to it. The time was when we fought pitched battles once or twice a year, killed each other all day long *secundem artem*, and then relapsed into gentlemanly repose and amity, undisturbed save by the *petite guerre* of the pickets. At that remote period, the present elderly, battered, and unexcitable warrior, used to rush "to horse" at the first roar of the cannon; for the roar in question preceded a general and decisive engagement, in which every man ought to be "on hand." Now we have changed all that, or rather the enemy have. Once, under Mc-Clellan, they seemed only bent on fighting big battles, and making a treaty of peace. Now they seem determined to drive us to the last ditch, and *into it,* the mother earth to be shovelled over us. Virginia is no longer a battlefield, but a living, shuddering body, upon which is to be inflicted the *immedicabile vulnus* of all-destroying war. So be it; she counted the cost, and is not yet at the last ditch.

All that talk about immedicable wounds and last ditches has diverted me from the contrast I was drawing between the past and present. Then, I meant to say, I always started up at the cannon's roar, expecting a decisive battle; now, so incessant and so indecisive is the fighting, I lie under my tree and smoke, and dream of other scenes, scarcely conscious that those guns are thundering yonder, and that many a brave fellow is uttering his last groan. Thus we harden. Do I think of "those blue eyes?" Well, the comrade dying yonder thinks of the pair *he* knows. Poor fellow! then I return to my reverie.

The war grows tedious; carnage bores one. "Bores!!!" This is, I think, about the fortieth day of fighting. We had the "seven days' battles around Richmond" in 1862. Is this campaign to be the "seventy days' battles around Virginia?" The game keeps up with wonderful animation; guns roaring, shell bursting, and listen! that long, sustained, resolute crash of the deadly small-arms! Suddenly it stops; but a good many brave fellows have "gone under" in that five minutes' work. This takes place at all hours of the day and night. Grant keeps "pegging away." To-day he seems to gain something, but to-morrow Lee stands like a lion in his path, and all the advantage is lost. We continue to re-pulse every attack along the bristling lines, as in 1862. Grant ends where McClellan began; upon the ground at least. We hold our own. "Lee's army is an army of veterans," writes the corre-spondent of a Northern journal; "it is an instrument sharpened to a perfect edge. You turn its flanks; well, its flanks are made to be turned. This effects little or nothing. All that we can reckon as gained, therefore, is the loss of life inflicted on the enemy, and of having reached a point thus near the objective, but no brilliant military results." Candid and true. They lose more heavily—the enemy—than we do, but our precious blood flows daily. Poor Charley——! A braver soul was never born into this world than his; and, since something happened to him, he has been quite reckless. He is dead yonder, on the slopes of Hanover, fighting his guns to the last. And that greater figure of Stuart; he has fallen, too! How he would have reigned, the King of Battle, in this hot campaign, clashing against the hosts of Sheridan in desperate conflict! What deathless laurels would he have won for himself in this hurly-burly, when the war grows mad and reckless! But those laurels are deathless now, and bloom in perennial splendour! Stuart is dead at the Yellow Tavern yonder, and sleeps at Hollywood; but as the dying Adams said of Jefferson, he "still lives"—lives in every heart, the greatest of the Southern cavaliers! His plume still floats before the eyes of the gray horsemen, and "history shall never forget him!"

There was Gordon, too—alive but the other day, now dead and gone whither so many comrades have preceded him. He fell in that same fierce onslaught on the enemy's cavalry, when they tried to enter Richmond by the Brook road, in that sudden attack which saved the capital. "I blamed Stuart once for his reckless attack with so small a force as he then had on so large a one as the enemy's," said a most intelligent gentleman of the neighbourhood to me not long since; "but now I know that he proved himself here, as everywhere, the great soldier, and that he thereby saved Richmond." And the gallant Gordon! how well I knew him, and how we all loved him! Tall, elegant in person, distinguished in address, with a charming suavity and gaiety, he was a universal favourite. Of humour how rich! of bearing how frank and cordial! of courage how stern and obstinate! Under fire, Gordon was a perfect rock; nothing could move him. In camp, off duty, he was the soul of good-fellowship. His bow and smile were inimitable, his voice delightful. He would present a bouquet to a lady with a little speech which nobody else could approach; and, at the head of the "Old First" North Carolina cavalry, he would have charged McClellan's massed artillery at

Malvern Hill. We used to tell him that his rapid rise to the rank of General was the result of his "personal, political, and pecuniary position;" but that alliterative accusation was only a jest. He won his rank by hard fighting and hard work; he gave the South all he had—his time, his toil, his brain; she demanded his life, and he gave that, too, without a murmur. Peace to that brave!

These memories seduce me. I am getting *triste*—blue. I do not like blue, having so many disagreeable associations connected with it; I prefer gray. Blue eyes and blue skies are exceptions, however. I differ with General Henry A. Wise, who said to me once, "I like a *gray day*." Hurrah for the sunshine, and up with the flag that has *"Vive la joie!"* for its motto. We need all the sunshine and gaiety that is attainable, for whatever may be thought of our friend General Ulysses Grant's genius as a soldier, he allows the gray people very little time for relaxation or amusement. I think McClellan is the better general, but the present generalissimo does "keep pegging away" with unusual regularity! There is another roar; but the artillery fire has slackened. Now the sound is heard only at intervals. The desultory "wood-chopping" of the sharpshooters comes from the woods and gradually recedes. Grant is moving.

## II.

We strike tents, shoulder arms—I do not, I only buckle on a sabre—cross the Chickahominy, and take up the line of march for the James river—hungry.

A tedious march down the right bank of the "Swamp," into the low grounds of Charles City, everywhere facing Grant; line of battle; fighting on the long bridge road; men throwing up earthworks with their bayonets in twenty minutes, whenever they stop; sun rising and setting; wind blowing; woods reverberating with shots; column still moving toward James river. Then the question is settled; General Grant is going to try the Petersburg line of advance on Richmond, with his base at City Point.

Judicious! General Lee said a year ago, I am told, that this was the quarter from which Richmond was most exposed. That terrible question of our "communications"—the Southern railroads! After all, it is bread and meat which will decide this war, or rather, I am afraid, the want of it. The granaries of the Gulf States are full, and we are starving. Who is to blame? History will answer that question. The time will come when the survivors of this army, or their children, will know why we are left to starve upon a microscopic ration—"so-called"—of meat, which just enables a man to carry a musket and cartridge-box without staggering and falling upon the march, or in battle, from exhaustion! Some day we will know that; meanwhile we go on starving, and try to do the work. Close up!

Over James river above Drury's Bluff—*not* "Fort Darling," nobody ever heard of that place—on pontoons. The artillery moves on all night; I and the most amiable of Inspector-Generals bivouac with saddles for pillows in a clover-field. We have just passed an ancient-looking house, but seeing no light, forebore from arousing the lady of the establishment, preferring to sleep al fresco, by the camp-fire. Yonder, through the gloaming, as I lie on my red blanket—from Chancellorsville—with feet to the rail fire, and my head on my English saddle, as I smoke—*not* after supper—yonder I see the old house. It is not a very imposing place. Set upon a handsome hill, amid waving fields, above the James, nearly opposite the Randolph house of "Wilton," it would be attractive in "good times." But now it is pulled to pieces and dust-covered. For the cannon of the Army of Northern Virginia have rolled by the door hour after hour, and the trampling hoofs of the cavalry have raised clouds of dust, hanging on the trees and walls. House, out-buildings, fences (broken down), grass-plat, box-rows—all disappear under the cloud. Dust is king there. We drop asleep with rosy visions; for, in passing the house, an Ethiopian friend named Richard, who subsequently kindled our rail fire for us, promised us breakfast. We rise at dawn, repair to the establishment, make our toilets (I always carry soap, brush, and towel in my haversack), and are shown into the drawing-room, to which the ladies have not descended, though they have sent polite messages touching breakfast.

It is with real historic interest that I gaze upon this old mansion. For this is "Ampthill," the former residence of the famous Colonel Archibald Cary of the first Revolution—the man of the low stature, the wide shoulders, the piercing eyes, and the stern will. He was of noble descent, being the heir apparent to the barony of Hunsdon when he died; sat in the Virginia Convention of 1776; lived with the eyes of his great contemporaries fixed on him—with the ears of George Washington, Thomas Jefferson, and George Mason, listening to hear him speak, and was the sort of man who will "stand no nonsense." When the question of appointing Patrick Henry Dictator was agitated, Cary said to Henry's brother-in-law, "Sir, tell your brother that if he is made Dictator, my dagger shall be in his breast before the sunset of that day!" There spoke "Cary of Ampthill," as they used to call him—a man who religiously kept his word, saying little and performing much. Hardest of the hard-headed, in fact, was this Ampthill Cary, and his contemporaries nicknamed him "Old Iron" therefor. He played a great part in old times— he is dead in this good year 1864, many a long day ago—but this is his house. Looking around at the wainscoted walls, the ample apartments, and with a view of the extensive out-buildings through the window, I come to the conclusion that those old Virginians had a tolerably good idea of "how to live." Here is a house in which a reasonable individual could be happy, provided he had a pleasing young personage of the opposite sex to assist him. Woodwork to the ceiling; wide windows; trees waving without, and green fields stretching far away to the horizon; pure airs from the river fanning the cheek, and moving gently the bright plumage of the singing birds perched amid the rustling foliage—Cary of Ampthill must surely have been a gentleman of taste. Is that him yonder, sitting on the porch and reading his old blurred "Virginia Gazette," containing the announcement of the proposed passage of a Stamp Act in the English Parliament? That must be "Old Iron." He wears ruffles at his breast,

knee-breeches, a coat with barrel sleeves covered with embroidery, a pigtail, and a cocked hat. His shoulders are broad,
his frame low, his eye piercing—and I think he is swearing as he
reads about the doings of parliament. He has apparently just returned from inspecting the blood-horses in his stables, and after
taking his morning julep, is reading the *Gazette*, and pondering
on the probable results of secession from England, with the
sword exercise which is sure to follow. But look! he raises his
head. A gun sounds from down the river, reverberating amid the
bluffs, and echoing back from the high banks around "Wilton,"
where his friend Mr. Randolph lives. It must be the signal of a
ship just arrived from London, in this month of June, 1764; the
*Fly-by-Night*, most probably, with all the list of articles which
Colonel Cary sent for—new suits for himself from the London
tailors (no good ones in this colony as yet), fine silks for the
ladies, wines from Madeira, and Bordeaux, and Oporto, new
editions of the "Tattler," or "Spectator," or "Tom Jones," all
paid for by the tobacco crop raised here at Ampthill. The *Fly-
by-Night* probably brings also the *London Gazette*, showing
what view is taken in England of the "rising spirit of rebellion"
in the colonies, and what the ministers think of the doctrine of
coercion. Our present Governor, Fauquier, is not wholly
"sound," it is thought, upon these questions, and Lord Dunmore
it is supposed will succeed him. A second gun! The Captain of
the *Fly-by-Night* seems to have anchored at the wharf, and the
swivel, announcing his arrival to his patrons, is making a jolly
racket. Again!—and there again! Bomb! bomb! bomb! bomb!
Can that be the *Fly-by-Night*, and is that Mr. Randolph galloping up in hot haste from the ferry opposite "Wilton?"

It is a courier who stops a moment to tell me that the Yankee
gunboats have opened below Drury's Bluff, and are trying to
force a passage through the obstructions. So my dream is broken;
I wake in the every-day world of 1864; the year 1764 has quite
disappeared; and Cary of Ampthill—where is his figure? That
is only my friend, the amiable Inspector-General, on the porch,
reaching a copy of the *Richmond Examiner*. I took his looped-up
felt for a cocked hat, and his officer's braid for the ante-revolu-

tionary embroidery! So the past disappears, but the winds are blowing, and the cloud-shadows float just as they did one hundred years ago. The fields are green again, the river breeze comes to me with its low sweet murmur, and the birds are singing in the trees as they sang for Cary of Ampthill.

"Gentlemen, will you walk in to breakfast?"

O most prosaic—but also most agreeable of announcements! The past and its memories fade; we are again in the present, as the most agreeable of odours indicates!

# II

## A FAMILY RIFLE-PIT

### AN INCIDENT OF WILSON'S RAID

IN WAR the bloody and the grotesque are strangely mingled; comedy succeeds tragedy with startling abruptness; and laughter issues from the lips when the tears upon the cheek are scarcely dry.

I had never heard of a "family rifle-pit" before June, 1864. I am going to give the reader the benefit of the knowledge I acquired on that occasion.

General Grant was then besieging Petersburg, or Richmond rather, if we are to believe the military gentlemen who edited the New York newspapers; and having failed to drive Lee from his earthworks, where the Virginian persisted in remaining despite every effort made to oust him, the Federal commander organized an enormous "raid" against the Southside and the Danville railroads, by which Lee was supplied. The result of this cavalry movement is known. Generals Wilson, Kautz, and others who commanded in the expedition, were successful in their object, so far as the destruction of a large part of the railroads went; but when they attempted to return to their infantry lines, below Petersburg, they "came to grief." Hampton and the Lees assailed them, forced them to abandon their artillery and ambulances on the old stage road near Reams' Station, and it was only by a resolute effort that the remnants of the Federal cavalry got home again.

It was a few days after the raid that the present writer rode, on duty, through the region which the opposing cavalry had fought over, looking with interest upon the marks of the hard struggle, on the dead horses, half-burnt vehicles, and remains of artillery carriages, with the spokes hacked hastily to pieces, and the guns dismounted. But these results of combat—of retreat and pursuit —are familiar to the reader, doubtless, and not of very great interest to the present writer.

The "Wilson and Kautz raid" would indeed have been forgotten long ago by him, but for the "family rifle-pit" mentioned above, and to this the attention of the worthy reader is now requested.

I heard all about it from a very charming lady who resided in a little house on the roadside, not very far from Reams'; and before me, as the bright eyes flashed and the red lips told the story, was the scene of the events narrated. In front, across the road, was a field of oats; beyond was a belt of woods; the country all around was a dead and dusty level, scorching in the sun. The house had a yard, and in this yard was a well with a "sweep," as they call it, I believe, in Dinwiddie, which is pronounced by the inhabitants Dunwoody, which "sweep" is a great beam balanced in the crotch of a tree, a bucket being suspended to one end of the beam by a pole, and hanging above the well, into which it is made to descend by working the pole downwards with the hands.

In the small house lived Mr.——, from Gloucester, with his wife and family of small children—all refugees. For a long time it seemed that the amiable household would remain quite undisturbed; they had scarcely seen a single blue-coat. But suddenly, one bright June morning, the road, the fields, the woods, the yard, the porch, and the mansion, swarmed with Federal cavalry, coming from the direction of Prince George.

It was soon ascertained that General Wilson was "riding a raid," without the fear of Confederates before his eyes; and had thus come to Reams' Station, on the Weldon Railroad, where a force of Rebel cavalry was expected to be encountered. Scouting parties had accordingly been thrown forward, a reconnoissance made, sharpshooters were advanced, the cavalry moved behind in column of squadrons, and the house and family of Mr.—— were captured, not to mention some old negroes, and very young ones—the latter clad, for the most part, in a single garment, adapted rather to the heat of the weather than to the production of an imposing effect.

The cavalry-men crowded to the well, swarmed through the grounds, and then commenced a scene well known to many a family in the South. The lives of venerable ducks were sacrificed, in spite of their piteous quacking; frightened chickens were chased and knocked over with sticks; calves were shot, and the hen-roost and dairy cleared with a rapidity and skill which indicated thorough practice. In ten minutes the yard was duck-less and chickenless; the dairy was crockless, the hen-roost innocent of eggs. The besom of destruction seemed to have passed over the whole, and the hungry bluebirds were cooking and devouring their spoil.

Unfortunately for Mr.——, they were not satisfied with poultry, butter, and eggs. They wanted hams—and an *officer*, Mrs.—— assured me, demanded her keys. When she assured him that her children required this food, the *officer's* reply was an insult, and the young lady was forced to deliver to him the key of her smoke-house, which was speedily rifled. Mrs.—— was looking on with bitter distress; but all at once her pride was aroused—the *Southern woman* flamed out!

"Take it if you choose," she said, with sarcasm; "I can easily send word to General Lee at Petersburg, and meat will be supplied me! There are twelve months' rations for the whole army in Richmond" (I hope the recording angel blotted out that statement!); "and if you *do* cut the railroad, General Lee's army will not suffer, but be just as strong and brave as ever!"

"That's foolish—it will ruin him!" said one of the men.

"You will see," was the reply. "Do you think General Lee could not prevent your coming here if he wished to? He *wants* you to come, for he expects to catch you all—every man—before you get away!"

This new and striking view of the subject seemed to produce

a deep effect upon the listeners. They paused in their depredations, looked doubtfully around them, and one of them, putting his hand before his mouth, said *aside* to a comrade:

"I believe what she says! Mr. Lee can get us all away from here quick enough, and I'm sorry that we ever come!"

Thirty minutes after the appearance of the enemy, the house and grounds were stripped. Then they disappeared on their way toward the Danville road.

Two or three days thereafter, it was known that General Wilson's column had cut the road, but were falling back rapidly before Lee and Hampton; that they had abandoned sixteen pieces of artillery, and were now striving, with exhausted men and horses, to cross the Weldon road and get back to their lines.

There was a very brave gentleman, of the Fifth Virginia Cavalry—Captain Thaddeus Fitzhugh—the same who had crossed the Chesapeake in an open boat, with a few men, and captured a detachment of the enemy, and a steamboat which he brought off and destroyed, in the fall of 1863. Captain Fitzhugh was sitting in the porch of Mrs.——'s house, conversing with the lady, when looking up, he saw a large body of the enemy's cavalry just across the wood. The odds were great, but the Captain did not retreat. He threw himself on horseback, leaped the fence toward the enemy, and firing his pistol at them, shouted:

"Come on, boys! Charge! Butler's brigade is coming!"

Having made this appeal to an imaginary squadron, the Captain rode across their front; but suddenly came the clatter of hoofs, the rattle of sabres, and some shots. Butler's brigade *had* arrived, and the Federal cavalry melted away into the woods so rapidly, that an old negro, hiding with his mule in the covert, said they "nuver see mule, nor nothin', hi! hi!"

General Butler—that brave soldier and most courteous of gentlemen—drew up his brigade; all was ready for the coming combat; and then it was that the question arose of the "family rifle-pit."

Nervous, unstrung, trembling at the thought that her children were about to be exposed to the enemy's fire, Mrs.—— ran out to the Confederate cavalry in front of her house, and seeing one of the officers, asked him what she should do. His reply was:

"Madam, I would advise you to shelter your family at once, as we expect to begin fighting at any moment."

"But I have no place, sir!" exclaimed the lady, in despair.

"There is probably a cellar——"

"No; the house has none!"

"Can't you get behind a hill, madam?"

The lady gazed around; the country was as flat as a table.

"There is not the least knoll, even, sir!"

"Then, madam," said the practical and matter-of-fact officer, "I can only suggest a rifle-pit; your husband and servants might dig it; and that will certainly protect you."

Odd as the suggestion may seem, it was immediately adopted, as the most commonplace and reasonable thing in the world.

The lady thanked the officer, hastened back to the house—and now behold the grand family hegira toward the field beyond the house!

First came Mr.—— and an old servant, carrying spades to dig the rifle-pit; next came the little family, who had hastily taken up whatever they saw first, and especially noticeable was the young heir of the house. Dimly realizing, apparently, that their absence might be eternal, he had secured a small tin cup and two dilapidated old hats, wherewith to comfort himself in exile; last of all, and in rear, that is, between her offspring and the bullets, came the beautiful young mother, full of anxious solicitude; trembling, but proud and defiant.

I should like to possess your portrait, could it have been taken at that moment, madam!—to look again to-day, in the hours of a dull epoch, upon the kind, good face which smiled so sweetly yonder, making sunshine in the pine woods of Dinwiddie.

And the family rifle-pit was dug by rapid hands; the lady and the children looking on with deep interest. Foremost among the spectators was the brave little urchin grasping his battered tin cup and tattered old hats, to the possession of which he seemed to attach a romantic value. Soon a pile of earth arose; a long trench had been dug; and the lady and her children took refuge therein at the moment when the crack of carbines resounded, and bullets began to hiss above the impromptu earthworks. It was not doomed to be tested by round-shot or shell from the enemy's cannon. They had abandoned their artillery from the impossibility of getting through with it; and only their carbine-balls whistled above the cowering inmates of the rifle-pit.

Then even these no longer came to make the mother's heart tremble for her children. Butler's men had charged; the enemy had given way; when the charming person who related to me this grotesque incident emerged from her place of refuge, not a single Federal cavalry-man was in sight. Only the dismantled grounds and the family rifle-pit remained to show that the whole was not some nightmare of darkness, which had flown with the coming of sunshine.

# III

## A FIGHT, A DEAD MAN, AND A COFFIN

### AN INCIDENT OF 1864

THE incident about to be narrated occurred in November, 1864, when Early with his 8,000 or 9,000 men had been compelled to retire up the Valley before Sheridan, with his 30,000 or 40,000; and when, in the excess of their satisfaction at this triumph of the Federal arms, the Federal authorities conceived the design of ferreting out and crushing in the same manner the band of the celebrated bandit Mosby—which result once achieved by the commander of the "Middle Department," the whole of Northern Virginia would be reduced under the sway of the Stars and Stripes.

To ferret out Colonel Mosby was a difficult task, however; and to crush him had, up to this time, proved an undertaking beyond the ability of the best partisans of the Federal army. Not that they had not made numerous and determined attempts to accomplish this cherished object. In fact, no pains had been spared. Mosby had proved himself so dangerous a foe to wagon trains, lines of communication, and foraging parties, that the generals whose trains were destroyed, whose communications were interrupted, and whose detached parties were captured, had on many occasions sworn huge oaths to arrest his "depreda-tions;" and more than once the most skilful partisan officers, in command of considerable bodies of picked men, had been sent into the wilds of the Blue Ridge, or to "Mosby's Confederacy"—

that is to say, the county of Fauquier—to waylay and destroy or capture this wily foe who had so long eluded them.

All had failed. Mosby refused to be captured or destroyed. If a large force came against him, he retreated to his mountain fastnesses—not a trace of his existence could be found. If the force was small, he attacked and nearly always cut to pieces or captured it. With his headquarters near Piedmont Station, on the Manassas railroad, east of the Ridge, he knew by his scouts of any movement; then couriers were seen going at full gallop to summon the men, scattered among the mountain spurs, or waiting at remote houses in the woods, to the previously specified rendezvous—at Markham's, Upperville, Paris, Oak Grove, or elsewhere; then Mosby set out; and he nearly always came back with spoils—that is to say, arms, horses, and prisoners.

In November, 1864, this state of things had become intolerable. Early had been forced to retire—that wolf with the sharp claws; but Mosby, the veritable wildcat, still lingered in the country as dangerous as ever. Immense indignation was experienced by the enemy at this persistent defiance; and an additional circumstance at this time came to add fuel to the flame of the Federal displeasure. Hitherto, the Confederate partisan had operated generally east of the Blue Ridge, between the mountains and Manassas, guarding that whole country. With the transfer of active hostilities, however, to the Valley, in the summer and fall of 1864, he had turned his attention more especially to that region. *There* were to be found the trains of Hunter and Sheridan, the wandering parties of "Jesse Scouts," clad in gray, whom he delighted to encounter: in the Valley not [north?] east of the Ridge was his most favourable field of operations—and, above all, it was there that his services were chiefly needed to protect the inhabitants from the depredations of these detached parties which spread such terror amid the population.

To the Valley Mosby accordingly directed his attention, and this region thenceforth became his main field of operations. Scarce a day passed without an attack upon some wandering party, upon some string of wagons, or upon the railroad by which the Federal army was supplied. These stirring adventures are the subject of a volume which will soon appear from the accomplished Major Scott, of Fauquier. The object of this chapter is to record the particulars of one of the fights referred to, in which a small band of Confederates under Captain Mountjoy, that accomplished partisan of Mosby's command, suffered a reverse.

Were it within the scope of the present article to draw an outline of the person and character of this brave gentleman—Captain Mountjoy—many readers, we are sure, would derive pleasure from the perusal of our sketch. Never was a braver heart than his—never a more refined and admirable breeding. Gallant-looking, cool, courteous, with his calm sad face overshadowed by the drooping hat with its golden cord; wearing sword and pistol like a trained cavalryman; not cast down by reverses, not elated by success—a splendid type of the great Mississippi race from which he sprung, and a gentleman "every inch of him." Mountjoy's was a face, a figure, and a bearing which attracted the eyes of all who admire in men the evidences of culture, resolution, and honour. But this is not the place to record the virtures of that brave true heart, gone now with many others to a land where war never comes. We proceed to record the incident which we have referred to.

It occurred, as we have said, in November, 1864, and the scene was a mansion perched upon a hill, with a background of woods, between the little village of Millwood and the Shenandoah.* This house was well known to Mosby, well known to many hundreds of Confederate soldiers, who—God be thanked! —never left its door without food, without receiving all that it was in the power of the family to give them, and that without money and without price.

A day or two before the incident about to be related, Mountjoy had gone with a considerable party of men, towards Charlestown; had made an attack; secured numerous horses and prisoners; and on this afternoon was returning towards Millwood—only by the river road—to cross the Shenandoah at Berry's ferry,

* Cooke spent the last years of his life near Millwood. The house referred to here is probably the one in which he later lived.—ED.

and secure his captures. Mountjoy had but one fault as an officer
—rashness. On this occasion he was rash. As he returned from his
scout, and arrived opposite the different fords, he permitted,
first one, then another, then whole squads of his men to cross to
their homes east of the Ridge, so that on reaching a point nearly
opposite Millwood, he had with him only fifteen men guarding
the numerous horses and prisoners.

Then came the hostile fate—close on his heels. The attack made
by him upon the enemy down the river had greatly enraged
them. They had hastily mustered a considerable force to pursue
him and recapture the prisoners, and as he reached Morgan's
Lane, near the Tilthammer Mill, this party, about one hundred in
number, made a sudden and unexpected attack upon him.

The force was too great to meet front to front, and the
ground so unfavourable for receiving their assault, that Mountjoy gave the order for his men to save themselves, and they
abandoned the prisoners and horses, put spurs to their animals,
and retreated at full gallop past the mill, across a little stream,
and up the long hill upon which was situated the mansion above
referred to. Behind them the one hundred Federal cavalrymen
came on at full gallop, calling upon them to halt, and firing vol-
leys into them as they retreated.

We beg now to introduce upon the scene the female *dramatis
personæ* of the incident—two young ladies who had hastened
out to the fence as soon as the firing began, and now witnessed
the whole. As they reached the fence, the fifteen men of Captain
Mountjoy appeared, mounting the steep road like lightning,
closely pursued by the Federal cavalry, whose dense masses completely filled the narrow road. The scene at the moment was
sufficient to try the nerves of the young ladies. The clash of
hoofs, the crack of carbines, the loud cries of "halt! halt!!
halt!!!"—this tramping, shouting, banging, to say nothing of
the quick hiss of bullets filling the air, rendered the "place and
time" more stirring than agreeable to one consulting the dictates
of a prudent regard to his or her safety.

Nevertheless, the young ladies did not stir. They had half
mounted the board fence, and in this elevated position were

exposed to a close and dangerous fire; more than one bullet burying itself in the wood close to their persons. But they did not move—and this for a reason more creditable than mere curiosity to witness the engagement, which may, however, have counted for something. This attracted them, but they were engaged in "doing good" too! It was of the last importance that the men should know where they could cross the river.

"Where is the nearest ford?" they shouted.

"In the woods there!" was the reply of one of the young ladies, pointing with her hand, and not moving.

"How can we reach it?"

"Through that gate."

And waving her hand, the speaker directed the rest, amid a storm of bullets burrying themselves in the fence close beside her.

The men went at full gallop towards the ford. Last of all came Mountjoy—but Mountjoy, furious, foaming almost at the mouth, on fire with indignation, and uttering oaths so frightful that they terrified the young ladies much more than the balls, or the Federal calvary darting up the hill.

Let us here, in parenthesis, as it were, offer a proof of that high-breeding we have claimed for Captain Mountjoy. A young lady expressed afterwards her regret that so brave a gentleman should have uttered an oath, and this came to his ears. He at once called to see her and said gravely, in his calm, sad voice. "I am sorry that I swore. I will try not to do so again, but I was very angry that day, as the men might have whipped the enemy in spite of their numbers, if I could only have gotten them to make a stand, and this was before *you*."

But that was when his blood was cool. At the moment when he brought up the rear of the men, Mountjoy was raging. Nevertheless he stopped in the very face of the enemy, besought the young ladies to leave the fence where they were exposing themselves to imminent danger, and then, still furious, he disappeared, most of all enraged, as he afterwards explained, that this stampede of his men and himself should have taken place in the presence of the young ladies.

The partisan had scarcely disappeared in the woods, when the enemy rushed up, and demanded which way the Confederates had taken.

"I will not tell you!" was the reply of the youngest girl.

The trooper drew a pistol, and cocking it, levelled it at her head.

"Which way?" he thundered.

The young lady shrunk from the muzzle, and said:

"How do I know?"

"Move on!" resounded from the lips of the officer in command, and the column rushed by, nearly trampling upon the ladies, who ran to the house.

Here a new incident greeted them, and one sufficiently tragic. Before the door, sitting his horse, was a trooper, clad in blue —and at sight of him the ladies shrunk back. A second glance showed them that he was bleeding to death from a mortal wound. The bullet had entered his side, traversed the body, issued from the opposite side, inflicting a wound which rendered death almost certain.

"Take me from my horse!" murmured the wounded man, stretching out his arms and tottering.

The young girls ran to him.

"Who *are* you—one of the Yankees?" they exclaimed.

"Oh, no!" was the faint reply. "I am one of Mountjoy's men. Tell him, when you see him, that I said, 'Captain, this is the first time I have gone out with you, and the last!'"

As they assisted him from the saddle, he murmured:

"My name is William Armistead Braxton. I have a wife and three little children living in Hanover—you must let them know——"

Then the poor fellow fainted; and the young ladies were compelled to carry him in their arms into the house, where he was laid upon a couch, writhing in great agony.

They had then time to look at him, and saw before them a young man of gallant countenance, elegant figure—in every outline of his person betraying the gentleman born and bred. They afterwards discovered that he had just joined Mosby, and that, as he had stated, this was his first scout. Poor fellow! it was also his last.

The scene which followed has more than once been described to the present writer, and it made a dolorous impression on his heart. The wounded man lay upon the couch, struggling against death, writhing with his great agony, and bleeding so profusely that the couch was saturated with his blood. Even in that moment, however, the instincts of gentle breeding betrayed themselves in the murmured words:

"My spurs will—tear the cover—lay me—on the floor."

This, of course, was not complied with, and the young ladies busied themselves attempting to bind up his wound.

While one was thus engaged, another hastened to unbuckle his belt, in order to secure his pistol. This was necessary, as the Federal cavalry was already trampling in front of the house, and shouting to the inmates.

Unable to undo the belt, the young lady quickly drew the pistol from its holster, secreted it in a closet, and turning round, saw that in this moment the dying man had rolled from the couch upon the floor, where he was exclaiming: "Lord Jesus, have pity upon me!"

She hastened back to him, and at the same instant the house was literally crowded suddenly with Federal soldiers, who burst open the doors, tore the ornaments from the mantelpiece, broke everything which they could lay their hands upon, and exhibited violent rage at the escape of the Confederates.

Those men were in *gray*. We neglected to state that fact. Mountjoy's men were in *blue*. Thus the opponents had swapped uniforms—the blue being gray, and the gray blue. This fact caused the capture of the wounded man's pistol. The young lady who had secreted it was kneeling by him, holding his hand —or rather he had caught her own, as wounded men will, and tightly held it—when a tall and very brutal-looking trooper, bending over the prostrate figure, saw the empty holster.

"Where is his pistol?" he thundered in a ferocious tone.

"What pistol?" said the young lady, firmly, and returning the brutal gaze without flinching.

"His pistol!—you have hidden it! Where is it?—give it up."

And he pushed the wounded man with his foot, nearly turning him over.

"You'll not get it from *me!*" exclaimed the young lady, looking boldly at him, every drop of her woman's blood aroused inflamed, and defiant at this cruel act.

"Give me the pistol!—or——"

And he drew his own, pointing it at her.

"I've not got it!"

Here the voice of a diminutive negro girl, who had seen the weapon secreted, and who took the Federal trooper in his gray coat for a Confederate, was heard exclaiming—

"La! Miss ——, 'tis in the closet, where you put it!"

And in an instant the man had rushed thither and secured it.

The house was now filled with men, rushing from top to bottom of it, and breaking to pieces every object upon which they could lay their hands. In the house at the time was Captain ——, a wounded officer of artillery, and Lieutenant ——, a staff officer, who had been surprised, and was now secreted in a closet. Captain ——'s room was visited, but he was not molested; Lieutenant —— was so skilfully concealed in his closet, against which a bed was thrust, that he was not discovered.

Smashed crockery, shattered parlour ornaments, followed spoons, knives, forks, shawls, blankets, books, daguerreotypes—these and many other movables speedily appeared in dwindling perspective; then they vanished.

Thus theft, insult, and outrage had their veritable carnival—but the young ladies did not heed it. They were absorbed by the painful spectacle of the wounded gentleman, who, stretched upon the floor of the dining-room below, seemed about to draw his last breath. He still held the hand of the young lady who had removed his pistol; to this he clung with an unrelaxing clutch; and the sight of her tearful face, as she knelt beside him, seemed to afford him the only satisfaction of which he was capable.

"Pray for me!" he murmured, clinging to her hand groaning; "pray for me, but pray to yourself!"

"Oh, yes!" was the reply, and the wounded man sank back, moaning, amid the crowd of jeering troopers trampling around his "fallen head!"

To these an honourable exception speedily revealed himself.

This was a young Federal officer, who came to the side of the wounded man, gazed first at him, then at the young lady, and then knelt down beside them.

The glazing eyes of the wounded man looked out from his haggard face.

"Who are you?" he muttered.

"I am Lieutenant Cole," was the reply, in a sad and pitying voice; "I am sorry to see you so dangerously wounded."

"Yes—I am—dying."

"If you have any affairs to arrange, my poor friend, you had better do so," said Lieutenant Cole; "and I will try and attend to them for you."

"No—the ladies here—will——"

There he paused with a hoarse groan.

"You are about to die," said the Lieutenant; "there is no hope. I am a Christian, and I will pray for you."

As he spoke he closed his eyes, and remaining on his knees, silent and motionless, was evidently offering up a prayer for the dying man, who continued to writhe and toss, in his great agony.

There are men whom we regret, but are proud to have for our enemies; this man was one of them.

When he rose his expression was grave; he threw a last glance at the sufferer, and then disappeared. His fate was sad, and seemed an injustice to so brave a gentleman. On the very next day he was captured by a party of Confederates, and while being conducted across the Blue Ridge thought that he discovered an opportunity to escape. Drawing his pistol, which by some negligence had been left upon his person, he fired upon his guard. The bullet missed its aim—and the guard firing in turn, blew out Lieutenant Cole's brains.*

* A singular coincidence comes to the writer's memory here. The mother of the young ladies whose adventures are here related, had on this day gone to attend the funeral of young Carlisle Whiting at the "Old Chapel" some miles distant. Young Whiting had been killed by a Federal prisoner, whom he was conducting south, near Front Royal. The prisoner's pistol had been overlooked; he drew it suddenly, and fired upon his guard, the bullet inflicting a mortal wound. [J.E.C.]

Cooke was destined to be buried in the graveyard of the Old Chapel mentioned here.—Ed.

At nightfall the Federal troops had torn the house to pieces, taken all which they could not destroy, and had vanished. Mountjoy had succeeded in getting off with his men. At six o'clock on the next morning poor Braxton breathed his last, still holding the hand of the young lady, which seemed to be all by which he had clung to life.

Then a strange and unexpected difficulty arose. It is safe to say that the young ladies of New York or Philadelphia, at that moment buried in slumbers in their happy homes, surrounded by every comfort—it is safe to say that they would have found it difficult then—will find it difficult now—to conceive even the great dilemma which their young rebel "sisters" were called upon to face. The death of a friend would have been sad to the young New Yorker or Philadelphian, but at least they would have seen his body deposited in a rosewood coffin; the head would have rested on its satin cushion; lace handkerchiefs raised to streaming eyes, in the long procession of brilliant equipages, would have been soothing to his friends, as indicating the general grief.

Here, in that good or bad year 1864, on the border, things were different. There were no equipages—no lace handkerchiefs —no satin, and rosewood, and silver—not even a coffin. In the midst of their grief for the loss of that brave soldier of one of the old Virginia families, their connexions, the young Confederate girls were met by this sudden obstacle—by this gross, material question, this brutal difficulty—where shall a coffin for the dead be procured? There lay the dead body pale, cold, terrible—how bury it as Christians bury their dead?

They did not cry or complain, but courageously set to work. Beside themselves, there were in the house two young cousins now, who had hastened to the place, Phil —— and George ——, at that time mere boys. These went to the mill, past which Mountjoy had retreated, and painfully raising upon their shoulders some broad and heavy planks lying there, bore them up the hill to the house. Then, accompanied by the youngest of the girls, they went to an old saw-mill near the river, gathered together a number of rails from old timber there, returned, and began their lugubrious work.

The details of their employment were as sombre as the employment itself. The dead body was first to be measured; and this was courageously undertaken by the youngest girl, who, placing one end of a cord upon the dead man's forehead, measured to his feet. The length was thus determined, and the boys set to work, assisted by the girl, sawing, hammering, and nailing together the rude box which was to contain all that remained of the poor youth.

The work absorbed them throughout the short November day, and only at nightfall was it finished. Then the fear seized upon them that they had made the coffin too long; that the corpse would not lie securely in it, and move when carried. A singular means of testing the length of the coffin was suddenly hit upon. The eldest of the young ladies, who had been watching the corpse during the work, now approached, and without shrinking, lay at full length in the coffin, which was then found to be amply large. Then the body was deposited in it—the pious toil had been accomplished.

Was not that painfully in contrast with the decent city "arrangements," which take from the mourner all the gross details —permitting his grief to hover serenely in the region of sentiment? This rude pine coffin differed from the rosewood; the funeral cortège which ere long appeared, differed, too, from the long line of shining carriages.

It consisted of three hundred horsemen, silent, muffled, and armed to the teeth, for the enemy were close by in heavy force. They appeared, without notice, about three hours past midnight, and at the head of them, we believe, was Mountjoy.

The body, still in its rude coffin, was lifted into a vehicle; some hasty words were exchanged with the young ladies, for a large force of the enemy was near Millwood within sight, a mile or two across the fields; then the shadowy procession of horsemen moved; their measured hoof-strokes resounded, gradually dying away; the corpse was borne through the river, ascended the mountain—and at sunrise the dead man was sleeping in the soil of Fauquier.

# IV

## GENERAL PEGRAM

### I.

THE writer's object in the present paper is to chronicle the events of a day in the pine-woods of Dinwiddie in 1865, and to mention a circumstance which impressed him forcibly at the time; nearly convincing him of the truth of "presentiments," and warnings of approaching death.

It was early in February of the year 1865, and General Grant had for some time been straining every nerve to force his way to the Southside railroad—when General Lee would be cut off from his base of supplies, and compelled to retreat or surrender his army. Grant had exhibited a persistence which amounted to genius; and the Federal lines had been pushed from the Jerusalem to the Weldon road, from the Weldon to the Vaughan and Squirrel Level roads, and thence still westward beyond Hatcher's Run, toward the White Oak road, running through the now well-known locality of Five Forks. On the western bank of the run, near Burgess's Mill, General Lee's extreme right confronted the enemy, barring his further advance.

The Confederate right was almost unprotected by cavalry. This unfortunate circumstance arose from the fact that after the destruction of the Weldon Railroad as far south as Hicksford, fifty miles from Petersburg, the cavalry was obliged to repair to that distant point for forage. Never was anything more unfortunate; but it was one of those misfortunes which no generalship

535

could prevent. By sheer force of numbers, General Grant had effected the destruction of the road; the Southside road could not supply forage; the cavalry horses must go to Hicksford or starve. Such was the explanation of the fact that General Lee's right was guarded only by a small regiment or two of horse, on picket.

Such was the "situation." Grant on the banks of Hatcher's Run; the Rowanty almost unguarded; the path open for cavalry to the Southside road; Five Forks, and the retreat of the Confederate army, looming in the distance. The passionate struggle which had for four years drawn to the great arena the eyes of all the world was about to be decided amid the sombre pines of Dinwiddie.

A few scenes in these pine woods at the crisis referred to may interest the reader. The narrative will probably convey a better idea of the "times as they were" than a more ambitious record—the familiar view being generally the best. While the infantry lines were closing in the death-grapple in front of Petersburg, the blue and gray horsemen were hunting each other in the Dinwiddie forests, and the game was not unexciting. The "events of a day" are here rapidly traced, just as they appeared to the writer. No tremendous exploits will be narrated or "thrilling adventures" recorded; but perhaps some of the actual colouring of the great war-canvas will be caught in the hasty memoir.

Returning from a tour of inspection at Hicksford, night surprised me not far from Nottoway river; and having crossed that turbulent stream at risk of drowning my horse, I spent the night at the hospitable mansion of Mr. D——, not far from Halifax bridge, on the Rowanty. The Federal forces were just beyond the stream, and no Confederate picket between; but the night passed undisturbed even by the prowling of a single Federal scout; and on the next morning the line of march was resumed for Petersburg by way of Malone's.

Two hundred yards to the left of Halifax bridge there suddenly appeared a number of "scattered" cavalry-men—gray—approaching at full gallop, evidently stampeded.

"What is the matter?"

"The Yankees have crossed with two regiments at Malone's!" from the hurrying horseman.

"Did you see them?"

"Yes, sir."

"Where is your regiment?"

"Back to Kirby's, and everything is ordered to Dinwiddie Court-House!"

This report was soon confirmed by the rest, and "full particulars," as the journals say, were given. A strong force of Federal cavalry had suddenly attacked the small regiment on picket at Malone's, and dispersed it, nearly capturing Gen. William H. F. Lee, who chanced to be there inspecting his lines. This force had steadily pressed on, the Confederates retiring; was now at Kirby's, and soon would be at Dinwiddie Court-House.

This was not eminently agreeable to myself personally. "Kirby's" was on the only road to Petersburg, except by way of Malone's—for the time rendered impracticable—and to reach my journey's end it seemed necessary to make the circuit by Dinwiddie Court-House. To attempt the road by Kirby's was certain capture; and in an undoubted bad humour the "solitary horseman," as Mr. James would say, turned to the left, crossed Stony Creek, struck into the "Flat Foot Road," and in due time drew near Roney's bridge, on the upper waters of the stream, near Dinwiddie. Within a quarter of a mile of the stream a soldier made his appearance, coming to meet me, and this individual informed me with the politest possible salute that I had better "look out, as the Yankees were at the bridge."

"At the bridge! Where?"

"At Roney's bridge, just in front, sir."

This was the "unkindest cut of all." I had made a wearisome circuit, reached a supposed place of crossing—and here were my blue friends again like a lion in the path, rendering it necessary to strike still higher up the stream. At this rate it seemed probable that I would be forced to return to Petersburg by way of Lynchburg and Richmond! Malone's—Kirby's—Dinwiddie—the enemy were everywhere.

A good military rule, however, is to "believe nothing you hear, and only half you see." The report that Federal cavalry was at the bridge in front was probable, but not certain. They might be Confederates; and taking the soldier with me, I proceeded to reconnoitre. As we reached the vicinity, the woods were seen to be full of dismounted cavalry, but whether these were Federal or Confederate, it was impossible to say. Drawing nearer, the men seemed to be the latter; nearer still, and the surmise was confirmed. Regulation *gray* had long disappeared—our cavalry were nondescript in costume—but the sharpshooters in front were *not* in blue.

One came out to meet me, carbine ready—a quite useless precaution it seemed—and the following dialogue ensued:

"What command?" I asked.

"General Lee's."

"Where are the Yankees?"

"Just over the bridge."

Then the road by Dinwiddie Court-House was blockaded! Meditating with melancholy resignation on this fact, I unconsciously turned my horse's head from the bridge, when my friend with the carbine made a quick step toward me, and catching his eye, I found the expression of that member doubtful, puzzled, but not friendly. In fact the carbineer had his weapon cocked, and was evidently ready to bestow its contents on me if I moved a step.

Then, for the first time, the truth flashed on me. I was wearing a blue "Yankee overcoat" concealing my Confederate uniform; my hat was nondescript; there was absolutely nothing to show that I was not some adventurous Federal officer who had crossed the stream below, come up the Flat Foot road in rear of the Confederates to reconnoitre, and was about to return with the information acquired. To prevent this, my friend with the carbine evidently intended to send a bullet after me as soon as I moved.

This comic situation was a safety valve for all ill-humour, and one of the men having run for his Lieutenant, I gave that officer my name and rank—which announcement was greeted, however, with a similar glance of doubt. A few words dissipated this.

"Where is General Lee, Lieutenant?"

"Just over the hill."

"I will go there."

And accompanied by the young officer, I found General W. H. F. Lee, who had been compelled with his one or two hundred men—the whole force of the regiment—to retire behind the stream. His sharpshooters were now posted to rake the bridge if the enemy appeared, and a mounted party had been sent toward Dinwiddie Court-House.

After a few moments' conversation with General Lee—that brave and courteous gentleman, whom I am glad to call my friend—I found that the reports of the cavalry-men were correct. The enemy's horse, in strong force, had driven him back to Dinwiddie, and were then at the Court-House. General Lee informed me, laughing, that in the charge he had been very nearly stampeded for the first time in his life, his horse, "Fitz Lee," an unruly animal of great power, having whirled round at the first volley from the enemy, and nearly carried his rider off the field! In great disgust at this unmilitary conduct, the General had mounted a more manageable courser.

Whilst the General was narrating these particulars, two young officers of his staff, Captains Lee and Dandridge, came in, after a hot chase. The former had been entirely surrounded, but kept the woods, taking advantage of every opening; and finally perceiving an interval between the rear of one Federal cavalry regiment and the head of column of another, he had put spurs to his horse, charged the opening, and jumped through. The latter officer was also "cut off," and manœuvred in a similar manner, when, as he turned a bend in the bridle-path which he was following, he came suddenly upon a body of foot-soldiers clad in *dark blue*, with burnished guns at the right shoulder shift, steadily advancing *southward*. This was enormously puzzling! Why should a Federal infantry battalion be going *south* at that moment? And then there was something singular in the uniform and equipments of the men—very unlike Federals. Their coats were of *navy* blue, of unfamiliar cut; and they had cut-lasses apparently in their belts.

Captain Dandridge had gazed at this party with astonishment for some moments, when all at once he was perceived, and an officer, apparently, beckoned to him. To go or not to go—that was the question; but he finally decided to approach, and did so. Then the mystery was quickly solved. The men in blue were a battalion of Confederate marines, and they were proceeding toward the Nottoway river to make a circuit, approach James river far below City Point, board and seize upon a Federal "ram," and then steam up the James, and destroy Grant's fleet of transports at City Point. This excellent scheme was thoroughly arranged; the torpedoes to be used were hidden in the woods of Nottoway ready for the party, when a deserter went over and informed the enemy, in consequence of which the expedition was abandoned.

We have seen how, by a singular chance, the battalion set out on its march, armed and prepared, the very day that the enemy's cavalry crossed the Rowanty. More singular still, they passed along *in rear* of the Federal cavalry without discovering them or being discovered. This, all things considered, was one of the most curious events of the war; as the scheme proposed for the destruction of the Federal transports was one of the boldest.

General W. H. F. Lee waited at Roney's bridge for some time, expecting an advance of the enemy's cavalry; but none coming, he sounded to horse, placed himself at the head of his small column of about eighty or a hundred men, and pushed out toward Dinwiddie Court-House to attack the raiders. Before he had advanced far, intelligence came that the enemy had evacuated the Court-House, and were falling back toward Cattail Creek, in the vicinity of which their infantry was stationed. General Lee immediately followed, came up with their rear at Cattail, and here a brief skirmish took place, just as night descended. The lines of Federal infantry which had advanced that day were discovered; and no further advance in that direction was attempted, the cavalry returning toward Dinwiddie.

An odd incident marked this rapid ride after the retiring

Federal cavalry. In the middle of the road we found two Confederate cavalry-men with a prisoner whom they had caught,
and the worthy in question attracted our attention. He was
clad in semi-military costume; a blue-gray overcoat of fine
cloth, with a long cavalry cape to it, decorated with a dazzling
row of buttons; an excellent new hat; and rode a superb horse,
which would have brought five or six thousand dollars in Confederate money.

As we came up—Captains Robert Lee, Philip Dandridge, and
myself—this gentleman complained in animated terms of the
immorality involved in capturing "a non-combatant;" he was not
a soldier, only the "correspondent of the *New York Herald*,"
and he hoped that he would immediately be released. This train
of reasoning, impressed upon his listeners in a most voluble and
eloquent voice, accompanied by animated gestures, did not seem
to convince anybody; and the men were directed to take the
prisoner back to Dinwiddie Court-House, and as he was evidently a man of decision and resources, "shoot him if he tried
to escape, making no attempt to recapture him."

He was accordingly started back, under convoy of the two
cavalry-men, and had proceeded about three or four hundred
yards, when our attention was attracted to him again by an
outcry in that direction. Turning round, we saw that something
curious was going on, and hastily spurred to the scene. Lo! as
we approached, there was the prisoner scudding across the field,
his cape floating in the wind, his horse at a full run, pursued by
carbine-balls! None struck him, however; and in a moment he
had disappeared in the belt of woods near at hand, in which lay
*perdus* the line of Federal infantry.

A few words from the chop-fallen cavalry-men and an old
negro, at a small house near by, explained everything. Three
or four Federal cavalry-men had been left behind by their comrades on the retreat, and had stopped at the house to ask the
way to their lines. While thus employed, the prisoner and his
escort came by; the Federal cavalry-men rushed forth to the
rescue "put their pistols" on the unsuspecting escort, and now
both rescuers and rescued were safe within their own lines!

The whole affair was truly laughable, and the gallant "correspondent" deserved his good fortune, since he made a true John Gilpin run for liberty. I did not grudge him the enjoyment thereof at all, but must confess to a keen feeling of regret at the loss of his horse. He appeared to be an excellent animal; and to "covet your neighbour's horse," if he chanced to be desirable, was in those days the besetting sin of every true cavalry-man!

II.

At nightfall General Lee retired from Cattail Creek toward Dinwiddie Court-House, the enemy having returned within their lines; and I determined to continue my way to Petersburg, where duty called me.

There was reason to doubt, however, the practicability of this journey—at least over the regular "Boydton road." Simultaneous with the advance of the Federal cavalry, their infantry had moved toward the Southside road; a severe engagement had taken place on the Quaker road; and the Federal infantry was known to have remained in its position, its left probably across, or resting upon the Boydton road. Now, as above intimated, it was necessary to follow this Boydton road to reach Petersburg that night. I determined to try, and so informed General Lee, who thereupon requested me to carry a dispatch which he had just written, to General Gordon, commanding the right of the army near Burgess', with an oral message, information, etc., in reference to the cavalry movement.

A small detachment of cavalry, belonging to Colonel Phillips' command, then on the right of the army, was placed at my orders; and setting out about night, we soon debouched upon the Boydton road, where at every step traces of the Federal forces were met with—the raiders having harried the whole region— and some prisoners captured. The vicinity of the bridge over Gravelly Run was thus reached, and beyond the bridge glimmered the fires of a picket.

The question of greatest interest was whether the picket was Federal or Confederate. The enemy's left was certainly near this point, but so was our right. The plain method of deciding was to try, and this was done—the cavalry detachment halting a hundred yards off. Riding on the bridge, I found the planking torn up, and in the centre a "yawning gulf;" at the same moment a voice came from beyond, ordering "halt!" The following dialogue then took place:

"Well, I have halted."

"Who are you?"

"Friends."

"Advance one."

"Impossible—the bridge is torn up."

"What command do you belong to?"

"What do *you* belong to?"

"I ask who you are!"

"Do you belong to Colonel Phillips' regiment?"

"No!"

This reply was discouraging. Colonel Phillips held the extreme right; this should be his picket; as it was *not*, the probabilities appeared to be in favour of the Federal picket view. Under the circumstances, the next course seemed to be a rapid "about face," the use of the spur, and a quick retreat, taking the chances of a bullet. The sudden click of a trigger interrupted these reflections, and my friend in the dark said briefly:

"I asked what command you belonged to!"

Something in the tone of the voice struck me as Southern, and I replied:

"Well, I don't believe you are a Yankee; I belong to General Lee's army."

"All right; so do we," was the answer. "You can come over at the ford yonder."

"What brigade is yours?"

"General Pegram's."

This reply ended all doubt. Pegram I knew was on Gordon's extreme right. Not finding General Gordon, I had been requested by General Lee to communicate with Pegram.

His headquarters were near the junction of the Boydton and Quaker roads; and having turned over the cavalry detachment to Colonel Phillips, I entered the old wooden building and found General John Pegram.

This gallant young officer had been my school-fellow and intimate friend in boyhood; and I had seen him every day almost until his departure for West Point. After graduating there he had entered the cavalry, served on the prairies, and in 1861 returned to offer his sword to Virginia, where he was received in a manner highly flattering, and placed in command of the forces near Rich Mountain. The unfortunate result of that campaign is known, and the proud and sensitive spirit of the young soldier was deeply wounded. In spite of the assurances of brave and skilful soldiers that the issue there was unavoidable, considering the great force brought against him, he persisted in brooding over it. "It would always be known as 'Pegram's surrender,'" he said. It was soon forgotten, however; greater events and greater disasters threw it in the background, and the young soldier fought his way to high repute in the Southern army. On the night when I met him, in February, 1865, he was commanding the advance brigade of General Lee's right wing, and had held his ground all day against the severest assaults of the enemy.

The cordial greeting of two friends, after long separation, over, General Pegram mounted his horse to ride with me to General Gordon's, beyond Burgess' mill, and on the way we dropped military affairs entirely, to revert to scenes which had taken place twenty years before, and speak of the "old familiar faces" and things long previous to the war. If it were necessary I could recall the entire conversation—the very words uttered by my companion—for the sad event of the next day engraved the whole upon my memory. In the voice of the speaker there was a peculiar sadness, a species of melancholy depression, which it was impossible not to observe. Something seemed to weigh upon his mind, and the handsome features of the young soldier (he was only about thirty), with the clear dark eye, the gallant moustache, and the broad, fine brow, were overshadowed by a heavy cloud. This obvious depression, however, did not render him cold or *distrait*—rather the contrary. He spoke of old friends and comrades with the greatest affection and kindness; referred with something very like womanly tenderness to a dear younger brother of his listener, dead many years before; and the pleasure which he derived from this return to the careless past was un-mistakable. But throughout all was that undertone of sadness which I remembered afterwards, and could not forbear regard-ing as the evidence of some mysterious presentiment.

This did not change at all when, after a ride of two or three miles we reached General Gordon's, and were shown to the General's chamber.* General G.'s cheery voice, as he smoked his cigar and discussed the events of the day, did not make my companion smile.

"Do you expect a renewal of the attack to-morrow, General?" I asked.

"Not on this side of the run, but I think it probable they will make a heavy attack on General Pegram in the morning."

The person thus alluded to was carefully examining a topo-graphical map at the moment; and his countenance and attitude exhibited unmistakable depression and languor. When we rose to go, the expression had not changed. As we shook hands, he addressed me by the name which he had used when we were school-fellows together, and said: "Come and see me whenever you can." And that pressure of the kind, brave hand, that utterance of the good friendly voice, was the last for me. On the next day the attack anticipated by General Gordon took place, and General Pegram was killed while gallantly leading his men.

Such was the soldierly ending of this brave young Virginian. He had been married only a few weeks to a young lady of rare beauty, and life seemed to open for him all flowers and sunshine; but the thunderbolt had struck him; his brave blood went to swell that great torrent poured out by the gallantest souls of the South.

This hasty sketch—beginning with jests, and ending in some-

---

* The General Gordon referred to here was General John B. Gordon. He should not be confused with General James B. Gordon, mentioned earlier in the book. The latter was dead at this time, having been killed at Yellow Tavern in 1864.—ED.

thing like tears—has aimed, in part, to record that presentiment which the young soldier seemed to have of his approaching fate. Wholly incredulous as the writer is of such warnings, it is impossible for him to banish from his mind the fancy that something conveyed to the young soldier a premonition of the coming event. But he did his duty all the same, dying in harness like a good soldier of the South.

# V

## LEE'S LAST BATTLES

### I.

GENERAL LEE's retreat from Petersburg will rank among the most remarkable events of history. As every circumstance connected with it will prove interesting hereafter, when the full history of this period comes to be written, I propose to record some particulars which came under my observation; and especially to describe the bearing of the illustrious Commander-in-Chief of the Confederate forces while passing through this tremendous ordeal.

An adequate record of this brief and fiery drama—played from the first to the last scene in a few April days—would involve the question of General Lee's soldiership. This question I have neither time nor space to discuss; but I am much mistaken if a simple statement will not set at rest for ever those imputations which have been cast, since the surrender, upon Lee's military judgment, by ignorant or stupid persons throughout the country. The facts ought to be placed on record. If General Lee continued, of his own choice, to occupy a position at Petersburg from which, as events soon showed, he could not extricate his army, it will go far to rob him of that renown which he had previously won; and if General Grant out-manœuvred and caught his great adversary by simple superiority of soldiership, he is the greater general of the two. The truth of the whole matter is that Lee was *not* surprised; that he foresaw clearly what was coming;

and acted from first to last under orders against which his military judgment revolted.

Orders were given by General Lee for the evacuation of Petersburg, and, consequently, of the State of Virginia, at least six weeks before General Grant broke through the Confederate lines. The military necessity for this movement was perfectly plain to all well-informed and intelligent persons, in the army and out of it. It was only the ignorant or the hopelessly stupid who cherished the hallucination that Lee could continue to hold his works around Petersburg against Grant's enormous force. Nevertheless there were a plenty who did think so, and who looked upon things there as a sort of "permanent arrangement." Lee, in the estimation of these persons, was the spoiled child of good fortune, greater than fate, and the Army of Northern Virginia could not be whipped. The Southern lines were to be held *en permanence*, and Grant was to "keep pegging away" until the crack of doom. Such was the fond delusion of all the "outside" class; those who were accurately informed, and took the "inside" view, knew better; and especially did General Lee know that unless he was speedily reinforced, he could not continue to hold his lines against the large and steady reinforcements sent to General Grant. "More men; give me more men!" was the burden of his despatches to the government. He had nearly fifty miles of earthworks to defend against three or four times his own numbers; and a child might have understood that if Grant continued to receive heavy reinforcements, and Lee none, while his army continued to diminish from casualties, the time would soon come when retreat or surrender would be the only alternatives. The reinforcements did not come, however. The Army of Northern Virginia went on dwindling, and Grant continued to increase his strength, until at the end of winter the result of the coming campaign no longer admitted of a doubt. The crisis had evidently come, and it was perfectly plain that Lee must evacuate Virginia. All his prominent Generals shared his views. One of them said: "If Grant once breaks through our lines, we might as well go back to Father Abraham, and say, 'Father, we have sinned.'" If anything was plain it was this: that if the immense line of Lee's works was broken anywhere, he was lost.

N. ROBERT'S SC.

GEN. LEE'S RETREAT FROM PETERSBURG.

It is certainly nothing very remarkable that under these circumstances General Lee should make an attempt to save his army—the only hope of the Confederacy. There was only one way to do it, and the opportunity of embracing that sole means was rapidly slipping away. General Lee must move, if he moved at all, on the line of the Southside Railroad toward Danville, and he must move at once; for General Grant, who knew perfectly well the necessities of his adversary, was pouring heavy columns toward Hatcher's Run, to intercept him if he made the attempt. The Federal army was kept ready day and night, with rations cooked and in haversacks, for instant pursuit; and each of the great opponents understood completely his adversary's design. General Grant knew that General Lee *ought* to retreat, and he had learned the important maxim that it is always best to give your enemy credit for intending to do what he ought to do. If Lee moved promptly toward Danville, every effort would be made to come up with and destroy him; if he did not retreat, time would be allowed the Federal army to gradually fight its way to the Southside road. Once lodged upon that great artery of the Southern army, Grant had checkmated his opponent.

Upon this obvious view of the situation, General Lee, in February, issued orders for the removal of all the stores of the army to Amelia Court-House, on the road to Danville. A movement of this sort is, of course, impossible of concealment, and the whole army soon knew that something was "in the wind." Government cotton and tobacco was hauled away from Petersburg; hundreds of the inhabitants left the place; all the surplus artillery was sent to Amelia Court-House, and even the reserve ordnance train of the army was ordered to the same point. Then suddenly, in the midst of all, the movement stopped. The authorities at Richmond had said, "Hold your position." Lee countermanded his orders and awaited his fate.

I say *awaited his fate*, because I am perfectly well convinced that from that moment he regarded the event as a mere question of time. No reinforcements reached him, while Grant grew stronger every day by reinforcements from Washington and Sherman's army—two corps from the latter—and soon he had at his command Sheridan's excellent force of 12,000 or 15,000 cavalry. He was pushing heavy columns, one after another, toward the Southside road, and at any moment a general attack might be expected all along the lines, while the *élite* of the Federal force was thrown against Lee's right. Such an assault, in his enfeebled condition, was more than General Lee could sustain, unless he stripped his works elsewhere of all their defenders; but a brave effort was made to prepare for the coming storm, and Lee evidently determined to stand at bay and fight to the last. The expected attack soon came. Grant rapidly concentrated his army (amounting, General Meade stated at Appomattox Court-House, to about 140,000 men) on Lee's right, near Burgess' Mill; his most efficient corps of infantry and cavalry were thrown forward, and a desperate attack was made upon the Confederate works on the White-oak road. A bloody repulse awaited the first assault, but the second was successful. At the same time the lines near Petersburg were broken by a great force, and the affair was decided. The Confederate army was cut in two; the enemy held the Southside Railroad, intercepting the line of retreat; and what Lee's clear military judgment had foreseen had come to pass. Between his 40,000 men and Danville were the 140,000 men of Grant.

## II.

I should think it impossible even for his worst enemy to regard the situation of this truly great man at the moment in question without a certain sympathy and respect. He was not Commander-in-Chief only, but the whole Southern Confederacy himself—carrying upon his shoulders the heavy weight of the public care. Every confidence was felt in the patriotism and sincere devotion of President Davis to the Southern cause—but there was a very general distrust of his judgment, and his administration had not made him popular. Lee, on the contrary, was the idol almost of the people; and it was to him that the South looked in this dark hour, calling on him for deliverance.

Up to this moment he had been in a condition to meet his great responsibility. In a campaign of unexampled fury, dragging its bloody steps from the Rappahannock to the Appomattox, he had held his lines against almost overwhelming assaults, foiling an adversary of acknowledged genius, commanding a superb army. Against this army, constantly reinforced, he had continued to hold the works around Petersburg, and protect the capital; and to him, amid the gloom and depression, all had looked as to their sole hope. There was no possibility of General Lee himself escaping a knowledge of this fact. It was in the faces and the words of men; in the columns of the newspapers; in the very air that was breathed. Good men wrote to him not to expose himself, for if he fell all was over. In brief words, the whole country agreed that in this man and his army lay the only hope of the Southern Confederacy.

If the reader realizes what I have thus tried to express, he may form some idea of the crushing ordeal through which General Lee was, on the 2d of April, called upon to pass.

The brief particulars about to be set down may furnish the candid historian of the future with material to form an unbiassed judgment of General Lee and his retreat. I am mistaken if the narrative, however brief and incomplete, does not show the great proportions and noble character of the individual—his constancy under heavy trials, and his majestic equanimity in face of a misfortune the most cruel, perhaps, which a soldier can be called on to bear.

Soon after sunrise on the 2d of April the Federal columns, in heavy mass, advanced from the outer line of works, which they had carried at daybreak, to attack General Lee in his inner intrenchments near Petersburg. When the present writer reached the vicinity of army headquarters, on the Cox road, west of the city, a Federal column was rapidly advancing to charge a battery posted in the open field to the right of the house, and at that time firing rapidly. General Lee was in the lawn in front of his Headquarters,* looking through his glasses at the column as it moved

---

\* This was the Turnbull house, west of Petersburg. It was set on fire by Union shells that day and was entirely destroyed.—Ed.

at a double quick across the fields; and knowing the terrible sig-
nificance of the advantage which the Federal troops had gained,
I looked at the General to ascertain, if possible, what he thought
of it. He never appeared more calm; and if the affair had been a
review, he could not have exhibited less emotion of any description. In full uniform, with his gold-hilted sword, and perfectly
quiet look, he appeared to be witnessing, with simple curiosity,
some military parade. But this "dress" costume was assumed, it is
said, with another view. He had dressed himself that morning, I
afterwards heard, with scrupulous care, and buckled on his finest
sword, declaring that if he was captured he would be taken in
full harness.

The movement of the Federal column became more rapid,
and the battery was soon charged; but it succeeded in galloping
off under a heavy fire of musketry. The column then pressed on,
and the Federal artillery opened a heavy fire on the hill, before
which the Southern guns—there was no infantry—withdrew,
General Lee retired slowly with his artillery, riding his well-
known iron gray; and one person, at least, in the company forgot
the shell and sharpshooters, looking at the superb old cavalier,
erect as an arrow, and as calm as a May morning. When he said
to an officer near, "This is a bad business, Colonel," there was no
excitement in his voice, or indeed any change whatsoever in its
grave and courteous tones. A slight flush came to his face, however, a moment afterwards. A shell from the Federal batteries,
fired at the group, burst almost upon him, killing a horse near by,
and cutting bridle-reins. This brought a decided expression of
"fight" to the old soldier's face, and he probably felt as he did
in Culpeper when the disaster of Rappahannock bridge ocurred
—when he muttered, General Stuart told me, "I should now like
to go into a charge!"

These details may appear trivial. But the demeanour of public
men on great occasions is legitimate, and not uninteresting matter for history. General Lee's personal bearing upon this critical
occasion, when he saw himself about to be subjected to the greatest humiliation to the pride of a soldier—capture—was admirably
noble and serene. It was impossible not to be struck with the

grandeur of his appearance—no other phrase describes it: or to refrain from admiring the princely air with which the old cavalry officer sat his horse. With his calm and thoughtful eye, and perfect repose of manner visible in spite of the restive movements of his horse, frightened by the firing, it was hard to believe that he saw there was no hope,—and for himself, would have cared little if one of the bullets singing around had found its mark in his breast.

### III.

In ten minutes the Federal troops had formed line of battle in front of the Headquarters, and a thin line of Confederate infantry manned the badly-constructed works on the Cox road. If the Federal line of battle—now visible in huge mass—had advanced at once, they would have found opposed to them only two small brigades, which would not have been a good mouthful. The amusing thing was to hear the "ragged rebels"—and they were very ragged—laughing as they looked at the heavy line apparently about to charge them, and crying: "Let 'em come on! we'll give 'em ——!" Gordon was meanwhile thundering on the left of Petersburg, and holding his lines with difficulty, and at night one point at least was gained. The surrender would not take place there. *Where* it would be was not yet decided.

Before morning the army had been moved to the northern bank of the Appomattox; the glare and roar of the blown-up magazines succeeded; and accompanied by the unwieldly trains, loaded with the miserable rubbish of winter quarters, the troops commenced their march up the Appomattox, toward the upper bridges.

General Lee was on his gray horse, leading his army in person; there were no longer any lines to defend, any earthworks to hold; the army was afloat, and instead of being depressed, they seemed in excellent spirits. But the drama had only commenced.

The great game of chess between Grant and Lee commenced on the morning of the 3d of April; the one aiming if possible to extricate his army, the other to cut off and capture, or destroy it.

The relative numbers of the opposing forces can only be stated in round numbers. I understood afterwards that General Meade stated the Federal force to amount to about one hundred and forty thousand men. That of General Lee did not exceed, if it reached, forty thousand. So great had been the drain upon this historic army from the casualties of the past year, from absence with and without leave, and other causes, that—deprived of all reinforcements—it was now weaker than it had probably ever been before. General Meade, it is said, expressed extreme astonishment to General Lee when informed of his small numbers, declaring that if General Grant had suspected this weakness, he would have long before broken through the Confederate lines. The statement was natural, and General Meade doubtless believed in the ability of the Federal army to have done so; but it is certain that General Grant made persistent and desperate attempts to accomplish this very object, in which his adversary, by rapid movements of his small force from point to point, and obstinate fighting, had invariably foiled him.

To return to the retreat. The Southern army had been so long cooped up in its hovels and casemates—moving only by stealth along "covered-ways"—that any movement anywhere was a relief. In addition to this, the troops had not yet had time to reflect. The sensation of being driven from their earthworks— now like home to them—was stunning; and the men did not at once realize the tremendous change which had all at once taken place in the aspect of affairs. No man seemed yet to have persuaded himself of the fact that "General Lee's Army," which only yesterday had held the long lines, in defiance of all comers, was to-day in full retreat, and bent first of all upon *escaping* from the enemy they had so often defeated.

Gradually, however, the unhappy condition of affairs began to dawn upon the troops; and all at once they looked the terrible fact in the face. *General Lee was retreating from Virginia*—most depressing of events!—and it was even a matter of very extreme doubt whether he could accomplish even that much. No troops were ever better informed upon military affairs than those of the South; and the private soldier discussed the chances with a topographical knowledge which could not have been surpassed by a general officer with a map before·him. I heard one brave tatter-demalion, evidently from the backwoods, say, "Grant is trying to cut off old Uncle Robert at Burkesville Junction;" and another replied, "Grant can get there first." There, in a few words, was the essence of the "situation."

General Grant held the Southside Railroad, and was pouring forward troops under Sheridan toward the Danville Railroad, to which he had a straight cut without a particle of obstruction, except a small force of cavalry—less than two thousand effective men—under General Fitz Lee. General Lee, on the contrary, was moving by a circuitous route on the north bank of the Appomattox, encumbered by a huge wagon-train, and having in front of him a swollen river, which proved a terrible delay to him at the moment when every instant counted. So great were the obstacles, that General Grant could have intercepted the Southern column, had he made extraordinary exertions, even at Amelia Court-House. General Lee did not succeed in reaching that point until *Wednesday, the 5th*—the bridges over the Appomattox being swept away or rendered useless by the freshet which had covered the low grounds and prevented access to them. The troops finally crossed on pontoons at two or three places; and, although suffering seriously from want of rations, pushed forward in good spirits to Amelia Court-House.

Up to this time there had been very few stragglers, the Virginia troops turning their backs upon their homes without complaint, and satisfied to follow "Old Uncle Robert" wherever he led them. The statement that desertions of Virginians had taken place is untrue. They marched with their brethren from the Gulf States cheerfully; and it was only afterward, when broken down by starvation, that they dropped out of the ranks. That some, seeing the sure fate before them—surrender, and, as they supposed, long incarceration in a Northern prison—left their ranks during the last hours of the retreat, is also true; but, a few hours after they thus left their colours, it was the general officers who looked out for avenues of exit through the Federal *cordon* closing around, to avoid the inevitable surrender; and who said to their men, "Save yourselves in any way you can."

The scene at Amelia Court-House on Wednesday was a curious one. The huge army trains were encamped in the suburbs of the pretty little village, and the travel-worn troops bivouacked in the fields. They were still in good spirits, and plainly had an abiding confidence in their great commander. The brigades, though thinned by their heavy losses at Petersburg, still presented a defiant front; and the long lines of veterans with bristling bayonets, led by Longstreet, Gordon, and Mahone, advanced as proudly as they had done in the hard conflicts of the past. The troops were still in excellent *morale*, and had never been readier for desperate fighting than at that moment. Men and officers were tired and hungry, but laughing; and nowhere could be seen a particle of gloom, or shrinking, or ill-humour—sure symptoms in the human animal of a want of "heart of hope." I will add that I saw little of it to the end.

The unavoidable delay in crossing the Appomattox had given General Grant time to mass a heavy force—as General Meade's report shows—at Burkesville Junction; and if it was General Lee's intention to advance on the east side of the Danville road, he gave it up. I believe, however, that such was never his design. His trains were directed to move through Cumberland, Prince Edward, and Campbell, toward Pittsylvania; and the army would naturally keep near enough to protect them, moving southward between the Junction and Farmville. While the troops were resting at Amelia Court-House, and waiting for the rear to come up, the Federal commander must have pushed forward with great rapidity. His cavalry was already scouring the country far in advance of the Confederate column, and the numbers and excellence of this branch of their service gave them a fatal advantage. The reserve train, containing nearly all the ammunition of the Southern army, was attacked and burned near Paynesville, and the fate awaiting other portions of the army train was foreseen. Its unwieldly size and slow movement made it an easy prey; and it was incessantly attacked, and large sections carried off or destroyed. So numerous were these captures, that nearly the whole subsistence of the army was lost; and from this time commenced the really distressing scenes of the march. The men were without rations, and had marched almost day and night since leaving Petersburg; their strength was slowly drained from them; and despondency, like a black and poisonous mist, began to invade the hearts before so tough and buoyant.

The tendency of military life is to make man an animal, and to subject his mind in a great measure to his body. Feed a soldier well, and let him sleep sufficiently, and he will fight gaily. Starve him, and break him down with want of sleep and fatigue, and he will despond. He will fight still, but not gaily; and unless thorough discipline is preserved, he will "straggle" off to houses by the road for food and sleep. Desertion is not in his mind, but the result is the same. The man who lags or sleeps while his column is retreating, close pressed by the enemy, never rejoins it. Such is the explanation of the phenomena exhibited on this retreat; and now why were the troops thus left without rations, and compelled to scatter over the country in search of enough food to preserve them from starvation?

The reply to that question is, that rations for his army were ordered to be sent to Amelia Court-House by General Lee; that trains containing the supplies were dispatched from Danville; and that these trains were ordered, *by telegraph from Richmond*, to come on to Richmond, and did so, when the bread and meat was thrown in the gutter, to make way for the rubbish of the Departments. The rubbish was preserved for subsequent capture, and the Army of Northern Virginia staggered on, and starved, and surrendered.

If any one demands the proof of this assertion, I will give it.*

## IV.

General Lee left Amelia Court-House on the evening of the 5th, and from this time the army was incessantly engaged, particularly with the Federal cavalry. On the 6th the enemy was encountered in force; and line of battle was formed to repulse them, if they advanced upon the trains then moving towards

* For a more judicious discussion of what happened to the supplies Lee was supposed to receive at Amelia Court House, see Douglas Southall Freeman, *R. E. Lee*, IV, Appendix IV-2, pp. 509 ff.—ED.

High Bridge. It was on this evening that Generals Ewell and
Anderson were suddenly attacked and their commands thrown
into great confusion, in the rear of the wagon-trains. These officers and others—including General Custis Lee, son of the General—were captured, and the drama seemed about to end here;
but it did not.

To the hostile fate which seemed to be pressing him to his
destruction, General Lee opposed a will as unconquerable as the
Greek Necessity with her iron wedge. The terrible results of this
disorganization of Ewell and Anderson were averted by a movement of infantry as rapid and unexpected as that of the Federal
cavalry. From the flanking column of Confederate infantry a
brigade was pushed across at a double-quick; and between the
disorganized troops of Ewell and the victorious enemy rose a
wall of bayonets, flanked by cannon. From this human rock the
wave went back; and though the lurid glare of the signals along
the Federal lines in the gathering darkness seemed the prelude to
another attack, none was made.

I have spoken briefly of this scene. It was one of gloomy pic-
turesqueness and tragic interest. On a plateau, raised above the
forest from which they had emerged, were the disorganized
troops of Ewell and Anderson, gathered in groups, unofficered,
and uttering tumultuous exclamations of rage or defiance. Rising
above the weary groups which had thrown themselves upon the
ground, were the grim barrels of cannon, in battery, to fire as
soon as the enemy appeared. In front of all was the still line of
battle just placed by Lee, and waiting calmly. General Lee had
rushed his infantry over just at sunset, leading it in person, his
face animated, and his eye brilliant with the soldier's spirit of
"fight," but his bearing unflurried as before. An artist desiring to
paint his picture ought to have seen the old cavalier at this moment, sweeping on upon his large iron gray, whose mane and tail
floated in the wind; carrying his field-glass half raised in his right
hand; with head erect, gestures animated, and in the whole face
and form the expression of the hunter close upon his game. The
line once interposed, he rode in the twilight among the disor-

dered groups above mentioned, and the sight of him raised a tumult. Fierce cries resounded on all sides; and with hands clenched violently and raised aloft, the men called on him to lead them against the enemy. "It's General Lee!" "Uncle Robert!" "Where's the man who won't follow Uncle Robert?" I heard on all sides; the swarthy faces, full of dirt and courage, lit up every instant by the glare of the burning wagons. Altogether, the scene was indescribable.

This took place on the evening of the 6th of April.* The main body of the Federal army was now closing round Lee, and it was only by obstinate and persistent fighting that he was able to continue his retreat. Everywhere the Federal forces were confronted by his excellently served artillery; and the thin lines of infantry, marching on the flanks of the trains, met and repulsed every attack with the old spirit of the Army of Northern Virginia. In hunger, and thirst, and weariness, and retreat, these veteran troops stood by their colours without a murmur, and fought as admirably as when carrying all before them, and flushed with victory. Others, however, were less constant; rather, let us say, less physically competent. They fell out of the ranks by hundreds, overcome by hunger and exhaustion; or, what was equally bad, they dropped their heavy guns and cartridge boxes, and straggled along, a useless, cumbrous mob. On the morning of the 7th, beyond Farmville, the Federal cavalry made continuous and desperate onslaughts on the train, throwing everything into confusion. The teamsters, always the least soldierly portion of an army, became panic-stricken, and the terrible roads increased a thousand-fold the difficulties of the march. Wagons were captured or abandoned all along, in spite of hard fighting, and from this time the retreat became a scene of disorder which no longer left any ground for hope. I intended to describe it, but the subject is too disagreeable. Let some other eye-witness place upon record these last scenes of a great tragedy.

* The battle on April 6, which Cooke does not name, was Sayler's Creek, the last major engagement in which the Army of Northern Virginia was engaged.—ED.

On the 7th, General Grant opened his correspondence with General Lee, stating that the result of the march, so far, must have convinced him of "the hopelessness of further resistance;" and this correspondence continued until the morning of the 9th, General Lee refusing to surrender the army. But his condition was hopeless. The Confederate forces were reduced to 7,800 muskets, and Grant had in General Lee's front 80,000 men, with a reserve of 40,000 or 50,000, which would arrive in twenty-four hours. These odds were too great; and although General Gordon drove them a mile with his thin line half an hour before the surrender, the Federal forces continued to close in and extend their cordon of infantry, cavalry, and artillery, until the Southern army was almost completely surrounded. Lee's line slowly fell back before this overwhelming force, and the moment seemed to have come when the "Old Guard" of the Army of Northern Virginia would be called upon to crown its historic fame by a last charge and a glorious death. These men would have died with Lee without a murmur, fighting to the last; but any such wanton sacrifice of human life, without any imaginable use, was far from the thoughts of the great soldier. He had fought as long as he could, and done all in his power to extricate his army from a position in which it had been placed by no fault of his. Now he did not hesitate in his course. At first he had recoiled from the idea of surrender when it was suggested to him by, I think, General Pendelton. This officer had informed him that his corps commanders were unanimously of opinion that surrender was inevitable; but he had exclaimed, greatly shocked, "Surrender! I have too many good fighting men for that!" Now the current had set too strongly against him, and he was forced to yield. The army, with less than eight thousand muskets, a very short supply of ammunition, and almost nothing to eat, was at Appomattox Court-House, in the bend of the James—wholly impassable without pontoons—and on every side the great force of General Grant was contracting and closing in. A Federal force had seized considerable supplies of rations, sent down by railroad from Lynchburg; and this force now took its position in front of the Confederate army, slowly moving by the left flank toward

James river. General Custer, who seemed to be greatly elated on this occasion, and to enjoy the result keenly, stated to Confederate officers that Grant's force amounted to eighty thousand men, and that a heavy reserve was coming up.

Under these circumstances General Lee determined to surrender his army, and did so, on condition that the officers and men should be paroled, to go to their homes and remain undisturbed by "United States authorities" as long as they remained quiet and peaceable citizens. Officers and men were to retain their private property, and the former their side-arms.

Such was the Convention between Lee and Grant.

## V.

The Army of Northern Virginia had surrendered! Strange, incredible announcement!

The effect which it produced upon the troops is hard to describe. They seemed to be stupefied and wholly unable to realize the idea. For Lee, the invincible, to yield up his sword was an incredible thing; and when the troops could no longer have any doubt, men who had fought in twenty battles, and faced death with unshrinking nerve, cried like children. To yield is a terrible thing—a bitter humiliation; and if the private soldiers felt it so keenly, we may imagine the feelings of the leader who was thus called upon to write that word "Surrender" at the end of so great a career. He had said once that he "intended for himself to die sword in hand;" but now not even this was permitted him. He must sacrifice his men or surrender, and he decided without difficulty or hesitation.

If there are any poor creatures so mean as to chuckle at this spectacle of a great man letting fall the sword which has never been stained by bad faith or dishonour, they can indulge their merriment. The men who had fought the illustrious leader upon many battle-fields—who had given and taken hard blows in the struggle—did not laugh that day.

The scenes which took place between General Lee and his men were indescribably pathetic. I shall not speak of them, except to say that the great heart of the soldier seemed moved to its depths. He who had so long looked unmoved upon good fortune and bad, and kept, in the midst of disaster and impending ruin, the equanimity of a great and powerful soul, now shed tears like a child.

"I have done what I thought was best for you," he said to the men. "My heart is too full to speak; but I wish you all health and happiness."

It may be asked why I have omitted from my sketch the scene of surrender. There was no such scene, except afterwards when the troops stacked arms and marched off. The real surrender was an event which was felt, not seen. It was nothing apparently; the mere appearance of a Federal column waving a white flag, and halting on a distant hill. But the tragic event was read in the faces of all. No guns in position with that column so near; no line of battle; no preparations for action! A dreamy, memorial sadness seemed to descend through the April air and change the scene. Silence so deep that the rustle of the leaves could be heard —and Longstreet's veterans, who had steadily advanced to attack, moved back like mourners. There was nothing visible in front but that distant column, stationary behind its white flag. No band played, no cheer was heard; the feelings of the Southern troops were spared; but there were many who wanted to die then.

This retreat was a terrible episode of military life, unlike any which the present writer ever before saw; but he does not regret having borne his part in its hardships, its sufferings, and its humiliations. He is glad to have seen the struggle out under Lee, and to have shared his fate. The greatness and nobility of soul which characterize this soldier were all shown conspicuously in that short week succeeding the evacuation of Petersburg. He had done his best, and accepted his fate with manly courage, and that erect brow which dares destiny to do her worst; or rather, let us say, he had bowed submissively to the decree of that God in whom he had ever placed his reliance. Lee, the victor upon many hard-fought fields, was a great figure; but he is no less grand in defeat, poverty, and adversity. Misfortune crowns a man in the eyes of his contemporaries and in history; and the South is prouder of Lee to-day, and loves him more, than in his most splendid hours of victory.

JOHN ESTEN COOKE.

Virginia, June, 1865.

# INDEX

Appomattox, Lee's army moved to, 553; Army of Northern Virginia hemmed in at, xxi, 560

Aldie, Pelham fights at, 121; Stuart and Bayard fight at, Oct., 1862, 279-81

Amelia Court House, Lee orders provisions sent to, 549; Lee moves on to, Apr. 5, 1865, 555; Confederates at, 555-57; Lee leaves, Apr. 5, 1865, 557; D. C. Freeman on, 557n.

Ashby, Turner, furnished inaccurate information leading to battle of Kernstown, 43; appearance, 61; early career, 62-65; sorrow at brother's death, 62-63; with Jackson at Winchester, spring, 1862, 63-65; death of his horse, 66; death, 67; not enough discipline, 69; enthusiasm, 69; praised by Jackson, 70; Cooke vs. Avirett on his behavior at withdrawal from Winchester, 64n.

Bagby, George W., criticism of Cooke, xvin.

Bateman, Kate, xv

Bayard, George D., captures Farley, 133; Farley waylays him, 184; fights Stuart at Aldie, Oct., 1862, 279-81; talks with Darrell, 418

Beaty, John Owen, biographer of Cooke, xi

Beauregard, Pierre G. T., Cooke first sees him at Manassas, summer, 1861, 73; with President Davis and Stuart en route to Fairfax Court House, 75; appearance, 76-77; popularity, 79-82; Cooke attached to his army, 1861, 202; reviews troops with Jerome Bonaparte at Centreville, 1861, 366-68; in command of the *Revolutionnaires*, 379-80

Bonaparte, Jerome, reviews forces at Centreville, 1861, 366-68

Bonham, Milledge L., Beauregard supersedes him at Manassas, June, 1861, 73; Cooke in his brigade, 1861, 203; *Revolutionnaires* placed under his command, 379-80; at Fairfax, 392

Bumpo, N., joins Confederate army at fifteen, 343; fights under Jackson in infantry, 343-48; fights under Stuart in cavalry, 348-50; becomes artillery officer, 350

Brown, John, at Harpers Ferry, xi, xvii, 378

Camp No-Camp, Confederates move out of, 460-64

Camp Qui Vive, Beauregard at,

564